# Intellectual Property: The Law in Canada

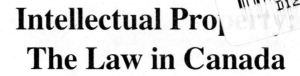

Elizabeth F. Judge

and

Daniel Gervais

THOMSON
™
CARSWELL

©2005 Thomson Canada Limited

**Library and Archives Canada Cataloguing in Publication**

Judge, Elizabeth F. (Elizabeth Frances), 1966-
Intellectual property : the law in Canada / Elizabeth F. Judge and
Daniel Gervais.

ISBN 0-459-24257-1

1. Intellectual property—Canada.   I. Gervais, Daniel J., 1963-   II. Title.

KE2779.J83 2005          346.7104'8          C2005-903410-6
KF2979.J83 2005

Composition: Computer Composition of Canada Inc.

The acid free paper used in this publication meets the minimum requirements of the American National Standard for Information Services — Permanence of Paper for Printed Library Materials. ANSI Z39.48-1984.

THOMSON
™
CARSWELL

**One Corporate Plaza**                          **Customer Relations:**
2075 Kennedy Road                               Toronto 416-609-3800
Toronto, Ontario              Elsewhere in Canada/U.S. 1-800-387-5164
M1T 3V4                                          Fax 1-416-298-5082

# Preface

This book covers all aspects of intellectual property law in Canada, including copyright, industrial designs, trade-marks and related torts such as the misappropriation of personality, patents, confidential information, plant varieties, integrated circuit topographies, and international intellectual property. The authors include extensive analysis of major Canadian cases, including all recent Supreme Court of Canada decisions and their contributions to the developing theory of Canadian intellectual property law. Throughout, the authors highlight continuing controversies, especially ones raised by new technologies. In copyright, they consider the effect of the Supreme Court's landmark decisions in *Théberge, CCH v. L.S.U.C.*, and *SOCAN* and provide commentary on the ongoing process of copyright reform, digital copyright issues, and topical issues such as the standard for originality, private copying and collective licensing. In patents, the authors discuss new developments in patentable subject matter including computer programs and life forms and the Supreme Court's recent decisions in *Harvard Mouse* and *Monsanto Canada v. Schmeiser*.

The book adopts an innovative format which blends the benefits of a treatise and casebook. We intend this book to be used by practising lawyers and in the curriculum for introductory and advanced law school courses. The book is suitable both for seminar style and lecture format courses.

For practitioners, this treatise provides succinct statements of the current law and analysis of the trends and debates. We have selected key passages from significant cases, and longer excerpts where the context and original wording is crucial. In addition to the major cases discussed in the text, we have also included ample citation of additional relevant cases as references for citation in litigation.

For instructors of intellectual property law, we have included many teaching materials, which accent issues raised by new technologies, such as peer-to-peer file sharing, internet service provider liability, traditional knowledge, biotechnology, and newer forms of intellectual property such as domain names and the protection of image. An extensive set of discussion questions is keyed to each topic area to facilitate class discussion and for practice by student study groups. Intellectual property law in practice can simultaneously involve multiple areas of intellectual property and applying these issues can be particularly challenging for new students of intellectual property law. An innovative chapter details such "overlaps" between intellectual property laws and is complemented by thematic questions designed to highlight these intricate overlaps and to teach students how to apply intellectual property laws to a particular factual scenario. Sample examination questions are also provided.

# Foreword

The law of intellectual property enjoys a new importance in the "information age" comparable to that formerly accorded to the law governing land and tangible assets when these were the rising stars of the commercial world. Knowledge and ingenuity, brand names and patents, copyright protection and the exclusive right to the exploitation of the products of the mind preoccupy the Canadian legal system today as never before. When I was called to the bar, the usual run of lawyers associated IP practice with Cratchett-type figures in stiff collars exchanging head notes of obscure English judgments. As recently as 1998, when the Supreme Court heard a case involving the IP bar, the judges were told that this was "a first" in twenty-five years, and therefore, counsel observed brightly, we should not anticipate another such case until 2023. "We'll be ready for it," growled one of my colleagues, without much enthusiasm. Since then the IP work of the Court has expanded rapidly, as have the IP practice groups in major law firms across the country and recognition in law schools of the central role played by intellectual property in modern legal practice. IP law is a subject whose day in the sun has arrived.

The authors bring both sophistication and depth of learning to their subjects. One of the longstanding problems with IP law has been its relative lack of accessibility. For years, Canadian lawyers had little other than English and American precedents for guidance. Earlier generations of Canadian judgments were often little more than cut and paste efforts (with notable exceptions, such as the opinions of President Thorson of the Exchequer Court). The standard Canadian texts (mostly written by the learned Dr. Harold G. Fox) were scholarly and accurate but in many instances presupposed that the reader knew more about the subject than was likely the case. In more recent years, better texts and commentaries have become available, but there has remained a real need for a straightforward exposition of the law relating to intellectual property and its underlying principles which could be read with profit by expert and novice alike without having to jump around the law library from one footnoted source to another.

This book fills that need admirably. Quoting extensively from primary sources, the important elements of IP law are expertly treated and the underlying policies, spoken and unspoken, are laid out. The text offers one-stop shopping for the harassed practitioner trying to come to grips with some difficult concepts as much as for the student who wants to drill down through the jurisprudence to understand and evaluate the theory that is supposed to hold it altogether. The authors make the essential points but offer a good many non-obvious insights into their subject matter as well.

Important international and comparative law references are included. This work is likely to become a standard text in the field and we are all the richer for it.

The Honourable Mr. Justice William Ian Corneil Binnie
Supreme Court of Canada
April 26, 2005

# Acknowledgements

The authors wish to express their gratitude to Monsieur Claude Théberge, the Canadian artist who created the painting *Le scénario*, for letting us reproduce one of his magnificent works as the illustration on the cover. We are indebted to I. Caley Ross for his diligent and thorough research assistance and to Johanne Auger at BCF in Montreal for her useful comments on the trade-mark section. The financial support of the Social Sciences and Humanities Research Council of Canada, the Law Foundation of Ontario, and Bell University Labs is also gratefully acknowledged.

# About the Authors

## *Daniel J. Gervais*

Dr. Daniel J. Gervais is Vice-Dean, Research and Oslers Professor of Technology and Intellectual Property Law at the Faculty of Law (Common Law) of the University of Ottawa. After studies in computer science and his LL.B., Professor Gervais obtained an LL.M. degree from the University of Montreal, a Diploma *magna cum laude* of Advanced International Studies from the IUHÉI in Geneva, Switzerland, and a doctorate *magna cum laude* from Nantes University (France). He became a member of the Bar of Quebec in 1985, where he finished first overall and obtained all available awards. He is also a member of the Law Society of Upper Canada. Prior to his teaching career, Dr. Gervais was successively Legal Officer at the GATT/World Trade Organization, where he was actively involved in the TRIPS Agreement negotiations; Head of Section at the World Intellectual Property Organization (WIPO); Assistant Secretary General of the International Confederation of Societies of Authors and Composers (CISAC); and Vice-President, International, of Copyright Clearance Center, Inc. (CCC), the largest reprographic rights organization in the world (revenue of C$150 million in 2003). He was also a consultant with the Paris-based Organisation for Economic Co-Operation and Development (OECD). In 2004, Professor Gervais was a Visiting Scholar at Stanford Law School. He is also the 2004 Trilateral Distinguished Scholar at Michigan State University College of Law. Professor Gervais recently lectured as Invited Professor at the Universities of Nantes and Grenoble (France) and will teach as Invited Professor at the University of Haifa (Israel) in the Spring of 2005. He also taught postgraduate courses in intellectual property law at the University of Amsterdam. He speaks French, English, Spanish and German (functional). Professor Gervais has published several peer-reviewed articles, in six languages, on various intellectual property topics. He is also the author of the reference book on the TRIPS Agreement published by Sweet & Maxwell in London (first edition 1998; second edition 2003). In 2003, he was awarded the Charles B. Seton Award by the Copyright Society of the USA (best paper), the first time the award was given to a Canadian national in the Society's 50-year history. His recent research was financed by grants from the Social Sciences and Humanities Research Council of Canada (SSHRC) and Bell University Labs. Professor Gervais is a member of the Board and National Law School Liaison of the International Commission of Jurists (ICJ Canada), a Board member of ALAI Canada; and a member of the Program Committee of the 45th Circuit (OCRI). He is also Associate Editor of the *Journal of World Intellectual Property*.

## *Elizabeth F. Judge*

Elizabeth F. Judge is an Assistant Professor at the University of Ottawa, Faculty of Law, Common Law Section, where she specializes in intellectual property, privacy and evidence law and is a member of the law and technology group. Her research has focused on the protection of personal information through tort, property and intellectual property law and other property that individuals can hold in themselves. She teaches courses on Intellectual Property, Evidence, Privacy and an advanced intellectual property seminar on Property of the Person. In the graduate programme, Professor Judge has taught graduate seminars on the jurisprudence and policy of law and technology and served as faculty coordinator for the Master of Laws with concentration in Law and Technology. She is a founding editor and Editor-in-Chief and Faculty Advisor for the *University of Ottawa Law & Technology Journal*. Dr. Judge has held SSHRC and Killam doctoral fellowship awards for graduate work in both English Literature and Law, and has taught in both Law and Literature. Prior to joining the Faculty of Law, she practised law in Washington, D.C., specializing in tax and complex insurance litigation. Professor Judge is a member of the Law Society of Upper Canada and is admitted to the Bars of the State of California, the District of Columbia and the United States Tax Court. She holds a Bachelor of Arts from Brown University (English and American Literature; Political Science) (Hons.), *magna cum laude*, a Juris Doctorate from Harvard Law School, *cum laude*, a Master of Arts (English) from the University of Toronto and a Master of Laws and a Doctor of Philosophy in English Literature from Dalhousie University. In 2001-2002, she served as a law clerk to the Honourable Mr. Justice Ian Binnie at the Supreme Court of Canada. She is an Associate Editor of the *Canadian Patent Reporter* and a member of the Advisory Boards of the Canadian Internet Policy and Public Interest Clinic (CIPPIC) and the Canadian Privacy Law Review Newsletter. Her publications include scholarship in law and literature. Professor Judge's research interests are in the areas of law and technology, including intellectual property, online privacy, personality rights, the property of personal information, and technology and the courts, as well as evidence, legal history, law and literature, and jurisprudence.

# Table of Contents

**CHAPTER 1: Introduction to Intellectual Property: Philosophies, Policies and History**

I.   Justifying Intellectual Property ............................................. 2
II.  Theories of Intellectual Property ........................................... 4

**CHAPTER 2: Copyright**

I.   Introduction .................................................................. 7
     1.   Common and Civil Law Traditions and Copyright ........... 10
     2.   Copyright Philosophy and the Idea of "Balance" .............. 12
II.  Work ........................................................................ 13
     1.   "Work" ................................................................ 13
     2.   "Fixation" ........................................................... 14
     3.   Ideas versus Expression ........................................... 15
     4.   Originality .......................................................... 16
          (a)   Canada's Middle Way ...................................... 21
     5.   Literary Works ..................................................... 25
          (a)   Quality ..................................................... 26
          (b)   Quantity .................................................... 27
          (c)   Computer Programs ........................................ 27
          (d)   A Note on the Future of Computer Program
                Protection by Copyright ................................... 28
     6.   Dramatic Works .................................................... 30
     7.   Musical Works ..................................................... 32
     8.   Artistic Works ..................................................... 33
     9.   Photographs ....................................................... 34
     10.  Architectural Works ............................................... 37
     11.  Compilations ...................................................... 37
III. Ownership ................................................................... 38
     1.   Employees ......................................................... 39
          (a)   Employees and the Meaning of Publication ............ 40
     2.   Photography ....................................................... 42
     3.   Crown Copyright .................................................. 44
     4.   Joint Authorship ................................................... 44
     5.   Collective Works .................................................. 45
IV.  Assignment/Transfer of Copyright ...................................... 46
     1.   Intangible versus Tangible ........................................ 46
V.   Terms of Protection ........................................................ 47
VI.  Infringement ............................................................... 48
     1.   General Aspects .................................................... 48
     2.   Reproduction ...................................................... 50

|  |  |  |  |
|---|---|---|---|
|  | a) | Publication | 53 |
|  | b) | Parallel Importation | 54 |
| 3. | | Communication to the Public/Public Performance | 54 |
| 4. | | Adaptation and Translation | 56 |
|  | (a) | A Note on Adaptation and Traditional Knowledge | 59 |
| 5. | | Rental | 60 |
| 6. | | Authorization | 60 |
|  | (a) | "Authorization" in the Context of the CRIA/Peer-to-Peer Litigation | 64 |
| 7. | | Moral Rights | 69 |
| 8. | | Secondary Violation | 72 |
| 9. | | Principal Defences | 74 |
| 10. | | Statutory Defences | 80 |
|  | (a) | A Hierarchy of Exceptions? | 81 |
|  | (b) | The Meaning of Fair Dealing | 84 |
|  | (c) | Other Possible Impacts | 88 |
|  | (d) | Parody and the "Public Interest" Defence | 90 |
|  | (e) | Other Exceptions | 97 |
| 11. | | Remedies | 98 |
| 12. | | Criminal Sanctions | 104 |
| VII. | | Copyright Registration | 113 |
| VIII. | | Related Rights | 114 |
| IX. | | Collective Management | 116 |
| 1. | | Overview | 116 |
| 2. | | The Four Legal Regimes of Collective Management in Canada | 118 |
|  | (a) | Music Performing Rights and Certain Neighbouring Rights | 118 |
|  | (b) | The General Regime | 119 |
|  | (c) | Retransmissions and Certain Uses by Educational Institutions (Section 71) | 121 |
|  | (d) | Private Copying | 122 |
|  |  | (i) A Note on Private Copying in the Digital Age | 122 |
| X. | | Points of Attachment and Foreign Works | 126 |
| XI. | | Database Protection | 127 |
| XII. | | Discussion Questions | 129 |

## CHAPTER 3: Industrial Designs

| | | | |
|---|---|---|---|
| I. | | Introduction | 141 |
| II. | | Object of the Protection | 142 |
| 1. | | Visual Appeal | 145 |
| 2. | | Originality | 149 |
| III. | | Registration, Ownership and Term of Protection | 155 |
| IV. | | Marking | 157 |

V.    Infringement, Remedies and Defences ................................    158
VI.    Discussion Questions .......................................................    164

**CHAPTER 4: Trade-Marks**

I.    Introduction .................................................................    165
      1.    Origin ................................................................    165
      2.    Constitutional Ground ............................................    167
      3.    Purpose and Theory of Protecting Trade-Marks ..............    189
II.    Object of the Protection ..................................................    192
      1.    General ..............................................................    192
      2.    Company Names ...................................................    197
      3.    Proposed Trade-Marks ............................................    198
      4.    Well-Known Trade-Marks ........................................    198
      5.    Official Marks .......................................................    212
      6.    Clearly Descriptive Trade-Marks ................................    217
            (a)    General .......................................................    217
            (b)    Place of Origin .............................................    231
            (c)    Secondary Meaning .......................................    235
            (d)    Loss of Distinctiveness ...................................    238
      7.    Prohibited or Invalid Trade-Marks .............................    246
            (a)    Names ........................................................    253
            (b)    Foreign Marks ..............................................    254
      8.    Confusion ............................................................    257
III.    "Use of a Trade-mark" ....................................................    275
IV.    Registration .................................................................    279
      1.    Who Can File for Registration ..................................    279
      2.    Procedure ...........................................................    280
      3.    Impact of Registration on Previous Users .....................    281
      4.    Expungement (Section 45) .......................................    282
V.    Licences and Assignments ...............................................    284
VI.    Infringement .................................................................    285
      1.    Infringement of Registered Marks ..............................    286
            (a)    Right to Use ................................................    286
            (b)    Depreciation of Goodwill ...............................    289
            (c)    Parallel Importation ......................................    295
      2.    Infringement of Any Mark .......................................    296
            (a)    Common Law ..............................................    296
            (b)    Section 7 ....................................................    311
      3.    Remedies .............................................................    317
            (a)    Injunctions Generally ....................................    317
VII.    Domain Names and Internet-Based Infringement ....................    323
VIII.    Discussion Questions .......................................................    333

## CHAPTER 5: Patents

| | | | |
|---|---|---|---|
| I. | | Introduction | 339 |
| | 1. | Origin | 339 |
| | 2. | Constitutional Ground | 340 |
| | 3. | Basic Principles | 340 |
| II. | | Object of Protection | 347 |
| | 1. | Subject-Matter | 348 |
| | | (a) Excluded Subject-Matter | 348 |
| | | (b) Computer Programs | 350 |
| | | (c) Life Forms | 355 |
| | 2. | Novelty | 384 |
| | 3. | Utility | 399 |
| | | (a) Sound Prediction | 401 |
| | 4. | Non-Obviousness | 408 |
| III. | | Application | 413 |
| | 1. | The Inventor | 413 |
| | 2. | Employees | 417 |
| | 3. | Disclosure | 423 |
| IV. | | Term of Protection | 425 |
| V. | | Infringement | 426 |
| | 1. | Generally | 426 |
| | | (a) Claim Construction Principles | 427 |
| | | (b) The Doctrine of Equivalents | 441 |
| | | (c) "Use" of a Patent | 449 |
| | | (d) Process Patents and Notice of Compliance Issues | 455 |
| | 2. | Defences | 460 |
| | 3. | Compulsory Licences | 465 |
| VI. | | Remedies | 474 |
| VII. | | Discussion Questions | 481 |

## CHAPTER 6: Confidential Information

| | | | |
|---|---|---|---|
| I. | | Introduction | 485 |
| II. | | Object of the Protection | 495 |
| | 1. | Trade Secrets | 497 |
| III. | | Employees | 499 |
| IV. | | Breach of Duty of Confidence, Elements and Defences | 512 |
| V. | | Remedies | 512 |
| VI. | | Information Submitted to Government | 513 |
| VII. | | Discussion Question | 518 |

## CHAPTER 7: Plant Varieties

| | | |
|---|---|---|
| I. | Introduction | 519 |
| II. | The Application Process | 523 |

III.    Scope and Duration of Rights ............................................ 523
IV.    Infringement and Remedies ............................................... 525
V.    Discussion Questions ...................................................... 525

**CHAPTER 8: Integrated Circuit Topographies**

I.    *Integrated Circuit Topography Act* ...................................... 527
II.    Discussion Question ...................................................... 528

**CHAPTER 9: International Intellectual Property**

I.    Substantive Instruments .................................................. 530
    1.    The Paris Convention ............................................. 532
    2.    The Berne Convention ............................................ 536
    3.    The Rome Convention (1961) ...................................... 539
    4.    The TRIPS Agreement ............................................. 540
        (a)    History ....................................................... 540
        (b)    The Logic of the TRIPS Agreement ..................... 545
        (c)    TRIPS Dispute-Settlement ............................... 547
        (d)    The Substantive Content of TRIPS ...................... 547
        (e)    General Provisions ......................................... 548
        (f)    Copyright ................................................... 548
        (g)    Trade-Marks ............................................... 549
        (h)    Geographical Indications ................................. 550
        (i)    Industrial Designs ........................................ 551
        (j)    Patents ..................................................... 551
        (k)    Integrated Circuits ....................................... 553
        (l)    Undisclosed Information ................................. 553
        (m)    Enforcement ............................................... 554
        (n)    Protection of Existing Subject-Matter .................. 555
    5.    NAFTA ........................................................... 556
    6.    The WIPO Treaties .............................................. 557
II.    Other Instruments ....................................................... 560
III.    The Role of Intellectual Property Treaties in Domestic Law ........ 562
IV.    Discussion Questions ..................................................... 573

**CHAPTER 10: Intellectual Property Overlaps**

I.    Copyright and Trade-Marks and Protection of Image ............... 576
    1.    Fictional Characters .............................................. 576
        (a)    Copyright Protection for Fictional Characters .......... 577
        (b)    Copyright and Trade-Mark Convergence .............. 579
    2.    The Tort of Misappropriation of Personality ................... 581
II.    Copyright and Industrial Designs ....................................... 590
III.    Copyright and Topographies ............................................ 597
IV.    Patents and Copyright ................................................... 597
V.    Trade-Marks and Industrial Designs .................................... 600

VI.   Patents and Trade-Marks ................................................... 604
VII.  Discussion Questions ....................................................... 614

**INDEX** .............................................................................. 625

# *Chapter* 1: Introduction to Intellectual Property: Philosophies, Policies and History

I. Justifying Intellectual Property

II. Theories of Intellectual Property

"Intellectual property" includes creations of the human mind. Intellectual property laws protect works of art and intellect in fields of art and science. Intellectual property is one example of intangible property (although not all intangible property is intellectual property, as for example, derivatives or stock options). Intellectual property protects the intangibles of creativity and innovation, rather than the physical property in which that creativity and innovation is expressed or manifested. The question of whether intellectual property is properly characterized as a kind of "property" is heavily debated. Intellectual property is akin to tangible property in many ways: it can be inherited, used as collateral, allocated in a settlement and treated as an asset in bankruptcy. However, there are two features that distinguish intellectual property from tangible property: it is *non-rivalrous* (meaning numerous people can use the idea at the same time without diminishing other's people enjoyment or ability to use the idea) and *non-exclusive* (meaning an idea cannot be physically limited to one person). Another distinguishing feature for some forms of intellectual property is that the owner has only a limited term "monopoly".

Intellectual property is generally divided into two broad categories, which apply internationally: of copyright and industrial design, and industrial property, including trade-marks, trade-names, geographical indications of source, patents, and confidential information. "Intellectual Property" is defined in s. 2(viii) of the Convention Establishing the World Intellectual Property Organization (WIPO) (which Canada ratified effective June 26, 1970) as follows:

> intellectual property" shall include the rights relating to:
>
> - literary, artistic and scientific works,
> - performances of performing artists, phonograms, and broadcasts,
> - inventions in all fields of human endeavour,
> - scientific discoveries, . . .
> - industrial designs,
> - trademarks, service marks, and commercial names and designations,
> - protection against unfair competition,

and all other rights resulting from intellectual activity in the industrial, scientific, literary or artistic fields.

In Canada, in addition to the *Copyright Act, Trade-marks Act and Patent Act,* other intellectual property statutes provide protection for industrial design, integrated circuit topographies and plant breed varieties. Intellectual property can also be legally protected through other laws such as torts (*e.g.,* misappropriation of personality, invasion of privacy), competition law, criminal law, and contracts.

Briefly, *copyright* protects artistic, dramatic, musical, architectural, and literary (including computer programs) original works. Related (or "neighbouring") rights include rights for performances, sound recordings, and communication signals. *Industrial design* protects original, visually appealing, aesthetic designs applied to useful articles. *Trade-marks and trade-names* protect marks (words and/or symbols) used to indicate the source of a good or service. *Patents* protect new, useful, non-obvious inventions and improvements.

## I. JUSTIFYING INTELLECTUAL PROPERTY

Consider a person who first comes up with a brilliant idea. Why should or shouldn't that person reap the reward of that idea? The pros and cons for this question arise from the peculiar characteristics of intellectual property as "non-rivalrous" and "non-exclusive." Thomas Jefferson's description of these qualities is one of the most famous:

> no one possesses the less, because every other posses the whole of it. He who receives an idea from me, receives instruction himself without lessening mine; as he who lites his taper at mine, receives light without darkening me. That ideas should freely spread from one to another over the globe, for the moral and mutual instruction of man, and improvement of his conditions, seems to have been peculiarly and benevolently designed by nature, when she made them, like fire expansible over all space, without lessening their density at any point, and like the air in which we breathe, move, and have our physical being; incapable of confinement or exclusive appropriation. Inventions then cannot, in nature, be a subject of property.[1]

"In nature," it is true, as Jefferson wrote, that intellectual property cannot be the subject of "property." Creativity and invention cannot be physically fenced in to exclude others and to limit the idea to the person who first thought of it, as such intangibles are "non-rivalrous" and "non-

---

[1] Thomas Jefferson, letter to Isaac McPherson, Monticello, August 13, 1813.

exclusive." These characteristics hold true, however, with respect to consumption but not with respect to the economic ability to exploit and profit from an idea. An infinite number of people can use an idea at the same time but an infinite number of people cannot all profit from the idea at the same time. An advantage of intellectual property, unlike physical property, is that we all can use an idea at the same time. Why then would the legal system not continue to allow full access to an idea by everyone at the same time? Why have statutes which grant the owner of intellectual property a legal right to exclude others, if in nature (without positive laws) we could all use the idea at the same time?

Since the inventor or creator of intellectual property cannot physically exclude people from an idea, without intellectual property statutes a next best way for a person to try to protect that intellectual property is to hide and hoard it. However, this is not a desirable result. From the creator's perspective, while hiding and hoarding an idea would keep others away from the ideas, it would limit the inventor's ability to profit and be rewarded for the idea if it could not be circulated. From society's perspective, hiding and hoarding by the creator is disadvantageous because the public would not learn of the idea and could not in turn build on it to make other creative expressions or inventive improvements. From a larger public policy perspective, hence, intellectual property laws seek to promote the dissemination and circulation of ideas by giving the creator some control over the ideas without having to resort to hiding and hoarding them; intellectual property laws provide rights in the intangibles which the "natural" non-rivalrous and non-exclusive qualities of intellectual property otherwise make difficult to protect. By rewarding inventors and creators, intellectual property rights provide an incentive to create and invent and, in turn, by encouraging the circulation of that intellectual production, increase the pool of human intellectual creations.

The balancing for intellectual property is a tricky one. The ideal is to protect intellectual property so people will create and disclose their ideas, but not over-protect it so that other people are prevented from accessing and building on those ideas and creating new ideas based on the inspiration of others. The Supreme Court has spoken of this "balancing" frequently in recent intellectual property cases, "between promoting the public interest in the encouragement and dissemination of works of the arts and intellect and obtaining a just reward for the creator (or, more accurately, to prevent someone other than the creator from appropriating whatever benefits may be generated)."[2]

---

[2] *Galerie d'Art du Petit Champlain inc. v. Théberge*, [2002] 2 S.C.R. 336, (sub nom. *Théberge v. Galerie d'Art du Petit Champlain inc.*) 210 D.L.R. (4th) 385, (sub nom. *Théberge v. Galerie d'Art du Petit Champlain inc.*) 17 C.P.R. (4th)

The *public domain* is the name given to the area that is free for the public to use and access. The public domain includes any aspect that is not protected by the intellectual property regime (for example, facts cannot be copyrighted) and all those rights that were covered by intellectual property but where the limited term monopoly has expired. The public domain is an important aspect of the production and dissemination of creativity and innovation. Creativity and innovation are built on the efforts of those who came before. Creators and users are not two mutually exclusive groups; instead all "creators" are "users" of other people's ideas and original work. The idea behind the public domain is that access to intellectual activity helps to create more intellectual activity. As the Supreme Court warned in *Théberge*, "Excessive control by holders of copyrights and other forms of intellectual property may unduly limit the ability of the public domain to incorporate and embellish creative innovation in the long-term interests of society as a whole, or create practical obstacles to proper utilization."[3]

## II. THEORIES OF INTELLECTUAL PROPERTY

A general description of intellectual property law would say it functions as an incentive and reward. But intellectual property theories emphasize these objectives in different ways. While there are numerous justifications for intellectual property, two main theories can be identified. Labour theory, based on John Locke's philosophy of property, has been a heavy influence on common law jurisdictions. Personality theory, based on Georg Hegel's philosophy, has been prominent in civil law jurisdictions. From a very broad perspective, labour theory posits that intellectual property is a *reward* for hard work (since work is less fun in general than playing on the beach) and an *incentive* for work (utilitarian theory). A variation of this labour theory is a "value-added" theory in which intellectual property rights are justified when labour produces something of value to others (so intellectual property rights are deserved only if an idea is worthwhile from society's perspective (in the short- or long-term)). The labour theory is based on the idea that without intellectual property protection, fewer people will devote their efforts to intellectual activities because they need the enticement and reward of the legal protection. Personality theory, by contrast, views original ideas and expression as an integral part of the creator's identity and essential to people's development. Intellectual property rights, under this view, are not positive rights that are granted by government but natural rights that arise

---

161, (sub nom. *Théberge v. Galerie d'art du Petit Champlain inc.*) 285 N.R. 267, 23 B.L.R. (3d) 1 (S.C.C.), at para 30, [*Théberge* cited to S.C.R.].

[3]   *Ibid.* at para 32

from the creator's individual relationship with the idea and which cannot be alienated from the creator without her permission.

Common law jurisdictions tend to emphasize the utilitarian or social dimensions of intellectual property while civil law jurisdictions tend to emphasize creative work as an extension of the author's personality and to provide extensive protections (especially with respect to copyright). But, the idea of ensuring that people have protection for their own intellectual creations but also access to other people's intellectual creations is integral to both continental and common law systems. For example, under the *Universal Declaration of Human Rights*, "everyone has the right to the protection of the moral and material interests resulting from any scientific, literary or artistic production of which he is the author" *and* "everyone has the right freely to participate in the cultural life of the community to enjoy the arts and to share in the scientific advancement and its benefits."[4] As these goals recognize, it is in the public interest to protect and encourage creation and to protect and permit access to creation. Ideally, intellectual property laws do both.

---

[4] United Nations, Universal Declaration of Human Rights, 10 December 1948, Article 27.

# *Chapter* 2: Copyright

I. Introduction

II. Work

III. Ownership

IV. Assignment/Transfer of Copyright

V. Terms of Protection

VI. Infringement

VII. Copyright Registration

VIII. Related Rights

IX. Collective Management

X. Points of Attachment and Foreign Works

XI. Database Protection

XII. Discussion Questions

## I. INTRODUCTION

Copyright is of federal competence according to s. 91(23) of the *Constitution Act, 1867*.[1] Initially, the *Copyright Act of the United Kingdom* applied in Canada. Canada's first complete code of copyright law in Canada, which substantially followed English copyright legislation, was enacted in 1921 and came into force three years later.[2] Canada's *Copyright Act* regulates copyright in Canada today.[3] In one of the most famous passages on copyright law, Justice Estey described copyright in *Compo Co. v. Blue Crest Music Inc.* as:

> [N]either tort law nor property law in classification, but is statutory law. It neither cuts across existing rights in property or conduct, nor falls between rights and obligations heretofore existing in the common law. Copyright legislation simply creates rights and obligations upon the terms and in the circum-

---

[1] *Constitution Act, 1867* (U.K.), 30 & 31 Vict., c. 3, reprinted in R.S.C. 1985, App. II, No.5.

[2] *Canadian Copyright Act*, S.C. 1921, c. 24.

[3] *Copyright Act*, R.S.C. 1985, c. C-42, online: Department of Justice Canada <http://laws.justice.gc.ca/en/C-42/index.html> [*Act*].

stances set out in the statute. This creature of statute has been known to the law of England at least since the days of Queen Anne when the first copyright statute was passed. It does not assist the interpretative analysis to import tort concepts. The legislation speaks for itself and the actions of the appellant must be measured according to the terms of the statute.[4]

As the Supreme Court of Canada said in *Bishop v. Stevens*,[5] this federal legislation alone controls copyright: ". . . copyright law is purely statutory law, which 'simply creates rights and obligations upon the terms and in the circumstances set out in the statute'."[6]

Justice Binnie returned to this principle in *Galerie d'art du Petit Champlain inc. v. Théberge*: "Copyright in this country is a creature of statute and the rights and remedies it provides are exhaustive."[7] Copyright derives from positive rather than natural law and there is no common law copyright in Canada.[8]

A substantial revision of the Canadian copyright legislation is ongoing in a three-phase process. The 1924 *Act* was significantly modified in 1988 with amendments addressing the protection of computer programs and choreographic works (Phase I). Subsequently, the act was amended to comply with obligations under *NAFTA* and the *TRIPS Agreement* (see the International Section). The *Act* was further amended in 1997 (Phase II). Phase III, focusing on digital copyright issues, is currently being considered.[8a]

In the *Copyright Act*, two types of rights are protected: economic rights and so-called "moral" rights. The economic rights are contained in section 3 of the *Act* and moral rights are found in section 14.1.

3. (1) For the purposes of this Act, "copyright", in relation to a work, means the sole right to produce or reproduce the work or any substantial part thereof

---

[4] *Compo Co. v. Blue Crest Music Inc.* (1979), [1980] 1 S.C.R. 357, 105 D.L.R. (3d) 249, 45 C.P.R. (2d) 1, (sub nom. *Blue Crest Music Inc. v. Compo Co.*) 29 N.R. 296 (S.C.C.) at 372-373 [*Compo* cited to S.C.R.].

[5] *Bishop v. Stevens*, [1990] 2 S.C.R. 467, 72 D.L.R. (4th) 97, 31 C.P.R. (3d) 394 (S.C.C.) [*Bishop v. Stevens* cited to S.C.R.].

[6] *Ibid.* at 477. See also *Compo, supra*, note 4. This principle is reinforced by s. 89 of the *Act*, which states that "no person is entitled to copyright otherwise than under and in accordance with this Act".

[7] [2002] 2 S.C.R. 336, (sub nom. *Théberge v. Galerie d'Art du Petit Champlain inc.*) 210 D.L.R. (4th) 385, (sub nom. *Théberge v. Galerie d'Art du Petit Champlain inc.*) 17 C.P.R. (4th) 161, (sub nom. *Théberge v. Galerie d'art du Petit Champlain inc.*) 285 N.R. 267 (S.C.C.) at 338, [*Théberge* cited to S.C.R.].

[8] *Act, supra*, note 3, s. 89.

[8a] Bill C-60, tabled in the House of Commons on June 20, 2005, purports to implement changes designed to adopt the Act to the Internet era.

in any material form whatever, to perform the work or any substantial part thereof in public or, if the work is unpublished, to publish the work or any substantial part thereof, and includes the sole right

a)   to produce, reproduce, perform or publish any translation of the work,
b)   in the case of a dramatic work, to convert it into a novel or other non-dramatic work,
c)   in the case of a novel or other non-dramatic work, or of an artistic work, to convert it into a dramatic work, by way of performance in public or otherwise,
d)   in the case of a literary, dramatic or musical work, to make any sound recording, cinematograph film or other contrivance by means of which the work may be mechanically reproduced or performed,
e)   in the case of any literary, dramatic, musical or artistic work, to reproduce, adapt and publicly present the work as a cinematographic work,
f)   in the case of any literary, dramatic, musical or artistic work, to communicate the work to the public by telecommunication,
g)   to present at a public exhibition, for a purpose other than sale or hire, an artistic work created after June 7, 1998, other than a map, chart or plan,
h)   in the case of a computer program that can be reproduced in the ordinary course of its use, other than by a reproduction during its execution in conjunction with a machine, device or computer, to rent out the computer program, and
i)   in the case of a musical work, to rent out a sound recording in which the work is embodied,

and to authorize any such acts.

14.1 (1) The author of a work has, subject to section 28.2, the right to the integrity of the work and, in connection with an act mentioned in section 3, the right, where reasonable in the circumstances, to be associated with the work as its author by name or under a pseudonym and the right to remain anonymous.

These two types of rights will be discussed further in greater detail.

Because the *Copyright Act* is the sole source of copyright in Canada, foreign precedents should be used with caution, including those of the United States.[9] In *Compo*, the Supreme Court wrote:

The United States *Copyright Act*, both in its present and earlier forms, has, of course, many similarities to the Canadian Act, as well as to the pre-existing Imperial *Copyright Act*. However, United States court decisions, even where the factual situations are similar, must be scrutinized very carefully because of

---

[9]   The United States became party to the Berne Convention (see the *International* section) in 1989. See also *Bishop v. Stevens, supra*, note 5.

some fundamental differences in copyright concepts which have been adopted in the legislation of that country. The United States statutes have not been based upon the international copyright treaties of the 19th and 20th centuries, being the Berne Convention of 1886 and the Rome Copyright Convention of 1928, as the United States of America did not become signatories thereto. Indeed it was not until the adoption by that country in 1955 of the Universal Copyright Convention of 1952 that the United States participated in the field of international copyright law other than by a collection of bilateral agreements.[10]

However,

This is not to say that Canadian copyright law lives in splendid isolation from the rest of the world. Canada has adhered to the *Berne Convention for the Protection of Literary and Artistic Works* (1886) and subsequent revisions and additions, and other international treaties on the subject including the *Universal Copyright Convention* (1952). . . . In light of the globalization of the so-called 'cultural industries', it is desirable, within the limits permitted by our own legislation, to harmonize our interpretation of copyright protection with other like-minded jurisdictions. That being said, there are some continuing conceptual differences between the *droit d'auteur* of the continental *civiliste* tradition and the English copyright tradition, and these differences seem to lie at the root of the misunderstanding which gave rise to the present appeal.[11]

## 1. Common and Civil Law Traditions and Copyright

Copyright in Canada has been fed by two streams. It is inspired by and derived from English traditions of economic rights, and influenced by civil law traditions with the inclusion of moral rights.

Economic rights are commonly more strongly associated with the English "copyright" tradition, and moral rights with the "*droit d'auteur*" civil law tradition. Justice Binnie, for the majority in *Théberge*, characterized these two traditions as follows:

Moral rights, by contrast, descend from the civil law tradition. They adopt a more elevated and less dollars and cents view of the relationship between an artist and his or her work. They treat the artist's *oeuvre* as an extension of his or her personality, possessing a dignity which is deserving of protection. They focus on the artist's right (which by s. 14.1(2) is not assignable, though it may be waived) to protect throughout the duration of the economic rights (even

---

[10] *Supra* note 4 at 367.
[11] *Théberge, supra,* note 7 at 345-46.

where these have been assigned elsewhere) both the integrity of the work and his or her authorship of it (or anonymity, as the author wishes).[12]

[. . .]

It is not altogether helpful that in the French and English versions of the Act the terms 'copyright' and '*droit d'auteur*' are treated as equivalent. While the notion of 'copyright' has historically been associated with economic rights in common law jurisdictions, the term '*droit d'auteur*' is the venerable French term that embraces a bundle of rights which include elements of both economic rights and moral rights. As Professor Strowel observes:

> [TRANSLATION] The expressions 'droit d'auteur' and 'copyright' speak volumes in themselves. It has been pointed out that the distinction between the copyright tradition and the 'droit d'auteur' tradition is based on a question of terminology: where the followers of the first tradition, the British and their spiritual heirs, talk about 'copyright' to refer to a right that derives from the existence of a 'copy,' an object in itself, the followers of the second tradition talk about 'author's right' (droit d'auteur) to refer to a right that stems from intellectual effort or activity brought to bear by an author, a creator. This is the fundamental difference: on the one hand, a right that is conceived of by reference to the author, the creative person, and, on the other, by reference to the copy of the work, the product of the creative activity that is protected against copying.

> (A. Strowel, *Droit d'auteur et copyright: Divergences et convergences: Étude de droit comparé* (1993) at pp. 19-20.)[13]

Continuing conceptual differences between the "*droit d'auteur*" of the continental *civiliste* tradition and the English copyright tradition exist. There is a tension between a natural law idea that views copyright as affirming pre-existing rights that authors have in their work and emphasizes the work as an intrinsic part of the author's personality, and a system based on the idea that copyright consists only of statutory rights and emphasizes economic rights. While the Canadian copyright legislation includes both economic and moral rights, recent Supreme Court jurisprudence has

> stressed the importance placed on the economic aspects of copyright in Canada: the *Copyright Act* deals with copyright primarily as a system designed to organize the economic management of intellectual property, and regards cop-

---

[12] *Ibid.* at 348.
[13] *Ibid.* at 367.

yright primarily as a mechanism for protecting and transmitting the economic values associated with this type of property and with the use of it.[14]

In Canada, the *Copyright Act* both creates and is definitive of rights. Copyright consists only of what is in the statute. *General* natural law or common law principles do not define the scope of copyright. To refer again to Justice Estey's words in *Compo*: "[C]opyright law . . . is statutory law. . . . Copyright legislation simply creates rights and obligations upon the terms and circumstances set out in the statute."

## 2. Copyright Philosophy and the Idea of "Balance"

In recent cases, the Supreme Court of Canada has been emphasizing that under this statutory scheme, copyright conceptually is about both authors' and users' rights and the balance between them. The Court has stressed that copyright "exceptions" *are* "users' rights" and "perhaps more properly understood as an integral part of the *Copyright Act* than simply a defence" or as mere "loopholes."[15]

In *Théberge*, and most recently in *CCH*, the Supreme Court of Canada has spoken of the dual objectives of copyright. The philosophy of copyright in Canada was set forth extensively in *Théberge*, where the Supreme Court of Canada described the important idea of "balance" in copyright.[16]

> The *Copyright Act* is usually presented as a balance between promoting the public interest in the encouragement and dissemination of works of the arts and intellect and obtaining a just reward for the creator (or, more accurately, to prevent someone other than the creator from appropriating whatever benefits may be generated).
>
> [. . .]
>
> The proper balance among these and other public policy objectives lies not only in recognizing the creator's rights but in giving due weight to their limited nature. In crassly economic terms it would be as inefficient to overcompensate artists and authors for the right of reproduction as it would be self-defeating to

---

[14] *Éditions Chouette (1987) inc. v. Despeuteaux*, [2003] 1 S.C.R. 178, 223 D.L.R. (4th) 407, 23 C.P.R. (4th) 417, 301 N.R. 220 (S.C.C.) at 215 [S.C.R.] and see *Théberge, supra* note 7 at 347-48.

[15] *CCH Canadian Ltd. v. Law Society of Upper Canada*, [2004] 1 S.C.R. 339, 236 D.L.R. (4th) 395, 30 C.P.R. (4th) 1, 317 N.R. 107 (S.C.C.) at 364-65 [*CCH* cited to S.C.R.].

[16] While *Théberge, supra*, note 7, was a 4-3 decision, its main findings on the philosophy of copyright law were confirmed by the Court in its unanimous decision in *CCH*.

undercompensate them. Once an authorized copy of a work is sold to a member of the public, it is generally for the purchaser, not the author, to determine what happens to it.

Excessive control by holders of copyrights and other forms of intellectual property may unduly limit the ability of the public domain to incorporate and embellish creative innovation in the long-term interests of society as a whole, or create practical obstacles to proper utilization.[17]

With respect to the difficulty of striking a balance for digital copyright, the Supreme Court has recently stated that the "capacity of the Internet to disseminate 'works of the arts and the intellect' is one of the great innovations of the information age," and that while the use of the Internet "should be facilitated rather than discouraged," this "should not be done unfairly at the expense of those who created the works of arts and intellect in the first place."[18]

## II. WORK

### 1. "Work"

Copyright protects "every original literary, dramatic, musical and artistic work" (s. 3(1), s. 2, s. 5(1)). Economic and moral rights under ss. 3 and 14 of the Act are defined in relation to a "work." The word "work" as it is defined in s. 2 of the Act includes every original production in the literary, scientific or artistic domain, whatever may be the mode or form of its expression. The Act also describes each of these types of works:

'artistic work' includes paintings, drawings, maps, charts, plans, photographs, engravings, sculptures, works of artistic craftsmanship, architectural works, and compilations of artistic works;

'dramatic work' includes
a)    any piece for recitation, choreographic work or mime, the scenic arrangement or acting form of which is fixed in writing or otherwise,
b)    any cinematographic work, and
c)    any compilation of dramatic works;

---

[17] *Théberge, supra*, note 7 at 355-56, retaken in *CCH, supra*, note 15 at 349-50.
[18] *Society of Composers, Authors & Music Publishers of Canada v. Canadian Assn. of Internet Providers*, [2004] 2 S.C.R. 427, (sub nom. *SOCAN v. Canadian Assn. of Internet Providers*) 240 D.L.R. (4th) 193, (sub nom. *SOCAN v. Canadian Assn. of Internet Providers*) 32 C.P.R. (4th) 1, 322 N.R. 306 (S.C.C.) at 448-49 [*SOCAN* cited to S.C.R.].

'literary work' includes tables, computer programs, and compilations of literary works;

'musical work' means any work of music or musical composition, with or without words, and includes any compilation thereof;

The key word in this definition is "original" and it has been the subject of many debates. It should first be noted that a work does not have to be published in order to be the subject of copyright. Published or not, an original work is protected under copyright law.

## 2. "Fixation"

Fixation is an important concept and similarly has been the subject of much controversy in the case law. Two seminal cases turned on the interpretation of fixation. In *Gould Estate v. Stoddart Publishing Co.*, the Ontario Court of Appeal held that oral statements made by Glenn Gould could not be protected by copyright.[19] His oral speech was not protected by copyright because, as the judges ruled, there was no fixation. Oral works can be the subject of copyright if they are fixed. However, where a speech is fixed, the person who orally speaks it may not be the author for purposes of copyright. In *Hager v. ECW Press Ltd.*, an oral interview was written down by the interviewer.[20] The court determined that there was copyright in the written interview, but it belonged to the interviewer, since that person was responsible for the fixation of the text. That rule is subject to fulfilling the originality requirement as defined in *CCH*. A mechanical transcription of a speech or words of an interviewee generally does not qualify for copyright protection (see the Originality Section below). Informal speeches and comments are not subject to copyright, but if it is properly recorded (fixed), a structured lecture or dictation could be.[21] To quote Lederman J. in *Gould*:

> The conversation between the two men was the kind that Gould would have with a friend. Indeed Gould and Carroll remained friends for a short while afterwards. Gould was not delivering a structured lecture or dictating to Carroll. Rather, Carroll engaged Gould in easygoing conversation out of which emerged comments which provided insights into Gould's character and personal life. Gould was making offhand comments that he knew could find their way into

[19] (1998), 39 O.R. (3d) 545, 161 D.L.R. (4th) 321, 80 C.P.R. (3d) 161 (Ont. C.A.), leave to appeal refused (1999), 82 C.P.R. (3d) vi (S.C.C.), affirming (1996), 30 O.R. (3d) 520, 74 C.P.R. (3d) 206 (Ont. Gen. Div.) [*Gould* (C.A.) cited to O.R.].
[20] (1998), [1999] 2 F.C. 287, 85 C.P.R. (3d) 289 (Fed.T.D.) [*Hager* cited to F.C.].
[21] See *Gould, supra,* note 19.

the public domain. This is not the kind of discourse which the Copyright Act intended to protect.[22]

The "fixation" notion was further clarified in *Canadian Admiral Corp. v. Rediffusion*, where the judge indicated the test for fixation: "a work must be expressed to some extent at least in some material form and having a more or less permanent endurance."[23]

However, music can be protected even if unfixed. The definition of "musical work" was modified in 1993.[24] Prior to 1993, a musical work had to be "printed, reduced to writing or otherwise graphically produced or reproduced."[25] This clearly required that music be fixed. The 1993 definition refers to any work of music or musical composition, with or without words. While the fixation requirement is not expressly excluded, this seems to be the intended result. In addition, under s. 15(1) a performer's performance of music is specifically protected even if unfixed. It would be strange that performers would receive a higher degree of protection than the author of the underlying musical work, because of the historical hierarchical "superiority" of copyright (as defined in ss. 3 and 14.1) over "neighbouring rights," including the rights of performers. This hierarchy is embodied in Article 1 of the 1961 *Rome Convention* (see the International section) and, to a certain extent at least, in s. 90 of the Act.[26]

Although the terminology used in the Act is not very clear, the test for fixation is to determine objectively if the work stayed somewhere long enough to have sunk into the mind of "recipients" (viewers, listeners, readers etc.). The rule appears to be not so much doctrinal in nature as the expression of obvious evidentiary difficulties in proving rights in, and infringement of, unfixed works.

### 3. Ideas versus Expression

Copyright protects expression and does not extend to protect ideas. Article 9(2) of the *TRIPS Agreement* (see the *International* section) incorporates this distinction. The *TRIPS* definition of the scope of copyright extends protection to "expression" (*i.e*, a form of expression covered under

---

[22] *Gould* (Ont. Gen. Div.), *supra* note 19, at 529-30.

[23] [1954] Ex. C.R. 382, 20 C.P.R. 75 (Can. Ex. Ct.) at 396 [*Rediffusion* cited to Ex. C.R.].

[24] *Copyright Act*, S.C. 1993, c. 23, s. 1(1).

[25] *Copyright Act*, *supra*, note 3, s. 2.

[26] Which was added to the *Act* by *An Act to Amend the Copyright Act*, S.C. 1997, c. 24, s. 90, together with the bulk of the new "neighbouring rights."

the definition of literary and artistic work) but specifically *excludes* "ideas, procedures, methods of operation or mathematical concepts."[27]

The case law gives more information on the subtleties of this distinction. For example, in *Moreau v. St. Vincent*, the plaintiff developed a system to distribute crossword puzzles to subscribers.[28] The defendant created new crossword puzzles with the same information as the plaintiff. In denying the plaintiff copyright in the system itself, the court emphasized the "elementary principle of copyright law that an author has no copyright in ideas but only in his expression of them. The law of copyright does not give him any monopoly in the use of the ideas with which he deals or any property in them."[29] There is no property in the use of ideas in a system or arrangement even if original: "[h]is copyright is confined to the literary work in which he has expressed them... [T]he plaintiff was attempting to protect the arrangement or system for conducting a competition that he said he had devised."[30] The plaintiff was entitled to copyright in the literary work in the article or writing, but not in the system described by that literary work.

Another example is found in *Fletcher v. Polka Dot Fabrics Ltd.* where the plaintiff designed patterns for cloth diapers called "Snappy Nappy."[31] The plaintiff argued that the defendant had copied the plaintiff's idea of putting a picture on diapers. The court determined that the idea of putting a drawing on a diaper was not protected but that the actual drawing used was protected by copyright. One of the best examples of this distinction is a recipe book. Copyright applies to the recipe as it is written but the idea of using one ingredient instead of another is not protected by copyright.

## 4. Originality

Originality is another, and perhaps the most important, foundational concept of copyright. If the work is "original" and there is "fixation" (where it is required), then a work is copyright protected. However, interestingly the Act does not define originality as such.

Courts faced both a qualitative and quantitative conundrum with respect to setting a threshold standard for originality. With respect to quality, if the

---

[27] *Agreement Establishing the World Trade Organization, Annex 1C: Agreement on Trade-Related Aspects of Intellectual Property Rights*, 15 April 1994, 1869 U.N.T.S. 299, online: WTO <http://www.wto.org/english/docs_e/legal_e/27-trips_01_e.htm> [*TRIPS* or *TRIPS Agreement*].

[28] [1950] Ex. C.R. 198, [1950] 3 D.L.R. 713, 12 C.P.R. 32 (Can. Ex. Ct.) [*Moreau* cited to Ex. C.R.].

[29] *Ibid.* at 203

[30] *Ibid.* at 203-04.

[31] (1993), 51 C.P.R. (3d) 241 (Ont. Small Cl. Ct.).

courts fixed the standard at the low end of the continuum, *any* writing, no matter how trivial, could be copyrighted such as gum wrappers, non-creative basic business templates or facts. If the courts fixed the standard at the high end of a quality continuum, courts would have to act as aesthetic arbiters to decide which expression is of a sufficiently high quality. With respect to quantity, if the courts again fixed the standard at the low end of the continuum, one letter or one word or one line could conceivably be copyrighted, which could limit other people's access to basic expressive building blocks. If the courts fixed the standard at the high end of the quantitative continuum, novels and encyclopaedias could be copyrighted, but short original expressions such as haiku could not.

Prior to 2004, two main theories of originality could be found in Canadian jurisprudence. The first, based on the UK case of *University of London Press v. University Tutorial Press Ltd.*, which dealt with the protection of exam questions, applied a theory which became known as the theory of "skill, labour and judgment".[32] As the name indicates, it required that a work manifest some "labour" and a minimum degree of skill or judgment on the part of the author. Originality "does not require that the expression must be in an original or novel form, but that the work must not be copied from another work."[33] However, even statistical tables, factual collections of data, routine exam questions or even accounting forms could be protected under this theory because there was no requirement for "creative" input under this test. As a logical corollary, a work copied from someone else would not be considered original under this theory because the labour was not the author's. In broad terms, this theory tended to protect against the misappropriation of one's work. The *London Press* view was present in a number of Canadian cases, though rarely the subject of a serious discussion.

For example, in *Kantel v. Grant*,[34] the judge interpreted originality to emphasize this sense that a work must "originate from" the author, rather than be original in the sense of "novel":

> The word 'original' does not in this connection mean that the work must be the expression of original or inventive thought. Copyright Acts are not concerned with ideas or the originality of ideas — in which there is no copyright; it is the language in which the idea is expressed which is the only thing protected, and it is that to which 'original' in the Act relates; the Act does not require that the expression must be in an original or novel form, but that the

---

[32] *University of London Press v. University Tutorial Press Ltd.*, [1916] 2 Ch. 601(Eng. Ch. Div.) [*London Press*].

[33] *Ibid.* at 608-609.

[34] [1933] Ex. C.R. 84 (Can. Ex. Ct.) [*Kantel*].

work must not be copied from another work — that it should originate from the author.[35]

The second theory for originality is that copyright requires a modicum of creativity. This theory was partly adopted in two decisions of the Federal Court of Appeal, namely *Tele-Direct (Publications) Inc. v. American Business Information Inc.*[36] and *Édutile Inc. v. Automobile Protection Assn. (APA).*[37] In *Tele-Direct*, which dealt with the protection of telephone directories, Décary J.A. wrote the following:

> [F]or a compilation of data to be original, it must be a work that was independently created by the author and which displays at least a minimal degree of skill, judgment and labour in its overall selection or arrangement. The threshold is low, but it does exist. If it were otherwise, all types of selections or arrangements would automatically qualify, for they all imply some degree of intellectual effort, and yet the Act is clear: only those works which are original are protected. There can therefore be compilations that do not meet the test.
> [. . .]
>
> It is true that in many of the cases we have been referred to, the expression 'skill, judgment *or* labour' has been used to describe the test to be met by a compilation in order to qualify as original and, therefore, to be worthy of copyright protection. It seems to me, however, that whenever 'or' was used instead of 'and', it was in a conjunctive rather than in a disjunctive way. It is doubtful that considerable labour combined with a negligible degree of skill and judgment will be sufficient in most situations to make a compilation of data original. One should always keep in mind that one of the purposes of the copyright legislation, historically, has been 'to protect and reward the *intellectual* effort of the *author* (for a limited period of time) in the work'. . . . The use of the word 'copyright' in the English version of the Act has obscured the fact that what the Act fundamentally seeks to protect is 'le droit d'auteur'. While not defined in the Act, *the word 'author' conveys a sense of creativity and ingenuity.* (emphasis in original)[38]

---

[35] *Ibid.* at 95.

[36] (1997), [1998] 2 F.C. 22, 154 D.L.R. (4th) 328, 76 C.P.R. (3d) 296, 221 N.R. 113 (Fed. C.A.) [*Tele-Direct* cited to F.C.], leave to appeal to S.C.C. refused (1998), 78 C.P.R. (3d) v (note) (S.C.C.).

[37] [2000] 4 F.C. 195, 188 D.L.R. (4th) 132, 6 C.P.R. (4th) 211 (Fed. C.A.) [*Édutile* cited to F.C.], leave to appeal to S.C.C. refused (2001), 267 N.R. 197 (note) (S.C.C.).

[38] *Tele-Direct, supra,* note 36 at 36-37.

Then the same Court used a somewhat different test for the skill and labour theory in *CCH*.[39] There the majority adopted a "recipe" approach, which allowed originality to be present as various combinations of "ingredients":

> It is widely accepted that an 'original' work must be independently produced and not copied. In attempts to further explain this cornerstone of copyright law, different judges and commentators have described the word 'original' with a host of words and phrases mentioned above, including various combinations of the terms 'labour', 'judgment', 'skill', 'work', 'industry', 'effort', 'taste' or 'discretion'. . . . To me, these are all possible ingredients in the recipe for originality, which may be altered to suit the flavour of the work at issue. Each term may help to determine whether a work is, in fact, original, but it is a mistake to treat any of these words as if they were statutory requirements. These are not, in themselves, prerequisites to copyright protection, but rather evidence of the sole prerequisite, originality. To determine whether or not the materials in issue are 'original' works, a principled and reasoned approach based upon evidence is required, not reliance on a particular word or phrase that merely seeks to explain the concept of originality. Moreover, I am not convinced that a substantial difference exists between an interpretation of originality that requires intellectual effort, whether described as skill, judgment and/or labour or creativity, and an interpretation that merely requires independent production.[40]

*Lifestyle Homes Ltd. v. Randall Homes Ltd.* is one case where the courts expected creativity as a criterion for originality.[41] The plaintiff wanted to protect the architectural plans for an undistinguished "cookie-cutter" house. The Act includes "architectural works" as an "artistic work." The court indicated that for this category a threshold of creativity is required to attract copyright protection.

> There is nothing in either the photos of the plaintiffs' houses or the photos of the defendant's houses that sets them apart from the common stock of ideas or that strikes the eye as uncommon. On the contrary, the designs are of a kind that one sees in great numbers in various cities and towns.[42]

---

[39] [2002] 4 F.C. 213, 212 D.L.R. (4th) 385 (Fed. C.A.) [*CCH* (C.A.) cited to F.C.], leave to appeal allowed (2002), 21 C.P.R. (4th) vi (S.C.C.), reversed [2004] 1 S.C.R. 339 (S.C.C.), additional reasons at (2004), 34 C.P.R. (4th) 1 (F.C.A.).

[40] *Ibid.* at 254-55.

[41] (1991), 70 Man. R. (2d) 124, 34 C.P.R. (3d) 505 (Man. C.A.) [*Lifestyle Homes* cited to Man. R.].

[42] *Ibid.* at para. 69.

Two underlying concerns are at play here. If copyright were extended to banal designs, then any contractor who incorporates these simple architectural elements would be infringing the plans; and, by corollary, a designer who wanted to avoid infringing copyright would have an incentive to design buildings with strange, and potentially unpractical and unliveable design elements.

In *Apple Computer Inc. v. Mackintosh Computers Ltd.*, the Federal Court of Appeal considered that originality depends on the scope that two authors have to exercise creative choice.[43] Thus, if one describes a project and asks two authors to create it and they create (and can only create) the same thing, the result cannot be the subject of copyright since there is no place for interpretation. But, if another person *could* come up with a different way of expressing the same idea, then each author's works (both satisfying the project but using different creative choices) could be copyright protected. Thus, for computer software, as in the *Apple Computer* case, the test would be applied to ask if two different software codes could be written to have a computer perform the same operation.

The interpretation of originality also varies from one country to another. The United States uses the creativity notion, as stated by the U.S. Supreme Court in *Feist Publications Inc. v. Rural Telephone Service Co.*[44] English courts apply the standard from *University of London Press*,[45] requiring that the work not be copied and come from the author. In Australia the concept of originality is even broader, requiring no creativity.[46] Yet, that test has been called into question by a number of more recent decisions[47] and s. 6 of the UK Act now states that only compilations that constitute the "author's own intellectual creation" are protected, a test which seems to be linked to creativity.

[43] (1987), [1988] 1 F.C. 673, 44 D.L.R. (4th) 74, 18 C.P.R. (3d) 129, 81 N.R. 3, 16 C.I.P.R. 15 (Fed. C.A.), varying (1986), [1987] 1 F.C. 173, 28 D.L.R. (4th) 178, 10 C.P.R. (3d) 1, 8 C.I.P.R. 153 (Fed. T.D.), additional reasons at (1987), 12 F.T.R. 287 (Fed. T.D.), affirmed [1990] 2 S.C.R. 209, 71 D.L.R. (4th) 95, 30 C.P.R. (3d) 257, 110 N.R. 66 (S.C.C.) [*Apple Computer* (Fed C.A.) cited to F.C.].
[44] *Feist Publications Inc. v. Rural Telephone Service Co.*, 499 U.S. 340, 111 S.Ct. 1282 (U.S. Kan., 1991) [*Feist*] (*Feist* involved factual compilations. The US Supreme Court ruled that choices about the selection and arrangement of facts can be sufficiently original, "so long as [the choices]. . . are made independently by the compiler and entail a minimal degree of creativity" at 1289).
[45] *Supra*, note 32.
[46] *Telstra Corp. v. Desktop Marketing Systems Pty Ltd.*, [2001] FCA 612, 51 I.P.R. 257 (Australia Fed. Ct.) [*Telstra* cited to I.P.R.].
[47] *Newspaper Licensing Agency Ltd. v. Marks & Spencer plc*, [2001] UKHL 38; [2003] 1 A.C. 551 and *Designers Guild Ltd. v. Russell Williams (Textiles) Ltd.* [2000] 1 WLR 2416; [2001] All E.R. 700 (UKHL).

The U.S. case of *Feist* involved rival telephone directories. The U.S. Supreme Court ruled that facts, such as an individual's telephone number, do not qualify as original for copyright purposes; however, compilations of facts can be original.

> No one may claim originality as to facts. . . . This is because facts do not owe their origin to an act of authorship. The distinction is one between creation and discovery: the first person to find and report a particular fact has not created the fact; he or she has merely discovered its existence. [. . .]

> Factual compilations, on the other hand, may possess the requisite originality. The compilation author typically chooses which facts to include, in what order to place them, and how to arrange the collected data so that they may be used effectively by readers. These choices as to selection and arrangement, so long as they are made independently by the compiler and entail minimal degree of creativity, are sufficiently original that Congress may protect such compilations through the copyright laws.[48]

In *Feist*, the U.S. court found that a basic telephone directory did not meet the required criterion of originality in spite of the amount of work and expense involved in compiling the data and presenting the names, addresses and numbers of subscribers in the usual alphabetical table format.

In Australia, the test established by *Telstra* stated that any work done with some skill, labour or judgment, or "sweat of the brow", to use the American description of the equivalent concept, was an original work protected under copyright, clearly rejecting any requirement of creativity.[49] The Australian court considered and rejected the *Feist* standard of requiring a minimal degree of creativity and instead ruled that copyright protection could be claimed "even if there was no creativity in the selection or arrangement of the data," a standard which the Australian court said was consistent with the English tradition.

### (a) Canada's Middle Way

In reversing the Federal Court of Appeal in *CCH*, a unanimous Supreme Court of Canada ostensibly opted for a third, middle path for the standard of originality. First, the Supreme Court declared that it preferred not to follow American jurisprudence, including the famous *Feist* case of 1991.[50] A first, quick reading of *CCH* might lead one to believe that the "Canadian"

---

[48] *Supra*, note 44 at 1288-89.
[49] *Supra*, note 46. (The High Court denied a motion for leave to appeal.)
[50] *CCH*, *supra*, note 15 at para. 22.

notion of originality is the following: one starts with the "test" of effort and labour (the work originates from the author, without "copying"), but to which test a requirement is added that the effort and labour must be neither mechanical[51] nor trivial.[52] At first glance, therefore, it seems that Canada is now situated between the two standards of sweat of the brow and creativity:

**High test**: Minimum of creativity

**Apparent Canadian test**: Non-mechanical and non-trivial effort and labour

**Low test**: Effort and labour

Why did the Supreme Court reject the criterion of creativity? Because, in the Court's words: "the creativity standard of originality is too high. A creativity standard implies that something must be novel or non-obvious — concepts more properly associated with patent law than copyright law."[53] Novelty and non-obviousness are indeed concepts drawn from patent law. However, it is not clear why the Court drew the conclusion that copyright creativity is equivalent to novelty or non-obviousness. These notions were used neither by the U.S. Supreme Court in *Feist* nor in relevant copyright decisions on originality from civil-law jurisdictions. The Supreme Court of Canada in *CCH* added that a notion of creativity was less practical than its "new" Canadian standard since, it said, "a standard requiring the exercise of skill and judgment in the production of a work avoids these difficulties and provides a workable and appropriate standard for copyright protection."[54] Yet, one could argue that this standard too raises practical problems. How can one prove the *quantity* of an author's work? Why should one? For a telephone directory, the issue is perhaps moot, but would poets or visual artists who create "rapidly" have a more difficult time proving originality under this standard? Would it raise difficult issues of proof if the author has

---

[51] *Ibid.* at para. 16. ("This exercise of skill and judgment will necessarily involve intellectual effort. The exercise of skill and judgment required to produce the work must not be so trivial that it could be characterized as a purely mechanical exercise.") See also para. 25.

[52] *Ibid.* at para. 88.

[53] *Ibid.* at para. 24.

[54] *Ibid.*

died? It may be hard to avoid subjective aspects to any standard of originality, so the choice of standard turns on which criterion is most easily applied and appropriate.

But it seems that the Supreme Court chose a "middle path" only in appearance. *Canada instead has taken on a standard essentially identical to those of our American neighbours and to the Continental systems.* This is clear for at least two reasons. First, the level of originality as defined by the Supreme Court is functionally almost impossible to distinguish from the "modicum of creativity" approach of *Feist*. Indeed, what makes it so that the effort and labour are neither mechanical nor trivial? The answer is precisely the presence of a modicum of creativity.[55]

The *Feist* standard of originality is in fact a "test" that is both easy to use and objective. It consists of measuring the *creative choices* of the author, defined as those that were dictated to the author neither by the eventual function of the work nor by the technique used, nor, in cases where the work is more technical in nature, by the applicable standards or practices. A simple way of conceiving of this "test" is as follows: would another author likely have created the same "work" in the same context? If the answer is yes, the work is of a mechanical or manual nature and there is no originality in the sense of copyright because there is no room for creative choices. If the answer is no, *i.e.*, if it is likely that another author would have reached a substantially different result, it is because there was a creative "space," a possibility to make choices, conscious or not, rational or not, that the first author would not have made, or at least not in the same manner. This is what is said not only in *Feist* but also in the rulings of the French Supreme Court (*Cour de cassation*),[56] which used this test in cases in which

---

[55] See Daniel Gervais, "*Feist* Goes Global: A Comparative Analysis of the Notion of Originality in Copyright Law" (2002) 49 Journal of the Copyright Society of the U.S.A. 949.

[56] A detailed analysis of those cases is presented in the article mentioned in the previous note. To summarize, the traditional originality test in France is that the work must express or reflect the author's personality, a fairly subjective notion to be sure. According to a French commentator, it was normal that such a subjective notion would emerge during the nineteenth century because "the modes of expression then in vogue — sculpture, painting and writings — is . . . the expression of (inner) turmoil ("tourmente") of the author, the emotional, subjective and non-rational aspect of human thought. In a way, what differentiates one work from another is its irrationality, a reflection of the author's own irrational mind." Jean Martin, "Le droit d'auteur applicable au logiciel" in Isabelle de Lamberterie, ed., *Le droit d'auteur aujourd'hui*: ouvrage collectif (Paris: Éditions du Centre National de la Recherche Scientifique,1991) 99 at 111 [translated by authors]. This approach, while understandable for the types of works mentioned (sculpture, writings and painting), does not mesh well with compilations and

a search for the presence of the author's personality became illusory or impossible. Finally, it is also the definition of originality that emerges from work related to the Berne Convention.

Second, the Supreme Court itself placed the standard that it has just set out in *CCH* on the same level as *Feist*. As proof, let us compare the definitions of originality in *Feist* with regard to data compilations and *CCH*:

---

databases. Yet, the protection of several types of compilations has been recognized by French courts: statistical studies (Trib. gr. inst. Paris, 18 January 1989, J. cl. 1989. No. 43760.); comparative tables of television audience ratings (Paris, 22 May 1990, J. cl. 1990. 23057.) or even specialized telephone directories (Paris, 18 December 1924, D.H. 1925, 30) and calendars (Paris, 14 April 1986, J. cl. 1986. 21169.; Somm. 152). The French "Supreme Court" made it clear that labour itself was insufficient (Cass. Civ. 1$^{re}$, 2 May 1989, J.C.P. 1990. II. 21392 (Annot. André Lucas) [*Coprosa*]) and that one had to look at the choice of the method used by the author of the compilation (Cass. crim., 18 May 1938, Gaz. Pal. 1938. II. 311; Cass. civ., 27 May 1942, 1, 124). In fact, recognizing that the classical test could not be used for newer types of works such as databases (compilations) and computer software, several French courts have tried to develop a new test or, more precisely, to elevate the classical test to a higher level of abstraction, by answering the following question: what is it that an author does to show her personality through a work? The fairly unanimous answer given by French courts is that creative choices make the difference. In a case involving a bilingual dictionary, the Court of Appeal of Paris found that "the *choices* and intellectual operations required to create the [dictionary] tend to give the resulting work a certain degree of originality, even when dealing with a technical type of work" (Paris, 21 March 1989, J. cl. 1989. 20923 at 8$^e$ [*Harrap's*] [translated by authors]). In *Harrap's*, the Court made it clear that the fact of sorting data that was difficult to generate in alphabetical order was not original. Originality can only follow from intellectually creative (as opposed to mechanical or dictated by the function or format) choices. A similar conclusion was reached by the same court a few years later concerning a repertory of Cajun words (Paris, 14 January 1992, Gaz. Pal. 1992. Jur. 604238 (Annot. Berenice Berhault).) and in a case involving a compilation of short stories based on traditional folklore (Paris, 23 September 1992, J. cl. 1992. 22611 [*Fayard*].) In *Fayard*, the Court found that "by *choosing* the stories, by narrating them with his own style and by *arranging* them according to a sequence *chosen by him and which was not necessary,* and by giving the book a specific structure, Mr. Guillois created a creative work." (*Ibid.* at 5$^c$.) [authors' translation, emphasis added].

| *Feist* | *CCH* |
|---|---|
| "Factual compilations . . . may possess the requisite originality. The compilation author typically **chooses** which facts to include, in what order to place them, and how to arrange the collected data so that they may be used effectively by readers. These **choices** as to selection and **arrangement**, so long as they are made independently by the compiler and entail a minimal degree of creativity, are sufficiently original that Congress may protect such compilations through the copyright laws."[57] | "Although headnotes are inspired in large part by the judgment which they summarize and refer to, they are clearly not an identical copy of the reasons. The authors must **select** specific elements of the decision and can arrange them in numerous different ways. Making these decisions requires the exercise of skill and judgment. The authors must use their knowledge about the law and developed ability to determine legal *ratios* to produce the headnotes. They must also use their **capacity for discernment** to **decide** which parts of the judgment warrant inclusion in the headnotes. This process is more than just a mechanical exercise."[58] |
| | Even if the summary often contains the same language as the judicial reasons, the act of **choosing** which portions to extract and **how to arrange them** in the summary requires an exercise of skill and judgment.[59] |

In short, the standard established in *Feist*, itself similar to the one current in France and elsewhere in the world with regard to more technical works, is essentially identical to the "new" Canadian standard, in spite of the apparent effort made by the Supreme Court to differentiate itself from foreign jurisprudence. This originality standard is premised on the author's creativity, defined here as non-mechanical and non-trivial effort, skill and labour.

## 5. Literary Works

Section 2 of the Act defines the types of works protected under copyright, and specifies that a "'literary work' includes tables, compilations [of

---

[57] *Supra*, note 44 at 1289 [emphasis added].
[58] *CCH*, *supra*, note 15 at para. 30 [emphasis added].
[59] *Ibid.* at para. 31 [emphasis added].

literary works], . . . [and] computer programs."[60] It is important to remember
that copyright protection applies only to the "expression", not the content
or underlying idea itself.[61] In *Goldner v. Canadian Broadcasting Corp.*, for
example, where the plaintiff wrote three unpublished papers on bowling,
the court stated that a person cannot hold copyright in an arrangement or
method of doing something but only in the expression of the method.[62] Thus
one could hold copyright in a literary work describing the best way to serve
a tennis ball, but that does not in turn give the author a monopoly to exclude
others from practicing their serves by following the method described.

## (a) Quality

Literary merit and quality are not factors when assessing if something
is a literary work.[63] This principle has the admirable result that copyright is
not made contingent on subjective assessments of the aesthetic value of a
particular literary work. Individual authors are not subject to the whims of
taste and judges are not required to be literary critics. The corollary, however, is that copyright is available to protect rather pedestrian and minimally
"literary" works. Contracts,[64] business forms and manuals,[65] menus,[66] and
brochures are "literary works" that are covered by copyright (provided
originality and other copyright requirements are met) just as Ondaatje's *The
English Patient* is a literary work. "Literary," as the House of Lords commented in *Ladbroke*, means something different in copyright law than it
does in everyday language references, and the merit of a work of literature
is not relevant to whether it is copyrightable as a "literary work". The Federal
Court of Canada, ruling on business forms in *Bulman Group Ltd. v. "One
Write" Accounting Systems Ltd.*, explained:

> '[L]iterary' is used in the statute in the sense of written or printed matter, and
> not in some dictionary sense of imparting ideas, information or knowledge.

---

[60] *An Act to Amend the Copyright Act and to Amend other Acts in consequence
thereof*, R.S.C. 1985 (4th Supp.), c. 10, s. 1(2).
[61] Legal protection for ideas may be available under misappropriation or other torts,
and under contract for "ideas", especially for those ideas disclosed in confidence.
[62] (1972), 7 C.P.R. (2d) 158 (Fed. T.D.), leave to appeal refused (1974), 13 C.P.R.
(2d) 230 (Fed. C.A.).
[63] *Ladbroke (Football) Ltd. v. William Hill (Football) Ltd.*, [1964] 1 All E.R. 465
(U.K. H.L.) [*Ladbroke*].
[64] *Arcon Canada Inc. v. Arcobec Aluminium Inc.* (1984), 7 C.P.R. (3d) 382 (Que.
Sup Ct.).
[65] See *Underwriters' Survey Bureau Ltd. v. American Home Fire Assurance Co.*,
[1939] Ex. C.R. 296 (Can. Ex. Ct.) [*Underwriters*].
[66] See *Tomas v. Boaden Catering Ltd.* (1995), 68 C.P.R. (3d) 275 (Fed. T.D.).

But, nevertheless, a mere printing or writing is not sufficient. For copyright to subsist, there must be, in a compilation of the commercial type here, a literary sense of functionally assisting, guiding, or pointing the way to some end.[67]

It should be noted, however, that while the quality of expression is not supposed to be a factor in evaluating whether a work is *copyrightable*, the quality of expression taken from a copyrighted work is a factor that courts consider when evaluating if a copyrighted work has been *infringed*.

### (b) Quantity

Some expression is not eligible for copyright protection because it is too minimal to satisfy the requirements of an "original literary work" under s. 2. In *Exxon Corp. v. Exxon Insurance Consultants International Ltd.*, the plaintiff claimed copyright in the invented work "Exxon," which formed part of the name of three of its companies. The corporation claimed that considerable time and labour was expended in arriving at the name "Exxon" and that even single words could be a literary work under the copyright legislation. The court rejected this claim, reasoning that "[Exxon] is a word which, though invented and therefore original, has no meaning and suggests nothing in itself. To give it substance and meaning, it must be accompanied by other words or used in a particular context or juxtaposition."[68] Copyright protection thus could not be granted for this single word.[69] However, the court suggested in *obiter dictum* that a single word used as a title might be protected by copyright as part of the larger work. Section 2 provides that a copyrightable work includes the title providing that the title is original and distinctive. A person cannot claim a copyright monopoly on individual terms in common use.[70]

### (c) Computer Programs

Computer programs are protected under copyright law as literary works. Section 2 defines computer programs as "a set of instructions or statements, expressed, fixed, embodied or stored in any manner, that is to be used directly or indirectly in a computer in order to bring about a specific result."[71] It is actually the code of a computer program that is protected. The output,

---

[67] (1982), 62 C.P.R. (2d) 149 (Fed. T.D.) at 153.
[68] [1982] 1 Ch. 119 (Eng. C.A.) at 130 [*Exxon*].
[69] *Ibid.*
[70] *Supra*, note 65.
[71] *Supra*, note 3. See text of "Literary works" section above on page 22.

if it takes an original musical or audiovisual form, may be protected as a separate work.

The seminal case on the protection of computer programs as literary works is *Apple Computer*. The findings of Reed J., which were essentially adopted by the Federal Court of Appeal and then by the Supreme Court, rejected the notion that computer programs should not be protected as literary works because they are functional works, sets of instructions designed to make a machine perform a certain task rather than communicate from one person to another. She considered source code, as written by the human programmer to be literary in form even though not meant to communicate an expression to another human being and that the executable (assembly or object) version of the program was a translation of that source code:

> An analogy can be drawn to the conversion of a text into morse code. If a person were to sit down and convert a text into the series of dots and dashes of which morse code is comprised, one might argue that the resultant notations were really instructions to the telegraph operator on how to send the message. But the message written in morse code, in my view, still retains the character of the original work. It is not a different literary work. Similarly, a text written in shorthand might be said to constitute a description of the oral sounds of the text if it were spoken aloud (shorthand being phonetically based), but that would not make it a different literary work from the longhand version.
>
> In my view the conversion of a work into a code, or the conversion of a work originally written in one code into another code constitutes a translation for the purposes of the Act.[72]

### (d) A Note on the Future of Computer Program Protection by Copyright

In Reed J.'s analogy, one should note that Morse Code, although in a different form from the written text (and, there, clearly it is accurate to state that the form does not matter) is still meant to be used in a communication between humans. Computer programs were a form of "expression" not meant to communicate or express anything to humans directly, but rather to make a machine perform its task. This may have an impact on the nature of copyright itself, as it moves away from "creative" expression towards the protection of purely functional works. It may affect, for example, the notion that copyright protects "artists".

The debate surrounding whether computer programs could, and should, be protected under copyright law was settled in part when programs were

---

[72] *Supra*, note 43 at 182.

expressly added to the Act.[73] Computer programs are explicitly listed as a "literary work" in the s. 2 definition. However, the question whether this protection is adequate or sufficient resurfaces regularly; in particular, the protection of computer programs under patent law has become commonplace in certain jurisdictions, including the United States.

While computer programs themselves are protected as literary works, it is actually the "code" which is the protected expression. Hence, if a company designs a program with similar functions to another program but with a different source code, they would not violate any copyright in the first code. There may, however, be separate copyright(s) in the audio, visual or audiovisual output of a program which may qualify for protection as an artistic work.

The protection of the code may also extend to non-literal infringement, in spite of the apparent emphasis of the statutory definition on a "set of instructions". There is a continuum that begins with the underlying idea(s) embodied in the program (which is not protected by copyright) and ends with the actual code. U.S. courts used various "tests" in such cases. In *Delrina Corp. v. Triolet Systems Inc.*,[74] the Ontario Court of Appeal discussed these tests and suggested a different approach which seems closer to the wording of the Canadian Act. It is a three-step process which begins with an analysis of whether copying has taken place, then considers whether what was copied was protected expression, and finally whether what was copied was a substantial part of the original program. (See the Infringement Section below.)

A further question may arise as programs known as "code generators" are increasingly used to generate code, i.e., potentially protected "expression". These programs embody programming rules and respond to input of data by (generally licensed) users of the programs. Is the code generated by a machine protected? If so, who is the author? If one accepts that there must be some minimally creative skill, labour and judgment, then whose skill and labour is involved? While the situation may be covered under a licence agreement (which, if it is in writing, may transfer the ownership of the code to one of the parties — see s. 13(4)) of the Act), assuming that the creator of the program that generates the code is the copyright owner of all output is not as simple an answer as it seems. Is it fair to assume that minimally creative skill and labour of the author of the code generator is sufficient to instil all resulting productions with originality under the Act, when the results (expressions) to be generated are impossible to foresee because they

---

[73] *Supra*, note 60. See above text in "Literary works" section.

[74] (2002), 58 O.R. (3d) 339, 17 C.P.R. (4th) 289, 23 B.L.R. (3d) 231 (Ont. C.A.), additional reasons at (2002), 22 C.P.R. (4th) 332 (Ont. C.A.), leave to appeal to S.C.C. refused (2002), [2002] S.C.C.A. No. 189, 21 C.P.R. (4th) vi (S.C.C.).

depend on the user's input? Then again, is it fair to assume that the user's inputs, which are general guidelines as to what the program to be generated should do, constitute sufficient skill, labour and judgement under the Act, when in fact the form of the resulting expression is totally decoupled from the form of the input, and seems to be more akin to creative "suggestions" as defined in *Kantel* or in *Tate v. Thomas*?[75] In *Tate*, it was held that suggesting the general outline of a work and even contributing ideas, lines and part of the plot was not sufficient to allow someone to claim authorship. A similar finding was made in *Neudorf v. Nettwerk Productions Ltd.*,[76] (concerning Sarah McLachlan's song "Steaming" from her album *Touch*). That Court found that the plaintiff's contribution, from which the "hook melody" was derived, was insufficient to make him a joint author; he only made "suggestions" about the song, which fell short of the legal standard for "original expression."[77]

One could of course deny copyright protection to all generated output, arguing that there is no direct human input and, in some cases, this may be an appropriate response, especially if a randomizer is used. However, in other cases, if a sufficient degree of predictability between the generator's skill and labour and the generated output can be established, then the author of the generator could be said to be the owner of copyright in the output, subject to an agreement in writing to the contrary. If, on the other hand, the generator may be considered a mere tool which the user of the program uses to create, then it is the user's skill, labour and judgement which are reflected in the work. Finally, there may be some situations where the resulting product embodies substantial contributions relevant to the final form from both the author of the generator and the user of the program. In that case, if the contributions are not distinct, the work would be a work of joint authorship (as defined in s. 2).[78]

## 6. Dramatic Works

Dramatic works are defined in s. 2 as:

'dramatic work' includes

---

[75] [1921] 1 Ch. 503.

[76] (2000), [2000] B.C.J. No. 1705, 8 C.P.R. (4th) 154, 2000 CarswellBC 1711 (B.C. S.C.) [*Neudorf* cited to C.P.R.].

[77] *Ibid.* at para. 2.

[78] This may pose practical difficulties because joint authors are tenants in common rather than joint tenants, thus requiring the consent of all authors, *e.g.*, to grant a license. See the "Ownership" section below.

(a)    any piece for recitation, choreographic work or mime, the scenic arrange-
       ment or acting form of which is fixed in writing or otherwise,

(b)    any cinematographic work, and

(c)    any compilation of dramatic works;[79]

A dramatic work must have "a story, a thread of consecutively related events."[80] The case law has developed this aspect by way of example. In *Tom Hopkins International Inc. (Tom Hopkins Champions Unlimited) v. Wall & Redekop Realty Ltd.*, the court upheld copyright in original instructional videos, which the plaintiff made on real estate sales, holding that these educational videos constituted dramatic works because they had a series of elements linked together by a topical thread.[81]

In *Hutton*, by contrast, the Alberta Court of Appeal decided that mere presentations of rock videos, interspersed with interviews, trivia contests, and banter by the VJ, did not constitute a dramatic work. There was "no attempt at pretence or storyline or dramatic incident."[82] Where there was no story line and no link between the different elements it would "be stretching any definition of dramatic work" to call it a "dramatic work." It should be noted that many authors want their music videos to be recognized as dramatic works since financial rights are typically higher for dramatic works.

The courts have also rejected claims that the playing of a sports game is a choreographed work. In *FWS Joint Sports Claimants v. Canada (Copyright Board)*, the judges determined there can be no copyright on a sporting event since it is unpredictable and incompatible with the notion of a choreographic piece of art.[83] Sporting events are unlike a play or ballet where the performance unfolds according to a plan. This result may suggest that so-called "reality television" does not constitute a story and is therefore not protected. However, in most cases, the reality is in fact "staged," and includes editing and creative input and narrative threads.

A predetermined sketch would constitute a dramatic work, as stated in *Kantel*:

---

[79] *Supra*, note 3, as re-en by *North American Free Trade Agreement Implementation Act*, S.C. 1993, c. 44, s. 53(2), as amended by *supra* note 60, s. 1(4).

[80] *Hutton v. Canadian Broadcasting Corp.* (1989), 102 A.R. 6, 29 C.P.R. (3d) 398, 27 C.I.P.R. 12 (Alta. Q.B.) at 443, affirmed (1992), 120 A.R. 291, 41 C.P.R. (3d) 45 (Alta. C.A.) [*Hutton* cited to C.P.R.]. See *Seltzer v. Sunbrock*, 22 F. Supp. 621 (U.S. Dist. Ct. C.D. Cal., 1938) at 628.

[81] [1984] 5 W.W.R. 555, 1 C.P.R. (3d) 348 (B.C. S.C.) (A.D.) [*Hopkins* cited to C.P.R.].

[82] *Supra*, note 80 at 444.

[83] (1991), [1992] 1 F.C. 487, 81 D.L.R. (4th) 412, 36 C.P.R. (3d) 483, 129 N.R. 289 (Fed. C.A.), leave to appeal refused (1992), 41 C.P.R. (3d) v (S.C.C.) [*FWS* cited to F.C.].

> The original manuscript, and even Exhibit A, grouped a series of predetermined incidents, songs, dialogues, and for want of a better name what I would call talks, in a fixed sequence, which gave to the sketch in its entirety the elements and characteristics of a dramatic composition.[84]

It should be noted that something which does not fall directly within the scope of a dramatic work could nevertheless be protected by copyright if it qualifies under another category, as for example artistic works.

## 7. Musical Works

Section 2 defines a musical work very broadly, as a result of 1993 amendments apparently designed to deal with the fixation requirement. As mentioned above in respect of the fixation requirement, it seems that music could be protected even if unfixed. The definition of "musical work" was modified in 1993.[85] Prior to 1993, a musical work had to be "printed, reduced to writing or otherwise graphically produced or reproduced."[86] This phrasing required that music be fixed. The 1993 definition instead refers to any work of music or musical composition, with or without words. While the fixation requirement is not expressly excluded, that would seem to be the intended result (see the earlier discussion in the "Fixation" section). Thus, music does not have to be in writing to be protected.

Music is somewhat different from other categories of copyright works because there are several layers of rights. In addition to the rights of the composer(s) and, if applicable, the lyricist(s), which are protected as full copyrights under ss. 3 and 14.1, there are "neighbouring rights" to the performer on the performance of the music (singer or musician) and to the maker (producer) of the sound recording (if applicable). For example a song might have at level one a composer of the music and a lyricist for the words; at level two, the musician; and at level three, the producer. Thus, to make a copy of a song (taken from a sound recording containing a performance of a musical work, and assuming the song is still protected by copyright), there would be three or more (there may be more than one author of the music, and more than one performer involved in its performance) authorizations required for a single act of reproduction (of the musical work, of the performance, and of the sound recording) even though to the average user all that seems to be involved is a single copy of a "song." Some of these authorizations may be obtained from collective societies (see the *Collective Management* section), or covered by an exception such as private copying

---

[84] *Supra*, note 34 at 94-95.
[85] *Supra*, note 12.
[86] *Supra*, note 3, s. 2.

(see the "Private Copying" subsection of the *Collective Management* section).

## 8. Artistic Works

A last but very vast category of works known as "artistic works" is defined in s. 2 to include:

> paintings, drawings, maps, charts, plans, photographs, engravings, sculptures, works of artistic craftsmanship, architectural works and compilations of artistic works.[87]

Contrary to what the name seems to imply, artistic merit, the artist's intention to create "art" and the actual aesthetic value (assuming it can be objectively evaluated) are not pertinent to whether something meets the classification of artistic works.[88] This paves the way for the protection of many newer forms of artistic expression. Although the artist's *intention* is not pertinent, there does have to be an objective *expression*.[89]

In *DRG Inc. v. Datafile Ltd.*, label designs with the numbers 0-9 and letters A-Z, which followed a colour-coded classification system for filing, were sufficient to constitute an artistic work. The Court found that the labels objectively were "visual expressions" which was sufficient to fulfill the requirements for an artistic work.[90] The Act does not require that the designs be ones which experts would evaluate as "artistic."

In another case alleging copyright in designs which were key parts of a system, a company invoked a violation of its copyright on color sticks used to teach arithmetic.[91] The coloured rods were used in conjunction with a teaching system that was described in an accompanying book. The court found that while copyright protected the originality in the ideas *as they were expressed in the book*, the sticks were only a practical device to present the

---

[87] *Supra*, note 3, s. 2.

[88] *George Hensher Ltd. v. Restawile Upholstery (Lancs.) Ltd.*, [1975] R.P.C. 31 (U.K. H.L.).

[89] *Aldrich v. One Stop Video Ltd.* (1987), 39 D.L.R. (4th) 362, 17 C.P.R. (3d) 27 (B.C. S.C.) [*Aldrich* cited to D.L.R.].

[90] (1987), [1988] 2 F.C. 243, 18 C.P.R. (3d) 538, 17 C.I.P.R. 136 (Fed. T.D.), affirmed (1991), [1991] F.C.J. No. 144, 35 C.P.R. (3d) 243, 117 N.R. 308, 1991 CarswellNat 1123 (Fed. C.A.).

[91] *Cuisenaire v. South West Imports Ltd.* (1967), [1968] 1 Ex. C.R. 493, 54 C.P.R. 1 (Can. Ex. Ct.), affirmed (1968), [1969] S.C.R. 208, 2 D.L.R. (3d) 430, 57 C.P.R. 76 (S.C.C.).

method in graphical form to children. Copyright therefore could not apply to the sticks themselves and others could reproduce them.

The singer Adam Ant's claim that his face makeup was an artistic work was rejected in *Merchandising Corp. of America v. Harpbond Ltd.*[92] His makeup consisted of two broad red lines of greasepaint with a light blue line between, running diagonally across the face from the nose to the jaw. The court distinguished between the actual makeup and the combination of the makeup and face of the person on whom it was applied:

> The surface upon which the startling make-up was put was Mr. Goddard's [Adam's] face and, if there were a painting, it must be the marks plus Mr. Goddard's face. If the marks are taken off the face there cannot be a painting. A painting is not an idea: it is an object; and paint without a surface is not a painting. Make-up, as such, however idiosyncratic it may be as an idea, cannot possibly be a painting for the purposes of the Copyright Act 1956.[93]

Would the same conclusion be reached when considering groups such as the *Cirque du Soleil*? Is it fair to say that makeup is so different from one face to another as to not be "reproducible"? Notably, the Supreme Court of Canada in *Théberge*, considering an interesting fact situation involving the physical transfer of ink (from an authorized reproduction poster of a painting) onto a different substrate (canvas) by the application of resin, ruled that the transfer was not a reproduction and thus did not infringe copyright. On the facts of that case, the artistic work, in other words, consisted of the ink and not the substrate: "the image 'fixed' in ink is the subject matter of the *intellectual* property and it was not reproduced. It was transferred from one display to another."[94] With clown makeup, the underlying face forms more of an integral part of the art than does, for example, the underlying backing in *Théberge*.

## 9. Photographs

Photographs are defined broadly under the Act. The technique or technology used does not matter, as long as the process is "analogous to photography" (s. 2). Like other works, photographs are subject to the same requirement of originality.

Picture this: A person is hired to take exact pictures of works of art in a museum for a book about an upcoming exhibition. The works of art are paintings which are protected by copyright. Does the photographer have a

---

[92] [1983] F.S.R. 32 (U.K. C.A.).

[93] *Ibid.*at 46.

[94] *Théberge, supra*, note 7 at para 38.

separate copyright in her photograph (*i.e.*, separate from the copyright in the paintings she is paid to take pictures of)? In the U.S. case of *Bridgeman Art Library v. Corel Corp.*,[95] a New York court determined that the photographs of the paintings could not give rise to a separate copyright since, the court reasoned, no creative choices were made. Any other competent photographer, given the same task, would have produced the exact same product. In fact, the photographer's assignment was to ensure that there was no personal or creative input from the photographer so that the underlying paintings could be reproduced as faithfully as possible. Interestingly, because there was a conflict of laws issue in the case, the court proceeded to analyze the facts under both U.S. and British law and came to the same conclusion under both.

Judge Kaplan wrote:

Plaintiff . . . argues that the photocopier analogy is inapt because taking a photograph requires greater skill than making a photocopy and because these transparencies involved a change in medium. But the argument is as unpersuasive under British as under U.S. law.

The allegedly greater skill required to make an exact photographic, as opposed to Xerographic or comparable, copy is immaterial. As the Privy Council wrote in *Interlego AG v. Tyco Industries, Inc.,* '[s]kill, labor or judgment merely in the process of copying cannot confer originality. . . .' The point is exactly the same as the unprotectibility under U.S. law of a 'slavish copy.'

Nor is the change in medium, *standing alone,* significant. The treatise relied upon by plaintiff for the contrary proposition does not support it. It states that 'a change of medium will *often* entitle a reproduction of an existing artistic work to independent protection.' And it goes on to explain:

'Again, an engraver is almost invariably a copyist, but his work *may* still be original in the sense that he has employed skill and judgment in its production. An engraver produces the resemblance he wishes by means which are very different from those employed by the painter or draughtsman from whom he copies; means which require a high degree of skill and labour. The engraver produces his effect by the management of light and shade, or, as the term of his art expresses it, the *chiaroscuro*. The required degree of light and shade are produced by different lines and dots; the engraver must decide on the choice of the different lines or dots for himself, and on his choice depends the success of his print.'

---

[95] 36 F.Supp.2d 191 (S.D.N.Y., 1999).

Thus, the authors implicitly recognize that a change of medium alone is not sufficient to render the product original and copyrightable. Rather, a copy in a new medium is copyrightable only where, as often but not always is the case, the copier makes some identifiable original contribution. In the words of the Privy Council in *Interlogo AG*, '[t]here must . . . be some element of material alteration or embellishment which suffices to make the totality of the work an original work.' Indeed, plaintiff's expert effectively concedes the same point, noting that copyright 'may' subsist in a photograph of a work of art because 'change of medium is *likely* to amount to a material alteration from the original work, unless the change of medium is so insignificant as not to confer originality . . .'

Here, . . . '[it] is uncontested that Bridgeman's images are substantially exact reproductions of public domain works, albeit in a different medium.' There has been no suggestion that they vary significantly from the underlying works. In consequence, the change of medium is immaterial.

Finally, the *amicus* argues that this result is contraindicated because public art collections in the United Kingdom charge fees for reproductions of photographic images of works in their collections, thus evidencing their view that the images are protected by copyright. But the issue here is not the position of an economically interested constituency on an issue that has not been litigated, at least in this century, but the content of the originality requirement of the British Copyright Act.

For all of the foregoing reasons, the Court is persuaded that its original that Bridgeman's transparencies are not copyrightable under British law was correct.[96]

With respect to originality, "choice, layout, and posture of the subject, the choice of camera angle and lighting, and ... the artistic work and personal efforts of the photographer" have been considered by courts when evaluating whether a photograph is original expression.[97] Applying these factors, the court in *Ateliers Tango* upheld the copyright of a freelance photographer who had been hired to take a picture of a tango dance troupe for promotional purposes. The photographer's research on locations, and creative choices involved in poses, camera angles, decor and picture angles satisfied the originality requirement.[98] The Court was convinced that another photographer could have produced a very different result.

---

[96]   *Ibid.* at 198-99 [footnotes omitted] [emphasis added].

[97]   *Ateliers Tango Argentin Inc. v. Festival d'Espagne & d'Amérique Latine Inc.* (1997), 84 C.P.R. (3d) 56 (Que. S.C.) at 66 [*Ateliers Tango*].

[98]   *Ibid.*

## 10. Architectural Works

"Architectural work" includes any building or structure or any model of a building or structure. Size and cost of an architectural work do not matter;[99] however, the definition of "architectural work of art" has been interpreted to require an "artistic character or design." That does not open the door to copyright being dependent on individual personal aesthetic judgments about particular designs. It is intended instead to forestall copyright monopolies on home plans which *are* indistinctive and which would effectively remove design elements which were available to all to use and place them under copyright.[100]

## 11. Compilations

Compilations are defined as a work resulting from the selection or arrangement of data or the selection or arrangement of literary, dramatic, musical or artistic works or parts of works. Originality of a compilation is assessed with respect to the *selection or arrangement*. A compilation can consist, therefore, of an original selection or arrangement of uncopyrightable information (such as facts) or works which are in the public domain (because, for example, the copyright term has expired) or can consist of an original selection or arrangement of copyrighted works (in which case the compiler must seek permission to include the works).

In *Feist*,[101] the U.S. Supreme Court found that compilations (of facts but the same rule applies to compilations of works, such as an anthology) are protected by a separate copyright only to the extent that the author of the compilation can prove the existence of her intellectual production, thought, and conception.[102] For example, in *Eckes v. Card Prices Update*,[103] a collection of the 5,000 most valuable baseball cards (out of approximately 18,000) was found to be protected due to the subjective selection and arrangement of information, and in view of the selection, the creativity and judgment exercised by the compilers in choosing the cards for the collection.

---

[99] *Robert D. Sutherland Architects Ltd. v. Montykola Investments Inc.* (1996), 73 C.P.R. (3d) 269, 150 N.S.R. (2d) 281 (N.S. C.A.).

[100] See *Viceroy Homes Ltd. v. Ventury Homes Inc.* (1991), 34 C.P.R. (3d) 385 (Ont. Gen. Div.), affirmed (1996), 69 C.P.R. (3d) 459 (Ont. C.A.); *Hay v. Sloan* (1957), 12 D.L.R. (2d) 397, 27 C.P.R. 132 (Ont. H.C.); *Netupsky v. Dominion Bridge Co.* (1971), [1972] S.C.R. 368, 24 D.L.R. (3d) 484, 3 C.P.R. (2d) 1 (S.C.C.).

[101] *Supra*, note 44. The case is discussed by the Federal Court of Appeal in *CCH, supra*, note 39. See the Originality section.

[102] See also the Database section.

[103] 736 F.2d 859 (2nd Cir., 1984).

In the U.K. case of *G.A. Cramp & Sons Ltd. v. Frank Smythson Ltd.*,[104] the plaintiff publishers tried to claim copyright in a pocket diary. In addition to the typical calendar pages, the diary was accompanied by a collection of tables including such conventional information as a calendar for the year, postal information, a selection of "days and dates" for the year, tables of weights and measures, comparative time tables, a sunset table, a percentage table, and the like. A former employee of the plaintiff, then employed by the defendant, copied seven of these tables from the plaintiff's diary and inserted them in a diary published by the defendant. The House of Lords held that copyright was not established, since the commonplace matter of the tables left no room for taste or judgment and their selection did not constitute an original literary work. The tables contained commonplace information and a standard selection and arrangement.

## III. OWNERSHIP

In principle, the author of a work is the first copyright owner (s. 13(1)).

However, the application of this simple principle may give rise to somewhat strange conclusions. For example in *Hager*, the court found that the copyright in an interview belonged to the person fixing the oral declarations of the interviewee.[105] The plaintiff was the author of a book on Canadian aboriginals which included a chapter on the singer Shania Twain. To research the book, the plaintiff interviewed Twain and recorded and made notes of their conversations. The defendant later published a book on Twain which included almost all the direct quotations from the plaintiff's book, as well as other material (re-worded) from the book. With respect to the direct quotes, the court held that the original interviewer of Shania Twain was the copyright holder. In *Gould*, discussed above with respect to fixation, the court indicated that oral declarations recorded by a journalist were not protected:

> [A] person's oral statements in a speech, interview or conversation are not recognized in that form as literary creations and do not attract copyright protection.[106]

The way to reconcile these two cases is to base copyright in the journalist's contribution. If a journalist merely notes oral statements made by another, with little prompting from the journalist, and reproduces those statements, then the journalist is not entitled to copyright protection in those

---

[104] [1944] A.C. 329 (U.K. H.L.).
[105] *Supra*, note 20.
[106] *Supra*, note 19.

words. To use *CCH* terminology, that work is "mechanical". However, in a structured interview, when a journalist actually directs the answers by asking specific questions that follow a logical pattern or train of thought, then there may be non-trivial, non-mechanical skill, labour and judgment involved which could meet the *CCH* test (see the Originality section). There may be additional creative input in the formatting of the interview for publication.[107]

Because the rule is that the author is the first owner of copyright, if a consultant is paid to develop a product, such as a website or computer software program, she remains the proprietor of the copyright on that work. The person paying for the service or the object obtains only a licence (implied or express) to use the copyrighted work, unless the first copyright owner transfers her rights in writing (s. 13(4)). Thus, absent an agreement to the contrary, if a company merely pays for a service, the developer holds the copyright and the company acquires only a licence to use the program. The developer is free to distribute this program as he wishes.[108] There are three key exceptions to this rule: employees paid to "create," photographs and similar works, and works created at Her Majesty's request.

## 1. Employees

Section 13(3) of the Act provides the following with respect to copyright in the employment context:

---

[107] In certain cases, it could be argued that a joint work was created. This thesis has some support in the United States, but seems harder to reconcile with the Canadian Act, especially as interpreted in *Slumber-Magic Adjustable Bed Co. v. Sleep-King Adjustable Bed Co.* (1984), 3 C.P.R. (3d) 81 (B.C. S.C.) at 115-116. However, see Hirsch, Andrea. S., "Copyrighting Conversations: Applying the 1976 Copyright Act to Interviews," (1981) 31 *Am. Univ. L. Rev.* 1071 (cited by Reed J. in *Hager*) and Ruhga, Vicki. L., "Ownership of Interviews: A Theory for Protection of Quotations," (1988) 67 Nebr. L. Rev. 675. In an interesting case, the Court of Appeals for the Ninth Circuit (which includes California) held that the Urantia Foundation — the assignee of a group known as the "Contact Commission", composed of a psychiatrist, Dr. William Sadler, and five or six followers — had a valid compilation copyright in The Urantia Book. According to the Foundation, spiritual beings known as "the Divine Counselor, the Chief of the Corps of Superuniverse Personalities, and the Chief of the Archangels of Nebadon" began channelling the teachings through one of Dr. Sadler's patients. The case is *Urantia Foundation v. Maaherra*, 114 F.3d 955 (9th Cir., 1997).

[108] *Pizza Pizza Ltd. v. Gillespie* (1990), 75 O.R. (2d) 225, 33 C.P.R. (3d) 515 (Ont. Gen. Div.) [*Pizza Pizza* cited to O.R.].

13(3) Where the author of a work was in the employment of some other person under a contract of service or apprenticeship and the work was made in the course of his employment by that person, the person by whom the author was employed shall, in the absence of any agreement to the contrary, be the first owner of the copyright, but where the work is an article or other contribution to a newspaper, magazine or similar periodical, there shall, in the absence of any agreement to the contrary, be deemed to be reserved to the author a right to restrain the publication of the work, otherwise than as part of a newspaper, magazine or similar periodical.

The employee situation is thus an exception to the general rule that the author is the first copyright owner (until evidence to the contrary is adduced). The employer becomes the first owner of the copyright unless there is an agreement to the contrary. Thus, if the creator is an "employee" and the work is created in the course of employment, then in order for the employee-creator to hold copyright the work must be subject to an "agreement to the contrary" (typically, a collective agreement). Problems arise with directors of corporations and other non-employed contributors. But courts are not tied to employment law standards and may determine that s. 13(3) applies if the above criteria are met.[109]

Courts apply similar criteria for distinguishing employees from independent contractors in the copyright context as they do for other areas of law. In the copyright context, courts normally consider four factors to determine whether someone is an employee or an independent contractor: 1) the property of the tools, 2) control or direction (relationship of subordination), 3) whether the author assumes all or part of the business risk (loss or profit) and 4) the degree of integration of the author into the business of the "employer."[110]

### (a) Employees and the Meaning of Publication

Under s. 13(3), authors of newspaper and similar articles retain a specific right to control that their article appears in the format for which they were employed to create. In *Robertson v. Thomson Corp.*,[111] a majority decision of the Court of Appeal for Ontario held that this was a personal

---

[109] See *B & S Publications Inc. v. Max-Contacts Inc.* (2001), 287 A.R. 201 (Alta. Q.B.).

[110] *Amusements Wiltron inc. v. Mainville*, [1991] R.J.Q. 1930, 40 C.P.R. (3d) 521 (Que. S.C.) [*Amusements* cited to R.J.Q.].

[111] (2004), [2004] O.J. No. 4029, 243 D.L.R. (4th) 257, 34 C.P.R. (4th) 161, 2004 CarswellOnt 4015 (Ont. C.A.), leave to appeal allowed (2005), 2005 CarswellOnt 1501 (S.C.C.) [*Robertson*].

right, independent of copyright, and as such non-transferable and only applicable to publication in a newspaper, not an online database. One could argue, however, that when a right is non-transferable, the legislature said so (*e.g.*, moral rights in s. 14.1(2)). One could imagine a transfer of this right to a collective society or union, for example.[112] In the same decision, the Court rightly held that a database containing hundreds of articles published in the *Globe and Mail* was not a reproduction of the newspapers, nor was it a newspaper or periodical (it is in fact the very opposite of a periodical), thus leaving it possible for employed authors to oppose publication (as defined in s. 2) in such a format. In the United States, following a similar decision in the case of *New York Times Co. v. Tasini*,[113] many freelance and even employed authors are now routinely asked to sign waivers of all non-assignable rights and to assign all economic rights to the publisher. It remains to be seen whether a similar practice will emerge in Canada, where it is present in sectors other than newspaper publishing.

The Court of Appeal for Ontario also noted in *Robertson*, though in *obiter dictum*, that the right to oppose "publication" would not include the right to oppose transmission on the Internet, which is a form of communication to the public,[114] noting that the definition of "publication" in s. 2.2 excludes public performance and communication to the public. However, the same definition applies to making copies available to the public, which happens when a work is uploaded on a publicly-available Internet server.[115] The question that remains is whether "copies" are made available in that way, as is also required by the definition. While the term "copies" is not defined, they need not be in tangible form, as the introductory paragraph of

---

[112] See, *e.g.*, *Writers' Union of Canada Certification Application, Re* (1998), 84 C.P.R. (3d) 329 (C.A.P.P.R.T), affirmed (2000), (sub nom. *Canada (Attorney General) v. Writers' Union of Canada*) 9 C.P.R. (4th) 477 (Fed. C.A.).

[113] (2001), 121 S.Ct. 2381 (U.S.S.C., 2001). The Court of Appeal for Ontario may have made too far-reaching a statement when it said in *Robertson, supra*, note 111, that the rights of a newspaper publisher in the U.S. were less than the rights of the freelance author (at para. 55). First, a work specifically ordered as a contribution to a collective work is considered a "work made for hire", the rights to which belong to the person for whom the work was prepared, under ss. 101 and 201(b) of the U.S. Act (U.S.C. Title 17). If the work is not specifically ordered, then the publisher, as the owner of the collective work, indeed only has the "privilege of reproducing and distributing the contribution as part of that particular collective work, any revision of that collective work, and any later collective work in the same series" (s. 201(c)). In *Tasini*, the U.S. Supreme Court held that making a database or CD-ROM was not a "revision" of the original contributions.

[114] See *SOCAN, supra*, note 18.

[115] See *Ibid.*

s. 3 confirms. Therefore, making a copy of a protected work on an Internet server could be said to constitute "publication." It is important to note, however, that publication must be done with the rightsholder's consent to be considered publication (except for infringement purposes).[116] A work published without consent would thus be considered an unpublished work for purposes of determining the term of protection, for example.[117]

## 2. Photography

A significant departure from the principles of authorship that underlie the Act, s. 10(2) provides that the owner of the "plate" of the photograph or of the initial photograph at the time the photograph was made is deemed to be the "author" of the photography. This means a corporation can be the "author" of a photograph, as contemplated in s. 10(2)(b). This exception to the normal rule of authorship was introduced in the Act in 1921 to simplify matters.[118] Prior to 1921, courts tried to determine the authorship of a photograph by examining who had supervised the making of the photograph and was its most "effective cause."[119] This was not necessarily the person operating the camera, in the same way that the director of a film is not necessarily behind the camera. The 1921 amendments were thus seen as a solution to a practical problem. The evolution of technology and industry practices may have transformed this "solution" into a problem, as most photographers are now also operators of the camera, though they may not own the "plate." A question which emerged in recent years is whether s. 10(2) applies to digital cameras, where no negative or plate exists. Would the owner of the memory card be considered the owner of the photograph? If a technologically neutral interpretation of the Act is preferred, the answer would be affirmative. The provision means that if someone with no background in photography were to provide a professional photographer with a roll of film, the "author" of the photograph in Canada would be the provider of the film, a most bizarre result. One who seeks copyright control is thus encouraged to bring one's own film when having a photographic portrait made, as the subject will be the "author" of the photograph!

A second important rule with respect to the authorship of photographs is contained in s. 13(2) of the Act, which states that if the plate was ordered and paid for by a third party, the third party is the first owner of copyright

---

[116] S. 2.2(3).
[117] See *Wing v. Van Velthuizen* (2000), [2000] F.C.J. No. 1940, 9 C.P.R. (4th) 449, 197 F.T.R. 126, 2000 CarswellNat 2873 (Fed. T.D.).
[118] *Supra*, note 2.
[119] *Nottage v. Jackson*, [1883] 11 Q.B.D. 627 (Eng. Q.B.).

(though not the author), unless there is an agreement to the contrary. Again the question whether this provision applies to digital photographs can be raised, given that s. 13(2) was defined with reference to a specific technology that produced a "plate."

It is important to note that s. 10(2) applies only to photographs, while s. 13(2) applies to photographs, engravings and portraits. If both are combined in a given situation, then authorship is determined under s. 10(2), including for purposes of s. 14.1 (moral rights), but first ownership is determined according to s. 13(2).

In a 1985 Ontario case, *Paul Couvrette Photographs v. Ottawa Citizen (The)*,[120] a photographer agreed with a model that if she would pose for free, she would get free prints, while the photographer in turn would get photographs to enhance his portfolio. Couvrette sued the *Ottawa Citizen* newspaper when it published the photos without his consent. The Court found that s. 13(2) applied because the model had waived her usual fee and that constituted consideration; under that section copyright belonged to the model who ordered the prints and the agreement that each could use the photographs in their respective portfolios did not constitute an "agreement to the contrary." At that time, the relevant part of s. 13(2) read, ". . . was made for valuable consideration. . . ."[121] However, s. 13(2) was amended in 1997[122] to add the words "and the consideration was paid," which may have reversed the *Couvrette* finding.

## Note De Lege Ferenda

In its 2004 report to Parliament, the Standing Committee on Canadian Heritage wrote the following on photography:

> The Committee feels that photographers should be given copyright protection in their works equal to that enjoyed by other artists. Historically, photographs have been treated differently from other categories of works because they were perceived to be more mechanical and less creative than other art forms. This idea is outmoded and inappropriately treats photographers differently from other artists.[123]

---

[120] (1985), 7 C.P.R. (3d) 552 (Ont. Prov. Ct.) [*Couvrette*].

[121] *Supra*, note 3, s. 13(2).

[122] *Supra*, note 26, s. 10(1).

[123] Standing Committee on Canadian Heritage, *Interim Report of Copyright Reform* (Report of the Standing Committee on Canadian Heritage) Sarmite D. Bulte, M.P. (May 2004) at 7, online: Parliament of Canada <www.parl.gc.ca/InfocomDoc/Documents/37/3/parlbus/commbus/house/reports/herirp01/her-irp01-e.pdf>. Sections 5 and 6 of Bill C-60, tabled on June 20, 2005, would repeal ss. 10 and 13(2) in their entirety.

### 3. Crown Copyright

In concordance with s. 12 of the Act, Crown documents are protected by copyright. As an exception to s. 13(1), when a work is prepared or published by or under the direction or control of Her Majesty or any government department, the copyright in the work belongs to the Crown, subject to an agreement to the contrary. This is again an exception to the normal authorship rules that the author is first owner.

To simplify things in many regards, the government has waived the enforcement of copyright in relation to laws and decisions and reasons of federally-constituted courts and administrative tribunals "provided due diligence is exercised to ensure the accuracy of the materials reproduced and the reproduction is not presented as an official version."[124] That is, the government retains copyright on these works but extends the public a licence to copy, with two provisos.

In the United States, there is no copyright on U.S. government publications.[125]

### 4. Joint Authorship

Ownership of copyrights gets more complicated when dealing with two or more authors. When a work is created in collaboration between two or more authors and the parts created by each one is not distinct from the parts created by others, the Act (s. 2) considers this a case of joint authorship. Sections 2, 6.2, 7 and 9 apply to this type of work. The authors are tenants in common (rather than joint tenants) of the work in equal parts.[126] This means that the consent of all authors is required to grant a licence and that the rights of each author will pass to her beneficiaries rather than to surviving authors.

A good example can be found in *ATV Music Publishing of Canada Ltd. v. Rogers Radio Broadcasting Ltd.* involving the Beatles' song "Revolu-

---

[124] *Reproduction of Federal Law Order*, S.I./97-5, C. Gaz.1997.II.444. Many provincial governments have adopted similar policies.

[125] *Copyrights*, 17 U.S.C. §105 (1983). See also *R. v. Bellman*, [1938] 3 D.L.R. 548 (N.B. C.A.).

[126] The leading cases on this point are *Lauri v. Renad*, [1892] 3 Ch. 402 (Eng. C.A.) and *Cescinsky v. Routledge & Sons, Ltd.*, [1916] 2 K.B. 325 (U.K.). They were mentioned with approval by the Supreme Court in *Underwriters' Survey Bureau Ltd. v. Massie & Renwick Ltd.*, [1940] S.C.R. 218, [1940] 1 D.L.R. 625 (S.C.C.), leave to appeal refused [1940] S.C.R. 219 (note) (S.C.C.) [*Massie & Renwick* cited to S.C.R.].

tion."[127] The defendants' song "Constitution" put original lyrics to the music of "Revolution." The defendant argued that "Revolution" was a collective work of Paul McCartney and John Lennon, with distinct parts, and that the plaintiffs had rights in the lyrics and therefore could not sue for the unauthorized use of the music. The case turned on whether the song was a single work or two (the music and the lyrics). The court found that where different people authored the music and lyrics to a song, there could be separate copyrights to those parts, as well as a copyright in the collective work. However, on the facts of this case, the court held that the music and lyrics could not be considered distinct and thus the whole "song" had been authored jointly by Lennon and McCartney:

> The defendants admit that the music used in the recording of 'Constitution' is the music to the song 'Revolution' by Lennon and McCartney. The defendants admit that the words to the song 'Revolution' were 'authored by Lennon and McCartney'. There is no evidence before me of any separate copyright of the words or of the music. There is no evidence before me that one was the author of the words and the other the author of the music. The evidence before me indicates only one copyright of the music with the words. Since the names of the two authors would indicate that there were two persons then it seems to me that the work herein falls within the definition 'work of joint authorship' for which there would be one copyright of which the plaintiff is the owner in Canada.[128]

As a result, either one could sue for infringement of the music (without the lyrics).

In *Thibault v. Turcot*,[129] the Quebec Superior Court found that when two people had collaborated to compose an "opéra comique," the one writing the music and the other the libretto, the work is one complete unit for the purpose of copyright.

## 5. Collective Works

A collective work parallels the concept of joint authorship, except here the parts contributed by the different authors *are* distinct from one another. Sections 2 and 14(2) apply to this type of work. In a collective work the distinct contribution of each author has its own copyright protection, whereas in joint authorship the authors hold a single copyright.

---

[127] (1982), 35 O.R. (2d) 417, 65 C.P.R. (2d) 109 (Ont. H.C.) [*ATV* cited to O.R.].
[128] *Ibid.* at 422.
[129] (1926), 34 R.L.N.S. 415.

In *Robertson v. Thomson Corp.*,[130] the Court of Appeal of Ontario held that "collective work" and "compilation" were interchangeable terms. While this conclusion is true of newspapers, it is not always applicable and thus should be applied with care outside the facts of this case, which involved a database of articles published in the *Globe and Mail*. The two terms are not generally synonymous. Certain "compilations" (for example, by an author of her own works) would not qualify as "collective works." The terms are defined separately in s. 2.[131] In most cases, the terms also have different purposes. The expression "collective work" is used to determine authorship, while "compilation" is used in the various definitions of the categories of works protected under the *Act*.

## IV. ASSIGNMENT/TRANSFER OF COPYRIGHT

It is possible to assign copyrights according to section 13(4); however, this must be done in writing.[132] The copyright owner can assign the whole copyright or only partial rights and can make the transfer subject to limitations, relating to geographical area, medium or market sector, or restrict it to a part of the copyright term. The statutory condition that the assignment or grant of an interest be in writing is a substantive legal requirement and not a simple rule of evidence.[133] A simple or bare licence (which does not confer an interest) does not need to be in writing and it can be implied.[134]

### 1. Intangible versus Tangible

It should be noted that copyright rights are distinct from the possession of the physical object which contains the copyrighted expression. In the case of *Dickens v. Hawksley*,[135] Charles Dickens's will left all his private papers to his sister-in-law, including an unpublished manuscript, and the residue of his property (including his copyrights) to his children. When the manuscript was later published the question arose whether the sister-in-law's possession of the physical manuscript meant that she had also inherited

---

[130] See *supra*, note 111.

[131] Interestingly, s. 101 of the *U.S. Copyright Act* (U.S.C. Title 17) specifically states that the term "compilation" includes collective works (but the reverse is not always true).

[132] *Supra*, note 110.

[133] *Motel 6 Inc. v. No. 6 Motel Ltd.* (1981), [1982] 1 F.C. 638, 127 D.L.R. (3d) 267, 56 C.P.R. (2d) 44 (Fed. T.D.) [*Motel 6* cited to F.C.].

[134] See *Roberston*, *supra* note 111 and the cases cited therein.

[135] [1935] Ch. 267 (Eng. Ch. Div.).

the copyright for the manuscript. The court rejected this idea, finding that property in the physical object is separate from the copyright. The same principle applies when a person sends a letter; she does not give up copyright in her words (assuming the letter constitutes original expression so as to be protected by copyright) by simply sending the physical letter to the recipient. More recently in *Théberge*, Justice Binnie for the majority distinguished the copyright holder's interest in the intangible expression from the purchaser's interest in the physical object containing the expression. This distinction between intangible and tangible property is an important aspect to how the copyright regime balances the author's, user's and general public's interests.

A licence can grant an *interest* in the work or simply allow an action with respect to that work. For example, as in *Bishop v. Stevens*, a licence can grant a right to institute proceedings against someone else, but only if it is in writing.[136] This is consonant with ss. 13(4) and (6), which require a writing for an assignment but also for any grant of an "interest".

The only right that can not be assigned is the moral right associated with the work (ss. 14.1 and 14.2). The moral right can, however, be waived. An assignment by itself does not constitute a waiver of moral rights. (See the "Moral Rights" section).

Independently of any agreement to the contrary, rights assigned by an author revert to his or her heirs 25 years after the author's death (s. 14), a process known as reversion.[137] While an agreement by the author to the contrary is void, an agreement by the heir(s) by which they agree in advance to assign the reverted rights seems to be valid.[138]

Finally, s. 57(3) provides that an assignment of copyright shall be adjudged void *against any subsequent assignee or licensee* for valuable consideration without actual notice, unless the prior assignment is registered.

## V. TERMS OF PROTECTION

In concordance with s. 6 of the Act the term of protection is the life of the author plus 50 years after his death, and until the last day of the fiftieth year following the death, after which time the work becomes part of the

---

[136] *Supra*, note 5.
[137] See *Kelley Estate v. Roy* (2002), (sub nom. *Winkler v. Roy*) 21 C.P.R. (4th) 539 (Fed. T.D.). For a discussion on the history of this provision in U.K. and Canadian law and its application in time (on timing, see s. 60(2) of the *Copyright Act*), see *Anne of Green Gables Licensing Authority Inc. v. Avonlea Traditions Inc.* (2000), 4 C.P.R. (4th) 289 (Ont. S.C.J.).
[138] See *Chappell & Co. v. Redwood Music Ltd.*, [1980] 2 All E.R. 817 (U.K. H.L.).

public domain. In the case of co-authors, according to s. 9(1), the 50-year term starts after the death of the last surviving co-author. In the case of collective works, the term of protection of each contribution is independent.

There are a few additional special rules. If the work is anonymous or created under a pseudonym, s. 6.1 provides that the term of protection is the shortest of 50 years after publication or 75 years after creation of the work. However, if the identity of the author is disclosed *during that term,* the normal term of protection applies.

The moral right attached to the work is subject to the same term of protection as economic rights.

In the case of photographs, if the author is a corporation (see the Ownership-Photographs section), the term of protection is 50 years from the making of the work (s. 10), unless the owner or majority shareholder of the corporation is a natural person, in which case the normal rule contained in s. 6 applies (s. 10(1.1.) and the term is based on the life of that natural person. This provision seems to be referring to the ownership or control of the corporation at the time the photograph is made (and, consequently, authorship determined according to s. 10(2)).

Under s. 23, neighbouring rights (under ss. 15, 18, 19 and 21) generally have a term of protection of 50 years from the relevant act (the performance or its first fixation, the first fixation of the sound recording, or the broadcast).

## VI. INFRINGEMENT

### 1. General Aspects

Section 3 of the Act sets out the economic rights of the author. The owner of a copyright work has the following exclusive rights.

The sole right:

- o   To produce or reproduce the work or any substantial part thereof in any material form whatever,
- o   to perform the work or any substantial part thereof in public or,
- o   if the work is unpublished, to publish the work or any substantial part thereof.

This includes the sole right

a)   to produce, reproduce, perform or publish any translation of the work,
b)   in the case of a dramatic work to convert it into a novel or other non-dramatic work,

c)      in the case of a novel or other non-dramatic work, or of an artistic work, to convert it into a dramatic work, by way of performance in public or otherwise,

d)      in the case of a literary, dramatic or musical work, to make any sound recording, cinematograph film or other contrivance by means of which the work may be mechanically reproduced or performed,

e)      in the case of any literary, dramatic, musical or artistic work, to reproduce, adapt and publicly present the work as a cinematographic work,

f)      in the case of any literary, dramatic, musical or artistic work, to communicate the work to the public by telecommunication,

g)      to present at a public exhibition, for a purpose other than sale or hire, an artistic work created after June 7, 1998, other than a map, chart or plan,

h)      in the case of a computer program that can be reproduced in the ordinary course of its use, other than by a reproduction during its execution in conjunction with a machine, device or computer, to rent out the computer program, and

i)      in the case of a musical work, to rent out a sound recording in which the work is embodied,

and to authorize any such acts.

The expression "produce or reproduce the work or any substantial part thereof in any material form whatever" constitutes the core copyright right, and the right which originally produced the name "*copy*-right." Copyright was, in its 1710 version in the *Statute of Anne*, a right given authors and publishers to prevent the reproduction of their books. As new ways to use books were invented or became important, new rights were added. For instance, the author of a play may not make much money from the sale of copies. It thus seemed fair to recognize an exclusive right to perform that play in public (especially in theatres that charge an admission fee). The same is true, of course, of musical works. The bulk of music revenues does not generally flow from the sale of sheet music.

Then, as technology allowed for the "distance" performance of such works by radio and then television, satellite, cable and now the Internet, new rights were added or rights were redefined by legislators or courts to cover these new forms of exploitation. As Binnie J. stated for the majority in *SOCAN*:[139]

This appeal raises the difficult issue of who should compensate musical composers and artists for their Canadian copyright in music downloaded in Canada from a foreign country via the Internet. In an era when it is as easy to access a Web Site hosted by a server in Bangalore as it is to access a Web Site with a server in Mississauga, where is the protection for the financial rights of the

---

[139] See *supra*, note 18 at paras. 1, 40-41.

people who created the music in the first place? Who, if anyone, is to pay the piper?
[. . .]

The capacity of the Internet to disseminate 'works of the arts and intellect' is one of the great innovations of the information age. Its use should be facilitated rather than discouraged, but this should not be done unfairly at the expense of those who created the works of arts and intellect in the first place.

The issue of the proper balance in matters of copyright plays out against the much larger conundrum of trying to apply national laws to a fast-evolving technology that in essence respects no national boundaries.

The general infringement rule is set forth in article 27 of the Act.

27. (1) It is an infringement of copyright for any person to do, without the consent of the owner of the copyright, anything that by this Act only the owner of the copyright has the right to do.

## 2. Reproduction

The reproduction right applies only if a *substantial part* of work is copied. This allows, for example, short quotes (at least of a larger work) to be taken without permission. How is substantiality evaluated? In the case of a scholarly or scientific book, is the index more important (per page) in terms of quality than other sections of the book? Substantiality is indeed a question that is related more to the quality rather than the quantity of what was taken.[140] To determine whether someone has copied a work a three-step test is applied. The plaintiff must establish: first, that she created or otherwise owns a copyright in a protected work; second, objective similarity between the plaintiff's work and the defendant's product (whether the defendant's product is itself a copyrighted work is immaterial); and third, that the defendant had access to the plaintiff's work. Access is presumed if the plaintiff's work was widely disseminated. However, this is a rebuttable presumption if the defendant can show the contrary.

Corollaries to this infringement test are that a truly independent creation is not a copy and two copyrights in similar works can subsist. In certain areas, such as certain forms of popular music, it is not unlikely that two

---

[140] *Breen v. Hancock House Publishers Ltd.* (1985), [1985] F.C.J. No. 957, 6 C.P.R. (3d) 433, 6 C.I.P.R. 129, 1985 CarswellNat 570 (Fed. T.D.); *Canadian Performing Right Society Ltd. v. Canadian National Exhibition Assn.*, [1934] O.R. 610 (Ont. H.C.).

creators can achieve similar results without copying from one another. For example, if a person marooned on a deserted island creates a song that, upon his return to "the mainland," has been created by someone else during his absence, neither author has infringed copyright.

In *Verge v. Imperial Oil Ltd.*, the Plaintiff alleged that he had created the *Hockey Night in Canada* jingle and that Imperial Oil had copied it from him.[141] However, Verge was unable to prove that Imperial Oil had ever had access to his work.

Unlike a patent, copyright does not confer a monopoly on the protected expression; rather, it is a negative right to prohibit others from copying the work or exercising the other exclusive rights under s. 3 of the *Act*. The "first creator" does not have priority if the second can show that her work was created independently. That burden is a heavy one for a defendant to discharge, however, if the first author's work was publicly available and accessible.

The defendant's burden of proof is especially heavy because, while an *independent* creation is not an infringement, an "*unconscious*" reproduction is considered a copy. In *Francis Day & Hunter Ltd. v. Bron*,[142] the Court ruled that unconscious copying could amount to an infringement, if the plaintiff could show that the defendant was familiar with the original work and that some causal connection linked that familiarity to the work complained of. Mere proof of similarity between the works and proof of access did not necessarily prove this, as it was a question of fact whether the similarity with the other facts is enough to prove the causal connection.[143]

---

[141] (1988), [1988] F.C.J. No. 971, 23 C.P.R. (3d) 159, 91 N.R. 103, 1988 CarswellNat 1015 (Fed. C.A.) [*Verge* cited to N.R.].

[142] (sub nom. *Day (Francis) & Hunter Ltd. v. Bron*) [1963] 2 All E.R. 16 (Eng. C.A.) [*Francis Day*]. It was mentioned with approval in several Canadian cases, including *Gondos v. Hardy* (1982), 64 C.P.R. (2d) 145 (Ont. H.C.).

[143] In the words of Lord Upjohn in *Francis-Day*:

> The authorities in question in each case treated the question of unconscious copying as purely a question of inference of fact which might be drawn in the circumstances of a particular case, and not as a presumption of law. . . .
> The truth is that the plaintiff in a copyright action must show that a substantial part of the original work has been reproduced. . .; and, although not expressed in the *Act*, it is common ground that such a reproduction, in the words of junior counsel for the plaintiffs, must be causally connected with the work of the original author. If it is an independent work, then, though identical in every way, there is no infringement. If a true infringer wrongly persuades the court that it is his own unaided work, the plaintiff fails, as do other plaintiffs when fraudulent defendants unhappily succeed (as, no doubt, they sometimes do) in persuading the court that they have not been fraudulent. (At 23-24). U.S. cases to the same effect include *Fred Fisher v.*

In *Francis Day*, Lord Diplock provided a good explanation of the notion of reproduction:

> [T]o constitute infringement of copyright in any literary, dramatic or musical work there must be present two elements: First, there must be sufficient objective similarity between the infringing work and the copyright work, or a substantial part thereof, for the former to be properly described, not necessarily as identical with, but as a reproduction or adaptation of the latter; secondly, the copyright work must be the source from which the infringing work is derived. ... There must be a causal connexion between the copyright work and the infringing work.[144]

The act of copying can often be inferred from the similarities between both works. In *Motel 6*, for example, the logo of a motel looked very much like a copy of a logo used by a well-known international motel chain.[145] This same situation occurred in *Visa International Service Assn. v. Visa Motel Corp.*[146] where the defendant had "created" a logo which was almost identical to the VISA logo of the well known credit card company. In such cases, access by the defendant can usually be presumed.

Some additional light on the exact meaning of "to produce or reproduce" under s. 3(1) was shed by the Supreme Court in *Théberge*. The case involved the transfer of ink from posters of an artistic painting onto canvas. The posters themselves had been made with the plaintiff artist's authorization, but the defendant then transferred the ink from the paper posters on to canvas so as to sell the posters as "quasi-paintings,"a more expensive form, without paying the plaintiff (the painter) any additional royalties. The artist argued that the transfer amounted to a production or reproduction of his

---

*Dillingham*, 298 F. 145 (S.D.N.Y., 1924), 147, in which Judge Learned Hand wrote: "Whether he unconsciously copied the figure, he cannot say, and does not try to. Everything registers somewhere in our memories, and no one can tell what may evoke it. On the whole, my belief is that, in composing the accompaniment to the refrain of "Kalua,", Mr. Kern must have followed, probably unconsciously, what he had certainly often heard only a short time before. I cannot really see how else to account for a similarity, which amounts to identity. So to hold I need not reject his testimony that he was unaware of such a borrowing." See also *Edwards & Deutsch Lithographing Company v. Boorman*, 15 F.2d 35 (7th Cir., 1926).

[144] *Supra*, note 142 at 27.

[145] *Supra*, note 133.

[146] (1984), 1 C.P.R. (3d) 109 (B.C. C.A.) at 121, affirmed (1984), 1 C.P.R. (3d) 109 at 112 (B.C. S.C.). See also *Boutin v. Bilodeau*, (sub nom. *Boutin v. Distributions C.L.B. Inc.*) [1994] 2 S.C.R. 7, 54 C.P.R. (3d) 160, (sub nom. *Boutin v. Distributions C.L.B. Inc.*) 168 N.R. 9 (S.C.C.), reversing (1992), 46 C.P.R. (3d) 395 (Que. C.A.).

painting. The majority of the Supreme Court disagreed. Binnie J for the majority, wrote:

> This is not to say that the Act recognizes only literal physical, mechanical reproduction. The legal concept has broadened over time to recognize what might be called metaphorical copying (transformation to another medium, e.g. books to films). It is recognized that technologies have evolved by which expression could be reproduced in ways undreamt of in earlier periods, such as evanescent and 'virtual' copies in electronic formats. Transformation of an artistic work from two dimensions to three dimensions, or *vice versa*, will infringe copyright even though the physical reproduction of the original expression of that work has not been mechanically copied. Equally, translations or transformations into another medium may be infringements of economic rights. Nevertheless, the important evolution of legal concepts in the field of copyright is not engaged by the facts here. This is a case of literal physical, mechanical transfer in which no multiplication (metaphorical or otherwise) takes place.
>
> It is of interest that our courts have not given an independent meaning to 'produce' as distinguished from '*re*produce' in s. 3(1) of the Act. Nor have the courts done so under the English Act. In fact, in that country, the word 'produce' was thought to be of such little consequence that it was eliminated from the Act by amendment in 1956.[147]

### (a) Publication

The introductory paragraph of s. 3 as well as subsections 3(1)(a) and 18(1)(a) provide a right to "publish" which should be linked to the definition of publication in s. 2.2. It includes, in respect of unpublished works, a right to make available copies of a work, which probably includes the Internet.[148] In the introductory paragraph of s. 3 and s. 18(1)(a), the right is clearly limited to a first publication. With respect to translation (s. 3(1)(a)), where there is no express statutory limitation, arguably the right is maintained after the first publication and it would then resemble a full right of "making available" as provided in the *WIPO Copyright Treaty* (see the International Section). However, subsections 3(1)(a) to (i) ostensibly define further the copyright contained in the introductory paragraph (which ends with "and *includes* the sole right to . . .". From that perspective, which seems more logical in context, the right of publication in respect of translations would

---

[147] *Supra*, note 7 at paras. 47-48.
[148] See under "Employees" in the Ownership section, *supra*. Bill C-60, tabled on June 20, 2005, includes making available as a form of communication to the public.

also be limited to first publication (as provided for in the introductory paragraph of s. 3), after which the usual rights (reproduction of a substantial part, performance in public, communication to the public, etc.) would apply.

## (b) Parallel Importation

Under trade-mark law, it is not an infringement to import and sell in Canada wares produced abroad where a trade-mark was lawfully affixed, even if such goods were not initially meant to be sold in Canada (where there may be an "exclusive distributor"), provided those goods and related services are the same as those that are sold in Canada by or with the authorization of the trade-mark holder (see Parallel Importation in Trade-Marks section[149]). However, in a recent decision,[150] the Federal Court found that one could not use this reasoning in the case of copyright infringement. The owner or exclusive licensee of the copyright owner in Canada would thus be able to prevent the sale of parallel imports bearing a copyright protected logo or other copyrighted work.

## 3. Communication to the Public/Public Performance

The two rights of communication to the public and public performance are related historically: as performance before a live audience was one of the first forms of exploitation to be covered by copyright, it made sense to create a right to provide protection when the performance took place at a distance through the use of Hertzian (radio) waves and the other types of communication technologies invented since then (television, cable, satellite and the Internet). In U.S. law the single concept of public performance is used and covers such distance performances.[151]

Section 3(1) of the Act first grants the holder of the copyrights the right to "perform in public." The term "in public" was defined in *Canadian Cable Television Assn. v. Canada (Copyright Board)* as the "usual meaning of the words 'in public', that is to say openly, without concealment and to the knowledge of all."[152] A distinction should be made between the communi-

---

[149] See *Consumers Distributing Co. v. Seiko Time Canada Ltd.*, [1984] 1 S.C.R. 583, (sub nom. *Seiko Time Canada Ltd. v. Consumers Distributing Co.*) 10 D.L.R. (4th) 161, 1 C.P.R. (3d) 1 (S.C.C.).

[150] *Kraft Canada Inc. v. Euro Excellence Inc.* (2004), [2004] F.C.J. No. 804, 33 C.P.R. (4th) 246, 252 F.T.R. 50, 2004 CarswellNat 5579 (F.C.).

[151] *Copyrights, supra*, note 125, § 106(4).

[152] [1993] 2 F.C. 138, 46 C.P.R. (3d) 359, 151 N.R. 59 (Fed. C.A.), leave to appeal refused (1993), 51 C.P.R. (3d) v (note) (S.C.C.) at para. 27 [*CCTA* cited to F.C.].

cation *to the* public and a performance *in* public, that is, in a place open to a public. As was noted by Létourneau J.C.A. in *CCTA*, above, "the words 'to the public' are broader than 'in public'."[153] Article 1721 of *NAFTA* defines "public" for the purposes of the right of communication to the public and public performance as

> any aggregation of individuals intended to be the object of, and capable of perceiving, communications or performances of works, regardless of whether they can do so at the same or different times or in the same or different places, provided that such an aggregation is larger than a family and its immediate circle of acquaintances or is not a group comprising a limited number of individuals having similarly close ties that has not been formed for the principal purpose of receiving such performances and communications of works.[154]

In *SOCAN*, the Supreme Court found that, in respect of the transmission of musical works on the Internet,

> It is an infringement for anyone to do, without the consent of the copyright owner, 'anything that, by this Act, only the owner of the copyright has the right to do' (s. 27(1)), including, since the 1988 amendments, the right 'to *communicate* the work to the public by telecommunication . . . and to *authorize* any such acts' (emphasis added) (s. 3(1)(*f*)). In the same series of amendments, 'telecommunication' was defined as 'any transmission of signs, signals, writings, images or sounds or intelligence of any nature by wire, radio, visual, optical or other electromagnetic system'(s. 2). The [Copyright] Board ruled that a telecommunication occurs when the music is transmitted from the host server to the end user. I agree with this.
> [. . .]
>
> At the end of the transmission, the end user has a musical work in his or her possession that was not there before. The work has, necessarily, been communicated, irrespective of its point of origin. If the communication is by virtue of the Internet, there has been a 'telecommunication'. To hold otherwise would not only fly in the face of the ordinary use of language but would have serious consequences in other areas of law relevant to the Internet, including Canada's ability to deal with criminal and civil liability for objectionable communications entering the country from abroad.

---

[153] *Ibid.* at para. 17.
[154] *North American Free Trade Agreement Between the Government of Canada, the Government of Mexico and the Government of the United States*, 17 December 1992, Can. T.S. 1994 No. 2, (entered into force 1 January 1994), online: International Trade Canada: <http://www.dfait-maeci.gc.ca/nafta-alena/agree-en.asp> [*NAFTA*].

The word 'communicate' is an ordinary English word that means to 'impart' or 'transmit' (*Shorter Oxford English Dictionary on Historical Principles* (5th ed. 2002), vol. 1, at p. 463). Communication presupposes a sender and a receiver of what is transmitted.[155]

## 4. Adaptation and Translation

A right of adaptation of dramatic works into non-dramatic works is granted in s. 3(1)(b); a right to turn novels and other non-dramatic works and artistic works into dramatic works is granted in s. 3(1)(c); and a right to make a sound recording or a film from any literary, dramatic or musical work is granted in s. 3(1)(d). Together these may be referred to as "adaptations" or derivatives. One could add the close category of translation, in respect of which an exclusive right is granted in s. 3(1)(a).

The adaptation right (though obviously not the translation right) poses an interesting dilemma, logically linked to the so-called idea/expression dichotomy (see the Work section). Copyright protects original expressions of thought, not the underlying ideas. And creators are all "standing upon the shoulders of giants," to refer to the famous words of Sir Isaac Newton. No one creates in a vacuum. All creativity is rooted in past experiences and shaped by expressions of previous creators internalized, consciously or not,[156] by each creator in her own way. Thus, while one often speaks of "users" and "authors", it is important to note that these are not mutually exclusive groups: scholars and artists build on and are inspired by the works of those who come before them.

The adaptation right is infringed when what is taken to create a derivative work exceeds the underlying idea and consists of all or part of the (protected) expression. Derivative works raise difficult questions with respect to the conflicting rights and interests of the author and copyright owner in the expression, the end user in the purchased object containing the expression, and the public generally to build on the work of those who come before them to have a vibrant creative culture. As Justice Binnie wrote in *Théberge*, adaptation raises "the conflict between the scope of the copyright holders' economic rights to control the end uses of . . . [the] work and the purchasers' rights as owners of the material object. . . ."[157] While the U.S. notion of derivative work does not expressly form part of the Act, Justice Binnie analyzed it as follows in *Théberge*:[158]

---

[155] *Supra*, note 18 at paras. 42, 45-46. See also note 148, *supra*.

[156] In *Francis Day, supra*, note 142, the English Court of Appeal indicated that even "unconscious" copying could be an infringement.

[157] *Supra*, note 7 at para. 72.

[158] *Ibid*. at paras. 49, 70-73 [emphasis in original].

The U.S. legislation expressly incorporates a definition of 'derivative work', as happens for example when a cartoon character is turned into a puppet, or a tragic novel is turned into a musical comedy. In such circumstances there is, in a sense, 'a production' rather than a reproduction. However, the examples of what might be called derivative works listed in ss. 3(1)(*a*) to (*e*) of our Act are consistent with the notion of reproduction because they all imply the creation of <u>new</u> copies or manifestations of the work.
[. . .]

Of relevance to the present discussion is the fact that the United States legislation, apart from entitling the copyright holder to control the 'reproduction'of his work, allows the copyright holder the right to authorize (or prohibit) the creation of 'derivative works'. The concept is formally defined in s. 101 of the *United States Code*, Title 17, as follows:

> A 'derivative work' is a work based upon one or more preexisting works, such as a translation, musical arrangement, dramatization, fictionalization, motion picture version, sound recording, art reproduction, abridgment, condensation, <u>or any other form in which a work may be recast, transformed, or adapted</u>. A work consisting of editorial revisions, annotations, elaborations, or other modifications which, as a whole, represent an original work of authorship, is a 'derivative work'.

The concept of a derivative work is found in the Berne Convention, and in the copyright legislation of the United States, England, Australia, New Zealand and Canada. All these provisions reflect a common progression in copyright legislation from a narrow protection against mere literal physical copying to a broader view which allows the copyright owner control over some changes of medium and adaptations of the original work. While the idea of 'derivative works' therefore has parallels in other jurisdictions, including Canada, the American statutory language is particularly expansive, including in particular the words 'any other form in which a work may be recast, transformed, or adapted', that have no precise counterpart in Canadian legislation.

The poster art industry in the United States has been actively litigating the broad statutory 'derivative works' provision against owners of the material objects that embody the copyrighted work. In *Mirage Editions*, . . . [856 F.2d 1341 (9th Cir. 1988)] for example, the copyrighted image was applied to a ceramic tile. The 9th Circuit Court of Appeals ruled that the ceramic was an infringing 'new' derivative work, a conclusion expressly rejected by the 7th Circuit Court of Appeals in *Lee v. A.R.T. Co.*, 125 F.3d 580 (1997), which concluded that the fixation did not infringe the copyright. Easterbrook J., for the 7th Circuit, reasoned that '[a]n alteration that includes (or consumes) a complete copy of the original lacks economic significance'(p. 581). He further found that there was no distinction between framing works of art, an acceptable practice under copyright law, and more permanent methods of display, such as re-fixing the art work on tile. The 9th Circuit has taken a different view: see *Mirage Editions, supra*. These cases and their progeny typically turn on conflicting interpretations of the words 'recast, transformed or adapted' in the U.S. statutory definition, but even under that more expansive U.S. definition of 'derivative works' the 7th Circuit concluded that permanently mounting the artwork on tile did not 'recast, transform, or adapt' the work. If these words appeared in our Act, there would presumably be a similar battle of statutory construction here, with the respondent saying the work was 'recast, transformed or adapted', and the appellants denying that characterization, but the conflict between the scope of the copyright holders' economic rights to control the end uses of his work and the purchasers' rights as owners of the material object is the same. In the absence of the 'recast, transformed or adapted' language (or equivalent) in our Act, however, the respondent is unable to rely on it as an additional basis of copyright liability. As Estey J. noted in *Compo, supra*, at p. 367:

> . . . United States court decisions, even where the factual situations are similar, must be scrutinized very carefully because of some fundamental differences in copyright concepts which have been adopted in the legislation of that country.

I should note that while there is no explicit and independent concept of 'derivative work' in our Act, the words 'produce or reproduce the work . . . in any material form whatever' in s. 3(1) confers on artists and authors the exclusive right to control the preparation of derivative works such as the union leaflet incorporating and multiplying the Michelin man in the *Michelin* case, *supra*. See generally, McKeown, *supra*, at p. 64. In *King Features Syndicate Inc. v. O .and M. Kleemann Ltd.*, [1941] A.C. 417 (H.L.), under a provision in the English Act similar to s. 3(1) of our Act, the plaintiff's copyright in the cartoon character 'Popeye the Sailor' was held to be infringed by an unauthorized doll, i.e., the two dimensional character was reproduced without authorization in a new three-dimensional form. See also W. J. Braithwaite, 'Derivative Works in Canadian Copyright Law' (1982), 20 *Osgoode Hall L.J.* 191, at p. 203. To the extent, however, that the respondent seeks to enlarge the protection of s. 3(1) by reading in the general words 'recast, transformed or adapted' as a freestanding source of entitlement, his remedy lies in Parliament, not the courts.

The adaptation itself may of course be subject to copyright if it meets the required conditions, including originality, in which case it would enjoy its own protection (a new term, etc.), without affecting the protection (or absence thereof, *e.g.*, if it is in the public domain) of the underlying work.

It is important to note that it is possible for a work to meet the requirements of the Act and be copyrightable even though it infringes another work's copyright. With respect to compilations, for example, if a person creates an original compilation of selected works which are under copyright but does not ask permission of the copyright owners of the individual works, the compiler would be able to exercise copyright rights in the compilation (and prevent others from reproducing a substantial part of the compilation), but would be subject to actions by anyone whose copyrights were infringed. The compiler, meanwhile, could bring a copyright infringement action against those who infringe the copyright in the compilation.

To take the example of a collective work, the majority decision of the Ontario Court of Appeal in *Robertson*[159] was understood by some commentators as meaning that a newspaper publisher, who is undoubtedly the owner of a copyright in a collective work, had a positive right to publish or reproduce the newspaper independently of the copyright rights of authors of contributions to the collective work. That is not so. The newspaper publisher has rights under s. 3, which he can duly enforce if a substantial part of the newspaper is reproduced, communicated to the public etc., but this right in the collective work is not a "licence to infringe" the works of others. The publisher, as any author of a collective work, is bound by the terms of contracts with authors of works incorporated in the collective work (contributors), as well as applicable exceptions (if any) and relations with employed authors as defined in s. 13(3). (See the Employees section in the Ownership Section.)

### (a)  A Note on Adaptation and Traditional Knowledge[160]

The case of *Roberton v. Lewis*[161] is similarly interesting. Two composers who had arranged old Scottish songs were found to have separate copyrights in their respective works. This case takes on a contemporary hue when one considers the tendency to reuse "traditional" material. Here are a few examples: On September 26th, 2001, *The Globe and Mail* published a full-page advertisement for a high-speed internet service. The ad shows a shaman, most likely from British Columbia's Tlingit nation, in full regalia performing the "Raven Dance". This dance is performed as part of an important ceremonial event. The ad also contains the word "GO" in large print and the caption "Actually, it's a huge world after all". The ad credits neither the Tlingit people nor the photographer (although he apparently had given his consent) or the dancer. The use of sacred aboriginal art is nothing new but it is on the increase. It is fairly common to see "dream catchers" hanging from rear-view mirrors in cars. In Australia, sacred aboriginal

---

[159] See *supra*, note 111.
[160] See also the relevant section in Part II.
[161] *Roberton v. Lewis*, sub nom. *Lady H. Robertson v. Harry Lewis* (t/a Virginia music) [1976] R.P.C. 169 (Ch.).

designs are often found on tea towels, rugs and restaurant placemats. In the United States, people routinely commercialize "Navajo rugs" mixing both sacred Navajo design and profane designs that have no connection to the Navajo nation. Millions of dollars worth of "Indian" crafts are imported from Asia to be sold in Canada and the United States. Another example is the taking of sacred Ami chants by the German rock group Enigma for its song "Return to Innocence," or the South African pop music in Paul Simon's album *Graceland*.

## 5. Rental

Because the rental of certain types of work led to widespread copying and thus interfered with normal commercial exploitation, Parliament added subsections 3(1)(h)[162] and 3(1)(i)[163] to give copyright owners the right to prevent the rental of computer programs and sound recordings. In the case of sound recordings, a separate rental right is given to the maker (producer) of the sound recording and the performing artist, under s. 18(1)(c) and 15(1)(c), respectively. These sections must be read in conjunction with s. 2.5, which defines what constitutes rental. The definition focuses on commercial rentals (having regard to the substance of the transaction, not its form). The expression "motive of gain" used in s. 2.5(1)(b) "is a much wider expression than that used in the 1931 statute 'without private profit' and it cannot be restricted to circumstances where the motive of gain is the main or the only motive."[164]

## 6. Authorization

The right to "authorize" any of the acts mentioned in s. 3 is a distinct right from the performance of those acts themselves.

One of the most interesting parts of the Supreme Court's decision in *CCH* is the Court's clarification of the notion of authorization. Prior to *CCH*, Canadian courts had said several times that to authorize was to "sanction, approve or countenance" but the exact meaning of these terms, especially "countenance," in cases of authorization by either simply providing means which could be used to infringe or by failing to check whether

---

[162] *Supra*, note 3, as re-en by *North American Free Trade Agreement Implementation Act*, *supra* note 79, s. 55(2), amended by *supra*, note 60, s. 3(3).

[163] *Supra*, note 60, s. 3(3).

[164] *C.A.P.A.C. v. Western Fair Assn.* (1951), (sub nom. *Composers, Authors & Publishers Assn. (Canada) v. Western Fair Assn.*) [1951] S.C.R. 596, [1952] 2 D.L.R. 229, 15 C.P.R. 45 (S.C.C.) [*C.A.P.A.C.* cited to S.C.R.].

use of the means would be infringing[165] was not entirely clear. The Chief Justice was very clear on this point in *CCH*: "Countenance in the context of authorizing copyright infringement must be understood in its strongest dictionary meaning, namely, 'give approval to, sanction, permit, favour, encourage.'"[166]

Providing the means to infringe (at least without additional evidence, such as intent to "approve" or direct knowledge of the direct infringer's purpose) was already found not to constitute an authorization both by Privy Council and the Supreme Court. In *Muzak Corp. v. Composers, Authors & Publishers Assn. (Canada)*[167] the Court found that Muzak, an American company that leased a library of electrical transcriptions containing musical works to a Canadian franchisee, did not authorize a public performance; and in *Vigneux v. Canadian Performing Right Society*,[168] the Privy Council had found that the supplier of a jukebox did not authorize public performances of musical works, since "[t]hey had no control over the use of the machine; they had no voice as to whether at any particular time it was to be available to the restaurant customers or not."[169]

Sometimes the means provided *can* be used for infringing purposes but also have non-infringing uses. The question of authorization in these cases should be based on a different test. A control-based test makes sense in a context where the means provided can be put to both legal and infringing uses by the user, the copyright equivalent of "dual use" technologies,[170] or "neutral technology," as the Supreme Court characterized it in *CCH*.[171] This is reminiscent of the *Sony*[172] standard, from a case where the U.S. Supreme Court held that using VCRs for "time-shifting" of television broadcasts was fair use. Time shifting refers to the practice in which users record a program to play back at a later time. VCRs, which can be used for infringing purposes, also have a substantial non-infringing use (watching rented or self-made tapes; watching non-copyrighted material and fair use) and, consequently, VCR manufacturers and distributors could not be held liable for contributory

---

[165] As when a city rents a hall for a theatrical performance. See *de Tervagne v. Beloeil (Town)*,[1993] 3 F.C. 227, 50 C.P.R. (3d) 419, (sub nom. *de Tervagne v. Beloeil (Ville)*) 65 F.T.R. 247 (Fed. T.D.).

[166] *CCH*, *supra*, note 15 at para. 38.

[167] [1953] 2 S.C.R. 182, 19 C.P.R. 1 (S.C.C.).

[168] [1945] 2 D.L.R. 1, 4 C.P.R. 65 (Canada P.C.) [*Vigneux* cited to D.L.R.].

[169] *Ibid.* at 11.

[170] An expression normally used in defence-related legislation and treaties, *e.g.*, *The Wassenaar Arrangement on Export Controls for Conventional Arms and Dual-Use Goods and Technologies*.

[171] *CCH*, *supra*, note 15 at paras. 37-46.

[172] *Sony Corp. of America v. Universal City Studios Inc.*, 464 U.S. 417 (U.S.S.C., 1984).

infringement, a notion that resembles the Canadian notion of authorization under copyright law.[173] Put differently, if a technology has a substantial and credible non-infringing use, then the "means provider" should not have a positive duty of ensuring copyright compliance, absent of course a supervisory role for different reasons (employer, etc.). This means that there is no duty on the part of a technology provider whose technology can credibly be used for a substantial non-infringing purpose to check whether users of that technology are complying with the Act. The provider should, however, not suggest or encourage infringing behaviour.[174] This seems to be what the Chief Justice had in mind when she wrote in *CCH* that "authorizing the mere use of equipment that could be used to infringe copyright"[175] did not amount to a violation of the right to authorize.

When applied to a library, as in *CCH*, a photocopy machine falls in the dual use category. Some photocopies may be non-infringing either because they constitute a reproduction of an insubstantial part (under s. 3 of the Act) or because they are covered by an exception such as s. 29. This also explains why the photocopy service was found not to constitute an authorization; most, if not all, the copies made were considered fair dealing for research and thus non-infringing.

This conclusion is reinforced in the Court's later decision in *SOCAN*, in which Binnie J. (for the majority) wrote:

> The operation of the Internet is obviously a good deal more complicated than the operation of a photocopier, but it is true here, as it was in the *CCH* case, that when massive amounts of non-copyrighted material are accessible to the end user, it is not possible to impute to the Internet Service Provider, based solely on the provision of Internet facilities, an authority to download copyrighted material as opposed to non-copyrighted material.

---

[173] However, the notion is used as a quasi-equivalent for the combined U.S. notions of contributory and vicarious copyright infringement, the basis for which is different. The choice of two distinct notions affords U.S. courts a higher degree of flexibility in tackling cases situated near or on the border between active and passive cases. It could be said that there is in fact a passive-active continuum.

[174] In *Vigneux, supra.* note 169, the test chosen, which was based only on actual control, was either too lenient or incomplete if one considers that a jukebox sold to a restaurant or public establishment may not have a very credible non-infringing use. The real question was whether the means provider had a duty to check whether his customer had obtained a SOCAN (or the equivalent at the time — see the Collective Management section) licence.

[175] *CCH, supra.* note 15 at para. 38. The Chief Justice adds that "this presumption may be rebutted if it is shown that a certain relationship or degree of control existed between the alleged authorizer and the persons who committed the copyright infringement."

[. . .]

The knowledge that someone *might* be using neutral technology to violate copyright (as with the photocopier in the *CCH* case) is not necessarily sufficient to constitute authorization, which requires a demonstration that the defendant did '[g]ive approval to; sanction, permit; favour, encourage' (*CCH*, para. 38) the infringing conduct.[176]

It is also important to point out that, after *CCH* and *SOCAN*, the right to authorize stands as a fully autonomous right under ss. 3 and 27. This has implications in terms of infringement (as it did in *CCH*), but may also have consequences in terms of licensing, tariffs, etc. In other words, it seems necessary to treat separately the performance of restricted acts (*i.e.* acts which, in the absence of an exception, require an authorization) and the authorization of such acts.

The notion of authorization, a "separate" right under s. 3, should be considered according to the following sequential analysis when applied in an infringement context.[177] One may proactively encourage (in a way that is likely to influence the direct infringer's conduct) or formally instruct another to perform a restricted act or expressly approve such an act (if the approving person is in a position to approve the behaviour of the person whose behaviour is thus approved). That constitutes active authorization. One may passively authorize an infringement. Here, one should distinguish between two types of "passive" situations. First, one may fail to exercise a duty to control (imposed by the existence of a type of relation that requires supervision and then to the extent that the performance of the restricted act was reasonably required or foreseeable as part of the functions subject to the duty to supervise). Second, if there is no duty to control, then the dual use analysis above applies: if someone simply provides dual use means to another, and does not expressly encourage (through advertising or otherwise) infringing behaviour, which would fall in the first ("active" part of the analysis), then that person cannot be said to have (passively) authorized the infringement.

---

[176] *Supra*, note 18 at paras. 123 and 127.
[177] Of course, a rightsholder may also "authorize" the performance of a restricted act. This would amount to the grant of a licence.

### (a) "Authorization" in the Context of the CRIA/Peer-to-Peer Litigation

The first Canadian court to apply the notion of authorization as defined in *CCH* was the Federal Court in *BMG Canada Inc. v. John Doe*.[178] Mr. Justice von Finckenstein applied the test as follows:

> As far as authorization is concerned, the case of *CCH Canada Ltd v. Law Society of Canada*, 2004 SCC 13, established that setting up the facilities that allow copying does not amount to authorizing infringement. I cannot see a real difference between a library that places a photocopy machine in a room full of copyrighted material and a computer user that places a personal copy on a shared directory linked to a P2P service. In either case the preconditions to copying and infringement are set up but the element of authorization is missing.[179]

If we apply the sequential analysis suggested above, one may, with respect, get to a somewhat different answer. The Federal Court chose the "passive authorization" analysis and then rightly applied the test applicable to a person who makes part of her hard drive available to others via a peer-to-peer (P2P) network without being in a supervisory role. Clearly that last part of the analysis is correct: a P2P user generally does not have a duty to supervise other Internet users. But the first part of the analysis, that is, whether a P2P user is actually passive, is more open to debate. This passive/dual use analysis would almost certainly apply to those who provide P2P software because a substantial number of P2P exchanges are legal (*e.g.*, even without discussing fair dealing, if the person is exchanging material in which he or she owns the right or which is in the public domain). File-sharers can be considered to be proactive. Their task is not limited to the making of a copy for "private use" — a notion which also needs clarification. They have to take *at least one additional step* to identify the file as available to other P2P users,[180] and that is consistent with *prima facie* infringement.

---

[178] (2004), [2004] F.C.J. No. 525, 239 D.L.R. (4th) 726, 32 C.P.R. (4th) 64, 250 F.T.R. 267, 2004 CarswellNat 2774 (F.C.) [*BMG*], affirmed by 2005 FCA 193. However, the Federal Court of Appeal expressly declined to confirm the copyright aspects of von Finckenstein J.'s decision. Bill C-60, tabled on June 20, 2005, would amend the Act to include as an infringing act the making available to the public "or to one or more persons in particular" (s. 15).

[179] *Ibid.* at para. 27.

[180] At least with knowledge and if the making available corresponds to a choice made by the user, even a default choice but one that was explained and agreed to by the user. A different conclusion would be arrived at if files were hacked or taken without the user's knowledge and consent.

One could argue that uploading is covered by either s. 29[181] or s. 80, but there are several reasons that go against this. The first deals with the notion of authorization; the second with the s. 80 exception; and the third with the possible role of the right of communication to the public.

First, it seems clear that if either the upload or download is an infringement (of the right of reproduction and/or the right of communication to the public), then the P2P user who made a file available may be said to have infringed the right to authorize, subject to the above-mentioned caveats. *BMG* takes a different approach and following that decision on this point would essentially render moot the notion of passive authorization.

Second, as to the right of reproduction and the infringement thereof, a number of questions remain unanswered in *BMG* and should be addressed before one can endorse Justice von Finckenstein's conclusion that s. 80 applies to a download. Granted, the factual issue of whether the copy from which the copy is made is legal or not does not seem to be a criterion under the relevant provisions of the Act. But that is not sufficient to find that s. 80 applies to downloads. That section applies when a copy is made on an "audio recording medium" (s. 80), which is defined in s. 79 as a "recording medium, regardless of its material form, onto which a sound recording may be reproduced and that is of a kind *ordinarily used* by individual consumers for that purpose, excluding any prescribed kind of recording medium." The notion of what is "ordinary" is a dynamic one and may itself be influenced by the fast growth of the P2P phenomenon. Yet, a determination that the hard drive of a PC is such an allowable medium must be made based on actual *evidence* that the practice is widespread to the point of "ordinariness." This evidence may exist, but it should be properly presented to a court before a determination is made.[182] But that is essentially an evidentiary matter. A second, more important condition must also be met for s. 80 to apply: if a PC is considered an allowable medium under s. 80, then the copy must be made for the "private use of the person making the copy." "Private"

---

[181] It is difficult to argue that, with respect to the average user, file-sharing of music is a form of research, even in light of the broad definition adopted in *CCH*.

[182] One could contrast the Federal Court's analysis (which does not even discuss this point) with the Copyright Board's decision on private copying, where a detailed analysis of the actual use of various media is made. See Copyright Board of Canada, *Tariff of Levies to Be Collected By CPCC in 2003 and 2004 on the Sale Of Blank Audio Recording Media, in Canada, in Respect of the Reproduction for Private Use of Musical Works Embodied in Sound Recordings, of Performer's Performances of such Works and of Sound Recordings in Which such Works and Performances are Embodied* (Decision) (December 12, 2003), online: Copyright Board of Canada <http://www.cb-cda.gc.ca/decisions/c12122003-b.pdf>.

in this and other copyright-related contexts can be defined as the opposite of "public," which, for purposes of copyright law, usually refers to one's family and close social acquaintances.[183] If the copy is originally downloaded for that (private) purpose and a hard drive is considered as an "audio recording medium," then arguably s. 80 indeed applies to the copy made available. In that case, if there is no direct infringement, the person who made the file available cannot be said to have authorised an infringement of the right of reproduction, provided no additional copy is made in making the file available to other users. But again, this must be determined by a court based on evidence on actual P2P usage.

Third, making a file available for P2P users to download may constitute a communication to the public and/or the authorization of such a communication,[184] an act not covered by s. 80, as is made clear in s. 80(2)(c). If one assumes that the community of P2P users who could access a file made available on the network constitutes a public,[185] independently of the fact that each user accesses the file as a point-to-point transmission, then it could be argued that a communication to that public takes place when the file is transmitted, and, consequently, that an authorization of that communication takes place when the file is identified by that person as available for other P2P users. In *SOCAN*, the Supreme Court held that a communication of a musical work "by virtue of the Internet" is a "telecommunication" within

---

[183]  See the *International* section.

[184]  Rothstein J.A. (dissenting) rejected this possibility in the Federal Court of Appeal's decision in *CCH* (C.A.), *supra*, note 39 at para 101. The majority pointed at a lack of evidence on this point and certainly did not close the door: "I accept that a series of sequential transmissions may infringe the right to communicate to the public. However, the question of whether a group of recipients is sufficiently large to constitute 'the public' can only be answered on a case-by-case basis, and there is insufficient evidence before this Court to make such a determination". See also note 178, *supra*.

[185]  There is little doubt, if one reads Article 1721 of *NAFTA*, *supra*, note 155: "*public* includes, with respect to rights of communication and performance of works provided for under Articles 11, 11bis(1) and 14(1)(ii) of the Berne Convention, with respect to dramatic, dramatico-musical, musical and cinematographic works, at least, any *aggregation of individuals* intended to be the object of, and *capable of perceiving, communications* or performances of works, *regardless of whether they can do so at the same or different times or in the same or different places*, provided that such an aggregation is larger than a family and its immediate circle of acquaintances or is not a group comprising a limited number of individuals having similarly close ties that has not been formed for the principal purpose of receiving such performances and communications of works" [emphasis added].

the meaning of s. 3(1)(f).[186] The Act does not contain a requirement that the communication be simultaneous.[187] Neither is technology, *i.e.*, the use of the Internet, a barrier to a finding of infringement either, as Internet broadcasting is clearly a form of communication to the public. The fact that the music cannot be heard because a file is transmitted is, however, a serious counter-argument to consider. Commercially speaking, a file download (for someone to listen to later) is more similar to a *distribution* than a communication. There is no right of distribution *per se* in the Canadian Act.[188] Because in the physical world distribution required the making of copies, it was arguably unnecessary to have an additional right of distribution.

Even if knowingly making a music file available to other P2P users is considered as a form of distribution and not a communication to the public, the s. 80 exception does not apply because one of the purposes of such copying would be to distribute, and in such a case s. 80(1) does not apply, as provided for in s. 80(2) (b), even in the context of non-commercial distribution. The only possible counterargument is if the intent and copying are not coextensive, *i.e.*, if the copy was made for private use and then later identified as available for other users. The Act does specify that a copy *made for* one of the purposes listed in s. 80(2) is not covered by the exception. The expression "made for" seems to require a simultaneousness of the intent with the copying. It is also worth noting that, while distribution is not expressly covered by the s. 3 rights, it is recognized as defeating the s. 80 exception, which tends to show that Parliament considered distribution to be illegal under s. 3.

When assessing a case of potential infringement of the right to authorize in relation to a specific device, Canadian courts might consider the distinction made in U.S. law between vicarious and contributory infringement. U.S. law on this point recognizes that one who does not directly infringe copyright may nevertheless infringe by contributing or encouraging infringement. In the case of a device that can be used to infringe copyright, the U.S. Supreme Court in *Sony*[189] decided that the makers of videotape

---

[186] *SOCAN, supra,* note 18.

[187] An argument reinforced by the fact that when simultaneousness is required, Parliament said so, as in s. 31(2)(c) of the Act.

[188] Contrary to, *e.g.,* the U.S. Act, § 106 of which reads in relevant part as follows: "Subject to sections 107 through 118, the owner of copyright under this title has the exclusive rights to do and to authorize any of the following: [. . .] (3) to *distribute copies* or phonorecords of the copyrighted work to the public by sale or other transfer of ownership, or by rental, lease, or lending." [emphasis added]. The Canadian Act contains a rental right in respect of sound recordings and computer programs.

[189] 464 U.S. 417 (U.S.S.C., 1984).

recorders (VCRs) were not liable under this doctrine because the VCR was capable of a substantial non-infringing use, namely time-shifting (for later viewing) of television broadcasts on a noncommercial basis. Sony was decided in the days of analog copies, the number of "generations" of which is limited by the progressive, cumulative loss in quality from one generation of copies to the next. The same cannot be said of digital copies, the thousandth of which should be of exactly the same quality as the "original." Courts in the United States issued injunctions to shut down a service known as "MP3.com," which consisted of a central server on which music files had been copied and made available for (free) download.[190] This was a clear case of direct infringement: MP3.com had copied music files without an authorization. Shortly thereafter, Shawn Fanning, a college student, launched Napster, a service which consisted not of copied music files but rather of an Internet "directory" of music files available on the personal computers of Napster users, who were using the software to make part of their computer's hard drive available to other Napster users. This created the first so-called "peer-to-peer" network for file-sharing. Napster had thus not directly copied or communicated the music. The U.S. Court of Appeals for the Ninth Circuit,[191] confirming the court of first instance,[192] found that Napster was liable under both contributory and vicarious infringement doctrines. The court concluded that almost all Napster users were "sharing" protected music files, that such sharing was not fair use and that Napster knew exactly what users of its software were doing.

In all these cases, the debate seemed to focus on the portion of uses that were non-infringing. In the presence of substantial non-infringing uses, U.S. courts have been very reluctant to find contributory or vicarious infringement. Napster was an easy target: by shutting down the central server, the brain as it were, the entire system fell apart. A variety of programs created since do not require a central server: they seek the content from one computer to the next until a match is found. These new peer-to-peer services are only computer programs, and a much harder target for legal action. This explains why the recording industry has been trying to use technology, such as Digital Rights Management, to make it harder to copy music files, while also targeting individual consumers who use peer-to-peer software, as in the above-mentioned CRIA litigation.

---

[190] *UMG Recordings, Inc. v. MP3.com, inc.*, 92 F.Supp.2d 349 (S.D.N.Y., 2000).

[191] *A & M Records, Inc. v. Napster, Inc.*, 239 F.3d 1004 (U.S. C.A. 9th Cir., 2000). (The Ninth Circuit includes the State of California.)

[192] *A & M Records, Inc. v. Napster, Inc.*, 114 F.Supp.2d 896 (U.S. N.D. Cal., 2000).

## 7. Moral Rights

Sections 14.1(1) and 28.2(1) of the Act work together to protect the so-called "moral right." An author's "moral rights" consists of two main rights: the right to be associated with the work (and conversely not be associated with it in the case of an anonymous or pseudonymous work); and a right to the "integrity" of the work within the scope of the definition found in article 28.2, *i.e.*, only if the work is, to the prejudice of the honour or reputation of the author, (*a*) distorted, mutilated or otherwise modified; or (*b*) used in association with a product, service, cause or institution. However, in the case of a painting, sculpture or engraving, the prejudice is deemed to have occurred as a result of *any* distortion, mutilation or other modification of the work. But (*a*) a change in the location of a work, the physical means by which a work is exposed or the physical structure containing a work, or (*b*) steps taken in good faith to restore or preserve the work, are not in and by themselves a distortion, mutilation or other modification of the work (s. 28.2(3)).

Moral rights stem from the civil law concept of *droit d'auteur* or "author's rights." In *Théberge*, Mr. Justice Binnie explained the statutory provision for the moral right in the context of Canada's dualist backdrop of common law "copyright" and civil law "droit d'auteur":

> [S]. 28.2(1) of the Act provides that even a purchaser of the tangible object may not 'distor[t], mutilat[e] <u>or otherwise modif[y]</u>' (emphasis added) the work 'to the prejudice of the honour or reputation of the author'. It seems clear, at least by negative implication, that a modification of a work by the purchaser which does *not* 'prejudice ... the honour or reputation of the author' was intended by Parliament to be within the purchaser's rights.

> In addition, as a secondary point, s. 28.2(3) of the Act provides that a change in 'the physical ... structure containing a work ... shall not, by that act alone, constitute a distortion, mutilation or other modification of the work.' To the extent a change in substrate can be said to change the 'physical structure' containing the respondent's work, it does not 'by that act alone' amount to a violation of a moral right either.

> The separate structures in the Act to cover economic rights on the one hand and moral rights on the other show that a clear distinction and separation was intended.
> [. . .]

> This is not to say that moral rights do not have an economic dimension (e.g., there may be an economic aspect to being able to control the personality-invested 'moral' rights of integrity and attribution) or to deny that there is a

moral rights aspect to copyright (e.g., a critic may reproduce parts of the text of a book when reviewing it, but it will be considered a breach of the author's economic rights unless his or her authorship is attributed). However, in terms of remedies, the distinction in the Act between the two sets of rights is clear.

My view is that Parliament intended modification without reproduction to be dealt with under the provisions dealing with moral rights rather than economic rights. To adopt a contrary view, i.e., to treat the modification of the substrate here as the violation of an economic right, would allow copyright holders other than the artist to complain about modification (despite the non-assignability of moral rights). It would allow an artist who objected to a 'modification' of an authorized reproduction both to sidestep the independent evaluation of a judge in unleashing a pre-judgment seizure in Quebec, and to sidestep at a trial anywhere in Canada the important requirement of showing prejudice to honour or reputation in order to establish an infringement of moral rights.

Could the *economic* rights of the sculptor of the descending geese at the Eaton Centre be said to be infringed (quite apart from his *moral* rights) because the seasonal 'combination' of geese plus Christmas ribbons could be considered a 'reproduction'? The be-ribboned flock incorporated the original artistic work in more than "substantial part", no doubt, but there was no 'reproduction' in any legal sense, any more than there was 'reproduction' when the appellants in this case contributed blank canvas to the 'combination' of ink layer and canvas. The sculptor rightly invoked his moral rights against the Eaton Centre, not economic rights.[193] (emphasis in original)

Indeed, in *Snow v. Eaton Center Ltd.*,[194] the artist Michael Snow opposed the modification of his artistic creation (which was a flock of carved Canadian geese hanging from the ceiling at the south entrance of the Eaton Centre in Toronto). The Eaton Centre wanted to put red bows on the birds for Christmas. The court determined there was a violation of the moral rights associated with the work, in part because the artist felt greatly offended by the modification. The court determined that the test comprises both a subjective and an objective evaluation of the prejudice. While the author must genuinely feel offended, the prejudice must be based on some objective foundation. The threshold for sculptures (as well as paintings and engravings) is now much lower under the Act than for other works: any distortion, mutilation or other modification is deemed infringing, according to s. 28.2(2) which was added to the Act in 1985.[195]

---

[193] *Théberge, supra*, note 7 at paras. 57-61.
[194] (1982), 70 C.P.R. (2d) 105 (Ont. H.C.) [*Snow*].
[195] *Supra*, note 60, s. 6.

Another interesting case is *Prise de parole Inc. v. Guérin, éditeur Ltée.*[196] An author opposed the reproduction of parts of his novel in a compilation. His claim was partly based on the (economic) right of reproduction, but also on his moral right. He asserted that leaving out parts of his novel he considered essential amounted to a mutilation of the work. His claim was rejected by the Federal Court:

> Under section 14.1(1) of the *Act* the author of a work has, subject to section 28.2, the right to the integrity of his or her work: these are moral rights. The Act also provides in section 14.1(2) that an author's moral rights may not be assigned but may be waived in whole or in part. The evidence does not show that in the case at bar Doric Germain waived his moral rights. To be able to make a claim based on the right to the integrity of his or her work, the author must show, as stated in section 28.2(1) of the Act, that the work was distorted, mutilated or otherwise modified to the prejudice of the author's honour or reputation. I note that section 28.2(1) does not require the plaintiff to prove prejudice to his honour or reputation; rather, it must be proved that the work was distorted, mutilated or otherwise modified 'to the prejudice of the honour or reputation of the author.' In my view, this nuance justifies the use of a subjective criterion — the author's opinion — in assessing whether an infringement is prejudicial.

> It has, moreover, been recognized by the courts that this concept has a highly subjective aspect that in practice only the author can prove. In *Snow v. Eaton Centre*, the court ruled as follows:

>> I believe the words 'prejudicial to his honour or reputation' in s. 12(7) [of the *Copyright Act*, R.S.C. 1970, c. C-30] involve a certain subjective element or judgment on the part of the author so long as it is reasonably arrived at.

> However, in my view the assessment of whether a distortion, mutilation or other modification is prejudicial to an author's honour or reputation also requires an objective evaluation of the prejudice based on public or expert opinion. In *Snow* the applicant proved this. In the case at bar, the evidence certainly shows that Doric Germain felt frustrated by the publication of a shortened version of his work. During his testimony, he talked at length about the changes the defendant had made to his work: a substantial amount of his novel was reproduced but with essential omissions such as the subplot and a number of details about northern Ontario that were an important part of his original work; in addition, the order in which the plot was presented was altered and the novel's divisions and subdivisions were left out or changed. In short, the author

---

[196] (1995), [1995] F.C.J. No. 1583, 66 C.P.R. (3d) 257, 104 F.T.R. 104, 1995 CarswellNat 769 (Fed. T.D.), affirmed (1996), [1996] F.C.J. No. 1427, 73 C.P.R. (3d) 557, 206 N.R. 311, 1996 CarswellNat 2215 (Fed. C.A.).

clearly demonstrated that his work was distorted, mutilated or otherwise modified.

It must still be determined whether the work was distorted to the prejudice of the author's honour and reputation. Doric Germain expressed his great disappointment at seeing his work so distorted that he would have preferred his name not to be associated with the defendant's collection. He also stated that he is well known in his circle, has a good reputation as an author and has already written four novels. He received a grant from the Ontario Arts Council, was invited by the province of Ontario to the Salon international du livre in Le Mans, France in 1989 and had his photograph published on the cover of *Liaison*, the main arts journal in Ontario. He was invited to tour Manitoba schools and at that time gave radio and television interviews. He is often asked to give lectures in schools, although when asked by counsel for the defendant whether the number of lectures he was asked to give fell after the publication of the *Libre expression* collection, he acknowledged that [TRANSLATION] 'I don't think it did any harm.' Doric Germain also acknowledged that he had not been ridiculed or mocked by his colleagues or the newspapers and that he had not personally heard any complaints after the *Libre expression* collection was published.

In short, although the author has shown that his novel was substantially modified without his knowledge and that he was shocked and distressed by this, the evidence has not shown that, objectively, as required by section 28.2(1) of the Act, his work was modified to the prejudice of his honour or reputation. Since this has not been proven, the plaintiff is not entitled to moral damages.

This decision seems to take a fairly limited view of the moral right. It reinforces the need expressed in *Snow* (a case which preceded the 1985 amendments, however) for the author's subjective "feeling" of a prejudice to his reputation or honour to be supported by objective elements.

The moral right cannot be assigned, but it can be waived contractually. Many publishing contracts now contain a standard moral right waiver.

Bill C-60, tabled on June 20, 2005, would provide moral rights for performers as well as authors.

## 8. Secondary Violation

Subsections 27(2) to (5) set out secondary violation of copyright. It is mostly self-explanatory.

27(2) It is an infringement of copyright for any person to
a)    sell or rent out,
b)    distribute to such an extent as to affect prejudicially the owner of the copyright,

c)     by way of trade distribute, expose or offer for sale or rental, or exhibit in public,

d)     possess for the purpose of doing anything referred to in paragraphs (a) to (c), or

e)     import into Canada for the purpose of doing anything referred to in paragraphs (a) to (c),

a copy of a work, sound recording or fixation of a performer's performance or of a communication signal that the person knows or should have known infringes copyright or would infringe copyright if it had been made in Canada by the person who made it.

(3) In determining whether there is an infringement under subsection (2) in the case of an activity referred to in any of paragraphs (2)(a) to (d) in relation to a copy that was imported in the circumstances referred to in paragraph (2)(e), it is irrelevant whether the importer knew or should have known that the importation of the copy infringed copyright.

(4) It is an infringement of copyright for any person to make or possess a plate that has been specifically designed or adapted for the purpose of making infringing copies of a work or other subject-matter.

(5) It is an infringement of copyright for any person, for profit, to permit a theatre or other place of entertainment to be used for the performance in public of a work or other subject-matter without the consent of the owner of the copyright unless that person was not aware, and had no reasonable ground for suspecting, that the performance would be an infringement of copyright.

The legislators had to correct a gap found within the protection granted by s. 27(1) of the Act. Although it is illegal to copy a work, the legislator had to prohibit the importation of and dealing in copied works when the reproduction took place in a foreign country.

Section 29(3) was introduced in 1997 in response to a number of cases dealing with the need to prove the infringer's knowledge.[197]

To determine whether a sale has taken place for the purposes of s. 29(2), normal principles of contract law apply. The sale must have taken place in Canada.

Note that under. 45(1)(a) importation for personal use is allowed.

---

[197] Including *McLelland & Stewart Ltd. v. Coles Book Stores Ltd.* (1974), 7 O.R. (2d) 426, 55 D.L.R. (3d) 362, 21 C.P.R. (2d) 266 (Ont. H.C.), affirmed (1974), 21 C.P.R. (2d) 270 (Fed. T.D.) and *Clarke, Irwin & Co. v. C. Cole & Co.*, [1960] O.R. 117 (Ont. H.C.).

## 9. **Principal Defences**

There are five principal defences to an allegation of copyright infringement: 1) no "copy" or other restricted act[198] (communication to the public, adaptation, rental etc.) took place; 2) only the idea, not its expression was taken; 3) only an "insubstantial part" was taken; 4) ignorance of the existence of protection; 5) existence of a licence or consent.

In addition, a defendant may challenge a plaintiff's title.

1) The defendant can use the definition of the term "copy" to argue that the piece that is alleged to have been copied does not have many similarities with the original work.[199]

2) The second defence is often applied in suits involving computer programs. As explained above in relation to the protection of computer programs as literary works (see above the Computer Program section) absent literal (cut-and-paste) copying it is difficult to determine whether the idea or the expression of a computer program was used. At its core, copyright is not a right against (unfair) competition; it is a statutory right to prevent certain acts with respect to the expression contained in a protected work. The expression of the idea cannot be copied but the idea can be expressed in another manner.[200] In *Hager*,[201] Reed J. used the expression "colourable imitation" in that context. In the case of *Delrina Corp. v. Triolet Systems Inc.*,[202] the Ontario Court of Appeal analyzed the level of protection of computer programs in the following way:

> It is a fundamental feature of the copyright law in all three countries [Canada, the United Kingdom and the United States] that it protects only original *expression*. It does not protect the idea underlying the expression. Frequent reference has been made to the following statement of Thorson P. in *Moreau v. St. Vincent*, [1950] Ex. C.R. 198 (Can. Ex. Ct.) at 203.
>
> > It is . . . an elementary principle of copyright law that an author has no copyright in ideas but only in his expression of them. The law of copy-

---

[198] Defined as an act which, absent a statutory exemption or licence, requires the copyright owner's consent.

[199] *Francis Day, supra*, note 142.

[200] *VIA Rail Canada Inc. v. Location VIA-ROUTE Inc.* (1992), 96 D.L.R. (4th) 347, 45 C.P.R. (3d) 96 (Que C.A.).

[201] *Supra*, note 20, at 298.

[202] (2002), 58 O.R. (3d) 339, 17 C.P.R. (4th) 289, 23 B.L.R. (3d) 231 (Ont. C.A.), additional reasons at (2002), 22 C.P.R. (4th) 332 (Ont. C.A.), leave to appeal refused (2002), 21 C.P.R. (4th) vi (S.C.C.).

right does not give him any monopoly in the use of the ideas with which he deals or any property in them, even if they are original. His copyright is confined to the literary work in which he expressed them. The ideas are public property, the literary work is his own. Everyone may freely adopt and use the ideas but no one may copy his literary work without his consent.

Although the idea/expression dichotomy is a common feature of copyright law in the three countries, it has been observed that it is applied with greater rigour in the United States, with the effect of enlarging the idea aspect of a work and, correspondingly, reducing the expression aspect. The result is a narrowing of the scope of copyright protection.

Accepting that there may be this difference in the law, it has been recognized in Anglo-Canadian law that the non-protection of ideas embraces the view that there is no copyright in any arrangement, system, scheme or method for doing a particular thing or process. Several English and Canadian decisions in support of this statement are set forth in Sookman, *Computer, Internet, and Electronic Commerce Law* (1991-) p. 3-151 at footnote 644.117.

I refer also to the *World Trade Organization* ('WTO') Agreement on Trade Related Aspects of Intellectual Property Rights ('TRIPS') which was incorporated into Canadian law by S.C. 1994, c. 47, s. 8. It provides in Art. 9.2 that '[c]opyright protection shall extend to expressions and not to ideas, *procedures, methods of operation* or mathematical concepts as such.' (Emphasis added.) I refer to the emphasized words as showing what, authoritatively, falls outside the scope of protectable expression. Cf. *Apotex Inc. v. Wellcome Foundation Ltd.* (2000), 10 C.P.R. (4th) 65 (Fed. C.A.) at 84.

The Court then refers to a U.S. test known as "abstraction-filtration-comparison," devised in *Computer Associates International Inc. v. Altai Inc.*[203] This test consists of the following elements: first, recognizing that each work is a combination of ideas and expression, one compares the plaintiff's program with the defendant's at various levels of abstraction, starting with the code and then "abstracting" towards the program's flow-chart, structure and, ultimately, the underlying ideas. Then each part of the respective program is analyzed to see whether what was taken (in each case) was the idea or its expression. Ideas are "filtered out." Finally, the expression (what is left in the sieve so to speak) is compared to the defendant's expression (program). The court must assess whether the defendant copied any of the protected expression and the copied portion's relative importance.

The Ontario Court of Appeal in *Delrina* did not espouse the test, but did not reject it entirely either:

---

[203]  23 U.S.P.Q.2d 1241 (U.S. 2nd Cir. N.Y., 1992).

The trial judge in his reasons (at pp. 57-65) referred extensively to *Computer Associates International Inc. v. Altai Inc.*, which discussed and applied the 'abstraction-filtration-comparison' method. However, following this, he said at (p. 37) '[w]hether a Canadian court should adopt the abstraction-filtration-comparison method in deciding an action for copyright infringement or some other similar method' it was clear that 'some method must be found to weed out or remove from copyright protection those portions which, for the various reasons already mentioned, cannot be protected by copyright.' This indicates that the trial judge did not necessarily apply the abstraction-filtration-comparison method, assuming it, for the moment, to be 'wrong.' Further, I see nothing wrong with his general 'weeding-out' observation.

Before referring to the trial judge's analysis of the evidence . . . I will say something more on 'the law' relating to the abstraction-filtration-comparison method. . . As I have said, it is a method of determining whether a part of a work is entitled to copyright protection in the process of determining whether a defendant has substantially reproduced a plaintiff's work.

The Court seemed to apply a reverse abstraction-filtration-comparison test, by first deciding whether there was copying, then whether what was copied was protected expression, and then whether a substantial part was taken. Only if all three conditions are fulfilled can it be said that an infringement has taken place. The Court's decision on this point seems fully consonant with the text of ss. 3 and 27 of the Act. This leaves the question of non-literal copying, where what is copied is not the code itself but the structure and flowchart of a program.[204] That structure or flowchart may itself be protected, provided it meets the necessary requirement of originality and is not simply a mechanical reflection of industry standards or the tools used.[205] This may happen, for example, where a different language is used (*e.g.*, a 4GL used to "reprogram" third-generation language code[206]). The *Copyright Act* does not prevent someone from programming a computer to

---

[204] See *Autodesk Inc. v. Dyason*, [1992] R.P.C. 575 (Australia H.C.).

[205] See the definition of originality and *CCH, supra*, note 15. Most programs contain standard sections or subroutines and/or standard programming tools and techniques. The protection available under copyright law does not extend to those elements. Most programs also contain non-standard elements and "good ideas", often referred to as "nuggets". These nuggets can often be copied without taking the actual code, but doing so could infringe copyright, if the nuggets meet the originality standard , are sufficiently expressed, and that expression is taken in substantial part. In practice, once the idea contained in a "nugget" of code is understood, it can generally be recoded (or expressed in such a different form) that a finding of infringement of copyright cannot be made.

[206] See *Prism Hospital Software Inc. v. Hospital Medical Records Institute* (1994), 97 B.C.L.R. (2d) 201, 57 C.P.R. (3d) 129 (B.C. S.C.).

perform the same function as another program, but it does prevent someone from following another program's original structure. The rule here is no different than that which applies to other literary works (of which computer programs form a part). A translation of a literary work from English into another language requires an authorization. One can copy aspects of a novel and infringe even if one does not copy the words of the text itself. If elements such as the novel's storyline and characters meet the originality requirement and appropriating them takes a substantial part of the novel, copying these elements would constitute an infringing use, in the same way that adapting a copyrighted novel into a motion picture (or any other form of adaptation) is infringement unless the owner authorizes these uses. This is true whether or not the new use results in an original, copyright protected work.[207]

In filtering out unprotected non-literal elements, a court should exclude any idea that cannot be expressed in a substantially different way. Because copyright does not protect ideas, if there is only one way to express an idea, then that single expression is not protected. This is sometimes referred to as the idea/expression merger. A term closely related to this doctrine is "scenes à faire," a phrase used to describe the fact that certain (originally theatrical) developments are expressed in one or a very limited number of stock "scenes." These scenes are not protected because copyright does not provide a monopoly on "ways or methods of expression"[208] only on the expression itself and these routine patterned "scenes" lack originality. In the same way that the basic building blocks of computer programming are open to anyone to use, the standard, clichéd, scenes in plots are also open to anyone. The exclusion is best described as an absence of originality (because one has taken standard "forms" of expression). An additional theoretical basis is in the policy of not protecting ideas, at least not under the *Copyright* Act.[209]

3) The definition of the "substantial part" is determined by the quality and not the quantity. For example if the index is taken from a book, this may be a substantial part even though it represents only a relatively small number of pages. The same could be said if only a few bars of music are taken but they are the essential melody. A case in point is *Hawkes and Son*

---

[207] See also *Hager, supra*, note 20.

[208] See Article 9(2) of the *TRIPS Agreement, supra* note 27 which is discussed in greater detail in the International Section.

[209] In appropriate cases, remedies based on other doctrines may be available. If an "idea" was appropriated between parties to a contract, there may be remedies available under contract law. In other cases, a fiduciary duty may apply. There is no statutory basis to extend copyright to protect ideas, however.

*(London), Ltd. v. Paramount Film Service, Ltd.*[210] which involved a military march used by Paramount in one of its "news reels," this one showing the opening of the Royal Hospital School at Holbrook, Suffolk, by the Prince of Wales in 1933. In the short film, boys of the school marched past while a band played a few bars from the plaintiff's song. The Court of Appeal found for the plaintiffs:

> The plaintiffs say, and it is not disputed, that they are the owners of the copyright in this musical march 'Colonel Bogey,' and that in the course of this film this march has been played and reproduced; it is reproduced to the extent, I think, of some 28 or more bars, and it takes something like 50 seconds to one minute to reproduce. On the other hand, the defendants say that it is quite true that this march has been reproduced in the film, but it was reproduced only as incidental to the other features of the day which were portrayed in this film; that it was entirely subordinate to the general purpose of the film; and that in any case the march, and this part of the march, played a subsidiary part, and only a subsidiary part, in this picture film. . .
> [. . .]
>
> [I]t is said, first, that there is no substantial part of this musical work taken, and that the cases show that we must look into the question of the degree and what was the nature of the reproduction. In one case to which Lindley L.J. refers, he points out that in that case a worsted work copy of an engraving was held not to be an infringement of the copyright therein. On the other hand, photographs of pictures have been held to infringe the copyright, although there is a vast difference between a photographic reproduction and the picture itself. Therefore, when one deals with the word 'substantial,' it is quite right to consider whether or not the amount of the musical march that is taken is so slender that it would be impossible to recognize it.
>
> In order that we might give the defendants every chance, we decided to go and see this film reproduced, and we have done so this morning, and it appeared plain to us that there is an amount taken which would be recognized by any person. We have evidence before us which must not be overlooked - evidence 'that certain small exhibitors do, if they can get hold of news films, use the sound track for the purpose of what we call a non-synchronous interlude, and that sort of thing,' and 'in the case of some of the smaller theatres, it was probably just a means of getting over the coming in and going out of the people; and they do not worry very much about the value of that sound.[']²¹¹
>
> Having considered and heard this film, I am quite satisfied that the quantum that is taken is substantial, and although it might be difficult, and although it may be uncertain whether it will be ever used again, we must not neglect the

---

[210] [1934] Ch. 593 (Eng. C.A.).
[211] *Ibid.* at 601, 603-04.

evidence that a substantial part of the musical copyright could be reproduced apart from the actual picture film.

The general approach based on quality rather than quantity of the taking was articulated in the U.K. case of *Ladbroke*[212] as follows:

> Did the appellants reproduce a substantial part of it? Whether a part is substantial must be decided by its quality rather than its quantity. The reproduction of a part which by itself has no originality will not normally be a substantial part of the copyright and therefore will not be protected. For that which would not attract copyright except by reason of its collocation will, when robbed of that collocation, not be a substantial part of the copyright and therefore the courts will not hold its reproduction to be an infringement.

The impact on the plaintiff's potential market is also relevant in determining "substantiality." In the case of *Leslie v. Young & Sons*,[213] in which only four pages out of a 40-page book had been taken, Lord Herschell explained that those four pages "may be the very thing that the presence or absence of which would most largely promote or retard the sale of the work."[214]

The Alberta Court of Appeal also considered the meaning of substantiality in the case of *Hutton v. Canadian Broadcasting Corp.*[215] The appellants had conceived and produced a pilot called "Star Tracks." In 1980, Star Tracks became the television series Star Chart, a co-production between the appellants and the CBC (Respondent). The respondent cancelled the show, as it was contractually entitled to do, and produced its own "version" of the show. The trial judge dismissed the claim for copyright infringement. The Court of Appeal agreed:

> To show infringement of these rights there must be proof of substantial similarity and copying.
> [. . .]

> The requirement of substantial similarity must be apparent when viewing the works as a whole. As was recently stated in *Preston v. 20th Century Fox Canada Ltd.* (1990), 33 C.P.R. (3d) 242 at 273 (F.C.T.D.):

> > Substantial similarity is not to be measured only by the quantity of matter reproduced from a copyrighted work, though that may be a significant

---

[212] *Supra*, note 63 at 481.

[213] [1894] A.C. 335 (U.K. H.L.).

[214] *Ibi.d* at 342.

[215] (1992), 120 A.R. 291, 41 C.P.R. (3d) 45 (Alta. C.A.) [*Hutton* cited to C.P.R.].

factor. . . . Of more import may be the quality of matter reproduced. At least in the case of literary or dramatic works assessing similarities may depend upon a number of factors.

Although it may be useful to compare components of each work, the overriding requirement for infringement is substantial similarity of the works as a whole and substantial similarity in the modes of expression.

The context in which the defendant uses the material may also be relevant. For example, British courts consider substantiality not only from the perspective of the plaintiff's work but also in terms of whether what was taken was substantial *in the defendant's work*.[216] This approach is hard to reconcile with a plain reading of s. 3 of the Canadian Act, however, which clearly refers to the reproduction or other use of a protected work or substantial part thereof (that is, evaluated from the plaintiff's perspective). Yet, the view that copyright can be used as a legal means to protect against simple misappropriation, where the value of the taking to the *defendant* is indeed relevant, has been accepted on a few occasions.

4) Under s. 39, reasonably justified ignorance of the protection of an object can be pleaded as a defence. Although this has never succeeded in Canada, reasonably justified ignorance may nonetheless contribute to the reduction of damages.[217] This defence is unavailable if the work is registered.

5) As for the last defence of licence or consent, it largely depends on the facts and the plaintiff's behaviour. If a person has obtained a licence or can infer consent from the acts (or omissions in appropriate circumstances) of the copyright owner, then no infringement has taken place.

### 10. Statutory Defences

A handful of statutory defences are set out in ss. 29 and following of the Act.

In this area, the Supreme Court in *CCH* seems to have altered or at least explained a number of key elements of the scope and role of exceptions under the Act.

---

[216] Starting with *Kelly v. Hooper* (1839), 4 Jur. 21, 1 Y. & C.C.C. 197, cited with approval though in a somewhat different context in *Latour v. Cyr*, [1951] Ex. C.R. 92, 15 C.P.R. 21 (Can. Ex. Ct.).

[217] *Dictionnaires Robert Canada SCC v. Librairie du Nomade Inc.* (1987), [1987] F.C.J. No. 1, 16 C.P.R. (3d) 319, 1987 CarswellNat 250 (Fed. T.D.), affirmed (1990), 37 F.T.R. 240 (note) (Fed. C.A.).

### (a) A Hierarchy of Exceptions?

An interesting part of the *CCH* decision is the apparent establishment of a hierarchy of exceptions. The Court considered, first, whether the actions of the Law Society were fair dealing under s. 29. Then the Chief Justice, in her analysis of s. 30.3, stated: "I concluded in the main appeal that the Law Society's dealings with the publishers' works were fair. Thus, the Law Society need not rely on the library exemption."[218] This may seem surprising because s. 30.2 specifically applies to libraries and photocopying. In other words, there was a provision apparently directly on point (though not yet in force at the time of the facts of the case), yet the Supreme Court considered its analysis unnecessary.

Does this means that specific exceptions are to be considered only as instances where Parliament chose to exempt conduct that was not otherwise "fair" under s. 29, 29.1 or 29.2? Indeed, the Act does define these three sub-sections not simply as exceptions but also as "fair dealing," whereas ss. 29.4 to 32.2 and s. 80 are labelled *only* as "exceptions" ("It is not an infringement of copyright. . ."). The Chief Justice says that fair dealing "can perhaps more properly [be] understood as users' *rights*." "Research," she adds, "must be given a large and liberal interpretation in order to ensure that *users' rights* are not unduly constrained."[219] Fair dealing may be considered as "upstream exceptions," and exceptions specific to a certain category of users (including s. 30.3) could thus be called "downstream exceptions."

It is important to note, however, that an analysis of s. 30.2 would also have required examining whether the copying was fair dealing (under s. 30.2(1)) or "research and private study" (under s. 30.2(2)). In other words, the Court had to decide whether the copying was for research and private study under either provision. Yet, one should consider the potential impact of a different approach on the conclusions reached by the Court in *CCH*. One could have taken the view that the analysis of s. 30.2(2) should happen first because it was directly on point. Yet, s. 30.2(2) would not have been helpful to the Law Society for two reasons. First, it entered into force in September 1999, after the copying on which the publishers had based their infringement claim (some of which dated back to 1993). Second, s. 30.3(2) clearly states that the photocopying exception only applies to certain types of works (which does not include books, such as Dean Bruce Feldthusen's textbook, *Economic Negligence*). Yet, the court could have found that (a) Parliament had provided for the liability of libraries in the context of photocopying (reprographic reproduction) in ss. 30.2 and 30.3; (b) that those

---

[218] *CCH, supra*, note 15 at para. 84.
[219] *Ibid.* at para 51. [Emphasis added].

exceptions did not apply in this case for the above-mentioned reasons: (c) that Parliament introduced those exceptions because a significant portion of the photocopying occurring in libraries was not fair dealing, and thus libraries needed an exemption (because otherwise they could be said to be authorizing the reproduction and thus be in violation of section 3 *in fine*). In other words, it would have been defensible to use s. 30.2(2) as an indirect definition of the scope of the "research and private study" exception when copies are made by a library for its patrons. The Court did not do so. Alternatively, the Court could have noted that its analysis of fair dealing was applicable only to pre-1999 instances of copying, and that since the entry into force of s. 30.2, and of s. 30.3 for self-service machines,[220] only those provisions applied. Again, the Court did not do so.[221] For all these reasons, and in light of the Court's insistence on the application of ss. 29 and 29.1, it seems that fair dealing indeed has special status among exceptions, and is placed on a normative level that is close or equal to the rights contained in s. 3. Let us consider whether that is the case and what some of the implications might be.

The expression "users' rights" is used several times in the decision.[222] In a different context, however, the Court speaks of users' "interests,"[223] specifically when referring to the equilibrium in the Act between the rights of authors and the interests of users. There are two ways to interpret this. First, one could argue that this is a jejune if not careless choice of words and that the Court used words it did not intend to use to mean different things. From that perspective, and in keeping with *obiter dictum* in *Théberge*,[224] all exceptions, including fair dealing, are just that (independently

---

[220] Section 30.3 has the added condition that a collective management regime must be in place, which was the case in *CCH*.

[221] It may be in part because of the strategy adopted by the litigants. Gibson J. noted at the trial level that ss. 30.2 and 30.3 had not been "argued in any substantive way before the court." ((1999), [2000] 2 F.C. 451, 179 D.L.R. (4th) 609, 2 C.P.R. (4th) 129 (Fed. T.D.), additional reasons at (2000), 4 C.P.R. (4th) 129 (Fed. T.D.), reversed (2002), 18 C.P.R. (4th) 161 (Fed. C.A.), leave to appeal allowed (2002), 21 C.P.R. (4th) vi (S.C.C.), reversed (2004), 30 C.P.R. (4th) 1 (S.C.C.), additional reasons at (2004), 34 C.P.R. (4th) 1 (F.C.A.)). Similarly, the Federal Court of Appeal had noted that the library exemption applied to the Great Library (all three members of the panel agreed on this point), but did not use it to interpret the scope of fair dealing ([2002] 4 F.C. 213, 18 C.P.R. (4th) 161, 212 D.L.R. (4th) 385 (Fed. C.A.), leave to appeal allowed (2002), 21 C.P.R. (4th) vi (S.C.C.), reversed (2004), 30 C.P.R. (4th) 1 (S.C.C.), additional reasons at (2004), 34 C.P.R. (4th) 1 (F.C.A.)).

[222] *CCH*, *supra*, note 15. See., *e.g.*, in paras. 48, 51, and 54.

[223] *Ibid.*, at para. 70.

[224] *Théberge*, *supra*, note 7 at paras. 30-32.

of the fact that some are presented as such in the statute while others are characterized as "fair dealing") and thus normatively inferior to the exclusive rights contained in s. 3. In fact, one could even argue that fair dealing is "inferior" in status to other exceptions because in addition to having to show an allowable purpose, one must also show that use was fair, a condition not found in other exceptions.[225] That is a reasonable reading of the Act. However, it is not obvious that this was the view that the Supreme Court wanted to express.

Another reading of the Court's view is as follows: under ss. 29 to 29.2, users have (something like) a "right" to use a work. The Court posits the existence of a conflict, as it were, between the author's exclusive right and the user's "right", and concludes that Parliament decided on public policy grounds to halt authors' rights at the wall of fair dealing. It bears emphasis that all fair dealing exceptions are *purpose*-driven (private study, research, criticism, review and news reporting), and not specific to a class of users. Under many other exceptions, a user has the burden of showing that she belongs to the category of users concerned. Even s. 80 may be said to be restricted to a class of users, those who make private copies.[226]

This interpretation of *CCH*, while it may be at odds with some previously held views about exceptions in the Act, seems consistent both with the repeated use of the expression "users' rights" and with the hierarchy of exceptions applied by the Supreme Court. It is also consistent with the broad interpretation of the term "research" adopted by the Court in light of the statute's purpose. Indeed, if ss. 29 to 29.2 create users' "rights", there is no reason to treat them as simple exceptions to a "norm of protection."[227] When reading *CCH*, one is drawn to the conclusion that the court weighted the authors' exclusive rights and the users' "right" to use the works on level plates of the proverbial scale.

This reading of *CCH* also reconciles the use of both "rights" and "interests" when discussing exceptions and fair dealing. Users have a "right" to deal fairly with a protected work. They also have a broader *interest* in the maintenance of equilibrium in the protection that copyright affords, part of which is, from their viewpoint, reflected in the right of fair dealing and in (other) exceptions but also in limitations on author's rights, as, for example, limits on the author's term of protection and the type of acts covered under s. 3.

---

[225] Categories of users include, for example, archives or libraries.

[226] S. 80(1) refers to the "the private use of the person who makes the copy." In the same vein, ss. 29.4 to 32.2 refer to the user who benefits from the exception. That is not the case under ss. 29 to 29.2.

[227] Conversely, when interpreting ss. 29.4 to 32.2 and s. 80, courts could be guided by the fact that these are "true exceptions."

This interpretation of *CCH* is consistent with a view that the Supreme Court was affirming and building on the copyright principles set out in the majority reasons of *Théberge,* which speaks repeatedly of balance and of achieving public policy objectives by recognizing creator's rights but "giving due weight to their limited nature."[228]

### (b)  The Meaning of Fair Dealing

An interesting part of the *CCH* decision is the broad interpretation of the term "research." This approach is fully consonant, however, with the interpretation discussed above, according to which fair dealing has a special status among copyright exceptions — compared to those under ss. 29.4 to 32.2 or s. 80 of the Act. The Supreme Court takes the view that it is necessary to interpret fair dealing broadly in light of the *Act*'s purpose. Against this backdrop, research, even when conducted by commercial entities or for-profit, still qualifies as research for purposes of fair dealing.[229]

For ss. 29 to 29.2 to apply, the dealing must not only be for an acceptable purpose (private study, research, criticism, review and news reporting), but it must also be *fair.* This is perhaps the area where the Court's decision, in confirming, with some clarifications, the Court of Appeal's approach, may have a significant impact. In the past, courts have used criteria such as the amount used and the amount actually necessary to accomplish the purpose and whether there would be economic competition between a work and the product of a fair dealing use. *CCH* adopts a (probably non-exhaustive) list of six criteria to determine fairness:

(1)    the purpose of the dealing;
(2)    the character of the dealing;
(3)    the amount of the dealing;
(4)    alternatives to the dealing;
(5)    the nature of the work; and
(6)    the effect of the dealing on the work.

The Court specifically adds that not all six criteria have to be applied in each case,[230] thus avoiding the situation in the United States where courts must go through each of the four statutory fair use criteria even when they

---

[228] *Théberge, supra,* note 7 at para. 31.
[229] *CCH, supra,* note 15 at para. 51.
[230] *CCH, supra,* note 15 at para. 53.

are unlikely to be relevant.[231] As a point of comparison, the four U.S. criteria are as follows:

(1) the purpose and character of the use, including whether such use is of a commercial nature or is for non-profit educational purposes;
(2) the nature of the copyrighted work;
(3) the amount and substantiality of the portion used in relation to the copyrighted work as a whole; and
(4) the effect of the use upon the potential market for or value of the copyrighted work.[232]

If one compares the two "lists," one notes that five of the six Canadian criteria actually mirror the four U.S. criteria, as follows:

| Canada "fair dealing" | United States "fair use" |
|---|---|
| (1) purpose of the dealing | Corresponds to above (1) in U.S. list. However in the U.S. the non-profit nature is relevant |
| (2) character of the dealing | Corresponds to above (1) |
| (3) amount of the dealing | Corresponds to above (3) except the substantiality |
| (5) nature of the work | Corresponds to above (2) |
| (6) effect of the dealing on the work | Corresponds to above (4), although more specific as to the kind of effect |

There is thus little doubt that with respect to fair dealing Canada's copyright legislation is now closely aligned with the United States' fair use doctrine. Canadian courts do, however, have significantly more flexibility in that, first, they do not have to apply all criteria in each case; and, second, criteria (1) and (6) are defined in a more open fashion than the corresponding U.S. criteria. An important distinction between the two systems is that for the dealing to be fair in Canada, it must be *for a designated purpose*. Yet, even on this point the two systems are fairly close. In *Harper & Row*, the

---

[231] The use of all four criteria seems to be mandated under 17 USC §107. The chapeau to this section states that "in determining whether the use made of a work in any particular case is a fair use the factors to be considered **shall include**. . ." (emphasis added).

[232] *Ibid.*

U.S. Supreme Court listed non-exhaustively the following purposes of fair use: "criticism, comment, news reporting, teaching (including multiple copies for classroom use), scholarship, or research."[233] The net result of *CCH* is that, under Canadian law, there is a flexible list of six criteria to determine fairness but an exhaustive statutory list of acceptable purposes, while under the U.S. fair use doctrine, there is a mandatory list of criteria to determine fairness but an open list of permissible purposes.

Given the high degree of parallelism between the criteria enunciated in *CCH* and the U.S. fair use criteria, one may wonder whether U.S. caselaw will heretofore be used to interpret the Canadian criteria. Given that similar words are used, the functional comparability of the two markets (except for their respective size), and the similarity of the legislative context in which the interpretive issue arises, this is certainly tempting. Yet, one should proceed with caution, because the origins and history of the two systems are distinct.[234] One obvious difference is that, in the United States, the Constitution itself not only gives Congress the power to adopt copyright legislation but states the purpose of that legislation, namely to "promote the progress of Science and the Useful Arts."[235] One would thus have to compare the statements of purpose that emerge from *CCH* and *Théberge* but also from, *e.g.*, *Compo*,[236] to decide the degree of compatibility between the philosophies that undergird the two systems.

While it is not possible to provide a full comparative analysis, a few key statements can be juxtaposed.

---

[233] *Harper & Row Publishers Inc. v. Nation Enterprises*, 471 U.S. 539 (U.S. N.Y., 1985) at 560.

[234] The classic statement of "caution" is found in *Compo, supra*, note 4 at 367: "The United States Copyright Act, both in its present and earlier forms, has, of course, many similarities to the Canadian Act, as well as to the pre-existing Imperial Copyright Act. However, United States court decisions, even where the factual situations are similar, must be scrutinized very carefully because of some fundamental differences in copyright concepts which have been adopted in the legislation of that country." The statement is repeated in *CCH, supra*, note 15 at para. 22.

[235] U.S. Const., art. I, § 8, cl. 8.

[236] See note 234.

| Canada | United States |
|---|---|
| [T]he purpose of copyright law was to balance the public interest in promoting the encouragement and dissemination of works of the arts and intellect and obtaining a just reward for the creator.[237] | [T]o promote the progress of science and useful arts. . .[238]<br><br>[C]opyright's purpose is to promote the creation and publication of free expression.[239] |
| [W]hen an author must exercise skill and judgment to ground originality in a work, there is a safeguard against the author being overcompensated for his or her work. This helps ensure that there is room for the public domain to flourish as others are able to produce new works by building on the ideas and information contained in the works of others.[240] | [I]n determining whether a fact-based work is an original work of authorship, [courts] should focus on the manner in which the collected facts have been selected, coordinated, and arranged. This is a straightforward application of the originality requirement. Facts are never original, so the compilation author can claim originality, if at all, only in the way the facts are presented.[241] |
| The Copyright Act is usually presented as a balance between promoting the public interest in the encouragement and dissemination of works of the arts and intellect and obtaining a just reward for the creator (or, more accurately, to prevent someone other than the creator from appropriating whatever benefits may be generated).[242] | [T]he Framers intended copyright itself to be the engine of free expression. By establishing a marketable right to the use of one's expression, copyright supplies the economic incentive to create and disseminate ideas.[243] |
| One of the purposes of copyright legislation has been to protect and reward the intellectual effort of the author.[244] | |

---

[237] *CCH, supra,* note 15 at para. 23.

[238] See note 235.

[239] *Eldred v. Ashcroft,* 537 U.S. 186, 123 S. Ct. 769 (2003) rehearing denied 538 U.S. 916, 123 S. Ct. 1505, (2003).

[240] *CCH, supra,* note 15 at para 23.

[241] *Feist Publications Inc. v. Rural Telephone Service Co., supra,* note 44 at para. 39.

[242] *Théberge, supra,* note 7 at para. 30.

[243] *Harper & Row, supra,* note 233 at 558.

[244] *Télé-direct, supra,* note 36.

> The Copyright Act, 1911, was passed with a single object, namely, the benefit of authors of all kinds, whether the works were literary, dramatic or musical.[245] See also Article 1 of the Revised Berne Convention.

It thus seems that U.S. cases on fair use *could* be used in appropriate cases, but with the required degree of caution. Such caution would require filtering out any extraneous elements such as distinct constitutional arguments (*e.g.*, based on the U.S. Constitution's First Amendment), and elements based on a perception of the basic tenets of copyright law that seem alien to the Canadian approach. In light of the above comparison, however, there should be few cases where the latter problem would arise.

### (c) Other Possible Impacts

Apart from the relative alignment of fair dealing with the US fair use doctrine, *CCH*'s approach could have a number of important impacts. The first, already discussed above, is that if fair dealing is a "right" or at least a special exception (whereas ss. 29.4 to 32.2 and s. 80 would contain "normal exceptions"), then fair dealing is normatively on a higher level than other exceptions — possibly on an equal footing with authors' exclusive rights. When interpreting the Act and, given a purposive approach to the Act, fair dealing should be interpreted broadly. By contrast, "normal" exceptions, it may be argued, should be interpreted more restrictively.[246] This point is debatable, however, and one could also argue that all the exceptions should be interpreted on the same footing, in spite of the important variations in the language used by Parliament, in a way that reflects the purpose of the Act, including the equilibrium between authors and users.[247] "Although the

---

[245] *Performing Right Society, Ltd. v. Hammond's Bradford Brewery Co.*, [1934] 1 Ch. 121 at 127, quoted with approval by McLachlin J. (as she then was) in *Bishop v. Stevens, supra*, note 5 at 478-79. Article 1 of the Berne Convention reads as follows: "The countries to which this Convention applies constitute a Union for the protection of the rights of authors in their literary and artistic works." (See International Section).

[246] As in *Sillitoe v. Mc-Graw Hill Book Co. (U.K.) Ltd.*, [1983] F.S.R. 545 (Eng. Ch.) at 558. See also R. Sullivan, *Sullivan and Driedger on the Construction of Statutes*, 4th ed. (Butterworths, 2002), at pp. 396-398. It may also have an impact on the burden of proof.

[247] See *Sullivan and Driedger on the Construction of Statutes, ibid.* at 166-67. See also *CCH, supra*, note 15 at para. 9.

desires and intentions of these individuals [any participant in the legislative process] obviously determine the content and form of bills, the 'mind' that approves them and enacts them into law is the corporate mind of the legislature."[248]

Second, the choice of a hierarchy of norms, in which fair dealing is normatively higher than other exceptions, seems to imply that an analysis of any allegedly infringing conduct should proceed sequentially, as the Court did in *CCH*, even if there is a more specific, directly applicable "normal" exception. One should first determine whether the conduct was fair under s. 29, 29.1 or 29.2 and only then proceed to other exceptions if required. If this is what the Court intended, it could have an impact on, *e.g*, tariffs that currently compensate rightsholders for exceptions other than fair dealing, in case some of the conduct to which the specific exception applies is heretofore considered "fair".

Part of the fairness requirement demands that one use only the part of a protected work needed for the (allowed) purpose. In *Zamacoïs v. Douville*, the notion of fair dealing with respect to reproducing the whole of a copyrighted work was rejected in the context of criticism.[249] A newspaper published a (scathing) review of an article about the treatment of animals during war and along with the critical comments printed the entire article. The court held that the notion of fair dealing did not apply to this use. The public interest in topical news was not implicated here because the poet-dramatist author treated the topic in a whimsical manner and the reproduction had the effect of eliminating a significant portion of the author's potential market.

Another condition, as noted *inter alia* in ss. 29.1(b) and 29.2 of the *Act*, is that fair dealing for the purposes of criticism, review or news reporting is available as a defence only if the source and other data (name of the author, etc.) are provided.

In higher education, presumably most of what professors, researchers and graduate students do outside of teaching could be considered research as defined in *CCH*. Perhaps a broad definition of "private study" could also be justified for the reasons enunciated in *CCH*. This would lead to the conclusion that occasional use of publicly available material for research or private study is a form of use covered under s. 29. Because *CCH* recognizes that the maker of the copy — in other words the person performing the s. 3 act which would otherwise require an authorization (in that case the Great Library) — can also benefit from the exception applicable to the person who is doing the research, it follows that lawyers, professors and educational institutions may be able to rely on the research and private study exception to make material available to students without permission. While this seems

---

[248] *Ibid*. at 204.
[249] [1943] 2 D.L.R. 257 (Can. Ex. Ct.).

consonant with *CCH,* the use must also be fair according to the criteria mentioned by the Supreme Court. Based on the fifth and sixth *CCH* criteria (the nature of the work and the effect of the dealing on the work), fairness would seem to apply differently to the occasional use of general material such as newspaper clippings or non-educational web pages, on the one hand, and to material produced specifically for the educational market, on the other.

## (d)  Parody and the "Public Interest" Defence

Fair dealing for the purpose of parody has never been successfully invoked in a Canadian court. The three more striking cases from the point of view of freedom of expression are:

1) *Rôtisseries St-Hubert Ltée v. Syndicat des travailleurs(euses) de la Rôtisserie St-Hubert de Drummondville (CSN)* (1986), 17 C.P.R. (3d) 461 (Que. S.C.)

At the time of a labour conflict, the defendants composed and distributed a pamphlet which declaimed against the working conditions of the plaintiff's employees. This blue pamphlet bore a stylized head of a long-toothed cock carrying a knife. A sticker, entitled "The real face of St. Hubert", portayed a deformed head of a cock and was distributed without the plaintiff's consent and stuck on the plaintiff's premises in Drummondville. Another sticker, entitled "I support St. Hubert" bore a complete reproduction of the St-Hubert's stylized head of a cock in its characteristic trapezium with St-Hubert's colors and a font similar to the one used by the corporation. Badges with the same characteristics were also distributed. The Union argued that it had the right to use the modified logo to express its dissatisfaction with the employer's behaviour and attitude, under Article 2(b) of the *Charter of Rights and Freedoms*. The Court rejected the argument as ill founded without giving reasons.

2) *Cie générale des établissements Michelin - Michelin & Cie v. CAW-Canada* (1996), (sub nom. *Cie Générale des Établissements Michelin-Michelin & Cie v. C.A.W.-Canada*) [1997] 2 F.C. 306, 71 C.P.R. (3d) 348 (Fed. T.D.)

> The Plaintiff Compagnie Générale des Établissements Michelin-Michelin & Cie. ['Michelin'] is a French corporation with worldwide interests in the manufacture, distribution and sale of tires and automotive accessories. Michelin also provides tourism services, including the production of tourist guides and maps.

[T]he Defendant, National Automobile, Aerospace, Transportation and General Workers Union of Canada [hereinafter 'CAW'] attempted to unionize the employees of Michelin . . . , at Michelin Canada's three tire plants in Granton, Waterville and Bridgewater, Nova Scotia. [. . .]

During the campaign, the CAW distributed leaflets, displayed posters and issued information sheets that reproduced the term 'MICHELIN'. The CAW also used in its campaign material Michelin's corporate logo, the Michelin Tire Man or 'Bibendum' design, a drawing of a beaming marshmallow-like rotund figure composed of tires.

The Defendants argued that their posters and leaflets depicting "Bibendum" were forms of expression protected by section 2(b) of the *Charter*.

Mr. Justice Teitelbaum concluded as follows:

The Defendants argue that their parody of the Plaintiff's "Bibendum" copyrighted design does deserve the label protected expression. . . . I agree with the Defendants that the use of a copyright by a union to parody a company logo in the midst of an organizing campaign does raise certain constitutional issues. I do, however, part company with the Defendants on the resolution of the constitutional question. I hold that the Defendants' right to freedom of expression was not restricted. The *Charter* does not confer the right to use private property[250] — the Plaintiff's copyright — in the service of freedom of expression. (footnotes omitted)

3) *British Columbia Automobile Assn. v. O.P.E.I.U., Local 378* (2001), 10 C.P.R. (4th) 423 (B.C. S.C.)

The British Columbia Automobile Association claimed that the defendant union, representing some of its employees, established websites that infringed the plaintiff's copyright in its website by copying from that site and incorporating various design elements, including registered trade-marks and other indicia, into the defendant's website. The British Columbia Supreme Court rejected the union's defence as follows:

It is not necessary for me to discuss the scope of this statutory provision for fair dealing for the purpose of criticism or review. I do not think the defendant's use satisfies the fair dealing defence for the simple reason that the website

---

[250] Here the judge draws a distinction with *Comité pour la République du Canada - Committee for the Commonwealth of Canada v. Canada* (1991), (sub nom. *Committee for the Commonwealth of Canada v. Canada*) 77 D.L.R. (4th) 385 (S.C.C.), reconsideration refused (May 8, 1991), Doc. 20334 (S.C.C.), in which public property was used for a protest.

> contains no criticism of the BCAA website and it does not, as required by the statute, mention the source and author of the BCAA website.
>
> The Union is entitled to have a website and use it as part of its struggle but that does not give it the right to breach the plaintiff's copyright. I have concluded that the first two Union websites breached the plaintiff's copyright in the 1997 BCAA site.

In other words, s. 29.1 allows criticism of a work, not of its author or owner.

Similar findings were made in other cases. An interlocutory injunction was granted in *Canadian Tire Corp. v. R.C.U., Local 1518 of United Food & Commercial Workers Union*,[251] enjoining a union to stop using the Canadian Tire logo with a slash across it. The Court, however, did not completely close the door:

> While there may be situations where the guarantee of freedom of expression in paragraph 2(b) of the *Canadian Charter of Rights and Freedoms* may properly limit the protection otherwise given to the owners of copyright, I do not believe this represents such a situation. The addition by the defendants of a diagonal line across the plaintiff's logo does not, it seems to me, amount to a sufficient expression of thought by the defendants as to override the plaintiff's copyright in its logo: see *The Queen v. James Lorimer & Co. Ltd.* (1984), 77 CPR 2(d) 262 at p. 273 (Fed. C.A.).

Similarly, in *R. v. James Lorimer & Co.*[252] the Federal Court of Appeal mentioned freedom of expression as a valid defence, though it found that it did not apply to the facts of the case:

> I agree with the learned Trial Judge that there is no merit in this defence. If, indeed, the constraints on infringement of copyright could be construed as an unjustified limitation on an infringer's freedom of expression in some circumstances, this is not among them. So little of its own thought, belief, opinion and expression is contained in the respondent's infringing work that it is properly to be regarded as entirely an appropriation of the thought, belief, opinion and expression of the author of the infringed work.

An interesting defence was recognized by courts in the United Kingdom, based on the public interest and the public's right to information. In the case of *Ashdown v. Telegraph Group Ltd.*,[253] a national U.K. newspaper argued that it had a right to publish the verbatim minute of a meeting with

---

[251] (1985), 7 C.P.R. (3d) 415 (Fed. T.D.).

[252] [1984] 1 F.C. 1065, 77 C.P.R. (2d) 262 (Fed. C.A.).

[253] (2001), [2001] 4 All E.R. 666, [2002] Ch. 149 (U.K. C.A. (Civ. Div.)).

the Prime Minister and a prominent politician, in spite of the fact that the meeting was held in confidence. The politician, Ms. Ashdown, sued *inter alia* for copyright infringement. The publisher contended that the court was obliged to take into consideration the right of freedom of expression.

The English Court of Appeal wrote:

> Freedom of expression is one of the essential foundations of society: see Handyside v United Kingdom (1976) 1 EHRR 737. The right applies to information which offends, disturbs or shocks: see *Handyside*. Exceptions to the principle of freedom of expression must be narrowly interpreted: see Sunday Times v United Kingdom (1979) 2 EHRR 245. Freedom of expression is of particular importance for the press, which has a vital 'watchdog' role in society. . . . Where matters of public interest are concerned it is difficult to show that interference with freedom of expression satisfies article 10 [of the *European Convention for the Protection of Human Rights and Fundamental Freedoms*, a schedule to the UK *Human Rights Act 1998*]. . . . The expression of opinions on matters of public interest, even if misguided, is protected. . . . There is little scope under article 10(2) for restrictions on political speech or debate on questions of public interest. . . .

> This is not a case of deprivation of property within the meaning of article 1 of Protocol 1 to the Convention because it would result not in the extinction of all the claimant's rights but only in a control of the use of property. The distinction is important to the question of whether compensation is to be paid. . . . Controls are compatible with the Convention if they are deemed necessary in the general interest.

After this interesting analysis, in which the court concludes that freedom of expression would trump copyright protection if there is a direct conflict, it reached the conclusion that this was not the case based on the facts before the court:

> [I]t is necessary to consider the impact of the public interest on the test of fair dealing. Are the facts of this case such that, arguably, the importance of freedom of expression outweighs the conventional considerations set out above so as to afford the Telegraph Group a defence of fair dealing? Is it arguable that it was necessary to quote verbatim the passages of which Mr Ashdown was the author in order to convey to the readers of the 'Sunday Telegraph' the authenticity of its reports of current events of public interest? . . . True it was that the basic facts in the articles may have been published already in the 'Financial Times', the 'Observer' and the radio interview on 'Resigning Issues'. But Mr Ashdown's own words gave the factual material a detail and authority which was novel. There had been previous publications that gave the public much of the information that was contained in the 'Sunday Telegraph' articles. . . . Tony

Blair and Paddy Ashdown privately agreed to try to persuade Labour and the Liberal Democrats to go into the next election on a joint policy manifesto, before the LibDem leader stood down. Details of the scheme are due to be revealed in Ashdown's diaries. Downing Street is seeking assurances that the diaries will not be published until after the next election. The diaries, a highly detailed account of Ashdown's top secret contacts with Labour, are described as explosive by one senior Liberal Democrat who has seen extracts. The source said: 'They were practising a massive deception on their respective parties.' There were a number of other newspaper articles to similar effect.

The accuracy of these accounts was challenged by Mr Blair. In these circumstances we consider that, just as there is scope for argument that the 'Sunday Telegraph's' publication was the reporting of current events, so it is arguable that the Telegraph Group were justified in making limited quotation of Mr Ashdown's own words, in order to demonstrate that they had indeed obtained his own minute, so that they were in a position to give an authentic account of the meeting. In this context the last of the criteria that we have just considered is of critical relevance. Can it be argued that the extensive reproduction of Mr Ashdown's own words was necessary in order to satisfy the reader that the account given of his meeting with Mr Blair was authoritative? We do not believe that it can. The statement by the 'Sunday Telegraph' that they had obtained a copy of the minute coupled with one or two short extracts from it would have sufficed. There may in law have been justification for the publication of the confidential information that was contained in the minute. That is not an issue which is before this court. We do not, however, consider that it is arguable that there was any justification for the extent of the reproduction of Mr Ashdown's own words. . . We do not consider it arguable that article 10 requires that the Telegraph Group should be able to profit from this use of Mr Ashdown's copyright without paying compensation.

As in the (Canadian) *Zamacoïs* case, it is much harder to invoke fair dealing when the whole work is taken. However, the principle of a public interest defence (apparently within the confines of fair dealing) seems to exist in U.K. law.

One could also mention the English case of *Hyde Park Residence Ltd. v. Yelland*[254] in which a security company appealed against the refusal of its claim for infringement of copyright and a finding that the defendant had a bona fide defence based on fair dealing or public interest. The defendant was a newspaper which had obtained and published the plaintiff's photographs, of Diana, Princess of Wales, and Dodi Al-Fayed the day before their fatal accident, without permission. The appeal was allowed. Interestingly, the Court of Appeal clearly stated that it had inherent jurisdiction to refuse

---

[254] (2000), [2001] Ch. 143, [2000] 3 W.L.R. 215 (Eng. C.A.) (U.K. C.A. (Civ. Div.)).

to enforce copyright in circumstances where it would otherwise offend against the policy of the law but added that the circumstances had to derive from the work itself, and not from the ownership of the copyright. Enforcement of copyright would thus be refused in the case of work that was, *inter alia*, immoral, contrary to family life or injurious to public health or safety, or incited acts that tended toward such conduct. Although the still photos were arguably of public interest, publication was unnecessary, as the information they contained could have been conveyed in a way that did not infringe copyright.

A defence based on the public interest was accepted by the same court in *Lion Laboratories Ltd. v. Evans*.[255] Two employees of a company that manufactured the device used by British police to monitor blood alcohol levels of drivers had published internal company correspondence that showed the models were defective. The company sued for breach of confidence and infringement of copyright. The Court found that there was a "well established" defence of public interest to actions for breach of confidence and copyright. In deciding whether the defence could be raised the court had to take into account (a) the wide difference between what was interesting to the public and what was in the public interest to make known; (b) the fact that the media had a private interest in publishing what appealed to the public in order to increase circulation; (c) that the public interest might be best served by the information being given to the police or other responsible body rather than to the press and (d) that a defendant ought not to be restrained merely because the matter the defendant sought to publish did not reveal misconduct.

While the following may be considered *obiter dictum*, in *SOCAN* the Supreme Court agreed to consider the function of exceptions in a broader societal context when the Court wrote:

> This Court has recently described the *Copyright Act* as providing 'a balance between promoting the public interest in the encouragement and dissemination of works of the arts and intellect and obtaining a just reward for the creator (or, more accurately, to prevent someone other than the creator from appropriating whatever benefits may be generated)' (*Théberge v. Galerie d'art du Petit Champlain* at para. 30, *CCH Ltd. v. Law Society of Upper Canada*, at para. 10). The capacity of the Internet to disseminate 'works of the arts and intellect' is one of the great innovations of the information age. Its use should be facilitated rather than discouraged, but this should not be done unfairly at the expense of those who created the works of arts and intellect in the first place.
> [. . .]

---

[255] (1984), [1985] Q.B. 526, [1984] 2 All E.R. 417 (Eng. C.A.).

Parliament did not say that the intermediaries are engaged in communication of copyright content *but* enjoy an immunity. Instead, s. 2.4(1)(*b*) says that such intermediaries are deemed, for purposes of the *Copyright Act*, not to *communicate* the work to the public at all. Whether or not intermediaries are parties to the communication for legal purposes other than copyright is an issue that will have to be decided when it arises.

The respondent contends that s. 2.4(1)(*b*) is an exemption from liability and should be read narrowly; but this is incorrect. Under the *Copyright Act*, the rights of the copyright owner and the limitations on those rights should be read together to give 'the fair and balanced reading that befits remedial legislation' (*CCH*, para. 48).

Section 2.4(1)(*b*) is not a loophole but an important element of the balance struck by the statutory copyright scheme. It finds its roots, perhaps, in the defence of innocent dissemination sometimes available to bookstores, libraries, news vendors, and the like who, generally speaking, have no actual knowledge of an alleged libel, are aware of no circumstances to put them on notice to suspect a libel, and committed no negligence in failing to find out about the libel. . . .
[. . .]

The 1988 amendments, including the predecessor to s. 2.4(1)(*b*), followed on the recommendation of an all party Sub-Committee on the Revision of Copyright of the House of Commons Standing Committee on Communications and Culture. Its report, entitled *A Charter of Rights for Creators* (1985), identified the need for a broader definition of telecommunication, one that was not dependent on the form of technology, which would provide copyright protection for retransmissions. This led to the adoption of the broad definition of communication in s. 3(1)(*f*). In conjunction with this, the Committee recommended, at p. 80, that those who participate in the retransmission 'solely to serve as an intermediary between the signal source and a retransmitter whose services are offered to the general public' should not be unfairly caught by the expanded definition. The ostensible objective, according to the Committee, was to avoid the unnecessary layering of copyright liability that would result from targeting the 'wholesale' stage (p. 80).
[. . .]

The Internet Service Provider, acting as an intermediary, does not charge a particular fee to its clients for music downloading (although clearly the availability of 'free music' is a significant business incentive).

I conclude that the *Copyright Act*, as a matter of legislative policy established by Parliament, does not impose liability for infringement on intermediaries who supply software and hardware to facilitate use of the Internet. (emphasis added; footnotes omitted)

### (e) Other Exceptions

There are two other categories of exceptions in the Act. While fair dealing applies to specific acts by any user, there are a number of user-specific exceptions in the Act, contained in ss. 29.4 to 30. Many apply only in the absence of a motive of gain (s. 29.3). Several exceptions are specific to "educational institutions," a term defined in s. 2 as applying only to non-profit institutions and government agencies. They cover manual reproductions or use of a projector (which may also cover multimedia projectors as devices "similar to overhead projectors" in s. 29.4 (1)(b)); certain public performances (s. 29.5); and the taping of news programs (s. 29.6) and other broadcasts (s. 29.7). Note the conditions imposed on educational institutions, in particular with respect to record keeping (s. 29.9) or payment of royalties (s. 29.6(2) and 29.7(2)). In addition, many of these exceptions (ss. 29.4 to 30) apply in a defined technological context and may not be compatible with the current use of technology for off-campus ("distance") education. (See, for example, the use of the language "on the premises" in ss. 29.4(1) *in fine*, 29.4(2) and 29.5.) There is also an all-encompassing exception for educational institutions (as well as other organizations, discussed below) concerning the live performance in public of music or a sound recording of music "in furtherance of an educational object" (s. 32.2(3)). Although this exception seems broader than s. 29.5, the section simply provides that an educational institution is not liable to pay compensation and thus is not worded as a true exception.

Libraries, archives and museums also benefit from specific exceptions (ss. 30.1 to 30.5). Note again the conditions imposed on these institutions, notably in terms of determining their patrons' intent (e.g. in s. 30.2(4)(a) and 30.21(3)(c)) and the other conditions imposed.

There is an exception allowing users of computer programs to make a copy of the program if necessary for compatibility with a particular computer and solely for the person's use, provided the copy is destroyed after the person ceases to be the owner of the copy (s. 30.6(a)). The making of a single backup copy is also permitted (s. 30.6(b)).

Under s. 30.8, a broadcaster who is otherwise authorized to broadcast or otherwise communicate a protected work to the public may make a royalty-free "ephemeral" copy of the material for broadcast purposes, subject to a series of detailed conditions, including record-keeping (s. 30.8(2)). "Ephemeral" is defined as no more than 30 days. After that time, a royalty is payable.

Section 32.2 also contains a number of additional "small exceptions," including the right for an author to reuse her material under certain conditions (s. 32.2(1)(a)); the right to reproduce an architectural work or a sculpture located in a public place (a feature of the Act no doubt useful for art students); to report on a public lecture or political speech; and to recite a "reasonable extract" of a work in public.[256] There are also specific exceptions, mostly concerning the use of music, in agricultural fairs and by religious, charitable and fraternal organizations (s. 32.2(2) and (3)).[257] However, this subsection is not worded as an exception proper but simply as an absence to pay "compensation." It is unclear whether s. 32.2(3) would prevent, *e.g.*, the issuance of an injunction or even damages other than "compensation."

Finally, under s. 30.7, the incidental and non-deliberate inclusion of protected subject matter is not an infringement. For example, if a protected work is accidentally included when filming a family gathering (if, for example, the radio is playing or the television is on or a copyrighted painting is hanging in the background) or when filming outside, that act would not infringe copyright.

## 11. Remedies

A few remedies are available in cases of copyright infringement. Section 34(1) of the Act states that the remedies available are: injunctions, damages, accounts and delivery up. Under s. 35, the copyright owner can ask for an account of profits made by the defendant *and* for damages. Section 35(2) provides the type of evidence that must be available by each party. An accounting of profits is usually considered an equitable remedy and thus subject to equitable defences. As the Federal Court of Appeal in a patent case explained about equitable remedies:[258]

> The learned Trial Judge declined to grant the equitable remedy of an accounting of profits. He cited the somewhat objectionable conduct by both parties, including the appellant's attitude in the development of his patent and the respondent's refusal to acknowledge the appellant's patent rights. The Trial Judge concluded that 'neither side's hands are entirely clean' and, therefore, felt equity did not favour either. Accordingly, he refused the remedy of accounting of profits. . . . Whatever the reason for, or merits of, the Trial Judge's refusal of an injunction, it is our view that, finding as we do that there could be potential

---

[256] It is difficult to define with precision the difference between the "reasonable extract" which is authorized under s. 32.2(1)(d) and the "substantial part" criterion of s. 3. It is not an infringement under s. 3 if the public performance concerns only an insubstantial part. Clearly, the reasonable extract must be more than an insubstantial part.

[257] See *C.A.P.A.C.*, *supra*, note 165.

[258] *Dableh v. Ontario Hydro*, [1996] 3 F.C. 751, 68 C.P.R. (3d) 129, 199 N.R. 57 (Fed. C.A.), leave to appeal refused (1997), 74 C.P.R. (3d) vi (S.C.C.) at para. 51 [*Dableh* cited to F.C.].

infringement, it is appropriate in a final judgment to grant a *quia timet* injunction. The 'clean hands' doctrine must be applied with some care, and it is now accepted that improper conduct by a party should not deprive him or her of an equitable remedy unless that conduct bears directly on the appropriateness of the remedy.

An accounting of profits was refused by the same court in another patent case because of the plaintiff's long delay in bringing the action.[259]

However, while the basis to ask for an accounting of profits in a patent infringement case is equitable — and *an alternative* to damages —, there is specific statutory authority in the *Copyright Act* to grant such a remedy *in addition to* damages. It could thus be argued that a successful defendant is entitled by law to both remedies, in spite of the apparent double recovery[260] because that is apparently the intent of Parliament.

Courts have occasionally granted punitive (exemplary) damages. In *Pro Arts*, Justice Labrosse of the Ontario High Court of Justice stated with reference to the general provision on remedies in the Act (now s. 34(1)):

> There is certainly no prohibition in the Act to an award of exemplary damages and if the plaintiff is entitled to all such remedies by way of damages and otherwise as are or may be conferred by law for the infringement of a right, it is my view that it was not the intention to exclude exemplary damages. Exemplary damages are well recognized at common law. There have also been numerous Canadian decisions where exemplary damages have been awarded: see *Underwriters' Survey Bureau Ltd. v. Massie & Renwick Ltd.* (1941), 1 C.P.R. 207, [1942] Ex. C.R. at p. 6, 2 Fox Pat. C. 39 (Exchequer Court) [varied

---

[259] *Invacare Corp. v. Everest & Jennings Canadian Ltd.* (1987), [1987] F.C.J. No. 233, 14 C.P.R. (3d) 156, 9 F.T.R. 241, 12 C.I.P.R. 173, 1987 CarswellNat 802 (Fed. T.D.), additional reasons at (1987), 15 C.P.R. (3d) 278 (Fed. T.D.).

[260] Courts have traditionally tried to avoid this double recovery. See *Netupsky v. Dominion Bridge Co.*, (1969), 9 D.L.R. (3d) 182, 70 W.W.R. 241, 61 C.P.R. 150 (B.C. C.A.), reversed on other grounds (1971), [1972] S.C.R. 368 (S.C.C.), *supra*, note 165; and *Pro Arts Inc. v. Campus Crafts Holdings Ltd.* (1980), 28 O.R. (2d) 422, 110 D.L.R. (3d) 366, 50 C.P.R. (2d) 230 (Ont. H.C.) at 386, in which Labrosse J. explained the principle as follows (under a previous version of the *Copyright Act* however):"Under s. 21 of the Act a legal fiction is created and the plaintiff is deemed to be the owner of the counterfeits and the plaintiff may take proceedings for the recovery of the infringing copies or for damages for conversion. . . .the remedies available to the plaintiff are cumulative and not alternative and damages may be awarded for conversion as well as for infringement and for the profits realized by the infringer. Damages for conversion will usually be based on the value of the article converted at the time of its conversion. However, the Court must avoid any overlap or duplication." [*Pro Arts* cited to D.L.R.].

1 C.P.R. 224, [1942] Ex. C.R. 1, 2 Fox Pat. C. 55]; *Standard Indust. Ltd. v. Rosen*, [1955] O.W.N. 262, [1955] 4 D.L.R. 363, 24 C.P.R. 41, 14 Fox Pat. C. 173 (Ontario High Court); *T.J. Moore Co. Ltd. v. Accessoires de Bureau de Que. Inc.* (1973), 4 C.P.R. (2d) 113 (Federal Court); and *MCA Can. Ltd.-MCA Canada Ltee v. Gillberry & Hawke Advertising Agency Ltd.* (1976), 28 C.P.R. (2d) 52 (Federal Court).[261]

Arguably, punitive damages have been used as a tool in cases where the plaintiff had difficulty in proving actual damages. Such was the case in *Standard Industries Ltd. v. Rosen*, cited by Justice Labrosse, in which Justice Spence of the same court explained:

> The problem of damages is a difficult one. The plaintiff's witnesses have given very indefinite evidence to the effect that changes in the plaintiff's catalogues in an attempt to circumvent the damaging pirating of its material had cost 'thousands of dollars.' How many thousands? [. . .]

> But the inability to show exact damages does not bar the plaintiff's recovery. It is perhaps the essence of such an action that the plaintiff would be unable to prove the actual incidence of deception and the danger is that the deception will occur without the plaintiff ever having any knowledge of it and the change in its business will be very difficult to pin down.

> In similar circumstances in *Underwriter's Survey Bureau Limited et al. v. Massie & Renwick Limited*, [1942], 1 D.L.R. 434, Ex. C.R. 1, 1 C.P.R. 207, McLean J. in the Exchequer Court considered an appeal from a Referee to whom the question of damages had been referred and who had granted, for what he characterized as nominal, general and exemplary damages, the sum of $5,000. McLean J. increased the amount to $10,000.

> I am of the opinion that I should allow $2,000 general damages, but I can treat the conduct of the defendant in proceeding at once to flout the judgment of Wilson J. in the first action only by awarding exemplary damages in the amount of $5,000.[262]

Sections 35 and 38.1 were meant to address this problem of proving actual damages. These sections may reduce a court's willingness, if not its authority, to grant punitive damages in addition to actual damages, an account of profits or, if the plaintiff so elects, statutory damages (see below). Punitive measures could still be appropriate in particularly egregious con-

---

[261] *Ibid.* at 381.

[262] (1954), [1955] 4 D.L.R. 363, 24 C.P.R. 41 (Ont. S.C.) at 375-76 [*Standard Indust.* cited to D.L.R.].

duct, but may then also be justified on a different basis, such as contempt of court.

The Supreme Court provided a detailed framework for punitive damages in the 2002 case of *Whiten v. Pilot Insurance Co.* (a contract case). Justice Binnie, for the majority, emphasized that punitive damages are an exception, which should be imposed only where there is "high-handed, malicious, arbitrary, or high reprehensible misconduct that departs to a marked degree from ordinary standards of decent behaviour," and where awarded, the amount should be "reasonably proportionate to such factors as the harm caused, the degree of the misconduct, the relative vulnerability of the plaintiff and any advantage or profit gained by the defendant." Punitive damages are awarded for the purposes of "retribution, deterrence and denunciation," and only where compensatory damages are insufficient for these purposes.[263]

Statutory damages (s. 38.1) were added to the Act in 1999.[264] Because it is not always cost effective or even possible to find a large number of infringing copies, a plaintiff may prefer to rely on damages set by law. Those damages can be set at any amount between $500 and $20,000, unless the defendant can show that she had no reasonable grounds to believe that she was infringing, in which case the minimum is set at $200. The amount is normally set per work, but can be reduced by the court if the total award would be "grossly out of proportion to the infringement" (s. 38.1(3)(b)). A special amount applies to a defendant who has failed to pay applicable royalties to a collective society (see the Collective Management section).

Under s. 34, a party may file a motion (with supporting affidavit) after the close of pleadings to obtain summary judgment. In *Wall v. Brunell*,[265] the Federal Court explained the burden of the parties to such a motion as follows:

> [A] responding party to a motion for summary judgment may not rest on the mere allegations or denials of its pleadings but must set out in affidavit material, or other evidence, specific facts showing that there is a genuine issue for trial. . . . The rule requires the respondent on a summary judgment motion to put his 'best foot forward' at the time the motion is heard. . . .

---

[263] [2002] 1 S.C.R. 595, 209 D.L.R. (4th) 257, 283 N.R. 1, 20 B.L.R. (3d) 165 (S.C.C.) at para 94. See also *Hill v. Church of Scientology of Toronto*, [1995] 2 S.C.R. 1130, 24 O.R. (3d) 865 (note), (sub nom. *Manning v. Hill*) 126 D.L.R. (4th) 129, 184 N.R. 1, (sub nom. *Hill v. Church of Scientology*) 30 C.R.R. (2d) 189 (S.C.C.).

[264] S.C. 1997, c. 24, s. 20(2)-(4).

[265] (1997), [1997] F.C.J. No. 608, 75 C.P.R. (3d) 429, 1997 CarswellNat 782 (Fed. T.D.), affirmed (2000), [2000] F.C.J. No. 841, 7 C.P.R. (4th) 321, 2000 CarswellNat 1184 (Fed. C.A.).

The requirement that the parties put their 'best foot forward' goes together with the requirement that the motions court 'take a hard look at the merits of the action at this preliminary state' to determine whether the moving party has succeeded in establishing that there is no genuine issue for trial. . . .

As noted by Madam Justice Tremblay-Lamer in *Milliken & Co. v. Interface Flooring Systems (Canada) Inc.*:[266]

In *Granville Shipping Co. v. Pegasus Lines Ltd. S.A.*, I considered all of the case law pertaining to summary judgment motions and I summarized the general principles as follows:

1.    the purpose of the provisions is to allow the Court to summarily dispense with cases which ought not proceed to trial because there is no genuine issue to be tried (*Old Fish Market Restaurants v. 1000357 Ontario Inc. et al.*);

2.    there is no determinative test (*Feoso Oil Limited v. Sarla*) but Stone J.A. seems to have adopted the reasons of Henry J. in *Pizza Pizza Ltd. v. Gillespie (Pizza Pizza)*. It is not whether a party cannot possibly succeed at trial, it is whether the case is so doubtful that it does not deserve consideration by the trier of fact at a future trial;

3.    each case should be interpreted in reference to its own contextual framework (*Blyth* and *Feoso*);

4.    provincial practice rules (especially Rule 20 of the Ontario *Rules*) can aid in interpretation (*Feoso* and *Collie*);

5.    this Court may determine questions of fact and law on the motion for summary judgment if this can be done on the material before the Court (this is broader than Rule 20 of the Ontario *Rules of Civil Procedure*) (*Patrick*);

6.    on the whole of the evidence, summary judgment cannot be granted if the necessary facts cannot be found or if it would be unjust to do so (*Pallman* and *Sears*);

7.    in the case of a serious issue with respect to credibility, the case should go to trial because the parties should be cross-examined before the trial judge (*Forde* and *Sears*). The mere existence of apparent conflict in the evidence does not preclude summary judgment; the court should take a 'hard look' at the merits and decide if there are issues of credibility to be resolved (*Stokes*); (citations omitted)

On a motion for summary judgment, it is for the moving party to establish that the other party's statement of claim, statement of defence or counterclaim discloses no genuine issue to be tried.

---

[266] [1998] 3 F.C. 103, 83 C.P.R. (3d) 470 (Fed. T.D.), additional reasons at (1998), 149 F.T.R. 125 (Fed. T.D.), affirmed (2000), [2000] F.C.J. No. 129, 5 C.P.R. (4th) 209, 2000 CarswellNat 177 (Fed. C.A.).

The copyright owner is deemed to be the owner of all infringing copies (s. 38) and "plates" (an "'old technology" reference) "used or intended to be used for the production of" infringing copies. This allows a right holder to apply for seizure of infringing goods (see ss. 34(4), 38(1)(b), 44.1, 44.2 and 44.4). Under the Quebec *Code of Civil Procedure*, infringing copies can be seized with a simple writ issued by a court clerk, without judicial approval. This procedure applies to an infringement of economic rights, not an infringement of moral rights.[267]

"Anton Piller" orders may also be granted when circumstances so warrant. Such orders, named after a United Kingdom case,[268] allow the plaintiff to enter a defendant's premises to inspect potentially infringing articles and documents relating thereto and remove them, a procedure resembling a search warrant, but conducted by a party in a civil case rather than law enforcement.

In *Pulse Microsystems Ltd. v. Safesoft Systems Inc.*,[269] the Manitoba Court of Appeal explained the origin and nature of Anton Piller orders as follows:

> The Anton Piller order is an exquisite example of creative judicial legislation. In *Anton Piller KG v. Manufacturing Processes Ltd*, the case from which the order takes its name, the English Court of Appeal approved a practice which had recently been adopted in the Chancery Division, in infringement of propriety rights cases, of making orders which Lord Denning M.R. noted 'have some resemblance to search warrants,' but with a difference. At p. 60 he pointed out:
>
>> Let me say at once that no court in this land has any power to issue a search warrant to enter a man's house so as to see if there are papers or documents there which are of an incriminating nature, whether libels or infringements of copyright or anything else of the kind. No constable or bailiff can knock at the door and demand entry so as to inspect papers or documents. The householder can shut the door in his face and say 'Get out.' That was established in the leading case of *Entick v. Carrington* (1765) 2 Wils.K.B. 275.
>
> Unable to authorize the plaintiffs or their agents to enter the defendants' premises against their will, the court, employing a kind of *Catch 22* logic, fashioned an order compelling the defendants to give permission to the plaintiffs to enter, inspect, copy and seize or remove documents and things. The defendants'

---

[267] See *Théberge, supra*, note 7.

[268] *Anton Piller KG v. Manufacturing Process Ltd.* (1975), [1976] 1 Ch. 55, [1976] 1 All E.R. 779 (Eng. C.A.).

[269] 134 D.L.R. (4th) 701, 110 Man. R. (2d) 163, 67 C.P.R. (3d) 202, [1996] 6 W.W.R. 1 (Man. C.A.).

refusal to comply does not entitle the plaintiffs to enter forcibly; but it makes the defendants liable to punishment for their contempt.

In approving the granting of these orders, Lord Denning M.R. cautioned (at p. 61):

> We are prepared, therefore, to sanction its continuance, but only in an extreme case where there is grave danger of property being smuggled away or of vital evidence being destroyed.

In *Nintendo of America Inc. v. Coinex Video Games Inc.*,[270] the Federal Court of Appeal described the four criteria to obtain an Anton Piller order:

- An extremely strong prima facie case.
- The plaintiff must establish that the resultant damage, potential or actual, will be very serious.
- There must be clear evidence that the defendants have in their possession infringing copies of plaintiff's material.
- The plaintiff must show there is a real possibility that the infringing material will be removed or disposed.

In addition, because of the draconian nature of the order, courts often impose strict safeguards and insist on a frank and full disclosure of all material facts from the plaintiff.

"Rolling" Anton Piller orders may be granted when the identity of the infringer is unknown.[271]

A slightly different procedure, the Mareva injunction, is used to prevent a defendant from dissipating assets so as to prevent the execution of a judgment. It is particularly relevant when the defendant is a foreign national or is otherwise planning to leave the court's jurisdiction or remove major assets from the jurisdiction. The plaintiff must also make a strong prima facie case.[272]

## 12. Criminal Sanctions

Though they are very rarely used, the Act also provides criminal sanctions. Section 42 reads as follows:

---

[270] (1982), [1983] 2 F.C. 189, 69 C.P.R. (2d) 122, 46 N.R. 311 (Fed. C.A.).

[271] See *Montres Rolex S.A. v. Balshin* (1992), [1993] 1 F.C. 236, 45 C.P.R. (3d) 174, 147 N.R. 297 (Fed. C.A.).

[272] See *Grenzservice Speditions GmbH v. Jans* (1995), 15 B.C.L.R. (3d) 370, 129 D.L.R. (4th) 733, 64 C.P.R. (3d) 129 (B.C. S.C.).

### (1) Offences and punishment

Every person who knowingly
(a)    makes for sale or rental an infringing copy of a work or other subject-matter in which copyright subsists,
(b)    sells or rents out, or by way of trade exposes or offers for sale or rental, an infringing copy of a work or other subject-matter in which copyright subsists,
(c)    distributes infringing copies of a work or other subject-matter in which copyright subsists, either for the purpose of trade or to such an extent as to affect prejudicially the owner of the copyright,
(d)    by way of trade exhibits in public an infringing copy of a work or other subject-matter in which copyright subsists, or
(e)    imports for sale or rental into Canada an infringing copy of a work or other subject-matter in which copyright subsists

is guilty of an offence and liable

(f)    on summary conviction, to a fine not exceeding twenty-five thousand dollars or to imprisonment for a term not exceeding six months or to both, or
(g)    on conviction on indictment, to a fine not exceeding *one million dollars or to imprisonment for a term not exceeding five years* or to both. (emphasis added)

### (2) Possession and performance offences and punishment

Every person who knowingly
(a)    makes or possesses any plate that is specifically designed or adapted for the purpose of making infringing copies of any work or other subject-matter in which copyright subsists, or
(b)    for private profit causes to be performed in public, without the consent of the owner of the copyright, any work or other subject-matter in which copyright subsists

is guilty of an offence and liable

(c)    on summary conviction, to a fine not exceeding twenty-five thousand dollars or to imprisonment for a term not exceeding six months or to both, or
(d)    on conviction on indictment, to a fine not exceeding one million dollars or to imprisonment for a term not exceeding five years or to both.

### (3) Power of court to deal with copies or plates

The court before which any proceedings under this section are taken may, on conviction, order that all copies of the work or other subject-matter that appear to it to be infringing copies, or all plates in the possession of the offender predominantly used for making infringing copies, be destroyed or delivered up to the owner of the copyright or otherwise dealt with as the court may think fit.

### (4) Limitation period

Proceedings by summary conviction in respect of an offence under this section may be instituted at any time within, but not later than, two years after the time when the offence was committed.

### (5) Parallel importation of books

No person may be prosecuted under this section for importing a book or dealing with an imported book in the manner described in section 27.1.

In *R. v. Aquintey*,[273] the Court analyzed whether the owner of a video rental store was guilty of renting out[274] infringing copies of audiovisual works for purposes of a criminal offence under s. 42(1)).

*(iii)  Were the copies seized from the defendant 'infringing' copies?*

Section 1 of the *Act* provides, in part, that 'infringing,' when applied to a copy of a work in which copyright subsists, means 'any copy . . . made . . . in contravention of this *Act*.' A copy of a work made without the authorization of the holder of the copyright in that work is made in contravention of the *Act*. The Crown's allegation is that that is what occurred in this case, and has named the person it says holds the copyright.

There is nothing in s. 42(1) that makes the identity of the owner of the copyright a matter that the Crown is required to prove. What the Crown must establish is that copyright subsists and that the copies are 'infringing' copies. A failure to establish the identity of the owner may have practical implications with respect to proving lack of authorization to copy, but in itself it has no legal significance: see *Musa v. LeMaitre*, an unreported decision of the Queen's Bench Division (Divisional Court) in England, dated December 4, 1986, per Brown L.J. at p. 16. In the case at bar, the averments as to the ownership of the copyright are surplusage. While, as I will presently explain, I am satisfied that the Crown has satisfactorily established the ownership of the copyrights in question, even if it had not the conclusion that the videotapes were infringing copies would be inescapable.
[. . .]

*(iv) Did the defendant act 'knowingly'?*

The final question is whether the defendant acted knowingly. In my opinion, he did. Knowledge, like any other state of mind, is susceptible of proof by

---

[273] (1998), 79 C.P.R. (3d) 318 (Ont. Prov. Div.),

[274] Prior to September 1, 1997, the equivalent terms read as "letting for hire". See 1997, c. 24, s. 24(1).

circumstantial evidence. Two circumstances are of particular importance in this case.

As I indicated earlier, these were 'blockbuster' movies in the Philippines. They were the product of a significant commercial enterprise. . . .

Further, the letter from Viva Video's attorney, dated January 9, 1995, addressed to the attention of the owner of 'Atin Ito Variety Store,' was found in a pile of documents beside the cash register near which the defendant was standing at the time of the seizure of the videotapes on May 9, 1995. I find, based on Mr. Hunter's evidence, that the letter had been opened. It beggars belief to imagine that the defendant, the sole proprietor of this store, had not read it. The contents of the letter, which were set out above, clearly put the defendant on notice that the Viva Video products he was renting might be unauthorized.

[. . .]

In all the circumstances, I find as a fact that the defendant knew that the copies of *Alfredo Lim, Demolisyon*, and *Costales* that he was offering for rent were unauthorized copies.

In *R. v. Laurier Office Mart Inc.*,[275] an Ottawa copyshop was accused of offering materials for sale that infringed copyright, contrary to s. 42(1) of the Act. University professors left course materials, consisting of books and articles, with the copyshop so that students could obtain photocopies for their personal use. The court rejected the alleged offences that involved materials which were photocopied before copyright certificates had been registered. For those materials, the Crown lacked evidence sufficient to satisfy the beyond reasonable doubt criminal standard that copyright existed at the time of the offence (see ss 5 (1) and 53(2)). Ratushny Prov. Div. J. then discussed whether the defendants acted "knowingly":

There is no evidence that the defendant had any actual knowledge that its copying services for the works violated the *Act* or even might be violating the *Act*. The evidence at trial was that none of the professors had been aware that what they were asking the defendant to do could be wrong. Ms Lucy White of the Canadian Copyright Licensing Agency, known as Cancopy,[276] testified that Cancopy, a federal not-for-profit corporation incorporated in 1986, is the only organization in Canada, except for a similar organization in Quebec, which serves as a national licensing body to protect copyright holders' rights. They have contracts with certain publishers and other copyright owners, giving them

---

[275] (1994), 58 C.P.R. (3d) 403 (Ont. Prov. Div.), affirmed (1995), 63 C.P.R. (3d) 229 (Ont. Gen. Div.). See also the discussion on the impact of *CCH* in the Exceptions section.

[276] Now known as "Access Copyright".

exclusive right to give consent to copy. They issue licences, collect royalties, help in enforcement of obligations under the *Copyright Act*, engage in education and, more recently, have been involved in a public awareness campaign, particularly with universities and their copy shops. Ms White agreed that in general, copy shop managers have a low level of awareness of copyright issues. She said that after the works were seized from the defendant's business premises on July 20, 1993, the defendant contacted Cancopy so as to obtain a licence to continue to provide its copying services to the University of Ottawa. On September 1, 1993, the defendant did obtain a licence. Since that date, the defendant has routinely and appropriately remitted royalties. The defendant, she said, still does not seem to grasp a lot of issues and has a lot of questions, but there is no problem with compliance.

The Crown does not dispute these facts, but argues that the test as to whether the defendant acted knowingly is an objective one, based on *R. v. Photo Center Inc.* (1986), 9 C.P.R. (3d) 425, 8 C.I.P.R. 8 (Que. S.C.), and *R. v. Sault Ste. Marie (City)* (1978), 85 D.L.R. (3d) 161 at pp. 170-82, 40 C.C.C. (2d) 353, [1978] 2 S.C.R. 1299. The Crown argues that as copyright notices are clearly evident on some of the works, for example, 'Submitted for publication: please do not quote without author's permission' and they are copies of copies with publishers' and authors' names, a reasonable person in the defendant's position in particular, whose business includes a lot of copying for the public, would be put on notice that copyright was being infringed and would take reasonable precautions.

In *Sault Ste. Marie*, Mr. Justice Dickson outlined the three often quoted categories of criminal offences: the full *mens rea* offence, meaning the accused's actual or subjective state of mind has to be proved; strict liability offences where no *mens rea* has to be proved but the accused can avoid liability if he can prove he took all reasonable steps to avoid the particular event; absolute liability offences where Parliament has made it clear that guilt follows proof of the prescribed act only. Mr. Justice Dickson expressly commented that most public welfare offences are not full *mens rea* offences, unless words such as 'knowingly' make them such.

The *Photo Center* case involved a charge under the *Copyright Act*. The court did consider a good faith, reasonable diligence defence, thereby treating the *Copyright Act* offence as being one of strict liability. However, I think it clear from *Sault Ste. Marie* and from the inclusion of 'knowingly' in s. 42(1) of the Act, that regardless of that section's status as a public welfare offence, *mens rea* is an essential element of that offence. I agree in this respect with *R. v. Harris* (1990), 34 C.P.R. (3d) 392, 81 Nfld. & P.E.I.R. 147, 19 A.C.W.S. (3d) 1232 (Nfld. Prov. Ct.), and *R. v. Biron* (1992), 127 N.B.R. (2d) 142, 19 W.C.B. (2d) 529 (N.B. Prov. Ct.), and I disagree that s. 42(1) is a strict liability offence.

The onus on the Crown to prove *mens rea*, is to prove the defendant's subjective state of mind, or in other words, that the defendant had actual knowledge it was violating the *Copyright Act*. Mr. Justice Dickson in *Sault Ste. Marie*, at p. 170, states it better, that the onus on the Crown is to prove that:

> . . . the accused who committed the prohibited act did so intentionally or recklessly, with knowledge of the facts constituting the offence, or with wilful blindness toward them. Mere negligence is excluded from the concept of the mental element required for conviction. Within the context of a criminal prosecution a person who fails to make such inquiries as a reasonable and prudent person would make, or who fails to know facts he should have known, is innocent in the eyes of the law.

There is no evidence that the defendant 'intentionally or recklessly, with knowledge of the facts constituting the offence,' violated the *Act*.

The Crown's alternate position, if this is a full *mens rea* offence, is that the defendant at the very least was wilfully blind, given the copyright notices on the works and the scale of its business. Wilful blindness is defined in *Biron* at pp. 149-50:

> Wilful blindness arises when a person who has become aware of the need for inquiry, declines to make the inquiry because he does not wish to know the truth and would prefer to remain ignorant. In such a situation, he is fixed with knowledge and his belief in another state of facts is irrelevant. (See *R. v. Sansregret*, [1985] 1 S.C.R. 570, 58 N.R. 123, 35 Man. R. (2d) 1, 18 C.C.C. (3d) 223.)

There is no evidence of wilful blindness. It is significant in this respect that after the works were seized but before the charges were laid, the defendant obtained a licence from Cancopy on September 1, 1993, and since that date continues to have a lot of questions but has compiled with all requirements.

Another case worth mentioning is *R. v. Farrell*,[277] in which the accused had sold counterfeit NIKE, FUBU, TOMMY HILFIGER and OAKLEY hats and OAKLEY sunglasses. The Crown, which had filed under both the *Trade-Marks Act* and the *Copyright Act*, took the position that these were strict liability offences with the onus being on the accused to satisfy the Court of his due diligence once the *actus reus* has been established. The Court dealt with the charges as follows:

---

[277] (2002), 19 C.P.R. (4th) 538 (N.B. Q.B.).

The Crown relies on the Quebec Superior Court decision in *R. v. Photo Centre Inc.* reported at (1986), 9 C.P.R. (3d) 425 (Que. S.C.), to advance the proposition that these are strict liability offences.

In *Photo Centre*, the accused had circulated videocassettes when he was unsure of their authenticity. The lawyer he had consulted had manifested doubts as to the legality of the product. He was convicted under paragraph 25(1)(c) of the *Copyright Act*. His conviction was upheld on appeal. The Court dealt with the elements of the due diligence defence to strict liability offences as set out in *R. v. Sault Ste. Marie (City)*, [1978] 2 S.C.R. 1299 (S.C.C.) and went on the quote from the decision of the Supreme Court of Canada in *R. v. Molis* , [1980] 2 S.C.R. 356 (S.C.C.) where Justice Lamer stated:

> *But I hasten to add that the defence of due negligence that was referred to in Sault Ste. Marie is that of due diligence in relation to the fulfillment of a duty imposed by law <u>and not in relation to the ascertainment of the existence of a prohibition or its interpretation.</u>* (emphasis added)

And then continuing with the *Photo Centre* decision at page 427, the *Quebec Superior Court* judge went on to say:

> Proceeding to render judgement on this appeal, the Court has no hesitation in recognizing the accused entertained no error with respect to the circulation. The accused perhaps had no knowledge of the law which prohibited the exercise, but ignorance of the law is not a defence. There remains the ignorance of the fact that the copied specimens could have been the subject of the protection of the law. Good faith is alleged in defence. But if the accused was ignorant of the fact that this protection encompassed the works that he was putting into circulation, it must then be shown that he took all reasonable precautions to so ascertain. Once knowledge was acquired, it must be proven that he acted with all reasonable diligence to terminate his faulty actions.
>
> What did he do? What other means or reasonable precautions which he took and what is the reasonable diligence that he used to cease his actions?
>
> As mentioned above, the accused had consulted a lawyer who indicated some doubt. This reticence emanating from a jurist, whose identity and knowledge were not disclosed, should nevertheless had roused the attention of the accused who should then have properly informed himself. The information from the municipal officer or an agent of Mounted Police was not in the nature of an expert consultation. Although it is true that the R.C.M.P. sees to the application of this law, one would have to be naïve to believe that each of its agents recognizes and can interpret the laws which it applies. Consequently, the precautions taken, if one

can so call them, were not of the reasonable quality referred to by the
Supreme Court of Canada in the decision of R. v. City of Sault Ste.
Marie. . . .

Finally, as soon as the accused commenced having doubts about the
legalities of his acts, he should similarly have used all reasonable diligence to desist and we are unaware at what stage of the circulation he
so applied himself.

In my view, the *Photo Centre* case has no application to the present situation.
Further, I am of the view that *Photo Centre* does not stand for the proposition
that offences under the *Copyright Act* are strict liability offences. It merely
deals with the actions required where it has been proven that an accused has
knowledge of an infringement and seeks to establish his innocence by showing
due diligence.
[. . .]

In this case the *mens rea* of the offences for which the accused is charged is
the knowledge that the Tommy Hilfiger, Nike, Oakley and FUBU articles he
was offering for sale were articles infringing the copyright in those works. The
Crown has not proved this knowledge beyond a reasonable doubt. In the
absence of proof of knowledge, it is open to the Crown to prove that the
accused's conduct amounted to willful blindness of the infringement of the
copyright in those works.

That the accused was offering for sale infringing copies is beyond dispute. This
was established through the evidence of Jack Hunter, an expert in the field, as
well as through exhibit 18 containing the copyright and trademark certifica-
tions.

The Crown must also prove the willful intent to deceive or defraud beyond a
reasonable doubt with respect to the four counts under the *Criminal Code of
Canada*, namely section 412.

Although the *actus reus* is not in issue, as indicated earlier, the Crown must
prove the *mens rea* of the accused beyond a reasonable doubt. The Crown
relies on its own cross-examination of the accused in asserting that the *mens
rea* has been proven beyond a reasonable doubt, particularly with the counts
relating to the Nike, Tommy Hilfiger and Oakley brands. It asserts that the
accused should have known that the quality of the Tommy Hilfiger and Nike,
in particular, were sub-standard, that the prices set for Tommy Hilfiger, Nike
and Oakley products, in particular, were lower than the actual retail prices.

Alternatively, the Crown contends that the accused was alerted to the counterfeit when he was informed by customers that the prices where too high. Or
alternatively, he should have been alerted to the counterfeit. It contends the

accused should have made inquiries from Mr. Dickson as to the retail value and/or authenticity of the articles, which he did not do.

The Crown finally contends that the accused's credibility was shaken when he acknowledged on cross-examination that he may have told Corporal Paradis one retail price after commission, rather than one before commission. The Crown suggests that because of this contradiction, the accused may not have been truthful with the rest of his evidence.

I reject those submissions. I find the accused testified in a candid and frank manner. He does not appear to be a sophisticated consumer. He testified he had never heard of FUBU or Oakley products before. He had heard of Tommy Hilfiger and Nike because of their notoriety. He has never seen a genuine Tommy Hilfiger or a genuine Nike product in any retail store. He would have never handled a genuine product of these brands. He would not have had anything by which he could have compared the products or the retail value to give him a hint as to their counterfeit status.

The Crown's own witness, Jack Hunter, conceded that some of the items were reasonably good copies and that the general public, unaware of the strict quality control requirements of these four manufacturers, could easily be led to believe that the articles were genuine.

I believe the accused when he asserts that he did not know that he was dealing with infringing products in which a copyright subsists. Having heard all of the evidence, I am satisfied that there was little, if anything, about these articles to raise the suspicion of an unsuspecting individual. I note that the prices of the Tommy Hilfiger, Nike and FUBU hats, in particular, were not so out of line with retail price as to arouse suspicion. As to the Oakley sunglasses, the price of $25.00 was considerably less than the retail which is often in excess of $100.00. But with the accused being an unsophisticated consumer and never having been exposed to these high-end sunglasses before, I believe him when he says he was unaware of their counterfeit nature.

The limitation period in s. 42(4) came into effect September 1, 1997[278] and increased the period to two years from the previously applicable period of six months under s. 786(2) of the *Criminal Code*.[279]

---

[278]  1997, c. 24, s. 24(3).

[279]  R.S.C. 1985, c. C-46. See, *e.g.*, *R. v. Shimming* (1991), 35 C.P.R. (3d) 397 (Sask. Prov. Ct.).

## VII.  COPYRIGHT REGISTRATION

Copyright registration is not required in Canada, in keeping with the Berne Convention (see the International section), which requires of its signatories that copyright be recognized "without formality." Many jurisdictions no longer maintain registries, but some countries, including Canada, keep optional registries. Although registration is only permissive, it does serve an important evidentiary function. Under section 53(2), the certificate of copyright registration is evidence that the copyright exists and that the person registered on the certificate is the owner of the copyright. Other evidence can be adduced to contradict the certificate and this can affect the evidentiary weight of the certificate. This evidentiary value of a copyright certificate is particularly useful in *ex parte* matters.

Section 34.1(1) of the Act should be mentioned in this context because it provides a rebuttable presumption, for infringement suits and only when the defendant puts the copyright or the plaintiff's title in issue, that copyright exists and that the author is the owner of the copyright. In *Circle Film Enterprises Inc. v. Canadian Broadcasting Corp.*,[280] the Supreme Court resolved the potential conflict between these two provisions. In that case, the *plaintiff* relied on the certificate as evidence of ownership while the *defendant* tried to rely on the statutory presumption that the author is the owner. The Supreme Court found that the production of a certificate of registration was prima facie evidence, as then provided by section 36(2)[281] of the Act, that the plaintiff was the owner of copyright, and that the certificate of registration served as evidence to the contrary sufficient to displace the presumption raised by section 34.1[282] in favour of the author. As there was no other evidence adduced on ownership other than the certificate, the plaintiff was successful.

In Canada, contrary to the United States, there is no substantive examination of applications for copyright registration.

---

[280] [1959] S.C.R. 602, 31 C.P.R. 57, 20 D.L.R. (2d) 211 (S.C.C.). See also *Grignon v. Roussel* (1991), [1991] F.C.J. No. 557, 38 C.P.R. (3d) 4, 44 F.T.R. 121, 1991 CarswellNat 208 (Fed. T.D.).

[281] Section 36(2) read as follows (before 1997): "A certificate of registration of copyright in a work shall be prima facie evidence that copyright subsists in the work and that the person registered is the owner of the copyright." (R.S.C. 1970, c. C-30, s. 36). The current provision, s. 53(2) reads: "A certificate of registration of copyright is evidence that the copyright subsists and that person registered is the owner of the copyright."

[282] The presumption at that time was contained in s. 20(3), providing that, "unless the contrary is proved," the work shall be "presumed to be a work in which copyright subsists" and the author shall be "presumed to be the owner of copyright." The presumption is now found in s. 34.1(1).

Assignments and licences may also be registered (s. 57(1)). An unregistered assignment is void against a subsequent assignee or licensee for valuable consideration without actual notice (s. 57(3)), provided the second contract is otherwise valid under applicable (provincial) rules.[283]

The Federal Court may amend or expunge an incorrect entry in the Register on application of the Registrar of Copyrights or of any interested person (s. 57(4)).

## VIII.  RELATED RIGHTS

Related rights are best illustrated through example. The example below shows the different levels and the rights attributed to each for a particular song.

| Level | Example | Related rights |
|---|---|---|
| Author of the song | Luc Plamondon | *Article 3* – Copyright in works<br>*Article 14* – Limitation where author is first owner of copyright |
| Performer | Céline Dion | *Article 15* – Copyright in performer's performance<br>*Article 19-20* – Right to remuneration/Conditions |
| Producer | SONY | *Article 18* – Copyright in sound recordings<br>*Article 19-20* – Right to remuneration/Conditions |
| Broadcasting organization | CBC | *Article 21* – Copyright in communication signals |

There are very few cases on these relatively new sections of the *Copyright Act*. Neighbouring or related rights are given to persons other than music composers and lyricists for their contribution to the dissemination of music. Performers, for historical reasons dating back to the 1950s, chose to obtain rights that "neighbour on" copyright without being a full copyright (i.e., as in ss. 3 and 14.1 of the Act). Performers' rights are like the neighbouring rights of record producers and broadcasters, even though performers could justify demands for full copyright by insisting on their "creative"

---

[283] See *Poolman v. Eiffel Productions S.A.* (1991), 35 C.P.R. (3d) 384 (Fed. T.D.).

contribution, especially notable in the fields of jazz and classical music, while producers and broadcasters typically add financial support and commercial know-how to the equation.

Neighbouring rights are characterized as "copyright" (e.g., in the Title of Part II of the *Copyright Act*, "Copyright in Performer's Performances, Sound Recordings and Communication Signals") partly for constitutional reasons: s. 91 of the *Constitutional Act* gives the federal government jurisdiction over "copyrights". In other jurisdictions, such as the United States, performers and broadcasters are mainly protected under a system of contractual and "guild" arrangements.

The existence and duration of neighbouring rights are independent of the existence of an underlying copyright in the music. The producer of a sound recording containing, *e.g.* sounds of waves or bird songs, would qualify for protection. A performer of music no longer protected under s. 3 (e.g. Mozart or Ravel) benefits from rights in her performance under s. 15.

The principal rights of a performer are to prevent the communication to the public and fixation (recording) of a live performance, and the reproduction and rental of a fixed performance, or its use for a "purpose other than that for which the performer's authorization was given" (s. 15(1)(b)(ii). Those rights do not apply to cinematographic (audiovisual) works once the performer has authorized the embodiment of her performance in the work (s. 17). In other words, the rights in s. 15 essentially apply to music only.

Sound recording "makers" (commonly known as the producers — see the definition of "maker" in s. 2) are given a right to prevent the first publication, reproduction and rental of their sound recordings (s. 18).

When sound recordings are used for broadcasting (and other forms of communication to the public) and public performance, the producer and performer are entitled to an "equitable remuneration" under s. 19, set by the Copyright Board.[284]

Broadcasters are given an exclusive right in their communication signal to fix (record), reproduce, retransmit or perform in public in a place where an entrance fee is required. The retransmission right applies only vis-à-vis other broadcasters. Retransmission by cable or comparable systems is covered by a compulsory licence regime under s. 31. Tariffs are set by the Copyright Board.[285]

The above rights are given to Canadian performers and producers and countries party to the *Rome Convention* of 1961, which protects neigh-

---

[284] See, *e.g.*, *Public Performance of Sound Recordings 1998 - 2002, Re* (2000), (sub nom. *NRCC Tariff 1.C (CBC-Radio), 1998 to 2002, Re v.*) 9 C.P.R. (4th) 504 (Copyright Bd.).

[285] See, *e.g.*, *Distant Radio & Television Signals Tariff, 2001-2003, Re* (2003), 25 C.P.R. (4th) 253 (Copyright Bd.).

bouring rights (see the International section). As of July 15, 2004, 77 countries were party to that Convention. However, the United States is not party to the Convention. Sections 18 and 20 rights (rights in sound recordings other than the right to "equitable remuneration" and broadcasters' rights) are extended to any member of the World Trade Organization

## IX.  COLLECTIVE MANAGEMENT

### 1.  Overview

A few types of copyright are managed collectively. A collective society is an organization that administers the rights of several copyright owners. It can grant permission to use their works and set the conditions for that use. Collective administration is widespread in Canada, particularly for music performance rights, reprography rights and mechanical reproduction rights, private copying and retransmission. Some collective societies are affiliated with foreign societies; this allows them to represent foreign copyright owners as well.

Collective management is a *method*, a tool that rightsholders choose when the individual exercise of their right(s) to authorize is impracticable. Rightsholders then *choose* to let users within a defined group or category use their own works and all those works within a repertoire in exchange for compensation set by mutual agreement or by the Copyright Board. A voluntary collective system has the advantage of reducing the legislative distortion of compulsory licensing (see below), which, in addition, must be compatible with Canada's obligations under the Berne Convention and the *WTO Agreement on Trade-Related Aspects of Intellectual Property Rights* (*TRIPS Agreement* (see the International section below)).

Bill C-32[286] introduced a definition of the expression "collective society" as follows:

> A 'collective society' means a society, association or corporation that carries on the business of collective administration of copyright or of the remuneration right conferred by section 19 or 81 for the benefit of those who, by assignment, grant of licence, appointment of it as their agent or otherwise, authorize it to act on their behalf in relation to that collective administration, and (*a*) operates a licensing scheme, applicable in relation to a repertoire of works, performer's performances, sound recordings or communication signals of more than one author, performer, sound recording maker or broadcaster, pursuant to which the society, association or corporation sets out classes of uses that it agrees to authorize under this Act, and the royalties and terms and conditions on which

---

[286] Assented to on April 25, 1997. It became S.C. 1997, c. 24.

it agrees to authorize those classes of uses, or (*b*) carries on the business of collecting and distributing royalties or levies payable pursuant to this Act. (Emphasis added)

In spite of this unified definition, the Act contains various legal regimes concerning the collective administration of copyright and neighbouring rights, including new regimes introduced in the 1997 ("C-32") amendments.

Collective societies can also be classified according to their field of activity, as was done by the Copyright Board when it listed existing Canadian collectives[287] and identified the following areas:

- Music (11)[288]
- Literary (6)
- Audiovisual and multimedia (5)
- Visual arts (4)
- Retransmission (8)
- Private copying (1)
- Educational rights (1)
- Media monitoring (1)

Another useful way of categorizing Collective Management Organizations is according to their rights acquisition regime, in one of the three following ways:

- Full voluntary system
- Voluntary system with legal back-up[289]
- Legal, compulsory (also known as "non-voluntary") licence[290]

Under a full voluntary system (such as SOCAN's) rightsholders must assign their rights or authorize the collective to act on their behalf. The law may provide a "backup" to a full voluntary system, usually in one of two ways. The law may limit the remedies available to rightsholders who do not opt in to a collective scheme. If a tariff is in place pursuant to a decision of the Copyright Board, remedies may, for example, be limited to the payment

---

[287] See <www.cb-cda.gc.ca>.

[288] The number in parentheses is the number of societies operating in the area in question mentioned on the Copyright Board's list.

[289] The back up could be a limit on the damages/royalties that can be claimed by non-participating rightsholders, or the extension of a voluntary scheme to non-participating rightsholders once a substantial number of rightsholders of a certain category have joined.

[290] See <http://www.ifrro.org/laws/index.html>.

of what would have otherwise been available under the tariff (see ss. 70.17). In some countries, the law provides that once a substantial number of rightsholders (substantiality is usually determined by an independent commission or tribunal) have joined a collective scheme, there is a presumption that this scheme encompasses all other rightsholders, domestic or foreign, except those who expressly decide to opt out. In other words, once a membership threshold has been reached, the law changes the full opt-in model into an opt-out model. This facilitates the acquisition of licensing authority for collectives, reduces their cost, and ensures uses can acquire licences that cover a much broader and possibly complete worldwide repertory of protected content. This system, known as extended repertoire or extended collective licensing, is mentioned repeatedly in a report on copyright reform issued by a parliamentary committee.[291]

Under a legal or compulsory license, rightsholders lose their right to authorize or prohibit a use that would otherwise infringe their right(s). Users obtain the right to use the protected work or other material, subject to the payment of remuneration. For example, s.31 (2) contains a compulsory license for cable retransmission of television programs.

## 2. The Four Legal Regimes of Collective Management in Canada

Collective management of rights in Canada is governed in four different ways, according to the right(s) involved. These regimes (since 1997) are as follows:

- Music performing rights (and certain neighbouring rights)
- General regime
- Retransmissions and certain uses by educational institutions; and
- Private copying.

## (a) Music Performing Rights and Certain Neighboring Rights

This type of collective management is regulated by Section 67 of the *Copyright Act*. Collective Management Organizations active in this field grant licences for the public performance and communication to the public of music (the underlying musical work, the performer's performance and

---

[291] Report of the Standing Committee on Canadian Heritage. Interim Report on Copyright Reform, May 2004.

the producer's sound recording). SOCAN is[292] the only collective representing authors of music (composers and lyricists), under section 3 of the Act for the public performance and communication to the public of their works. Performers and producers do not have an exclusive right (that is, a right to exclude or interdict) but rather a right to a payment fixed by the Copyright Board and known as an "equitable remuneration". Authors voluntarily *assign* their copyrights to SOCAN. The *Act* imposes collective management of the rights to remuneration.[293] The Neighbouring Rights Collective of Canada (NRCC) is a non-profit umbrella collective, created in 1997, to administer the rights of performers and makers of sound recordings. This is done through its member collectives.

Collective management of rights for dramatic and literary works contained in sound recordings (notably through ArtistI[294]) is voluntary.

In fixing tariffs in this area, the Act imposes specific criteria to be applied by the Copyright Board.[295]

### (b) The General Regime

We refer to the regime that governs Collective Management Organizations in Section 70.1 and following as the "general" regime because it applies to all voluntary licensing schemes other than those of Section 67. It is important to note, however, that in terms of financial flows, Section 67 CMOs collect (and distribute) more money than all Section 70.1 collectives combined.

This general regime could apply to the collective management of the rights of reproduction, adaptation, rental, publication and public performance in the area of copyright (section 3) and to the rights of performers (including first fixation of their performances, reproduction and communication to the public of live performances under section 15) and to certain rights of sound recording producers (section 18) and broadcasters (section 21). In practice, it applies to:

---

[292] Officially, "The Society of Composers, Authors and Music Publishers of Canada". It was formed in 1990, but its predecessors have been around in some form or another in Canada since 1925. In 1990, SOCAN was created as a result of the merger of two former Canadian performing rights societies: The Composers, Authors and Publishers Association of Canada (CAPAC) and the Performing Rights Organization of Canada (PROCAN).

[293] S. 19(1) and (2) of the *Copyright Act*, *supra*, note 3.

[294] ArtistI is the collective society of the *Union des artistes* (UDA) for the remuneration of performers' rights. See <http://www.uniondesartistes.com>.

[295] Section 68(2).

- Reprography, where the two main societies are the Canadian Copyright Licensing Agency (Access Copyright)[296] and the Société québécoise de gestion collective des droits de reproduction (COPIBEC)[297]
- Mechanical rights, and CMOs such as (a) the Society for Reproduction Rights of Authors, Composers and Publishers in Canada (SODRAC), which "administers royalties stemming from the reproduction of musical works"[298]; and (b) the Canadian Musical Reproduction Rights Agency (CMRRA), "a Canadian centralized licensing and collecting agency for the reproduction rights of musical works in Canada."[299] Mechanical reproduction is a term of art used to describe the reproduction of musical works for the production of sound recordings. When music is used in an audiovisual context, such as a motion picture or advertising, the licence required is known as a "synchronization" right because music and images are "synchronized." While mechanical reproduction is generally governed by a tariff, which may be set by the Copyright Board, synchronization licences are usually negotiated case-by-case.
- The visual arts and Collective Management Organizations such as the Canadian Artists' Representation Copyright Collective (CARCC/CARFAC), "established in 1990 to create opportunities for increased income for visual and media artists. It provides its services to artists who affiliate with the Collective. These services include negotiating the terms for copyright use and issuing an appropriate license to the use."[300] This includes SODRAC and the Société de droits d'auteur en arts visuels (SODART) "created by the Regroupement des artistes en arts visuels du Québec (RAAV) and responsible for collecting rights

---

[296] "The Canadian Copyright Licensing Agency (CANCOPY) represents writers, publishers and other creators for the administration of copyright in all provinces except Quebec. The purpose of the collective is to provide easy access to copyright material by negotiating comprehensive licences with user groups, such as schools, colleges, universities, governments, corporations, etc. permitting reproduction rights, such as photocopy rights, for the works in CANCOPY's repertoire." <http://www.accesscopyright.ca>.

[297] "La *Société québécoise de gestion collective des droits de reproduction* (COPIBEC) is the collective society which authorizes in Quebec the reproduction of works from Quebec, Canadian (through a bilateral agreement with CANCOPY) and foreign rights holders. COPIBEC was founded in 1997 by *l'Union des écrivaines et écrivains québécois* (UNEQ) and the *Association nationale des éditeurs de livres* (ANEL)." <http://www.copibec.qc.ca>.

[298] Online: <http://www.sodrac.com>.

[299] Online: <http://www.cmrra.org>.

[300] Online: <http://www.carfac.ca>.

on behalf of visual artists. It negotiates agreements with organizations that use visual arts, such as museums, exhibition centres, magazines, publishers, audio-visual producers, etc. SODART issues licences to these organizations and collects royalties due to the artists it represents."[301]

Collective Management Organizations operating under the general regime can file tariffs for approval by the Board[302] or conclude agreements with users[303] that will take precedence over tariffs.[304] A CMO may, under this regime, file a copy of an agreement concluded with a user with the Board, which prevents the application of Section 45 of the *Competition Act* (dealing with conspiracies to limit competition). However, the Commissioner of Competition may ask the Copyright Board to examine the agreement if he considers it is contrary to the public interest.[305] The Board may also be asked to determine the royalty applicable in individual cases (arbitration).[306]

### (c) Retransmissions and Certain Uses by Educational Institutions (Section 71)

This is a legal (non-voluntary licence) regime. The criteria that apply to tariff fixing procedures under this regime are different than those of the general regime. The Section 71 regime, also known as the "particular cases regime", applies to:

- The retransmission of a distant signal;
- The retransmission regime, which includes, since the 1997 amendments, the making and conservation beyond one year of a copy of a news program or commentary by an educational institution and the public performance of the copy;
- The making of a copy of a work at the time it is communicated to the public by an educational institution and keeping the copy beyond 30 days to decide whether to perform the copy and the public performance (primarily to students) of the copy.

---

[301] Online: <http://www.raav.org/sodart>.
[302] S. 70.13 and following.
[303] S. 70.12(b).
[304] S. 70.191.
[305] S. 70.5(2) to (5).
[306] S. 70.2. If an agreement between the parties, the Board shall not proceed (section 70.3).

There are eight CMOs who operate in whole or in part under this "particular cases regime."

Non-member rightsholders may claim royalties collected on the basis of an approved tariff, subject to conditions applicable to member rightsholders.[307]

### (d) Private Copying

A specific regime was put in place concerning the private copying of sound recordings.[308] It does not concern licensing as such, but rather a remuneration designed to compensate rightsholders for a use of works (and objects of neighbouring rights) that is otherwise considered non-infringing.[309]

Relevant collectives created the Canadian Private Copying Collective (CPCC), "which is responsible for distributing the funds generated by the levy to the collective societies representing eligible authors, performers and makers of sound recordings. The member collectives of the CPCC are: the Canadian Mechanical Reproduction Rights Agency (CMRRA), the Neighbouring Rights Collective of Canada (NRCC), the Société de gestion des droits des artistes-musiciens (SOGEDAM), the Society for Reproduction Rights of Authors, Composers and Publishers in Canada (SODRAC) and the Society of Composers, Authors and Music Publishers of Canada (SOCAN)." The media currently covered by the private copying tariff include CD-R and CD-RW, CR-R audio and Mini Disc, and non-removable memory permanently embedded in a digital audio recorder (including flash memory and hard drives), such as Apple's iPod. The Federal Court of Appeal ruled in December 2004 that the levy on permanently embedded memory in digital audio recorders is invalid.[310]

### (i) A Note on Private Copying in the Digital Age

Section 80 of the Act established an exception to copyright infringement allowing the copying of music for private use under certain conditions. For

---

[307] S. 76. See also *S.A.R.D.E.C. Designation Application, Re* (1998), (sub nom. *Societe des Auteurs, Recherchistes, Documentalistes & Compositeurs designation application, Re*) 86 C.P.R. (3d) 481 (Copyright Bd.).

[308] S. 79-88 of the Act.

[309] S. 80(1).

[310] *Canadian Private Copying Collective v. Canadian Storage Media Alliance*, 2004 FCA 424 (F.C.A.) [CPCC 2004].

example, music cannot be uploaded to a publicly available server for its telecommunication to the public (s. 80(2)(c)) or distribution (s. 80(2)(b)).

Another important condition is that the private copy must be made on an "audio recording medium" (s. 80(1)), which s. 79 defines as a recording medium "of a kind ordinarily used by individual consumers for" the purpose of reproducing music. How should one interpret this condition? One could argue that the expression "ordinarily used" should be seen as static and that it refers to technology that was ordinarily used for that purpose at the time of entry into force of that provision. However, that would essentially defeat the entire purpose of the provision because digital and computer technology evolves quickly. The provision should rather be construed in a "technologically neutral" way, which means that it is dynamic and applies to technologies as they become ordinarily used for the purpose of copying music. This is the approach taken by the Copyright Board in its third decision on private copying tariffs, in which it decided that DVDs were not "ordinarily used" for the purpose of copying music: "Consequently, the Board is not persuaded, at this time, that a DVD qualifies as an audio recording medium ordinarily used by consumers to private copy music. As previously explained, this determination means that copying music onto a DVD infringes copyright."[311]

In its first private copying decision for the years 1999-2000, the Board had agreed that recordable CDs were "ordinarily used" for copying music, in spite of the fact that the evidence submitted showed that approximately 8% of those CDs were used to copy music (at the time). The Board wrote in that respect: "'Ordinary' is used to describe anything from that which is regular, normal or average, to what is merely recurring or consistent. Therefore, the ordinary character of an occurrence is not necessarily a function of quantity, but rather a matter of consistency".[312] Justice Linden of the Federal Court of Appeal affirmed the decision. Justice Linden stated:

> The key point is whether the Board had to decide the meaning of 'ordinarily used' by looking at the products generally, as contended for by the applicant, or by considering the use by individual consumers of that product. In my view, it is the usage by individual consumers that must be ordinary, not the use of the product generally, because of the insertion of the words 'by individual

---

[311] *Private Copying 2003-2004, Tariff of Levies to be Collected by CPCC, Re* (2003), 28 C.P.R. (4th) 417 at para 150 (Copyright Bd.); reversed in part by *CPCC 2004*, ibid.

[312] Reported at (1999), (sub nom. *Private Copying 1999-2000, Tariff of Levies to be Collected by CPCC, Re*) 4 C.P.R. (4th) 15 at para 80 (Copyright Bd.), affirmed (2000), (sub nom. *AVS Technologies Inc. v. Canadian Mechanical Reproduction Rights Agency*) 7 C.P.R. (4th) 68 (Fed. C.A.).

consumers', which have to be given some meaning. If these words were not there, the applicants' contention would have been more solidly grounded.[313]

In other words, copying onto a medium that does not qualify as an "audio recording medium" is not covered by the exception. While this seems correct when reading the Act, it creates an interesting quandary. For a new medium, not in existence when ss. 79 and 80 came into force, to become "ordinarily used", there must be a phase where that medium is not (yet) ordinarily used. In other words, a phase of increasingly important use (though not yet widespread enough to be considered "ordinary") not protected by the exception. Did Parliament mandate infringement before the exception applies? Does it make sense to consider smaller scale use infringing while massive (ordinary) use is not?

There are many possible answers. One is to consider that indeed use prior to attaining "ordinary status" is infringing. That conclusion may be valid for use that clearly is not on its way to becoming ordinary" but seems less logical in a case where empirical data show steadily increasing use that may well become "ordinary". One could read an "implied exception" in s. 80 for the latter scenario, based on the fact that Parliament cannot possibly have 'mandated' infringement, but that seems a stretch of both letter and intent of s. 80. Another option is to read s. 80 in the broader context of the Act. Section 80 must be read, first, in conjunction with ss. 82-88. In other words, the exception in s. 80 is linked to a compensation mechanism (that being said, the exception applies even in the absence of an applicable tariff). Second, there are other exceptions in the Act. As the Supreme Court did in *CCH*, even in the face of a specific exception, fair dealing might apply.

The correct interpretation of s. 80 is that it is independent of other exceptions, including s. 29 and following. Thus, when, based on credible empirical data, use of a new medium is "on its way" to becoming ordinary to copy music, that use could be considered fair dealing, at least for certain types of uses and users. When the use in question reaches "ordinary status", s. 80 (and the corresponding right to the use of the compensation mechanism for blank media) applies.

Another crucial limitation which restricts the scope of both the exception and the levy is the fact that it only applies to a *medium*. Is a recording medium, such as a hard disk, flash memory etc, incorporated permanently in a device an audio recording medium?

In December 2004, the Federal Court of Appeal maintained tariffs set by the Copyright Board on certain types of blank media but rejected a $25

---

[313] *AVS Technologies v. Canadian Mechanical Reproduction Rights Agency* (2000) 7 C.P.R. (4th) 68 at para 6 (Fed. C.A.).

tariff on portable devices such as Apple's® iPod®[314]. The decision hinges precisely on the statutory definition of "medium". While the private coping *exception* applies to any "audio recording medium", defined in s. 79 as "a recording medium, regardless of its material form, onto which a sound recording may be reproduced and that is of a kind ordinarily used by individual consumers for that purpose, excluding any prescribed kind of recording medium", the possibility of imposing a levy only applies to "blank media, defined as "an audio recording medium onto which no sounds have ever been fixed, and (b) any other prescribed audio recording medium." The Court parsed the definitions in the following terms:

> I do not believe that it was open to the Board to establish a levy on memory embedded in digital audio recorders. In my respectful view, Part VIII of the Act and the definition of 'audio recording medium' gave the Board no such authority.

> The Board established the levy on the basis that it could, in effect, look through the device being sold and reach the permanently embedded memory found therein. The Board twice noted that the levy sought by the CPCC, and approved by it was on 'memory in devices' but not on 'devices' The conceptual difficulty inherent in the exercise on which the Board embarked in certifying a levy on the memory embedded in a device, but not on the device itself, is illustrated by the tariff which it certified . . .

> Although the Board purported to establish a levy on the embedded memory, it acknowledged that this memory could not, looked at on its own, allow for the establishment of the levy; the device into which the memory was embedded had to be considered.

> [. . .] According to the Board, permanent memory embedded in an MP3 player comes within the definition, whereas the identical memory embedded into other devices does not.

> [. . .] It is the device that is the defining element of the levy and not the memory incorporated therein. The Board cannot establish a levy and determine the applicable rates by reference to the device and yet assert that the levy is being applied on something else.

> One can readily understand why the Board wanted to go as far as it could to bring MP3 players within the ambit of Part VIII. The evidence establishes that these recorders allow for extensive private copying by individuals. Their use can potentially inflict on rightsholders harm beyond any 'blank audio recording medium' as this phrase has been understood to date. However, as desirable as

---

[314] *CPCC 2004, supra,* note 310.

bringing such devices within the ambit of part VIII might seem, the authority for doing so still has to be found in the Act.

The Board found this authority in the definition of 'audio recording medium'. It focussed on the phrase 'regardless of its material form' to hold that Parliament intended that a levy be established on a medium, regardless of its incorporation into a device. In the words of the Board, 'A medium that is incorporated into a device remains a medium'

There are a number of problems with the Board's analysis. First, according to the Board's own reasoning, a memory does not become an 'audio recording medium' unless and until it is incorporated into the appropriate device . . . It is therefore difficult to see how such a memory can be said to remain a medium when embedded into a device.

Second, upon being incorporated into a device, a memory undergoes no change in form. It is therefore difficult to see how the Board can rely on the phrase 'regardless of its material form' to justify its conclusion. Furthermore, to rely on this phrase, the Board first had to identify an 'audio recording medium'. According to its own reasons, a memory is not an 'audio recording medium' unless and until embedded into a digital audio recorder.

It is apparent that the phrase on which the Board relied to 'see through' a digital audio recorder and reach the memory embedded therein does not support its conclusion when regard is had to its own findings. (Notes and references omitted.)[315]

This would lead one to the conclusion that Internet downloads onto a computer hard disk or portable device are not covered by the exception contained in s. 80 and thus constitute an infringement of the reproduction rights contained in ss. 3, 15 and 18, unless a specific exception, such as fair dealing, applies. An application for leave to appeal has been made to the Supreme Court of Canada.

## X. POINTS OF ATTACHMENT AND FOREIGN WORKS

Foreign works are protected in Canada on the same terms as works by Canadians, providing that it is from a country which is member of the Berne Convention or the WTO. This concept is referred to as national treatment. (See the *International* section.)

To be protected in Canada (see section 5(1.2)), a work, performance or sound recording must have one of the required points of attachment. These

---

[315] *Ibid.* at paras. 148-157.

points of attachment create a link between Canada (or another country party to a treaty which imposes national treatment obligations on Canada) and the object of the protection, the rightsholder, or both.

Section 5 contains the points of attachment for copyright in works (ss. 3 and 14.1). They are: citizenship, ordinary residence, and first publication (as defined in s. 5(1)(c) and 5(1.1).

For performers rights contained in s. 15 (see the Related Rights section), the points of attachment are linked to the country where the performance takes place, the place from which it is broadcast, or where the performance is fixed on a sound recording the maker (producer) of which is a Canadian citizen or a citizen or resident of an eligible country (section 15(2)).

For producers of sound recordings rights contained in s. 18, the points of attachment are the citizenship or residence of the maker/producer and the country of first publication (s. 18(2).

For the right to remuneration for the public performance and communication to the public of sound recordings contained in s. 19, the points of attachments are somewhat more restrictive. The producer of the sound recording must be a Canadian citizen (or permanent resident) or of a country party to the Rome Convention (see the International Section) or where *all* the fixations done for the sound recording occurred in Canada or a Rome Convention member State.[316] The United States is not and is unlikely to become (for domestic political reasons) party to the Rome Convention.

## XI. DATABASE PROTECTION

Databases are collections of data or other materials. The selection and arrangement of material may be protected by copyright if it meets the originality requirement (see the Originality section). However, such protection only protects the owner of copyright against reproduction of a substantial part of what is protected, that is, not the data but rather their selection or arrangement. This has prompted demands in many countries to adopt specific protection above and beyond copyright protection to allow database makers to prevent the extraction and reuse of data compiled by them.

Canada does not protect databases under a separate regime, as was stated in *Tele-Direct*.[317] In 2002-2004, the United States was moving towards the protection of databases under a statutory (federal) tort of misappropriation. The European Union granted databases protection under a *sui generis* right defined in the *Directive 96/9/EC of the European Parliament*

---

[316] Section 20(1). The international scope of the right to remuneration may in certain cases be extended or limited by the Minister (ss. 20(2) - (4)).

[317] *Supra*, note 36.

*and of the Council of 11 March 1996 on the legal protection of databases.*
Article 7(1) of the EU Databases Directive provides that:

> Member States shall provide for a right for the maker of a database which
> shows that there has been qualitatively and/or quantitatively a substantial in-
> vestment in either the obtaining, verification or presentation of the contents to
> prevent extraction and/or re-utilization of the whole or of a substantial part,
> evaluated qualitatively and/or quantitatively, of the contents of that database.

## Note De Lege Ferenda

In a report issued in October 2002 under the authority of s. 92 of the
*Copyright Act* entitled "Supporting Culture and Innovation: Report on the
Provisions and Operation of the *Copyright Act*", Canadian Heritage and
Industry Canada, the two government departments jointly responsible for
the operation of the *Act*, commented on this issue as follows:

*Issue: Whether the Act should be amended to provide for some form of protec-
tion for non-original databases.*

A database is a collection of digitized information, facts, works or other material
that has been arranged in such a way that a user can retrieve items having
certain characteristics or meeting certain criteria. Organizations, such as publishers, commercial enterprises, hospitals, educational institutions, libraries and
archives, expend considerable resources in developing and maintaining databases, whether for commercial or non-commercial, internal or external use.
Providing appropriate legal protection for databases can therefore provide
important incentives to invest in their creation and use.

A work that results from the selection or arrangement of works or data may
itself be protected as a "compilation" as defined in the *Copyright Act*. From
this definition, many databases receive copyright protection with its attendant
rights, exceptions and term of protection. Exactly which databases benefit from
copyright protection remains unclear, however. Recent court decisions suggest
that the selection and arrangement of the underlying works or data must be
sufficiently "original" to qualify for protection. The fact that considerable effort
or money was invested in the creation of the database may be irrelevant. A
broader issue is whether copyright protection, with its particular rights, exceptions and term of protection, is the most appropriate way to protect databases.
(footnotes omitted)

## XII.  DISCUSSION QUESTIONS

### Tangible versus Intangible

**Q:**    Historia is researching the 20th-century poet Philippa. Philippa died in 1984 and her will named her Daughter as her sole beneficiary. At an auction, Historia bought a group of ribbon-tied letters which Philippa had written to her brother Alex in 1978. Alex is still alive and Historia asks only him for permission to reproduce the letters in a scholarly book that Historia is writing about Philippa. Alex writes back with his approval. Historia includes the full text of 25 letters. Has Historia infringed copyright?

### Originality

**Q:**    In *CCH v. LSUC*, the Chief Justice for a unanimous court describes the originality standard set out there of "skill and judgment" as requiring more than "sweat of the brow" but which does "not, however, go as far as . . . requiring that a work possess a minimal degree of creativity to be considered original" (para 22). Can you think of examples of original expression which would satisfy the originality requirement of "skill and judgment" but which would *not* have a "minimal degree of creativity"? In other words, would a "minimal degree of creativity" impose a higher requirement for originality than the "skill and judgment" standard of *CCH v. LSUC*?

**A:** Arguably, one answer might be based on examples from *CCH v. LSUC* with respect to legal publishers' headnotes, topical indexes, or case summaries for legal judgments. In a similar context, the Second U.S. Circuit Court of Appeals remarked that the "dominant editorial value" for publishers of judicial opinions is faithfulness to the original and thus the "creative is the enemy of the true" (*Matthew Bender & Co. v. West Publishing Co.*, 158 F.3d 674 (U.S. 2nd Cir. N.Y., 1998), 688, *cert. denied* 526 U.S. 1154, 119 S. Ct. 2039 (1999)). While a legal publisher might not be able to show creativity and novelty, or even aim for "novelty," competent legal editors would exercise skill and judgment in writing the headnotes. Another example is an alphabetical list of unusual surnames. The resulting alphabetical lists (and there could be several plausible variations in the alphabetical order of the same group of surnames) might require skill and judgment but not be "creative."

**Q:**    Avery Programmer is a Canadian computer programmer and an enthusiastic fan of Wallace Blakely. Blakely, a Romantic era artist who painted in the late eighteenth- and early nineteenth-centuries, was a versatile artist, acclaimed for his poetry, engravings, drawings, and fabric design.

Blakely is especially known for the graphic layouts of his poetry and prose which he personally designed. Blakely's work includes small scale extremely detailed images which form the first letter in the first line of his poems and his short prose. Programmer created a comprehensive web site celebrating the work of Blakely (www.blakelygallery.com). All Blakely's works are in the public domain. Programmer spent years tracking down original images by Blakely. He searched a large number of sources to find the images, including archives, private collections, universities, auction catalogues, and periodicals. The website is a particularly useful resource for those interested in Blake's work because most of the original Blakely images are not available to the general public to view. The scanned images on Programmer's website are high quality digital copies and most of the images are not readily available elsewhere in digital format. Programmer has now discovered that a rival website has been created (www.aboutblakelyart.com). Programmer visited the site and discovered his digital images had been copied onto the rival site. Programmer specifically identified 35 images which match Programmer's (pixel by pixel) and are not available anywhere else. The rival website by Wallace Simile is a commercial site which sells advertising and products such as posters, pens, and notecards with Blakely images on them. Does Programmer have copyright in his digital images? Did Simile infringe it?

**Q:**    Raj borrows a book from his university library which was published in 1824 and contains a short novel in English that was written in 1820. The novel and book are in the public domain. Raj writes out the whole book in long hand on paper. Does Raj have copyright in the book? Has Raj infringed copyright? Does either answer change if Raj photocopies the entire 1824 book? What if he scans the book and makes aesthetic enhancements to the resulting electronic version? What if Raj adds scholarly editorial footnotes? Or includes this work in his collection of "Forgotten Early Nineteenth-Century Short Novels" and publishes the anthology? What if Raj photographs the original book and takes care to choose a complementary background, and selects lighting that increases the legibility of the printed letters and makes the watermarks and stains on the original book page more easily visible? What if Raj translates the novel into Italian?

**A:** Copyright exists in original literary works. Under the definition of originality in *CCH v. LSUC*, originality requires that a work "must have originated from the author, not be copied, and must be the product of the exercise of skill and judgment that is more than trivial" (para. 28). Raj copied the book so it does not even meet the requirement that a work must "originate from" the author. Raj, however, has not infringed copyright since the work is already in the public domain. The book was published in 1824 so any editorial or publisher enhancements are no longer protected by copyright either. Neither answer changes if Raj photocopies the entire book. Such "sweat of the brow" labour is not sufficient for purposes of copyright originality. In each instance there is no infringement because the work is in the public domain. Raj's editorial enhancements arguably could be original enough to meet the *CCH v. LSUC* standard, if they require skill and judgment. A parallel would be the topical index to a collection of law cases or headnotes to judicial decisions, discussed in *CCH v. LSUC*. If there is originality in the selection or arrangement of Raj's collection of novels, that could be copyrightable. Copyright law recognizes that photography and translations are not trivial mechanical skills. Both the photograph and the translation "originates from" Raj. For the photograph, if the choice of background and lighting show "skill and judgment" then Raj would meet the originality requirement. Similarly, with translations, the translator must select word choices, consider nuances, and struggle with idioms.

**Q:**    Two expert restoration painters have worked painstakingly for ten years to restore a famous painting originally painted on the ceiling of a church in 1507 and depicting a religious scene. Restorio and Preservio have worked jointly over all parts of the painting and have collaborated extensively on materials, pigments and techniques. Both Restorio and Preservio have years of training and experience and academic background in art restoration. Over the ten years, Restorio and Preservio have added brush strokes to almost the entire surface of the ceiling. The painting had been restored twice before by other painters in 1750 and 1834, but those eighteenth- and nineteenth-century restorations, although well intentioned and meant to retain the integrity of the original, had destroyed some of the underlying paint, changed the outlines of some of the original image, and failed to match the original colours. Restorio and Preservio are trying to restore the painting to as close to the original 1507 painting as they can. Those scholars and art historians who have seen the results have judged the result to be almost identical to the original. These assessments, however, are inevitably subjective given the limited evidence which exists about the original paintings and the damage done to the original in the eighteenth- and nineteenth-century restoration attempts.

*Assume Canadian copyright law applies. Do Restorio and Preservio have copyright in the painting on the ceiling? When Restorio and Preservio are finished restoring the ceiling, does Peter Public infringe any rights that Restorio, Preservio, or anyone else might have when Public draws a picture of the ceiling using only historical descriptions, written in prose, of the 1507 ceiling painting as his source material (and without viewing the restored ceiling)? Explain your conclusion and reasons fully.*

## Literary Works

**Q:**    Would a gum wrapper be a copyrightable work? What factors would you consider?

## Translations

**Q:**    Ezra Pond is a Canadian poet. He has been working on poetic translations of prose written in Portuguese by a living Canadian author, Jorge Mantillo. Pond did not get copyright permission to translate this prose. Ezra Pond is a clever poet. Unfortunately, he is not very adept at foreign languages. His "translated" poetry is lyrical but not an accurate word-for-word translation. There are many basic errors where Pond used English words that sounded similar to Portuguese ones but did not have similar definitions. He titled the poem, "Homage to Jorge Mantillo."

Is Pond's poem a copyrightable work? How would you decide? Does Pond's poetry infringe the translation right of the original author? Does it matter that Pond tried to be correct and missed? What if Pond was inspired by the Portuguese prose but intended to write a poem that would be a tribute to the original author but not a translation? Is the question whether Pond's poem has a separate copyright the same question as whether Pond's poem infringes the copyright of Mantillo's original work?

**Q:**    Consider someone who creates a unique tool which can be used in turn to create an artistic work or musical work (as for example, special paint brushes or a prized violin). Should the creator of the tool have any rights in the works that are produced from those tools (paintings, music)? Should the creator of the tool have joint (or collective) authorship in the output? What if the works produced by that tool are different than the works produced by a standard version (for example, a Stradivarius violin)? Would that, or should that, entitle the creator of the tool to copyrights in the output produced by that tool?

## Dramatic Works

**Q:**    Bailey Barnum is in charge of a small travelling circus in Canada. The circus includes trapeze artists, clowns, acrobats, and animal trainers. The acts are scheduled for a 90-minute show. Some acts are in the centre ring and perform alone. Sometimes there are three acts all performing at the same time in three separate rings. The order of the acts and the length of time of each act is set in advance. Some acts include improvisational elements. The clowns and mimes and jugglers change their act depending on audience reaction. For some acts, members of the audience participate. Could this circus be copyrighted as a dramatic work?

**Musical Works**

**Q:**    You are an intellectual property lawyer in Canada. The Canadian musical composer John Sage approaches you seeking help protecting one of his musical compositions, titled 3'22". There are three movements to the piece. In each movement, no musical instruments are played and no words are sung. Sage instructs people who are going to perform the piece that they should wear a tuxedo and sit on stage on a piano bench in front of a piano for the full three minutes and twenty-two seconds. The performer should be accompanied by a page turner who will turn the sheets of music at the completion of each movement. There are no musical notes scored on the music sheet, but the length of each individual movement of the piece is marked on the sheets. The piano, the person turning the pages, and the person on the piano bench are the only things on stage. Sage's vision is that the piece causes the audience to notice the environmental sounds in the auditorium and become more sensitive to the ambient noise that is around us daily. Sage has spoken about the piece on many occasions. He refers to it as music. The piece 3'22" has been performed hundreds of times since it debuted ten years ago. Some of those performances were sound recorded. Sage's typical audience members are people aged 35 to 55 who appreciate classical music. They tend to be quiet and respectful in the audience. Sage performs in concert halls.

   An alternative music band, Roxy, has just put out a new studio album "Fanland" and is on a promotional concert tour in which they are performing music from their studio album. Track eight, of ten tracks, on the studio CD is titled, "Tribute to John Sage." It consists of 1'40" of silence. The album was recorded in a soundproof studio. Roxy performs this piece in concert after the intermission. With the house lights darkened, the band members walk on stage with their guitars and stand on stage silently. They move their guitars to the other hand after 45 seconds, and move one step forward after another 20 seconds. They do not play their musical instruments for the one minute and forty seconds period. In the concerts, the lights come up after this time period and then the band plays another song from the studio album. Roxy also puts out a new live album featuring performances from their promotional tour. The sound recording of the Winnipeg performance of 1'40" is included as track ten of the ten tracks on the live album. Roxy's typical audience members are teenagers and people in their twenties. Roxy's audience members tend to be enthusiastic, and they like to shout and clap when Roxy performs. On tour, Roxy performs in outside arenas.

Sage contacted Roxy and accused them of infringing his copyright. Roxy's lead singer replied, "What part of the silence do you think I have stolen? My silence is original silence."

**a)**    *Sage would like you to register the copyright in Canada. To do so, you will need to identify any copyrightable material Sage might have and the best choice(s) of work or subject matter of neighbouring rights to describe it under the Copyright Act. You will also need to identify the author, and ensure the other requirements for copyright are met. Explain your choices fully. Advise Sage whether he should register the copyright in the piece.*

**b)**    *Sage would like to know if Roxy has infringed any copyright rights that Sage might have. Discuss fully, addressing the likelihood of success of any action and the remedies Sage should seek. Consider any defences that Roxy might have.*

**c)**    *Sage would like to know whether Roxy or anyone else has copyright rights in 3'22" or "Tribute to John Sage."*

**Artistic Works**

**Q:**    A large energy company coined a word which is used in the corporate names of its head company and subsidiaries. The word is TODAPOTENCIA. The word appears with unusual lettering with the letter "O" appearing as open hands with water running through them. Another energy company adopts the same word for their promotional materials. The second company does not copy the unusual lettering or the design of the hands and water.

Is the made-up word a copyrightable literary work? Is the design, with the lettering, hands, and water, a copyrightable artistic work? Does the second company infringe any copyrights when it adopts the word but not the design elements?

**Q:**    Priscilla Parker has designed a new boardgame. She has written up the rules in an instruction book. She has also created a design for the board game itself which includes the usual square blocks to move the game pieces around the pieces. The square blocks loop around a forest scene with mythical figures which Parker has designed and painted. What aspects of the boardgame (if any) could Parker have copyright in? What kind of copyright works would there be?

**Photographs**

**Q:**    Image appropriation art is post-modernist art which takes another artist's work and reuses it in another context as a way to explore the meaning and limits of "originality" and "authorship." Sherrie Levine is an appropriation artist. She has said the purpose of her art is to explore the ideas of originality, place the old work in a new context and to call attention to the relative absence of women artists in the early 20th century Modernist movement in art. Sherrie Levine does this by re-photographing original photographs by such photographers as Walker Evans and Edward Weston. She references the original artist in the title of her works, which are in the format "After [original artist]" number [_____]. The original and re-photographed photographs are extremely hard to distinguish. Levine's photographs are head-on photos of the original photo and have the same subject matter, lighting, and composition. Walker Evans was a Depression era photographer. In 1936, Evans photographed sharecroppers in Alabama. Evans's photographs are still under copyright. The photographs are held by a museum and the copyright is owned by Evans's estate. In the late 1970s, Sherrie Levine rephotographed Walker Evans's photographs of a sharecropper family using an exhibition catalogue as her source. In 2001, Michael Mandiberg scanned Sherrie Levine's photographs and included those images in his websites www.afterwalkerevans.com and www.aftersherrielevine.com. The photographs on the two websites appear to be identical. Mandiberg has said his purpose is to spark discussion and thought on our relationship with digital images and the dissemination of art. Mandiberg's site also has "Certificates of Authenticity" which can be printed out in pdf format and signed by the website *user*. Mandiberg states on his website that he has an "explicit strategy to create a physical object with cultural value, but little or no economic value."

Are Sherrie Levine's photographs of Walker Evans's photographs original copyrightable works?

Are Michael Mandiberg's digital images of Sherrie Levine's photographs original copyrightable works?

Do Sherrie Levine's photographs infringe copyright? If so, are there any defences or exemptions which apply?

Do Mandiberg's digital images infringe copyright? If so whose copyright(s) and are there any defences or exemptions which apply?

Does a user infringe copyright by downloading Mandiberg's digital images and printing them out? If so, whose copyright(s) and are there any defences or exemptions which apply?

## Photographs and Architectural Works

Q:    Jill grew up in Manitoba and comes to Ottawa for the first time this past summer. She takes a photograph of the Supreme Court Building. The photograph is a typical tourist picture, taken from the front lawn and including the whole building. Jill took some time to compose the picture, made sure the building was centred in the frame, and that the statues of Justice and Truth were visible. Jack arrives in the fall on his visit to Ottawa. Jack grew up in Halifax and has never met Jill or seen her photographs. Jack takes a photograph of the Supreme Court of Canada building. He too frames the building in the centre of the shot. Jack experiments with different settings on his auto-focus telephoto/wide lens camera. Jill's photo and Jack's photo are conventional amateur photographs of the building, similar to each other and to other photographs taken by tourists over the years. Is Jill's photograph an original copyrightable work? Is Jack's? If Jill's photograph is copyrightable, does Jack's photograph infringe Jill's copyright? Has either Jill or Jack infringed the copyright in the original architectural design for the design of the Supreme Court building (assume that the designer has been dead less than 50 years).

## Originality and Authorship

**Q:**    Designer creates a software program which will automatically generate short poems on a specific theme and in a particular form (e.g. haiku, free verse, etc.) selected by a user. User selects "blue dog" as a theme and chooses the category of a sonnet (a 14-line single-stanza rhyming poem). The software produces a sonnet about a blue dog titled "Blue Dog". Who is the author of the software program and what factors would you consider to evaluate if it could be copyrighted? Is the computer-generated poem a copyrightable literary work? How would this be analysed and what information would you consider? If this computer-generated poem can be a copyrightable literary work, who is the author of the poem? Under *CCH v. LSUC*, originality requires non-mechanical and non-trivial effort, skill and labour. Given the computer assistance, is this "Blue Dog" sonnet "mechanical"?

**Q:**    Horatio is a novelist who is beginning to work on his fifth novel. He has his basic plot outlined, which will be a detective story about the mystery of a fictional unsolved nineteenth-century murder. His neighbour Marlowe comes over for dinner one evening and suggests that Horatio set his next novel in England and that it should involve a travelling circus. Marlowe also says he thinks Albion would be a great name for the detective. Horatio publishes his 300 page novel a year later. It is called Albion's Circus and is about a murder of a trapeze artist in England in 1860 which the detective John Albion solves. Horatio's novel becomes a best seller. Marlowe sues Horatio for a percentage of the royalties on the grounds that Marlowe is a joint author. Marlowe argues his suggestions for the novel were critical to the novel's popularity. You are the judge. How would you rule on the question of joint authorship and why?

**Q:** Canadian song-writer Nellie Wayne has written forty songs that have been in the top ten of the recording charts and five have gone on to be number one. Many of these songs have been performed by the well-known singer Dionne Franklin but some have been performed by unknown singers and topped the charts. One morning Wayne woke up and had a new song in her head. She has said in interviews that she thinks she dreams music. She writes down the song immediately and it becomes an instant success in a version sung by Franklin. Does this song meet the originality requirement? Do intellectual property theories and/or public policy justify granting an intellectual property to Wayne? Why, or why not?

**Moral Rights**

**Q:** Elisa purchased an original oil painting by Cooper Carlisle entitled "Avian Hope". Carlisle is a Canadian painter who paints brightly coloured abstract images of fish, birds, and other animals which are asymmetrically placed on the canvas. Carlisle is very particular about the frames of his paintings and personally selects each frame for his paintings and personally places the wire hanging for mounting. Carlisle recently described "Avian Hope" to a magazine interviewer as a picture of a heron with its wings spread in flight and flying up toward the trees and symbolizing hope. Elisa bought the painting to hang in the busy lobby of a corporate office building. When Elisa saw the painting in place, she decided it would look better upside down and she re-hung it. It is hard to pick out the bird image in the painting when viewed upside down and if it can be picked out it looks like the bird is crashing into the ground. Elisa is pleased because the yellow in the painting is now at the top at the painting and no longer clashes with the red furniture in the lobby. People going by in the lobby who stand and look at the painting sometimes wonder what it is supposed to be. Other people who view it say they like the bright colors. Carlisle argues his moral rights have been violated. Does Carlisle have a persuasive argument?

**Infringement**

**Q:** Freddie Forger sees the original "Avian Hope" by Carlisle hanging in Elisa's lobby. He has a phenomenal ability to remember visual images. Freddie goes home to his studio and does an oil painting from memory which is indistinguishable from "Avian Hope". All the brush strokes on the canvas were done by hand by Freddie. Has Freddie infringed copyright? If so, whose?

**Q:**   Mr. Magoo also sees the original "Avian Hope" by Carlisle hanging in Elisa's lobby. Magoo also has a phenomenal ability to remember visual images. Magoo goes home to his studio and does an oil painting from memory of "Avian Hope." Unfortunately, Magoo is near-sighted and wasn't wearing his glasses when he saw "Avian Hope." Magoo duplicates exactly what he saw with his near sighted vision, which is an interesting picture but it doesn't look at all like "Avian Hope." Magoo wanted to make an exact reproduction. Has Magoo infringed copyright?

**Q:**   Juanita is at a newsstand looking at this week's celebrity gossip magazines. She sees one with a particularly funny article about a movie star couple on vacation at a theme park, with photographs of the couple wearing costumes. Juanita thinks her friends would enjoy the article and photos. She takes pictures of the four magazine pages and sends them electronically to ten of her friends. Has Juanita infringed copyright?

**Q:**   Red Star Greeting Card Company designed a best-selling new-pet card depicting a skinny man with a long neck and grey hair next to a greyhound breed dog, which is lanky and has grey fur, with the sentiment inside "They say you get to look like your pet after awhile." The lead designer of Whatever Occasion Card Company sees the card and wants to market a "new pet" card of its own. The company copies the same phrase "They say you get to look like your pet after awhile" for the inside of the card but they change the font and print the words in red instead of black. They also substitute a photograph of an auburn-haired woman with her orange tabby cat as the design for the front of the card. Whatever Occasion claims they were inspired by Red Star's card but only borrowed the idea. Has Whatever Occasion infringed Red Star's copyright in the greeting card?

**Fair Dealing**

**Q:**   An author of a wildly popular children's book series has just finished her seventh novel in the fantasy series featuring a young girl with magical powers, her wizard friend, and her flying squirrel. The latest book by J.K. Rowlands is over 900 pages long and is called "The Mystery of Lark Angel Run." As a marketing strategy, her publisher has placed an embargo on any news reporting of the novel until October 31$^{st}$. One newspaper, "Magic Express," receives a copy of the manuscript in the mail from an anonymous source, flown in by an owl, and publishes a summary of the book. The summary is four newspaper pages long and includes some direct quotations from the novel. The summary is written by a freelance journalist. Is there copyright in the summary? If so, who is the author? Have any rights by Rowlands been infringed?

**Q:**    Celine Scholar is a professor specializing in cultural studies. She is currently researching tabloid newspapers that focus on celebrity gossip stories. Scholar has been going to a local convenience store which has a photocopier and has been copying the entire issues of each week's tabloid gossip papers. She has been doing this for twelve weeks. Does Scholar have a copyright defence to infringement of the newspaper's copyrights? Does the convenience store have a copyright defence to infringement of the newspaper's copyrights?

**Multiple Issues**

**Q:**    Some universities are using a program to detect plagiarism in student academic papers and examinations. Students turn their papers in electronically, the papers are added to a database, and the program checks for similarities between papers. One company's process is to archive a full copy of the original work. The company also makes a "digital fingerprint" of students' papers which is used to compare subsequent papers for plagiarism. The company argues the digital fingerprint conveys only a "fact" about plagiarism and is neither the original work nor the same expression as the original work.

Does this practice raise copyright concerns? What factors would you consider as you evaluate this? Based on the reasoning of *Apple Computer* and the Morse Code analogy relied on there, does the "digital fingerprint" infringe copyright? Does the company have copyright in the "digital fingerprint" which is generated automatically by a computer program? The company provides this commercial service to educational institutions. Based on *CCH*, could the company argue fair dealing? Could the company argue consent? Is there copyright in the database compilation?

**Q:**    SYNO Music Inc. asks you to sue Michael Song, the famous composer. They believe that, in spite of some notable differences in the melody and lyrics, Mr. Song's latest opus, "I love you", is a copy of a song written by a composer and performer who has an exclusive (written) contract with SYNO, Céline Voice. Ms. Voice's song, which she recorded on a CD released in July 2004, is called "Never Without You". Mr. Song's CD, which is also called "I Love You", was released in Canada in August 2004.

What will SYNO Music Inc. have to show to be successful? What remedies should they be considering asking for?

If Mr. Song wants to show to the Court that "Never Without You" is very similar to many songs published prior to 2004, can he make a copy of those songs to file with the Court without obtaining the right to make those copies?

**Q:**    Madam Justice Veritas of the Court of Canada recently came to give a lecture at the Faculty of Law. Her speech, the written text of which she had in front of her, was recorded with her permission by the cable TV channel CanTV, then broadcast on that channel. Madam Justice Veritas was very proud of her speech, which she wrote herself. CanTV also sells copies of the videocassette of Justice Veritas's speech. Taking as a given that Madam Justice Veritas had not signed a written contract with anyone whatsoever, answer the following questions based on the *Copyright Act* and provide your reasons.

a)    Is the speech a protected work?

b)    Who is the author of the speech?

c)    Who is the primary holder of the rights to the speech?

d)    Does CanTV hold any right whatsoever to the speech as recorded on videocassette?

e)    Does CanTV hold any right whatsoever to the television broadcast of the speech?

CanTV also makes the speech available on its Web site, where anyone with Web access can view it free of charge.

f)    Does CanTV have to obtain permission from Madam Justice Veritas or someone else to place the speech on a Web site and make it accessible in this way?

# *Chapter* 3: Industrial Designs

I. Introduction

II. Object of the Protection

III. Registration, Ownership and Term of Protection

IV. Marking

V. Infringement, Remedies and Defences

VI. Discussion Questions

## I. INTRODUCTION

Under the *Copyright Act*, an artistic work such as a sculpture or other three-dimensional work of art is protected (subject to the originality requirement) without any formality. Registration is possible but not mandatory. This is advantageous for creators, who are automatically protected, but disadvantageous for the public. The lack of registration may make it difficult to identify information such as the author or other rightsholder in a protected work and the date of creation, which in turn can create transaction costs for users who wish to determine if a work is covered by copyright and, if so, how to contact the rightsholder(s) to obtain an authorization (licence). Because there is no requirement under the *Copyright Act* that a work be published and no central depository of copyrighted material in Canada, a user or creator may find herself accused of infringing a pre-existing work which she was not aware even existed. She may be able to defeat the claim because a finding of infringement requires evidence of access to the protected work (see the Copyright Section[1]).

The legislative protection offered by the *Industrial Design Act* works differently. In certain cases, where an artistic work is used in a more industrial context, to create a "useful article," defined as "any thing that is made by hand, tool or machine" that "has a utilitarian function",[2] *i.e.*, a "function other than merely serving as a substrate or carrier for artistic or literary

---

[1]  The interface between industrial designs and copyright is discussed in the Intellectual Property Overlaps section.

[2]  *Industrial Design Act*, R.S.C. 1985, c. I-9, s.2, online: Department of Justice Canada <http://laws.justice.gc.ca/en/I-9/text.html>.

matter,"[3] separate legislation called the *Industrial Design Act* (hereinafter "the Act") provides intellectual property protection for aesthetic features applied to such useful articles. To benefit from this protection, certain additional formalities and requirements have been imposed by Parliament.

The Act defines a "design" or "industrial design" as "features of shape, configuration, pattern or ornament and any combination of those features that, in a finished article, appeal to and are judged solely by the eye." It is the aesthetic or non-utilitarian functions of the article, its externally visible features, which are protected under the Act. This is made clear by s. 5.1(a), which reads as follows: "No protection afforded by this Act shall extend to (a) features applied to a useful article that are dictated solely by a utilitarian function of the article."

The use of the word "pattern" in the definition shows that two-dimensional designs, such as drawings, may also be protected and that the Act is not limited to three-dimensional designs. The term "ornament" does not require that the design necessarily beautify the article. A design simply needs to "distinguish the appearance" of that article.[4]

## II. OBJECT OF THE PROTECTION

Industrial design protection covers *aesthetic* designs that are *applied* to *useful* articles. The Act requires that the designs be aesthetic, meaning there is visual appeal. Designs which are required by the utilitarian function or are the only design which can achieve the function of the object are not protected (s. 5.1(a)). Apart from the utilitarian function of the article, which is not protected under the Act, it is similarly not possible to protect a method or principle of manufacture or construction (s. 5.1(b)).[5] Thus, if the only way to make an object is with a mould that produces a hollow centre, the

---

[3]  See *2426-7536 Quebec Inc. v. Provigo Distribution Inc.* (1992), 50 C.P.R. (3d) 539 (Que. S.C.). See also the copyright/industrial design part of the Overlaps section.

[4]  See *DRG Inc. v. Datafile Ltd.* (1991), [1991] F.C.J. No. 144, 35 C.P.R. (3d) 243, 117 N.R. 308, 1991 CarswellNat 1123 (Fed. C.A.) (". . .it would be a strange result indeed if, by the operation of section 46 (now 64) of the *Copyright Act*, designs would come under or be excluded from the protection of the *Copyright Act* depending on whether they were 'ugly' or 'beautiful'. A 'beautiful' industrial design would be protected for a maximum of ten years under the *Industrial Design Act*, while an 'ugly' industrial design would be protected during the life of its author and a period of fifty year after his death under the *Copyright Act*. Such an absurd result cannot be sanctioned by this Court.").

[5]  See also *Angelstone Ltd. v. Artistic Stone Ltd.*, [1960] Ex. C.R. 286, 33 C.P.R. 155 (Can. Ex. Ct.).

feature of the hollow centre itself would result from the manufacture method and not be subject to protection. To take a simple illustration, if a bird bath has a basic design with a sturdy pedestal base and a bowl, those elements are dictated by the object's form and not subject to protection. If, however, the designer adds aesthetic ornamentation, such as flowers, bird figures, or scrollwork, along the rim of the bowl, those features could be protected because they are visually appealing aesthetic ornamentation. While merely functional aspects of the design cannot be protected, the visual design of a functional object can be; however, an aesthetic design which completely overlaps with the functional aspects can not be protected. An article may be useful and have ornamental features (*e.g.,* a chair or tableware). However, in *Amp Inc. v. Utilux Pty. Ltd.*,[6] a case dealing with electrical terminals, the English Court of Appeal held that function is not protectable, and that when function and shape completely overlap, and are indistinguishable, the protection stops. The House of Lords noted that where the object of the design was practical efficiency, the design could be denied protection.[7] The design had to be meant to "appeal to the eye."[8]

The Act does not give monopolies in the article itself, the function of the article, the method or process of making the article or the materials used.

In *Clatworthy*, a case dealing with a display stand,[9] the Exchequer Court of Canada explained the scope of protection for industrial design and the difference between a protected pattern (design) and the underlying object on or to which it is affixed:

> The design or configuration of the display stand made and sold by the defendant is the same as the plaintiff's, except that ornamentation work on the outside of the base and on the top of the standard is different; as a whole the plaintiff's display stand is said to be of a Grecian pattern while the defendant's is Gothic. To the casual observer the distinction in this respect would hardly be noticeable, although in the opinion of Mr. Smeal who was the author of the complete designs of both display stands, they would not be confusing to any persons understanding anything about designing, and are readily distinguishable on account of the different ornamental work deliberately applied to each by him,

---

[6]  (1971), [1971] F.S.R. 572, [1972] R.P.C. 103 (U.K. H.L.) [*Utilux*].

[7]  See also *Carr-Harris Products Ltd. v. Reliance Products Ltd.* (1969), 58 C.P.R. 62 (Can. Ex. Ct.), affirmed (1970), 65 C.P.R. 158 (S.C.C.).

[8]  See also *Dek-Block Ontario Ltd. c. H. Beaudry Blocs de béton ltée* (1993), 1993 CarswellQue 1447 (Que. S.C.) and *Kestos Ltd. v. Kempat Ltd.* (1935), 53 R.P.C. 139 (Eng. Ch. Div.).

[9]  *Clatworthy & Son Ltd. v. Dale Display Fixtures Ltd.*, [1928] Ex. C.R. 159 (Can. Ex. Ct.), affirmed [1929] S.C.R. 429, [1929] 3 D.L.R. 11 (S.C.C.) [*Clatworthy*]. See also *Renwal Manufacturing Co. v. Reliable Toy Co.*, [1949] Ex. C.R. 188, 9 C.P.R. 67 (Can. Ex. Ct.) [*Renwal Manufacturing* cited to Ex. C.R.].

in order that they might be in contrast. The ornamental work applied to each is well known to the art though in detail they are quite different; the general configuration of both display stands, are the same.

[. . .]

According to the statute the design must, it would seem, be something capable of application to any article of manufacture or other article, for the ornamentation thereof. The words 'to the ornamenting of any article of manufacture or other article to which an industrial design may be applied or attached' are used in more than one section of the statute.

[. . .]

I think it is clear that a design within the Act[10] may be some ornament, printed, woven or produced on such articles as textile fabrics, paper hangings, floor cloths, lace, etc., or some ornament produced in such things as metal articles, glass or tiles. The Act seems confined to designs applicable to manufactured articles, and the application of such design to such articles; it does not apply to the things to which a design is applied.

It is the concept of the design which must be applied to the article; the design itself need not be literally "applied" on top of the article. Hence, the Act protects ornamental design affixed to the article as well as the shape of the article as long as the shape is aesthetic. The observations of Parker J. in *Pugh v. Riley Cycle Co. Ltd.* have frequently been cited by Canadian courts in support of this more expansive interpretation of the term "applied":[11]

A design to be registrable under the Act must be some conception or suggestion as to shape, configuration, pattern, or ornament. It must be capable of being applied to an article in such a way that the article to which it has been applied will show to the eye the particular shape, configuration, pattern, or ornament, the conception or suggestion of which constitutes the design.

It has also been decided that a building or structure is not an article to which a design may be applied.[12]

---

[10]   At the time, designs were protected under the *Trade-Marks and Designs Act,* later replaced by the *Industrial Design and Union Label Act* (R.S.C. 1952, c. 150) and then *the Industrial Design Act,* R.S.C. 1970, c. I-8.

[11]   (1912), [1912] 1 Ch. 613, 29 R.P.C. 196 (U.K. H.L.) at 202 [R.P.C.].

[12]   See *2426-7536 Quebec Inc. v. Provigo Distribution Inc., supra,* note 3.

## 1. Visual Appeal

The protection applies to features that "appeal to and are judged solely by the eye" (s. 2). Industrial design protection is limited to visual features, but the design does not have to be "beautiful" to qualify, only visually appealing. Whether the design is "visible" and "aesthetic" is assessed from the perspective of the potential purchaser.[13] The question is whether a design would attract a buyer to the object and the visual appeal has to be assessed by looking at the prospective buyer. By corollary, therefore, the design must be plainly visible to the purchaser.

In *Mainetti S.P.A. v. E.R.A. Display Co.*,[14] a case dealing with the protection of a skirt hanger, and the design of the clamps to hold the skirt, the court acknowledged that *functional* objects, such as skirt hangers, can have aesthetic designs (provided they are not dictated by the form). Designs can be influenced by function as long as the design is not dictated solely by the form. Nevertheless the court denied protection to the skirt hanger design because, although there were ornamental aspects to the skirt clamps, the design was not visible to consumers. Walsh J. wrote the following:

> In the case of *Dunlop Rubber Co. v. Golf Ball Developments. Ltd.* (1931), 48 R.P.C. 268, Farwell J., at pp. 277-78, states:
>
>> The second thing is that the test of a design is the eye and the eye alone. Now there is, I think, no possible doubt that 'the eye' in that section means the eye of the Court, because the Court has ultimately to determine these questions, and it is the eye of the Court and the eye of the Court alone which has to be the judge of the design in question. That I think is plain from the language of the Section, and it is made even plainer by the authorities to which I have been referred. The eye is the eye of the Court, but the Court is entitled to be assisted and instructed by evidence so that when in applies its eye to the test, it may have a mind to direct its eye which is instructed by the proper evidence. Such instruction may certainly be given to the Court by persons who are competent to do it with regard to the prior art; that is to say, the Court is entitled to be told what the designs earlier than the registered Design represent, the differences or similarities between the earlier designs and the registered Design and the alleged infringing design. Evidence of that sort to instruct the Court is clearly relevant, and the Court must clearly pay attention to it.
>
> This case is also authority for the use of expert evidence.
> [. . .]

---

[13] See *Utilux*, supra note 6.
[14] (1984), [1984] F.C.J. No. 230, 80 C.P.R. (2d) 206, 2 C.I.P.R. 275, 1984 CarswellNat 579 (Fed. T.D.) [*Mainetti* cited to C.P.R.].

It has been established that in comparing designs one should not look at differences but rather resemblances. Certainly now that the various minor and deliberately created differences have been shown to the Court it is not difficult to distinguish defendant's hangers from plaintiff's but if these differences had not been pointed out I would have reached the conclusion that these were merely different versions of a hanger made by the same manufacturer. I say this even though, as has been pointed out, all hangers must bear certain resemblances because of the function they are to serve but this has not and does not prevent original designs being made for them. I conclude that, applying the three tests set out in the case of *R. v. Premier Cutlery Ltd., supra*, defendant's design does infringe that of plaintiff. It can be confused with it at first glance. It is unlikely that defendant's design would have had any existence independently of plaintiff's registered design which inspired it. With respect to the third test there is no evidence of any other prior design to which it could be said to be nearer than to plaintiff's design. I conclude therefore that it should be expunged from the register.

[. . .]

'A design can exist even with functionality', see *R. v. Premier Cutlery Ltd.* (1980), 55 C.P.R. (2d) 134 at p. 147, which relies on the Carr-Harris case, [*Carr-Harris Products Ltd.* v. *Reliance Products Ltd.* (1969), 58 C.P.R. 62, 42 Fox Pat. C. 9], which dealt with such a simple object as tent pegs, as has been indicated. In it Cattanach J. stated at p. 81:

> Since the design for the plaintiff's tent peg is, in my opinion, a design for the ornamentation of tent pegs that is applied by making the tent pegs in the shape dictated by the design it follows that making a tent peg in that shape is ornamentation applied to that tent peg.

> Accordingly the attack on the validity of the plaintiff's design as not being a design for ornamentation also fails.

At p. 82 he states:

> The next attack is that the plaintiff's registered design is merely a functional shaping of the peg.

> The protection given to the plaintiff by its registered design is a monopoly for one particular and specific appearance as applied to its tent pegs and in my opinion that appearance follows as a result of the tent peg's overall shape. While utility sets rough limits to variation in shape or form I do not think that the use and function of a tent peg dictated the shape of the plaintiff's design as a whole but rather that the plaintiff succeeded in departing from the commonplace form which results from the requirements of utility alone and achieved a distinctive appearance.

While at first sight this might appear to rule out rejection of the hanger registrations on the ground of functionality, a close examination of this statement discloses that it depends on the conclusion that the plaintiff had succeeded in departing from a commonplace form resulting from requirements of utility alone and had achieved a distinctive appearance. In the present case neither party pressed for a finding that both registrations should be expunged on the grounds that they were primarily functional rather than decorative, since such a finding if applied to one of the designs would also be applicable to the other, but were in agreement that the Court has the right to consider this question, and this despite the admission that plaintiff's design is valid save for the issue raised under s. 14 of the Act and so is defendant's design as well save for the effect of the prior registration of plaintiff's design. It must be remembered that the *Industrial Design Act* as in the case of the *Patent Act*, R.S.C. 1970, c. P-4, and *Trade Marks Act*, R.S.C. 1970, c. T-10, is primarily for the protection of the public against being misled into the belief that an infringing article is in fact that of the party whose design, patent or trade mark has been registered. It is only secondarily intended to protect the commercial interests of the parties litigating an alleged infringement, serious as those interests may be. The facts of the present case are unusual in that the hangers are not only not sold to the general public, but they are not even visible until removed from the skirt which is hung on them. They are then either thrown away by the vendor or, if given to the purchaser with the garment, they are first seen by the purchaser at the time when the garment is removed from them. All the ornamentation and design on the ends of the hangers is hidden under the skirts until they are removed with only the top of the clip on each end showing, and of course the centre hook. The arms of the hanger and the designs on the ends of the arms leading to the hooks remain hidden under the skirt when it is hung on them and it is the function of the design and the spring which the arms provide which holds the skirt out flat for better display free of sagging and wrinkles. It is reasonable to conclude that not even the dress manufacturers themselves who buy these hangers to display and sell the skirts on them have any but the slightest interest in the ornamental design at the ends of the arms. There is a clear distinction to be made, therefore, between ornamental design applied to such hangers and design applied to objects such as chairs, water pitchers, teapots, and perhaps even tent pegs which are visible in use, the artistic design of which may appeal to a purchaser quite aside from the useful function which they serve.

I find therefore that both designs are primarily functional and that a hanger of this sort where the more significant design features are hidden and which is not intended to be admired by or sold to the public at large in any event should not have been subject to Industrial Design registration and should be expunged from the register pursuant to s. 22(1) of the *Industrial Design Act*.

In the end result therefore plaintiff's action against defendant must be dismissed, but defendant's claim in its defence that the validity of its registration should be upheld is also dismissed. Both parties will henceforth be free to manufacture and sell their hangers in competition with each other and purchaser will buy one or the other on the basis of price, quality, and the success with which competing models accomplish the function which is their primary purpose, which may well be the basis on which the customers, the dress manufacturers, have been purchasing one or the other hanger in any event, and such competition is certainly not against the public interest.

A similar finding was made by the Federal Court in *Gandy v. Canada (Commissioner of Patents)*: [15]

The only feature of the design which the Applicant argues to be original is the arrangement of flanges that would be entirely concealed from view in an assembled sign. They would be open to the view of the person acquiring the extrusions for purposes of assembling a frame. In rejecting the application, the examiner relied expressly on the following passages from the decision of the House of Lords in *Amp Inc. v Utilux Pty. Ltd.*[[1972] R.P.C. 103 per Lord Reid at 108 and Lord Morris of Borth-y-Gest at 113] which related to designs of terminals incorporated within electrical appliances.

> . . . So the design must be one which appeals to the eye of some customers. And the words 'judged solely by the eye' must be intended to exclude cases where a customer might choose an article of that shape not because of its appearance but because he thought that the shape made it more useful to him.
>
> . . .
>
> In the present case the terminal was simply devised so that it should 'do the job'. It was to perform the function that was defined by Hoover's requirements. The terminal is I think to be considered as and looked at as a unit. But if its constituent parts are considered I think that on the evidence each one was solely devised so that it should correctly perform its own particular function. There was nothing extra. There was nothing that could be regarded as any kind of embellishment. First and last and all the time the key-note was functional success. The terminals, unseen in the machines for which they were required (save by those who make or service the machines), had only to pass the test of being able to perform their functions. They would be judged by performance and not by appearance.

In the *Utilux* case[16] cited by the Federal Court, the House of Lords had concluded that if the shape of an article was not there to appeal to the eye

---

[15]   (1980), [1980] F.C.J. No. 118, 1980 CarswellNat 859 (Fed. T.D.), affirmed (1980), 47 C.P.R. (2d) 118 (Fed. C.A.).

[16]   *Supra*, note 6.

but solely to make the article work then it was excluded from statutory protection.

Design features that are not visible when the user uses the object or looks at it are not protected. Thus, a computer chip which has a very attractive design when highly magnified is not protected because first, the chip is not ordinarily visible to a purchaser of the retail product (such as a laptop) and second, the chip's design cannot be appreciated by the naked eye. Design features which are unseen except by those who make the parts, assemble them, or service the finished article are not protected. Similarly, design features which appeal to other senses than the eye are not protected.

## 2. Originality

In addition to an *aesthetic* design, the Act also requires that the design be *original*. Originality has been extensively analysed with respect to copyright protection (see Originality section in Copyright). In copyright, the Supreme Court has ruled in *CCH Canadian Ltd. v. Law Society of Upper Canada* that the standard for originality is non-mechanical and non-trivial skill and judgment.[17] Under Industrial Design, originality is treated differently and is closer to the notion of "novelty" in patent law than it is to the idea of originality under copyright (although the other requirements for patent law are not analogous). The Act does not define originality as such but does provide an indication of the meaning of the term in the context of the Act, which seems different than the meaning of the same term in the *Copyright Act,* where originality is based on creative choices.

Originality for industrial design requires that the design be objectively different from preceding designs and "originate from" the designer.

In *Clatworthy*, the Exchequer Court of Canada discussed originality as follows:

> [. . .] It is required that a design be original, and that it was not in use by any person other than the proprietor, to his knowledge, at the time of his adoption of it. Invention or utility is not a requirement to a valid registration, and the general principles of Patent Law are not applicable here.
> [. . .]

> [. . .] Display stands had been made and sold by the defendants since 1910, the general configuration and purpose of some of them, was the same as the plaintiff's design here in question, except that they particularly lacked ornamental work, being very plain in design and without casters. The general

---

[17]  [2004] 1 S.C.R. 339, 236 D.L.R. (4th) 395, 30 C.P.R. (4th)1, 317 N.R. 107 (S.C.C.).

characteristics and the principle of construction was the same. The underslung base of the plaintiff's design was stressed before me, but the defendant, in the latter part of 1925 or early in 1926, and prior to the plaintiff's registration, obtained a display stand manufactured in the United States with this form of base and having the general outlines of the plaintiff's display stand, and he then placed it in the hands of his designer to produce a display stand similar to it. Practically the same display stand was advertised in February, 1925, in a trade journal published by Hugh Lyons & Co., Ltd., of Lansing, Michigan, featuring display stands. Below is a figure of the display stand obtained by the defendant in the United States prior to the plaintiff's registration, showing an underslung base without ornamentation, and it is said of Romanesque style.

In my opinion there is nothing more whatever in the plaintiff's design, than is shown in the above figure (*omitted*) excepting the ornamental work; that is not by itself claimed as a design, and none of it as such is original. It is a method of construction and not a configuration, pattern, or ornament that the plaintiff claims. It is well settled, I think, that however constructed, an article of the same configuration is equally within or without the scope of a registered design. A design cannot be rendered original merely by a change in the mode of the construction of the article. I cannot reach the conviction that this is the sort of thing to which protection should be granted. No design should be counted as original unless it is distinguishable from what previously existed, by something which is essentially original. The introduction of ordinary trade variants into an old design cannot make it new or original. The requirement of novelty or originality by the statute, precludes the introduction of ordinary trade variants from making a design new or original if it is not new or original without them. The public is entitled to its choice of ordinary trade variants for use in any particular instance, and no registration should prevent its using or not using trade knowledge of this kind.

I might appropriately quote from Bowen L.J. in *Le May v. Welch* [(1885) 28 Ch. Div. 24 at p. 34.], where a registered design for a shirt collar was in question. He said: —

> In order to enable the respondents to maintain the registration, they must be, or claim to be, the proprietors of a new or original design. In the present case is there any new or original design shown by this drawing? In considering whether the design is new or original, we must remember in the first place that we are dealing with a design which purports to found itself on shape, and to deal with outline; and secondly that we are considering the question with reference to an article of dress of the very simplest and least complicated kind, an article of dress which may well vary in form in every town in England, and in every year in which collars are worn. We must not allow industry to be oppressed. It is not every mere difference of cut, every change of outline, every change of length or breadth, or configuration, in a simple and most familiar article of a

dress like this which constitutes novelty of design. To hold that would be to paralyze industry and to make the Patents, Designs, and Trade-Marks Act a trap to catch honest traders. It cannot be said that there is a new design every time a coat or waistcoat is made with a different slope or a different number of buttons. Tailoring would become impossible if such were the law, and it does not appear to me that such is the law. There must be, not a mere novelty of outline, but a substantial novelty in design having regard to the nature of the article. Now in the present case is there substantial novelty? That is an issue of fact to be decided by the view. Mr. Higgins says, and in that I am disposed to agree with him, that a new combination of old elements of design will satisfy the Act, and he asks us to find such novel combination in the presence, for the first time, in his article, of three characteristics; the absence of band, the downward curved opening and the large share of collar above the button. Now the answer which seems to go to the root of his contention is this, that if you take the specimen which the Lord Justice has dwelt upon as the most conspicuous instance, you will see that Mr. Higgins' contention is not well founded. The plaintiff's collar it is true, differs from A.H.K. 1 by exaggerating one or more of the characteristics which are there combined; but I can find in it no other novelty. It would be a most dangerous view of this Act to allow a design which presents no other element of novelty than this, to have the benefit of registration.[18]

In that case, the court stated that a known design that is applied for the first time to new subject matter can qualify as an original design.

In *Cimon Ltd. v. Bench Made Furniture Corp.*,[19] the same court had to decide whether a sofa was validly protected under the Act, and, in the affirmative, whether the Defendant's sofa infringed the Plaintiff's design. The court discussed the meaning of "originality" under the *Industrial Design Act*:

[T]here is no doubt in my mind that Furniture Craft Corporation, acting under the control of the defendant, Edwards, inspired by the success of the new Cimon sofa, to which the registered design here in question had been applied, early in 1962 produced a line of sofas and of chairs calculated to look as much like the Cimon sofa as possible with a view to sharing in the Cimon success.

I might also say, at this point, that it is perfectly clear that Furniture Craft Corporation, acting under the direct control of Edwards, produced and sold sofas and chairs in accordance with the copies so developed until after the Toronto Furniture Show in January 1963. It is also clear, in so far as the

---

[18]  *Supra*, note 9.
[19]  (1964), [1965] 1 Ex. C.R. 811, 48 C.P.R. 31 (Can. Ex. Ct.) [*Cimon* cited to Ex. C.R.].

defendant company is concerned, that, very shortly after Furniture Craft Corporation ceased to produce them, the defendant company, under the direction of the defendant Edwards, started producing sofas and chairs to which the same design had been applied, has been doing so ever since, and intends to do so as long as it is commercially advantageous to do so.

I shall deal first with the claim for infringement of the registered design because, as indicated above, it is conceded by the plaintiffs that, if the design in question is capable of being registered under the *Industrial Design and Union Label Act*, there is no cause of action for infringement of copyright. [. . .]

These provisions have been the subject of authoritative comment in Clatworthy [. . .]:

> To be entitled to registration the 'design' must be original.[. . .] Just what is contemplated by 'originality' the Act does not make clear. Under the English Act a design, to be registrable, must be 'new or original.' As that Act uses both words it has, in a number of cases, been sought to draw a distinction in meaning between them, and it has been held that 'every design which is original is new, but every design which is new is not necessarily original.' *In re Rollason's Design*, (1897) 14 R.P.C. 909.

In *Dover, Limited v. Nürnberger Celluloidwaren Fabrik Gebrüder Wolff*, [1910] 2 Ch. 25, at p. 29, Buckley, L.J., defines 'original' as applied to designs, as follows: —

> The word 'original' contemplates that the person has originated something, that by the exercise of intellectual activity he has started an idea which had not occurred to any one before, that a particular pattern or shape or ornament may be rendered applicable to the particular article to which he suggests that it shall be applied. If that state of things be satisfied, then the design will be original although the actual picture or shape or whatever it is which is being considered is old in the sense that it has existed with reference to another article before.

And further on he says: —

> There must be the exercise of intellectual activity so as to originate, that is to say suggest for the first time, something which had not occurred to any one before as to applying by some manual, mechanical, or chemical means some pattern, shape, or ornament to some special subject-matter to which it had not been applied before.

The above quotations, in my opinion, set out what is called for by our *Act*.

[. . .]

There is, however, a fairly definite indication in other sections as to just what class of design is intended. [. . .] no person (during the existence of the exclusive right and without a licence) shall for purposes of sale 'apply' the design or a fraudulent imitation thereof 'to the ornamenting' of 'any article of manufacture. . .' The sort of design that can be registered is therefore a design to be 'applied' to 'the ornamenting' of an article. It must therefore be something that determines the appearance of an article, or some part of an article, because ornamenting relates to appearance. And it must have as its objective making the appearance of an article more attractive because that is the purpose of ornamenting. It cannot be something that determines the nature of an article as such (as opposed to mere appearance) and it cannot be something that determines how an article is to be created. In other words, it cannot create a monopoly in 'a product' or 'a process' such as can be acquired by a patent for an invention. There is, moreover, nothing in the legislation that limits the type of design that may be registered (as was suggested in argument) to those providing for something that is applied to an article after the article comes into existence. Section 11 contemplates a 'design' being 'applied' to the 'ornamenting' of any article. It is not restricted to a 'design' being 'applied' to an 'article'.

[. . .]

If, therefore, my understanding of the ambit of the Act is to be determined by my reading of the statutes without reference to the cases decided thereunder, I have no difficulty in concluding that the Cimon design is not objectionable as being a design for shape or configuration and is not objectionable as being a claim for an article or product. The fact that a design relates to shape or configuration of an article is not, in itself, an objection to its registration. As long as it is a design to be applied 'to the ornamenting' of an article, it is eligible for registration even though it requires that its purpose of 'ornamenting' be accomplished in whole or in part by constructing the article, or parts of it, in a certain shape or shapes. See *In re Clarke's Design* [[1896] 2 Ch. 38 at p. 43 per Lindley L.J., 'A design applicable to a thing for its shape can only be applied to a thing by making it in that shape.'] (This is quite a different thing from claiming the shape or configuration that an article necessarily assumes if it is to serve a certain purpose or if it has been constructed in accordance with a certain process.) The Cimon design is furthermore not a design for an article. It is not a design for sofas or for some particular kind of sofa. It is truly a 'design' for the ornamentation of sofas that can be applied by making the sofas in certain shapes. The distinction was expressed in *In re Clarke's Design* [[1896] 2 Ch. 38] by Lindley L.J., at page 43, as being 'the difference between the shape of a thing and a thing of that shape'. The distinction is narrow but is fundamental.

To summarize as to my view of the effect of the Canadian legislation on this branch of the case, my conclusion, from an examination of the legislation without reference to the cases, is that

(a) the defendants' contention that, under the Canadian Act, there can be no registration for shape or configuration of an article is unsound inasmuch as there can be registration of a design to be applied for the ornamenting of an article by making it in a particular shape or configuration; and

(b) the defendants' contention that, under the Canadian Act, there can be no registration of an article of manufacture as such is sound.

It follows that I do not agree with the defendants' contention that registration of a design to be applied by making an article in a particular shape or configuration is registration of the article itself.

Originality is assessed at the time of "adoption" (usually the time of creation) of the design (see s. 6(3))[20] and is evaluated with respect to the design, not the article itself. The statute requires that the applicant make a "declaration of originality," stating that the design was "not, to the proprietor's knowledge, in use by any person other than the first proprietor a the time the design was adopted by the first proprietor" (s. 4(1)(b)). This is reinforced by s. 6 which provides that the design shall be registered if it is "not identical with or does not so closely resemble any other design already registered as to be confounded therewith."

As noted in *Dover Ltd. v. Nurnberger Celluloidwaren Fabrik*, quoted originally in *Clatworthy, supra*, and subsequently in *Cimon, supra*, "original" contemplates that the "person has originated something, that by the exercise of intellectual activity he has started an idea which had not occurred to any one before, that a particular pattern or shape or ornament may be rendered applicable to the particular article to which he suggests that it shall be applied."

The requirement is one of "substantial originality". Simple trade variants are not original for the purposes of the Act.[21] Expert evidence is often adduced, especially to determine common trade knowledge.[22]

It is also useful to read the words of Lamont J. in *Clatworthy*:[23]

[T]o constitute an original design there must be some substantial difference between the new design and what had theretofore existed. A slight change of

---

[20] See *Bata Industries Ltd. v. Warrington Inc.* (1985), [1985] F.C.J. No. 239, 5 C.P.R. (3d) 339, 5 C.I.P.R. 223, 1985 CarswellNat 552 (Fed. T.D.).

[21] *Ibid.*

[22] See *Phillips v. Harbro Rubber Co.* (1920), 37 R.P.C. 233 (U.K. H.L.).

[23] See S.C.C. decision, *supra*, note 9 at 433.

outline or configuration, or an unsubstantial variation is not sufficient to enable the author to obtain registration. If it were, the benefits which the *Act* was intended to secure would be hampered, if not indeed paralysed.

The originality requirement for the purposes of industrial designs is thus closer to the novelty test of patent law. This is understandable. In both cases, third parties can check the register and determine what is protected. What is required to avoid infringement is an article that is objectively different. What is required to obtain a separate industrial design, in addition to objective novelty, is a novel aesthetic feature.

This interpretation is confirmed by Article 25(1) of the *TRIPS Agreement* (see the International Section), which provides in part as follows:

> Members may provide that designs are not new or original *if they do not significantly differ from known designs or combinations of known design features.* Members may provide that such protection shall not extend to designs dictated essentially by technical or functional considerations. [emphasis in original]

## III. REGISTRATION, OWNERSHIP AND TERM OF PROTECTION

Section 4 of the Act requires that the proprietor of a design, whether the first proprietor or a subsequent proprietor, apply to register the design by paying the prescribed fees and filing an application with the Minister in the prescribed form including a drawing or photograph of the design and a description of the design and the above-mentioned declaration of originality.

Section 7 provides for the issuance of a certificate of registration. The certificate is prima facie evidence of "the originality of the design, of the name of the proprietor, of the person named as proprietor being proprietor, of the commencement and term of registration, and of compliance with this Act." (s. 7(3)).[24]

The application for registration must be filed in Canada no more than one year after the publication of the design in Canada or elsewhere (s. 6(3)).[25] "Publication" in this context may be defined as making an article available to the public in a commercial context or offering it for sale. In

---

[24] See *Altomare c. Gad Furniture Industries Ltd.* (1989), 25 C.I.P.R. 307 (Que. S.C.).

[25] See *Industrial Design Application No. 1998-2666, Re* (2003), 25 C.P.R. (4th) 373 (Can. Pat. App. Bd. & Pat. Commr.).

*Algonquin Mercantile Corp. v. Dart Industries Canada Ltd.*,[26] Mahoney J. said in that respect:

> One must instead look to the design itself, 'publication' being properly defined as offering the design, or making it available, to the public. 'Public,' in turn, has many meanings but, for purposes of the definition of 'publication,' must be taken to include those persons who are actually interested in taking advantage of the design or who are regarded by the design owner as likely to be interested. Disclosure of the design with a view to obtaining orders for an article to be made according to it is a publication of the design.

> In its dealings with the merchandisers, the plaintiff made no formal arrangements to ensure the confidentiality of its design. It was reasonable to expect that the merchandisers would not reveal the design to the general public, but they could also be expected to discuss it within their own organizations. In short, the level of confidentiality which characterized these dealings was the same as that which ordinarily attaches to any private commercial proposition. Such confidentiality does not prevent a disclosure from being a publication of the design; therefore, the disclosure to the merchandisers more than one year before registration rendered the registration improper, and it should be expunged.

Section 12 of the Act provides the following on ownership:

(1)    The author of a design is the first proprietor of the design, unless the author has executed the design for another person for a good and valuable consideration, in which case the other person is the first proprietor.

(2)    The right of another person to the property shall only be co-extensive with the right that the other person has acquired

When compared to s. 13(2) of the *Copyright Act*, it seems that the good and valuable consideration does not need to be a payment (see the Ownership section under Copyright). Salary paid to an employee is good and valuable consideration[27] and when employees are paid to design, the design belongs to the employer if the employer is engaged in an ornamental business.[28] A doubt subsists, however, in cases where the design was not part of the employee's functions or where the employer is not engaged in the

---

[26]  (1983), [1984] 1 F.C. 246, 71 C.P.R. (2d) 11 (Fed. T.D.), affirmed (1984), 1 C.P.R. (3d) 75 (Fed. C.A.), leave to appeal refused (1984), 57 N.R. 392 (note) (S.C.C.) [*Algonquin* cited to F.C.]. See also *Slim Line Design Ltd. v. Pacific Northwest Manufacturing Inc.* (1999), 86 C.P.R. (3d) 498 (B.C. S.C.).

[27]  See *Renwal Manufacturing, supra*, note 9.

[28]  See *Comstock Canada v. Electec Ltd.* (1991), 38 C.P.R. (3d) 29 (Fed. T.D.) and *Lazarus v. Charles* (1873), L.R. 16 Eq. 117, 42 L.J. Ch. 507.

business of creating designs. As in patent law, it may be safer to assume that in such a case the benefit of the doubt should be given to the employee.

The protection is valid for ten years from the date of registration (s. 10(1)). The regulations provide that the proprietor must pay maintenance fees before five years from the registration date to maintain the exclusive right.

Industrial designs may be assigned (s. 13(1)) or an exclusive licence "to make, use and vend and to grant to others the right to make, use and vend the design, within and throughout Canada or any part thereof" (s. 13(2) and (3)). Subsections 13(1) and (3) refer to the recordal of assignments and exclusive licenses, using the expression "shall be", which seems to imply that recording the transaction is mandatory. (See Rule 19.)[29] While the Act does not provide the sanction for failure to comply, it seems reasonable to conclude that an unrecorded assignment of license remains valid *inter partes*, but it may not be opposable to third parties, especially in a court action.[30]

Under ss. 22 to 24, the Federal Court has exclusive jurisdiction to make, expunge or vary an entry in the Register.[31] Causes of expungement include a showing that the registered proprietor is not the proprietor as determined by the Act; that the design was published more than a year prior to the application; or that the registered design was not roper subject-matter under the Act.[32] The Burden of proof is on the applicant, as the certificate of registration is *prima facie* valid.

## IV. MARKING

Prior to June 9, 1993, s. 14 of the Act imposed a marking requirement (the letters "Rd"). Failure to mark was a fatal objection to the validity of registration.[33] Marking is no longer mandatory for designs registered after Jun 9, 1993, but it is still possible to mark protected designs with the capital letter "D". This defeats a defence of not being aware that a design was registered (s. 17).

---

[29]  *Industrial Design Regulations*, SOR/99-460 allows evidence either in the form of an affidavit OR a copy of the document effecting the assignment of licence. This seems to imply that the transaction need not be in writing. This is reinforced by the fact that other intellectual property statutes state clearly when a writing is required.

[30]  See also s. 15(2).

[31]  See *Epstein v. O-Pee-Chee Co.*, [1927] Ex. C.R. 156, [1927] 3 D.L.R. 160 (Can. Ex. Ct.).

[32]  See *Kaufman Rubber Co. v. Miner Rubber Co.*, [1926] Ex. C.R. 26, [1926] 1 D.L.R. 505 (Can. Ex. Ct.).

[33]  See *Allaire v. Hobbs Glass Ltd.*, [1948] Ex. C.R. 171, 9 C.P.R. 3 (Can. Ex. Ct.).

## V. INFRINGEMENT, REMEDIES AND DEFENCES

Section 11 delineates the exclusive right provided by the registration:

1)   During the existence of an exclusive right, no person shall, without the licence of the proprietor of the design,

   (*a*)   make, import for the purpose of trade or business, or sell, rent, or offer or expose for sale or rent, any article in respect of which the design is registered and to which the design or a design not differing substantially therefrom has been applied; or

   (*b*)   do, in relation to a kit, anything specified in paragraph (*a*) that would constitute an infringement if done in relation to an article assembled from the kit.

(2)   For the purposes of subsection (1), in considering whether differences are substantial, the extent to which the registered design differs from any previously published design may be taken into account

The best way to determine similarity is by visually comparing the articles side-by-side as the Federal Court of Appeal discussed in *Algonquin*:

> The conclusions of the trial Judge on this issue are to be found in vol. 3 of the Appeal Book at p. 449 and read as follows:
>
> > Whether one design infringes another is a question to be determined by the eye of the Court. In their details, the visual aspects of the various elements making up the registered design and the Defendant's appliance, e.g., legs, handles, surface layout, are very different. To my eye, the defendant's appliance does not look very much like the registered design at all. There is no merit to the allegation that it is a fraudulent imitation. I find no infringement.
>
> In the submission of the appellant the conclusion that: 'To my eye, the defendant's appliance does not look very much like the registered design at all' is not the proper test to be applied since it is too stringent and requires too high a standard. In the appellant's view, the proper test for the trial Judge to have applied to the evidence before him was whether the respondent's design was substantially different from that of the appellant or conversely, does the respondent's Family Griddle have the essential or salient design features of the appellant's Breakfast Nook, and if so, it is the appellant's submission that there is infringement. The appellant submitted a further threefold test which, in his view, would have been a proper test to apply to the facts of this case since originality of the registered design over the prior art is also an issue. That test is:

1.    Would the respondent's Family Griddle design be confused with the Breakfast Nook Design?
2.    Would the respondent's design have had any existence but for the appellant's design?
3.    Is the respondent's design nearer to the appellant's than to any other prior design?

On the other hand, the respondent submits that the proper approach by the Court to the question of infringement of a registered industrial design was enunciated by the House of Lords in *Holdsworth v. M'Crea* (1867), L.R. 2 H.L. 380 at 388, and reaffirmed by the House of Lords in *Hecla Foundry Co. v. Walker, Hunter & Co.* (1889), 14 App. Cas. 550 at 555, 6 R.P.C. 554, where Lord Herschell said:

> It seems to me, therefore, that the eye must be the judge in such a case as this, and that the question must be determined by placing the designs side by side, and asking whether they are the same, or whether the one is an obvious imitation of the other. I ought, perhaps, to qualify this by saying that, as a design to be registered must, by sect. 47, be a 'new or original design, not previously published in the United Kingdom,' one may be entitled to take into account the state of knowledge at the time of registration, and in what respects the design was new or original, when considering whether any variations from the registered design which appear in the alleged infringement are substantial or immaterial.

He cites also the case of *Dunlop Rubber Co. v. Golf Ball Devs. Ltd.* (1931), 48 R.P.C. 268 at 277-78, where Farwell J. enunciated the proper legal test to be applied as follows:

> One has to see the finished article if possible to see in what way the design does appeal to the eye. The second thing is that the test of a design is the eye and the eye alone. Now there is, I think, no possible doubt that 'the eye' in that section means the eye of the Court, because the Court has ultimately to determine these questions, and it is the eye of the Court and the eye of the Court alone which has to be the judge of the design in question. That I think is plain from the language of the Section, and it is made even plainer by the authorities to which I have been referred. The eye is the eye of the Court, but the Court is entitled to be assisted and instructed by evidence so that when it applies its eye to the test, it may have a mind to direct its eye which is instructed by the proper evidence. Such instruction may certainly be given to the Court by persons who are competent to do it with regard to the prior art; that is to say, the Court is entitled to be told what the designs earlier than the registered Design represent, the differences or similarities between the earlier designs and the registered Design and the alleged infringing design. Evi-

dence of that sort to instruct the Court is clearly relevant, and the Court must clearly pay attention to it.

It is the respondent's position that the 'substantially different' test advocated by the appellant is not the test which has been applied in Canada. In the view of counsel, that test was introduced by statute in the United Kingdom with the passage in 1949 of the *Registered Designs Act*, 1949 (U.K., 12, 13 & 14 Geo. 6), c. 88. It is his further submission that the threefold test, supra, advocated by appellant's counsel is not the test applied by Canadian Courts. The Canadian jurisprudence bears out the position taken by counsel for the respondent. While no definition of design appears in the *Industrial Design Act*, the Courts have defined the word 'design' as used in that *Act*. In the case of *Clatworthy & Son Ltd. v. Dale Display Fixtures Ltd.*, [1929] S.C.R. 429 at 431, [1929] 3 D.L.R. 11, Lamont J. speaking for the Supreme Court of Canada said:

> No definition of a 'design' is given in the *Act*. The word must, therefore, be taken in its ordinary signification which Lindley, L.J., in In re Clarke's Design, [1896] 2 Ch. 38, at p. 43, stated means: 'Something marked out — a plan or representation of something.' A 'design' is, therefore, a pattern or representation which the eye can see and which can be applied to a manufactured article.

This test was applied by President Jackett (as he then was) in the Exchequer Court case of *Cimon Ltd. v. Bench Made Furniture Corp.*, [1965] 1 Ex. C.R. 811, 30 Fox Pat. C. 77, 48 C.P.R. 31 at 49 and 50, where he stated:

> The sort of design that can be registered is therefore a design to be 'applied' to 'the ornamenting' of an article. It must, therefore, be something that determines the appearance of an article, or some part of an article, because ornamenting relates to appearance. And it must have as its objective making the appearance of an article more attractive because that is the purpose of ornamenting. It cannot be something that determines the nature of an article as such (as opposed to mere appearance) and it cannot be something that determines how an article is to be created. In other words, it cannot create a monopoly in 'a product' or 'a process' such as can be acquired by a patent for an invention. There is, moreover, nothing in the legislation that limits the type of design that may be registered (as was suggested in argument) to those providing for something that is applied to an article after the article comes into existence.

This decision was relied on by the trial Judge in this case and, in my view, he did not err in applying the *Cimon* test to the facts of this case.[34]

---

[34]  *Algonquin Mercantile Corp. v. Dart Industries Canada Ltd.* (1984), 1 C.P.R. (3d) 75 (Fed. C.A.), leave to appeal refused (1984), 57 N.R. 392 (note (S.C.C.).

The court must take care to avoid giving significant weight to features or elements of the finished article not part of the registered design. The correct test is "to look at the designs as a whole viewed as through the eyes of a consumer."[35]

In *L.M. Lipski Ltd. v. Dorel Industries Inc.*,[36] Reed J. explained the test and the role of designs other than those of the plaintiff's and the defendant's as follows:

> [I]s the Dorel bed guard so different from the Lipski bed guard so as not to be an infringement of the latter's industrial design? [. . .]

> Counsel for the plaintiff (and for the defendant) cited three tests for infringement of an industrial design. Counsel for the defendant cited the tests set out by Mr. Justice Walsh in *Mainetti S.P.A. v. E.R.A. Display Co.* (1984), 80 C.P.R. (2d) 206 (Fed. T.D.), at page 222. These tests are summarized in the headnote [at p. 207] as:

> (i)    whether one design could be confused with the other;
> (ii)   whether the alleged infringing article would have any existence in terms of the design applied to it, but for the registered design;
> (iii)  whether the alleged infringing article was nearer the original design than any other prior designs. . .

> The first test, that of likely confusion, must be elaborated upon in order to understand the headnote's meaning. Mr. Justice Walsh discussed the test as follows, at page 222:

>> . . .now that the various minor and deliberately created differences have been shown to the Court it is not difficult to distinguish defendants' hangers from plaintiff's but if these differences had not been pointed out I would have reached the conclusion that these were merely different versions of a hanger made by the same manufacturer. [Emphasis by Reed J.]

> Counsel for the plaintiff referred to the test as expressed by Mr. Justice Mahoney in *Algonquin Mercantile Corp. v. Dart Industries Can. Ltd.*, [1984] 1 F.C. 246, at page 250; (1983), 71 C.P.R. (2d) 11 (T.D.), at pages 13-14, affirmed (1984), 1 C.P.R. (3d) 75 (F.C.A.):

>> Whether one design infringes another is a question to be determined by the eye of the Court. In their details, the visual aspects of the various

---

[35]  See *Benchairs Ltd. v. Chair Centre Ltd.* (1973), [1973] F.S.R. 123, [1974] R.P.C. 429 (Eng. C.A.).

[36]  [1988] 3 F.C. 594, 20 C.P.R. (3d) 226 (Fed. T.D.) [*Lipski* cited to F.C.].

elements making up the registered design and the defendant's appliance, e.g., legs, handles, surface layout, are very different. To my eye the defendant's appliance does not look very much like the registered design at all. [emphasis by Reed J.]

The authorities cited by the plaintiff which mirror the second and third test set out by Mr. Justice Walsh in the *Mainetti* case, are respectively, *Cimon Ltd. et al v. Bench Made Furniture Corpn et al*, [1965] 1 Ex. C.R. 811 and *House of Faces, Inc. et al. v. LeBlanc et al.* (1984), 2 C.P.R. (3d) 177 (Ont. H.C.). [. . .]

In the *House of Faces* case, at page 181, Mr. Justice Montgomery of the Ontario High Court stated:

While the respondent's trays differ in small detail they would, in my view, be compared with the applicants' trays. The respondent's design is nearer to that of the applicants' than any prior user.

In my view there is infringement of industrial design established on the material before me.
[emphasis by Reed J.]

In the present case, the defendant's design differs from the plaintiff's in three aspects: the circles (rondels) in the two upper corners of the plaintiff's bed guard (which are a motif common to many Lipski products) do not appear in the defendant's design; the defendant has added an additional support piece to the middle of each half of the bed guard so that the elongated openings, in the guard, are eight rather than four in number; the raised plastic pattern in the centre of the defendant's bed guard differs from that of the plaintiff's (the defendant's is an exact copy of the centre pattern of the DMKA guard). At the same time that these differences exist, the overall appearance of the defendant's bed guard as well as most of the rest of its detail is an exact copy of the plaintiff's bed guard. An interlocutory injunction application is not the place to decide the very issues in dispute, but it is clear that there is a very good argument that the defendant has copied a substantial portion of the plaintiff's design. In addition, there is no doubt that it was the plaintiff's design which inspired the defendant's. Without the plaintiff's design the defendant's would never have existed. It is also clear that the defendant's design is a copy of the plaintiff's with certain deliberate modifications; the defendant's design is clearly closer to the plaintiff's design than to any prior design (except the DMKA model).

The defendant argues that the plaintiff's design was not the inspiration for the Dorel product; rather the DMKA bed guard played this role; and, it is argued, the defendant's product is closer to the DMKA bed guard than to the plaintiff's. I do not think the defendant can escape an action for infringement on the ground that he copied a copy of a copy of the registered design rather than the design itself. It is the similarity of appearance and form which creates an infringement. A copy of a copy is still a fraudulent imitation of the original.

A court is thus justified in not only comparing designs on the articles side-by-side but also comparing them with previously published designs (s. 11(2)).

The main activities that constitute infringement if unauthorized by the proprietor or an agent or licensee thereof are making (for any purpose); importing (for trade or business-this exempts personal items brought back by travellers); selling, renting or offering or exposing publicly (see the meaning of publication above) for one of those purposes.

Infringement occurs in respect of a "finished article" (see the definition of design in s. 2). This means that using the same shape, configuration, pattern or ornament on a different article will not infringe the registered design.

Section 11(1)(b) is designed to prohibit the circumvention of a protected design by the importation of kits assembled by the buyer. Because in such a case there is no sale of the infringing design (the design is only complete and visible after assembly), there is no infringement of s. 11(1)(a).[37]

Remedies include relief by way of injunction and the recovery of damages or profits, for punitive damages, and for the disposal of any infringing article or kit (s.15.1). Care should be taken in referring to cases decided prior to the introduction of s. 15.1 in the Act in 1993. The relevant principles on interlocutory injunctions are explained in the Remedies section of the Trade-marks chapter. However, it is worth noting these words of caution, when dealing with an industrial design:

> I will concede that the rule might not be as stringently applied when dealing with other fields of intellectual property as in copyright and industrial design. The subject matter in these instances has often an ephemeral lifespan where market saturation is quickly reached and where the winds of fashion which favour an owner's venture into hopefully exceptional gains will have an equally exceptional fickleness about them. If at the same time, the competing product appears in the eye of the Court to be an obvious knock-off and where piggy-back conclusions may be more easily reached, the Court will not hesitate for the sake of pure equity, to grant injunctive relief. It means in effect that the plaintiff has not only established a strong *prima facie* case but has also met the test of irreparable injury of a kind which may not be compensated in damages.[38]

---

[37] See *Dorling v. Honnor Marine Ltd.* (1963), [1965] Ch. 1, [1964] 1 All E.R. 241, [1964] R.P.C. 160 (Eng. C.A.).

[38] *Zivin v. Gilbro Ltd.* (1988), 19 C.P.R. (3d) 516 (Fed. T.D.).

Defences include showing that the design was not properly registered (see above), that the defendant's design differs substantially from the registered design, taking account of other registered design; that the plaintiff is not entitled to a remedy with respect to equitable remedies due to laches or unclean hands); that the plaintiff is not the proprietor or that the proprietor is not a party to the action; that the use of the design was licensed; that the registration has lapsed for failure to pay the prescribed fee (see s. 10); that more than three years have passed since the infringement (s. 18); and estoppel. There is also a partial defence (to remedies other than an injunction) available to a defendant who can show that he did not know and had no reasonable grounds to suspect that the design was registered (s. 17(1)). The defence is not available if all or substantially all the articles were marked and their labels or packaging with the capital letter "D" in a circle and the name, or the usual abbreviation of the name, of the proprietor of the design (s. 17(2)). This is mostly seen as an incentive to mark protected designs. Any notice given to the defendant prior to his use of the design would defeat the defence.

## VI. DISCUSSION QUESTIONS

**Q:**    Kris Kringle designs a nutcracker which works well to break open almonds, walnuts, pecans, and other nuts for human consumption. The nut cracker is in the shape of the Nut Cracker ballet figure. Can Kringle get industrial design protection for the design of his nut cracker? What must he do to get industrial design protection? Kringle makes 75 copies of the nut crackers. Does Kringle have copyright protection in the design for his nut cracker figure?

**Q:**    Can one obtain industrial design protection for t-shirts on which there is a copy of a painting made by a contemporary artist (who is still alive)? If so, who could apply?

**Q:**    If Kim creates a new knife which, due to the original design of its blade, cuts fruit and vegetables better than existing products, can he obtain industrial design protection? Would any other form of protection be available (instead or in addition)?

**Q:**    Kim also produced a new spoon whose handle is very intriguing, though it does not add much to the spoon's functionality. If anything, it is harder for a person to hold the spoon. If Kim only produces one copy of his new knife (a prototype) to show it at a trade fair, can he obtain protection for it under the *Industrial Designs Act*? Under any other Act?

# *Chapter* 4: Trade-Marks

I. Introduction

II. Object of the Protection

III. "Use" of a Trade-Mark

IV. Registration

V. Licences and Assignments

VI. Infringement

VII. Domain Names and Internet-Based Infringement

VIII. Discussion Questions

## I. INTRODUCTION

### 1. Origin

A (trade) mark is a word, symbol, drawing, shape, packaging, or colour(s) or a combination of the preceding used to distinguish the products or services of a person or organization from those of another in the market. The purpose of the *Trade-marks Act*[1] is two-fold: first, to protect the public by indicating the source of goods and services in order that purchasers can identify the level of quality they seek and receive a similar product or consistent service over time; and second, to protect the trade-mark owner against commercial misappropriation of the mark and/or the goodwill associated with the mark. The value of a mark stems from the mental link that is created over time in the minds of prospective buyers between particular goods or services and a particular source. By distinguishing the source of goods and services, trade-marks function to protect consumers; and by notifying consumers of source, trade-marks also are an important intangible asset for businesses. Trade-marks are used in relation with goods — usually referred to as "wares" in trade-mark law — such as running shoes, soft drinks or cars, and in relation with services, such as telecommunications or banking. Marks have become much more than a simple identification tool; they now represent a certain reputation or associate a certain lifestyle with a service or product through advertisement.

---

[1] R.S.C. 1985, c. T-13, online: Department of Justice Canada <http: laws.justice.gc.ca/en/t-13/105826.html> [*Trade-marks Act*].

165

Intellectual property law protects the value of the "mental link" created over time between a product or service and a given mark. This mental link can be referred to as the "goodwill" associated with a mark. Trade-marks form part of the intangible assets of those who own them, and sometimes the mark is one of the most significant assets a company owns. Trade-marks such as Coca-Cola®, Nike® (and its swoosh logo) or Microsoft®[2] are "balance sheet heavyweights"; a strong trade-mark can be the single most important asset that a company has. Many people will buy a product or service because consciously or unconsciously they associate qualities such as value, excellence, or efficiency, with the trade-mark. The capacity of a mark to raise these associations is why a strong trade-mark is invaluable — it directs a potential buyer towards a company's own product or service rather than those of a competitor. Trade-marks are influenced both by seller's perceptions about buyer psychology and the public's perceptions of goods and services and how they are differentiated.

Trade-marks serve an important informational purpose. The legal protection of marks gives companies an incentive to invest in making their marks more easily recognized and more easily remembered by consumers so consumers can identify which particular good or service they want and consumers save time searching for the appropriate product or service.

To take a simple example, personal computers today are mostly made from very similar parts, sometimes originating from the same manufacturer. These parts are packaged into PCs and sold under various trade-marks. To see the marks of the companies that manufactured the actual parts of the machine, one would have to open the computer and check on the parts themselves — and even then the name is not always indicated. In some cases, those manufacturers (*e.g.,* Intel) are well-known. In other cases, they are completely unknown to the average buyer. Yet, while the machines themselves are often technically similar, prices are not. Nonetheless, consumers do not always purchase the least expensive model. They buy based on a certain reputation or feeling of confidence and they rely on marks as a short hand for information about products. They may believe that a product is better (or better value), though often this perception is not based on personal experience or actual empirical evidence. In other cases, a particular manufacturer may have obtained high marks from a consumer magazine or other agency. When the magazine or agency is non-governmental, the fact that a consumer relies on the study is, in turn, itself reliance on that magazine or organization's "good name", *i.e.,* its trade-mark.

---

[2] While this symbol is not formally regulated by the *Trade-Marks Act*, the established international practice is to use the ® only next to a registered trade-mark, while the ™ can be used next to what one considers a trade-mark, whether it be unregistered, applied for or registered.

Trade-marks help to differentiate brands. Consumers may have objective or subjective reasons for preferences. For example, a given brand of denim jeans may objectively wear longer, fit better, have longer lasting stitching, or better quality cotton denim; or, a consumer may subjectively prefer the commercials, the image or the identity of one brand over another. Brand differentiation can be particularly important to companies where the objective intrinsic differences between products of a given type are not great. For example, salt or bleach are fairly standard commodities, but purchasers, through trade-marks, may respond differently to one brand of salt than another and may associate more desirable characteristics with that brand, even though governmental regulations ensure that various brands of salt are safe. Marks can also be important when companies expand product lines or services. Consumers may try a new product from a trusted company and can save time by not researching quality.

Trade-marks function differently than other types of intellectual property. Ordinarily, intellectual property gives creators and inventors rights, as an incentive or reward to create or invent, and the object of the intellectual property protection is the creation or invention. With trade-marks, the intellectual creation of the trade-mark itself does not give the creator of the mark a monopoly in the mark itself. Instead, trade-mark rights result when a trade-mark is used (not when the mark is created). Trade-mark law grants an exclusive right to use the mark *in association with the designated good or service*. The "use" requirement is integral to balancing in trade-mark law, allowing competitors to have access to functional or generic aspects (for example, the name of the good itself or the functional shape, which cannot be marks), and individuals to access marks for non-commercial expressive purposes.

One of the first trade-mark cases was *Millington v. Fox* which dates back to 1838. In that case, the judge concluded that it would be unfair to let a defendant sell its product as being that of another person.[3] A few years later, *Perry v. Truefitt* established that the common law prohibited a company from benefiting from the goodwill of another.[4]

## 2. Constitutional Ground

Trade-marks are of federal jurisdiction. Unlike copyrights and patents, which are explicitly listed as federal powers under s. 91 (ss. 91(23) and 91(22) respectively), the constitutional ground for trade-marks is found in the general federal power under s. 91(2) of the *Constitution Act, 1867,* for

---

[3] (1838), 3 My. & C. 338 (Eng. Ch.).
[4] (1842), 49 E.R. 749 (Eng. Rolls Ct.).

"the Regulation of Trade and Commerce".[5] Though most of the subject matter is covered in the *Trade-marks Act*, it should be noted that some other statutes have an effect on trade-marks. For example, the *Competition Act* regulates some parts of trade-mark law, notably in the areas of misleading advertising and abuse of monopolies.[6] The *Criminal Code* also deals with certain commercial crimes.[7] Finally, there is also a substantial portion of trade-mark law regulated by the provinces: the tort of passing off is of provincial jurisdiction. This tort was partly incorporated into section 7 of the *Trade-marks Act,* which gave rise to a series of interesting constitutional debates.

In *Vapor Canada Ltd. v. MacDonald*, the Supreme Court analyzed the validity of this "codification" of the tort.[8] A substantial portion of Chief Justice Laskin's reasons is worth quoting here, and of particular interest is the fact that s. 7(e) was declared *ultra vires*:

> Section 7 of the *Trade Marks Act* is the first of five sections of the Act (ss. 7 to 11) that are subsumed under the sub-title 'Unfair Competition and Prohibited Marks'. It stands alone, however, among those sections in not being concerned with trade marks or trade names. It alone gives any substance to the 'Unfair Competition' portion of the sub-title. Section 7 had a forerunner in s. 11 of the *Unfair Competition Act*, 1932 (Can.), c. 38.

> That Act, like the present *Trade Marks Act*, which replaced it, was concerned with the regulation of the use of trade marks and with a scheme of registration and protection therefor; and although it contained a sub-title 'Unfair Competition', covering ss. 3 to 11 thereof, the only provision that related to unfair competition was s. 11. This section was in these words:

> *11.*    No person shall, in the course of his business,

> (a)    make any false statement tending to discredit the wares of a competitor;
> (b)    direct public attention to his wares in such a way that, at the time he commenced so to direct attention to them, it might be reason-

---

[5] *Constitution Act, 1867* (U.K.), 30 & 31 Vict., c. 3, reprinted in R.S.C. 1985, App. II, No.5, online: Department of Justice Canada <http://laws.justice.gc.ca/en/const/index.html>.

[6] R.S.C. 1985, c. C-34, online: Department of Justice Canada <http://laws.justice.gc.ca/en/c-34/text.html>.

[7] R.S.C. 1985, c. C-46, online: Department of Justice Canada <http://laws.justice.gc.ca/en/c-46/text.html>.

[8] (1976), (sub nom. *MacDonald v. Vapor Canada Ltd.*) [1977] 2 S.C.R. 134, 66 D.L.R. (3d) 1, 7 N.R. 477, 22 C.P.R. (2d) 1 (S.C.C.), [*MacDonald* cited to S.C.R.].

ably apprehended that his course of conduct was likely to create confusion in Canada between his wares and those of a competitor;

(c)    adopt any other business practice contrary to honest industrial and commercial usage.

It is evident from a comparison of s. 7 of the present *Trade Marks Act* and s. 11 of the Act of 1932 that the former has expanded the acts proscribed by the latter and indeed has added in s. 7(*c*) and (*d*) provisions not found in s. 11. Section 7(*e*) differs from its predecessor equivalent s. 11(*c*) in three respects. It has added the words 'do any other act' to what is proscribed, it has introduced the disjunctive in place of the conjunctive when referring to 'honest industrial or commercial usage' and it has added the qualifying words 'in Canada'. There is, however, a more significant difference between the old s. 11 and the present s. 7. There was no provision in the 1932 Act for civil enforcement of the proscriptions of s. 11 at the suit of persons injured by their breach. There was, of course, provision there, as in the present *Trade Marks Act*, for enforcement of its *trade mark* provisions at the suit of an injured person. The provisions of s. 20 of the 1932 Act giving the then Exchequer Court of Canada 'jurisdiction to entertain any action or proceeding for the enforcement of any of the rights conferred or defined by this Act' were not urged in this Court in this case as providing a civil remedy in support of s. 11 equivalent to that expressly ordained by s. 53 of the present *Trade Marks Act* in support of s. 7 as well as in support of other substantive provisions of the Act.

[. . .]

The contention of the appellants and of the supporting intervenants, briefly put, was that s. 7(*e*), if not also the whole of s. 7, was legislation in the relation to property and civil rights in the province or, alternatively, legislation in relation to matters of a local or private nature in the province, within s. 92(13) or (16) of the *British North America Act*. The respondent and the Attorney-General for Canada supported s. 7(*e*) as being (1) legislation in relation to the regulation of trade and commerce within s. 91(2) of that Act; (2) supportable as legislation in implementation of a Canadian international obligation arising out of a treaty or convention, and thus falling within federal power for the peace, order and good government of Canada in relation to a matter not coming within s. 92; and (3) legislation in relation to the criminal law within s. 91(27).

This last mentioned basis of validity deserves no more than a brief statement of reasons for rejecting it. Assuming that s. 7(*e*) (as, indeed, the other subparagraphs of s. 7) proscribe anti-social business practices, and are thus enforceable under the general criminal sanction of s. 115 of the *Criminal Code* respecting disobedience of a federal statute, the attempt to mount the civil remedy of s. 53 of the *Trade Marks Act* on the back of the *Criminal Code* proves too much, certainly in this case. The principle which would arise from such a result would provide an easy passage to valid federal legislation to provide and govern civil relief in respect of numerous sections of the *Criminal Code* and would, in the light of the wide scope of the federal criminal law power, debilitate provincial legislative authority and the jurisdiction of provincial Courts so as to transform our constitutional arrangements on legislative power beyond recognition. It is surely unnecessary to go into detail on such an extravagant posture. This Court's judgment in *Goodyear Tire and Rubber Co. of Canada Ltd. v. The Queen*[[1956] S.C.R. 303], upholding the validity of federal legislation authorizing the issue of prohibitory order in connection with a conviction of a combines offence, illustrates the preventive side of the federal criminal law power to make a conviction effective. It introduced a supporting sanction in connection with the prosecution of an offence. It does not, in any way, give any encouragement to federal legislation which, in a situation unrelated to any criminal proceedings, would authorize independent civil proceedings for damages and an injunction.

[. . .]

I did not understand counsel to urge that s. 7, or s. 7(*e*) alone, should be supported under the criminal law power by excluding s. 53 as a means of enforcement. If that had been the argument, it would have meant a concession by the respondent and the intervening Attorney-General for Canada that s. 53 should be regarded as inapplicable to s. 7(*e*). No such concession was made.

The contentions of the appellants and the remaining two contentions of the respondent, supported as they are by the intervenors, require a more extensive canvass of the scope of legislative power than I have made in disposing of the submission under the criminal law power. I approach this canvass by examining first what it is that the legislation in question does, and what the legal position (not the constitutional position necessarily) was and would be apart from the challenged legislation.

I think it fair to look upon s. 7 as embodying a scheme, one limited in scope perhaps but nonetheless embodying an array of connected matters. I shall come later to what appeared to be a fundamental underpinning of the respondent's position and that of the Attorney-General for Canada, namely, that s. 7 or at least s. 7(*e*) must not be construed *in vacuo*, but must itself be brought into account as a segment or a piece of a tapestry of regulation and control of industrial and intellectual property.

It was not disputed that the common law in the provinces outside of Quebec and the *Civil Code* of Quebec governed the conduct or aspects thereof now embraced by s. 7 and embraced earlier by s. 11 of the Act of 1932. To illustrate, s. 7(*a*) is the equivalent of the tort of slander of title or injurious falsehood, albeit the element of malice, better described as intent to injure without just cause or excuse, is not included as it is in the common law action: see Fleming on Torts (4th ed. 1971), at p. 623. Section 7(*b*) is a statutory statement of the common law action of passing off, which is described in Fleming on Torts, *supra*, at p. 626 as 'another form of misrepresentation concerning the plaintiff's business . . . which differs from injurious falsehood in prejudicing the plaintiff's goodwill not by deprecatory remarks but quite to the contrary by taking a free ride on it in pretending that one's own goods or services are the plaintiff's or associated with or sponsored by him'. It differs from injurious falsehood in that 'it is sufficient that the offensive practice was calculated or likely, rather than intended, to deceive'.

Section 7(c) is a curious provision to be armed with a civil sanction by way of damages when one already exists in the ordinary law of contract. The provision refers to substitution of other goods for those ordered or requested, but there is always the right to reject upon discovery of the substitution, and if the substituted goods are knowingly accepted there would appear to be no relief. If s. 7(c) purports to give additional relief even if the substituted goods are knowingly accepted, where are the damages? Or does the provision envisage damages arising from failure to deliver the proper goods in time? If so, there is the usual remedy for breach of contract. I can see s. 7(c) in the context of a regulatory regime subject to supervision by a public authority, but its presence under the sanction of a private civil remedy merely emphasizes for me federal intrusion upon provincial legislative power.

Section 7(d) appears to be directed to the protection of a purchaser or a consumer of wares or services, in contrast with s. 7(a) which involves slander of title or injurious falsehood *qua* a competitor in business. It involves what I would term deceit in offering goods or services to the public, deceit in the sense of material false representations likely to mislead in respect of the character, quality, quantity or composition of goods or services, or in respect of their geographic origin or in respect of their mode of manufacture, production or performance. If any aggrieved person would have a cause of action under s. 53 in respect of damages suffered by him by reason of a breach of s. 7(d), it would ordinarily be expected to arise through breach of contract. One can envisage, of course, a statutory tort of deceit under s. 7(d), but this hardly adds to its constitutional propriety as federal legislation. Whether sounding in contract or in tort, it is not limited to those bases of relief in respect of enterprises or services that are otherwise within federal legislative competence. Again, the issue of a violation of s. 7(d) could as easily arise in a local or intraprovincial transaction as in an interprovincial one; there is nothing in s. 7 (d) that emphasizes any interprovincial or transprovincial scope of the prohibition in s. 7(d) so as to establish some connection with federal legislative authority under s. 91(2) of the *British North America Act*.

Section 7(e) is, in terms, an additional proscription to those enumerated in subparagraphs (a) to (d) of s. 7. Its vagueness is not, of course, a ground of constitutional invalidity, but I am satisfied that it does have subject matter, as the facts of this very case demonstrate. It would encompass breach of confidence by an employee by way of appropriating confidential knowledge or trade

secrets to a business use adverse to the employer. So too, it would appear to be broad enough to cover the fruits of industrial espionage.
[. . .]

The fact that s. 7(e) has subject matter, whether as embodying claims cognizable at common law or as providing a statutory basis for a civil cause of action, does not differentiate it, in constitutional terms, from s. 7(a) (b) (c) and (d). As a class of prescriptions, additional to those in the preceding catalogues, it appears to me to be simply a formulation of the tort of conversion, perhaps writ large and in a business context.
[. . .]

Turning to the cases which have dealt with s. 7, I know of none in which the constitutionality of that provision or of any of its parts has been passed upon prior to the present case. Some at least of the cases may be said or thought to assume the validity of s. 7 or the part thereof involved, as for example *Canadian Converters Co. Ltd. v. Eastport Trading Co. Ltd.*[(1968), 70 D.L.R. (2d) 149]. The cases are instructive, however, for revealing the scope of s. 7, and how it either squares with or overlays or extends, where it does so at all, the common law and the civil law on the matters with which that section deals.
[. . .]

[I]n the *Eldon Industries* case, which involved claims for relief in respect of the copying of a toy by a competitor of the plaintiffs, Schroeder J.A., speaking for the Ontario Court of Appeal had this to say (at pp. 106-106, 107-108):

> It has not been suggested that the defendants' conduct was brought within the prohibition of s. 7(a) of the Act nor has it been claimed that they offended in any respect against the provisions of s. 7(d). Paragraphs (b) and (c) of s. 7 declare in codified form the common law tort of passing off one person's wares for those of another. Paragraph (b) relates to the wrongful act of passing off one's wares as and for those of another by directing public attention to the wares (not necessarily in compliance with an order or request) as, *e.g.*, by giving one's products a particular marking, shape or appearance which has become recognized in the public eye as indicative of another source, and thereby creating confusion or a likelihood of confusion in the minds of the public. Paragraph (c), on the other hand, points to a particular kind of passing off — substituting wares or services for those ordered or requested, as when a product manufactured by A is ordered and the vendor supplies a product made by B as answering the description.
>
> A claim founded on the alleged marking or appearance of wares contrary to s. 7(b) is doomed to failure unless the claimant establishes that the marking or appearance has become recognized by the public as having a particular origin. . . .

. . .

Considerable argument was addressed to us as to the effect to be given to s. 7(*e*) of the *Trade Marks Act*. I am in agreement with the conclusion of the learned Judge of first instance that s. 7(*e*) must be read in conjunction with paras. (*a*), (*b*), (*c*) and (*d*) of that section: *A.C. Spark Plug Co. v. Canadian Spark Plug Service*, [1935] Ex.C.R. 57, [1935] 3 D.L.R. 84; *Kitchen Overall & Shirt Co. v. Elmira Shirt & Overall Co.*, [1937] Ex.C.R. 230, [1938] 1 D.L.R. 7. These cases were decided under s. 11 of the *Unfair Competition Act*, 1932 (Can.) c. 38, which had codified the common law of passing off, and s. 7 of the *Trade Marks Act* is substantially a re-enactment of s. 11 of the *Unfair Competition Act* with some additions thereto. Section 7(*e*), therefore, must be read *ejusdem generis* with s. 7(*a*), (*b*), (*c*) or (*d*). The principles governing cases of product simulation have been carefully evolved both at common law and in equity and are now stated in statutory form in s. 7(*a*) to (*d*). They were never intended to yield to a subjective or unknown standard embraced in the words 'any other business practice contrary to honest industrial or commercial usage in Canada', which would be the effect of the provisions in s. 7(*e*) if removed from the contextual influence of the foregoing clauses of the section. . . .

[. . .]

There is one judgment of this Court, *S. & S. Industries Inc. v. Rowell* [[1966] S.C.R. 419], which is of particular importance in any assessment of the scope of s. 7 and, especially of s. 7 (*a*) and (*e*), as it bears on validity. There was no constitutional question raised in that case which involved two points first, whether the appellant's patent was invalid and second, whether the respondent was entitled to damages for what was in essence slander of title or injurious falsehood. In delivering the judgment of the Court, Martland J. said this (at pp. 422-3):

> The appellant's submission was that the respondent, in order to recover damages, must bring his claim within the requirements of the common law action, which has been described as 'injurious falsehood', 'slander of goods', and 'trade libel'. This assumes, probably correctly, that the respondent's cause of action, if one existed, arose in the Province of Ontario and would be governed by the laws of that Province. I will deal with the appellant's argument upon that basis, although, as will appear later, my opinion is that the respondent's claim for damages in this case can properly be founded upon a federal statute, and, accordingly, it is not necessary to decide that point in this case.

> That a claim could be made at common law, provided the necessary conditions of liability were established, for damages resulting from the threat of legal proceedings in respect of alleged infringement of an

invalid patent or trade mark has been established by English authorities. . .

After noting the appellant's submission that malice (in the sense of want of just cause or excuse for making the untrue statements) was a necessary ingredient of the cause of action, Martland J. continued as follows:

> In England the matter of threats of proceedings for alleged patent infringement was dealt with by statute, in s. 32 of the *Patents Act of 1883*, but no similar provision is included in the Canadian *Act*. The respondent, however, relies upon the provisions of s. 7(*a*) of the *Trade Marks Act*, c. 49, Statutes of Canada 1952-53, as creating a statutory cause of action, similar in nature to the action for injurious falsehood, limited to claims in respect of statements made by a competitor, but in which malice is no longer an ingredient. . . .
>
>                          . . .
>
> There is no express requirement that the false or misleading statements be made with knowledge of their falsity, or that they be made maliciously. To interpret these provisions as though such elements were implied would be to construe them as merely restating rules of law which already existed. I do not think this approach is a proper one [. . .]
>
> In my opinion, the natural meaning of s. 7(*a*) is to give a cause of action, in the specified circumstances, in respect of statements which are, in fact, false, and the presence or absence of malice would only have relevance in relation to the assessments of damages.
>
> The circumstances of this case bring the respondent within the provisions of s. 7(*a*) and accordingly, in my opinion, the appeal should be dismissed with costs.

[. . .]

The Court in the *S. & S. Industries* case did not pronounce upon s. 7(*e*), and its concern with damages under s. 7(*a*) was in the context of a patent issue, and hence in respect of a matter on which Parliament is expressly authorized to legislate.

Overall, whether s. 7(*e*) be taken alone or, more properly, as part of a limited scheme reflected by s. 7 as a whole, the net result is that the Parliament of Canada has, by statute, either overlaid or extended known civil causes of action, cognizable in the provincial courts and reflecting issues falling within provincial legislative competence. In the absence of any regulatory administration to oversee the prescriptions of s. 7 (and without coming to any conclusion on whether such an administration would in itself be either sufficient or necessary to effect a change in constitutional result), I cannot find any basis in federal power to sustain the unqualified validity of s. 7 as a whole or s. 7(*e*) taken alone. It is not a sufficient peg on which to support the legislation that it applies throughout Canada when there is nothing more to give it validity.

The cases to which I have referred indicate some association of s. 7(*a*), (*b*) and (*d*) with federal jurisdiction in relation to patents and copyrights arising under specific heads of legislative power, and with its jurisdiction in relation to trade marks and trade names, said to arise (as will appear later in these reasons) under s. 91(2) of the *British North America Act*. If, however, this be enough to give a limited valid application to those subparagraphs it would not sweep them into federal jurisdiction in respect of other issues that may arise thereunder not involving matters that are otherwise within exclusive federal authority. Certainly, it would not engage s. 7(*e*) which, as interpreted in the cases which have considered it, does not have any such connection with the enforcement of trade marks or trade names or patent rights or copyright as may be said to exist in s. 7(*a*), (*b*) and (*d*). Even if it be possible to give a limited application to s. 7, in respect of all its subparagraphs, to support existing regulation by the Parliament of Canada in the fields of patents, trade marks, trade names and copyright, the present case falls outside of those fields because it deals with breach of confidence by an employee and appropriation of confidential information.

It was emphasized again and again by counsel for the respondent that s. 7(*e*) deals with predatory practices in competition, in a competitive market, that it postulates two or more aspirants or competitors in business and that it involves misappropriation and a dishonest use, in competition, of information or documents so acquired. This may equally be said of the tort of conversion where it involves persons in business or in competition. The fact that Parliament has hived off a particular form of an existing tort or has enlarged the scope of the liability does not determine constitutionality. The relevant questions here are whether the liability is imposed in connection with an enterprise or an activity, for example, banking or bills of exchange, that is itself expressly within federal legislative power; or, if not, whether the liability is dealt with in such a manner as to bring it within the scope of some other head of federal legislative power.

This depends not only on what the liability is, but as well on how the federal enactment deals with its enforcement. What is evident here is that the predatory practices are not under administrative regulation of a competent federally-appointed agency, nor are they even expressly brought under criminal sanction in the statute in which they are prohibited. It is, in my opinion, difficult to conceive them in the wide terms urged upon the Court by the respondent and by the Attorney-General of Canada when they are left to merely private enforcement as a private matter of business injury which may arise, as to all its elements including damage, in a small locality in a Province or within a Province. I do not see any general cast in s. 7(*e*) other than the fact that it is federal legislation and unlimited (as such legislation usually is) in its geographic scope.

Indeed, the very basis upon which s. 7(*e*) is analyzed by the respondent, namely, that it postulates two or more competitors in business, drains it, in my opinion, of the generality that would have been present if the legislation had established the same prescriptions to be monitored by a public authority irrespective of any immediate private grievance as to existing or apprehended injury.

The source of authority for s. 7(*e*), alleged to be in s. 91(2) of the *British North America Act*, may now be examined.

[. . .]

Having regard to the way in which the issue of validity came to this Court, I think the proper approach is to inquire whether s. 7(*e*), taken alone, can be supported as valid federal legislation, and, if not, whether it can be supported as part of a scheme of legislative control that Parliament may establish. In this connection I would not characterize the *Trade Marks Act* as the Federal Court of Appeal did in associating ss. 7 to 11 of the Act as representing 'a set of general rules applicable to all trade and commerce in Canada, including a statutory version of the common law rule against passing off'. I have already noted that ss. 8 to 11 belong to trade mark enforcement, and if we are left with s. 7 to represent *general* rules applicable to all trade and commerce in Canada, the generality resides only in the fact that s. 7 has no geographic limitation. This is the beginning of the problem not the end.

Two decisions of the Privy Council lie at the base of the Federal Court's conclusion on the validity of s. 7 including s. 7(*e*); they are *Citizens Insurance Co. v. Parsons* [(1881), 7 App. Cas. 96], and *Attorney-General of Ontario v. Attorney-General of Canada* [[1937] A.C. 405]. The conclusion was stated as follows:

> Against the background of these authorities, my conclusion is that a law laying down a set of general rules as to the conduct of business men in their competitive activities in Canada is a law enacting 'regulations of trade as a whole or regulations of general trade and commerce within the sense of the judgment in Parsons case'. From this point of view, I can see no difference between the regulation of commodity standards and a law regulating standards of business conduct; and, in my view, if there is anything that can be general regulation of trade as a whole it must include a law of general application that regulates either commodity standards or standards of business conduct.

> In my opinion the *Trade Marks Act*, as a whole, is a law of general application regulating standards of business conduct in Canada and is, therefore, within the powers conferred on Parliament by section 91(2) of the *British North America Act, 1867*. It is therefore unnecessary for me to consider the other grounds advanced for supporting the validity of section 7(*e*).

I am quite prepared, in considering the scope of federal legislative power in relation to the regulation of trade and commerce, to look at the *Parsons* case in the widest aspects of its pronouncements on what that scope is. The attenuation of this broadly phrased power cannot be attributed to the *Parsons* case but to a sequential course of decision which, in my view, failed to redeem the promise of what the *Parsons* case said. The *Parsons* case itself, on its facts, may even now be taken to have been correctly decided in so far as it concerned the validity of provincial legislation respecting contracts of insurance in the province, and the prescription of statutory conditions for policies of fire insurance on property in the province. It should not be forgotten that this Court had sustained the validity of the legislation, albeit with two dissents, when the case was before it: see (1880), 4 S.C.R. 215. In sustaining the provincial enactment, this Court was careful to emphasize the sweep and primacy of the federal trade and commerce power but found its limits not to be transgressed by the provincial legislation under consideration. Thus Ritchie J. said (at p. 242):

> No one can dispute the general power of parliament to legislate as to 'trade and commerce,' and that where, over matters with which local legislatures have power to deal, local legislation conflicts with an Act passed by the Dominion parliament in the exercise of any of the general powers confided to it, the legislation of the local must yield to the supremacy of the Dominion parliament; in other words, that the provincial legislation in such a case must be subject to such regulations, for instance, as to trade and commerce of a commercial character, as the Dominion parliament may prescribe. I adhere to what I said in *Valin v. Langlois*, that the property and civil rights referred to, were not all property and all civil rights, but that the terms 'property and civil rights' must necessarily be read in a restricted and limited sense, because many matters involving property and civil rights are expressly reserved to the Dominion parliament, and that the power of the local legislatures was to be subject to the general and special legislative powers of the Dominion parliament, and to what I there added: 'But while the legislative rights of the local legislatures are in this sense subordinate to the right of the Dominion parliament, I think such latter right must be exercised, so far as may be, consistently with the right of the local legislatures; and, therefore, the Dominion parliament would only have the right to interfere with property and civil rights in so far as such interference may be necessary for the purpose of legislating generally and effectually in relation to matters confided to the parliament of *Canada*.'

> I think the power of the Dominion parliament to regulate trade and commerce ought not to be held to be necessarily inconsistent with those of the local legislatures to regulate property and civil rights in respect to all matters of a merely local and private nature, such as matters connected with the enjoyment and preservation of property in the province, or matters of contract between parties in relation to their property or deal-

ings, although the exercise by the local legislatures of such powers may be said remotely to affect matters connected with trade and commerce, unless, indeed, the laws of the provincial legislatures should conflict with those of the Dominion parliament passed for the general regulation of trade and commerce. . . .

[. . .]

The plain fact is that s. 7(*e*) is not a regulation, nor is it concerned with trade as a whole nor with general trade and commerce. In a loose sense every legal prescription is regulatory, even the prescriptions of the *Criminal Code*, but I do not read s. 91(2) as in itself authorizing federal legislation that merely creates a statutory tort, enforceable by private action, and applicable, as here, to the entire range of business relationships in any activity, whether the activity be itself within or beyond federal legislative authority. If there have been cases which appeared to go too far in diminution of the federal trade and commerce power, an affirmative conclusion here would, in my opinion, go even farther in the opposite direction.

What is evident here is that the Parliament of Canada has simply extended or intensified existing common and civil law delictual liability by statute which at the same time has prescribed the usual civil remedies open to an aggrieved person. The Parliament of Canada can no more acquire legislative jurisdiction by supplementing existing tort liability, cognizable in provincial Courts as reflective of provincial competence, than the provincial legislatures can acquire legislative jurisdiction by supplementing the federal criminal law [. . .]

One looks in vain for any regulatory scheme in s. 7, let alone s. 7(*e*). Its enforcement is left to the chance of private redress without public monitoring by the continuing oversight of a regulatory agency which would at least lend some colour to the alleged national or Canada-wide sweep of s. 7(*e*). The provision is not directed to trade but to the ethical conduct of persons engaged in trade or in business, and, in my view, such a detached provision cannot survive alone unconnected to a general regulatory scheme to govern trading relations going beyond merely local concern. Even on the footing of being concerned with practices in the conduct of trade, its private enforcement by civil action gives it a local cast because it is as applicable in its terms to local or intraprovincial competitors as it is to competitors in interprovincial trade.

While s. 7(e) was declared *ultra vires*, doubt continues to exist as to the constitutional validity of s. 7(b). In *S.C. Johnson & Son Ltd. v. Marketing International Ltd.*,[9] Jackett C.J. wrote the following comment:

[9] (1978), [1979] 1 F.C. 65, 41 C.P.R. (2d) 35, 3 B.L.R. 298, 20 N.R. 451 (Fed. C.A.) at para. 11, affirmed (1979), [1980] 1 S.C.R. 99, 105 D.L.R. (3d) 423, 44 C.P.R. (2d) 16, 29 N.R. 515 (S.C.C.) [*S.C. Johnson* cited to F.C.].

With reference to s. 7(*b*), I do not think that it is necessary to discuss the evidence. It is largely of the kind that speaks for itself. I should say, however, that, if it were concluded that the evidence establishes a case that falls within the words of s. 7(*b*), I should have thought that, having regard to the reasoning on which the decision in *MacDonald v. Vapor Can. Ltd.* is founded, the claim based thereon might have to be dismissed on the ground that s. 7(*b*) is ultra vires.

In another case,[10] which dealt not with s. 7 but rather with s. 31.1(3) of the *Combines Investigation Act* R.S.C. 1970, c. C-23,[11] the Federal Court

---

[10] *Rocois Construction Inc. v. Quebec Ready Mix Inc.*, (sub nom. *Canada (A.G.) v. Qué. Ready Mix Inc.*) [1985] 2 F.C. 40, (*sub nom. Canada (A.G.) v. Qué. Ready Mix Inc.*) 25 D.L.R. (4th) 373, (sub nom. *Pilote Ready Mix Inc. v. Rocois Construction Inc.*) 8 C.P.R. (3d) 145, (sub nom. *Canada (A.G.) v. Qué. Ready Mix Inc.*) 24 C.C.C. (3d) 158, (sub nom. *Canada (A.G.) v. Qué. Ready Mix Inc.*) 32 B.L.R. 213 (Fed. C.A.) at para. 34, affirmed (sub nom. *Qué. Ready Mix Inc. v. Rocois Construction Inc.*) [1989] 1 S.C.R. 695, (sub nom. *Qué. Ready Mix Inc. v. Rocois Construction Inc.*) 60 D.L.R. (4th) 124, (sub nom. *Qué. Ready Mix Inc. v. Rocois Construction Inc.*) 25 C.P.R. (3d) 304 (S.C.C.) [*Quebec Ready Mix* cited to F.C.].

[11] Which then read as follows:

31.1 (1) Any person who has suffered loss or damage as a result of:

(*a*) conduct that is contrary to any provision of Part V, or

(*b*) the failure of any person to comply with an order of the Commission or a court under this Act,

may, in any court of competent jurisdiction, sue for and recover from the person who engaged in the conduct or failed to comply with the order an amount equal to the loss or damage proved to have been suffered by him, together with any additional amount that the court may allow not exceeding the full cost to him of any investigation in connection with the matter and of proceedings under this section.

(2) In any action under subsection (1) against a person, the record of proceedings in any court in which that person was convicted of an offence under Part V or convicted of or punished for failure to comply with an order of the Commission or a court under this Act is, in the absence of any evidence to the contrary, proof that the person against whom the action is brought engaged in conduct that was contrary to a provision of Part V or failed to comply with an order of the Commission or a court under this Act, as the case may be, and any evidence given in those proceedings as to the effect of such acts or omissions on the person bringing the action is evidence thereof in the action.

(3) For the purposes of any action under subsection (1), the Federal Court of Canada is a court of competent jurisdiction.

(4) No action may be brought under subsection (1),

(*a*) in the case of an action based on conduct that is contrary to any provision

of Appeal declared that, in order to be *intra vires* Parliament, a civil remedy had to be genuinely integral with the overall plan of supervision. The Court added that the precise balance of governmental regulation and private enforcement was a matter of policy for Parliament, and that Court interference with that would be an unwarranted extension of judicial control into the political domain. MacGuiguan, J.A., wrote:

> Since the result in *Vapor Canada* was a negative one, and the Court did not find it necessary to reflect generally on justifying a civil remedy under the trade and commerce power beyond the point to which it was necessary for decision in that case, it would be hard to establish a general theory of the trade and commerce power based on *Vapor Canada.* There was a similar negative result in *Labatt Breweries of Can. Ltd. v. A.-G. Can. et al.,,* [[1980] 1 S.C.R. 914], published just after trial judgment here, where a divided Court found *ultra vires* federal labelling provisions as to the alcoholic contents of 'light beer'. The principal judgment may fairly be said to be that of Estey J., who put the trade and commerce issue in the case this way (at pp. 939, 943-44 [S.C.R.]):
>
>> The impugned Regulations in and under the *Food and Drugs Act* are not concerned with the control and guidance of the flow of articles of commerce through the distribution channels, but rather with the production and local sale of the specified products of the brewing industry. There is no demonstration by the proponent of these isolated provisions in the *Food and Drugs Act* and its Regulations of any interprovincial aspect of this industry. The labels in the record reveal that the appellant produces these beverages in all Provinces but Quebec and Prince Edward Island. From the nature of the beverage, it is apparent, without demonstration, that transportation to distant markets would be expensive, and hence the local nature of the production operation. This distinction between the flow of commerce, and production and local sale, if I may say so with respect, is pointedly made by Pigeon, J., in *Reference re Agricultural Products Marketing Act*, [[1978] 2 S.C.R. 1198] at p. 1293:

---

> of Part V, after two years from
>   (i) a day on which the conduct was engaged in, or
>   (ii) the day on which any criminal proceedings relating thereto were finally disposed of,whichever is the later; and
> (*b*) in the case of an action based on the failure of any person to comply with an order of the Commission or a court, after two years from
>   (i) a day on which the order of the Commission or court was violated,
> or
>   (ii) the day on which any criminal proceedings relating thereto were finally disposed of,
> whichever is the later.

> In my view, the control of production, whether agricultural or industrial, is *prima facie* a local matter, a matter of provincial jurisdiction. Egg farms, if I may use this expression to designate the kind of factories in which feed is converted into eggs and fowl, are local undertakings subject to provincial jurisdiction under section 92(10) *British North America Act*. . .

and at p. 1296: 'Marketing' does not include production and, therefore, provincial control of production is *prima facie* valid. . .

. . . . .

> In the end, the effort of the respondent here is simply to build into these Regulations a validity essentially founded upon the embryonic definition of the application of the trade and commerce heading in the *Citizens Insurance* case,[(1881), 7 App. Cas. 96]. That observation and the subsequent references thereto are all predicated upon the requirement that the purported trade and commerce legislation affected industry and commerce at large or in a sweeping, general sense. In the context of the *Food and Drugs Acts*, it follows that even if this statute were to cover a substantial portion of Canadian economic activity, one industry or trade at a time, by a varying array of regulations or trade codes applicable to each individual sector, there would not, in the result, be at law a regulation of trade and commerce in the sweeping general sense contemplated in the *Citizens Insurance, supra,* case. That, in my view, is the heart and core of the problem confronting the respondent in this appeal. Thus, the provisions regulating malt liquors relate either to a single industry or a sector thereof, while other regulations appear to concern themselves in a similar way with other individual industries; the former being condemned by the *Citizens Insurance* case, and the latter does not rescue the malt liquor Regulations by reason of the *Board of Commerce* case, [(1881), 7 App. Cas. 96].

> I conclude, therefore, in this part, that the impugned sections as they relate to malt liquors cannot be founded in the trade and commerce head of jurisdiction.

Clearly it was the lack of generality of the regulation, resulting from the peculiarly local production for a local market, that determined the result for Estey J. and the three Judges concurring with him. But, again, there is no larger delineation of the law which could serve as a sure guide in other cases.

One of the clearest indications that section 7(b) may be unconstitutional can be found in *Motel 6 Inc. v. No. 6 Motel Ltd.*[12] where the court stated:

> The provisions of the common law have been given statutory effect by s. 7(*b*) but those provisions have in fact been extended to some extent by the section and also by its predecessor s. 11 of the late Unfair Competition Act, R.S.C. 1952, c. 274
>
> [. . .]
>
> [W]hen commenting on the *Noshery* case in the *MacDonald v. Vapor Canada* case, supra, quite erroneously attributed to me a diametrically opposed view of the effect of s. 7(*b*). Chief Justice Laskin, 22 C.P.R. (2d) 1 at p. 18, made the following statement on the subject:
>
>> In *The Noshery Ltd. v. The Penthouse Motor Inn Ltd. et al.* (1969), 61 C.P.R. 207, Addy, J., then in the Ontario Supreme Court, differed from both of the foregoing cases in the holding that s. 7(b) applied only as between competitors.
>
> Nowhere in the *Noshery* case is it stated or implied that s. 7(*b*) applies only as between competitors. [. . .]
>
> It is not every day that the shoe is on the other foot and that a trial Judge can enjoy the rare luxury of having the last word on any point. Although it might, at first glance, appear to be of comparatively minor importance, the change effected in 1953 by substituting 'service of another' for 'services of a competitor' might, if the section is ultimately found to be constitutional, prove to have a very direct bearing on the outcome of the present case, since all of the plaintiff's motels are in the U.S.A. and all of the defendant's are in Canada and, therefore, the parties could not, in my view, be considered as competitors.
>
> Even though the wording of s. 7(*b*) has to some limited extent broadened the scope of the common law action of passing off, it has not changed the nature of the action nor any of its other essential elements nor is any suggestion to that effect to be found in any reported case that I know of. The right which is the subject-matter of the action is still the property in the business and goodwill likely to be injured. The action still concerns an invasion of a right in that property and not of a right in the mark or name improperly used. The fact that the statutory provision might be broader in its scope than the common law action would not tend to relate it more intimately to 'the general regulatory scheme governing trade marks.' On the contrary, the broader the brush the less suitable it would be to fill in the fine lines of the narrow and carefully circum-

---

[12] (1981), [1982] 1 F.C. 638, 127 D.L.R. (3d) 267, 14 B.L.R. 241, 56 C.P.R. (2d) 44 (Fed. T.D.) [*Motel 6* cited to F.C.].

scribed provisions of trade mark registration and control, even if used by a skilful artist.

Having dealt with the nature of an action under s. 7(*b*), one must examine its place in the context of our constitution.

Patents and copyrights are specifically enumerated subjects of federal jurisdiction under Heads 22 and 23 of s. 91 of the *British North America Act*, 1867. Trade marks, however, are in a completely different category. As previously stated, federal legislative power on this subject draws its constitutional validity from the general power of the federal authority to regulate trade and commerce in the areas of inter-provincial and external trades (Head 2 of s. 91). Section 7(*b*) itself certainly does not, in any way, focus on inter-provincial or external trade or on the regulation of trade throughout Canada and, therefore, in the factual situation of the case at bar, if it is to be considered as having any constitutional validity whatsoever that validity must be founded somehow on trade mark law.

In order for the federal authority, pursuant to Head 2 of s. 91, to validly exercise its power on any subject which is also clearly within the field of property and civil rights normally reserved to provincial Legislatures, the subject-matter must be necessarily incidental to the power to regulate trade and commerce.

It seems to follow that, in order for any supplementary legislation which does not directly deal with trade marks but which must find its validity in the area of trade mark legislation, must be essentially or fundamentally required for or, at the very least, be necessarily or intimately related to the regulation or control of trade marks. I feel that it is in this sense that the Supreme Court of Canada stated that the provision must be 'connected with a general regulatory scheme to govern trade marks' or 'support existing regulation by the Parliament of Canada in the fields of patents, trade marks, trade names and copyright' or possess 'some association with federal jurisdiction in relation to trade marks and trade names'. The connection must be intimate and important, the support, real and substantial and the association that of blood brothers for I dare not, in this day and age, qualify the association as that of intimate bedfellows. A mere incidental relationship or a matter which is nothing more than an accessory, adjunct, appendage or adornment will not meet the required test. Otherwise, the uniform would enjoy a more favourable legal status than the body it has been tailored to clothe.
[. . .]

In a passing off action, again to quote Chief Justice of Canada, the 'enforcement is left to the chance of private redress without public monitoring by the continued oversight of a regulatory agency' and it is 'unconnected with any general regulatory scheme to govern trade marks', while the *Trade Marks Act* is characterized by a public registry and administrative controls not applicable in any way to s. 7(*b*).

[. . .]

The three main grounds on which a mark may be attacked were discussed in the earlier portions of these reasons. They are quite different from those on which an action of passing off under s. 7(*b*) or at common law can be maintained. Similarly, even though a passing off action should fail on the merits, the mark could still be found to be invalid on any one or all of the three main grounds of attack provided for in the Act, and the registration ordered to be vacated.

The areas where there are substantial differences between a passing off action under s. 7(*b*) and an action to invalidate a trade mark might be summed up as follows: the 'chose' or right protected, the cause of action, the grounds on which the action is founded, the nature of the evidence to be adduced and the time to which the evidence must be related. On the other hand, I cannot find any real common denominator of a passing off action under s. 7 in any of the above-mentioned actions. I, therefore, fail to see how an action under s. 7(*b*) nor how s. 7(*b*) itself can be said to 'round off federal legislation regarding trade marks'. Finally, when a trade mark is declared to be invalid, this constitutes a decision in rem. A judgment in a passing off action on the other hand, by its very nature, can never, under any circumstances, be considered an in rem decision.

I conclude that s. 7(*b*) of the *Trade Marks Act* is *ultra vires* the federal legislative authority and this Court is without jurisdiction to try the issue either on the basis of that section or a fortiori on the basis of the common law action of passing off. That portion of the plaintiff's claim will, accordingly, be dismissed.

A number of other subsequent trial decisions shed doubt on *Motel 6*, however.[13] In fact, in a later case, *Asbjorn Horgard A/S v. Gibbs/Nortac Industries Ltd.*,[14] the Federal Court of Appeal ruled that the *Trade-marks Act* as a whole satisfied the criteria for constitutional validity under the s.

---

[13] See *Wyeth Ltd. v. Novopharm Ltd.* (1986), [1986] F.C.J. No. 51, (sub nom. *Novopharm Ltd. v. Wyeth Ltd.*) 26 D.L.R. (4th) 80, 8 C.P.R. (3d) 448 (Fed. C.A.); *Riello Canada Inc. v. Lambert* (1986), [1986] F.C.J. No. 243, 9 C.P.R. (3d) 324, 3 F.T.R. 23, 1986 CarswellNat 611 (Fed. T.D.), additional reasons at (1987), 15 C.P.R. (3d) 257 (Fed. T.D.); and *Imperial Dax Co. v. Mascoll Corp.* (1978), 42 C.P.R. (2d) 62 (Fed. T.D.).

[14] *Asbjorn Horgard A/S v. Gibbs/Nortac Industries Ltd.*, [1987] 3 F.C. 544, 38 D.L.R. (4th) 544, 14 C.P.R. (3d) 314, 80 N.R. 9 (Fed. C.A.), additional reasons at (1987), (sub nom. *Asbjorn Horgard A/S v. Gibbs/Nortac Industries Ltd. (No. 2)*) 81 N.R. 1 (Fed. C.A.), reconsideration refused (1987), 16 C.P.R. (3d) 112 (Fed. C.A.) [*Asbjorn* cited to F.C.].

91(2) trade and commerce power, and that, by protecting goodwill, section 7(b) specifically is *intra vires* because it is rationally and functionally connected to the trade-marks scheme.

In *Asbjorn*, the Federal Court of Appeal seemed to reverse the *Motel 6* conclusion and declared section 7(b) *intra vires*, on the basis of *Quebec Ready Mix*.[15] MacGuigan J.A., said the following:

> Subsection 7(*b*) is a statutory statement of the common law action of passing off, which consisted of a misrepresentation to the effect that one's goods or services are someone else's, or sponsored by or associated with that other person. It is effectively a 'piggybacking' by misrepresentation.
> [. . .]
>
> At common law the right to a trade mark thus arose through the use of a mark by a business to identify its products to the public. There was no need for the business to register its mark in order to protect its right to use the trade mark and prevent the misuse of its trade mark by other businesses. The passing off action was the enforcement mechanism available for the protection of trade mark rights. Without the passing off action, common law trade mark rights would have little value.
>
> The Canadian Act, as the statutory history set out by Laskin C.J.C. in the *MacDonald* case, supra, showed, has traditionally been concerned with the protection of unregistered as well as registered trade marks. In this it is like the *Copyright Act*, [R.S.C. 1970, c. C-30] whose coverage is broader than registered copyright. In both Acts what registration does is to provide additional benefits over and above those available at common law.
> [. . .]
>
> In s-s. 7(*b*) Parliament has chosen to protect the goodwill associated with trade marks. In this way, as Chief Justice Laskin put it, it 'rounds out' the statutory scheme of protection of all trade marks. As such, the civil remedy which it provides in conjunction with s. 53 is 'genuinely and *bona fide* integral with the over-all plan of supervision': *Rocois Construction, supra,* at p. 172 C.P.R., p. 79 F.C., p. 226 N.R. It has, in sum, a rational functional connection to the kind of trade marks scheme Parliament envisaged, in which even unregistered marks would be protected from harmful misrepresentations.
>
> In my view, s-s. 7(*b*) is clearly within federal constitutional jurisdiction under subs. 91(2) of the *Constitution Act, 1867*.

The finding of constitutionality of section 7(b) made in *Asbjorn* was later approved by a different bench of the Federal Court of Appeal in *Dumont*

---

[15] *Supra* note 10.

*vins & spiritueux Inc. c. Celliers du monde Inc.*[16] but with an interesting nuance:

> It seems to me to follow from these reasons that paragraph 7(*b*) is valid in so far as the passing off action is connected to a trade mark, registered or not, but that it would not be valid in a case such as the one at bar in which the passing off action, as a result of the fact that the absence of an unregistered trade mark is *res judicata*, is not connected to any trade mark. In my opinion, the same reasoning applies to paragraph (*c*).

Then, the Trial Division of the Federal Court refused to apply *Asbjorn* to an analysis of the validity of section 7(a),[17] and this "trend" to minimize the *Asbjorn* findings continued in other cases.[18] In *Benisti Import-Export Inc. c. Modes TXT Carbon Inc.*,[19] Prothonotary ("Master") Morneau reviewed recent cases as follows:

> In *Mattel Canada Inc. v. GTS Acquisitions Ltd.* (1989), 25 C.I.P.R. 192 at pp. 193-94, 28 C.P.R. (3d) 534 (F.C.T.D.), my colleague Giles, even states that paragraph 7(*a*) of the Act covers any intellectual property matter. He states:
>
>> I dismissed the motion because the injunctive relief sought against the plaintiff was in part beyond the jurisdiction of this Court. The reasons of Chief Justice Laskin in *MacDonald v. Vapour Can. Ltd.,* [1977] 2 S.C.R. 134, 22 C.P.R. (2d) 1, 7 N.R. 477, 66 D.L.R. (3d) 1, as explained by Mr. Justice MacGuigan in *Asbjorn Horgard A/S v. Gibbs/Nortac Industries Ltd.*, [1987] 3 F.C. 544, 13 C.I.P.R. 263, 14 C.P.R. (3d) 314, 38 D.L.R. (4th) 544, 80 N.R. 9, 12 F.T.R. 317 (note) (C.A.), indicated that s. 7 of the *Trade Marks Act*, R.S.C. 1970, c. T-10 is within the jurisdiction of the Parliament of Canada only to the extent that it forms

---

[16] (sub nom. *Dumont Vins & Spiritueux Inc. v. Celliers du Monde Inc.*) [1992] 2 F.C. 634, (sub nom. *Dumont Vins & Spiritueux Inc. v. Celliers du Monde Inc.*) 42 C.P.R. (3d) 197, (sub nom. *Dumont Vins & Spiritueux Inc. v. Celliers du Monde Inc.*) 139 N.R. 357 (Fed. C.A.) [*Celliers du Monde* cited to F.C.]. *Asbjorn* was also adopted in the more recent case of *Kirkbi AG v. Ritvik Holdings Inc. / Gestions Ritvik Inc.* (2003), [2003] F.C.J. No. 1112, 228 D.L.R. (4th) 297, 26 C.P.R. (4th) 1, 2003 CarswellNat 3408 (F.C.A.), leave to appeal allowed (2004), 30 C.P.R. (4th) vii (S.C.C.) [*Kirkbi AG* cited to D.L.R.].

[17] *Safematic Inc. v. Sensodec Oy* (1988), [1988] F.C.J. No. 401, 20 F.T.R 132, 21 C.P.R. (3d) 12, 1988 CarswellNat 582 (Fed. T.D.).

[18] See, *e.g., Promotions Atlantiques Inc. v. Hardcraft Industries Ltd.* (1987), [1987] F.C.J. No. 703, 17 C.P.R. (3d) 552, 13 C.I.P.R. 194, 1987 CarswellNat 640 (Fed. T.D.).

[19] (2002), [2002] F.C.J. No. 240, 20 C.P.R. (4th) 125, 2002 CarswellNat 409 (Fed. T.D.) [*Benisti* cited to C.P.R.].

part of a scheme for the regulation of intellectual property. Therefore, s. 7(*a*) of the *Trade Marks Act* cannot be read as generally prohibiting the making of false or misleading statements tending to discredit the business, wares or services of a competitor, but only as prohibiting the making of such false and misleading statements in association with a trade mark or other intellectual property.

Counsel for the plaintiff made much of the Supreme Court of Canada decision in *MacDonald v. Vapor Canada Ltd.*, [1977] 2 S.C.R. 134, 22, C.P.R. (2d) 1.

The ratio of this judgment has to do with the constitutional invalidity of s. 7(*e*) of the Act. So what is said in this judgment about the scope of the other provisions of the Act is in the nature of *obiter dictum*. Moreover, although the following passage from p. 172 does not refer to 'industrial designs', we cannot clearly and obviously dismiss the proposition of the defendant's counsel in this case that the Supreme Court in *MacDonald* wished to emphasize the major intellectual property vehicles and was not consciously trying to rule out 'industrial designs', which it discusses earlier at p. 165. These two extracts read as follows:

At p. 165:

> It is said, however, that s. 7, or s. 7(*e*), in particular, may be viewed as part of an overall scheme of regulation which is exemplified by the very Act of which it is a part and, also, by such related statutes in the industrial property field as the *Patent Act*, R.S.C. 1970, c. P-4, the *Copyright Act*, R.S.C. c. C-30 and the *Industrial Design Act*, R.S.C. 1970, c. I-8.

At p. 172:

> The position which I reach in this case is this. Neither s. 7 as a whole, nor section 7(*e*), if either stood alone and in association only with s. 53, would be valid federal legislation in relation to the regulation of trade and commerce or in relation to any other head of federal legislative authority. There would, in such a situation, be a clear invasion of provincial legislative power. Section 7 is, however, nourished for federal legislative purposes in so far as it may be said to round out regulatory schemes prescribed by Parliament in the exercise of its legislative power in relation to patents, copyrights, trade marks and trade names. The subparagraphs of s. 7, if limited in this way, would be sustainable, and, certainly, if s. 7(*e*) whose validity is alone in question here, could be so limited, I would be prepared to uphold it to that extent. I am of opinion, however . . .

The fact that it is easier to extend the protection of s. 7 of the Act to some matters expressly referred to in section 91 of the *Constitution Act, 1867* (heads 22 and 23 in section 91, that is, patents of invention and discovery and copyrights) might not be as meaningful as the plaintiff's counsel hopes, since s. 7 itself is in a statute the subject matter of which does not fall with the express powers of s. 91 of the *Constitution Act, 1867*.

The plaintiff also referred the Court to the Federal Court of Appeal decision in *Asbjorn Horgard A/S v. Gibbs/Nortac Industries Ltd.*, [1987] 3 F.C. 544, 14 C.P.R. (3d) 314. Although the Court refers in that judgment to the Supreme Court decision in *MacDonald*, the ratio of *Asbjorn* is addressed to the constitutional validity of s. 7(*b*) of the Act, and not s. 7(*a*). In *Asbjorn*, then, the Court was not centrally concerned by anything other than the ratio that it had to decide. Accordingly, this judgment is of limited value in the debate that concerns us.

To summarize, in *MacDonald*, the Supreme Court declared section 7(e) unconstitutional.[20] There is no final word as to the validity of other paragraphs of section 7, especially subsections (a), (b) or (c), though it seems fair to conclude that while (a) is constitutionally dubious,[21] (b) and (c) would likely survive a challenge before the Supreme Court, though perhaps with some weight given to the cautionary note sounded by the Federal Court of Appeal in *Celliers du Monde*,[22] in particular the need for the plaintiff to show that the passing off is connected to a trade-mark. A plaintiff may always rely on the torts of passing off, slander of title, injurious falsehood[23] or trade libel in provincial law. To do so, however, a litigant will have to seek relief in a provincial court rather than the federal court.[24] A provincial court may always rely in parallel on section 7 of the *Trade-marks Act*. One disadvantage of proceeding at the provincial level is that an injunction will only be enforceable in the province concerned.

---

[20] *Supra*, note 8.

[21] It was already applied by the Supreme Court in *Rowell v. S. & S. Industries Inc.*, [1966] S.C.R. 419, 56 D.L.R. (2d) 501, 48 C.P.R. 193 (S.C.C.), but its constitutionality was not discussed.

[22] *Supra*, note 16.

[23] See Christopher Wadlow, *The Law of Passing Off*, 3rd ed. (Sweet & Maxwell, 2004) at 383 - 424.

[24] See *Consumers Distributing Co. v. Seiko Time Canada Ltd.* (1980), 29 O.R. (2d) 221, 112 D.L.R. (3d) 500, 11 B.L.R. 149, 50 C.P.R. (2d) 147 (Ont. H.C.), affirmed (1981), 34 O.R. (2d) 481, 128 D.L.R. (3d) 767, 60 C.P.R. (2d) 222 (Ont. C.A.), reversed on different grounds by [1984] 1 S.C.R. 583, (sub nom. *Seiko Time Canada Ltd. v. Consumers Distributing Co.*) 10 D.L.R. (4th) 161, 1 C.P.R. (3d) 1, 54 N.R. 161, 3 C.I.P.R. 223 (S.C.C.) [*Seiko*].

## 3. Purpose And Theory Of Protecting Trade-Marks

There are several key concepts in trade-mark law relating to the purpose, and which, in turn, define and restrict the scope of trade-mark protection. First, a primary purpose of protecting trade-marks is to *protect consumers*. Granting trade-mark owners a right to sue for infringement of their mark safeguards the public while allowing the trade-mark owners to *protect their intangible asset*. Second, owners of marks get an exclusive right to *use* the mark *in association with* the designated goods or services. A mark, in other words, is not protected *per se* as an isolated object but rather as an indicator of *source* to distinguish one person's goods (or services) from another person's. Trade-mark law does not provide absolute property rights in the mark itself.

In a 1998 case involving the PINK PANTHER mark,[25] the Federal Court of Appeal discussed the purpose and policy of trade-mark law and outlined these key concepts:

> The protection of trade-marks as property is based in the common law action for passing off. Historically, the marketplace has been very concerned with guaranteeing consumers the quality of goods that they had come to rely upon in the course of trade. To further that guarantee, the common law developed the tort of passing off, which helped to assure that a person was representing his or her goods as being his or her own goods and not the goods of someone else. A necessary element of the tort of passing off was always an attempt to deceive. When this attempt to deceive caused confusion and damage, it was actionable. While the rationale for the tort was to protect the public, it was not the consumer who sued, but the owner of the trade-mark who brought the action, thereby protecting the public, as well as its own interest.
>
> Today, even though the common law remedies are still available, trade-marks are protected statutorily and the action for passing off has been codified in paragraph 7(c) of the Act. The Act however, offers a wider ambit of protection than the old common law. First, the plaintiff in an infringement proceeding (or the opponent in an opposition proceeding) need not show that the goods or services are marketed in the same area as the old common law did. The registered trade-mark is valid across Canada and, along with it the owner possesses the right to its exclusive use in association with specified wares or services

---

[25] *United Artists Pictures Inc. v. Pink Panther Beauty Corp.*, (sub nom. *Pink Panther Beauty Corp. v. United Artists Corp.*) [1998] 3 F.C. 534, (sub nom. *United Artists Corp. v. Pink Panther Beauty Corp.*) 225 N.R. 82, (sub nom. *United Artists Corp. v. Pink Panther Beauty Corp.*) 80 C.P.R. (3d) 247 (Fed. C.A.) [*Pink Panther* cited to F.C.]. Leave to appeal allowed (1998), (sub nom. *United Artists Corp. v. Pink Panther Beauty Corp.*) 235 N.R. 399 (note) (S.C.C.), but appeal discontinued.

nationwide. As well, no damages need to be proven, nor indeed must an attempt to deceive be made out in order to succeed.

[. . .]

The question posed by the existence of intellectual property regimes has been defined as one of where to draw the line between the right to copy and the right to compete. This is a question about what is truly worthy of the status of property and what is in reality an element of the marketplace which should be open to all competitors to use in their efforts to succeed. I find this question a profitable one to keep in mind. For example, Henderson discusses the rationale behind protection for certain things and not others. He wrote:

> The main reason that we do not protect ideas *per se* is because they are commonplace. To protect an idea at its preliminary or 'bare idea' stage could stultify economic progress. And, most importantly, ideas, *per se*, are relatively useless.

When deciding property issues it is always a matter of balancing the public right to competition with the private right to ownership. I do not find that this is limited to questions of intellectual property; an owner does not have unlimited rights with respect to personalty or realty. Consideration of the public interest is advanced through statute and through the common law (*e.g.* the tort of nuisance). When considering these types of questions the Court must be cognizant of the fact that the market relies on individuals who, through their labour and ingenuity, bolster the strength of our economy. That strength benefits us all. We must be careful when we determine property rights so that the line is drawn fairly between the right to the exclusive use of an idea and the right of individuals to compete and earn a livelihood. This dilemma is neatly summarized by Madame Justice McLachlin when she says:

> We must stop thinking of intellectual property as an absolute and start thinking of it as a function - as a process, which, if it is to be successful, must meet diverse aims: the assurance of a fair reward to creators and inventors and the encouragement of research and creativity, on the one hand; and on the other hand, the widest possible dissemination of the ideas and products of which the world, and all the individuals in it, have such great need.[Madam Justice Beverley McLachlin, "Intellectual Property - What's it all About?", in Gordon F. Henderson, ed., *Trade-Marks Law of Canada*. (Toronto: Carswell, 1993) at 397].

The scheme of the *Act*, consonant with a source theory of property rights, allows for the registration of trade-marks in relation to the marketing of wares or services. Pursuant to section 30 of the Act, the registrant of the mark must specify the wares or services in relation to which he or she is registering the mark. As well, section 40 of the Act demands that the registration can only be effected when the mark itself has actually been used. A person may propose a mark for registration, but, until it has been used, the trade-mark cannot be registered. That 'use' is a defined term in the *Act* and does not refer to a state of being in operation. [subsection 4(1)]

What is important is that the trade-mark be associated in the minds of the public with the goods produced by the trade-mark owner. It is the association of a trade-mark with a particular source which is the key to understanding the rights protected by the Act.

This notion of source in relation to the goods is also fundamental to the definition of 'distinctive' set out in the Act. [section 2]

Again, the *Act* makes clear that what is being protected is not the exclusive right to any mark that a person might think of, but the exclusive right to use it in association with certain products or services. Where there is no use of the mark, or where the consumer is unable to rely on the mark to distinguish one person's products or services from another person's products or services, then no protection is warranted. In *Western Clock Co. v. Oris Watch Co.* [[1931]Ex. C.R. 64], Audette J. of the Exchequer Court made this comment:

> Distinctiveness is of the very essence and is the cardinal requirement of a trade-mark, which is used to distinguish the goods of a trader from the goods of all other traders.

The rights conferred by registration of a trade-mark are spelled out in sections 19 and 20 of the *Act*. These deal with actual infringement and deemed infringement. The right of exclusive use of the trade-mark granted by section 19 is valid only with respect to the wares and services stated in the registration. Section 20 of the Act prohibits the use of trade-marks which are confusingly similar to registered trade-marks, and their use is deemed to be an infringement. The question of confusion refers us back to section 6 of the Act.

A trade-mark is a mark used by a person to distinguish his or her wares or services from those of others. The mark, therefore, cannot be considered in isolation, but only in connection with those wares or services. This is evident from the wording of subsection 6(2). The question posed by that subsection does not concern the confusion of marks, but the confusion of goods or services from one source as being from another source. It is for this reason that marks which rely on geographic origins or generally descriptive words (*e.g.* the fictional marks Pacific Coffee or Premium Soda) are not afforded a wide ambit of protection. Even though proposed marks might be similar to them, the public is not likely to assume that two products that describe themselves as being 'Pacific' or 'Premium' necessarily originate from the same source. Because confusion is not likely, protection is not necessary.

In summary, trade-marks have a dual function. Not only do trade-marks allow for a manufacturer to distinguish goods or services from those of a competitor, in turn becoming an asset for that company, but trade-marks also help to alleviate consumer confusion as to the source of those goods or services.

## II. OBJECT OF THE PROTECTION

Traditional intellectual property rights take the form of monopolies granted to various creators and inventors. These rights have been variously theorized as rewards for creating or inventing a new product and as incentives to create and invent more. However, the object of trade-mark protection is somewhat different. Courts take account not only of the trade-mark holder's interests but also those of the consumers concerned. In most cases, with the exception of a right in respect of the depreciation of goodwill (section 22 of the *Trade-marks Act*), which seems to be a pure rightsholder right, courts usually do not enforce a trade-mark if there is no evidence of a consumer interest in, for example, avoiding possible confusion between two products or services. That is, at least in theory, a trade-mark has been explicitly thought of as legislation protecting consumers than as a right belonging only to the creator. This distinction between trade-marks and copyright and patents is eroding, however, as courts speak more about the public's interests in the context of copyright and patent, and of the trade-mark holder's property interests in the mark.

## 1. General

The law contains a limited substantive definition of the concept of "mark" and a list of types of marks, as we shall see below. However, one could also refer here, as a guide at least, to the definitions contained in the World Trade Organization's *Agreement on Trade-Related Aspects of Intellectual Property Rights* (TRIPS Agreement).[26] The TRIPS Agreement came into force in 1995 and applied to Canada the same year as it is a WTO member country (see the International section). Article 15 of the TRIPS Agreement defines a mark as follows:

---

[26] WTO, *Agreement on Trade-Related Aspects of Intellectual Property Rights,* Annex 1C of the Marrakesh Agreement Establishing the World Trade Organization, signed in Marrakesh, Morocco, on 15 April 1994, online: WTO, <http://www.wto.org/english/docs_e/legal_e/27-trips.pdf> [*TRIPS* or *TRIPS Agreement*].

Any sign, or any combination of signs, capable of distinguishing the goods or services of one undertaking from those of other undertakings, shall be capable of constituting a trademark. Such signs, in particular words including personal names, letters, numerals, figurative elements and combinations of colours as well as any combination of such signs, shall be eligible for registration as trademarks. Where signs are not inherently capable of distinguishing the relevant goods or services, Members may make registrability depend on distinctiveness acquired through use. Members may require, as a condition of registration, that signs be visually perceptible.

The definition contained in s. 2 of the *Trade-marks Act* reads as follows:

"trademark" means

a)    a mark that is used by a person for the purpose of distinguishing or so as to distinguish wares or services manufactures, sold, leased, hired or performed by him from those manufactured sold, leased, hired or performed by others,
b)    a certification mark,
c)    a distinguishing guise, or
d)    a proposed trade-mark

A *certification mark* is certification given by a third party guarantying a certain origin and quality.

"certification mark" means a mark that is used for the purpose of distinguishing or so as to distinguish wares or services that are of a defined standard with respect to

a)    the character or quality of the wares or services,
b)    the working conditions under which the wares have been produced or the services performed,
c)    the class of persons by whom the wares have been produced or the services performed, or
d)    the area which the wares have been produced or the services performed,

from wares or services that defined standard.

A *distinguishing guise* is the shape, wrapping or packaging distinctive to the product. The particular shape (and colour) of the bottles of Perrier® (and older bottles of Coca-Cola®) come to mind. According to s. 2:

"distinguishing guise" means

a)    a shaping of wares or their containers, or

b)    a mode of wrapping or packaging wares

the appearance of which is used by a person for the purpose of distinguishing or so as to distinguish wares or services manufactured, sold, leased, hired or performed by him from those manufactured, sold, leased, hired or performed by others;

The protection does not extend to functional elements (see s. 13(2)), as was demonstrated in a recent case involving LEGO blocks. Sexton J.A., for the majority wrote:

> Indeed, in my view, s. 13(2) reinforces the concept that the doctrine of functionality invalidates a mark which is primarily functional. It makes clear that the public is not constrained from using any utilitarian features of a distinguishing guise. It follows that if a distinguishing guise is wholly or primarily functional, then the public is not constrained from using the distinguishing guise in its entirety. Thus a distinguishing guise which is primarily functional provides no rights to exclusive use and hence no trade-mark protection. In other words the fact that the distinguishing guise is primarily functional means that it cannot be a trade-mark.[27]

The concept of a *proposed trade-mark* was created by the legislature to allow entities to apply for the registration of their trade-marks before using them. In some countries, use of a trade-mark is not required in order to obtain its registration. This possibility of registration before use is specifically addressed in the *TRIPS Agreement* definition mentioned above. In Canada and the United States, an application may be filed for a proposed mark, but the mark will only be registered once use of the mark in commerce has begun (see the Registration section). Special rules apply to holders of foreign registrations. This difference between Canadian law and the law of most of Canada's trading partners prompted the creation of this special category of "proposed trade-marks", defined in s. 2 of the *Trade-marks Act* as follows:

> "proposed trade-mark" means a mark that is proposed to be used by a person for the purpose of distinguishing or so as to distinguish wares or services manufactured, sold leased, hired or performed by him from those manufactured, sold, leased, hired or performed by others.

---

[27] *Kirkbi AG, supra*, note 16 at para. 59. See also *Remington Rand Corp. v. Philips Electronics N.V.* (1995), [1995] F.C.J. No. 1660, 64 C.P.R. (3d) 467, 191 N.R. 204, 1995 CarswellNat 1846 (Fed. C.A.), leave to appeal refused (1996), 67 C.P.R. (3d) vi (note) (S.C.C.) (refusing protection for triple-headed rotary electric shavers).

The *Trade-marks Act* does not define "mark" itself so questions have been raised as to which sensory indicators can qualify as protected marks. Marks traditionally have been visual signals, such as signs and logos or even packaging. Colours, another example of a visually perceptible mark, can also be marks, provided they are not functional.[28] However, since a trade-mark is, conceptually, anything that can serve to distinguish a product or service of one undertaking from those of another, sounds (*e.g.*, jingles) and even odours (*e.g.*, perfumes) could *in theory* be protected as marks. But courts have been unwilling to extend the concept of mark this far and have indicated that the trade-mark must be visible in order to be protected. The *TRIPS Agreement* also mentions visual perceptibility as a possible condition of protection. In *Playboy Enterprises Inc. v. Germain*, the court decided that a "mark" which was only aurally and not visually associated with the good could not be registered as a trade-mark.[29] The case was brought by the publisher of the well-known men's magazine against a company preparing to sell "hair pieces, hair tinting preparations, hair tonics, hair sprays and shampoos" under the PLAYBOY trade-mark. No labels or stickers with the PLAYBOY mark were affixed to the hairpieces; instead, customers and purchasers when shown or buying the hairpieces were verbally told that the goods were "PLAYBOY" hairpieces. The Court rejected the aural use of the word PLAYBOY as use of mark and found that a mark had to be represented visually. Pinard J. wrote:

> I am of the opinion that, use of a verbal description is not use of a trade mark within the meaning of the *Trade Marks Act*. A 'mark' must be something that can be represented visually.

> In *Wrights' Rope Ltd. v. Broderick & Bascom Rope Co.*, [1931] 4 D.L.R. 368, Ex. C.R. 143, MacLean J., then President of the Court, had to deal with the meaning of the word 'mark' in relation to the *Trade- Mark and Design Act*, R.S.C. 1927, c. 201, and he said at pp. 144 and 145:

> > It is reasonable I think to reach the conclusion that a coloured strand woven into a wire fabric is a 'mark' which may be used by any person carrying on the manufacture of wire rope, 'such use being for the purpose

---

[28] See *Parke, Davis & Co. v. Empire Laboratories Ltd.*, [1964] S.C.R. 351, 45 D.L.R. (2d) 97, 43 C.P.R. 1 (S.C.C.), affirming (1963), [1964] Ex. C.R. 399, 38 D.L.R. (2d) 694, 41 C.P.R. 121 (Can. Ex. Ct.) [*Parke, Davis* cited to S.C.R.].

[29] (1987), 16 C.P.R. (3d) 517 (Fed. T.D.) [*Playboy Enterprises*]. See also *Cullman Ventures Inc. c. Quo Vadis International Ltée* (2000), [2000] F.C.J. No. 1763, (sub nom. *Cullman Ventures Inc. v. Quo Vadis International Ltd.*) 9 C.P.R. (4th) 330, 2000 CarswellNat 2640 (Fed. T.D.).

of distinguishing the article manufactured or produced, or offered for sale by him' within the words of the Act and their literal meaning.

The modern word 'mark' has its origin in the Anglian word 'merc' which had the meaning of 'a sign.' 'Mark' is defined in the Oxford Dictionary as 'A sign affixed or impressed for distinction.' It is defined in Webster's New International Dictionary as 'an affixed, impressed or assumed distinguishing sign or token.' In the same work a mark is said to be 'a character, device, label, brand, seal, or the like, put on an article to show the maker or owner, to certify quality, for identification,' etc. Then, again, it is no distortion of language to say that a yellow coloured strand of wire as an element of a woven wire rope falls within the designation of a 'business device' as mentioned in the said section of the Act; such device being one 'adopted for use by any person in his trade for the purpose of distinguishing the same as his manufacture or product.'

In *Insurance Corp. of B.C. v. Registrar of Trade Marks*, (1979) 44 C.P.R. (2d) 1, [1980] 1 F.C. 669, Cattanach J. of the Federal Court of Canada also dealt with the meaning of the word 'mark' in relation to the *Trade Marks Act;* at pp. 7 and 8, he stated:

There remains the concluding word 'mark' in s. 9(1)(e). It does not have similar precise connotations as do the preceding words although it does have a minor heraldic significance in that there are marks of cadency such as the Prince of Wales label to signify the first son. In common parlance however a mark is a device, stamp, label, brand, inscription, a written character or the like indicating ownership, quality and the like. [. . .]

A certification mark, distinguishing guise and proposed trade mark are individually and specifically defined in the same section. The word 'mark' is not and resort may therefore be had to dictionaries to ascertain the meaning of the word 'mark' in its ordinary sense which is the sense in which I think the word 'mark' is used in the context of s. 9(1)(n).

Therefore, in order to be deemed to be used in association with wares, at the time of the transfer of the property in or possession of such wares, the trade mark must be something that can be seen, whether it is marked on the wares themselves or on the packages in which they are distributed or whether it is in any other manner so associated with the wares that notice of the association is then given to the person to whom the property or possession is transferred.[30]

Apart from odours (scent marks), purely aural marks (sound marks), which are not visually perceptible, and, as will be discussed, motion marks,

---

[30] *Ibid.* at 522-523.

is everything else protectable? It would seem that way. Unusual marks can be registered, providing the visual perceptibility requirement is met. Thus, a phone number for a pizza delivery service,[31] seams in jeans,[32] the top part of a key,[33] or a particular colour of pill (in a particular shape and size)[34] could all be registered because the visual perceptibility requirement did not pose a difficult hurdle. We will see that fictional characters too are protected under trade-mark law, although the less "graphic" a character is, the less protection fictional characters seem to have (see the Fictional Characters section). With respect to music, visual perceptibility did not bar the registration of music because sheet music can be used to "visually represent" the musical mark. One registration exists in Canada for a mark which has been described as a series of notes (Registration No. TMA359,318). This registration, however, protects only the visual representation of the notes themselves and not the sound of the notes when played and thus does not indicate that sound marks can be registered. Scent is likewise unregistrable as its visual representation is difficult and the perception of scent is subjective. Similarly, motion marks are also not registrable as the motion does not exist in a fixed form and instead is considered to be a series of separate marks.

## 2. Company Names

A distinction should be made between a trade-name and a trade-mark. Section 2 of the *Trade-marks Act* defines a trade-name as "the name under which any business is carried on, whether or not it is the name of a corporation, a partnership or an individual" (s. 2). For example, a company may be formed under the name "Holmes Watson Advisers Inc.", as its trade-name, yet sell wares or offer services under the trade-mark "Sherlock-Detection." Likewise, someone could open a small store for tennis equipment and call it Fifteen-Love. Fifteen-Love is a trade-name. If the store owner then started her own line of tennis apparel and called the line "Fifteen-Love" clothing, Fifteen-Love would be a trade-mark used to distinguish that line of sportswear from other companies' lines.

---

[31] *Pizza Pizza Ltd. v. Canada (Registrar of Trade Marks)*, [1989] 3 F.C. 379, 101 N.R. 378, 26 C.P.R. (3d) 355, 24 C.I.P.R. 152 (Fed. C.A.).

[32] *Santana Jeans Ltd. v. Manager Clothing Inc.* (1993), [1993] F.C.J. No. 1283, 72 F.T.R. 241, 52 C.P.R. (3d) 472, 1993 CarswellNat 388 (Fed. T.D.).

[33] *Dominion Lock Co. v. Schlage Lock Co.* (1961), 22 Fox Pat. C. 102, 38 C.P.R. 88 (Reg. T.M.).

[34] *Smith, Kline & French Canada Ltd., Re*, [1987] 2 F.C. 633, 9 F.T.R. 129, 12 C.I.P.R. 204 (Fed. T.D.).

A trade-name can cause confusion with a trade-mark even if it is not used as a trade-mark. Section 6(1) of the *Act*, specifically provides for this possibility:

> For the purposes of this Act, a trade-mark or trade-name is confusing with another trade-mark or trade-name if the use of the first mentioned trade-mark or trade-name would cause confusion with the last mentioned trade-mark or trade-name in the manner and circumstances described in this section.

To determine whether confusion exists, s. 6(5) provides a list of useful criteria, to which we return below under the Confusion Section. One may use one's name as a trade-name (s. 20(1)(a)) but not as a trade-mark if it falsely suggests a connection with any living individual (see s. 9(1)(k) and the Prohibited Marks Section). If s. 9(1)(k) does not apply, the name can only be registered as a mark once it has become distinctive (see ss. 12(1)(a) and 12(2) (and ss. 14 and 15) and the Secondary Meaning Section).

### 3. Proposed Trade-Marks

As previously mentioned, it is possible to apply for registration of a trade-mark without having used it in Canada. Applications for a proposed mark effectively give the applicant inchoate rights that are enforceable upon use. Proposed trade-marks do not apply to distinguishing guise. Use is required in order to obtain registration (see s. 40(2) of the Act).

### 4. Well-Known Trade-Marks

Even if a trade-mark is neither used nor registered in Canada, applicable international conventions protect well-known international trade-marks.[35]

---

[35] Including Article 6*bis* of the *Paris Convention* for *the Protection of Industrial Property* of March 20, 1883, online: WIPO <http://www.wipo.int/clea/docs/en/wo/wo020en.htm> and Articles 16(2) and (3) of the *TRIPS Agreement, supra,* note 26 (see also the International Section). Article 6*bis* of the *Paris Convention* provides:

> The countries of the Union undertake, ex officio if their legislation so permits, or at the request of an interested party, to refuse or to cancel the registration, and to prohibit the use, of a trademark which constitutes a reproduction, an imitation, or a translation, liable to create confusion, of a mark considered by the competent authority of the country of registration or use to be well known in that country as being already the mark of a person entitled to the benefits of this Convention and used for identical or similar

The applicable principles were enunciated by the Federal Court of Appeal as follows:

> The use of trade-marks was adopted to distinguish one person's goods from those of another, on the market, and to prevent one person selling his goods as those of another. The system was designed to encourage honest trading, and the protection of the buying public. One may safely say that our Trade-Marks Act was not enacted to encourage in Canada the adoption of foreign registered marks, even if there were no user by the foreign registrant here. That would cause confusion and deception, just the thing that trade-marks were supposed to avoid, and it would be a fetter upon trade, another thing quite foreign to the purposes of trade-marks. Trade-mark legislation was designed as much for the benefit of the public, as for the users of trade-marks.

> If such a practice were knowingly permitted by all countries, the use of trade-marks would end in hopeless confusion and bring about a result which trade-marks were originally supposed to avoid. Happily the tendency is always towards the protection of marks registered in another country. In fact a convention exists to-day, to which many important countries are parties, which provides for a system of international registration. In so far as possible each country should I think respect the trade-marks of the other country, or else international trade and public interests would suffer. I think knowledge of foreign registration and user, of a mark applied to the same class of goods, as in this case, and particularly where the foreign user is in a contiguous country using the same language, and between which travel is so easy, and advertising matter so freely circulates, should in most cases be a bar to registration knowingly, of that mark here. This should be particularly true where, as in this case, the plaintiff's advertising, circulating substantially in Canada, might very likely mislead the public into thinking that the defendant's goods were the same as the advertised goods of the plaintiff. The conspicuous presentation of the word mark on the label would influence the eye to that conclusion, notwithstanding the less conspicuous but clearly printed matter on the label, indicating the name of the maker of the goods. That rule would impose no hardship on any person. Conceivably there might be instances when this principle might well be ignored. The case of innocent user and registration is quite a different thing altogether and need not here be considered. Again if the plaintiff had neglected to apply for registration here for a long number of years after his registration in the United States possibly a different view might be taken of the case. That might be construed as a deliberate abandonment of this market, or of the mark

---

goods.

Article 16(2) of *TRIPS* provides:

> In determining whether a trademark is well known, Members shall take account of the knowledge of the trademark in the relevant sector of the public, including knowledge in the Member concerned which has been obtained as a result of the promotion of the trademark.

in this market. I do not think that contention can yet fairly be made. The defendant registered the mark, in Canada, within four months, after the plaintiff registered in the United States.[36]

The concept of marks "made known" in Canada, contained in s. 5 of the *Trade-marks Act*, is used to achieve the purpose of protecting certain foreign marks. It reads as follows:

A trade-mark is deemed to be made known in Canada by a person only if it is used by that person in a country of the Union, other than Canada, in association with wares or services, and

(*a*)    the wares are distributed in association with it in Canada, or
(*b*)    the wares or services are advertised in association with it in
      (i)    any printed publication circulated in Canada in the ordinary course of commerce among potential dealers in or users of the wares or services, or
      (ii)    radio broadcasts ordinarily received in Canada by potential dealers in or users of the wares or services,

and it has become well known in Canada by reason of the distribution or advertising.

Section 5 must be read in conjunction with sections 16(1) and 30(c), which allow the owner of a mark thus made known in Canada to apply for its registration; s. 38(2), which allows him or her to oppose an application by someone else; and s. 18(1) which allows him or her to obtain the expungement of an invalid trade-mark from the register.

A separate regime applies to foreign registered trade-marks that have not been made known in Canada (see the Registration Section and ss. 16(2) and 31).

A mark can only be made known in Canada if it is used (not merely registered) in association with wares or services in a member country of the Paris Union (see the International section for a list of countries).[37] In addition, if the wares are not distributed in Canada, the trade-mark owner must

---

[36] *Williamson Candy Co. v. W. J. Crothers Co.*, [1924] Ex. C.R. 183 (Can. Ex. Ct.) at 191-2, affirmed [1925] S.C.R. 377, [1925] 2 D.L.R. 844 (S.C.C.) [*Williamson Candy*]. Quoted with approval in *Andres Wines Ltd. v. E. & J. Gallo Winery* (1975), [1976] 2 F.C. 3, 25 C.P.R. (2d) 126 (Fed. C.A.) [*Andres Wines* cited to F.C.]. See also *Bartons Inc v. Mary Lee Candy Shoppes Ltd.*, [1950] Ex. C.R. 383, 13 C.P.R. 37 (Can. Ex. Ct.).

[37] See *Ditta F.R.A. Di Mignone v. Johnson & Johnson Ltd.* (1974), 13 C.P.R. (2d) 105 (Fed. T.D.).

prove advertisement in a "printed publication circulated in Canada in the ordinary course of commerce" or in radio broadcasts "ordinarily received in Canada by potential dealers in or users of the wares or services" (s. 5). In *Robert C. Wian Enterprises Inc. v. Mady*,[38] a case dealing with the mark BIG BOY, Cattanach J. explained the meaning of "printed publication" as follows:

> [I]t is necessary to assume that the plaintiff did establish that the two trade marks of which it is the registrant under the United States law were 'used' by the plaintiff in the United States previous to April 12, 1955, in association with hamburger sandwiches or indeed in respect of other goods or services, and, on that assumption, consider whether such wares or services were advertised previous to April 12, 1955, as required by s. 5 of the Canadian *Trade Marks Act*, in association with those trade marks in
>
> (a)    any printed publication circulated in Canada in the ordinary course of commerce among potential dealers in or users of such wares or services, or
> (b)    radio broadcasts, as defined in the *Radio Act*, ordinarily received in Canada by potential dealers in or users of such wares or services.
>
> As far as printed publications circulated in Canada in the ordinary course of commerce among potential dealers in or users of the plaintiff's wares or services are concerned, the evidence is meagre indeed. I reject any consideration of menus, napkins, bags, comic books and the like, which got into the hands of Canadians who patronized United States restaurants, on the ground that such articles were not publications circulated in Canada in the ordinary course of commerce. (In my view circulation of publications in the 'ordinary course of commerce' is accomplished by putting the publications into the hands of members of the public either as subscribers or as persons purchasing from news stands or other 'outlets' that exist for getting such publications into the hands of the public.)

A trade-mark may be well-known in Canada and yet fail to meet the test of s. 5. Hence in a case concerning the mark MARINELAND,[39] which the evidence showed was known by many Canadians because of travel to the United States, the Court found against the mark owner:

---

[38] [1965] 2 Ex. C.R. 3, 49 D.L.R. (2d) 65, 46 C.P.R. 147 (Can. Ex. Ct.).
[39] *Marineland Inc. v. Marine Wonderland & Animal Park Ltd.*, [1974] 2 F.C. 558, 16 C.P.R. (2d) 97 (Fed. T.D.) [*Marineland* cited to F.C.]. To the same effect, see *Stink Inc. v. Salt & Pepper Holdings Ltd.* (2001), [2001] F.C.J. No. 787, 13 C.P.R. (4th) 140, 2001 CarswellNat 1026 (Fed. T.D.); *Valle's Steak House c. Tessier* (1980), [1981] 1 F.C. 441, 49 C.P.R. (2d) 218 (Fed. T.D.); and *Motel 6, supra* note 12.

With respect to advertising in printed publications, the appellant directed its message to the market in the United States. Except in two isolated instances, there was no direct advertising by the appellant in publications printed in Canada and the advertising in publications originating elsewhere came to segments of the Canadian public by reason of 'spill over'. In my view that advertising did not result in the general recognition of the trade mark which is requisite to it becoming 'well known' as the trade marks mentioned as illustrated in the extract from *Wian v. Mady* quoted above.

After having given careful consideration to all of the evidence, I am led to the conclusion that it fails to meet the high standard of proof required to establish that the appellant's trade mark had become 'well known in Canada' in accordance with section 5 of the *Act* and as set forth in *Wian v. Mady (supra)* and *E & J Gallo Winery v. Andres Wines Ltd. (supra)*.

When the advertising is done through broadcasts, what matters is that such broadcasts be *received* by, but not necessarily emitted from, a Canadian source. In the case of *Andres Wines*,[40] the Federal Court of Appeal came to the following conclusion:

> The question to be determined on this attack is, therefore, whether the mark, 'SPANADA' was, at the material time, adapted to distinguish the wine of the respondent from that of others and as the mark appears to have an inherent distinctiveness the question, as I see it, becomes that of whether it has been established by the evidence that this inherently distinctive mark is not adapted to distinguish the wine of the respondent. The basis put forward for reaching a conclusion that the mark is not adapted to distinguish the respondent's wine is that it is already known as the trade mark of the appellant in respect of similar wares. But for this purpose it is not necessary, in my opinion, that the evidence should be sufficient to show that the mark is well known or has been made well known in Canada within the meaning of section 5, or by the methods referred to in that section. Such proof, coupled with use in the United States, would be sufficient to entitle the appellant to registration and to a monopoly of the use of the mark.
> [. . .]

> [T]he balance of probabilities weighs heavily in favour of the conclusion that the telecasts, as a whole, of commercial messages referring to the appellant's SPAÑADA wine by United States border television stations in the period between January 1970 and November 2, 1970 were received in Canada not only by a few but by a very large number of television viewers in Canada and further that the trade mark 'SPAÑADA' had become known to many people in Canada. I venture to think it probable that the advertising would have a

---

[40] *Supra*, note 36 at paras. 7 and 18. The case distinguishes *Marineland, supra*, note 39.

particular ring to people who were familiar with the Spanish custom referred to in the advertising and who would for that reason be more likely than others to pay particular attention to and remember the mark. The same people would probably be more likely than others to purchase the wine on the market.

While the *Trade-marks Act* may not protect certain well-known marks that are not "made known" according to s. 5, there are other ways to obtain protection. One is to rely on the tort of passing off and/or misappropriation rather than the Act. For example, in *Orkin Exterminating Co. v. Pestco Co. of Canada*,[41] a decision based largely on U.S. precedents, the Ontario Court of Appeal found that a Canadian company (Pestco), which decided to use the name ORKIN in the Yellow Pages to generate business for its pest control services (otherwise sold under the mark PESTCO) could not do so nor could it apply for registration of the mark ORKIN in Canada because of confusion with the mark of a U.S. company operating in the same field. The Court wrote:

> Orkin, and its predecessors, have been carrying on business in the United States since 1901 and the name Orkin has been associated with the business since that time. . . . The Orkin logo, which is a red diamond with 'Orkin' in capital letters inside it, has been used in connection with the company's business as the primary trade mark and logo of the business since the 1930s.
>
> Orkin is now, and at all times material to this proceeding has been, one of the largest pest control companies in the world. It is highly regarded by its customers, which include Canadian customers, for the 'excellent' and dependable service which it provides. The trial Judge said that:
>
>> The evidence is uncontradicted that Orkin enjoys an outstanding reputation for reliability and competence. Its integrity is such that many of its customers have left keys to their residences with the company so those residences can be serviced in their absence.
>
> The company has gone to great lengths over the years to establish and maintain a high standard of service through its employee training and product development programmes and its service guarantees.
>
> Orkin's business has expanded steadily over the past 80 years. It began in Georgia in 1901. By 1967 (which is an important year for this proceeding since it was then that Pestco began using the name Orkin) it was carrying on business in the southern United States as well as in some northern central states — Ohio, Indiana, Illinois, Wisconsin, Iowa and Michigan. It had at that time established

[41] (1985), 50 O.R. (2d) 726, 19 D.L.R. (4th) 90, 5 C.P.R. (3d) 433 (Ont. C.A.) [*Orkin* cited to D.L.R.].

operations in Cincinnati, Columbus, Cleveland, Detroit, Grand Rapids, Jackson, Kalamazoo, Saginaw and Milwaukee.

Orkin spent substantial sums of money advertising its name, logo and business in the United States through radio, television, newspapers and billboards. [. . .]

As far as Orkin's reputation in Canada is concerned the following matters may be noted. Canadians travelling in the United States are exposed to Orkin's extensive advertising and use of its trade marks in that country. There was evidence adduced that millions of Canadians travel in the United States every year, particularly in the southern vacation states, where Orkin's operations are extensive. Canadians in Canada are exposed to Orkin's advertising and articles appearing in American publications which circulate here. Examples of publications in which such articles and advertisements have appeared are: Fortune, 1952; Newsweek, 1964; Business Week, 1964; Time, 1964; United States News and World Report, 1964; Supermarket News, 1975, 1977 and 1978; and National Geographic, 1977.

Mr. Geiger estimated that over the past three or five years, thousands of Canadians have used Orkin services on a regular basis in connection with property owned or rented by them in the United States. Some of these received the bills for the service at their homes in Canada. Advertising material accompanied the bills.
[. . .]

Still concerned with principle and policy, the affected interests which must be considered are, in addition to the interests of Orkin in not having its reputation exposed to the risk resulting from Pestco's activities and in being able to use its trade name in Ontario, those of Pestco and the public in the absence of unreasonable restraints on freedom of trade, and the additional interest of the public not to be confused with respect to the source of the services which they buy. In the recent judgment of the Supreme Court of Canada in *Consumers Distributing Co. v. Seiko Time Can. Ltd.*[1984] 1 S.C.R. 583 at pp. 595 and 598, 10 D.L.R. (4th) 161 at pp. 171 and 173, 1 C.P.R. (3d) 1 at pp. 11 and 13, Estey J. said for the Court:

> The common law principles relating to commerce and trade generally proceed on the basis of a recognition of perceived benefits to the community from free and fair competition.
>
> . . . . .
>
> The role played by the tort of passing off in the common law has undoubtedly expanded to take into account the changing commercial realities in the present-day community. The simple wrong of selling one's goods deceitfully as those of another is not now the core of the action.

It is the protection of the community from the consequential damage of unfair competition or unfair trading.

Bearing in mind that Pestco has a virtually infinite range of names and symbols from which to choose, it is difficult to see the enjoining of it from using the name and logo of a well-established company in the same business as an unreasonable restraint on its freedom to carry on business as it sees fit. The public are entitled to be protected from such deliberate deception and Orkin, which has laboured long and hard and made substantial expenditures to create the reputation which it now has, which reputation has spread to Ontario, is entitled to the protection of its name from misappropriation. The spectre of Orkin having a monopoly in Ontario in its name and distinctive logo, even though it is not now carrying on business here, is considerably less troubling than the deceptive use of its name and symbol by another.
[. . .]

As far as freedom of trade and the reasonable expectations of business people are concerned, the interests of a dishonest defendant are entitled to less weight than those of a defendant who has acted in good faith. This has been recognized by the Supreme Court of the United States in the common law of unfair competition with respect to a use of the same trade mark as that of the plaintiff in an area remote from where the plaintiff carries on business. In *Hanover Star Milling Co. v. Metcalf* (1916), 240 U.S. 403, at p. 415, Mr. Justice Pitney said the following for the Court:

> In the ordinary case of parties competing under the same mark in the same market, it is correct to say that prior appropriation settles the question. But where two parties independently are employing the same mark upon goods of the same class, but in separate markets wholly remote the one from the other, the question of prior appropriation is legally insignificant, *unless at least, it appear that the second adopter has selected the mark with some design inimical to the interests of the first user, such as to take the benefit of the reputation of his goods, to forestall the extension of his trade, or the like.*

(Emphasis added in original)

In the later case of *United Drug Co. v. Theodore Rectanus Co.* (1918), 248 U.S. 90 at p. 100, Mr. Justice Pitney, once again for the Court, said:

> Undoubtedly, the general rule is that, as between conflicting claimants to the right to use the same mark, priority of appropriation determines the question. [Cases cited.] But the reason is that purchasers have come to understand the mark as indicating the origin of the wares, so that its use by a second producer amounts to an attempt to sell his goods as those of his competitor. The reason for the rule does not extend to a case where the same trade-mark happens to be employed simultaneously by two

manufacturers in different markets separate and remote from each other, so that the mark means one thing in one market, and an entirely different thing in another. It would be a perversion of the rule of priority to give it such an application in our broadly extended country that *an innocent party who had in good faith employed a trade-mark in one state*, and by the use of it had built up a trade there, being the first appropriator in that jurisdiction, might afterwards be prevented from using it, with consequent injury to his trade and good will at the instance of one who theretofore had employed the same mark, but only in other and remote jurisdictions, upon the ground that its first employment happened to antedate that of the first-mentioned trader.

(Emphasis added in original)

I need not, and do not, say that the defendant's bad faith alone will confer a cause of action on a foreign plaintiff . . . but it surely must be a relevant factor to take into account in adjusting competing interests. The significance of a defendant's state of mind has for some time been an important factor with respect to several different torts.
[. . .]

Trademark protection based upon reputation alone is in the interest of fairness to the trademark owner. It prohibits others from pirating well-known marks which have benefited from the creative efforts and financial nurturing of the trademark owner. Encouragement of international trade and the peaceful interaction between countries is a further benefit. Finally, protection serves the interests of consumers for it protects them against deception in the market place. More and more countries are recognizing the benefits of discouraging the growth of a local industry that relies upon the misappropriation of trademarks.
[. . .]

(Hoffman and Brownstone, "Protection of Trademark Rights Acquired by Intenrational Reputation without use or Registration," 71 The Trademark Reporter 1 at pp. 1-2 and 4 (1981).)
[. . .]

I now consider the facts of the present case in light of the principles I have discussed. Orkin concedes that the competing rights of the parties have to be determined as of 1967, when Pestco started using the Orkin name in Ontario, but submits that the trial judge's reference to the 'time of the commencement of this action' is an immaterial error because of the goodwill that Orkin has enjoyed in Ontario from at least 1967 to the present. [. . .] I accept 1967 as the time for determining the competing rights with respect to 'Orkin Exterminating Company' and 'Orkin' and 1976 with respect to the logo.

In 1967 Orkin's reputation in Ontario, based on its customers in Ontario and advertising of various kinds was, in the circumstances, of sufficient strength to make Orkin's rights superior to those of Pestco. Its reputation has grown steadily since 1967.

What are the circumstances? A very cogent circumstance is Pestco's decision in 1967 to use the Orkin name in Ontario. This is evidence from which it may be inferred that the name Orkin had commercial value at that time in Ontario and is a circumstance that has been observed in several cases to be an important indication of goodwill in a 'foreign' territory: see [. . .] *Restatement of the Law of Torts*, Tentative Draft No. 8 (1963), at p. 113: 'If he imitates the other's trademark or tradename knowingly and acts in other ways to convey the impression that his business is associated with the other, the inference may reasonably be drawn that there are prospective customers to be misled.'

Related to the foregoing is the evidence of the telephone calls that came in on Pestco's Orkin line. There may not have been many of them but they were steady. There is a reasonable basis for inferring that these calls came from Ontario customers who knew the plaintiff and thought they were calling the plaintiff. I say this because, since Pestco has never advertised or otherwise publicly used the name Orkin Exterminating Company, the only way in which a customer would have been attracted to Pestco under this name would have been to look up the name in the telephone directory. The use of the name in the white pages of the directory requires prior knowledge and familiarity with the name so that it could be located alphabetically. This prior knowledge could only have resulted from Orkin's reputation and goodwill previously imbued in the mind of the customer. The alphabetical location of the name in the yellow pages, in the years that it did appear there, would most likely have been used mainly by people with some prior knowledge of Orkin.

There was no noticeable drop in the number of calls for Orkin received by Pestco during the seven-year period from 1970 to 1976 when there was no yellow page listing of Orkin by Pestco. [. . .] The only way that a customer could have called Pestco during this period would have been to look up the name Orkin Exterminating Company alphabetically in the white pages which, as I have indicated, would have required a prior knowledge of Orkin and sufficient goodwill to attract the customer.
[. . .]

In the light of all these considerations, I am satisfied that from the beginning of its 'use' of Orkin in 1967 Pestco acquired no rights against Orkin and that in 1967 Orkin, if it had known of the misappropriation, could have obtained an injunction against Pestco to protect its rights in Ontario. Orkin's rights, because of its steadily increasing reputation in Ontario, were even more solidly based in 1976 when Pestco began to use the Orkin logo.

One of the determining factors seems to have been the clear attempt to misappropriate the goodwill Orkin had among Canadian customers. There was no other plausible explanation as to why the defendant could have listed its services under that name. The defendant obviously believed that Orkin had goodwill in Canada and its increase in sales seemed to justify the claim. Interestingly, the court's findings do not rely on the *Trade-marks Act* and are, as was mentioned above, largely based on U.S. cases.

A similar set of findings was made in *Hilton Hotels Corp. v. Belkin*,[42] in respect of the HILTON mark before there were any hotels operating under that trade-mark in Canada. In the case of *Coin Stars Ltd. v. K.K. Court Chili & Pepper Restaurant Ltd.*,[43] a British Columbia court issued an injunction against a Vancouver restaurant because the targeted clientele could confuse the restaurant with a Hong Kong-based establishment. The Court stated:

> The plaintiff, Coin Stars Limited ('Coin Stars') operates a restaurant under the Chinese name and trade mark pronounced KIN KWAN KOK, and the English name and trade mark PEP 'N CHILLI. The English name and the Chinese name bear no relationship to one another. Coin Stars, a Hong Kong company, is the owner and operator of two restaurants — one which it has operated in Hong Kong since 1981, the other which it has operated in Macau since 1989. Both the Chinese name and the English name are used in association with both restaurants.
>
> On June 6, 1990, Coin Stars licensed the British Columbia company, Pep 'N Chilli Restaurant Ltd. ('Pep 'N Chilli') the exclusive use of the Chinese name, the English name and a particular logo in Canada. Pep 'N Chilli licensed the marks for the purpose of opening and operating a Pep 'N Chilli restaurant in Vancouver. Pep 'N Chilli has applied to register the English name and the Chinese name in the name of Coin Stars and to register Pep 'N Chilli Restaurant Ltd. as the registered user of these trade-marks in the Canadian Trade-Marks Office.
>
> [. . .]
>
> The plaintiffs have presented a vast array of tourist guidebooks, trade-magazine publications, and various affidavits which support the conclusion that the Hong Kong restaurant, in particular, is a restaurant which has gained an international reputation as a fine dining establishment. It is one of the more popular restaurants in Hong Kong, specializing in Szechuan style cuisine. It caters to expa-

---

[42] (1955), 17 W.W.R. 86, 24 C.P.R. 100 (B.C. S.C.). See also *Sund v. Beachcombers Restaurant Ltd.* (1961), 27 D.L.R. (2d) 434, 36 C.P.R. 2 (B.C. C.A.), leave to appeal refused (1962), 21 Fox Pat. C. 119 (S.C.C.).

[43] (1990), [1990] B.C.J. No. 1622, 50 B.L.R. 306, 33 C.P.R. (3d) 186, 1990 CarswellBC 367 (B.C. S.C. [In Chambers]) [*Coin Stars* cited to C.P.R.].

triates, displays a particularly European atmosphere and is well-known for its superior service and lavish interior design.

[. . .]

I find that the plaintiffs' reputation or good-will goes far beyond mere knowledge of the restaurant in the minds of some travellers and recent Vancouver immigrants. Based on the affidavit evidence before me, I am satisfied there is strong evidence that the Coin Stars Hong Kong restaurant has developed a substantial reputation for fine dining which is associated or identified with the Chinese name and the English name. There is strong evidence that the Hong Kong restaurant is one which is well-known in Vancouver, either as a result of individuals from Hong Kong who have immigrated to Vancouver and settled here or as a result of business and tourist travel between the two cities. In either case, former residents of Hong Kong or travellers to Hong Kong have patronized the Hong Kong restaurant. They know the restaurant's reputation and associate the reputation with the Chinese name or the English name or both.

Statistically, the connection between Hong Kong and Vancouver is very strong. The plaintiff's affidavit material establishes that there is a great deal of travel and communication between the two cities. Canadians living in or visiting Hong Kong would be exposed to the plaintiff's advertising featuring the Chinese name and the English name and would be exposed to the reputation of the restaurant by word of mouth in Hong Kong. As the affidavits indicate, members of the Chinese community place great emphasis on restaurant dining. Quite apart from what a Canadian will learn reading tourist guides and trades magazines, he or she will learn a great deal of the reputation of the Hong Kong restaurant by word of mouth. Their knowledge of the Hong Kong restaurant will be passed on.

Finally, I find that the defendants' use of the Chinese name, a translation of the Chinese name, and the defendants' use of the words 'Chili & Pepper' — which are similar to the English name — is evidence from which I may infer that these trade names have commercial value in British Columbia. The defendant's use of these names is an important indication of the good-will which attaches to those names in British Columbia: *Orkin, supra.*

While the trade-marks have not yet been registered in Canada, I am satisfied that the plaintiffs have established a 'presence' within jurisdiction, in the sense considered by the Court in *Orkin.*

Well-known foreign marks can thus be protected as "marks made known" under the *Trade-marks Act,* assuming they meet the requirements laid down in s. 5, or under the tort of passing off as it was applied in *Orkin.* When well-known foreign marks not used in Canada are protected under the "marks made known" regime of the Act, apart from the different use requirement, the protection is subject to the same requirements as any other marks. In *United Artists Pictures Inc. v. Pink Panther Beauty Corp.*, the Federal Court of Appeal failed to find a likelihood of confusion between the Pink Panther character and PINK PANTHER shampoo.[44] Commenting on the protection of well-known marks, the Court wrote:

> This line of thinking is more fully developed in the *Seagram* case [(1990), 33 C.P.R. (3d) 454]. Seagram Real Estate Ltd. wished to register a trade-mark using that title along with a designed logo. The Trial Judge found that the various trade-marks registered by the opponent, the well-known liquor producer called Seagram's, all incorporating the word Seagram, were very famous. Nevertheless, this did not automatically result in protection of that mark over every conceivable field of activity. He stated:
>
>> In my view, unless in their over-all assessment I should conclude there is a likelihood of confusion, the appellants' marks are not entitled to extended protection simply because they have become well-known, indeed famous, in association with the manufacture and sale of alcoholic beverages.
>
> This conclusion is consonant with the overall purpose of the Act, which is to provide the registered owner of a trade-mark with its exclusive use in association with specified wares and services. We must remember that the registration of a trade-mark does not grant the registrant ownership of the words or images in that mark. The Trial Judge commented as well on the consideration to be given the nature of the wares involved. He stated:
>
>> Under the *Trade-marks Act* the correspondence of the classes of goods or services in association with which the disputed trade mark is used is no longer the vital question it once was. It is one of the matters to be taken into consideration with the other factors set out in s. 6. Nevertheless, some regard must be had to the class of goods or services to which the mark is applied, and it is still pertinent whether the goods are cheap or expensive and whether they are purchased quickly or after careful consideration.
>
> In the final analysis, the trade-marks were not found to be confusing, despite the fame of the registered mark. Much of the reasoning was based on the wide divergence of the types of wares involved — alcoholic beverages on one side

---

[44] *Supra*, note 25. On famous marks, see also *Veuve Clicquot Ponsardin c. Boutiques Cliquot Ltée*, 2004 FCA 164, (2004) 35 C.P.R. (4th) 1 (F.C.A.), leave to appeal allowed (2004), 35 C.P.R. (4th) vi (S.C.C.), which will be heard by the Supreme Court of Canada in October 2005. The case in part involves whether and how future plans are relevant to determining a likelihood of confusion, and the Supreme Court's decision may affect how famous marks are recognized in Canada.

and real estate on the other. It was not likely that a consumer would confuse the manufacturer of alcoholic products as being the same person involved in the real estate business.

This Court has recently reviewed the law relating to confusing trade-marks in *Miss Universe Inc. v. Bohna* [(1994), 58 C.P.R. (3d) 381 (Fed. C.A.)]. In that case the respondent had tried to register the mark 'Miss Nude Universe' for use in association with, *inter alia*, beauty pageant services. The appellant opposed the registration on the grounds that it was confusing with its own mark 'Miss Universe', used in association with an internationally renowned beauty contest. The Trial Judge [[1992] 3 F.C. 682] had found that the services were dissimilar enough to make confusion unlikely. Décary J.A., speaking for the Court, found that the Trial Judge had erred in not recognizing the scope of protection that should be accorded to the appellant's mark. Because of the wide scope of protection given to strong marks, he should have concentrated on the similarities in the services offered, and not on the differences. Justice Décary stated:

> The trial judge has erred, in my view, in ignoring the evidence that both trade-marks were used or to be used, respectively, in precisely the same industry or business and in concentrating rather on differences. . . .

The wide scope of protection afforded by the fame of the appellant's mark only becomes relevant when applying it to a connection between the applicant's and the opponent's trade and services. No matter how famous a mark is, it cannot be used to create a connection that does not exist.
[. . .]

The marks, while not identical, are very similar. The appellant submitted that the absence of the definite article in the mark 'Pink Panther' designated a panther that is pink, as opposed to the respondent's mark which refers to a particular pink panther, the one associated with the series of movies. While certainly not a major factor, this matter must be taken into account.

The trade-mark owned by United Artists is clearly a famous and inherently distinct one. It has been in use in Canada for thirty or more years. While this may not be a very long time, it cannot be denied that it is a longer time than the mark proposed by the appellant, which has not been used at all.

The Trial Judge's conclusions with respect to the differences in nature of the wares and the nature of the trade are accurate. He found both of these to be quite dissimilar. I agree, but I would underscore the differences to a greater extent. In my view, the Trial Judge has erred in finding that the factors were fairly balanced between the respondent and the appellant, and in finding in favour of United Artists by virtue of the fame of their mark. There is no doubt that 'The Pink Panther' is a famous and strong trade-mark. If it does not have inherent distinctiveness, then it certainly has acquired a great deal of distinctiveness in the thirty years or so that it has been part of popular culture. However, the issue to be decided is not how famous the mark is, but whether there is a likelihood of confusion in the mind of the average consumer between United Artists' mark and the one proposed by the appellant with respect to the goods and services specified. That question must be answered in the negative. There is no likelihood of confusion as to the source of the products. The key factor here is the gaping divergence in the nature of the wares and in the nature of the trade. It is not a fissure but a chasm.

United Artists produces movies. It does not manufacture or distribute beauty products. United Artists' products are not likely to be made available in the same places of trade as the appellant's products. Shampoo is not sold in movie theatres or video stores. Videos are not available in beauty parlours. These are facts recognized by the Trial Judge, but they bear emphasizing. What the Trial Judge did not give sufficient weight to is that, not only were the wares in each case completely disparate, but there is no connection whatsoever between them. As I stated earlier, where no such connection exists a finding of confusion will be rare.

One wonders whether a trip to the Disney Store might change the Court's mind! Yet here we see the necessity for the plaintiff to show not only that it owns a trade-mark but that there is actual or potential consumer confusion. Even owners of well-known marks must be able to show to the court's satisfaction that at least a significant likelihood of confusion exists. Given current marketing practices, such as the increasing use of character merchandising on a broader range of goods outside the typical entertainment field, consumers may come to expect (or at least not be surprised) that a single company will be selling disparate products (like shampoo and movies) and the likelihood of confusion when similar marks are used on different products may increase.

## 5. Official Marks

Official marks are also protected under the *Trade-marks Act*, but are not subject to the standard procedures required to register trade-marks. The objective of the official marks scheme is to identify the official mark (for example, a badge or crest) with a single institution, so as to avoid the public confusion that might result if those marks are used by other groups (which might misleadingly suggest official endorsement), and to prevent people from commercially exploiting public symbols by appropriating the esteem and respect in those official marks for their own profits. The term "official mark" may be misleading. It is not limited to marks used by institutions such as universities, governments, and the military. Canada's official marks system differs from many other jurisdictions in extending also to marks used by a "public authority," which in practice is a term of wide application.

Official marks are "adopted" rather than "registered" and are not subject to an examination process. Upon request from a "public authority," the Registrar of Trade-Marks simply "gives public notice" of the adoption and use of such a mark. Publication gives notice to the public of the official mark but there is no opportunity for opposition, although official marks can be challenged in court. The bars that apply to *registering* a trade-mark (*e.g.*, s. 12's bar against clearly descriptive or confusing marks) do not apply to the process of *adopting* official marks. Once an entity is recognized as a "public authority" by the Registrar, there are virtually no limits on the official marks that can be subject to a public notice and in which the entity will then have exclusive rights.[45] A public authority, for example, can adopt an official mark that is confusingly similar to a trade-mark that is already registered. Official marks are not limited to use of the mark in association with designated wares or services, but are instead rights in the official mark itself. Official marks are perpetual: there are no time limits or fees for renewal, and there are no provisions for removing unused or indistinctive official marks.

Once the notice is given, it becomes impossible for others to "adopt" and use that mark (for any purpose) or any mark so nearly resembling it as to be likely to be mistaken therefore.[46] Because the term "adopt" is used in s. 9, any person who had used or registered a mark prior to the public notice of adoption and use of an official mark may continue to use it.[47] In effect, a trade-mark owner who has a registered mark that resembles an official mark effectively has his rights frozen at the time of publication of the official

---

[45] See *Assn. of Architects (Ontario) v. Assn. of Architectural Technologists (Ontario)* (2002), (sub nom. *Ontario Assn. of Architects v. Assn. of Architectural Technologists of Ontario*) 19 C.P.R. (4th) 417 (Fed. C.A.), leave to appeal refused (2003), 23 C.P.R. (4th) vii (S.C.C.); Colin P. McDonald "Official Marks: Are There Any Limits to This Branding Power" (2004), 17 I.P.J. 83.

[46] See s. 9(1)(n)(iii) of the Act, *supra*, note 1. In *Canadian Rehabilitation Council for the Disabled DBA Easter Seals/March of Dimes National Council v. Rehabilitation Foundation for the Disabled DBA Ontario March of Dimes*, (2004) 35 C.P.R. (4th) 270 (F.C.), 2004 FC 1357, the Federal Court ruled that a licensee using an official mark under licence from another public authority does not constitute adoption and use of the official mark by the licensee for purposes of s. 9(1)(n)(iii).

[47] See *Canadian Olympic Assn. v. Allied Corp.* (1989), (sub nom. *Assoc. Olympique Canadienne v. Allied Corp.*) [1990] 1 F.C. 769, 28 C.P.R. (3d) 161, 105 N.R. 388, 26 C.I.P.R. 157 (Fed. C.A.), affirming (1987), [1987] F.C.J. No. 532, 16 C.P.R. (3d) 80, 13 F.T.R. 93, 14 C.I.P.R. 126, 1987 CarswellNat 662 (Fed. T.D.) [*Allied Corp*].

mark: prior use of the registered mark can continue but cannot be extended.[48] An official mark will also prevail over a pending application to register a mark. Once the Registrar gives notice of the adoption and use of an official mark, no one else can register that mark.

In *Canadian Olympic Assn. v. Allied Corp.*, the court reviewed the governing principles around ss. 9 and 12 of the Act.[49] The question was whether an applicant could register the mark "Olympian." Public notice that the Canadian Olympic Association would be using the same mark as an official mark came after the applicant had already adopted, but not yet registered, the mark. The court ruled that s. 9 prohibited the registration of the mark:

> Section 9 of the *Act* as a whole deals with adoption, and the prohibition against adoption is in the future tense ('No person shall adopt'). Subparagraph 9(1)(n)(iii) therefore forbids the adoption of a trade mark 'so nearly resembling as to be likely to be mistaken for' a mark adopted by a public authority in respect of which the Registrar 'has . . . given' (past tense) public notice. Consequently, it does not retroactively prohibit the adoption of marks. It is only prospective in operation.

> I do not see that this interpretation is affected by s. 11, since that provision forbids only use of a mark adopted contrary to s. 9. A mark adopted before the giving of public notice would not be adopted contrary to s. 9.

> Section 12 of the *Act*, dealing with registration, speaks in the present tense ('a mark of which the adoption is prohibited by section 9'). It therefore renders unregistrable a not yet registered mark, the adoption of which would now run afoul of s. 9, even if that mark had been adopted and used prior to the giving of public notice under s. 9.

---

[48] See, for example, *Royal Roads University v. R.* (2003), 27 C.P.R. (4th) 240 (F.C.). Royal Roads University and Canada Investment and Savings (a Crown agency) were both using the slogan "You Can Get There From Here" in their respective advertising campaigns. In sequence, Royal Roads adopted and used the mark, the Crown agency used the slogan, and then the Registrar gave notice of the university's adoption of the slogan as an official mark. MacKay J. ruled that the Crown agency's use of the slogan could continue because it preceded the Registrar's notice under s. 9 of the university's adoption of that slogan as an official mark.

[49] *Supra*, note 47. See also *Assn. of Architects (Ontario) v. Assn. of Architectural Technologists (Ontario)* (2002), (sub nom. *Ontario Assn. of Architects v. Assn. of Architectural Technologists of Ontario*) 19 C.P.R. (4th) 417 (Fed. C.A.), leave to appeal refused (2003), 23 C.P.R. (4th) vii (S.C.C.).

In sum, the formulas of the adoption and registration provisions are not parallel. Whatever rights to the use of a mark may flow from its adoption are undisturbed by the subsequent adoption and use of a confusingly similar official mark; the right to register the mark is, however, prohibited from the time of the giving of the public notice.

However, since what is at issue in the case at Bar is not the continued use by the appellant of its trade mark but rather its registration, it is clear from what I have said that it cannot now register the mark. In other words, since its adoption would not be possible now (not since March 5, 1980), its adoption may be said to be now prohibited by s. 9, and thus it falls under the interdiction of s. 12 as to registration.

The expression "public authority" is not defined in the Act. Based on available jurisprudence, a public authority can be defined as a person or administrative body entrusted with functions to perform for the benefit of the public, with a significant degree of governmental control, and operating for the public benefit, not for its private profit. A "public authority," however, can use an official mark for non-profit as well as commercial purposes.

The Canadian Olympic Association was found to be such a "public authority":

> The appellant's public character is manifest. What it does is done, not for the profit of its members, but entirely for the benefit of Canada and Canadians in response to generally recognized national needs. It is accepted, by the Canadian community, as the entity having the exclusive right to do a number of those things in and in relation to Canada and Canadians. It has been accorded, by its incorporation, the power necessary to do those things. By accepting the appellant's self-proclaimed exclusive role, the Canadian community has entrusted the appellant with functions to perform for the public's benefit as effectively as if by legislative mandate.
>
> In reaching the conclusion that the appellant is a public authority within the contemplation of subpara. 9(1)(n)(iii) of the *Trade Marks Act*, I do not regard the stated objects in the letters patent as determining the issue except to the extent that they are public, not private, objects. If it were otherwise, the appellant would fail at that hurdle. What is crucial is that the appellant does, in fact, pursue those objects; that the Canadian community wants them pursued; that the appellant is, in fact, the only entity exercising the power to pursue them and is accepted by the community as exercising that power as of right.[50]

---

[50] *Canadian Olympic Assn. v. Canada (Registrar of Trade Marks)* (1981), [1982] 2 F.C. 274, 59 C.P.R. (2d) 53 (Fed. T.D.), affirmed (1982), [1983] 1 F.C. 692, 139 D.L.R. (3d) 190, 67 C.P.R. (2d) 59 (Fed. C.A.) [*Canadian Olympic* cited to

By contrast, the Federal Court of Appeal recently held that a charity's mere compliance with the laws that generally govern charities is not enough governmental control to make that charity a "public authority."[51]

Canadian law also includes a concept of "national trade-mark" for legends and symbols used in the agri-food industry. The relevant provisions are in the *Canada Agricultural Products Act* [*CAPA*] and *Meat Inspection Act*.[52] The concept of a "national trade-mark" is not defined or referenced in the *Trade-marks Act*, however, and its possible overlap with official marks is not clearly delineated. It has never been examined in any reported Canadian court decision. While the two statutes concerned similarly provide for an exclusive right to "use," the rights in such marks do not stem from the *Trade-marks Act* (though the definition of "use" in the *Trade-marks Act* could serve as a guide). The scope of the rights, which are vested in the Crown, is defined in the two Acts concerned. Article 16 of *CAPA*[53] makes it illegal to

*a)*     apply or use a legend, word, mark, symbol or design or any combination thereof that resembles an agricultural product legend or a grade name; or

*(b)*     market, or possess for the purpose of marketing, an agricultural product to which there is applied or in connection with which there is used a legend, word, mark, symbol or design or any combination thereof that resembles an agricultural product legend or a grade name.

---

F.C.]. See also *Insurance Corp. of British Columbia v. Canada (Registrar of Trade Marks)* (1979), 44 C.P.R. (2d) 1 (Fed. T.D.), 13.

[51] *Canadian Jewish Congress v. Chosen People Ministries Inc.* (2003), [2003] F.C.J. No. 980, 231 D.L.R. (4th) 309, 27 C.P.R. (4th) 193, 2003 CarswellNat 1881 (Fed. C.A.). In other recent decisions on the interpretation of public authorities, the Federal Court held in *Canadian Post Corp. v. Post Office* (2000), [2001] 2 F.C. 63, 8 C.P.R. (4th) 289 (Fed. T.D.), that "public authority" is not restricted to Canadian public authorities, and in *College of Chiropodists (Ontario) v. Canadian Podiatric Medical Assn.*, 2004 FC 1774, (2004) 248 D.L.R. (4th) 277, 37 C.P.R. (4th) 219 (F.C.), that a professional association serving member interests and not acting as a regulatory body was not under governmental control and was not a "public authority."

[52] *Canada Agricultural Products Act*, R.S.C. 1985, c. C-0.4, s. 15, online: Department of Justice Canada <http://laws.justice.gc.ca/en/c-0.4/text.html> [*CAPA*] and *Meat Inspection Act*, R.S.C. 1985, c. M.3.2, s. 4, online: Department of Justice Canada <http://laws.justice.gc.ca/en/m-3.2/text.html>.

[53] See also s. 5 of the *Meat Inspection Act*.

## 6. Clearly Descriptive Trade-Marks

## (a) General

A trade-mark that gives a clear, or a deceptively misleading, description of the product or service cannot be registered per s. 12(1)(b) of the Act until and unless it becomes distinctive:

12. (1) Subject to section 13, a trade-mark is registrable if it is not

a)    [. . .]
b)    whether depicted, written or sounded, either clearly descriptive or deceptively misdescriptive in the English or French language of the character or quality of the wares or services in association with which it is used or proposed to be used or of the conditions of or the persons employed in their production or of their place of origin;
c)    [. . .]

Registrability is also subject to the narrower prohibition contained in s. 10. Section 10 prohibits the adoption or use (see the Use of a Trade-mark Section) of a trade-mark that, by ordinary and *bona fide* commercial usage becomes recognized in Canada as designating the "*kind, quality, quantity, destination, value, place of origin or date of production* of any wares or services," "in association with such wares or services or others of the same general class or use *in a way likely to mislead*, nor shall any person so adopt or so use any mark so nearly resembling that mark as to be likely to be mistaken therefore."[54]

However, a trade-mark that may give a strong indication or first impression of the product or service can be protected and registered. Merely suggestive trade-marks can be registered but clearly descriptive trade-marks cannot (unless they meet the requirements of s. 12(2)). When is a mark more than suggestive to the point of becoming "clearly descriptive"? The name of the product or service, for example, CAR for a car or BANK for banking services) is clearly descriptive, but so too are several other types of marks.

In a 1986 decision, the Chairman of the Trade-Marks Opposition Board had to decide whether the mark SELECTION was valid for wines.[55] He first considered the meaning of the term in various dictionaries:

---

[54] See s. 12(2) and the Secondary Meaning Section below. See also the Prohibited or Invalid Trade-Marks Section.

[55] *Rideout Wines Ltée v. Vins Brights Ltée* (1986), [1986] T.M.O.B. No. 243, 10 C.I.P.R. 254, 1986 CarswellNat 552 (T.M. Opp. Bd.) [*Rideout Wines* cited to C.I.P.R.].

[T]he word 'selection' appears to have two related principal meanings, these being the act, instance or process of selecting or choosing, or the fact or state of being selected or chosen. As what appears to be more of a secondary meaning, the word 'selection' is defined as a thing or group of things which has been selected or chosen with care. In my view, it is the latter meaning of the word 'selection' which arguably conveys the impression that something is superior in some way or other to those which have not been selected or chosen.

He then proceeded to apply the proper test, namely the first impression on a prospective buyer:

Having regard to the above, the issue is whether the average purchaser of Selection wines would, as a matter of immediate impression, be led to believe that the wines are superior or better relative either to other wines of the applicant or to wines of other companies. In this regard, it is the immediate impression created by the trade mark which must be considered and not the impression which one might have if one's mind dwells at length on the meaning of the trade mark in order to ascertain if the mark suggests a possible reference to quality: see *Charles Yeates & Co. v. Independent Grocers Alliance Distributing Co.*, (1962), 37 C.P.R. 173 at pp. 183-84, [1962] Ex. C.R. 36, 1 Fox Pat. C. 188 at p. 198. Further, it should be noted that certain words may be laudatory in relation to certain wares but not in relation to others as in *Henry Thorne & Co. v. Sandow Ltd.* (1912), 29 R.P.C. 440, where the Court concluded that the trade mark HEALTH as applied to 'cocoa' was a laudatory epithet and ought to be removed from the Register of Trade Marks.

I am of the opinion that many purchasers of wine when first encountering the trade mark SELECTION would not, as a matter of first impression, perceive the trade mark as having any reference whatsoever to the character or quality of the wine. Nevertheless, given the fact that the noun 'selection' does not posses a wide variety of meaning, I consider it equally likely that many purchasers of wine would immediately react to the applicant's trade mark SELECTION by believing that the wine had been selected by the applicant from amongst its wines as being one which is of superior quality.

As there is no evidence before me from which I could conclude that only a relatively small proportion of those purchasers of the applicant's wares would perceive the trade mark SELECTION as having a laudatory connotation, and bearing in mind that the legal burden is upon the applicant to establish the registrability of its trade mark, I have concluded that the trade mark SELECTION possesses a laudatory connotation and thereby signifies an enhancement of the character or quality of the applicant's wine and, as a consequence, is clearly descriptive or deceptively misdescriptive of the character or quality of the wares within the scope of s. 12(1)(*b*) of the *Trade Marks Act*.

The first impression of a hypothetical purchaser test is sometimes difficult to apply, especially when lawyers argue for hours or even days about what a consumer's first impression would be. The test is also flexible, as the buyer of a bottle of shampoo's first impression before buying one product rather than another may last only a second or two, while the first impression of the buyer of a car may be a somewhat "longer" one, due to the time usually spent making a purchase. But even then, courts do not presume that the average consumer is going to spend days parsing the exact meaning of a mark. If the mark gives a wrong description likely to deceive, it cannot be registered under s. 12(1)(b), subject to s. 12(2). If it is clearly descriptive, then it is improper for the manufacturer or distributor or other user of the mark, as the case may be, to have a monopoly on a word that clearly describes the product or service, unfair both towards consumers and competitors. Quite logically, and for the same reason, when a mark that was otherwise not clearly descriptive becomes a common word to describe a product or service it loses its distinctiveness (see the Loss of Distinctiveness Section).

In another decision,[56] the Trade-mark Opposition Board[57] explained the difference between clearly descriptive marks, which may be registered in certain cases after they have become distinctive, and inherently distinctive marks as follows:

> As the [Federal] Court of Appeal wrote in *AstraZeneca AB v. Novopharm Ltd.*, 2003 FCA 57 at paragraph 16:
>
>> [. . .] A mark actually distinguishes by acquiring distinctiveness through use, resulting in distinctiveness in fact. A mark that is 'adapted so to distinguish' is one that does not depend upon use for its distinctiveness because it is inherently distinctive. A coined or invented word mark falls into this category: *Standard Coil Products (Canada) Ltd. v. Standard Radio Corp.* , [1971] F.C. 106 (T.D.), at 115; *The Molson Companies Limited v. Carling O'Keefe Breweries of Canada Limited*, [1982] 1 F.C. 175 (T.D.), at 278-79.
>
> Principles to be applied when considering this issue are:
>
> 1.   The trade-mark applicant must satisfy the tripartite test enunciated in *Phillip Morris v. Imperial Tobacco Ltd.* (1985), 7 C.P.R. (3ᵈ) 254 (F.C.T.D.) at page 270. See: *AstraZeneca v. Novopharm, supra* at paragraph 19. The third part of the tripartite test requires that the association

---

[56] *Apotex Inc. v. Astra Aktiebolag* (2004), [2002] T.M.O.B. No. 115, 2004 CarswellNat 2239 (T.M. Opp. Bd.).

[57] See the Registration section.

between the mark and the product enables the owner of the mark to distinguish his product from that of others.

2.    Colour alone has not been viewed as being inherently distinctive. See: *AstraZeneca v. Novopharm*, at paragraph 18.

3.    Proof of actual distinguishment is not an easy burden to discharge. See: *AstraZeneca v. Novopharm*, at paragraph 20.

4.    Where the active ingredient in the pharmaceutical product is not claimed as the trade-mark, and the trade-mark sought to be registered is the colour and shape of the tablet, the applicant must show that the colour and shape distinguishes the tablet from the tablets of other manufacturers. See: *AstraZeneca v. Novopharm*, at paragraph 22.

5.    It is incumbent on the trade-mark applicant to show that physicians, pharmacists or patients can and do use the proposed trade-mark in choosing whether to prescribe, dispense or request the product. See: *Novopharm Ltd. v. Astra Aktiebolag* (2000), 6 C.P.R. (4th) 16 (F.C.T.D.); aff'd (2001) 15 C.P.R. (4th) 327 (F.C.A.).

6.    It is not fatal to an application that consumers may also use means other than the mark for identifying the product with a single source. As Mr. Justice Evans, as he then was, wrote in *Novopharm Ltd. v. Bayer Inc.* (1999), 3 C.P.R. (4th) 305 at paragraph 79; aff'd (2000) 9 C.P.R. (4th) 304 (F.C.A.):

> [. . .] Thus, while pharmacists rely mainly on the brand name and other identifying indicia on the stock bottles and packaging containing the product, or the inscription on the tablets, which is not part of the mark, if there is evidence that to any significant degree they also recognized the product by its appearance (excluding the markings on the tablet because they are not part of the mark), this may be sufficient to establish the distinctiveness of the mark.

Theoretically, the concept of a "clearly descriptive trade-mark" is simple to understand: does the mark clearly describe the product or service? However, in practice the high volume of sometimes inconsistent cases on the difference between clearly descriptive and suggestive marks indicates that the distinction is blurred.

For instance, in *S.C. Johnson & Son Ltd.*,[58] the Supreme Court decided that the word OFF was descriptive of the bug repellent spray sold under that mark because "although the word 'off' is used elliptically with regard to a repellent, it describes the wares or their effect." In his reasoning, Pigeon J. said the following:

---

[58] *S.C. Johnson, supra*, note 9.

In the case of *Gen. Motors Corp. v. Bellows*, [[1949] S.C.R. 678], where this Court upheld the finding that the initial registration of the trade mark 'Frigidaire' was invalid because it was descriptive, Rand J. said (at pp. 688-689):

> . . . Mr. Robinson argued that 'Frigidaire' in this sense is not descriptive of the 'character' of the article, but I must say I can imagine no term more so. In our mastery of environment we have devoted a great deal of attention to foods, a most important treatment of which has been their preservation against high temperatures. What is the essence of the idea of a refrigerator?

> Unquestionably, that of cold air for preservation; not the precise mode of operation by which the conserving effect is achieved but the effect itself, which is the functional property of the article itself; all the rest is implied. The air must obviously be held within a container, but the result, however brought about, is what is looked at. If evidence of that were needed, it is furnished by the material filed in the case. Forty-five names are shown to have appeared in the trade of which the following are examples: 'Iced-Aire', 'Frigice', 'North-Eaire', 'Frostair', 'Airgard', 'Sanidaire', 'Coolair' and 'Friguator'. These indicate that both words of the combination have some degree of effectiveness, and that would seem to follow from their commonness. The claim goes apparently to the monopoly of the word 'aire'. The affidavit of Shannon asserts that the company has taken successful proceedings against the use of 'Ideal-Aire', 'Filtaire', 'Governaire'; and with a similar exclusiveness of adjectives signifying coldness in combinations, the company would have successfully withdrawn from use virtually the entire group of the most apt and descriptive words for this class of goods.

These observations apply with even greater force to Johnson's attempt to monopolize the word 'off' with reference to insect repellents. They did not start with 'BUGZOFF' to which someone else had already laid claim. They sought to appropriate the most meaningful part of that combination. Now that it has been abandoned by the firm which had registered it in 1946, they are trying to prevent the use of that same combination by a competitor selling the same product in different form, that is an impregnated cloth instead of a liquid, foam or aerosol. There is clearly no substantial difference between 'BUGZOFF' and respondent's 'Bugg Off', and insecticides cannot be considered as being in a different category of wares.

Out of the many trade mark cases denying valid registration by reason of the descriptive character of an elliptical expression, the following appear worthy of special mention:

In *Re Keystone Knitting Mills' Ld App.* [(1928), 45 R.P.C. 421 (C.A.)], 'Charm' disallowed for hosiery. '. . . one has to look at the word . . . , not in its strict grammatical significance, but as it would represent itself to the public at large . . .' (Per Lord Hanworth M.R. at p. 426).

In *Re Nat. Machinery Co.'s App.* [(1941), 58 R.P.C. 128 (C.A.)], 'Dex' rejected for bolts as meaning 'deck bolts'.

In *Re Minnesota Mining & Manufacturing. Co. App.* [(1948), 65 R.P.C. 229], (Jenkins J.) 'Scotchlite' disapproved for light-reflecting materials.

In *Re Cabin Crafts Inc.'s App.* [(1955), 72 R.P.C. 333], (Lloyd-Jacob J.) 'Needletuft' refused for knitted fabrics and carpets.

In *Re Colgate-Palmolive Coy.'s App.* [[1957] R.P.C. 25], (Lloyd-Jacob J.) 'Brisk' denied for dentifrices.

In *T.A.D. Avanti Inc. v. Phone-Mate, Inc.* [(1978), 199 U.S.P.Q. 648 (Cal. Dist. Court)], 'Vox' held descriptive in respect of telephone answering units as meaning 'voice actuated'.

Compare *S.C. Johnson* with *Imperial Tobacco Ltd. v. Rothmans, Benson & Hedges Inc.*, where the trade-marks CUSTOM CUT and COUPE MESURE used in association with tobacco products were not deemed clearly descriptive as a matter of first impression of the character or quality of the wares.[59]

Then, in *Canadian Parking Equipment v. Canada (Registrar of Trade Marks)*,[60] the court held that the name AUTOMATIC PARKING DEVICES OF CANADA was descriptive of the "parking devices" but not of the service, which was to "install the parking devices," and hence the court allowed the mark for "servicing of parking lot and access control equipment." A peculiar distinction was thus made on the basis that the name was clearly descriptive *of the product* but not of the *service* rendered by the company.

If that last case may seem odd, the comments of the judge in *Clarkson Gordon v. Canada (Registrar of Trade Marks)* may be more perplexing.[61] The Court had to decide whether the mark AUDITCOMPUTER was clearly

---

[59] (1992), [1992] F.C.J. No. 1032, 45 C.P.R. (3d) 354, 58 F.T.R. 106, 1992 CarswellNat 667 (Fed. T.D.), affirmed (1993), [1993] F.C.J. No. 1099, 51 C.P.R. (3d) 169, 159 N.R. 399, 1993 CarswellNat 1893 (Fed. C.A.) [*Imperial Tobacco* cited to C.P.R.].

[60] (1990), [1990] F.C.J. No. 1008, 34 C.P.R. (3d) 154, 39 F.T.R. 63, 1990 CarswellNat 834 (Fed. T.D.) [*Canadian Parking* cited to C.P.R.].

[61] (1985), [1985] F.C.J. No. 430, 5 C.P.R. (3d) 252, 5 C.I.P.R. 167, 1985 CarswellNat 544 (Fed. T.D.) [*Clarkson Gordon* cited to C.P.R.].

descriptive of "services of examining and testing bookkeeping records by computer and consulting with respect to such examination and testing."

> I cannot find that the word 'AuditComputer' has a clearly descriptive content. It is an awkward and cumbersome (and for that reason one wonders how effective as a trade mark) combination of two words. On first reading, the word appears to be meaningless. To the extent that it does signify anything, it would appear that it might describe a type of computer. Or it might describe a mechanism for verifying the accuracy or efficiency of the functioning of a computer or computer programs. But, the coined word does not clearly describe a 'computer-assisted audit'. This becomes obvious when one considers that to get from the prospective trade mark the meaning contended for, one has to separate the two words of which it is formed, reverse them and add a verb between.

> While I accept that coined words do not by that fact alone escape the requirements of s. 12(1)(b) of the *Trade Marks Act*, [. . .]it will always be more difficult to prove that such words are clearly descriptive of a character or quality of the product to which they relate than is the case with 'uncoined' words.

These decisions emphasize that a mark should be considered as a whole, rather than parsed and dissected. A mark must be considered in its totality. In the case of a composite mark, consisting of both word and design elements, the mark will not be registrable if the word elements are clearly descriptive under s. 12(1)(b) and the word elements are the dominant feature of the mark. Whether the word elements are "dominant" is assessed based on the first impression of a prospective consumer considering the visual impression of the mark in its totality.[62]

Commenting on *S.C. Johnson*, in *Professional Publishing Associates Ltd. v. Toronto Parent Magazine Inc.*,[63] Strayer J. found TODAY'S PARENT to be clearly descriptive of a parenting magazine:

> I am satisfied that the trademark TODAY'S PARENT is clearly descriptive of the character of the magazine on which it appears. Such a title, when used in association with a magazine, would surely convey to most readers or listeners the information that this is a magazine dealing with matters of interest to those who are currently and fairly regularly engaged in the responsibilities of parenthood. This would in turn imply that it is a magazine intended for parents of children below the age of majority. In my view this case is even clearer than the situation in *S.C. Johnson & Son Ltd et al. v. Marketing Int'l Ltd.*(1979), 44 C.P.R. (2d) 16, 105 D.L.R. (3d) 423, [1980] 1 S.C.R. 99, where the Supreme

---

[62] *Best Canadian Motor Inns Ltd. v. Best Western International Inc.*, (2004), [2004] 3 F.C.R. 114, 30 C.P.R. (4th) 481, 246 F.T.R. 113 (F.C.).

[63] (1986), [1986] F.C.J. No. 158, 9 C.P.R. (3d) 207, 8 F.T.R. 207, 1986 CarswellNat 863 (Fed. T.D.) [*Professional Publishing* cited to C.P.R.].

Court of Canada held that the word 'Off' used in connection with an insect repellant was descriptive of such wares. Counsel for the plaintiff relied strongly on *GWG Ltd. v. Canada (Registrar of Trade Marks)* (1981), 55 C.P.R. (2d) 1 (F.C.T.D.), where Cattanach, J., held that the word 'kidfitters' was not clearly descriptive of clothing for children. I reviewed that decision carefully and I am satisfied that it turned on the facts as found by the learned trial judge. He found an ambiguity in the term which did not make it 'clearly' descriptive. I can find no comparable ambiguity in the words 'Today's Parent' as applied to a magazine. The trademark was therefore not registrable.

In a split decision, the Federal Court of Appeal found the words CHILL-ABLE RED not to be descriptive of a wine.[64] The Court again distinguished *S.C. Johnson*, although this time on the basis that OFF was a common word and CHILLABLE was not.

The appellant's counsel submitted, however, that the decision of the Supreme Court of Canada in the case of *S.C. Johnson & Son Ltd. et al. v. Marketing International Ltd*, [[1980] 1 S.C.R. 99; (1979) 44 C.P.R. (2d) 16] has had the effect of rendering inoperative [. . .] earlier decisions of the Exchequer and Federal Courts. With respect, I do not agree with that submission. In the *S.C. Johnson* case *supra*, the Supreme Court held that the mark 'Off' was not registrable because it was an elliptical use of the word in association with an insect repellent and was descriptive of the wares or their effect. The Court held that in seeking to register the mark 'Off', the applicant was in effect claiming a monopoly of a common word of the language, a word commonly used in connection with a variety of wares in related categories all exhibiting the common purpose of getting rid of something. Pigeon J. writing the judgment of the Court enumerated a number of trade marks ending with 'Off' presently on the register to show the widespread use of the word in that sense. Mr. Justice Pigeon also referred to a number of dictionary meanings of the word 'Off'.

In my opinion, the factual differences which are readily apparent in the case at bar serve to distinguish it from the *S.C. Johnson* case *supra*. The word 'Chill-able' is not a common word of the language. Likewise, there is no suggestion that it forms a part of a number of registered trade marks so as to show widespread use. Accordingly, I have concluded that the *S.C. Johnson* decision does not alter the previous jurisprudence insofar as the particular facts of this case are concerned.

---

[64] *Jordan & Ste-Michelle Cellars Ltd. v. T.G. Bright & Co.*, [1984] 1 F.C. 964, 81 C.P.R. (2d) 103, 2 C.I.P.R. 45, 57 N.R. 214 (Fed. C.A.) [*Jordan & Ste-Michelle* cited to F.C.].

An example of a suggestive trade-mark can be found in *Reed Stenhouse Co. v. Canada (Registrar of Trade Marks).*[65] The court determined that the mark PET PLAN used as a comprehensive system of health insurance for domestic animals merely suggested that the product was associated with animals without stating what the link was. As noted above, a suggestive trade-mark can be registered. Another related example concerns the mark GRO-PUP for dog food which the Exchequer Court found suggestive but not clearly descriptive.[66] In its decision, the Court said the following:

> Is the word 'Gro-Pup' descriptive or misdescriptive of the character or quality of the wares, namely, dog food, in connection with which it is intended to be used? After giving the matter my best consideration and examining carefully the authorities referred to by counsel as well as others not cited, I have reached the conclusion that the word 'Gro-Pup' is not descriptive and that its registration as a trade mark is not excluded [. . .].

> [. . .]

> As I have said, I do not think that the word 'Gro-Pup' is descriptive of the article to which it is to be applied, namely, dog food; it is at the utmost suggestive of the result which it is liable to produce. The word, in my opinion, is registrable [. . .].

It is important to bear in mind when reviewing the cases that the prohibition contained in s. 12(1)(b) applies to marks that are "*clearly* descriptive or *deceptively* misdescriptive in the English or French language of the character or quality of the wares or services in association with which it is used or proposed to be used or of the conditions of or the persons employed in their production or of their place of origin." "Clearly" is "not a tautological use" in the statutory section and means "plain," "self-evident," and "easy to understand."[67] The terms "clearly descriptive" and "deceptively misdescriptive" refer to, among other characteristics, the character or quality of the services themselves. The test as to whether or not a proposed trade-mark is "clearly descriptive" is one of first impression; the first impression as determined by the court is that of a hypothetical prospective purchaser

---

[65] (1992), [1992] F.C.J. No. 887, 45 C.P.R. (3d) 79, (sub nom. *Reed Stenhouse Co. v. Registrar of Trademarks*) 57 F.T.R. 317, 1992 CarswellNat 711 (Fed. T.D.).

[66] *Kellogg Co. v. Canada (Registrar of Trade Marks)* (1939), [1940] Ex. C.R. 163, [1939] 3 D.L.R. 65 (Can. Ex. Ct.) [*Kellogg Co.* cited to Ex. C.R.].

[67] *Thomson Research Associates Ltd. v. Canada (Registrar of Trade Marks)* (1982), 67 C.P.R. (2d) 205 (Fed. T.D), affirmed (1983), 71 C.P.R. (2d) 287 (Fed. C.A.), per Mahoney J.; *Canadian Parking, supra* note 60; and *GWG Ltd. v. Canada (Registrar of Trade Marks)* (1981), 55 C.P.R. (2d) 1 (Fed. T.D.).

of wares or service.[68] The term "deceptively" was introduced when this prohibition was "moved" from s. 26(1)(c) of the *Unfair Competition Act* to the *Trade-marks Act*. This shift was discussed in *Atlantic Promotions Inc. v. Canada (Registrar of Trade Marks)*.[69] Cattanach J. explained it in the following manner:

> By virtue of paragraph 26(1)(c) of the *Unfair Competition Act* registration was prima facie, denied to word marks that 'were clearly descriptive or misdescriptive of the character or quality of the wares'. The adverb 'clearly' also modified the adjective 'misdescriptive'.
>
> In paragraph 12(1)(b) of the *Trade Marks Act* the word 'clearly' as modifying the word 'misdescriptive' has been replaced by the word 'deceptively' so that it now reads 'deceptively misdescriptive'.
>
> The change was deliberate.
>
> Many words may be 'clearly misdescriptive' of the wares with which they are used in association but are not necessarily 'deceptively misdescriptive'.
>
> In my view the proper test to be applied to the determination as to whether a trade mark in its entirety is deceptively misdescriptive must be whether the general public in Canada would be misled into the belief that the product with which the trade mark is associated had its origin in the place of a geographic name in the trade mark.
>
> Whether a trade mark is deceptively misdescriptive is as much a question of fact as is whether one trade mark is confusing with another.

The terms said to be clearly descriptive or deceptively misdescriptive must be in French or in English. In *Gula v. B. Manischewitz Co.*, the term TAM TAM was found to be descriptive in Yiddish (meaning "tasty"), but not in English or French.[70] However, the English or French languages under s. 12 are "considered in their entirety and not as including only the vocabulary in current use in this country, a vocabulary that is extremely difficult to define especially in these days when communication media are no longer confined within national boundaries," as Justice Pigeon stated in *Home Juice Co. v. Orange Maison Ltée*.[71]

The concept of limiting the scope of description to only French and English may seem outdated considering Canada's multicultural environ-

---

[68] *Clarkson Gordon, supra*, note 61.

[69] (1984), [1984] F.C.J. No. 606, 1984 CarswellNat 831 (Fed. T.D.).

[70] (1947), [1948] 4 D.L.R. 581, 8 C.P.R. 103 (S.C.C.).

[71] (1970), 1 C.P.R. (2d) 14 (S.C.C.), 16.

ment and the confusion that could come from other languages. Courts have on many occasions accepted arguments concerning confusion with well-known foreign marks, thus indicating a willingness to consider confusion in cultures and languages other than French or English (see the Well-known Marks Section). Yet, under the current wording of s. 12(1)(b), descriptiveness in languages other than the two official languages cannot be considered. This limitation with respect to French and English, however, does not apply to instances of descriptiveness contained in s. 10, or s. 10.1 with respect to certain names of varieties of plants. Nor does it apply to s. 12(1)(a). Nevertheless, in *Nishi v. Robert Morse Appliances Ltd.*,[72] the Federal Court did not accept evidence that NISHI is a Japanese surname, recognized as such by many Canadians:

> On the first ground raised, the registrar recognized that the trade mark sought to be registered was indeed Mr. Nishi's name. He acknowledged, however, that the word also meant 'west' in the Japanese language. On that point, the registrar took judicial notice that some Canadians would be fluent in the Japanese language and would recognize 'nishi' as meaning 'west'. The registrar emphasized that his principal role was to determine whether or not 'Nishi' was *primarily merely* a surname. The appellant's documentary evidence before the registrar of telephone directories containing entries of the surname Nishi did little to convince him of the proliferation of the surname in Canada. The registrar concluded that albeit a number of people in Vancouver *might* recognize 'Nishi' as a surname, the same could not be said of the majority of Canadians or even a majority of Canadians in a significant area such as British Columbia. Furthermore, he does not seem convinced that of those who would recognize the name, a greater number would identify it as a surname rather than the word meaning 'west'.

> The following is what the registrar had to say with regard to the above issue [at pp. 113-5]:

>> With respect to the opponent's first ground of opposition, the onus or legal burden is on the applicant to show that its applied for trade-mark is registrable. In considering this issue, I am guided by the decision of Mr. Justice Cattanach in *Gerhard Horn Investments Ltd. v. Registrar of Trade Marks* (1983), 73 C.P.R. (2d) 23 (F.C.T.D.). At page 30 of the reported reasons, Mr. Justice Cattanach states as follows:

>>> The first and foremost consideration is whether the word or words sought to be registered in the name is the name or surname of a living individual or an individual who has recently died.

---

[72] (1990), 34 C.P.R. (3d) 161 (Fed. T.D.).

Mr. Nishi's affidavit clearly satisfies that requirement.

The subsequent issue to decide is whether or not NISHI is *primarily* merely a surname. The applicant's evidence establishes that NISHI is a word in the Japanese language meaning 'west.' Thus, NISHI is not merely the surname of an individual. However, it is still necessary to determine whether or not NISHI is *primarily* merely a surname.
[. . .]

The opponent's evidence includes excerpts from telephone directories for a number of Canadian cities containing entries for the surname Nishi. Most of the listings (including those for such major Canadian cities as Montreal, Edmonton and Victoria) include only one entry for the surname Nishi. The Toronto directory has eleven such entries and the Vancouver directory has over seventy. Directories for other cities in British Columbia (including Victoria) contain only one or two entries each. The opponent also apparently seeks to rely on the Nishi affidavit to establish some measure of public recognition for Mr. Nishi. However, Mr. Nishi fails to evidence activities which indicate he has acquired any measure of fame in Canada.

The opponent submits that the foregoing establishes that the mark NISHI is precluded from registration by virtue of Section 12(1)(a) of the *Act*. In this regard, the opponent relies on the opposition decision in *Juneau v. Chutes Corporation* (1986), 11 C.P.R.(3d) 260. However, in that case, the Chairman of the Opposition Board found that the surname Juneau was not a rare surname in the Province of Quebec and went on to state at page 264 of the decision as follows:

> On the other hand, I would think that a majority of Canadians, and particularly those residing in the Province of Quebec, would immediately respond to the trade mark JUNEAU as having a surname significance as opposed to having any of the geographic significances put forward by the applicant.

By way of contrast, the opponent has only evidenced that Nishi is not a rare surname in Vancouver. The evidence strongly suggests that it is a rare surname elsewhere in Canada and, in particular, elsewhere in the Province of British Columbia.

Thus, it can be said that a number of people in Vancouver might recognize Nishi as a surname. But it cannot be said that a majority of Canadians, or even a majority of Canadians in a significant area of Canada (*e.g.* - British Columbia), would recognize Nishi as a surname.

It can also be said that some Canadians (although not many) would recognize 'nishi' as a Japanese word. But I am unable to say that the numbers of Canadians recognizing Nishi as a surname would be significantly greater than the numbers recognizing it as a Japanese word meaning 'west'. I therefore cannot conclude that NISHI is *primarily* merely a surname and the opponent's first ground is therefore unsuccessful.

A similar result was reached in *Standard Oil Co. v. Canada (Registrar of Trade Marks)* concerning FIOR as a proposed trade-mark for use on wares described as direct reduction iron ore.[73] The Registrar of Trade-marks had refused the application because FIOR appeared in Toronto and Montreal telephone directories as a surname and had no dictionary meaning. The court reasoned:

> The next stage in considering the problem of applying section 12(1)(a) to the word 'FIOR' is to consider whether 'FIOR' is 'primarily' the surname of a living person. (Note that the French version uses the word 'principalement' where the English version uses 'primarily'.) In other words, is the chief, main or principal character of 'FIOR' that of a surname or is it principally or equally a word invented to be used as a trade mark?

> Certainly, from the point of view of the people called 'Fior' and their immediate circle of friends and acquaintances, the answer is that 'Fior' is principally if not exclusively a surname, and from the point of view of the trade mark advisers of the appellant, the answer is that it is principally if not merely an invented word. The test, for the purposes of section 12(1)(a) is not, in my view, the reaction of either of these classes of persons. The test must be what, in the opinion of the respondent or the Court, as the case may be, would be the response of the general public of Canada to the word. My conclusion is that a person in Canada of ordinary intelligence and of ordinary education in English or French would be just as likely, if not more likely, to respond to the word by thinking of it as a brand or mark of some business as to respond to it by thinking of some family of people (that is, by thinking of it as being the surname of one or more individuals). Indeed, I doubt very much whether such a person would respond to the word by thinking of there being an individual having it as a surname at all.

> I am, therefore, of the view that it is probably not 'primarily' a word that is a surname of an individual at all, but it is certainly not primarily 'merely' such a word.

---

[73] [1968] 2 Ex. C.R. 523, 55 C.P.R. 49 (Can. Ex. Ct.). See also *Calona Wines Ltd. v. Canada (Registrar of Trade Marks)* (1977), [1978] 1 F.C. 591, 36 C.P.R. (2d) 193 (Fed. T.D.) (the mark was FONTANA); and *Galanos v. Canada (Registrar of Trade Marks)* (1982), 69 C.P.R. (2d) 144 (Fed. T.D.) (the mark was GALANOS).

I have probably been influenced in coming to the conclusion that I have expressed as to how the word 'primarily' in section 12(1)(a) should be applied by the fact that applying the provision solely by reference to the existence of a dictionary meaning of a proposed trade mark would make practically every invented word vulnerable to attack as a proposed trade mark by anyone assiduous enough to pursue his searches for its use as a surname somewhere in the world (or, indeed, in a country such as Canada even if the search were restricted to Canada). I cannot believe that section 12(1)(a) was intended virtually to eliminate the creation of new words for purposes of proposed trade marks. [footnotes omitted]

Can one question the court's interpretation? If the adverb "primarily" is comparative in nature, and thus could be said to refer to cases where a word is used as a surname compared to cases where the same word is used in a different context, then when the evidence shows that a name is mostly used as a surname, the standard of s. 12(1)(a) could be said to have been met. Indeed, "primarily" seems to refer to actual use, not the first impression of hypothetical buyers (which is the proper test under s. 12(1)(b)), who might think of the term as a mark. In fact, many surnames have become famous marks. Such a comparative use test was used in *Elder's Beverages (1975) Ltd. v. Canada (Registrar of Trade Marks).*[74] The Court stated:

Here it was established by the respondent, as he is entitled to so establish, that a search through the telephone directories of 21 major cities in Canada listed 354 persons bearing the surname 'ELDER'.

The word 'ELDER' is therefore a surname.

The appellant established that the word 'ELDER' has dictionary meanings, three of which predominate:

(1)    a low tree or shrub;
(2)    a) a parent, a forefather, a predecessor, one who is older, a senior (usually in the plural);
       b) a member of a senate, governing body or class consisting of men of venerable age (now chiefly historical), and
(3)    in the Presbyterian churches, one of a class of lay officers who, with the minister, compose the Session, and manage the church affairs.

I do not think that the term 'elder' is restricted to the Presbyterian church but is popularly adopted by churches of other denominations to describe lay officers.

---

[74] [1979] 2 F.C. 735, 44 C.P.R. (2d) 59 (Fed. T.D.) at paras. 27-33.

This being so the word 'ELDER' is not 'merely' a word that is a surname of an individual.

The question therefore narrows to whether it is 'primarily' such a word.

In my opinion *the two characters of the word 'ELDER', one as a surname and the other as a dictionary word, are each of substantial significance and therefore it cannot be said that the word is 'primarily' a surname.* [emphasis added]

As can be seen from the above, the cases that have interpreted the notion of descriptiveness are not always fully consistent with one another. What is certain is the floor for descriptiveness. The exact name of a product or service is obviously descriptive. Beyond that, the exact distinction between clearly descriptive and merely suggestive is fuzzy. If a mark has been in use for a considerable period of time and evidence can be provided to show that it accomplishes its function of distinguishing one company's wares or services from those of others, then it likely is only suggestive.

There are two different instances in which the descriptive character of a mark is relevant in the *Trade-marks Act*. Under s. 10, if a *mark* has *become* descriptive by ordinary and bona fide commercial usage of the kind, quality, quantity, destination (purpose), value, place of origin or date of production, then it cannot be adopted (by another person) or used (by anyone) in a way that is likely to mislead the public. In such a case, the public protection element of trade-mark law takes precedence over the protection of the mark's owner. This happens when the mental link associated with a mark is no longer tied to a particular source but to a *kind of* product or service. The prohibition under s. 10 cannot be cured, contrary to other forms of loss of distinctiveness. (See the eponym section below.)

Under s. 12, no one can register a mark that is clearly descriptive or deceptively misdescriptive in English or French. Temporally speaking, this is the converse of the s. 10 prohibition. The prohibition in section 10 applies to a mark that *has become* descriptive. Then both the adoption and any misleading use are prohibited. Section 12 prohibits only the registration (not the use) of a clearly descriptive (or deceptively misdescriptive) term; but if, through use, that term becomes associated with a particular source of products or services (*i.e.*, fulfills the function of a mark), then it will be registrable (s. 12(2)). It acquires "secondary meaning" (see the eponym section below).

## (b) Place of Origin

Under s. 12(1)(b), one of the ways in which a mark can be clearly descriptive or deceptively misdescriptive is with respect to the place of origin of the goods. In such a case, s. 10 may also apply (see the previous section on Descriptive Trade-marks, General).

The test is the first impression of the average consumer, in a category of consumers likely to purchase the product or service. There are relatively few cases where a court found a word to be clearly descriptive (or deceptively misdescriptive) of a place of origin. In *Dower Brothers Ltd. v. Canada (Registrar of Trade Marks)*, the Exchequer Court found that FRENCH, when used in conjunction with ROOM would not suggest a place of origin for shoes.[75] Similarly, in *Syndicat National de la Parfumerie Francaise v. Andrew Jergens Co.*, the Registrar of Trade-marks found that a perfume sold under the mark MEMORIES OF PARIS was not deceptively misdescriptive as to its place of origin even though it was not manufactured in France.[76] However, in a different case the words MONSIEUR DE PARIS were found to be deceptively misdescriptive as to the place of origin of perfumes, Paris having a well-known reputation as a source of perfumes.[77] Yet, in *Chocosuisse Union des Fabricants-Suisses de Chocolate v. Hiram Walker & Sons Ltd.*, the court found that the words SWISS CHOCOLATE created a first impression not of origin but of a type of chocolate.[78]

Contrast this with a case where a fairly liberal interpretation of the first impression test was used in *Cathay Restaurants Ltd. v. Chin*.[79] The Court concluded:

> The plaintiff submitted that the word CATHAY has no meaning today but I do not think that can be taken as a fact where the word undoubtedly has an ancient meaning and is used with that meaning in poetic works. Since it is the ancient name of China it must, I think, be taken as meaning China in the minds of the public at large. In a trade mark it thus connotes something more than other kinds of expressions which, even if suggestive of oriental character, have no meaning whatever, whether ancient or modern in either the English or the French language. In the trade mark CATHAY HOUSE, as applied to a restaurant and to the Chinese food sold or served there, it appears to me to proclaim and describe the Chinese character of the establishment and to be clearly

---

[75] [1940] Ex. C.R. 73, [1940] 2 D.L.R. 96 (Can. Ex. Ct.). Compare with *Institut National des Appellations d'Origine des Vins & Eaux-de-Vies v. T.G. Bright & Co.* (1985), 5 C.P.R. (3d) 454 (T.M. Opp. Bd,), affirmed (1986), (sub nom. *T.G. Bright & Co. v. Institut national des appellations d'origine des vins & eaux-de-vie*) 9 C.P.R. (3d) 239 (Fed. T.D.).

[76] (1970), 64 C.P.R. 286 (Reg. T.M.).

[77] *Syndicat National de la Parfumerie Francaise v. Laboratoire Jean-Pierre Ltée* (1977), 34 C.P.R. (2d) 272 (Reg. T.M.).

[78] (1983), 77 C.P.R. (2d) 246 (T.M. Opp. Bd.).

[79] (1966), [1968] 1 Ex. C.R. 3, 51 C.P.R. 160 (Can. Ex. Ct.) at para. 13 [*Cathay Restaurants* cited to Ex. C.R.].

descriptive of the Chinese character of the food and services in association
with which it is used.

There are also several cases concerning alcoholic beverages, and they
do not all seem easy to reconcile. In *Labatt Breweries of Canada Ltd. v.
Carling Breweries of Canada Ltd.*,[80] the Trade-Marks Office accepted an
opposition to the registration of HEIDELBERG for beer:

> The opponent raised as a ground of opposition that the mark HEIDELBERG
> was not registrable in association with alcoholic brewery beverages on the
> grounds that the mark was clearly descriptive in the English or French language
> of the place of origin of the wares. Notwithstanding this ground of opposition
> and the evidence filed by the opponent, the applicant did not file any evidence
> that the 'alcoholic brewery beverages, namely, beer, ale, lager, porter and stout'
> on which the mark HEIDELBERG is intended to be used in Canada are not
> brewed in Heidelberg, West Germany. There was no evidence by the applicant
> that the applicant intended to brew the wares in Canada. The applicant gave
> no reason why the mark HEIDELBERG was chosen as the trade mark for use
> in relation to the alcoholic brewery beverages which are the subject of this
> application.

> Although the application for the mark HEIDELBERG as applied to the wares,
> 'alcoholic brewery beverages, namely, beer, ale, lager, porter and stout' is
> based on proposed use, the applicant could reasonably be expected to know
> whether the brewery beverages that the applicant proposed to sell under that
> mark were to be produced in Canada or elsewhere.

> The opponent also raised as part of its grounds of opposition that if the mark
> HEIDELBERG was not clearly descriptive of the place of origin of the wares
> that the mark HEIDELBERG was deceptively misdescriptive of the place of
> origin of the wares. Assuming that the alcoholic brewery beverages to be sold
> under the mark HEIDELBERG are brewed and sold only in Canada is the mark
> HEIDELBERG deceptively misdescriptive in the English or French language
> of the place of origin of the wares. Different countries by reason of geography,
> soil, weather and expertise have become associated with various alcoholic
> products. Scotland is noted for scotch whiskey; Canada is noted for rye whis-
> key; France is noted for wines; Germany is noted for alcoholic brewery bev-
> erages. Use of the mark HEIDELBERG in association with alcoholic brewery
> beverages is likely to lead a person in Canada of ordinary intelligence and
> ordinary education in English or French to respond to the mark HEIDELBERG
> by thinking of it as a brand of alcoholic brewery beverage emanating from
> Germany, or Heidelberg in particular.

---

[80] (1974), 18 C.P.R. (2d) 33 (Reg. T.M.).

It is my finding, therefore, that the mark HEIDELBERG is prohibited from registration by s. 12(1)(b) as being either clearly descriptive or deceptively misdescriptive of the place of origin of the wares.

In another case,[81] the use of CASABLANCA for wines not originating from Morocco was found to be deceptively misdescriptive, as was the use of BRIGHTS FRENCH HOUSE for wines not originating in France.[82]

Compare these decisions with the case of *Der Stabilisierungsfonds für Wein v. T.G. Bright & Co.*:

> The opponent's first ground of opposition is that the applicant's trade mark is deceptively misdescriptive of the place of origin of the applicant's wines. In the recent decision *Les Promotions Atlantique Inc. v. Registrar of Trade Marks* (July 9, 1984, unreported, T-1971-03) Cattanach J. stated at p. 3 that 'the proper test to be applied to the determination of whether a trade mark in its entirety is deceptively misdescriptive must be whether the general public in Canada would be misled into the belief that the product with which the trade mark is associated had its origin in the place of a geographic name in the trade mark'. In my view, since the evidence in the present case does not establish that the general public is even aware that there are places in Germany called Oberhausen, it certainly cannot be concluded that the general public in Canada would be misled into the belief that wines associated with the applicant's trade mark OBERHAUS had their origin in the places in Germany called Oberhausen. On the basis of the evidence, I can only conclude that the average member of the general public or the average purchaser of wines would be likely, as a matter of first impression, to react to the mark OBERHAUS as simply being a coined and fanciful word. Accordingly, I reject the opponent's first ground of opposition.[83]

A similar result was reached in another case concerning the mark HOCHTALER for wines.[84]

While there may seem to be some discrepancies among these results, the answer depends in large part not on the test to be applied, which under s. 12(1)(b) is one of first impression, but on the facts of each case and the evidence presented to the Trade-Mark Office or the court by the parties. Evidence of a first impression is not always easy to adduce. In cases where an opposition is filed as to place of origin, the burden is to show not only a misdescriptive character but an element of consumer deception. Many of

---

[81] *T.G. Bright & Co. v. Canada (Registrar of Trade Marks)* (1985), 4 C.P.R. (3d) 64 (Fed. T.D.).

[82] *Institut National des Appellations d'Origine des Vins & Eaux-de-Vie v. T.G. Bright & Co., supra*, note 75.

[83] (1985), 4 C.P.R. (3d) 526 (T.M. Opp. Bd.).

[84] *Der Stabilisierungsfonds für Wein v. Andres Wines Ltd.* (1985), 5 C.P.R. (3d) 256 (T.M. Opp. Bd.).

the apparent differences among the cases reflect the nature of the evidence introduced in support of the opposition.

It is important to note that s. 12(1)(b) is a bar to *registration*, not use. Section 10 may, however, apply as well. If a mark is not prohibited under section 10, the user of a mark covered by s. 12(1)(b) may still have common law rights, such as the tort of passing off, in the unregistered mark and will be able to secure registration if it can meet the s. 12(2) or s. 14 test. (See the Secondary Meaning section below.)

In respect specifically of wines and spirits, ss. 11.14 and 11.15 prohibit the adoption and use as a trade-mark of certain protected "geographical indications" for wines and spirits. "Geographical indications," as defined in s. 2, identify a place of origin and are used where a "quality, reputation or other characteristics" of the wine or spirit are "essentially attributable" to the place of origin. The *Trade-marks Act* contains an important exception for certain indications considered generic (see s. 11.18). These sections were recently being reviewed in light of an agreement between Canada and the European Union with respect to wines and spirits signed in 2003.[84a] Canada agreed to phase out a list of certain generic names for wines and spirits in ss. 11.18(3) and (4) of the *Trade-marks Act*, so that the names (including Bordeaux, Marsala, Burgundy, and Champagne) can be protected as geographical indications in Canada.

## (c) Secondary Meaning

A trade-mark must be distinctive of its owner.[85] The message to the public must indicate a "single source";[86] that is, the public must believe that the mark indicates that the product or service sold under a particular mark comes from a single source, which in turn helps to ensure that there are no sudden and unexpected changes in the quality of goods and services (variations due to the availability of ingredients or components are always possible).

This section deals with marks which were clearly descriptive *a priori* or consist of a person's name, but which, through use, have become distinctive. The concept of acquired distinctiveness is also important in another respect: a non-functional distinguishing guise will only be registrable once it has become distinctive, according to s. 13 of the *Trade-marks Act*.[87] A

---

[84a]  See SOR/2004-85.

[85]  *Aladdin Industries Inc. v. Canadian Thermos Products Ltd.* (1972), [1974] S.C.R. 845, 6 C.P.R. (2d) 1 (S.C.C.) [*Aladdin Industries*].

[86]  *Wilkinson Sword (Can.) Ltd. v. Juda* (1966), [1968] 2 Ex. C.R. 137, 51 C.P.R. 55 (Can. Ex. Ct.) [*Wilkinson Sword*].

[87]  See *Kirkbi AG, supra*, note 16.

descriptive trade-mark, as defined in s. 12(1)(b), can be registered if it has become distinctive pursuant to s. 12(2) of the *Trade-marks Act* — subject, however, to s. 10 (see the Descriptive Marks section, *supra*, and the text below).

In order to become distinctive, one must establish a strong link between the product or service and the mark. The general name of the actual product or service can never become distinctive. For example, the name "orange" will never be protected as a trade-mark when used in connection with oranges because it cannot acquire secondary meaning in that context. This avoids the problems that would ensue if one owner could have a monopoly on the word(s) in common use for the name of the good or service itself. However, ORANGE could be a perfectly acceptable trade-mark for cars or telephone services, for example. Coined words tend to be more inherently distinctive. In *Standard Coil Products (Can.) Ltd. v. Standard Radio Corp.*,[88] Cattanach J. held as follows:

> If a trade mark is a coined or invented word it is obviously adapted to distinguish but if a trade mark is prima facie not distinctive, as for example a laudatory epithet or descriptive of the character of quality of the wares, then it becomes a question of fact if the trade mark actually distinguishes the wares.
>
> The concluding words in s. 2(f) 'or is adapted so to distinguish them' are obviously introduced to cover the circumstances of a proposed trade mark or one that has not enjoyed a long and extensive use. The word 'or', as used in this context, is disjunctive. Therefore a word which is a proposed trade mark or one that has enjoyed limited use must be inherently distinctive to be registered, whereas a trade mark that is not inherently distinctive may be registered if it is established, as a fact, that it actually distinguishes the wares of its owner.

The jurisprudence of the Trade-Marks Opposition Board is to the same effect:

> 'Distinctive' in relation to a trade mark means a trade mark that actually distinguishes the wares or services in association with which it is used by the owner from the wares or services of others or is adapted to distinguish them. The words 'adapted to distinguish' refer to the inherent capability of a trade mark to distinguish the wares or services of the trade mark owner without the need of establishing acquired distinctiveness.[89]

---

[88] [1971] F.C. 106, 1 C.P.R. (2d) 155 (Fed. T.D.) at paras. 87-8, affirmed (1976), 26 C.P.R. (2d) 288 (Fed. C.A.) [*Standard Coil* cited to F.C.].

[89] *Hoechst Canada Inc. v. Sandoz Canada Inc.* (1995), 60 C.P.R. (3d) 559 (T.M. Opp. Bd.). See also *Boston Pizza International Inc. v. Boston Chicken Inc.* (2003), [2003] F.C.J. No. 395, 224 D.L.R. (4th) 475, 24 C.P.R. (4th) 150, 301 N.R. 190, 239 F.T.R. 160 (note), 2003 CarswellNat 583 (Fed. C.A.).

In *John Labatt Ltd. v. Molson Cos.*,[90] Molson used the word GOLDEN to identify one of its products. However, the adjective is arguably descriptive of the color of the beer. The court found that it had become distinctive, after many years of use. The court also stated the basic principle as follows:

> Once a descriptive word has acquired distinctiveness, it has, by definition, lost its generic character when used in association with the wares or services with which it has become identified; the acquired meaning distorts the ordinary meaning.

By contrast to ss. 12(1)(a) and (b), s. 10 contains a prohibition on registration *and* use as a trade-mark which cannot be overcome by showing distinctiveness. Presumably, in the cases mentioned in s. 10, it would be impossible to acquire distinctiveness. Section 10 prohibits registration and use as a trade-mark of a word which, by ordinary and *bona fide* commercial usage has become recognized in Canada as designating the *kind, quality, quantity, destination, value, place of origin or date of production* of any wares or services, for wares or services or others of the same general class or use it in a way likely to mislead the public. The prohibition extends to any mark so nearly resembling that mark as to be likely to be mistaken therefor.

In another case involving the same two breweries, the Trade-Mark Office found that the use of the word EXPORT on beer was not prohibited under ss. 10 or 12.[91] The main consideration was its "secondary" nature:

> In so far as the opponent's third ground of opposition is based on ss. 10 and 12(1)(e) of the *Act*, I consider that the prohibition in s. 10 must be applied to the trade mark as a whole and, in the present case, the component 'export' does not so dominate the applied for trade mark that contravention of s. 10 by that component would render the mark as a whole unregistrable.

An example of a case where s. 10 was found to apply concerns a prohibition on the use of HABANOS for cigars.[92] The court justified its finding because of a resemblance with HABANA, a recognized designation of Cuban origin. It stated:

---

[90] (1987), [1987] F.C.J. No. 1102, (sub nom. *Molson Cos. v. John Labatt Ltd.*) 19 C.P.R. (3d) 88, 91 N.R. 148, (sub nom. *Molson Cos. v. John Labatt Ltd.*) 15 C.I.P.R. 161, 1987 CarswellNat 698 (Fed. C.A.), leave to appeal refused (1988), (sub nom. *Molson Cos. v. John Labatt Ltd.*) 19 C.P.R. (3d) vii (note) (S.C.C.).

[91] *John Labatt Ltd. v. Molson Cos.* (1983), 2 C.P.R. (3d) 150 (T.M. Opp. Bd.).

[92] *Benson & Hedges (Canada) Ltd. v. Empresa Cubana Del Tabaco* (1975), 23 C.P.R. (2d) 274 (Reg. T.M.) at 279.

The issue for determination under this ground of opposition is whether the word 'Habanos' is a prohibited mark within the meaning of s. 10.

There is no evidence that the word 'Habanos' is recognized in Canada as designating the kind, quality, quantity, destination, value, place of origin or date of production of any wares or services. However, the evidence reveals that the words 'Havana' and 'Habana' are commonly used in Canada on cigars or packages of cigars to denote that the cigars are made in Cuba or that the cigars are made from tobacco leaf grown in Cuba and I am satisfied on the basis of the evidence adduced that 'Habana' is recognized in Canada as designating cigars made in Cuba or cigars that are made from tobacco leaf grown in Cuba. There is, in my opinion, a very close resemblance between the expressions 'Habanos' and 'Habana' in appearance, in sound and in the ideas conveyed so that the expression 'Habanos' might well be mistaken for 'Habana'. Moreover cigars are of the same general class as the wares claimed in the application namely, leaf tobacco and processed tobacco and I therefore come to the conclusion that the word 'Habanos' in association with tobacco products (not including cigars) is a prohibited mark under s. 10 of the *Trade Marks Act* in that 'Habanos' so nearly resembles 'Habana' as to be likely to be mistaken therefor.

The relevant date to consider for purposes of s. 10 is the date when an applicant (for registration) or user first started to use the mark.[93]

### (d) Loss of Distinctiveness

Distinctiveness is a requirement both for acquiring and maintaining trade-mark rights. Marks must continue to be distinctive of the owner and continue to indicate source. While a clearly descriptive mark may become distinctive, the converse is also possible; that is, it is possible for a distinctive trade-mark to become clearly descriptive or generic. Section 2 contains a definition of 'distinctive', which "in relation to a trade-mark, means a trade-mark that actually distinguishes the wares or services in association with which it is used by its owner from the wares or services of others or is adapted so to distinguish them."

A mark must be distinctive of its *owner*. A single-source rule applies to trade-marks. A trade-mark is not or no longer distinctive if there is more than one origin or if the origin is not the owner. Thus, problems often occur when a trade-mark is sold or its use entrusted to a licensee and the message to the public does not adequately indicate who the owner is. Sections 48(1) and (2) and 50(1) are also relevant in that context:

---

[93] See *John Labatt Ltd. v. Molson Cos.*, *supra*, note 91, and *242183 Ontario Ltd. v. Black Forest Inn Inc.* (1984), 3 C.P.R. (3d) 23 (T.M. Opp. Bd.).

48(1) A trade-mark, whether registered or unregistered, is transferable, and deemed always to have been transferable, either in connection with or separately from the goodwill of the business and in respect of either all or some of the wares or services in association with which it has been used.

(2) Nothing in subsection (1) prevents a trade-mark from being held not to be *distinctive if as a result of a transfer thereof there subsisted rights in two or more persons to the use of confusing trade-marks and the rights were exercised by those persons.* [emphasis added]

50(1) For the purposes of this Act, if an entity is licensed by or with the authority of the owner of a trade-mark to use the trade-mark in a country and the owner has, under the licence, direct or indirect control of the character or quality of the wares or services, then the use, advertisement or display of the trade-mark in that country as or in a trade-mark, trade-name or otherwise by that entity has, and is deemed always to have had, the same effect as such a use, advertisement or display of the trade-mark in that country by the owner.

A mark is distinctive only if it distinguishes the goods or services in association with which it is used by its owner from goods or services of anyone else (including a distributor, etc.). Section 50 allows trade-mark owners to count the use, advertisement or display of a mark by a licensee, providing the owner has direct or indirect control of the character or quality of the wares of services.[94] (See section V. Licences and Assignments.)

Section 48(1) contains the phrase "and deemed always to have been transferable" because it is difficult to conceive transferring a trade-mark without goodwill and courts had been reluctant to recognize the validity of such transfers in the past.[95] United Kingdom law requires a determination by the registrar that the transfer is not against the public interest, in the sense that there will be no deception as a result of the transfer. The Canadian Act does not contain the same requirement, although Laskin C.J. in *Madger v. Breck's Sporting Goods Co.* stated that our law is to the same effect.[96] This is another application of the general trade-mark principle that "[T]he system was designed to encourage honest trading, and *the protection of the buying public.*"[97] If there is confusion/deception as a result of the transfer, the mark

---

[94] See *Petro-Canada c. 2946661 Canada Inc.* (1998), (sub nom. *Petro-Canada v. 2946661 Canada Inc.*) [1999] 1 F.C. 294, (sub nom. *Petro-Canada v. 2946661 Canada Inc.*) 83 C.P.R. (3d) 129, (sub nom. *Petro-Canada v. 2946661 Canada Inc.*) 154 F.T.R. 1 (Fed. T.D.).

[95] *Cheerio Toys & Games Ltd. v. Dubiner* (1965), [1966] S.C.R. 206, 55 D.L.R. (2d) 313, 48 C.P.R. 226 (S.C.C.).

[96] (1975), [1976] 1 S.C.R. 527, 63 D.L.R. (3d) 645, 17 C.P.R. (2d) 201, 3 N.R. 601 (S.C.C.) [*Breck's* cited to S.C.R.].

[97] *Williamson Candy, supra*, note 36 (Emphasis added).

may lose its distinctiveness. As Laskin C.J., explained at paras. 11 and 12 in the *Breck's* case:

> Prior to its introduction [of s. 47 — now s.48], the requirement of distinctiveness, in the sense of identification of the source or origin of the goods with which the trade mark was associated, was supported by a requirement that there be no deception or confusion of the public in the message conveyed by the trade mark. Thus it was that an assignment of a trade mark could only be valid if it was assigned together with the entire goodwill of the business in the goods for which the trade mark was registered. It is enough to refer here to the judgments *in Great Atlantic and Pacific Tea Co. Ltd. v. Canada (Registrar of Trade Marks)* [[1945] Ex. C.R. 233] and *Wilkinson Sword (Canada) Ltd. v. Juda, supra,* in which the various considerations affecting the validity of an assignment were considered. It is important to notice that *an assignment as aforesaid would not invariably support the assignee's claim to trade mark protection if there was a deception of the public in the message that the trade mark conveyed in its use by the assignee,* that is, if the public would take from it that the trade mark was still distinctive of the origin of the goods being in the assignor rather than being distinctive merely of the place of manufacture.
> [. . .]
>
> Further, if the appellant's contention is in truth that it can obtain an assignment in gross of a trade mark indicative of a certain manufacturing origin and *use it as a seller's mark in respect of wares which it does not manufacture but which it has continued to obtain from the very manufacturer with the mark attached thereto by the latter, I do not see how in this respect the requirement of distinctiveness under the Canadian legislation is satisfied,* especially in view of the distributorship agreements between the appellant and Mepps. [emphasis added]

In *Breck's*, fishing equipment was manufactured by the first owner of the trade-mark. The mark was assigned to a U.S. company, then to a Canadian company. The source of the goods was a French company. The Canadian company, which became the owner of the mark, continued to purchase goods from the French company. The source didn't change but the ownership changed, thus creating the confusion. The Supreme Court did not accept the argument that the mark used to identify the origin of the good somehow "morphed" to identify the seller/distributor of the good instead of the manufacturer.[98]

*United Artists Pictures Inc. v. Pink Panther Beauty Corp.* is also instructive in that regard.[99] The court explained:

---

[98] See also *Waxoyl AG v. Waxoyl Canada Ltd.* (1984), 3 C.P.R. (3d) 105 (Fed. T.D.).

[99] *Supra*, note 25 at paras. 15 and 16.

It has been suggested that the common law action sought to protect the consumer's expectation of quality which resided in those marks. (See Gordon F. Henderson, An Overview of Intellectual Property, in *Trade-marks Law in Canada*, Gordon F. Henderson (ed.) (Toronto: Carswell, 1993), at pp. 3-4.) Thus, courts have held, in the past, that marks could not be assigned (*Re Sinclair (John) Ld. — In the Matter of a Trade Mark of* (1932), 49 R.P.C. 123 (Ch. D.)), or licensed (*Bowden Wire Ld. v. Bowden Brake Co. Ld* (1914), 31 R.P.C. 385 (H.L.)), and a manufacturer's mark could not be converted into a seller's mark (*Pinto v. Badman* (1891), 8 R.P.C. 181 (C.A.)). These propositions, however, have been undone by modern amendments to trade-marks legislation, allowing marks to be more amenable to commercial practice. In so doing, *the emphasis has shifted from a guarantee theory of protection to a source theory. In other words, what the registered mark does nowadays is to ensure that the wares or services are the wares and services of a particular person and no one else, that is, the source of the goods is guaranteed.*

The question posed by the existence of intellectual property regimes has been defined as one of where to draw the line between the right to copy and the right to compete. (See Henderson, supra, at 9.) *This is a question about what is truly worthy of the status of property and what is in reality an element of the marketplace which should be open to all competitors to use in their efforts to succeed.* [emphasis added]

The main qualification to the single source rule is the concept of "single entity", *i.e.*, when a mark does not distinguish one of the members of a corporate "family", but rather the family as such. In that case, there is no deception if some wares come from one member of the family and similar wares from another member of the family. This principle is clearly visible in *Moore Dry Kiln Co. v. United States Natural Resources Inc.*[100] Three different U.S. companies as well as a Canadian company were selling dry kilns under the trade-mark MOORE. The trial judge, whose findings were adopted by the Federal Court of Appeal, concluded:

A massive volume of documentary evidence dredged up from the parties' files establishes to my complete satisfaction that, at least from the change of name from Moore-Cawston to Moore Canada in 1943 until some time in 1964 or 1965, Moore Florida, Moore Oregon and Moore Canada were held out to the public in Canada as a single enterprise rather than as separate entities with individual identities. Enquiries from potential customers in the territory of one to another of the companies were referred to the one actually doing business

---

[100] (1975), 23 C.P.R. (2d) 35 (Fed. T.D.) at paras. 11, 19 and 29, affirmed (1976), [1976] F.C.J. No. 608, 30 C.P.R. (2d) 40, 12 N.R. 361, 1976 CarswellNat 478 (Fed. C.A.). See also *Sarco Canada Ltd. v. Sarco Co.*, [1968] 2 Ex. C.R. 537, 56 C.P.R. 80 (Can. Ex. Ct.).

in that territory but the customers were left with the clear impression they were doing business with the same company. Technical advice and support services were freely exchanged. Personnel was transferred from one to another and back again. Through advertisements in trade journals, calendars, stationery, invoices, technical and general product bulletins, operating manuals for and plaques and labels on equipment, Moore Dry Kiln Company was promoted in Canada as a single worldwide entity. *That image was also promoted at trade shows and conventions in Canada and elsewhere attended by Canadian customers.* A common heritage harking back to Lafayette Moore was emphasized through the slogans: 'Moore Since 1879' and 'Oldest and Largest Manufacturers of Lumber and Veneer Dryers' and variations thereof.

[. . .]

Little, if anything, was made of the individual corporate entities in the plaintiff's advertising programme. They were represented as, in fact, they were: simply the vehicles by which Williams carried on his single business enterprise, Moore Dry Kiln Company.
[. . .]

The word 'Moore' in association with the wares, as at September 26, 1972, in Canada, did not distinguish the plaintiff's wares from the wares of Moore Florida or, for that matter, from those of Moore Oregon. It was distinctive of the wares of a trading enterprise known to the public as Moore Dry Kiln Company whereof the plaintiff was a component without individual identity in the public mind. (emphasis added).

The distinctiveness of a trade-mark supposes there is a perceived unique source to the product regardless of the judicial entity or entities behind it. Even if a soft drink is bottled at different plants, consumers within a given market expect the same product in each can or bottle.

Hence, if different products or products of different quality are sold using the same trade-mark and there is no way for consumers to tell the difference, the trade-mark is diluted and the owner may lose the distinctiveness of his or her mark. In *Wilkinson Sword*,[101] a British company manufacturing razor blades was selling blades in Canada, some of which were manufactured in the U.K., others in Canada. The Court concluded as follows:

In my view, it is beyond dispute that, on the facts that have been placed before the Court, the trade marks in question did not during the relevant period 'actually distinguish' the plaintiff's razor blades from the wares of others and I must therefore hold that the trade marks were not 'distinctive' at any time

---

[101] *Supra*, note 86.

during that period. Accordingly, I hold that their registrations were invalid by virtue of section 18(1) (b).

[. . .]

Whether or not the individual members of the purchasing public were aware of the United Kingdom company's name is immaterial — the theory is that those who had shown a preference for the goods sold under the marks had learned to have confidence in the manufacturer of such wares regardless of whom he might be.

[. . .]

In the period during which this situation prevailed, I can only infer that the trade marks in question signified to the Canadian purchasing public that the goods associated with tile marks in question were manufactured by whatever manufacturer in England had been making the goods that they had been buying in association with such trade marks for over forty years. . . .

There is not one bit of evidence to indicate that the trade marks 'actually', at any relevant time, indicated, to the Canadian purchasing public, that the wares to which they were attached were wares of the plaintiff — either as manufacturer or seller — or even that such wares were wares manufactured or sold by some unidentified person other than the manufacturer of the wares in association with which the marks had been used in Canada from 1920 to 1963. The trade marks in question, at no time, distinguished wares of the plaintiff as manufacturer or vendor from wares of the United Kingdom company or any other person.

In *Heintzman v. 751056 Ontario Ltd.*, an Ontario piano manufacturer had outsourced production to Asia without informing consumers.[102] The judge stated:

The function and purpose of a trademark is to indicate the source from which goods emanate. If a mark is associated with a high quality product, its presence will assure the purchaser that the goods are likely to be of that quality. The mark, at least, allows a purchaser to tell whether or not the goods have come from a source in which he or she has confidence.

[. . .]

---

[102] (1990), [1990] F.C.J. No. 1033, 34 C.P.R. (3d) 1, 38 F.T.R. 210, 1990 CarswellNat 819 (Fed. T.D.). The situation is different when the quality of goods is identical or at least comparable. See *Jean Patou Inc. v. Luxo Laboratories Ltd.* (1998), [1998] F.C.J. No. 1910, 158 F.T.R. 16, 1998 CarswellNat 2682 (Fed. T.D.), affirmed (2001), [2001] F.C.J. No. 67, 281 N.R. 181, 2001 CarswellNat 69 (Fed. C.A.).

Not only were the efforts to notify the public virtually non-existent, there was clearly a deliberate attempt by the respondents to camouflage the fact that a change of source had occurred.

Another way to lose distinctiveness is to let the mark become generic, *i.e.*, a word that identifies a type of goods or services rather than their source. Certain words can in fact become "partly generic" in that they are sometimes used to identify a type of product, and, in other cases, products from a specific manufacturer. For example, the Federal Court in *Aladdin Industries* did not accept that the word THERMOS had become completely descriptive.[103] The court stated:

> [T]he evidence establishes two facts of major importance insofar as this case is concerned. The first is that at the date the proceedings were commenced the words 'thermos' and 'thermos bottle' had come into popular use in Canada and, when used in relation to the common kind of vacuum bottles, the kind found in the average home, were used and understood by persons of average education and intelligence in ordinary society as generic words descriptive of that class of bottle, and they had fallen into the day-to-day English and French languages of the Canadian people as synonymous with 'vacuum bottle' in English and 'bouteille isolante' in French, and as descriptive of the common household vacuum bottle.
>
> Before I state the second fact I will say that I am not convinced that on a question whether in Canada a particular word is a generic or descriptive word in the English or French languages, or as to what its meaning is, (other than technical words and words having special meaning in a profession, trade, etc.), a judge must decide the question solely on the evidence which is adduced and cannot use his own knowledge of the word and of the way persons use and respond to it in conversation in ordinary society. If I were to use my own knowledge and experience respecting the use of the word 'thermos' in conversation, it would support my conclusion above stated. However, as I have the impression that counsel's view was that my findings should be based upon the evidence adduced, I have endeavoured to make my findings solely on that evidence and inferences therefrom, without being influenced by any personally subjective feelings I may have.
>
> The second fact so established, in my opinion, is that as of the date the proceedings were commenced an appreciable portion of the population in Canada knew and recognized the respondent's trade mark 'THERMOS' and its significance, and that to them it was distinctive of the respondent's vacuum bottles.

---

[103] *Aladdin Industries Inc. v. Canadian Thermos Products Ltd.*, [1969] 2 Ex. C.R. 80, 57 C.P.R. 230 (Can. Ex. Ct.), affirmed (1972), [1974] S.C.R. 845 (S.C.C.) [*Aladdin Industries* cited to Ex. C.R.].

They were influenced, no doubt, by the 20,000,000 of the respondent's bottles bearing the trade mark which were sold in Canada in the period 1935-64 in competition with imported and other bottles, and by the extensive advertising by the respondent and by the millions of 'directions for use', etc., in connection with the respondent's bottles and trade mark, which reached the public and purchasers of vacuum bottles.
[. . .]

It is my opinion, also, that many of the public are aware of the dual use and meaning of the word 'thermos' and that they use it in its generic sense or in its trade mark sense, as the case may be, as circumstances may call for. In day-to-day conversation such persons may use the word in a generic sense without adding 'brand' or 'vacuum bottle', and without having in mind a bottle of a particular manufacturer; but when they go to a store to buy a vacuum bottle they will have in mind that the name 'THERMOS' on a bottle has a significance which distinguishes bottles made by the respondent and sold under that brand name from bottles bearing some other brand or no brand.

Once the distinctiveness is lost, so are most rights in the mark in respect of confusion. The non-distinctive mark can be struck from the Register.[104] The trade-mark owner must begin using the mark and thereby try to re-establish its distinctiveness before his or her rights can re-emerge.

Conversely, two different products can be sold under the same mark if each indicates the source.[105] As stated in *White Consolidated Industries Inc. v. Beam of Canada Inc.*, the most important thing is the message sent to the consumer or relevant public.[106]

To emphasize again, the purpose of the Act is two-fold: protecting the public and also protecting the trade-mark owner. The Act gives the trade-mark owner rights against commercial misappropriation of the mark and/or the goodwill associated with the mark. The *purpose* and the *value* of a mark is the mental link that is created over time in the minds of prospective buyers between a mark and the goods or services of a particular source. When the owner of the mark uses that link unfairly, such as by degrading the quality (without adequately informing the public), courts have tended to find that the mental link has been severed and the owner loses his or her rights in the mark.

---

[104] See *Sarco Canada Ltd. v. Sarco Co.*, *supra*, note 100; *Mayborn Products Ltd. v. Canada (Registrar of Trade Marks)* (1983), [1984] 1 F.C. 107, 70 C.P.R. (2d) 1 (Fed. T.D.).

[105] *Gray Rocks Inn Ltd. v. Snowy Eagle Ski Club Inc.* (1971), 3 C.P.R. (2d) 9 (Fed. T.D.).

[106] (1991), [1991] F.C.J. No. 1076, 39 C.P.R. (3d) 94, 47 F.T.R. 172, 1991 CarswellNat 214 (Fed. T.D.). See also *Breck's*, *supra* note 96.

In *Bousquet v. Barmish Inc.*,[107] for example, Barmish used the trademark CACHAREL, which was well established in France by Bousquet. However, since Bousquet did not sell or promote the product in Canada and Barmish acquired a reputation using Cacharel in Canada, Bousquet lost the right to use the trade-mark in Canada.

The notion of confusion between distinctive marks also has a territorial element, as stated in s. 6(2) of the Act:

> The used of a trade-mark causes confusion with a trade-name if the use of both the trade-mark and trade-name *in the same area* would be likely to lead to the inference that the wares or services associated with those trade-marks are manufactured, sold, leased, hired or performed by the same person, whether or not the wares or services are of the same general class. [emphasis added]

Two distinct businesses in two different areas can operate under the same distinctive name if no confusion is created as to the source of the product or service.[108] Depending on the nature of the wares or services, the "same area" may not necessarily be all of Canada. However, if there is evidence of confusion between two marks, as in *Motel 6*, the second will be banned.[109]

## 7. Prohibited or Invalid Trade-Marks

Sections 9, 10 and 10.1 of the *Trade-marks Act* list marks that cannot be used to designate a product or service. They contain prohibitions in relation to the registration, the adoption and the use of a mark:

> 9. (1) No person shall adopt in connection with a business, as a trade-mark or otherwise, any mark consisting of, or so nearly resembling as to be likely to be mistaken for,
>
> a)    the Royal Arms, Crest or Standard;
> b)    the arms or crest of any member of the Royal Family;
> c)    the standard, arms or crest of His Excellency the Governor General;
> d)    any word or symbol likely to lead to the belief that the wares or services

---

[107] (1991), [1991] F.C.J. No. 813, 37 C.P.R. (3d) 516, 48 F.T.R. 122, 1991 CarswellNat 878 (Fed. T.D.), affirmed (1993), 46 C.P.R. (3d) 510 (Fed. C.A.).

[108] *Great Lakes Hotels Ltd. v. Noshery Ltd.*, [1968] 2 Ex. C.R. 622, 56 C.P.R. 165 (Can. Ex. Ct.). Section 32(2) of the Act states that the Registrar may impose a territorial restriction on the use of the trade-mark, *i.e.*, the region where it has become distinctive. This applies with respect to distinguishing guise and secondary meaning.

[109] *Supra*, note 12.

in association with which it is used have received, or are produced, sold or performed under, royal, vice-regal or governmental patronage, approval or authority;

e) the arms, crest or flag adopted and used at any time by Canada or by any province or municipal corporation in Canada in respect of which the Registrar has, at the request of the Government of Canada or of the province or municipal corporation concerned, given public notice of its adoption and use;

f) the emblem of the Red Cross on a white ground, formed by reversing the federal colours of Switzerland and retained by the Geneva Convention for the Protection of War Victims of 1949 as the emblem and distinctive sign of the Medical Service of armed forces and used by the Canadian Red Cross Society, or the expression "Red Cross" or "Geneva Cross";

g) the emblem of the Red Crescent on a white ground adopted for the same purpose as specified in paragraph (f) by a number of Moslem countries;

h) the equivalent sign of the Red Lion and Sun used by Iran for the same purpose as specified in paragraph (f);

h.1) the international distinctive sign of civil defence (equilateral blue triangle on an orange ground) referred to in Article 66, paragraph 4 of Schedule V to the Geneva Conventions Act;

i) any territorial or civic flag or any national, territorial or civic arms, crest or emblem, of a country of the Union, if the flag, arms, crest or emblem is on a list communicated under article 6ter of the Convention or pursuant to the obligations under the Agreement on Trade-related Aspects of Intellectual Property Rights set out in Annex 1C to the WTO Agreement stemming from that article, and the Registrar gives public notice of the communication;

i.1) any official sign or hallmark indicating control or warranty adopted by a country of the Union, if the sign or hallmark is on a list communicated under article 6ter of the Convention or pursuant to the obligations under the Agreement on Trade-related Aspects of Intellectual Property Rights set out in Annex 1C to the WTO Agreement stemming from that article, and the Registrar gives public notice of the communication;

i.2) any national flag of a country of the Union;

i.3) any armorial bearing, flag or other emblem, or any abbreviation of the name, of an international intergovernmental organization, if the armorial bearing, flag, emblem or abbreviation is on a list communicated under article 6ter of the Convention or pursuant to the obligations under the Agreement on Trade-related Aspects of Intellectual Property Rights set out in Annex 1C to the WTO Agreement stemming from that article, and the Registrar gives public notice of the communication;

j) any scandalous, obscene or immoral word or device;

k) any matter that may falsely suggest a connection with any living individual;

l)    the portrait or signature of any individual who is living or has died within the preceding thirty years;

m)    the words "United Nations" or the official seal or emblem of the United Nations;

n)    any badge, crest, emblem or mark
   i)    adopted or used by any of Her Majesty's Forces as defined in the National Defence Act,
   ii)    of any university, or
   iii)    adopted and used by any public authority, in Canada as an official mark for wares or services,
   in respect of which the Registrar has, at the request of Her Majesty or of the university or public authority, as the case may be, given public notice of its adoption and use;

n.1)    any armorial bearings granted, recorded or approved for use by a recipient pursuant to the prerogative powers of Her Majesty as exercised by the Governor General in respect of the granting of armorial bearings, if the Registrar has, at the request of the Governor General, given public notice of the grant, recording or approval; or

o)    the name "Royal Canadian Mounted Police" or "R.C.M.P." or any other combination of letters relating to the Royal Canadian Mounted Police, or any pictorial representation of a uniformed member thereof.

10. Where any mark has by ordinary and *bona fide* commercial usage become recognized in Canada as designating the kind, quality, quantity, destination, value, place of origin or date of production of any wares or services, no person shall adopt it as a trade-mark in association with such wares or services or others of the same general class or use it in a way likely to mislead, nor shall any person so adopt or so use any mark so nearly resembling that mark as to be likely to be mistaken therefor.

Section 9 prohibits royal arms, official crests, flags, badges, etc., from being adopted in connection with business. Section 10 further prohibits marks which designate the general kind, quality, quantity, destination, value, place or origin, etc., of goods or services from being adopted as marks in association with goods or services of the same general class. The objective of s. 10 is to avoid having monopolies on marks which signify the general name of the good or service, as opposed to merely the source of that good or service. In this way, marks that are generally adopted by a trade remain available to all traders to use. Sections 9 and 10 are "absolute" prohibitions (within the parameters of those sections, *e.g.* the lack of consent of the interested party — s. 9(2)(a)). The prohibition in s. 9 is against "adoption", *i.e,* beginning to use.[110] The prohibition in s. 10 is against adoption and also

---

[110] See *Canadian Olympic Assn. v. Bowling Proprietors' Assn. of British Columbia* (1986), [1986] F.C.J. No. 197, 1986 CarswellNat 1048 (Fed. T.D.); *Cdn. Olympic*

use, but in the latter case, according to the language used in the section, only to the extent that use would be misleading. However, the difference between adoption and use is mostly relevant in respect of marks already in use when they begin to conflict with a new mark covered under ss. 9 or 10. Section 9(1) also prohibits adoption as a trade-mark "or otherwise", which would include, for example, company names.

In the case of s. 10, the mark would likely have *become non-distinctive* and thus unable to be properly used as a mark if under "ordinary and *bona fide* commercial usage" it has "become recognized in Canada as designating the kind, quality, quantity, destination, value, place of origin or date of production of any wares or services." (See the Descriptive Marks section above.)

Section 9 contains three types of prohibition. Sections 9(1)(a) to (h.1), (i.2), (j), (m) and (o) contain absolute prohibitions to protect public national and international authorities. Sections 9(1)(k) and (l) contain absolute prohibitions to protect private persons, which is discussed in the Names Section, below. Finally, s. 9(1)(e), (i), (i.1), (i.3), (n) and (n.1) contain so-called contingent prohibitions. These marks are protected subject to notices published in the *Trade-Marks Journal* or under Article 6*ter* of the *Paris Convention* (see the International section and the Official Marks section *supra*). A public authority is a person or administrative body entrusted with functions to perform for the benefit of the public and not for private profit. By contrast, the prohibitions contained in s. 12(1)(c) to (h) apply only to registration, not adoption or use. Sections 12(1)(a) and (b) contain only a "relative" prohibition, which not only is limited to registration but can be overcome by showing an acquired distinctiveness, which is also known as secondary meaning, as of the date of filing for registration. (See s. 12(2) and the Acquired Distinctiveness section below). Section 12 reads as follows:

> 12. (1) Subject to section 13, a trade-mark is registrable if it is not:
>
> (a) a word that is primarily merely the name or the surname of an individual who is living or has died within the preceding thirty years;
> (b) whether depicted, written or sounded, either clearly descriptive or deceptively misdescriptive in the English or French language of the character or quality of the wares or services in association with which it is used or proposed to be used or of the conditions of or the persons employed in their production or of their place of origin;

---

*Assn. v. Pace Setter Swim & Gym Wear Inc.* (1987), 15 C.P.R. (3d) 565 (T.M. Opp. Bd.); and *Canadian Olympic Assn. v. Mufty Bears Ltd.* (1986), 9 C.P.R. (3d) 65 (T.M. Opp. Bd.). But see *Allied Corp.*, *supra*, note 47 — this case is discussed below.

c)   the name in any language of any of the wares or services in connection with which it is used or proposed to be used;

d)   a word that is primarily merely the name or the surname of an individual who is living or has died within the preceding thirty years;

e)   whether depicted, written or sounded, either clearly descriptive or deceptively misdescriptive in the English or French language of the character or quality of the wares or services in association with which it is used or proposed to be used or of the conditions of or the persons employed in their production or of their place of origin;

f)   the name in any language of any of the wares or services in connection with which it is used or proposed to be used;

g)   confusing with a registered trade-mark;

h)   a mark of which the adoption is prohibited by section 9 or 10;

i)   a denomination the adoption of which is prohibited by section 10.1.

j)   in whole or in part a protected geographical indication, where the trade-mark is to be registered in association with a wine not originating in a territory indicated by the geographical indication; and

k)   in whole or in part a protected geographical indication, where the trade-mark is to be registered in association with a spirit not originating in a territory indicated by the geographical indication.

(2) A trade-mark that is not registrable by reason of *paragraph (1)(a) or (b)* is registrable if it has been so used in Canada by the applicant or his predecessor in title as to have become distinctive at the date of filing an application for its registration

When is a word "clearly descriptive" to the point that it cannot be used as a trade-mark?[111] Section 12(1)(b) provides that a trade-mark can be registered if it is *not,* when depicted, written or sounded, clearly descriptive or deceptively misdescriptive in the English or French language of the character or quality of wares or services in association with which it is used. The test is one of "first or immediate impression from the perspective of the everyday consumer of or dealer in the wares" and "must not be based on research into or critical analysis of the meaning of the words."[112] Dictionaries, as the court in *Aladdin Industries* cautioned, "do not always reflect the true meaning of words."[113]

In *A. Lassonde Inc. v. Canada (Registrar of Trade-marks)* the mark BANANORANGE was contested.[114] The Court found that it did not violate

[111] See also the Descriptive Trade-Marks Section, *supra.*

[112] *Imperial Tobacco, supra,* note 59 at para. 18, McGillis J.

[113] *Supra,* note 103 at 81.

[114] (2000), [2000] F.C.J. No. 128, (sub nom. *A. Lassonde Inc. c. Canada (Registraire des marques de commerce)*) 5 C.P.R. (4th) 517, 180 F.T.R. 177, 2000

s. 10, because it did not explicitly say what the product was, but was in violation of s. 12 because it was clearly descriptive of the composition of the product and the intrinsic nature of the product. The court rejected the appellant's arguments that the dictionary provided additional definitions for the word "banana" by analogy as a military medal or twin-rotor helicopter. Instead, the impression of a potential buyer on hearing or seeing the mark BANANORANGE would be of those mixed fruits and, since that was clearly descriptive of the product, the mark was therefore not registrable under s. 12(1)(b).

In *Canadian Shredded Wheat Co. v. Kellogg Co.*, the plaintiff had patents on a shredded wheat manufacturing process and sold the product as "shredded wheat biscuits" and registered the trade-marks.[115] When the patents expired, Kellogg also sold "shredded whole wheat biscuits", which were similar in appearance to the plaintiff's product. Lord Russell wrote, "a word or words to be really distinctive of a person's goods must generally speaking be incapable of application to the goods of anyone else," and consequently found that the term SHREDDED WHEAT could not be a trade-mark as it was both purely descriptive and the name of the article of manufacture.[116] Similarly, in *Linoleum Manufacturing Co. v. Nairn*,[117] a company which invented and patented a new floor covering made of solidified oil and which coined the word "linoleum" to describe it could not prevent a competitor company from marketing their solidified oil floor product as "linoleum" after the patents expired. The only term for the good itself during the time that the patents gave the original makers a monopoly was "linoleum," and thus the inventor company could not claim exclusive trade-mark rights in a word which described the good itself and did not distinguish source. The word or words commonly used to designate the general name of the good are available to a competitor firm which can market a similar product once the patents expire. An inventor of a process or product, in other words, should coin both a trade-mark, as well as a general name for the product.

In *Channell Ltd. v. Rombough*,[118] the Supreme Court did not accept O'CEDAR as a mark for furniture polish:

> We think it is clear that the word 'cedar,' being a word in common use, could, notwithstanding the registration of the trade-mark 'O'Cedar,' be employed for

---

CarswellNat 274 (Fed. T.D.), affirmed (2001), [2001] F.C.J. No. 1096, 281 N.R. 365, 2001 CarswellNat 1475 (Fed. C.A.).

[115] (1938), [1938] 2 D.L.R. 145, 55 R.P.C. 125 (Ontario P.C.).

[116] *Ibid.*, at 145.

[117] (1878), 7 Ch. D. 834 (Eng. Ch. Div.).

[118] (1924), [1924] S.C.R. 600, [1925] 1 D.L.R. 233 (S.C.C.).

the sale of goods of which the oil of cedar was a component part. It would be in this connection a word descriptive of a quality or of the character of the goods.

It does not appear necessary to refer to many authorities in support of this proposition. They are quoted in abundance in the judgments under appeal. That a word in common use as the name of a thing cannot be appropriated as a trade-mark is shown by the decision of the Judicial Committee in *Standard Ideal Co. v. Standard Sanitary Mfg. Co.*[[1911] A.C. 78]. As was said in that case, a common English word having reference to the character and quality of the goods cannot be an apt or an appropriate instrument for distinguishing the goods of one trader from those of another. And the mere prefixing of the letter 'O' to such a word as cedar certainly does not make it so distinctive that registration gives to the appellants the right to complain of the use of it by another manufacturer to describe a polish whereof oil of cedar is one of the ingredients.

Mr. Henderson argued that the word 'cedar' used in the trade-mark in question had acquired a secondary meaning as signifying the appellants' goods. We have carefully read the evidence and can find nothing in support of this contention. No doubt the trade knew that the appellants were manufacturing a polish under the name 'O'Cedar,' as they were aware that other manufacturers were using the word 'cedar,' but there is nothing here to indicate that the latter word as used had become in any way distinctive of the appellants' goods.

One question is whether a mark with some functional aspects is clearly descriptive. Considering this issue, the Federal Court of Appeal in *Pizza Pizza Ltd. v. Canada (Registrar of Trade Marks)* held that a phone number was registrable as a mark for a take-out pizza delivery business and not in violation of s. 12(1)(b) of the *Trade-marks Act* because the number did not clearly describe the product or service provided.[119] It is true, the court acknowledged, that the numerical combination of a telephone number has functional aspects, but that is not its sole function and the number, allotted by the telephone company (albeit probably one the company helped select because of its mnemonic qualities) is unrelated to the goods themselves.

*Parke, Davis* also considered the notion of functional use in the context of pharmaceuticals where the company tried to trade-mark the coloured bands on pill capsules. The Supreme Court rejected this as, "the law appears to be well settled that if what is sought to be registered as a trade-mark has a functional use or characteristic, it cannot be the subject of a trade-mark,"

---

[119] [1989] 3 F.C. 379, 26 C.P.R. (3d) 355, 101 N.R. 378, 24 C.I.P.R. 152 (Fed. C.A.).

and here the coloured band functioned to seal the cap to the body of the drug capsule.[120]

The topic of functional use also comes up with respect to distinguishing guise marks. According to s. 13, to be registrable a "distinguishing guise" must be distinctive at the time of registration and exclusive use of the distinguishing guise mark is "not likely unreasonably to limit the development of any art or industry." In a case considering the functional aspects of a distinguishing guise mark, *Remington Rand Corp. v. Philips Electronics N.V.*, Phillips had registered the triangular arrangement of three shaving heads on rotary electric shavers as a distinguishing guise mark for their shavers and tried to prevent Remington Rand from marketing a similarly configured triple headed rotary shaver on the grounds that it infringed Philips's mark. The marks, however, were expunged because the court held that such an arrangement of the three cutting heads was primarily functional.[121]

## (a) Names

People can use their own name or names of persons who are living or have died within the preceding thirty years as trade names and register them when such names become distinctive (s. 12(2)). The example of TIM HORTON'S shops may be the best known, but other examples include several brands of perfumes, cosmetics, clothing and athletic equipment.[122] Section 12(1)(a) must be read in conjunction with s. 9(1)(k), which prohibits adoption of a mark which "falsely" suggests a connection with any living individual. There is a parallel prohibition on the use of portraits or signatures in s. 9(1)(l), which extends also to individuals who died in preceding thirty years and does not contain the requirement of falsehood. Both prohibitions in s. 9 are subject to a "consent" limitation, contained in s. 9(2)(a).

The word "falsely" in s. 9(1)(k) is important. For instance, if an individual has agreed to "sponsor" a particular product or service, then the connection suggested is not false. But consent, which excludes the prohibition (see s. 9(2)(a)), is not the only way to avoid falsehood.

In *Carson v. Reynolds*, the two above mentioned sections were used to prevent the use of HERE'S JOHNNY, a signature introduction for the late U.S. television show host Johnny Carson on the *Tonight Show*, as a mark

---

[120] *Supra*, note 28 at para. 6.

[121] *Supra*, note 27.

[122] Tim Horton was a famous hockey player for the Toronto Maple Leafs. He died in 1974.

for portable toilets.[123] The court banned the use of this name because contrary to s. 12(1)(a) of the Act it was primarily merely the name of a living person, and contrary to s. 9(1)(k) of the Act it created a misleading link between the product and Johnny Carson.

In *Canada (Registrar of Trade Marks) v. Coles Book Stores Ltd.*, the court determined that the word COLES was "primarily" a surname, rather than one dictionary definition of "cole" meaning cabbage.[124] Section 12(1)(a) thus applied.

The registration of a mark does not prevent a person from using one's own name as a trade-*name*, defined in s. 2, as the name "under which any business is carried on, whether or not it is the name of a corporation, a partnership or an individual." However, as provided for in s. 20(1)(a), the name cannot be used as a trade-*mark*, within the parameters of s. 9(1)(k) and 12(1)(a). One could thus use one's name as the name of a company but could not sell goods or offer services and advertise under that name if s. 9(1)(k) applied. In the case of s. 12(1)(a), registration will not be possible until secondary meaning (see Distinctiveness Section) can be shown pursuant to ss. 12(2) and 32.

### (b) Foreign Marks

According to s. 14, foreign marks can be registered in Canada even if s. 12 would normally constitute a bar to such registration. That section contains specific criteria that apply to foreign registered marks, namely it must not:

(*a*)    be confusing with a registered trade-mark;

(*b*)    be without distinctive character, having regard to all the circumstances of the case including the length of time during which it has been used in any country;

(*c*)    contrary to morality or public order or of such a nature as to deceive the public; or

(*d*)    a trade-mark of which the adoption is prohibited by section 9 or 10.

The test under ss. (1)(a), (c) and (d) are similar to those used in respect of Canadian marks.[125] There is a question, however, as to whether the

---

[123] [1980] 2 F.C. 685, 115 D.L.R. (3d) 139, 49 C.P.R. (2d) 57 (Fed. T.D.).

[124] (1972), [1974] S.C.R. 438, 23 D.L.R. (3d) 568, 4 C.P.R. (2d) 1 (S.C.C.).

[125] See *Canadian Council of Professional Engineers v. Lubrication Engineers Inc.* (1984), [1985] 1 F.C. 530, 1 C.P.R. (3d) 309 (Fed. T.D.), affirmed (sub nom. *Lubrication Engineers Inc. v. Canadian Council of Professional Engineers*) [1992] 2 F.C. 329, (sub nom. *Lubrication Engineers Inc. v. Canadian Council*

"distinctive character" requirement of s. (1)(b) is identical to the "distinctiveness" that Canadian marks must acquire under, for example, ss. 12(2) or 13 or the "inherent distinctiveness" of s. 6(5)(a). The latter expression refers to distinctiveness that either does not need a substantial amount of time to be acquired, which is usually the case for non-descriptive coined words,[126] or has been acquired through extensive use in Canada.[127] That leaves open the question of identity of the distinctive character and distinctiveness standards. The Federal Court of Appeal has taken the view that these words have different meanings, and that for a mark to be "not without distinctive character" (s. 14 (1)(b)) is a less stringent standard than the "full" distinctiveness required in other parts of the Act:

> The effect of s. 14 is that a foreign registered trade-mark must still satisfy certain threshold conditions in order to be eligible for registration in Canada. One of those conditions is that the trade-mark must have a 'distinctive character'. This is a less demanding test than distinctiveness but it still requires some evidence of use in Canada (*W.R. Grace & Co. v. Union Carbide Corp.* (1987), 14 C.P.R. (3d) 337 ay p. 346):
>
> > Thus, I think that it can be said that in reference to trade marks, the term 'distinctive character' means those trade marks which have the traits or characteristics of distinctive trade marks. To revert to the definition, set forth above, the characteristic of distinctive trade marks in Canada is that they actually distinguish the wares or services of the owner from the wares or services of others or are adapted to distinguish them. To put it another way, if a mark to some extent *in fact distinguishes* the wares or services of the owners from those of others, *the mark is not without distinctive character.* In the context of this case, the trade mark being descriptive, it may not be sufficiently distinctive <u>to have acquired a secondary meaning in Canada</u> to satisfy the definition of distinctive. None the less, it may have some distinctiveness. If that is so, <u>it is not without distinctive character in Canada.</u> [emphasis added in original].

Use in Canada seems to be implicit in the passage which I have emphasized above. However, the question was specifically addressed by McKeown J. in *Supershuttle International, Inc. v. Canada (Registrar of Trade-Marks)* (2002), 19 C.P.R. (4th) 34 (F.C. T.D.):

---

*of Professional Engineers*) 41 C.P.R. (3d) 243, (sub nom. *Lubrication Engineers Inc. v. Canadian Council of Professional Engineers*) 140 N.R. 318 (Fed. C.A.).
[126] See *Standard Coil, supra,* note 88.
[127] See *Alticor Inc. v. Nutravite Pharmaceuticals Inc.* (2003), [2003] F.C.J. No. 930, 27 C.P.R. (4th) 99, 235 F.T.R. 53, 2003 CarswellNat 1697 (Fed. T.D.).

In this case the applicant submitted there was no need for the mark to be
have been used or made known in Canada under this section [14(1)(b)].
However, I disagree, since the language of the provision explicitly uses
the words 'in Canada', stating that a trade-mark is registrable if 'in
Canada ... it is not without distinctive character'. In my view, this
language suggests a requirement of at least some knowledge of the mark
in Canada. Knowledge or use exclusively in another country would be
insufficient.

While there may be some difference between distinctive character and the
distinctiveness of a mark, the jurisprudence is consistently to the effect that
distinctiveness can only be acquired by use in Canada. It is not obvious why
the demonstration of 'distinctive character' should not be subject to the same
condition. The following comments of Tomlin J. in *Impex Electric Ltd. v.
Weinbaum* (1927), 44 R.P.C. 405, at p. 410 have frequently been cited in the
Federal Court:

> For the purpose of seeing whether the mark is distinctive, it is to the
> market of this country alone that one has to have regard. For that purpose
> foreign markets are wholly irrelevant, unless it be shown by evidence
> that in fact goods have been sold in this country with a foreign mark on
> them, and that the mark so used has thereby become identified with the
> manufacturer of the goods.
> [Several cases where the above was cited are mentioned]

The result is that foreign registered trade-marks which are not inherently distinctive may well see their registration in Canada at risk in expungement
proceedings unless they can show some degree of acquired distinctiveness
through use in Canada. Since the date at which distinctiveness is to be assessed
for purposes of s. 18 is the date at which expungement proceedings are begun,
delay in using the marks following registration works against the registrant. In
this case, there is a gap of some three years between the date of registration
and the date of expungement proceedings. It may well have been possible for
the BOSTON CHICKEN mark to acquire distinctiveness had it been used in
Canada in that period of time.[128]

The *Boston Pizza* case has been interpreted as not requiring use in
Canada in order to acquire distinctiveness, when the mark is *a priori* inher-

---

[128] *Boston Pizza International Inc. v. Boston Chicken Inc.* (2003), [2003] F.C.J. No.
395, 24 C.P.R. (4th) 150, 301 N.R. 190, 239 F.T.R. 160 (note), 2003 CarswellNat
583 (Fed. C.A.) at paras. 11-14 [*Boston Pizza* cited to C.P.R.]. See also *Supershuttle International Inc. v. Canada (Registrar of Trade-Marks)* (2002), [2002]
F.C.J. No. 530, 19 C.P.R. (4th) 34, 218 F.T.R. 306, 2002 CarswellNat 789 (Fed.
T.D.); and *Alticor Inc. v. Nutravite Pharmaceuticals Inc., supra*, note 127.

ently distinctive, for example a coined word.[129] Indeed, a mark which, because it is a non-descriptive coined word or expression, is "inherently" capable of distinguishing the goods or services of one undertaking from those of another would seem to meet the requirement of s. 14(1)(b), especially because that subsection specifically refers to use in another country. The inherent ability of the mark to distinguish must be assessed from a Canadian standpoint, however, as the "in Canada" language in s. 14(1) specifies.

An apparent difficulty in statutory interpretation stems from the fact that s. 18 requires that any mark be distinctive at the time "proceedings bringing the validity of the registration into question are commenced." The difficulty is only apparent. First, the two dates are different: the "distinctive character" of s. 14 is assessed as of the date of application because s. 14 is a "notwithstanding" provision linked to s. 12, which specifically refers to the date of filing. Second, according to the definition of "distinctive" in s. 2, a mark is distinctive provided it "actually distinguishes the wares or services in association with which it is used by its owner from the wares or services of others *or is adapted so to distinguish them.*"

## 8. Confusion

Confusion is perhaps the most important concept in trade-mark law. It essentially defines the scope of the rights of the trade-mark owner. The fundamental principle of trade-mark law, as enunciated in 19th century cases, is that it is unfair to let a defendant sell its product as being that of another person and to let one undertaking benefit from the goodwill of another. But the test as to whether a product or service is marketed as those of another, or as to whether one company is trying to unfairly appropriate another's goodwill, is not based on the perception of the trade-mark owner but rather on the perception of prospective buyers. In most cases, the trade-mark owner will have to show the existence of actual consumer confusion, or in cases where the *Act* or the common law lower the threshold, only the likelihood of confusion resulting from a defendant's use of an identical or similar mark to the trade-mark owner's.

Section 12(1)(d) of the Act states that a mark that creates confusion with a registered trade-mark or a commercial name is not registrable. The

---

[129] *WCC Containers Sales Ltd. v. Haul-All Equipment Ltd.* (2003), [2003] F.C.J. No. 1266, 28 C.P.R. (4th) 175, 238 F.T.R. 45, 2003 CarswellNat 5181 (F.C.).

date at which confusion exists is the filing date of the application.[130] The confusion must be in relation to the *origin* of the product; that is, a consumer mistakenly thinks it comes from one company when in reality it comes from another. Section 6(2) provides that the use of a trade-mark causes confusion with another trade-mark if using both in the same area would be likely to lead consumers to infer that the goods or services came from the same source, even if the goods or services are different.[131] Section 6(5) provides courts with a guide to determine whether a trade-mark is confusing. It states:

> In determining whether trade-marks or trade-names are confusing, the court or the Registrar, as the case may be, shall have regard to all the surrounding circumstances including:
>
> a)    the inherent distinctiveness of the trade-marks or trade-names and the extent to which they have become known;
> b)    the length of time the trade-mark or trade-names have been in used;
> c)    the nature of the wares, services or business;
> d)    the nature of the trade; and
> e)    the degree of resemblance between the trade-marks or trade-names in appearance or sound or in the ideas suggested by them.

The criteria stated in s. 6(5) can be simplified to five basic concepts to establish confusion: strength, length of use, type of merchandise and service, nature of commerce and resemblance. These criteria do not all have equal weight and appropriate importance must be given to each criteria based on the circumstances of each case.[132]

> To decide whether the use of a trade-mark or of a trade-name causes confusion with another trade-mark or another trade-name, the Court must ask itself whether, as a matter of first impression on the minds of an ordinary person having a vague recollection of that other mark or name, the use of both marks or names in the same area in the same manner is likely to lead to the inference that the services associated with those marks or names are performed by the same person, whether or not the services are of the same general class.

---

[130] See *George Weston Ltd. v. Humpty Dumpty Foods Ltd.* (1989), [1989] F.C.J. No. 401, (sub nom. *Humpty Dumpty Foods Ltd. v. George Weston Ltd.*) 24 C.P.R. (3d) 454, 24 C.I.P.R. 14, (sub nom. *Humpty Dumpty Foods Ltd. v. George Weston Ltd.*) 27 F.T.R. 219, 1989 CarswellNat 514 (Fed. T.D.).

[131] *Miss Universe Inc. v. Bohna* (1994), [1995] 1 F.C. 614, 58 C.P.R. (3d) 381, 176 N.R. 35 (Fed. C.A.); *Molson Breweries, A Partnership v. John Labatt Ltd.*, (sub nom. *Molson Breweries v. John Labatt Ltd.*) [2000] 3 F.C. 145, 5 C.P.R. (4th) 180, 252 N.R. 91 (Fed. C.A.), leave to appeal refused (2000), 7 C.P.R. (4th) vi (S.C.C.).

[132] *Ibid.*

In determining whether there is a likelihood of confusion, the Court shall have regard to all the surrounding circumstances, including those described in subsection 6(5) above.

The onus is always upon an applicant for the registration of a trade-mark to establish that, on the balance of probabilities, there is no likelihood of confusion with a previously used and registered trade-mark.[133] [footnotes omitted]

When considering the *strength* of a trade-mark, the trade-mark has to be considered both as a whole[134] and in its entire context.[135] As Thorson J. explains:

Trade marks may be similar when looked at in their totality even if differences may appear in some of the elements when viewed separately. It is the combination of the elements that constitutes the trade mark and gives distinctiveness to it, and it is the effect of the trade mark as a whole, rather than of any particular element in it, that must be considered.[136]

A simple rule of thumb to evaluate the strength of a mark is to determine whether the use of that mark in connection with goods or services different from those with which it is currently used would lead the public to believe there is a connection between the "new" product or service and the trademark owner. A strong mark can be used in connection with goods or services that differ widely from the original goods or services and still cause the public to believe there is a connection with the original source. A strong trade-mark will have a broader protection than a weak mark. For example, a coined word used as a trade-mark often has a greater distinctiveness and, hence, a broader scope of protection than a common word used as a trademark. Trade-marks consisting of common words are weak.[137] When marks are weak, smaller differences are enough to avoid confusion.[138]

---

[133] *Ibid.*

[134] *Battle Pharmaceuticals v. British Drug Houses Ltd.*, [1944] Ex. C.R. 239, [1944] 4 D.L.R. 577, 4 C.P.R. 48 (Can. Ex. Ct.), affirmed (1945), [1946] S.C.R. 50 (S.C.C.) [*Battle Pharmaceuticals* cited to Ex. C.R.].

[135] *Simmons Ltd. v. A to Z Comfort Beddings Ltd.* (1991), [1991] F.C.J. No. 546, (sub nom. *Park Avenue Furniture Corp. v. Wickes/Simmons Bedding Ltd.*) 37 C.P.R. (3d) 413, (sub nom. *Park Avenue Furniture Corp. v. Wickes/Simmons Bedding Ltd.*) 130 N.R. 223, 1991 CarswellNat 1119 (Fed. C.A.).

[136] *Supra*, note 134.

[137] *General Motors Corp. v. Bellows* (1949), [1949] S.C.R. 678, [1950] 1 D.L.R. 569, 10 C.P.R. 101 (S.C.C.).

[138] *Commercial Union Assurance Co. plc v. Canadian Co-operative Credit Society Ltd.* (1992), [1992] F.C.J. No. 450, (sub nom. *Canadian Co-operative Credit*

The *length of use* can be a determining factor in regards to confusion. In *Panavision Inc. v. Matsushita Electric Industrial Co.*, the court concluded that the two marks that had existed side by side for a period of ten years, without any evidence of confusion during this period could not be said to be confusing.[139] The longer two marks have coexisted, the more difficult it will be to convince a court that there exists a likelihood of confusion without evidence of actual confusion.[140]

The *type of merchandise and service* can be very determinative in establishing confusion. If two marks operate in distinct fields, there is a smaller likelihood of confusion. For example, in *Clorox Co. v. Sears Canada Inc.*, the judge stated that fruit-cake and barbecue sauce which both used the name MASTERPIECE were different types of merchandise and that confusion was unlikely.[141] "Masterpiece" is a very general word, with limited strength as a trade-mark. Furthermore, in *Joseph E. Seagram & Sons Ltd. v. Canada (Registrar of Trade Marks)*, the court found that the mark SEAGRAM was only protected in the field of alcoholic beverages and that use of that name for a real estate company would not create consumer confusion.[142]

The *nature of commerce* test relates to the methods and strategies of commercialization. The court illustrated the importance of the channels of distribution and targeted clientele in *Tiger Brand Knitting Co. v. John E. Fetzer Inc.*[143] In this case the court had to determine whether there could be

---

*Society Ltd. v. Commercial Union Assurance Co. PLC*) 42 C.P.R. (3d) 239, (sub nom. *Canadian Co-operative Credit Society Ltd. v. Commercial Union Assurance Co. PLC*) 56 F.T.R. 1, 1992 CarswellNat 176 (Fed. T.D.); *Panavision Inc. v. Matsushita Electric Industrial Co.* (1992), [1992] F.C.J. No. 19, 40 C.P.R. (3d) 486, (sub nom. *Matsushita Electric Industrial Co. v. Panavision Inc.*) 53 F.T.R. 228, 1992 CarswellNat 1018 (Fed. T.D.).

[139] *Ibid.*

[140] See *ConAgra Inc. v. McCain Foods Ltd.* (2001), [2001] F.C.J. No. 1331, 14 C.P.R. (4th) 288, 210 F.T.R. 227, 2001 CarswellNat 1941 (Fed. T.D.).

[141] [1992] 2 F.C. 579, 41 C.P.R. (3d) 483, 53 F.T.R. 105 (Fed. T.D.), affirmed (1993), [1993] F.C.J. No. 508, 49 C.P.R. (3d) 217, 155 N.R. 159, 1993 CarswellNat 1903 (Fed. C.A.).

[142] (1990), [1990] F.C.J. No. 909, (sub nom. *Joseph E. Seagram & Sons Ltd. v. Seagram Real Estate Ltd.*) 33 C.P.R. (3d) 454, (sub nom. *Seagram (Joseph E.) & Sons Ltd. v. Canada (Registrar of Trademarks)*) 38 F.T.R. 96, 1990 CarswellNat 826 (Fed. T.D.).

[143] (1989), [1989] F.C.J. No. 439, 26 C.P.R. (3d) 551, 24 C.I.P.R. 8, (sub nom. *John E. Fetzer Inc. v. Tiger Brand Knitting Co.*) 31 F.T.R. 87, 1989 CarswellNat 513 (Fed. T.D.). See also *Alticor Inc. v. Nutravite Pharmaceuticals Inc.*, *supra*, note 127.

confusion between Detroit Tigers (a professional baseball team) merchandise labeled as TIGER and a brand of clothing called TIGER:

> The opposition chairman failed to recognize that the logos differed, that they are pitched to different consumers in different settings and with different channels of distribution.
>
> The singular common element in respect of the marks is the word 'tiger'. So long as this is the only similarity and there are other distinguishing features in the competing marks, the protection of the statute cannot be invoked. [. . .]
>
> The primary focus of the court must be on the likelihood of confusion and the motive of any party is never more than a minor or secondary consideration. In the final analysis, however, no judgment can be made without an appreciation of the manner in which the competing parties intend to market their products. Evaluation of the likelihood of confusion cannot be done in a vacuum.

The degree of *resemblance* is evaluated by considering the whole mark, though when the mark is composed in part of a common word, courts tend to focus on the other elements.[144] For example, in *Pepsi-Cola Co. v. Coca-Cola Co.*, Davis J. stated: "What is protected by law is the whole mark as registered but a part of the mark may be so taken and used as to amount to a substantial taking of the whole."[145] Consideration was then given to the fact that "cola," the similar element of the compound marks, was not distinctive.

While the *Trade-marks Act* codifies the elements to be taken into account in s. 6, their respective weight in each case and the conclusion to be reached is largely a factual matter, as explained by Thorson J. in *Battle Pharmaceuticals*:[146]

> The Courts have realized the difficulty involved when a Judge seeks to project himself into the minds of other persons in order to ascertain what the effect of certain circumstances would be likely to have on them and, with a view to reducing the extent of the subjective attitude to a given problem of this kind, have laid down certain principles, both general and specific, as guides to be followed. Cases in which trade marks have been held to be similar are

---

[144] Even when part of it is disclaimed (see s. 35 , the Registration Section and *Globetrotter Management Ltd. v. General Mills Inc.*, [1972] F.C. 1187, 8 C.P.R. (2d) 143 (Fed. T.D.)).

[145] (1939), [1940] S.C.R. 17, [1940] 1 D.L.R. 161 (S.C.C.), affirmed [1942] 2 D.L.R. 657, [1942] 2 W.W.R. 257, 1 C.P.R. 293 (Canada P.C.). See also *Sealy Sleep Products Ltd. v. Simpson's-Sears Ltd.* (1960), 33 C.P.R. 129 (Can. Ex. Ct.) (The common "word" in both marks was "pedic").

[146] *Supra*, note 134.

numerous [. . .]. Such cases are not helpful except so far as they express or illustrate guiding principles, for each case is peculiar to itself so far as the actual trade marks involved in it are concerned. This view, frequently expressed in the authorities, was recently clearly stated by the Judicial Committee of the Privy Council in *Coca-Cola Co. of Canada Ltd. v. Pepsi-Cola Co. of Canada Ltd.*, [1942] 2 D.L.R. 657 at pp. 661-2, where Lord Russell said:

> Except when some general principle is laid down, little assistance is derived from authorities in which the question of infringement is discussed in relation to other marks and other circumstances.

It is possible to have confusion between wares and services.[147]

The Act includes an exception which allows otherwise confusing marks to be registered if the applicant owns all the marks in question (s. 15). These marks are cross-referenced in the registry entries and are known as associated trade-marks.

To which consumer does the confusion test apply? The court first should consider the issue of confusion from the standpoint of the likely consumer and not the average consumer, especially for goods sold in specialized markets or via specialized channels. For example, in the case of pharmaceuticals, the group of "consumers" includes pharmacists and doctors,[148] but it may also include the end-users/patients.[149] In *Hudson's Bay Co. v. Baylor University*,[150] the Federal Court of Appeal discussed the "likely consumer" test:

> The appellant makes the point that the 'minority of sports fanatics' referred to by the Trial Judge in this passage may well constitute the class of consumers which must be borne in mind in addressing the issue of confusion in this case.

---

[147] *Building Products Ltd. v. B.P. Canada Ltd.* (1961), 21 Fox Pat. C. 130, 36 C.P.R. 121 (Can. Ex. Ct.).

[148] *Ayerst, McKenna & Harrison Inc. v. Apotex Inc.* (1983), 41 O.R. (2d) 366, 146 D.L.R. (3d) 93, 72 C.P.R. (2d) 57 (Ont. C.A.); *Smith, Kline & French Canada Ltd. v. Novopharm Ltd.* (1983), 72 C.P.R. (2d) 197 (Ont. H.C.); *Syntex Inc. v. Novopharm Ltd.* (1983), 74 C.P.R. (2d) 110 (Ont. H.C.); *Syntex Inc. v. Apotex Inc.*, [1984] 2 F.C. 1012, 1 C.P.R. (3d) 145, 55 N.R. 135 (Fed. C.A.) .

[149] *Ciba-Geigy Canada Ltd. v. Apotex Inc.*, [1992] 3 S.C.R. 120, 95 D.L.R. (4th) 385, 44 C.P.R. (3d) 289, 143 N.R. 241 (S.C.C.) [*Ciba-Geigy* cited to S.C.R.]. However, in cases where only the outer packaging is perceived, the colour of the pill may not be directly relevant. See *Astrazeneca AB v. Novopharm Ltd.* (2001), 15 C.P.R. (4th) 476 (Fed. T.D.), additional reasons at (2002), 18 C.P.R. (4th) 88 (Fed. T.D.), affirmed (2003), 24 C.P.R. (4th) 326 (Fed. C.A.), leave to appeal refused (2003), 26 C.P.R. (4th) vi (S.C.C.).

[150] (2000), (sub nom. *Baylor University v. Hudson's Bay Co.*) 8 C.P.R. (4th) 64, 257 N.R. 231 (Fed. C.A.).

It is well established that the issue of confusion arising from the sale of wares under competing trade-marks must be determined by reference to persons who are likely to purchase those wares. In *Cheung Kong (Holdings) Ltd. v. Living Realty Inc.*, [[2000] 2 F.C. 501, 4 C.P.R. (4th) 71, (F.C.T.D.).] Evans J. said:

> Counsel for the opponent referred me to cases for the more general proposition that the test for confusion is whether the 'average consumer' might be confused, and that this hypothetical person was to be identified in the context of the actual consumers of the product associated with the mark. Thus, whether a mark is likely to cause confusion is a question that is to be asked, not in the abstract, but in respect of the particular market in which the wares or services are offered.

> Thus, in *Canadian Schenley Distilleries Ltd. v. Canada's Manitoba Distillery Ltd.* (1975), 25 C.P.R. (2d) 1 (F.C.T.D.), Cattanach J. said (at page 5):

>> To determine whether two marks are confusing one with the other it is the persons who are likely to buy the wares who are to be considered, that is those persons who normally comprise the market, the ultimate consumer.

> McKeown J. expressed the same view in *McDonald's Corp. v. Coffee Hut Stores Ltd.*[(1994), 55 C.P.R. (3d) 463 (F.C.T.D.)] in relation to the use of surveys.
> [. . .]

> The evidence of Mr. Warrington is that the market for collegiate merchandise in Canada is primarily clothing (sweatshirts, T-shirts and caps) purchased and worn by males between ages 15 to 40, who have a particular interest in sport. His evidence in this respect is consistent with the evidence of the Hudson's Bay Company which is to the effect that it also sells collegiate clothing, bearing U.S. university designations such as UCLA, Michigan, Georgetown etc., through its sporting goods department and that typical purchasers are male, between the ages of 10 and 25. [footnotes omitted]

Another consideration is which language the relevant consumer speaks. In *Ferrero S.p.A. c. Produits Freddy Inc.*,[151] the court had to pronounce on the confusion found between NUTELLA and NOIXELLE (the French word "noix" means "nut"):

> [T]he issue of likelihood of confusion is one of concrete fact to be verified in real life and not one to be inferred from the constitutionally bilingual nature of

---

[151] (1988), 22 C.P.R. (3d) 346, 24 C.I.P.R. 189 (Fed. C.A.).

the country. The bilingual nature of the country has resulted in translated versions of trade marks having become commonplace. In those areas where the trade marks are worded in the local language, the buying public may more easily be confused by two trade marks which appear to be translated version one with the other but this ought not to bring about an inappropriate extension of the protected domain of a trade mark.

In that case, however, the Federal Court of Appeal found that there was no likelihood of confusion because both marks were invented words and NOIXELLE was an approximation, not a translation of NUTELLA. In addition, it was unlikely that the average bilingual consumer would dissect the words in the same way as a professional translator.

Language often becomes a cause of confusion, as in *Boy Scouts of Canada v. Alfred Sternjakob GmbH & Co. KG*, a case in which a company wanted to sell products under the mark SCOUT & DESIGN, which the plaintiff alleged caused confusion with the Scout movement.[152] Joyal J. came to the following conclusion:

> It will be noted that in the French idiom, the word 'scout' is the equivalent of the English word 'scout'. This meaning, however, is limited to the genus scout as applied to the scout movement. In French, the word 'scout' has no other etymology. The word has no association with Buffalo Bill or a hunter of football talent.

> The dictionary meaning in French of the word 'scout' or 'scoute' is 'jeunes garçons, jeunes filles faisant partie d'une association de scoutisme', i.e., young boys and young girls engaged in the scout movement. [Le Petit] Robert gives us a similar meaning of the word. From this it is clear to me that the French word 'scout' not only connotes the scout movement but is by definition exclusive to it. By definition, there is no other ascribable meaning to it.

> *Quaere*, in those circumstances, to what extent this court should take this factor into consideration. It could be argued that the criteria in the *Trade Marks Act* and the evidential findings thereunder as to confusion or deception should be measured not only with reference to English-speaking experience but to French-speaking experience as well. This would result in an enquiry as to the connotation or otherwise of certain words in a bilingual context, with each language having equal presence.

> It is a fact that the policy of the Trade Marks Office and the practice of counsel and of agents before it are to check into and analyse the descriptive, misdescriptive, misleading, distinguishing and confusing consequences which flow

---

[152] (1984), [1984] F.C.J. No. 1111, 2 C.P.R. (3d) 407, 4 C.I.P.R. 118, 1984 CarswellNat 604 (Fed. T.D.) [*Boy Scouts of Canada* cited to C.P.R.].

from a French or English adaptation of any particular word or the use of it as a registered trade mark.

The wares of the applicant under the 'scout' label are to be sold throughout Canada. The evidence discloses that they will be sold through outlets including young people's stores and department stores. They will be advertised and displayed for sale in the French-speaking market. In that market the name 'scout' is descriptive of the scout movement and by inference is identified with the appellant's purposes and programmes. In that market the word 'scout' or 'scoute' has but one definition and but one connotation.

From that base, it is but one tiny leap to consider the actual wares with which the applicant proposes to use the SCOUT label. The wares are described as 'school bags, travel bags, city bags, suitcases and trunks'. The exhibits filed by the applicant consisting of facsimiles and photographs of SCOUT-labelled products in use in Europe show bags very much of the rucksack or backpack variety and are depicted against an outdoor background of physical activity including hiking, picnicking, bicycling, walking and camping. The image this creates has remarkable similarity not only with the image one might have of scout programmes and activities in Canada but with the actual and constant generic character of such programmes and activities.

I would agree that the exclusive meaning and connotation of the French 'scout' on the one hand, and the similarity of wares proposed by the applicant with those in use by the appellant constitute in a sense a stacking process. Neither element taken alone would be a determinant. Both taken together lead me to conclude that the proposed mark would be confusing if not deceptive.

In reaching this conclusion, I have had regard to the provisions of s. 6 of the *Trade Marks Act* and to the considerations imposed by s. 6(5) and of paras. (a) to (e) thereof.

The Trade-marks Office commented on the *Boy Scouts of Canada* case in a later decision:

[I]t is evident that the question of confusion should be assessed in a bilingual context in which both the English and French languages are accorded equal importance. It appears to me that there are two basic ways in which this goal might be accomplished: i) assess the question of confusion in the context of unilingual francophones, unilingual anglophones and bilingual persons and then if two trade marks are confusing to the average member of any of these groups conclude that the trade marks are confusing, or ii) assess the question of confusion in the context of bilingual persons only. The former approach would appear to be flawed in that it is inconsistent with the long established principle that trade marks which are descriptive in English or French of the wares or services with which they are associated are weak and only entitled to a narrow ambit of protection: see, e.g., *General Motors Corp. v. Bellows* (1949), 10 C.P.R. 101. If one followed the former approach, one would have to conclude that most trade marks which are descriptive in the English language only are still strong because they would have no meaning for an average unilingual francophone and *vice versa*. This could effectively permit individuals to obtain monopolies in descriptive words which would clearly be contrary to the public interest and to the intent of the *Trade Marks Act*. The latter approach of considering the question of confusion in the context of bilingual persons only is somewhat artificial in that only a minority of Canadians are actually bilingual; however, because of the above discussed flaw with the former approach, I consider it much more reasonable to follow the latter approach.[153]

Compare the *Produits Freddy* (Nutella) case with *Monsport Inc. v. Vêtements de Sport Bonnie (1978) Ltée*, where the issue was that of confusion between MONSPORT and BONSPORT.[154] The judge made the following findings, following a typical s. 6(5) analytical method:

Jurisprudence has also established that the plaintiff must be able to show that a likelihood of confusion between the marks exists; he is not required to prove that confusion has actually occurred. It is important to note however, that the court is entitled to draw negative conclusions about the plaintiff's case if, despite a substantial period of co-existence in the market-place, no instances of actual confusion are established: Freed & Freed Ltd. v. Registrar of Trade Marks (1950), 14 C.P.R. 19, [1951] 2 D.L.R. 7, [1950] Ex. C.R. 431.

One may now, in the light of the above-mentioned general principles, consider the application of the subparagraphs of s. 6(5) of the *Trade Marks Act* to the particular facts of this case.

*(a) The inherent distinctiveness of the trade marks or trade-names and the extent to which they have become known*

Neither of the trade marks in question has a high degree of inherent distinctiveness. Furthermore, the word 'sport' is a very common word and has a high degree of descriptiveness in either official language when used in association with sport clothes. Even if it were argued that the term 'mon sport' would have no meaning to a unilingual anglophone, the meaning of the use of the suffix 'sport' in association with sport clothes must be considered to be unmistakable.

---

[153] *Vins La Salle Inc. v. Vignobles Chantecler Ltée* (1985), 6 C.P.R. (3d) 533 (T.M. Opp. Bd.) at 535-36. See also *SmithKline Beecham Corp. c. Pierre Fabre Médicament* (1998), [1998] T.M.O.B. No. 141, 1998 CarswellNat 3245 (T.M. Opp. Bd.).

[154] (1988), [1988] F.C.J. No. 1077, 22 C.P.R. (3d) 356, 23 F.T.R. 222, 21 C.I.P.R. 207, 1988 CarswellNat 612 (Fed. T.D.) [*Monsport* cited to C.P.R.].

Even if the purchasers in question were assumed to have virtually no knowledge of the French language, the words 'mon' and 'bon' are ones that are most likely to be known in Canada by someone with even the most minimal contact with the French language. The phrases 'bon voyage' and 'bon appetit' are virtually part of the English language and the term 'mon amour' is quite widely known. They now might almost be considered as part of English usage in Canada.

The trader who uses a trade mark which incorporates an element that is common to the trade and highly descriptive such as the word 'sport' cannot expect a broad ambit of protection for the trade mark. . .

[. . .]

*(b) The length of time the trade marks or trade names have been used*

The marks have been used for almost the same length of time. The plaintiff commenced using MONSPORT in the fall of 1982, and the defendant commenced using its mark some seven months later. The plaintiff hence cannot benefit from a long period of exclusive use to allow the court to draw the inference that its trade mark has become widely known.

*(c) The nature of the wares, services or business*

The wares of the parties are in the same general class, but there are some significant differences between the way they are currently marketed. As the plaintiff indicated in its authorities, it must not be forgotten that once a registration is obtained with respect to certain wares, the registrant is entitled to use the mark in association with those wares in any way in which it sees fit. It is not limited to a consideration of the way it has used the trade mark in association with the wares in the past.

[. . .]

*(d) The nature of the trade*

Both parties' wares are not very expensive items. It can be assumed that parties involved in their purchase will not spend an inordinate amount of time in the selection of the wares, or in consideration of the trade mark: *General Motors Corp. v. Bellows* (1947), 8 C.P.R. 1, [1948] 1 D.L.R. 375, [1947] Ex. C.R. 568. On the other hand, sportswear tends to be an area in which trade marks are of great importance and there are tremendous brand loyalties which are built up by speciality sport manufacturers such as Adidas, as was mentioned by the defendant's principal on discovery.

It is also relevant that even if the plaintiff's wares were sold in department stores, they might never be sold in the same area of the store as are the defendant's products. If the major thrust of the plaintiff's products is in fact the serious athlete, the plaintiff's wares would not be in competition with the defendant's wares which are a fashion item and presented to a different consumer, albeit under the same roof.

Where the marks under consideration are quite weak, smaller differences in the other subsections of s. 6 of the *Trade Marks Act are* sufficient to avoid a finding that the marks are confusing: *M & K Stereo Plus Ltd. v. Broadway Sound Plus Ltd.* (1985), 5 C.P.R. (3d) 390.

As to the geographical areas in which the parties market their wares, both parties are either currently selling or intend to sell across Canada.

*(e) The degree of resemblance between the trade marks or trade names in appearance or sound or in ideas suggested by them*

Both parties provided expert evidence with respect to the trade marks and the differences and similarities which exist between them. This evidence may be helpful in a comparison of the marks, but the question of the confusion in the mind of the public falls to be determined by the court, and is not a matter for expert evidence: Freed & Freed, supra, and Coca-Cola Co. of Canada Ltd., supra.

A determination of the matter is easier when the French consumer is considered. The words have very different meanings and no speaker of the French language would likely be confused as to the difference between the two marks. There is also some visual difference between the two marks, especially as the defendant uses the trade mark in a design form which is a dominant feature of the mark.

To the English speaking consumer, the mark might have a totally different impact. Both these trade marks have a meaning in French. . .

[. . .]

Even if the consumer faced with the marks MONSPORT and BONSPORT & Design does not have even the most rudimentary knowledge of French, there is a clearly recognizable common element shared by these two marks: the English word 'sport'. Any resemblance which is based on this descriptive element is not to be considered. As to the prefixes, they are phonetically different and are not totally foreign sounds to the English speaker, e.g., the proper name 'Mondale', the words 'bonfire' and 'bond'. The evidence offered by the plaintiff's linguistic expert leans too heavily on analytical auditory comparisons of the two marks, where it cannot be denied that the written aspect of the trade mark occurs more frequently in today's commercial environment.

They are both weak marks, and have been used in respect of similar wares over a four year period, and there is no proof of any instance of confusion ever having occurred, despite the fact that the wares may even be currently sold in the same department stores. The clothing trade is so vast, that even small differences in wares are probably sufficient to distinguish the wares of one party from those of another. Consumers in the market for casual wear readily distinguish between sweat-clothes designed for comfort and those designed for the more active person. They appear to be fairly distinct markets.

It would not seem that an Anglophone would have much more difficulty than a francophone in distinguishing the two trade marks. The sounds are not totally similar in English and, on the other hand, are quite distinguishable when written.

Although it is not necessary that the plaintiff show *mala fides* on the part of the defendant, it was conclusively established that there was nothing reprehensible in the defendant's conduct. The defendant's mark is in fact a contraction of its corporate name which it has been using for a long time. If anything, the plaintiff waited too long to commence this action. Having learned about the existence of the defendant at least as early as 1984, it did not institute its action until April, 1986.

In effect, the plaintiff has failed to discharge the onus of establishing that, in the circumstances of this case, the use of the two marks are likely to cause confusion in the market-place.

While anglophone, francophone and bilingual consumers are relevant,[155] those speaking other languages thus far have not been, at least under the standard confusion test.[156] In *Krazy Glue Inc. v. Group Cyanomex S.A. de C.V.*, the court determined that the confusion between KOLA LOKA and KRAZY GLUE would not be significant since only a portion of Canadians speak Spanish.[157] McGillis J. wrote:

> I have found as a fact that only a minimal proportion of the Canadian population speaks Spanish as a mother tongue or understands Spanish sufficiently to be capable of making the translation. I therefore conclude, on the basis of the facts established by the evidence, that the average consumer, having a vague or imperfect recollection of the registered trade-mark KRAZY GLUE, would find no degree of resemblance whatsoever in the ideas suggested by KOLA LOKA and KRAZY GLUE. Furthermore, I would have reached the same conclusion

---

[155] *Pierre Fabre Medicament v. SmithKline Beecham Corp.*, [2001] 2 F.C. 636, (sub nom. *Pierre Fabre Médicament c. SmithKline Beecham Corp.*), 11 C.P.R. (4th) 1, (sub nom. *Pierre Fabre Médicament v. Smithkline Beecham Corp.*) 271 N.R. 72, 200 F.T.R. 97 (note) (Fed. C.A.).

[156] See, however, the Well-Known Marks section.

[157] (1992), [1992] F.C.J. No. 957, 45 C.P.R. (3d) 161, (sub nom. *Jadow (B.) & Sons Inc. v. Grupo Cyanomex, S.A. de C.V.*) 57 F.T.R. 278, 1992 CarswellNat 1028 (Fed. T.D.).

even if the evidence tendered on appeal had established the existence of Spanish communities in Toronto and Quebec City. The mere fact that ethnic enclaves exist in two urban centres in the country would not be sufficient to displace the well-established average consumer test. Rather, such a fact, if established on the evidence, would constitute only an additional element to be considered in addressing the central question of the likelihood of confusion.

One may hope that, with the growing number of communities speaking foreign languages, and in keeping with passing-off decisions concerning well known foreign marks, the confusion test will be extended to other languages in appropriate cases (especially where a geographically determined market is relevant within the country — see s. 6(2): "in a certain area"). It should be noted that the *Trade-marks Act*, under section 12(1)(c), prohibits the registration as a mark of the name of the wares or services "in any language".

It is also worth noting that when a clearly descriptive mark or a mark based on a person's name becomes distinctive only in a part of the country, under s. 32(2), a registration may be obtained for that part of the country, as was the case for the mark ORANGE MAISON, the registration for which was limited to the province of Quebec in *Home Juice Co. v. Orange Maison Ltée*.[158]

Confusion can exist with only parts of a mark, such as in *Pernod Ricard v. Molson Breweries*, where the dispute concerned RICARD and RICKARD'S RED.[159] The court in that case indicated that the most important part of a mark was usually the first part. Consumers are likely to think that the product of a different company using the same first part of the mark is part of a "family" of products originating from the first company. Confusion can exist within such families of trade-marks. For example, McDonalds identifies all its products with "Mc" therefore any other person using "Mc" may be causing confusion as to the origin of the product, depending on factors such as nature of the goods (e.g. food or not) and distribution channels.[160]

---

[158] [1970] S.C.R. 942, 16 D.L.R. (3d) 740, 1 C.P.R. (2d) 14 (S.C.C.).

[159] (1992), [1992] F.C.J. No. 706, 44 C.P.R. (3d) 359, (sub nom. *Molson Breweries v. Pernod Ricard*) 56 F.T.R. 53, 1992 CarswellNat 1025 (Fed. T.D.) [*Ricard* cited to C.P.R.].

[160] *McDonald's Corp. v. Coffee Hut Stores Ltd.* (1996), [1996] F.C.J. No. 774, 68 C.P.R. (3d) 168, 199 N.R. 106, 1996 CarswellNat 711 (Fed. C.A.) (no confusion between MCBEANS for specialty coffee and tea and products of the famous fast food chain); *McDonald's Corp. v. Yogi Yogurt Ltd.* (1982), 66 C.P.R. (2d) 101 (Fed. T.D.) (confusion likely between proposed MCYOGURT mark and those of McDonalds); *McDonald's Corp. v. Silverwood Industries Ltd.* (1992), [1992] F.C.J. No. 70, (sub nom. *McDonald's Corp. v. Silcorp Ltd.*) 41 C.P.R.

In the *Ricard* case, Denault J. wrote:

> The test of confusion is one of first impression. The trade marks should be examined from the point of view of the average consumer having a general and not a precise recollection of the earlier mark. Consequently, the marks should not be dissected or subjected to a microscopic analysis with a view to assessing their similarities and differences. Rather, they should be looked at in their totality and assessed for their effect on the average consumer as a whole: *Ultravite Laboratories Ltd. v. Whitehall Laboratories Ltd.*, (1965), 44 C.P.R. 189 at pp. 191-2, 53 D.L.R. (2d) 1, [1965] S.C.R. 734; *Oshawa Group Ltd. v. Creative Resources Co. Ltd.* (1982), 61 C.P.R. (2d) 29 at p. 35, 46 N.R. 426 *sub nom. Oshawa Group Ltd. v. Registrar of Trade Marks* (F.C.A.); *Cantine Torresella S.r.l. v. Carbo* (1987), 16 C.P.R. (3d) 137 at p. 146, 14 C.I.P.R. 234 (F.C.T.D.).

> Although the marks are not to be dissected when determining matters of confusion, it has been held that the first portion of a trade mark is the most relevant for purposes of distinction: *Molson Companies Ltd. v. John Labatt Ltd.* (1990), 28 C.P.R. (3d) 457 at p. 461, 32 F.T.R. 152, 19 A.C.W.S. (3d) 1369 (F.C.T.D.); *Conde Nast Publications Inc. v. Union des Editions Modernes* (1979), 46 C.P.R. (2d) 183 at p. 188 (F.C.T.D.). I believe the following words of President Thorson in the case of *British Drug Houses Ltd. v. Battle Pharmaceuticals* (1945), 4 C.P.R. 48 at pp. 57- 58, [1944] 4 D.L.R. 577, [1944] Ex. C.R. 239 (Ex. Ct.), to be particularly useful in explaining why attention should be drawn to the first portion of the appellant's mark in this case:

>> . . . the Court should rather seek to put itself in the position of a person who has only a general and not a precise recollection of the earlier mark and then sees the later mark by itself; if such a person would be likely to think that the goods on which the later mark appears are put out by the same people as the goods sold under the mark of which he has only such a recollection, the Court may properly conclude that the marks are similar.

> In my view, the average consumer of ordinary intelligence, experiencing imperfect recollection, might not be particularly alerted to the distinction between the respondent's mark and the first word of the appellant's mark. Consequently, I feel that there is a potential for consumers believing that the *respondent* has launched a new product to which it has added the identifier 'red' for the purpose of distinguishing it from its other products.

---

(3d) 67, (sub nom. *McDonald's Corp. v. Silcorp Ltd.*) 139 N.R. 319, 1992 CarswellNat 1357 (Fed. C.A.) (no confusion between MAC'S SNACKS Design for restaurant and McDonalds restaurants; SUPER MAC'S or MAC'S PLUS for grocery and convenience stores or MAC'S for convenience store).

When the products are starkly different, the likelihood of confusion is very slim. For example, LEXUS as a mark for cars and LEXUS for food items are not likely to make the consumer believe that the car maker started making food.[161]

In the *Pink Panther* case, the Federal Court of Appeal had to decide whether the mark PINK PANTHER on shampoo bottles, though not written in pink and with no drawing of a pink panther, could cause confusion with the cartoon "star" of the well known United Artists Corp. movies starring Peter Sellers. Emphasizing that the "concentration of the source of the wares or services must inform any consideration of section 6 of the *Act*," the Court applied the criteria under s. 6 to determine whether a likelihood of confusion exists.[162] This discussion serves as a useful review of the confusion analysis:

(a) the inherent distinctiveness of the trade-marks or trade-names and the extent to which they have become known

The first item listed under subsection 6(5) is the strength of the mark. This is broken down into two considerations: the inherent distinctiveness of the mark, and the acquired distinctiveness of the mark. Marks are inherently distinctive when nothing about them refers the consumer to a multitude of sources. Where a mark may refer to many things or, as noted earlier, is only descriptive of the wares or of their geographic origin, less protection will be afforded the mark. Conversely, where the mark is a unique or invented name, such that it could refer to only one thing, it will be extended a greater scope of protection.

Where a mark does not have inherent distinctiveness it may still acquire distinctiveness through continual use in the marketplace. To establish this acquired distinctiveness, it must be shown that the mark has become known to consumers as originating from one particular source. [. . .]

(b) length of time in use

The length of time that a mark has been used is obviously a factor which will contribute to confusion on behalf of the consumer in determining the origin of wares or services. A mark that has been in use a long time, versus one newly arrived on the scene, is presumed to have made a certain impression which must be given some weight. It is important to remember that 'use' is a term defined by the Act and, therefore, has a special meaning.

---

[161] *Toyota Jidosha Kabushiki Kaisha v. Lexus Foods Inc.* (2000), [2001] 2 F.C. 15, 194 D.L.R. (4th) 491, 9 C.P.R. (4th) 297, 264 N.R. 158 (Fed. C.A.), leave to appeal to S.C.C. refused (2001), 275 N.R. 385 (note) (S.C.C.).

[162] *Supra*, note 25.

### (c) nature of the wares, services or business

Clearly, where trade-marks are similar, the degree to which the wares or services which bear those marks are similar will be a large factor in determining whether confusion is likely to result. Similarity in wares or services cannot be a *sine qua non* in a determination of confusion, as subsection 6(2) dictates that confusion may result 'whether or not the wares or services are of the same general class.' However, the ultimate test is confusion, and where one product does not suggest the other it will be a strong indication that confusion is unlikely. The nature of the wares, services and business, therefore, though not always controlling, are certainly of significance. [. . .]

The relevant factors under this heading will include not only the general class of goods that are involved, but also the quality and price of those goods. The consideration of price stems from the assumption that a consumer will be more careful when purchasing an expensive item, such as an automobile, than where inexpensive goods are concerned. In the former case, there is less likelihood of confusion even in the case of identical marks because a shopper will be assumed to undertake a judicious inquiry of the wares or service that he or she is purchasing, and not rely simply upon the hasty impression of a trade-mark or trade-name. With less expensive goods or services, more reliance may be placed on those marks and less care taken to ensure that the product is truly from the source which the consumer expects.

[. . .]

### (d) nature of trade

Similar to the nature of the wares or services is the consideration of the nature of the trade in which those wares or services circulate. The risk of confusion is greater where the wares or services, though dissimilar, are distributed in the same types of stores or are of the same general category of goods. For example, if both items are in the general category of household products and are sold in similar places, then confusion is more likely. However, where one mark refers to household products and the other to automotive products, and they are distributed in different types of shops, there is less likelihood that consumers will mistake one mark for the other.

The nature of the trade extends the analysis to the type of trading environment as well. Where one product is traded on a wholesale level and the other through retail outlets, this must be taken into consideration. This relates both to the environment and to the nature of the consumer. A professional consumer purchasing at the wholesale level is less likely to be confused than a casual shopper in a retail setting. [. . .]

(e) similarity in appearance, sound and idea suggested

Obviously, where the marks are identical this analysis is not needed. But where the marks are similar, the Registrar or the Court must assess the likely impression made by the marks on the public. While the marks must be assessed in their entirety (and not dissected for minute examination), it is still possible to focus on particular features of the mark that may have a determinative influence on the public's perception of it. [. . .]

[. . .]

(f) all the surrounding circumstances

The overriding, general consideration is 'all the surrounding circumstances.' This obviously includes the specific factors listed above, but allows the Judge or the Registrar the flexibility to take account of any fact peculiar to the situation at hand. In many cases the five factors explicitly enumerated will comprise 'all the surrounding circumstances.' In particular cases there may, for example, be a history of competition between the marks without resulting in any confusion. Of course, any evidence of actual confusion will always be relevant. As well, survey evidence may be entered where it has been conducted in an objective manner, so that the results have some probative value.

One important circumstance is the presentation of the trade-mark in the context of the product itself. The 'get-up', or the way that a product is packaged, and as a consequence the way the mark is presented to the public, is an important factor in determining whether confusion is likely. [. . .]

Where the surrounding circumstances are also important is in determining how much weight each of the enumerated factors should be given. [some footnotes omitted]

In the end, because of notable differences in the nature of the wares and channels of trade used, the Court concluded that confusion was unlikely, adding that:

[W]e owe the average consumer a certain amount of credit, a sufficient amount of which was not forthcoming from the Trial Judge. While the public might be confused by a product which used the name Pink Panther and simultaneously depicted a pink cat, the use of the words alone cannot be said to give rise to such confusion. Indeed one of the surrounding circumstances that the Trial Judge should have adverted to is the fact that much of the fame which this Court and the Court below attach to the respondent's mark stems not from the words 'The Pink Panther' but from the associated music and cartoon images.

The statement of applicable principles made by the Federal Court of Appeal seems correct, but one wonders whether the merchandising wave of the last several years, especially for clothing and countless assorted products and services using cartoon characters, would lead a court to a different conclusion if the issue were addressed again. Additionally, one could argue that the "amount of credit" owed consumers should be different when dealing with a product like shampoo, where the time spent making a purchase decision is likely to be limited, as opposed to a car or a major appliance. This is clearly one of the relevant surrounding circumstances and also forms part of the nature of trade criterion. As O'Reilly, J. put it in *Tradition Fine Foods Ltd. v. Oshawa Group Ltd.*: "The average consumer is one who has only a vague or imperfect knowledge or recollection of one of the trade-marks in issue. One should consider the consumer's first impression."[163] The test is usually that of the "unaware ordinary consumer," at least for everyday consumption goods.[164]

## III. "USE" OF A TRADE-MARK

Use is a central concept in Canadian trade-mark law both to gain and to maintain rights against third parties, and it is essential to be able to determine when a trade-mark is used. A trade-mark cannot actually be registered until a declaration of *use* is filed, although one can apply for registration in respect of a proposed trade-mark.[165] "Use" defines the scope of several trade-mark owner rights against third parties under ss. 19-22 (with respect to registered marks). On the other hand, after three years of non-use, a third party may apply to the Registrar for expungement of a trade-mark under s. 45 (see the Expungement Section below). Lack of use in Canada, coupled with an intent to abandon, a registered mark is a ground for invalidating the mark (s. 18(1)(c)).

Section 4 of the Act sets out a definition of "use":

(1)   A trade-mark is deemed to be used in association with wares if, at the time of the transfer of the property in or possession of the wares, in the normal course of trade, it is marked on the wares themselves or on the packages in which they are distributed or it is in any other manner so

---

[163] (2004), [2004] F.C.J. No. 1244, 33 C.P.R. (4th) 289, 2004 CarswellNat 2302 (F.C.).

[164] See *Centre de distribution de la piscine Trans-Canada Inc. c. Cibelle piscines & clôtures Inc.*, [1988] R.D.J. 68 (Que. C.A.), 74.

[165] A statement of use may also be filed with the initial application if the mark is already in use (s. 30(b)). If the mark is only a proposed mark, the declaration of use must be filed before the mark can be registered (s. 40 (2)).

associated with the wares that notice of the association is then given to the person to whom the property or possession is transferred.

(2)   A trade-mark is deemed to be used in association with services if it is used or displayed in the performance or advertising of those services.

(3)   A trade-mark that is marked in Canada on wares or on the packages in which they are contained is, when the wares are exported from Canada, deemed to be used in Canada in association with those wares.

The definition contains several important points. First, the use must be in the "normal course of trade," which typically begins with the manufacturer and ends with the consumer.[166] In most cases regarding wares, use means that the mark appears on the wares or their packaging[167] at the time of sale and delivery.[168] The user in a typical distribution chain is usually the manufacturer, especially when the manufacturer is known by the purchasing public, usually through advertising. There may, however, be cases where a (foreign) manufacturer builds special products for the Canadian market and consumers come to associate the mark with the Canadian distributor.[169] Finally, in appropriate cases the public can also differentiate between the mark of a distributor, even if affixed on the goods, and the manufacturer. Cigar smokers understand that the mark HAVANA HOUSE (the name of a distributor) affixed on cigars does not mean that the distributor manufactures Cuban cigars.[170] The claimed use must also be legal.[171] Finally, certain special requirements apply to the "use" of official marks under s. 9.[172]

---

[166] *Manhattan Industries Inc. v. Princeton Manufacturing Ltd.* (1971), 4 C.P.R. (2d) 6 (Fed. T.D.).

[167] S. 4(1) allows the mark to be associated with the wares "in any other manner" but this does not extend to simple verbal use of the mark. See *Playboy Enterprises, supra*, note 29. Use on comparative brochures, as opposed to the wares themselves or their packaging is not "use" for the purposes of the Act. See *Clairol International Corp. v. Thomas Supply & Equipment Co.*, [1968] 2 Ex. C.R. 552, 55 C.P.R. 176 (Can. Ex. Ct.) [*Clairol* cited to Ex. C.R.]. This case is discussed in the Depreciation of Goodwill Section.

[168] See *Aerosol Fillers Inc. v. Plough (Canada) Ltd.* (1980), [1981] 1 F.C. 679, 53 C.P.R. (2d) 62, 34 N.R. 39 (Fed. C.A.).

[169] See *Proll Toys Inc. v. Magnus Organ Distributors Ltd.* (1982), 73 C.P.R. (2d) 34 (T.M. Opp. Bd.).

[170] See *Havana House Cigar & Tobacco Merchants Ltd. v. Skyway Cigar Store* (1999), [1999] F.C.J. No. 1749, 3 C.P.R. (4th) 501, 251 N.R. 215, 1999 CarswellNat 2449 (Fed. C.A.) [*Havana House* cited to C.P.R.].

[171] *McCabe v. Yamamoto & Co (America)*, [1989] 3 F.C. 290, 23 C.P.R. (3d) 498, 25 F.T.R. 186, 23 C.I.P.R. 64 (Fed. T.D.).

[172] See *Canada Post Corp. v. Post Office* (2000), [2001] 2 F.C. 63, 8 C.P.R. (4th) 289, 191 F.T.R. 300 (Fed. T.D.); and *Société des Loteries du Québec c. Club Lotto International C.L.I. Inc.* (2001), [2001] F.C.J. No. 94, (sub nom. *Société*

The statutory rules to satisfy "use" are different for wares versus services. In respect of *wares* (s. 4(1)), there must be proof of at least one normal commercial transaction.[173] Advertising,[174] symbolic sales, the distribution of catalogues,[175] maintaining a passive (as opposed to e-commerce enabled) website,[176] and the distribution of samples[177] (unless that distribution involves a transfer of ownership and the trade-mark user can show actual preparation of the market[178]), press coverage, or testing are not sufficient to constitute use. The locus (time and place) of the transaction is determined by applicable provincial (common law/civil law) rules. Putting a trade-mark on another company's products as a form of "sponsoring" is not "use" within the meaning of the Act. The mark must be used to distinguish the actual product (a company could "sponsor" products from different manufacturers).[179]

With respect to use of a mark for *services*,[180] advertising and making services available in Canada is sufficient to constitute use under s. 4(2).[181]

---

*des Loteries du Québec v. Club Lotto International C.L.I. Inc.*) 13 C.P.R. (4th) 315, (sub nom. *Société des loteries du Québec v. Club Lotto International C.L.I. Inc.*) 204 F.T.R. 21, 2001 CarswellNat 182 (Fed. T.D.).

[173] See *Gordon A. MacEachern Ltd. v. National Rubber Co.* (1963), [1964] Ex. C.R. 135, 39 D.L.R. (2d) 668, 41 C.P.R. 149 (Can. Ex. Ct.); and *Mr. Goodwrench Inc. v. General Motors Corp.* (1994), [1994] F.C.J. No. 555, 55 C.P.R. (3d) 508, 77 F.T.R. 142, 1994 CarswellNat 312 (Fed. T.D.).

[174] See *Parker-Knoll Ltd. v. Canada (Registrar of Trade Marks)* (1977), 32 C.P.R. (2d) 148 (Fed. T.D.).

[175] See *J.C. Penney Co. v. Gaberdine Clothing Co.* (2001), [2001] F.C.J. No. 1845, 16 C.P.R. (4th) 151, 213 F.T.R. 189, 2001 CarswellNat 2865 (Fed. T.D.).

[176] See *Pro-C Ltd. v. Computer City Inc.* (2001), 55 O.R. (3d) 577 (Eng.), 205 D.L.R. (4th) 568, 14 C.P.R. (4th) 441 (Ont. C.A.), leave to appeal to S.C.C. refused (2001), 171 O.A.C. 399 (note) (S.C.C.).

[177] See *King Features Syndicate Inc. v. Lechter*, [1950] Ex. C.R. 297, 12 C.P.R. 60 (Can. Ex. Ct.); *Andres Wines, supra* note 36; *Dubiner v. Heede International Ltd.* (1975), 23 C.P.R. (2d) 128 (Reg. T.M.); *Grants of St. James's Ltd. v. Andres Wines Ltd.* (1969), 58 C.P.R. 281 (Reg. T.M.); *Molson Cos. v. Halter* (1976), 28 C.P.R. (2d) 158 (Fed. T.D.); *Renaud Cointreau & Cie v. Cordon Bleu International Ltd.* (2000), [2000] F.C.J. No. 1414, (sub nom. *Cordon Bleu International ltée v. Renaud Cointreau*) 188 F.T.R. 29, 2000 CarswellNat 2137 (Fed. T.D.).

[178] See *Fetherstonhaugh & Co. v. ConAgra Inc.* (2002), [2002] F.C.J. No. 1716, (sub nom. *ConAgra Foods, Inc. v. Fetherstonhaugh & Co.*) 23 C.P.R. (4th) 49, 225 F.T.R. 193, 2002 CarswellNat 3549 (Fed. T.D.).

[179] See *British Petroleum Co. v. Bombardier Ltd.*, [1973] F.C. 480, 10 C.P.R. (2d) 21 (Fed. C.A.).

[180] This is a term that should be defined broadly. See *Gesco Industries Inc. v. Sim & McBurney* (2000), 195 D.L.R. (4th) 239, 9 C.P.R. (4th) 480, 262 N.R. 132

Section 4(3) states that marking a product or its packaging in Canada is deemed a commercial transaction in Canada when the product is exported. This allows Canadian companies who export their goods to benefit from the *Act* even if, according to usual contract principles, the sale is deemed to have taken place in a foreign country.

Conceptually, the "user" of a mark is the "source" that the consumer consciously or unconsciously identifies with the mark and which guides individual purchasing decisions. It does not matter whether the source is a specific corporate or physical entity. Given the mark's expressive function of indicating source, the consumer expects that a particular mark will entail a particular product or service (see the Loss of Distinctiveness Section).

When dealing with a typical product distribution chain, generally the user is thus the manufacturer.

> The wares sold f.o.b., the United States for the Canadian market indicated as the origin of those wares the United States vendor, manufacturer. In the market place the wares distinguished the United States supplier. It would be contrary to the principles of international trade to deny the owner of the mark whose wares cross the border for sale in this country the benefits of trade mark use in this country. Many internationally known marks are sold through distributors in Canada. The mark is still that of the original supplier not that of the distributor.[182]

However, the distributor can register the trade-mark, if and only if, the trade-mark used by the distributor is distinctive of the distributor and not the manufacturer.[183]

Sometimes the owner of a registered mark would like to update the appearance of a mark in order to appeal to a different target market or reflect changing tastes or fashions or revise a mark that was based on cultural stereotypes. Whether a mark is in "use," however, is evaluated against the appearance of the mark in the registry. When the owner is using an updated mark which deviates significantly from the registered mark, the registered mark can be attacked for lack of use or abandonment. However, trade-mark law allows some flexibility and does not require that the mark in use be completely identical to the mark on the registry. If the updated or revised

---

(Fed. C.A.). In respect of use of services generally, see *Porter v. Don the Beachcomber*, [1966] Ex. C.R. 982, 48 C.P.R. 280 (Can. Ex. Ct.); and *Wenward (Canada) Ltd. v. Dynaturf Co.* (1976), 28 C.P.R. (2d) 20 (Reg. T.M.).

[181] See *Marineland Inc. v. Marine Wonderland & Animal Park Ltd.*, *supra*, note 39.

[182] From the editorial note in *Manhattan Industries Inc. v. Princeton Manufacturing Ltd.*, *supra*, note 166.

[183] *Havana House*, *supra*, note 170.

mark can be recognized by the public as maintaining an identity with the registered mark and does not lead to confusion, use of the updated mark will count as continued use of the registered mark.[184]

"Use" is also the term used to delineate certain rights of the trade-mark owner, in ss. 19-22 (See the Infringement Section below).

## IV. REGISTRATION

In order to register a mark, one must go through several steps: file an application, use the mark,[185] and wait for any opposition. Section 16(1) provides for registration of marks used or made known in Canada:

16. (1) Any applicant who has filed an application in accordance with section 30 for registration of a trade-mark that is registrable and that he or his predecessor in title has used in Canada or made known in Canada in association with wares or services is entitled, subject to section 38, to secure its registration in respect of those wares or services, unless at the date on which he or his predecessor in title first so used it or made it known it was confusing with

(a) a trade-mark that had been previously used in Canada or made known in Canada by any other person;
(b) a trade-mark in respect of which an application for registration had been previously filed in Canada by any other person; or
(c) a trade-name that had been previously used in Canada by any other person.

## 1. Who Can File for Registration

In order to register a trade-mark in Canada, it must be used in Canada or made known (see the Well Known Marks Section) in Canada. The user is the person entitled to file under s. 30(b). (See the Use of a Trade-Mark Section.) In a distribution chain, the user is usually the manufacturer. The distributor can register a mark only if it distinguishes the *distributor*.[186]

---

[184] *Promafil Canada Ltée v. Munsingwear Inc.* (1992), 44 C.P.R. (3d) 59 (Fed. C.A.), leave to appeal refused (1993), 156 N.R. 240 (note) (S.C.C.) where the Court ruled that the use of a corpulent formally attired penguin counted as use of the registered slim penguin mark.
[185] If use precedes the date of the application, then it will be indicated in the application (s. 30(b)); otherwise, if the application is for a proposed mark, a declaration of use will be filed at a later date, but prior to the issuance of a certificate of registration (s. 40(2)).
[186] *Havana House, supra,* note 170.

## 2. Procedure

The *Trade-marks Act* and its applicable *Rules* clearly lay out the registration procedure. First an application has to be filed pursuant to s. 30. The initial application must state the date of first use of the mark, if applicable, in Canada (s. 30(b)), unless the provision applies concerning foreign marks made known in Canada (s. 30(c)) or registered in the country of origin of the applicant *and* used in a foreign country member of the Paris Union (s. 30(d) and see the International Section), or unless the application is for a proposed trade-mark (s. 30(e)). The Registrar will then examine the application in light of compliance with s. 30, registrability of the mark (s. 12) and the applicant's entitlement to register the mark (s. 16) and, once approved, publish ("advertise") it in the *Trade-Marks Journal* (s. 37).[187] However, prior to publication, s. 35 (disclaimer of rights to exclusive use of a portion of the mark, for example a descriptive word included as part of the mark)[188] may apply. Section 36 (abandonment) or s. 37 (trade-mark is unregistrable in Registrar's opinion) may also apply.[189]

During a two-month period following publication (advertisement), the application is subject to opposition by "any person" pursuant to s. 38.[190] Opposition proceedings are held before the Registrar and both the applicant and opponent can submit evidence and make submissions. The application is allowed if no one opposes it within the time period or if the Registrar decides the opposition in favour of the applicant. Parties can appeal the Registrar's decision to the Federal Court under s. 56(1). Once the application has been allowed by the Registrar, the trade-mark can then be registered, and the certificate of registration issued. For applications involving proposed trade-marks, a declaration of use must be provided before the registration can be completed (s. 40(2)).

Once registration is granted, a certificate is issued which is valid for 15 years (ss. 40 and 46). It is renewable indefinitely as long as the trade-mark remains in "use." The Registrar can require evidence of use; this request can be initiated at any time by the Registrar or on written request made at least three years after the registration date (s. 45)).

---

[187] The *Journal* is circulated to trade-mark "agents" (see ss. 28(1)(f), 28(2) and 65(c.1)) as well as many corporate counsels and law firms across the country.

[188] See *Canadian Jewish Review Ltd. v. Canada (Registrar of Trade Marks)* (1961), 37 C.P.R. 89 (Can. Ex. Ct.). A disclaimer cannot be used to cure a deceptively misdescriptive mark or a confusing mark.

[189] As to the Registrar's discretion, see *Koffler Stores Ltd. v. Canada (Registrar of Trade Marks)*, [1976] 2 F.C. 685, 28 C.P.R. (2d) 113 (Fed. T.D.).

[190] See note 197, *infra*.

Registration has some advantages over the rights which accrue under common law by the use of a mark. The owner of a registered mark has the right to exclusive use *nationally* of the mark in association with the designated goods or services and the right to prevent others from using confusing marks throughout Canada. A registered mark is also presumed to be valid. The validity of a trade-mark can be attacked on the grounds that it was not registrable at the time it was registered, it is not distinctive, or it has been abandoned (s. 18),[191] but the party seeking to invalidate the mark bears the onus of proof.

## 3. Impact of Registration on Previous Users

Many, probably most, trade-marks used in Canada are unregistered. They are the names used by businesses, in certain cases as long as decades, but which, for one reason or another, were never registered. These marks are protected at common law (see the Passing Off Section) in the area where they are used. What happens when someone else *registers* the same or a similar mark? It is important to note, first, that one advantage of registration is that the protection is national, even if the mark is not used in all regions, provinces and territories.[192]

A previous, usually unregistered, user of the same or a similar mark is permitted to oppose the registration of a trade-mark or contest the validity of registration (once issued) of a mark for a period of five years following the trade-mark's registration.[193] In this time period, the previous user only has the burden to prove use of her mark at the time of the advertisement (s. 17 (1)). After five years, however, that previous owner has to show that the owner of the registered mark acted in bad faith, defined in this context as meaning with knowledge of the existence of the previous user (s. 17(2)).[194]

Under s. 21 of the *Act*, where it is not contrary to public interest, the Federal Court can permit the first user of the trade-mark to continue using the confusing mark in a given area, with adequate restrictions, such as no national advertising, and "with an adequate specified distinction from the registered trade-mark." In such a case, the first user must be in good faith,[195] and the parties should ideally be in different territorial areas.[196]

---

[191] On abandonment, see *Promafil Canada Ltée v. Musingwear Inc., supra*, note 184.

[192] See the words "throughout Canada" in s. 19.

[193] See *Kores of Canada Ltd. v. Hebert* (1969), 60 C.P.R. 177 (Can. Ex. Ct.).

[194] See *Lee v. Michael Segal's Inc.*, [1972] F.C. 53, 5 C.P.R. (2d) 204 (Fed. T.D.).

[195] See *Kayser-Roth Canada (1969) Ltd. v. Fascination Lingerie Inc.*, [1971] F.C.

## 4. Expungement (Section 45)

Section 45 of the Act is used very often. Its purpose is ostensibly to provide a tool to remove unused marks, sometimes referred to as "dead-wood," from the Register maintained under ss. 26 and 28. This provides a means to preclude people from hoarding marks and to free up marks that were registered but are not in use for potential productive use by someone else. Expungement of unused registered marks is also useful where someone else wants to register a new mark that would otherwise be blocked from registration because it is confusingly similar to a previous registered mark.) Any person[197] who genuinely believes that a registered trade-mark is not in use can ask the Registrar to send a notice under s. 45, requiring evidence by affidavit of use of the trade-mark at any time within the three-year period preceding the date of the notice.[198] The Registrar can decide not to send a notice if there is a good reason not to do so, such as when the section is used to harass the owner of a registered mark.[199] When a notice is sent, the owner of the registration has three months to prove use of the trade-mark; a single *bona fide* commercial use of the mark in the time period will suffice. If the owner fails to prove use, the trade-mark is expunged,[200] unless a justification of special circumstances is provided. (see s. 45(3)).[201] Three factors are considered to determine if there are special circumstances: the length of time the mark has not been used, if the reasons for non-use are beyond the control of the owner, and whether there is a serious intention to

---

84, 3 C.P.R. (2d) 27 (Can. Ex. Ct.), amended (1971), 3 C.P.R. (2d) 27 at 33 (F.C.).

[196] See *Steinberg v. Belgium Glove & Hosiery Co.* (1953), 19 C.P.R. 56 (Can. Ex. Ct.); and *Ensemble folklorique des farandoles de Chicoutimi c. Folie's de Paris* (1998), 1998 CarswellQue 669 (Que. S.C.).

[197] According to s. 2, this term includes any lawful trade union and any lawful association engaged in trade or business or the promotion thereof, and the administrative authority of any country, state, province, municipality or other organized administrative area.

[198] Under s. 45(1), the Registrar may also act *ex officio* at any time.

[199] See *Parke, Davis, supra*, note 28.

[200] See *Gesco Industries Inc. v. Sim & McBurney, supra*, note 180.

[201] See *John Labatt Ltd. v. Cotton Club Bottling Co.* (1976), 25 C.P.R. (2d) 115 (Fed. T.D.). In *Cassels Brock & Blackwell LLP v. Montorsi Francesco E Figli - S.p.A.*, 2004 FC 753, (2004) 35 C.P.R. (4th) 35 (F.C.), the Federal Court of Canada held that the hearing officer did not exceed the jurisdiction under this section by determining that special circumstances, reasonably based, excused a period of non-use and that the mark should be maintained on the Register while *concurrently* directing a second notice under s. 45 be issued requiring the registered owner to show compliance.

use the mark again.[202] Special circumstances, such as a regulatory prohibition or absence of authorization on the sale of goods during the relevant period, could constitute such a justification.

Under circumstances defined in s. 50, use by a licensee will be deemed use by the owner (see the Licensing & Assignment Section).[203]

A broader mechanism than s. 45 is available under s. 57 which accords exclusive original jurisdiction to the Federal Court to order that register entries be struck out or amended so that the entries accurately define the registered owner's rights. Under s. 57, the Federal Court may strike from the Register a trade-mark "which is not a trade-mark"[204] or amend any registration that does not accurately express or define the existing rights of the registered owner.[205] This would include cases where the wrong person (*e.g.*, a distributor not considered as the source of the product) registered the mark.[206] In equity, defences of laches and acquiescence may be available, provided the respondent has "clean hands".[207]

Although s. 45 is narrower in scope than s. 57,[208] it can be used by "any person," while an application under s. 57 must be made by an "interested person." An "interested person" is defined in s. 2 as including "any person who is affected or reasonably apprehends that he may be affected by any entry in the register, or by any act or omission or contemplated act or omission under or contrary to this *Act*" and the Attorney General. In *Feingold v. Demoiselle Juniors Ltd.*,[209] the Exchequer Court provided the following analysis of an "interested person":

> The question is merely one of *locus standi*, and to answer the question it must be assumed that the word mark 'DEMOISELLE JUNIOR' is wrongly on the

---

[202] *Canada (Registrar of Trade-marks) v. Harris Knitting Mills Ltd.* (1985), 4 C.P.R. (3d) 488 (Fed. C.A.).

[203] See *United Distillers Glenmore, Inc. v. El Toro Restaurant & Pizzeria Ltd.* (1996), 70 C.P.R. (3d) 346 (T.M. Bd.).

[204] *Elgin Handles Ltd. v. Welland Vale Manufacturing Co.* (1964), [1965] 1 Ex. C.R. 3, 43 C.P.R. 20 (Can. Ex. Ct.).

[205] See *MacKenzie v. Busy Bee Enterprises International Ltd.* (1976), [1977] 2 F.C. 124, 32 C.P.R. (2d) 196 (Fed. T.D.).

[206] See *Uniwell Corp. v. Uniwell North America Inc.* (1996), [1996] F.C.J. No. 336, 66 C.P.R. (3d) 436, 109 F.T.R. 81, 1996 CarswellNat 311 (Fed. T.D.).

[207] See *Ling Chi Medicine Co. (H.K.) Ltd. v. Persaud* (1998), [1998] F.C.J. No. 861, 81 C.P.R. (3d) 369, 232 N.R. 61, 1998 CarswellNat 1169 (Fed. C.A.).

[208] See *Molson Cos. v. Halter, supra*, note 177 and *United Grain Growers Ltd. v. Lang Michener*, [2001] 3 F.C. 102, 269 N.R. 385, 12 C.P.R. (4th) 89 (Fed. C.A.), leave to appeal to S.C.C. allowed (2001), 14 C.P.R. (4th) vii (S.C.C.).

[209] (1947), [1948] Ex. C.R. 150, 7 C.P.R. 25 (Can. Ex. Ct.). See also *John Labatt Ltd. v. Carling Breweries Ltd.* (1974), 18 C.P.R. (2d) 15 (Fed. T.D.).

Register. Can the plaintiffs, carrying on the same type of business in the same area as the defendants, having a trade name and a word mark similar (as I have found) to the defendant's word mark, reasonably apprehend that the goodwill of its business may be adversely affected if the defendant's mark remains on the Register?

In Kerly on Trade Marks, 6th ed., pp. 324 to 331, the author reviews the decisions in the English Courts as to who are persons aggrieved or interested. He refers to the case of *Apollinaris Co.'s Trade-Marks*, (1891) 2 Ch. 186, where Fry J., in delivering judgment in the Court of Appeal said:

> Further, we are of opinion that, wherever one trader, by means of his wrongly registered trade mark, narrows the area of business open to his rivals, and thereby either immediately excludes, or with reasonable probability will in the future exclude, a rival from a portion of that trade into which he desires to enter that rival is an 'aggrieved person'.

Reference is also made in Kerly on Trade Marks to the case of *Powell's Trade Mark*, (1893) 2 Ch. 388, (1894) A.C. 8. In that case Lord Herschell J., in giving judgment, said:

> Wherever it can be shown, as here, that the applicant is in the same trade as the person who has registered the trade mark, and wherever the trade mark, if remaining on the register, would or might limit the legal rights of the applicant, so that by reason of the existence of the entry on the register he could not lawfully do that which, but for the existence of the mark upon the register he could lawfully do, it appears to me he has a *locus standi* to be heard as a person aggrieved.

Applying the principles of these cases, I find that the plaintiffs engaged in the same line of business and in the same area as the defendant, and possessing a trade name and a word mark similar to that of the defendant's word mark, may very reasonably apprehend that the goodwill of their business may be adversely affected by the continuance on the Register of the defendant's word mark; and that, therefore, the plaintiffs are 'persons interested' and entitled to take these proceedings.

## V. LICENCES AND ASSIGNMENTS

Trade-marks can be assigned (s. 48) and can be licensed (s. 50). An assignee must change the message of the mark to notify the public that the mark is distinctive of a new source of goods. The quality of the goods that the mark is used in association with can change providing that the mark is made distinctive of those goods and the public is notified.[210]

A crucial component of trade-marks is that the quality of a product bearing a given trade-mark cannot be different from one producer to the next. Section 50 gives trade-mark owners whose marks are used under licence a certain degree of flexibility by permitting some licensee uses of a mark to have the same effect as use by the owner. It is important to note that s. 50(1) requires the trade-mark owner to have direct or indirect control of the character or quality of the wares or services, which means "actual control rather than a mere potential to control."[211] Typical trade-mark licensing agreements thus contain quality control provisions.[212]

As emphasized earlier, the trade-mark owner must ensure that the connection between the mark and source in the consumers' minds is not severed, and this risk is raised when assigning a mark or licensing it to a third party. If the link is severed, the mark loses its distinctiveness and will lose protection. (See also the Loss of Distinctiveness Section.) As the Supreme Court said in *Breck's*: "The assignment of a trade-mark must maintain the associative character of the assigned mark in identifying goods."[213]

There is a rebuttable presumption under s. 50(2) that where the public is notified of changes in source resulting from licensing the owner has licensed those uses and controls the character or quality of the goods or services.

## VI. INFRINGEMENT

There are two main categories of infringement: in the first category is infringement of any trade-mark, whether registered or not, based on the common law tort of passing off and general civil liability in Quebec, and partly codified in s. 7 of the Act, and in the second category are three specific

---

[210] *Heintzman v. 751056 Ontario Ltd.*, *supra*, note 102 (trade-mark used in association with high-quality pianos assigned and used in association with low quality instruments).

[211] *Cheung Kong (Holdings) Ltd. v. Living Realty Inc.* (1999), [2000] 2 F.C. 501, 4 C.P.R. (4th) 71 (Fed. T.D.). See also *Petro-Canada c. 2946661 Canada Inc.* (1998), (sub nom. *Petro-Canada v. 2946661 Canada Inc.*) [1999] 1 F.C. 294, (sub nom. *Petro-Canada v. 2946661 Canada Inc.*) 83 C.P.R. (3d) 129 (Fed. T.D.).

[212] There is, however, no strict need that the license be in writing if evidence of actual control can be adduced. See *Wells' Dairy Inc. v. UL Canada Inc.* (2000), (sub nom. *Wells' Dairy Inc. v. U L Canada Inc.*) 7 C.P.R. (4th) 77 (Fed. T.D.).

[213] *Supra*, note 96.

instances of infringement that apply only to registered marks, provided for in sections 19, 20 and 22.

## 1. Infringement of Registered Marks

### (a) Right to Use

The exclusive right to use a registered trade-mark in Canada is granted to the owner of the registered trade-mark by ss. 19 and 20 of the Act. The notion of "exclusive right to *use*" has been further developed in the jurisprudence (see the Use of a Trade-mark section). While some commentators have argued the opposite, it seems logical to apply the same definition of "use" (as contained in s. 2 and refined by case law) both as the criteria for those seeking to register a mark and as the definition of the scope of their rights.[214]

Section 19 grants a right valid "throughout Canada," regardless of where the mark is in fact used, unless the mark was registered pursuant to s. 12(2) or s. 13 and has become distinctive only in part of the country (s. 32(2)). The registered mark is prima facie valid, as stated in s. 19.[215] Under s. 19, the registered trade-mark and the product or service in association with which it is used (covered by the certificate of registration) must be identical to the infringing mark and the product and service in association with which it is used; no evidence of confusion is required.[216]

Under s. 20, the exclusive right is expanded to "confusing" trade-marks and trade-names.[217] The notion of confusion and the test to be applied, based on s. 6, is discussed in the Confusion Section.[218]

---

[214] See H.G. Richard et al., *Canadian Trade-Marks Act Annotated* (Carswell, looseleaf), at p. 20-4C.

[215] See also *Parke, Davis, supra*, note 28; *Charles Yeates & Co. v. Independent Grocer's Alliance Distributing Co.* (1961), [1962] Ex. C.R. 36, 37 C.P.R. 173 (Can. Ex. Ct.); and *Nestle Enterprises Ltd. v. Edan Food Sales Inc.* (1991), [1992] 1 F.C. 182, 37 C.P.R. (3d) 480, 50 F.T.R. 30 (Fed. T.D.).

[216] See *Bonus Foods Ltd. v. Essex Packers Ltd.* (1964), [1965] 1 Ex. C.R. 735, 49 D.L.R. (2d) 320, 43 C.P.R. 165 (Can. Ex. Ct.); and *Lovable Brassiere Co. v. Lovable Knits Inc.* (1971), 1 C.P.R. (2d) 128 (Can. Ex. Ct.).

[217] See *Mr. Submarine Ltd. v. Amandista Investments Ltd.* (1987), [1988] 3 F.C. 91, 19 C.P.R. (3d) 3 (Fed. C.A.).

[218] See *Lovable Brassiere Co., supra*, note 216; *Canadian Council of Blue Cross Plans v. Blue Cross Beauty Products Inc.*, [1971] F.C. 543, 3 C.P.R. (2d) 223 (Fed. T.D.); and *Sprint Communications Co. Ltd. Partnership v. Merlin International Communications Inc.* (2000), [2000] F.C.J. No. 1861, 197 F.T.R. 44, 9 C.P.R. (4th) 307, 2000 CarswellNat 2792 (Fed. T.D.), additional reasons at 2001 FCT 358 (Fed. T.D.).

The mechanism of ss. 19 and 20 is thus as follows: no one can use, as defined in s. 2 of the Act, meaning use of the mark for the purpose of distinguishing his or her wares or services *as* his or her wares or services (see the Use of a Trade-Mark Section),[219] a registered trade-mark in respect of wares or services listed on the certificate of registration, unless the alleged infringer can invalidate the mark, which is presumed valid. When the two identities of marks and wares or services are present, the owner of the registered mark does not have to prove consumer confusion. Under s. 20, the exclusive right of the owner of the registered mark is expanded to cases where a confusing mark is used, in which case infringement is deemed.[220] Section 20 expands the scope of s. 19 to count as infringement cases where the allegedly infringing mark is not identical to the registered mark or is used in respect of goods or services not listed but still likely to cause confusion. In practice, s. 20 is often invoked in parallel with a passing off claim, under common law or s. 7, the latter statutory ground being the sole basis for passing off jurisdiction if the claim is brought before the Federal Court.

Even though s. 20 is often characterized as an exclusive right to "use" a registered mark (as defined in ss, 2 and 4), ss. 20 does not expressly require evidence that an infringing mark was "used" by the defendant but rather that the defendant "sold, distributed or advertised wares or services in association with a confusing trade-mark or trade name." Under ss. 2 and 4, "use" requires (in respect of goods) that (a) a transfer of possession or property in the normal course of trade; and (b1) at the time of which the mark is on the wares themselves or on the packages in which they are distributed; or (b2) the mark is in any other manner so associated with the wares that "notice of the association" is given to the buyer (which does not necessarily imply confusion). For services, use is defined more simply as use or display in the performance *or* advertising of the services.

---

[219] See *Pepper King Ltd. v. Sunfresh Ltd.* (2000), [2000] F.C.J. No. 1455, 8 C.P.R. (4th) 485, 194 F.T.R. 293, 2000 CarswellNat 2191 (Fed. T.D.).

[220] See *Molson Canada v. Oland Breweries Ltd./Brasseries Oland Ltée* (2002), 214 D.L.R. (4th) 473, 59 O.R. (3d) 607, (sub nom. *Molson Canada v. Oland Breweries Ltd.*) 19 C.P.R. (4th) 201 (Ont. C.A.). The Trial Division of the Federal Court went as far as to find that s. 20 created a presumption in favour of the trademark owner. See *Culinar Inc. v. Gestion Charaine Inc.* (1987), 19 C.P.R. (3d) 54 (Fed. T.D.) at para. 12: "In proving that its rights have been infringed, the plaintiff can also count on the protection of the Act, as s. 20 creates a presumption in favour of anyone who has a registered mark against any person who sells, distributes or advertises services in association with a confusing trade name, whatever the class of wares or services."

By the operation of s. 4(3) relating to exports, a use outside Canada may be deemed use in Canada and lead to a finding of infringement.[221]

Section 6(2) defines the scope of this right with respect to confusing marks: confusion is likely when use of the marks "in the same area would be likely to lead to the inference that the wares or services associated with those trade-marks are manufactured, sold, leased, hired or performed by the same person, whether or not the wares or services are of the same general class." Contrary to s. 19, which applies throughout Canada, a combined reading of ss. 20 and 6(2) leads to the conclusion that confusion must be present in a given area.

Section 20 provides two defences which give a person a right to use even when a trade-mark is registered by another. First, s. 20(1)(a) of the Act allows a person to use his or her personal name as a trade-name in good faith; an example of the application of this section is found in *Hurlburt Co. v. Hurlburt Shoe Co.*[222] Second, s. 20(1)(b) allows a person to use the geographic name of his or her location or an accurate description of the type or quality of the merchandise or service, if either is done in good faith and the use is not as a trade-mark. However, if a person uses (a) his name as a trade-name or (b) the geographical name of its place of business or (c) an accurate description of the character or quality of his or her wares or services in a manner likely to have the effect of depreciating the goodwill attaching to the trade-mark, then the s. 20 safeguard no longer applies and a finding of infringement may be made.[223] The test to exclude the exception contained in s. 20(1)(b) is not one of confusion but rather of depreciation of goodwill,[224] an expression used also in s. 22. Confusion is a different concept, which Parliament uses several times in the Act, but not in s. 22. Logically, the identical term of depreciation, used in the same Act in closely related provisions, must share a similar meaning.

---

[221] See *Coca-Cola Ltd. v. Pardhan* (1997), 77 C.P.R. (3d) 501 (Fed. T.D.), affirmed (1999), 172 D.L.R. (4th) 31, 85 C.P.R. (3d) 489 (Fed. C.A.), leave to appeal to S.C.C. refused (2000), [1999] S.C.C.A. No. 338, 2000 CarswellNat 721 (S.C.C.).

[222] [1925] S.C.R. 141 (S.C.C.).

[223] See *Guccio Gucci S.p.A. v. Meubles Renel Inc.* (1992), [1992] F.C.J. No. 536, (sub nom. *Meubles Domani's v. Guccio Gucci S.p.A.*) 43 C.P.R. (3d) 372, (sub nom. *Meubles Domani's v. Guccio Gucci S.p.A.*) 160 N.R. 304, 1992 CarswellNat 664 (Fed. C.A.).

[224] The comments of Walsh J. in *Johnson & Johnson Ltd. v. Philippe-Charles Ltd.* (1974), 18 C.P.R. (2d) 40 (Fed. T.D.) can be interpreted as saying the opposite, but his statement, namely that "when purchasers are confused, this has the effect of depreciating the goodwill," is *obiter dictum* and in addition does not seem to define the notion of depreciation of goodwill.

## (b)  Depreciation of Goodwill

As mentioned previously, the *Trade-marks Act* serves the purposes of protecting consumers and creates an intangible right for the owners of the mark. Section 22 of the Act is the only section in the Act that creates a right essentially in favour of the trade-mark owner and which does not also have the purpose of protecting the public. Section 22 applies even in the absence of consumer confusion.

To define the scope of the notion of the depreciation of goodwill, which also limits the exception contained in s. 20(1), one must first define "goodwill". Goodwill is the value of a trade-mark, its power to draw a buyer towards one company's product or service rather than that of a competitor. In one of the most important decisions dealing with s. 22, *Clairol International Corp. v. Thomas Supply & Equipment Co.*,[225] Thurlow J. defined goodwill as follows:

> The goodwill attached to a trade mark is that portion of the goodwill of the business of its owner consisting of the whole advantage, whatever it may be, of the reputation and connection which may have been built up by years of honest work or gained by lavish expenditure of money and that is identified with the goods distributed by the owner in association with the trade mark.[226]

In *Clairol*, the plaintiffs were the owner of the trade-mark MISS CLAIROL, registered for use in association with hair tinting and colouring compositions. The defendants were registered users of the trade-marks REVLON and COLORSILK, the former registered for use in association with cosmetic products and the latter for use in association with hair colour preparations. The defendants placed on the market advertising brochures and packages bearing the trade marks REVLON and COLORSILK but also containing colour comparison charts in which both the trade marks MISS CLAIROL and HAIR COLOR BATH also appeared. One column of the chart was headed REVLON COLORSILK HAIR COLOR and contained a list of colours with numbers. Under the heading MISS CLAIROL HAIR COLOR BATH appeared a list of numbers that corresponded to numbers used by the plaintiffs to identify their colour shades. On the packages in question the marks REVLON and COLORSILK appeared prominently but on one of the sides there appeared a chart consisting of two columns, the

---

[225] *Clairol, supra*, note 167.

[226] *Idem.* See also *Inland Revenue Commissioners v. Muller & Co.'s Margarine*, [1901] A.C. 217 (U.K. H.L.), 224. "[Goodwill] is the benefit and advantage of the good name, reputation and connection of a business. It is the attractive force which brings in custom" (per Lord Macnaghten).

first headed REVLON COLORSILK and containing a list of names of shades with identifying numbers and the second in smaller type headed MISS CLAIROL HAIR COLOR BATH and containing a list of the plaintiffs' colour identification numbers. Clairol sued, and this was the first time that s. 22 was invoked in court.

Having defined "goodwill" as mentioned above, the Court proceeded to consider:

> [W]hat is meant by 'depreciate the value' of such goodwill. To my mind this means simply to reduce in some way the advantage of the reputation and connection to which I have just referred, to take away the whole or some portion of the custom otherwise to be expected and to make it less extensive and thus less advantageous. As I see it goodwill has value only to the extent of the advantage of the reputation and connection which its owner enjoys and whatever reduces that advantage reduces the value of it. Depreciation of that value in my opinion occurs whether it arises through reduction of the esteem in which the mark itself is held or through the direct persuasion and enticing of customers who could otherwise be expected to buy or continue to buy goods bearing the trade mark. It does not, however, as I see it, arise. . . from danger of loss of exclusive rights as a result of use by others as this in my view represents possible loss of exclusive rights in the trade mark itself rather than reduction of the goodwill attaching to it.
> [. . .]
>
> [The defendant] is prohibited by the statute from using, in the sense that I have indicated, the trade mark of another in a manner likely to have the effect of depreciating the goodwill attaching thereto. He may of course put information on his wares for the purpose of telling customers about his own wares in order to get the customers to buy them in preference to those of the owner of a particular trade mark. In general how he may do that is left to his own ingenuity and provided the means adopted are honest means no one can challenge him. But he may not put his competitor's trade mark on his goods for that purpose or for the purpose of carrying a message to customers who are familiar with the goods identified by the trade mark in order to facilitate their purchase of his own goods and thus to reduce the chance that new customers hearing of the goods identified by the mark would buy them in preference to his or that old customers familiar with the goods identified by the trade mark would have continued buying the goods of the owner of the mark. In short he may not use his competitor's trade mark for the purpose of appealing to his competitor's customers in his effort to weaken their habit of buying what they have brought before or the likelihood that they would buy his competitor's goods or whatever binds them to his competitor's goods so as to secure the custom for himself, for this is not only calculated to depreciate and destroy his competitor's goodwill but is using his competitor's trade mark to accomplish his purpose.

Thurlow J.'s interpretation is thus that when consumers are led to buy
one product rather than a competitor's because the competitor's trade-mark
is used for comparative purposes on the wares or packaging then the goodwill is depreciated. The "use" made must, however, qualify as use defined
by s. 4 of the Act, which is different for wares and services. This interpretation was adopted in a number of subsequent cases.

An even broader interpretation was adopted in *Source Perrier S.A. v.
Fira-Less Marketing Co.*[227] The defendant was selling bottled water under
the name PIERRE EH! as a political satire directed at then former Prime
Minister Pierre Trudeau. The bottles were similar to Perrier's, the well
known sparkling mineral water. The bottles were used as part of a parody
and no intent to compete against Perrier was shown to be present. Nonetheless, the manufacturer Source Perrier sued under s. 22 and successfully
obtained an interlocutory injunction. In its judgement, the Court said:

> [T]he plaintiff's counsel argued that the 'Pierre Eh!' product [. . .] is [. . .] likely
> to reflect adversely on the Perrier reputation having regard to the fact that the
> plaintiff is a French company and is in no way involved in any political activities
> in Canada. He fears, in particular, that members of the public may well form
> the impression that Perrier has sanctioned or condoned such political spoof,
> and that there may well be members of the public who do not regard it as
> amusing.
> [. . .]

> [T]he defendant is depreciating the value of the goodwill attached to Perrier's
> marks contrary to the provisions of subsection 22(1) of the Act. The fact that
> the defendant intends to produce a spoof does not take away from the deception
> created in the minds of the customers. The defendant is clearly attempting to
> cash in on the well-established reputation of Perrier, and the deception, in my
> view, tends to dilute the quality of its trade marks, to impair its business integrity
> established over the years, and to cause injury to its goodwill.

> Undoubtedly, a customer approaching the 'Pierre Eh!' bottle and examining
> the labels will discover the spoof, but confusion is not the test to be used under
> section 22, 'the test is the likelihood of depreciating the value of the goodwill
> attaching to the trade mark, a result which would not necessarily flow from
> deception and which might result without deception being present'. [the court
> cites *Clairol* here]
> [. . .]

> The defendant submits that the plaintiff's right to the protection of its trade
> marks must be balanced with the defendant's rights to freedom of opinion and

---

[227] [1983] 2 F.C. 18, 70 C.P.R. (2d) 61 (Fed. T.D.) [*Source Perrier* cited to F.C.].

expression and relies on paragraph 2(*b*) of the *Canadian Charter of Rights and Freedoms*[. . .]

[. . .]

The defendant argues that parody and satire are deserving of substantial freedom and that a finding of infringement should not be made where the satiric product does not fulfill and does not intend to fulfill the demand for the original product and where the parodist has not appropriated more from the original product than is necessary to conjure up the satire.

[. . .]

In my view, the most liberal interpretation of 'freedom of expression' does not embrace the freedom to depreciate the goodwill of registered trade marks, nor does it afford a licence to impair the business integrity of the owner of the marks merely to accommodate the creation of a spoof. It must be borne in mind that this application for an injunction does not originate from the targets of the parody — those in the political trade are expected to be blessed with a broad sense of humour — but from the owner of the trade marks.

The court was unwilling to recognize the freedom of expression interests of the parodist in a situation where the mark was, in a sense, used gratuitously because the subject of the parody was *not* the owner of the mark; that is, the owner of the mark should not have to bear a loss associated with the mark being exploited to make a point about another subject entirely.

In other decisions, the application of s. 22 was more restrictive (that is, depreciation of goodwill more difficult to prove) by requiring that use under s. 22 be use of the same mark in association with the same goods or services. For example, in *Nintendo of America Inc. v. Camerica Corp.*, a competitor of Nintendo, the well known maker of video games, had put the word NINTENDO on some products.[228] The Court found that: "[T]he appearance of the plaintiffs' trademarks on the packaging of Game Genie and the Codebook cannot be construed as a measure taken by the defendants to encourage consumers to buy their product in preference to Nintendo's."

In three cases, various courts refused to apply s. 22 to prevent a union from using the employer's logo or other trade-mark on their posters, flyers or websites.[229] In one of those cases, the Court found that the term "use"

---

[228] (1991), [1991] F.C.J. No. 58, 34 C.P.R. (3d) 193, 42 F.T.R. 12, 1991 CarswellNat 872 (Fed. T.D.), affirmed (1991), 44 F.T.R. 80 (note) (Fed. C.A.) [*Nintendo* cited to C.P.R.].

[229] *Cie générale des établissements Michelin - Michelin & Cie v. CAW-Canada* (1996), [1997] 2 F.C. 306, (sub nom. *Cie Générale des Établissements Michelin-Michelin & Cie v. C.A.W.-Canada*) 71 C.P.R. (3d) 348 (Fed. T.D.); *Rôtisseries St-Hubert Ltée c. Syndicat des travailleurs(euses) de la Rôtisserie St-Hubert de*

defined in s. 2 must have, unless the contrary is indicated, the same meaning every time it is used in the Act. This seems consistent with traditional statutory interpretation principles,[230] especially when, as is the case here, the same term is used in the same part of the Act (infringement of registered marks): "The term 'use' cannot have another significance than that given to it in ss. 2 and 4 of the Act, that is: 'a use in association with wares or services'. This definition of the term 'use' does not make s. 22 ineffective."[231] The court added that the union had not "used" the plaintiff's trademarks in "association with wares or services." They did not "use" the trademarks in the ordinary course of trade. Furthermore, they did not use the trade-marks as registered. Although it is true that the union organizing effort could bring financial reward to the union, distributing leaflets was itself not a "commercial activity." The court also concluded that s. 22 applied to the use of the trade-mark as registered, not to that of a similar or confusing trade mark.

In *British Columbia Automobile Assn.*,[232] the Court commented that s. 22 was a "unique provision capable of substantially divergent interpretation which has not definitively been interpreted by an appellate court in this country." The same comment was made in *Future Shop Ltd. v. A. & B. Sound Ltd.*[233] Then in the *Michelin* case, which analyzed *Clairol* in great detail, Teitelbaum J., commented that *Clairol* had "yet to be *definitively* interpreted by an appellate court."

In *ITV Technologies Inc. v. WIC Television Ltd.*,[234] Tremblay-Lamer J. analysed most of the cases dealing with s. 22 and concluded:

> Based on this jurisprudence, I believe that two conditions are necessary for WIC to successfully invoke s. 22. First, the public must make a connection between the marks of the two parties. Second, the use by [the Defendant] of [the Plaintiff's] marks must have the probable effect of creating a negative impression on the mind of the public such that it will impair the goodwill attached to [the Plaintiff's] trade-marks.

---

*Drummondville (CSN)* (1986), 17 C.P.R. (3d) 461, [1987] R.J.Q. 443 (Que. S.C.); and *British Columbia Automobile Assn. v. O.P.E.I.U., Local 378*, 85 B.C.L.R. (3d) 302, [2001] 4 W.W.R. 95, 10 C.P.R. (4th) 423 (B.C. S.C.).

[230] R. Sullivan, *Statutory Interpretation* (Irwin Law, 1997) at 69.

[231] *Rôtisseries St-Hubert Ltée c. Syndicat des travailleurs(euses) de la Rôtisserie St-Hubert de Drummondville (CSN), supra*, note 229.

[232] *Supra*, note 229.

[233] 93 B.C.L.R. (2d) 40, [1994] 8 W.W.R. 376, 55 C.P.R. (3d) 182 (B.C. S.C.).

[234] (2003), [2003] F.C.J. No. 1335, 29 C.P.R. (4th) 182, 239 F.T.R. 203, 2003 CarswellNat 4812 (F.C.), affirmed 2005 FCA 96 (F.C.A.).

One can certainly agree that if Parliament wanted "use" to be defined differently in one section of the Act (as opposed to the definition contained in s. 2), it would have said so. When the use is for a different purpose, it said so, as in s. 20(1)(b) when it specifically said "use other than as a trade-mark". In s. 22(2), the expression "use of the trade-mark" reappears, which tends to support the view that ss. 22 applies when someone's mark is used "as a mark" (as defined in ss. 2 and 4 — see under "Right to Use" above), thereby not (necessarily) creating a likelihood of confusion (which is covered in s. 20) but reducing the value of the goodwill. From this perspective, ss. 20 and 22 provide complementary causes of action. The complementarity seems to have been made part of the *Trade-Marks Act* in s. 20(1) *in fine*, where the exception to the application of s. 20 for bona fide use is restricted by the requirement that it not "depreciate the value of the goodwill" attaching to the registered mark.[235]

The notion of "depreciation" is more difficult to define. Its focus is not confusion; nor is it non-commercial parody or satire. Rather, depreciation refers to use by a person, in most cases a competitor, in the course of trade of another's person's mark(s) in a way that is likely to affect negatively the reputation and worth of a mark, a reflection of the "built-in effort" of the plaintiff over the years. Section 22 does not deal with libel, injurious falsehood[236] and other matters best left to tort law. Nor is its main target comparative advertising; if done properly and without undue negative inference, comparative advertising should be allowed. Such advertising may reduce the business of the trade-mark owner, but s. 22 outlaws depreciation, not fair competition. A consumer may well decide to opt for a different product

---

[235] A similar point of view is articulated, though from a slightly different perspective, in M. Bibic and V. Eatrides, "Would Victoria's Secret Be Protected North of the Border? A Revealing Look at Trademark Infringement and Depreciation of Goodwill" (2003), 93 *Trademark Reporter* 904, 927-8:[A]pplying textual analysis and reading the provision together with sections 19 and 20 reveals a clear and complete scheme of protection for trade-mark owners. Section 19 declares the exclusive right of the trade-mark owner, while sections 20 and 22 are complementary causes of action. A trade-mark owner can bring an action under section 22 where its trade mark is being "used" as a 'trade-mark,' but not necessarily in a confusing manner. A trade-mark owner can also bring an action under section 20 where there is no technical 'use,' but the sales, distribution or advertisements by the alleged infringer must be in a confusing manner. When viewed as such, Parliament's intentions are clear. Each section builds on the other, and addresses different aspects of the potential misappropriation of the registered owner's rights.

[236] Disparagement is actionable as injurious falsehood only if falsity, malice and special damages are all met. See note 23, *supra*.

because of its features and/or price without thinking less of the reputation of another company.

The notion of depreciation of goodwill is not the equivalent of the U.S. concept of "dilution".[237] In *Moseley (dba Victor's Little Secret) v. V Secret Catalogue, Inc.*,[238] a case dealing with the mark VICTORIA'S SECRET, the U.S. Supreme Court found that this right created a cause of action for dilution of the distinctive quality of a famous mark in cases of injury to the economic value of a famous mark, but that objective proof of actual harm (as opposed to a presumption of harm arising from a subjective "likelihood of dilution" standard) was required.[239] Among the key differences between the U.S. notion of dilution and the Canadian "depreciation of goodwill" are the fact that the protection against dilution applies essentially to famous marks, while s. 22 applies to any registered mark, and the fact that the U.S. right focuses on the reduction of the capacity of the famous mark to identify the goods of its owner, not loss of goodwill. The concepts are related but not identical and U.S. cases should thus be used with great caution.

### (c) Parallel Importation

Wares that are produced abroad and have lawful trade-marks can be imported and sold in Canada, providing that the wares are the same as the ones sold in Canada which the trade-mark holder has authorized. This is true even where there is an "exclusive distributor" in Canada.[240] However, where a product is imported that is not the same quality as the domestic product, the imported product cannot be sold as being the same as the domestic one.[241] The Federal Court has recently ruled that the rules applying to parallel importation are different under copyright law, and that the copyright owner can prevent the sale of parallel imports of copyright protected works, including copyrighted logos.[242] (See the Parallel Importation section in Copyrights.)

---

[237] A specific right under the *Federal Trademark Dilution Act* (FTDA); part of the *Lanham Trade-Mark Act*, 15 U.S.C.A. §§ 1125(c)(1) and 1127.

[238] 537 U.S. 418, 123 S.Ct. 1115 U.S. Sup. Ct. (2003).

[239] For a discussion of the evidentiary requirements post-*Moseley*, see *Savin Corp. v. Savin Group*, 391 F.3d 439 (2nd Cir., 2004).

[240] *Seiko, supra*, note 24.

[241] *H.J. Heinz Co. of Canada v. Edan Foods Sales Inc.* (1991), 35 C.P.R. (3d) 213 (Fed. T.D.).

[242] *Kraft Canada Inc. v. Euro Excellence Inc.* (2004), [2004] F.C.J. No. 804, 33 C.P.R. (4th) 246, 252 F.T.R. 50, 2004 CarswellNat 5579 (F.C.).

## 2. Infringement of Any Mark

There are two possibilities to consider for legal actions that apply to infringement of any mark, including unregistered marks. One is an action in tort based on the common law notion of passing off; the second is the statutory version or "codification" found in s. 7 of the *Trade-marks Act*. Both apply to all marks, whether registered or not. In fact, from a common law perspective, the registration of a trade-mark is essentially a confirmation of title. Rights actually accrue through use.

### (a) Common Law

The tort of passing off has a long history, and early British cases mentioned in the introduction of this Part constitute its first real major steps. The constitutive elements of the tort have changed over the years, and for our purposes, we should focus on two decisions by the Supreme Court which redefined those parameters. The first, *Seiko*, ensured a parallelism between Canadian law and evolutions in U.K. law.[243] The second, *Ciba-Geigy*, one of the most interesting "comparative law" decisions by the high Court, reinterpreted the tort in a Canadian context and linked it to its civil law cousin, the law of unfair competition, part of the general regime of civil liability.[244] We will examine these two cases and then some recent developments of interest.

In *Seiko*, the Supreme Court proceeded to examine the history and purpose of passing off. It is worth quoting at some length from Estey J.'s analysis:

> From a factual viewpoint, the position advanced by the respondent, if it should be adopted, would have the following consequences:
>
> 1. The Canadian public would be deprived of the right, or option, to purchase the Seiko watch, a product of Hattori of Japan, on the alternative basis that the watch would be unsupported by the maker's warranty; and,
>
> 2. A monopoly would be effectively established by the application of the doctrine of passing off in these circumstances, equivalent to that normally authorized by the issuance of a patent of invention under the *Patent Act* of Canada, except that here the monopoly would be for an unlimited term.

---

[243] *Supra*, note 24.
[244] *Supra*, note 149.

These startling results themselves call for an examination of the principles of tort law to determine whether or not there is indeed, in these circumstances, room for the application of the doctrine of passing off, sometimes referred to as a branch of injurious falsehood. The common law principles relating to commerce and trade generally proceed on the basis of a recognition of perceived benefits to the community from free and fair competition. This is variously illustrated in the older authorities, for example, in *Nordenfelt v. Maxim Nordenfelt Guns and Ammunition Co.*,[1894] A.C. 535 (H.L.), per Lord Macnaghten, at p. 565:

> The true view at the present time I think, is this: The public have an interest in every person's carrying on his trade freely: so has the individual. All interference with individual liberty of action in trading, and all restraints of trade of themselves, if there is nothing more, are contrary to public policy, and therefore void.

Later, in *Attorney General of Australia v. Adelaide Steamship Co.*, [1913] A.C. 781, Lord Parker of Waddington, discussing this same principle, stated, at p. 794:

> Monopolies and contracts in restraint of trade have this in common, that they both, if enforced, involve a derogation from the common law right in virtue of which any member of the community may exercise any trade or business he pleases and in such manner as he thinks best in his own interests.

There are well known and important exceptions to this general rule where the law countenances, and indeed sometimes imposes, restrictions on this right to free competition and trade, including restrictions imposed by purchasers of goodwill upon vendors, deceitful trade practices calculated to injure others, defamation of trade and profession, improper or unfair use of trade information of a former employee, the protection of trade secrets, monopolies granted by patent including Letters Patent on inventions, and statutory monopolies or regulated trades and professions. Any expansion of the common law principles to curtail the freedom to compete in the open market should be cautiously approached. This must be the path of prudence in this age of the active legislative branch where the community's trade policies are under almost continuous review. This by no means calls for judicial abdication of the role of adjusting the common law principles relating to proper trade practices to the ever-changing characteristics and techniques of commerce. Reticence to curtail this general rule, however, is found even in *Erven Warnick BV v. J. Townend & Sons (Hull) Ltd.*, [1979] A.C. 731, [1979] 2 All E.R. 927, where Lord Diplock stated, at p. 933:

> . . . but in an economic system which has relied on competition to keep down prices and to improve products there may be practical reasons why

it should have been the policy of the common law not to run the risk of hampering competition by providing civil remedies to everyone competing in the market who has suffered damage to his business or goodwill in consequence of inaccurate statements of whatever kind that may be made by rival traders about their own wares. The market in which the action for passing off originated was no place for the mealy mouthed: advertisements are not on affidavit; exaggerated claims by a trader about the quality of his wares, assertions that they are better than those of his rivals, even though he knows this to be untrue, have been permitted by the common law as venial 'puffing' which gives no cause of action to a competitor even though he can show that he has suffered actual damage in his business as a result.

In the most recent edition of *Salmond on Torts* (17th ed.) at pp. 400-01, the learned author discusses passing off in these terms:

149. INJURIOUS FALSEHOOD: PASSING OFF.

To sell merchandise or carry on business under such a name, mark, description, or otherwise in such a manner as to mislead the public into believing that the merchandise or business is that of another person is a wrong actionable at the suit of that other person. This form of injury is commonly, though awkwardly, termed that of passing off one's goods or business as the goods or business of another and is the most important example of the wrong of injurious falsehood, though it is so far governed by special rules of its own that it is advisable to treat it separately. The gist of the conception of passing off is that the goods are in effect telling a falsehood about themselves, are saying something about themselves which is calculated to mislead. The law on this matter is designed to protect traders against that form of unfair competition which consists in acquiring for oneself, by means of false or misleading devices, the benefit of the reputation already achieved by rival traders. Normally the defendant seeks to acquire this benefit by passing off his goods as and for the goods of the plaintiff . . . . [Emphasis added.]

At p. 403, the learned author examines the basis for the concept of passing off:

The courts have wavered between two conceptions of a passing-off action — as a remedy for the invasion of a quasi-proprietary right in a trade name or trade mark, and as a remedy, analogous to the action on the case for deceit, for invasion of the personal right not to be injured by fraudulent competition. The true basis of the action is that the passing off injures the right of property in the plaintiff, that right of property being his right to the goodwill of his business.

He concludes, at p. 404:

Indeed, it seems that the essence of the tort lies in the misrepresentation that the goods in question are those of another; . . .

The role played by the tort of passing off in the common law has undoubtedly expanded to take into account the changing commercial realities in the present-day community. The simple wrong of selling one's goods deceitfully as those of another is not now the core of the action. It is the protection of the community from the consequential damage of unfair competition or unfair trading. Professor Fleming, in his work the *Law of Torts* (6th ed.), reviews this development at p. 674:

> The scope of the tort has been increasingly expanded to reach practices of 'unfair trading' far beyond the simple, old-fashioned passing-off, consisting of an actual sale of goods accompanied by a misrepresentation as to their origin, calculated to mislead the purchaser and divert business from the plaintiff to the defendant.

The learned author later resumes the discussion at p. 676:

> But not all harmful competition is unfair or unlawful. Most important, the countervailing public interest in free competition often demands priority: most prominently in the claim to use one's own surname honestly in business even at the cost of some confusion with a competitor, and in the use open to all of generic and descriptive, as distinct from fanciful, terms unless they have acquired a so-called secondary meaning by exclusive association with the plaintiff. [Emphasis added.]

The learned author of Prosser, *The Law of Torts* (4th ed.), also discusses passing off as a species of unfair competition, at pp. 957-58:

> One large area of unfair competition is what may be called for lack of a better generic name false marketing, which used to be called 'passing off,' and still quite often goes by that designation. It consists of the making of some false representation to the public, or to third persons, likely to induce them to believe that the goods or services of another are those of the plaintiff. This may be done, for example, by counterfeiting or imitating the plaintiff's trade mark or trade name, his wrappers, labels or containers, his vehicles, the badges or uniforms of his employees, or the appearance of his place of business. The test laid down in such cases has been whether the resemblance is so great as to deceive the ordinary customer acting with the caution usually exercised in such transactions, so that he may mistake one for the other. The older rule was that there must be proof of a fraudulent intent, or conscious deception, before there could be any liability, and this is still occasionally repeated; but the whole trend of the later cases is to hold that it is enough, at least for purposes of injunctive relief, that the defendant's conduct results in a

false representation, which is likely to cause confusion or deception, even though he has no such intention.

[. . .]

[T]he respondent goes on to urge that the circumstances here demonstrated fall within a doctrine referred to in argument, and, indeed, in some of the literature on the subject, as the 'extended action' in passing off. This doctrine is said to have evolved from the progressive discussions of the action for passing off in three cases in the United Kingdom: *A. G. Spalding & Bros. v. A. W. Gamage Ltd.* (1915), 32 R.P.C. 273; *Bollinger v. Costa Brava Wine Co. (No. 1)*, [1959] 3 All E.R. 800, [1960] R.P.C. 16, and *(No. 2)*,[1961] 1 All E.R. 561961] R.P.C. 116 (Ch. Div.); and *Warnink, supra*.

In the *Spalding* case, supra, the House of Lords considered a course of commercial conduct by a defendant in the marketing of a discontinued product of the plaintiff (soccer balls), as the 'improved' product recently brought to the market by the plaintiff. The defendant thereafter sought to rectify any harm done by its first advertisement by a second advertisement, which made reference to a description of the discarded balls using terms which the Court found had been long associated by the public with the plaintiff's product. Lord Parker of Waddington discussed the tort of passing off, at p. 284, as follows:

> A cannot, without infringing the rights of B, represent goods which are not B's goods or B's goods of a particular class or quality to be B's goods or B's goods of that particular class or quality. The wrong for which relief is sought in a passing-off action consists in every case of a representation of this nature.

> My Lords, the basis of a passing-off action being a false representation by the defendant, it must be proved in each case as a fact that the false representation was made.

and then described the test to determine the presence of the tort of passing off on the same page as:

> . . .whether the defendant's use of such mark, name, or get-up is calculated to deceive.

It should be added at this point that 'calculated to deceive' means, in the words of Lord Diplock, that such deception or confusion is a 'reasonably foreseeable consequence' of the conduct in question. See *Warnink, supra,* at pp. 932-33 [All E.R.].

On the facts of that case the trial Judge and the House of Lords concluded that the acts of the defendant were 'hardly consistent with fair or honest trade' and concluded: 'There is nothing in the subsequent advertisements pointing to a

desire on the part of the Defendants to undo the harm they had done by their
first advertisements. Indeed, I am not sure that the subsequent advertisements
are not so framed as to strengthen a belief induced by the first. . . [advertise-
ments].'
[. . .]

The principles of passing off were said to have been further expanded or
modernized in the United Kingdom in the decision of Danckwerts J. in *Bollinger v. Costa Brava Wine Co. (No. 1), supra*, where the issue was whether
plaintiffs associated with the marketing of champagne produced in the district
of France bearing that name could obtain an injunction prohibiting the marketing in the United Kingdom of a Spanish wine said to have similar characteristics, under the name 'Spanish Champagne'. Unlike the *Spalding* case, the
defendant was not faced with an allegation of marketing the discarded goods
of the plaintiff under a deceptive description indicating to the buying public
that the goods were regular products of the plaintiff. Moreover, the defendant
did not represent that the goods were identical with, or the same as, the goods
which the plaintiff was marketing in the U.K. In *Bollinger (No. 1)*, the defendant
advised the public that the wine came not from France but from Spain. The
key issue was whether the defendant could arrogate to its wine the word
'Champagne', and thereby succeed to any benefits which had accrued to the
plaintiff by reason of the word 'Champagne', having become known in the
market as associated with wine produced by the plaintiffs from grapes grown
in the District of Champagne in France. In meeting this issue, Danckwerts J.
discussed the inclusion of the concept of unfair competition in the action of
passing off at p. 805:

> The well-established action for 'passing off' involves the use of a name
> or get-up which is calculated to cause confusion with the goods of a
> particular rival trader, and I think that it would be fair to say that the law
> in this respect has been concerned with unfair competition between
> traders rather than with the deception of the public which may be caused
> by the defendant's conduct, for the right of action known as a 'passing-
> off action' is not an action brought by the member of the public who is
> deceived but by the trader whose trade is likely to suffer from the
> deception practised on the public but who is not himself deceived at all.

As to the immediate issue of the right in the plaintiffs to prevent the defendant
from using the geographic name, which had been used without any special
right or grant in law by the plaintiffs, the Court in finding for the plaintiffs
stated at pp. 810-11:

> There seems to be no reason why such licence should be given to a
> person, competing in trade, who seeks to attach to his product a name or
> description with which it has no natural association so as to make use of
> the reputation and goodwill which has been gained by a product genu-

inely indicated by the name or description. In my view, it ought not to matter that the persons truly entitled to describe their goods by the name and description are a class producing goods in a certain locality, and not merely one individual. The description is part of their goodwill and a right of property. I do not believe that the law of passing off, which arose to prevent unfair trading, is so limited in scope.

Danckwerts J. found the plaintiff had developed a goodwill or reputation in the market by associating its product with the region of origin. Deliberate employment of this name by another trader for the purpose of enhancing the trade operations of such other trader was, in the Court's view, the appropriation of another's right of property, namely his goodwill. This term goodwill is used in the sense that the word was used by Lord Macnaghten in *Inland Revenue Commrs. v. Muller & Co.'s Margarine Ltd.*, [1901] A.C. 217 at 224: 'It is the attractive force which brings in custom.' In reaching this result, the Court in *Bollinger* relied upon *Draper v. Trist,* [1939] 3 All E.R. 513, where Lord Goddard stated at p. 526:

> In passing off cases, however, the true basis of the action is that the passing off by the defendant of his goods as the goods of the plaintiff injures the right of property in the plaintiff, that right of property being his right to the goodwill of his business.

That extension of the action of passing off, if it is an extension, does not reach the circumstances of this appeal.

In *Seiko*, the Supreme Court again emphasizes the dual nature of trade-mark law: protection of the trade-mark owner and protection of the public and the "trade" more generally, and seems to be indicating that the second element is growing in importance: "The simple wrong of selling one's goods deceitfully as those of another is not now the core of the action. It is the protection of the community from the consequential damage of unfair competition or unfair trading." The Court seems reluctant to broaden passing off to encompass other forms of unfair trading, a matter probably best left to statutes dealing with business practices. Passing off is, as the name indicates, passing off one's goods as someone else's. In a different version, known as reverse palming off,[245] one passes off someone else's goods (presumably of a higher quality) as one's own.

---

[245] Passing off is also sometimes referred to as "palming off". See *Bell'O International LLC v. Flooring & Lumber Co.* (2001), 11 C.P.C. (5th) 327 (Ont. S.C.J.), additional reasons at (2001), 2001 CarswellOnt 2277 (Ont. S.C.J.). Reverse palming off is, as the name indicates, the opposite. The concept is well developed in U.S. law. See, *e.g., Dastar Corporation v. Twentieth Century Fox Film Corporation,* 539 U.S. 23, 123 S.Ct. 2041 (U.S. Sup. Ct. 2003). It is also enshrined

At the time *Seiko* was decided, Canada had essentially adopted the *Warnink* definition of passing off as consisting of five elements: (1) misrepresentation (2) by a trader in the course of trade (3) to prospective customers of his or ultimate consumers of goods or services supplied by him, (4) which is calculated to injure the business or goodwill of another trader, and (5) which causes actual damage to the business or goodwill of the trader bringing the action.

In *Ciba-Geigy*,[246] the Court "simplified" the tort and also explained how it resembled its civil law cousin. Again, it is worth reading from Gonthier J.'s reasons:

> This Court must determine whether, in a passing-off action dealing with prescription drugs, a plaintiff may argue that the public affected by the risk of confusion includes, in addition to physicians, dentists and pharmacists, the patients who consume the drugs, or is instead limited exclusively to the health care professionals in question.
>
> [. . .]

IV — Analysis

*A. Passing-Off Action*

*(1)* General Principles Developed by the Courts

The concept of passing-off was developed in 1842 in *Perry v. Truefitt* (1842), 6 Beav. 66, 49 E.R. 749, which seems to have been the first case in which the expression 'passing-off' appeared: 'A man is not to sell his own goods under the pretence that they are the goods of another man' (p. 752 E.R.). In *Singer Manufacturing Co. v. Loog* (1880), 18 Ch. D. 395 (C.A.), aff'd (1882), 8 App. Cas. 15 (H.L.), James L.J. described passing-off and its origins, at pp. 412-13:

> . . . no man is entitled to represent his goods as being the goods of another man; and no man is permitted to use any mark, sign or symbol, device or other means, whereby, without making a direct false representation himself to a purchaser who purchases from him, he enables such purchaser to tell a lie or to make a false representation to somebody else who is the ultimate customer. . . . [H]e must not, as I said, make directly, or through the medium of another person, a false representation that his goods are the goods of another person.

---

in the *Lanham Act* (U.S. trade-mark law) in 15 U.S.C. §1125(a), rules dealing with false designation or origin.

[246] *Supra*, note 149.

The House of Lords has set out the requirements for a passing-off action on many occasions. In *Erven Warnink B.V. v. J. Townend & Sons (Hull) Ltd.*, [1980] R.P.C. 31, Lord Diplock identified five conditions, [. . .].

More recently, in *Reckitt & Colman Products Ltd. v. Borden Inc.*, [1990] 1 All E.R. 873, Lord Oliver reaffirmed, at p. 880:

> The law of passing-off can be summarised in one short general proposition, no man may pass off his goods as those of another. More specifically, it may be expressed in terms of the elements which the plaintiff in such an action has to prove in order to succeed. These are three in number. First, he must establish <u>a goodwill or reputation attached to the goods or services which he supplies</u> in the mind of the purchasing public <u>by association with the identifying 'get-up'</u> (whether it consists simply of a brand name or a trade description, or the individual features of labelling or packaging) under which his particular goods or services are offered to the public, such that the get-up is recognised by the public as distinctive specifically of the plaintiff's goods or services. Second, he must demonstrate <u>a misrepresentation</u> by the defendant to the public (whether or not intentional) leading or likely to lead the public to believe that goods or services offered by him are the goods or services of the plaintiff. . . . Third, he must demonstrate that he suffers or, in a quia timet action, that he is likely to suffer <u>damage</u> by reason of the erroneous belief engendered by the defendant's misrepresentation that the source of the defendant's goods or services is the same as the source of those offered by the plaintiff. [Emphasis added.]

The three necessary components of a passing-off action are thus: the existence of goodwill, deception of the public due to a misrepresentation and actual or potential damage to the plaintiff.
[. . .]

A manufacturer must therefore avoid creating confusion in the public mind, whether deliberately or not, by a get-up identical to that of a product which has acquired a secondary meaning by reason of its get-up.

Outside the common law countries passing-off has no exact lexicological equivalent and in general is not a delict as such. In France, for example, it is one aspect of unfair competition to which civil liability sanctions apply. The passing-off rules in Quebec are derived largely from the common law. Remedies may be sought in federal as well as provincial law:

> [TRANSLATION] Unlawful or unfair competition causing an unjust injury to another person falls within civil liability under art. 1053 C.C. Actions for damages for unfair competition are heard under not only the

federal legislation but also the general principles of delictual civil liability.

(Nadeau and Nadeau, *Traité pratique de la responsabilité civile délictuelle* (1971), at p. 221.)

### *(2)* Purposes of the Passing-Off Action and Target Clientele

In considering those upstream and downstream of the product, two separate aspects must be distinguished. I refer in this regard to the persons who manufacture or market the products, on the one hand ('the manufacturers'), and on the other to those for whom the products are intended, the persons who buy, use or consume them ('the customers').

It is clear that however one looks at the passing-off action, its purpose is to protect all persons affected by the product.

#### (a) *Protection of Manufacturers*

This corresponds to the third point mentioned by Lord Oliver. The right to be protected against the 'pirating' of a brand, trade name or the appearance of a product is linked to a kind of 'ownership' which the manufacturer has acquired in that name, brand and appearance by using them.

In *Pinard v. Coderre*, [1953] Que. Q.B. 99, Marchand J.A. of the Quebec Court of Appeal noted at p. 103:

> [TRANSLATION] It would seem that the first occupant of this name or these words acquired a right to use them exclusive of all other persons, comparable in many ways to a true right of ownership. [Emphasis added.]

Accordingly, to begin with, from what might be called the individual or manufacturer's standpoint, the passing-off action is intended to protect a form of ownership.

There is also the concept of ownership, protected by the passing-off action in relation to goodwill, a term which must be understood in a very broad sense, taking in not only people who are customers but also the reputation and drawing power of a given business in its market. In *Consumers Distributing Co. v. Seiko Time Canada Ltd., supra*, Estey J., at p. 598, cites *Salmond on the Law of Torts* (17th ed. 1977), at pp. 403-4:

> The courts have wavered between two conceptions of a passing-off action — as a remedy for the invasion of a quasi-proprietary right in a trade name or trade mark, and as a remedy, analogous to the action on

the case for deceit, for invasion of the personal right not to be injured by fraudulent competition. The true basis of the action is that <u>the passing-off injures the right of property in the plaintiff</u>, that right of property being his right to the goodwill of his business.

. . .

Indeed, it seems that the essence of the tort lies in the misrepresentation that the goods in question are those of another; . . . [Emphasis added.]

It will then be necessary to look at the relationship between the various merchants or manufacturers, and it is at that point that questions of competition have to be considered. As Chenevard says (*Traité de la concurrence déloyale en matière industrielle et commerciale* (1914), vol. 1, at pp. 6-7), [TRANSLATION] '[c]ompetition is the soul of commerce; it requires unceasing effort and as such is the chief factor in economic progress'. Drysdale and Silverleaf (*Passing-Off: Law and Practice* (1986)) are substantially of the same opinion, at p. 1:

In countries with a free market system the proper functioning of the economy depends upon competition between rival trading enterprises. It is the mechanism of competition which controls the price, quality and availability of goods and services to the public.

However, merchants must observe certain rules which, quite apart from being legal, are ethical at the least:

[TRANSLATION] Just as an effort made to dislodge an opponent from the position he occupies, to attract sales to oneself by offering better goods on better terms, is legitimate when only fair methods are used, so such conduct is objectionable when it infringes the rules of honesty and good faith that underlie commercial transactions.

(Chenevard, *supra*, at p. 11.)

[. . .]

The purpose of the passing-off action is thus also to prevent unfair competition. One does not have to be a fanatical moralist to understand how appropriating another person's work, as that is certainly what is involved, is a breach of good faith.

Finally, another more apparent, more palpable aspect, a consequence of the preceding one, must also be mentioned. The 'pirated' manufacturer is very likely to experience a reduction in sales volume and therefore in his turnover because of the breaking up of his market. When such a situation occurs in the ordinary course of business between rival manufacturers that is what one might call one of the rules of the game, but when the rivalry involves the use of dishonest practices, the law must intervene.

### (b) *Protection of Customers*

In the Anglo-Saxon legal systems, [TRANSLATION] 'the person chiefly concerned is the competitor affected by the unfair act' (Mermillod, *Essai sur la notion de concurrence déloyale en France et aux États-Unis* (1954), at p. 176). He is frequently in fact the first party affected by the practice or aware of it.

However, '[i]t should never be overlooked that . . . unfair competition cases are affected with a public interest. A dealer's good will is protected, not merely for his profit, but in order that the purchasing public may not be enticed into buying A's product when it wants B's product' (*General Baking Co. v. Gorman*, 3 F.2d 891 (1st Cir. 1925), at p. 893). Accordingly, 'the power of the court in such cases is exercised, not only to do individual justice, but to safeguard the interests of the public' (*Scandinavia Belting Co. v. Asbestos & Rubber Works of America, Inc.*, 257 F. 937 (2d Cir. 1919), at p. 941). The ordinary customer, the consumer, is at the heart of the matter here. According to the civilian lawyer Chenevard, *supra*, at p. 20, in a case of unfair competition it is [TRANSLATION] 'the buyer who is the first to be injured'.

The customer expects to receive a given product when he asks for it and should not be deceived. It often happens that products are interchangeable and that a substitution will have little effect. However, the customer may count on having a specific product. There are many reasons for such a choice: habit, satisfaction, another person's recommendation, the desire for change, and so on. I have no hesitation in using the classic saying, taken from popular imagery: 'the customer is always right'. Merchants must respect his wishes, choices and preferences as far as possible. Where this is simply not possible, no substitution must be made *without his knowledge*. That is the minimum degree of respect which manufacturers and merchants, who we should remember depend on their customers, should show.

There is no shortage of fraudulent or simply misleading practices: one may think, for example, of products having a similar get-up, the use of similar labelling, use of the same trade name, counterfeiting, imitation of packaging. These are all possible ways of attempting, deliberately or otherwise, to mislead the public. The courts and authors have unanimously concluded that the facts must be weighed in relation to an 'ordinary' public, 'average' customers:

> . . . you must deal with the ordinary man and woman who would take ordinary care in purchasing what goods they require, and, if desiring a particular brand, would take ordinary precautions to see that they get it.

(Neville J. in *Henry Thorne & Co. v. Sandow* (1912), 29 R.P.C. 440 (Ch. D.), at p. 453.)

The average customer will not be the same for different products, however, and will not have the same attitude at the time of purchase. Moreover, the attention and care taken by the same person may vary depending on the product he is buying: someone will probably not exercise the same care in selecting goods from a supermarket shelf and in choosing a luxury item. In the first case, the misrepresentation is likely to 'catch' more readily.

In *The Law of Passing-Off* (1990),[247] Wadlow gives the following definition at p. 351:

> The term 'get-up' is normally used in passing-off to mean the whole visible external appearance of goods in the form in which they are likely to be seen by the public before purchase. If the goods are sold in packages, then their get-up means the appearance of the pack taken as a whole. If they are sold or displayed unpackaged, then the get-up relied on can only be that inherent in the goods themselves.

The look, the appearance, the get-up of a product play a crucial role in the purchase process since they are the chief means at the manufacturer's disposal to attract customers. The importance of visual impact is well known: what appeals to the eye is crucial.

The product's appearance or its packaging — shape, size or colour — may be characteristic of a particular manufacturer and have the effect of marking out the product or making it recognizable as his own. In the mind of the customer appearance is not always linked to a trade mark, that is, the consumer may rely on the appearance rather than the trade mark to indicate the use of the product. For example, when he needs removable self-stick notes, he will look for small blocks of yellow paper. He may not know the name of the product or manufacturer, but he does not need to in order to recognize what he wants to buy. What he has noticed and what he has retained is the specific colour of the merchandise; or he will know that a particular product contained in a tin with an exotic bird on the lid is polish, without necessarily having to know the trade name or brand, and when he wishes to purchase *that polish* it is the image of the bird on the packaging that will assist him in recognizing the product. With a few exceptions, the external features of a product are not sought for themselves, but because they are the means of recognizing the satisfactory product, for example. They are a source of information associated with reputation for a consumer or a group of customers. Appearance is thus useful not only in product recognition but also to distinguish one product from another with the same uses.

---

[247] The same definition appears in the third edition (2004), at p. 663.

Of course, it may be that appearance is associated with a specific brand in the consumer's mind. When he wishes to have a product of that brand he will look for that get-up.

The question now is as to who lies beyond the product, that is who must be protected, who must not be confused by manufacturers, for example, by a similar appearance. As business is organized at present, it is very seldom that an individual deals directly with the manufacturer or producer: he is not generally the immediate customer. The route taken by a product between the time of its manufacture, to use a broad term, and the time it reaches the consumer can be compared to a chain made up of several links which must all be there and be in a particular order. Manufacturer, wholesaler, retailer and consumer are all links in this chain.

The first person who buys the product is not generally the one for whom it is ultimately intended. Assuming that there are three links in the chain, with the producer and the consumer at the two ends, the 'retailer' (grocer, bookseller, garage owner and so on) is an intermediary between the producer and the consumer. I would without hesitation describe him as a 'trade customer', that is a person who obtains a product not for his own use but with a view to passing it on to a third person in the course of his business. There is little need to dwell at length on the case of such merchant intermediaries, who are in fact part of the manufacturer's or producer's clientele. There may at times be some question whether the passing-off action really affects them as customers. The closer they are, that is the more direct contact they have with the manufacturer or producer, the less likely they are to be misled. This is indeed what Viscount Maugham found in *Saville Perfumery Ld. v. June Perfect Ld.* (1941), 58 R.P.C. 147 (H.L.), at pp. 175-76: 'It is, for example, quite a common occurrence . . . to find that retail traders are not misled while ordinary customers are'.

Outside the field of pharmaceutical products, the courts and authors have unquestionably recognized that the consumer, or the person who might be called the ordinary customer — the last link in the chain — is also part of the 'clientele' in whose minds any confusion must be avoided.

The English common law has long recognized this principle very explicitly. I shall again quote a passage from James L.J. mentioned above to emphasize the use of certain terms:

> . . . no man is permitted to use any mark, sign or symbol, device or other means, whereby, without making a direct false misrepresentation himself to a purchaser who purchases from him, he enables such purchaser to tell a lie or to make a false representation to somebody else who is the ultimate customer. [Emphasis added.]

> (*Singer Manufacturing Co. v. Loog, supra,* at p. 412.)

Further, when Lord Diplock in *Erven Warnink B.V. v. J. Townend & Sons (Hull) Ltd., supra,* set out the conditions for the passing-off action at p. 93, he used the very words 'ultimate consumers'.

There is no question that confusion, which is the essence of the tort of passing-off, must be avoided in the minds of all customers, whether direct — here one thinks of the retailers — or indirect — in that case the consumers. Proof of reputation or secondary meaning and of misrepresentation has never been limited by the courts to direct customers of the person claiming a right.

In civil law jurisdictions, including Quebec, the concept of a clientele is expressed still more broadly where misrepresentation is involved, as indicated by this passage from the reasons of Pelle tier J.A. in *République française v. S. Hyman Ltd.* (1920), 31 Que. K.B. 22, at p. 23:

> [TRANSLATION] [What is at issue is] the means of enforcing the principle that while a person may sell his own goods as he wishes, he is not entitled to offer them for sale in such a way as to lead buyers and the public in general to think that the goods he is selling are those legitimately manufactured and sold by someone else. [Emphasis added.]

Nadeau and Nadeau, *supra,* at p. 224, state in connection with passing-off:

> [TRANSLATION] 'It is not necessary to establish that buyers have been misled, but simply that an attempt was made to mislead *the public*'. (Emphasis added.) This language indicates that it is necessary to avoid confusing anyone who has an actual or potential, immediate or remote, connection with the product. The tendency in Anglo-Saxon law appears to be to discontinue use of the expression adopted by Lord Diplock, 'ultimate consumers', and, as he himself has increasingly done, to refer to the concept of the public. (See *inter alia* Wadlow, *supra,* and Fleming, *The Law of Torts* (7th ed. 1987), at pp. 675-76.)

Moreover, we must not lose sight of the fact that the ordinary clientele includes 'consumers'. I use this word in its juridico-sociological meaning, which to Western minds in the late 20th century inevitably implies the need for protection. The passing-off action is entirely consistent with the plethora of present-day protectionist provisions, even though it existed long before they did!

*Ciba-Geigy* teaches, first, that the three constitutive elements of the "modern" tort of passing off are the existence of goodwill, deception of the public due to a misrepresentation, and actual or potential damage to the plaintiff.[248] When a strong misrepresentation case is made, damage to the

---

[248] There is no need to show an *intent* to deceive. See *Eli Lilly & Co. v. Novopharm*

reputation may be presumed.[249] The "public" whose deception is relevant varies according to the product concerned. With respect to pharmaceuticals, the Supreme Court concludes in that case that doctors, pharmacists and also patients are relevant consumers.[250] The case also shows that passing off can result from any element, including the get-up, which is intended to communicate a message to the prospective consumer and attract his or her attention or jolt his or her memory in hopes of orienting his or her purchasing decision.

A proper analysis of the tort of passing off in Canadian law should focus on cases decided after *Ciba-Geigy*, in light of the re-scoping resulting from that Supreme Court decision. The discussion in *Seiko* about free competition also remains relevant.

Some of those recent cases added a few additional elements. For instance, a number of cases decided since *Ciba-Geigy* have concluded that it is sufficient to prove a likelihood of confusion or deception;[251] that is, there is no need to establish intention or actual results. In addition, it is well established that the plaintiff does not need to have a commercial presence in Canada or in the same jurisdiction as the defendant, in order to bring this kind of action (see the Well-Known Marks section) and the two parties need not be in competition.[252]

## (b) Section 7

The federal government tried to codify this tort in s. 7 of the *Trade-Marks Act*. The constitutionality of s. 7 is discussed in detail in the Consti-

---

*Ltd.* (1997), 147 D.L.R. (4th) 673, 73 C.P.R. (3d) 371 (Fed. T.D.), affirmed (2000), 10 C.P.R. (4th) 10 (Fed. C.A.), leave to appeal refused (2001), 275 N.R. 200 (note) (S.C.C.).

[249] See *Law Society (British Columbia) v. Canada Domain Name Exchange Corp.* (2004), [2004] B.C.J. No. 1692, 243 D.L.R. (4th) 746, 34 C.P.R. (4th) 437, 2004 CarswellBC 1858 (B.C. S.C.).

[250] See also *ibid*.

[251] See *Vine Products Ltd. v. MacKenzie & Co. (No. 2)*, [1969] R.P.C. 1 (Eng. Ch. Div.) — the so-called "Sherry" case; *Institut national des appellations d'origine des vins & eaux-de-vie v. Andres Wines Ltd.* (1987), 60 O.R. (2d) 316, 40 D.L.R. (4th) 239, 16 C.P.R. (3d) 385, 14 C.I.P.R. 138 (Ont. H.C.), affirmed (1990), 30 C.P.R. (3d) 279 (Ont. C.A.), leave to appeal refused (1991), 1 O.R. (3d) xi (note) (S.C.C.); *Walt Disney Productions v. Fantasyland Hotel Inc.*, 20 Alta. L.R. (3d) 146, [1994] 9 W.W.R. 45, 56 C.P.R. (3d) 129 (Alta. Q.B.), affirmed (1996), 38 Alta. L.R. (3d) 441 (Alta. C.A.); and *Sony of Canada Ltd. v. Hi-Fi Express Inc.* (1982), 38 O.R. (2d) 505, 138 D.L.R. (3d) 662, 67 C.P.R. (2d) 70 (Ont. H.C.).

[252] *King Features Syndicate Inc. v. Lechter, supra*, note 177.

tutional Ground section. The Supreme Court has declared s. 7(e) unconstitutional and other subsections are in doubt. Section 7 reads as follows:

   7. No person shall

a)   make a false or misleading statement tending to discredit the business, wares or services of a competitor;

b)   direct public attention to his wares, services or business in such a way as to cause or be likely to cause confusion in Canada, at the time he commenced so to direct attention to them, between his wares, services or business and the wares, services or business of another;

c)   pass off other wares or services as and for those ordered or requested;

d)   make use, in association with wares or services, of any description that is false in a material respect and likely to mislead the public as to
  ii)   the character, quality, quantity or composition,
  iii)   the geographical origin, or
  iv)   the mode of the manufacture, production or performance of the wares or services; or

e)   do any other act or adopt any other business practice contrary to honest industrial or commercial usage in Canada.

When invoking s. 7(a), whose constitutionality may still be in doubt (see the Constitutional Ground section), it is not necessary to demonstrate the defendant's bad faith. The onus is on the plaintiff to prove (a) the parties are competitors; (b) the existence of an (objectively) false or misleading declaration; (c) its likely or demonstrated effect of discrediting the plaintiff's business, its wares or its services; and (d) damage. It is comparable, in certain respects at least, to the tort of slander of title or trade libel. However, while traditionally courts look for *mala fides* as an element of an action at common law,[253] bad faith is not required for s. 7(a).[254] Section 7(a) has also been invoked against threats of an infringement action in respect of an invalid mark or patent,[255] for which an action also exists at common law.[256]

Section 7(b) is generally considered a codification of the tort of passing off and cases dealing with the tort at common law are applicable, as are the

[253] See, e.g., *Halsey v. Brotherhood* (1881-82), L.R. 19 Ch. D. 386 (Eng. C.A.), affirming (1880) L.R. 15 Ch. D. 514 (Eng. Ch. D.).

[254] See *Rowell v. S. & S. Industries Inc.*, [1966] S.C.R. 419, 56 D.L.R. (2d) 501, 48 C.P.R. 193 (S.C.C.).

[255] See *ibid*.

[256] See *ibid* and *Wren v. Weild* (1869), L.R. 4 Q.B. 730 (Eng. Q.B.); *Halsey v. Brotherhood* (1880), 15 Ch. D. 514; and *Royal Baking Powder Co. v. Wright, Crossley & Co.* (1901), 18 R.P.C. 95 (Eng. C.A.).

*Ciba-Geigy* teachings (see the Common Law Section), as was decided by courts in a number of provinces[257] and by the Federal Court of Appeal:

> Section 7(b) is the equivalent statutory expression of the common law tort of passing off, with one exception: in order to use paragraph 7(b) a person must prove that they have a valid and enforceable trade-mark, whether registered or unregistered. The thing that distinguishes the common law action of passing-off from a passing-off action under paragraph 7(b) of the *Act* is that in the common law action a litigant need not rely on a trade-mark to make use of the action. To bring a passing off action under the *Act*, one must have a valid trade-mark within the meaning of the *Act*.[258]

Section 7(c) constitutes an extension of the tort of passing off to include direct substitution, as explained by Stone J.A. in *Searle Canada Inc. v. Novopharm Ltd.*:[259]

> In *Ciba-Geigy*, Gonthier J. undertook a brief review of the general principles governing the common law action of passing-off. I have no doubt that these same principles apply to an action in passing-off under paragraph 7(c) of the *Trade-marks Act*. At pages 131-132, the learned Justice traced the concept to *Perry v. Truefitt* (1842), 49 E.R. 749. He drew attention to two subsequent English decisions: *Singer Manufacturing Company v. Loog* (1880), 18 Ch. D. 395 (C.A.); affd (1882), 8 App. Cas. 15 (H.L.); *Reckitt & Colman Products Ltd v Borden Inc*, [1990] 1 All ER 873 (H.L.). He next referred to the decision of the Supreme Court of Canada in *Oxford Pendaflex Canada Ltd. v. Korr Marketing Ltd. et al.*, [1982] 1 S.C.R. 494 . . .
>
> In order to succeed in its passing-off action under paragraph 7(c) of the *Trade-marks Act*, the appellant would have to show that its get-up had acquired a secondary meaning or reputation in the mind of the public such that the public identifies that get-up with the appellant; or at least with some manufacturing source, (as to which see e.g. *John Wyeth & Bro. Ltd. v. M. & A. Pharmachem Ltd.*, [1988] F.S.R. 26 (Ch. D.), at page 29). In addition, confusion in the minds of the public would need to be shown. Moreover, the appellant would have to

---

[257] See *Petals Inc. v. Winners Apparel Ltd.* (1999), 2 C.P.R. (4th) 92 (Ont. S.C.J.); *Law Society (British Columbia) v. Canada Domain Name Exchange Corp., supra* note 250; *Saskatoon Star Phoenix Group Inc. v. Noton*, [2001] 9 W.W.R. 63, 12 C.P.R. (4th) 4 (Sask. Q.B.). This is also true in Quebec. See *Kisber & Co. v. Ray Kisber & Associates Inc.* (1998), (sub nom. *Kisber & Co. v. Ray Kisber & Associates Inc.*) 82 C.P.R. (3d) 318 (Que. C.A.).

[258] *Asbjorn Horgard A/S v. Gibbs/Nortac Industries Ltd., supra* note 14. This case was decided prior to *Ciba-Geigy* but the passage was quoted with approval by the same court in 2003 in *Kirkbi AG, supra* note 16 at para. 38.

[259] [1994] 3 F.C. 603, 56 C.P.R. (3d) 213, 171 N.R. 48 (Fed. C.A.).

show that the respondent induced or enabled others to pass off its oral dosage formulations as the appellant's oral dosage formulations.

Section 7(d) requires a false or misleading designation; it must however be important.[260] If a bottle of water states that it contains 591ml and it actually contains 590ml, this does not constitute an important detail. There are relatively few cases dealing with that subsection, and its successful application is rare. One case in which it was raised and decided in the plaintiff's favour, though at the interlocutory stage, is *Fournier Pharma Inc. v. Apotex Inc.*:[261]

> [T]he evidence demonstrates that the fenofibrate product in APO-FENO MI-CRO is not micronized.
>
> The plaintiffs argue that the defendant has deliberately used the words 'micronized formulation' in its product monograph and on its labels, even though the fenofibrate used in its product is not micronized. The defendant only made the necessary changes to its product monograph and product labels on May 12, 1999.
>
> The plaintiffs argue that the use of the word MICRO suggests 'micronized formulation' and is misleading, especially when used with a product that is not micronized. They submit that a survey of 100 pharmacists, conducted by themselves, demonstrates that 25% of the respondents, in answer to an open ended question, responded that they thought APO-FENO MICRO was micronized. A further 48% responded similarly, when questioned more directly. They concluded that a total of 73% of respondents, therefore, expressed an opinion that APO-FENO MICRO was micronized.
>
> The plaintiff argues that the defendant has deliberately copied the colour of the brand name, to facilitate substitution at the pharmacy.
> [. . .]
>
> At this stage, there is no evidence of actual confusion. However, I am prepared to accept that the plaintiff has met the low threshold of satisfying the court that there may be a likelihood of confusion by the defendant's use of the word MICRO under subsection 7(b) of the *Trade-marks Act*.

---

[260] *Valle's Steak House c. Tessier, supra,* note 39.

[261] (1999), [1999] F.C.J. No. 1689, 2 C.P.R. (4th) 351, 1999 CarswellNat 1945 (Fed. T.D.). See also *Procter & Gamble Pharmaceuticals Canada Inc. v. Novopharm Ltd.* (1996), [1996] F.C.J. No. 915, 68 C.P.R. (3d) 461, 1996 CarswellNat 947 (Fed. T.D.).

I am also prepared to accept that the plaintiff's claim that the use of the word 'MICRO' in the description of the defendant's wares is likely to mislead the public, for the reasons set out in paragraphs (i) or (iii) of subsection 7(d) of the *Trade-Marks Act*, is not frivolous or vexatious.

In *Balanyk v. University of Toronto*,[262] the limited constitutional validity of the provision was once again made clear:

> The Supreme Court of Canada has said in *obiter* that s.7(d) depends for its validity on being applied to a subject matter coming within federal legislative authority under s.91 of the *Constitution Act, 1867*; *Vapor Canada Ltd. v. MacDonald*, above, at pp.148 and 157. Balanyk has pleaded no facts in relation to these causes of action which takes the matter out of the common law of deceit or misrepresentation, which is within the legislative authority of the provinces, into the legislative authority of Parliament, such as trademarks.

Section 7(d) is often invoked in conjunction with s. 52(1) of the *Competition Act*, which reads as follows:

> 52. (1) No person shall, for the purpose of promoting, directly or indirectly, the supply or use of a product or for the purpose of promoting, directly or indirectly, any business interest, by any means whatever,
>
> (a)  make a representation to the public that is false or misleading in a material respect;
>
> (b)  make a representation to the public in the form of a statement, warranty or guarantee of the performance, efficacy or length of life of a product that is not based on an adequate and proper test thereof, the proof of which lies on the person making the representation;
>
> (c)  make a representation to the public in a form that purports to be
>
> (i)  a warranty or guarantee of a product, or
>
> (ii)  a promise to replace, maintain or repair an article or any part thereof or to repeat or continue a service until it has achieved a specified result if the form of purported warranty or guarantee or promise is materially misleading or if there is no reasonable prospect that it will be carried out; or
>
> (d)  make a materially misleading representation to the public concerning the price at which a product or like products have been, are or will be ordinarily sold, and for the purposes of this paragraph a representation as to price is deemed to refer to the price at which the product has been sold by sellers generally in the relevant market unless it is clearly specified to be the price at which the product has been sold by the person by whom or on whose behalf the representation is made.

---

[262]  (1999), 1 C.P.R. (4th) 300 (Ont. S.C.J.).

Also potentially relevant are ss. 408 to 410 of the *Criminal Code*. These provisions are:

408. One commits an offence who, with intent to deceive or defraud the public or any person, whether ascertained or not,

(*a*)   passes off other wares or services as and for those ordered or required; or

(*b*)   makes use, in association with wares or services, of any description that is false in a material respect regarding
(i)   the kind, quality, quantity or composition,
(ii)   the geographical origin, or
(iii)   the mode of the manufacture, production or performance of those wares or services.

409. (1) Every one commits an offence who makes, has in his possession or disposes of a die, block, machine or other instrument designed or intended to be used in forging a trade-mark.
(2) No person shall be convicted of an offence under this section where he proves that he acted in good faith in the ordinary course of his business or employment.

410. Every one commits an offence who, with intent to deceive or defraud,

(*a*)   defaces, conceals or removes a trade-mark or the name of another person from anything without the consent of that other person; or

(*b*)   being a manufacturer, dealer, trader or bottler, fills any bottle or siphon that bears the trade-mark or name of another person, without the consent of that other person, with a beverage, milk, by-product of milk or other liquid commodity for the purpose of sale or traffic.

A few defences can successfully be used in passing off actions. A defendant may rely on doctrines such as "unclean hands" — it is not possible for a party with "dirty hands" to ask for an equity remedy such as an injunction.[263] Another defence is the use of one's own name.[264]

Prior use is a valid defence to a claim of passing off and should be accompanied by a counterclaim in appropriate cases as the prior user normally has superior rights.[265]

---

[263] See *Brewster Transport Co. v. Rocky Mountain Tours & Transport Co.* (1930), [1931] S.C.R. 336, [1931] 1 D.L.R. 713 (S.C.C.).

[264] *Hurlburt Co. v. Hurlburt Shoe Co.*, *supra*, note 222; *Hunt's Ltd. v. Hunt* (1925), 56 O.L.R. 349 (Ont. C.A.).

[265] *J. & A. McMillan Ltd. v. McMillan Press Ltd.* (1989), 27 C.P.R. (3d) 390 (N.B. C.A.).

In some cases an express disclaimer may be sufficient to defeat an action in passing off. In *Home Shoppe Ltd. v. National Development Ltd.*,[266] an identical product was sold under a different name and with an explicit statement that the product was the same but at a lesser price. The court determined that this did not constitute passing off.

## 3. Remedies

For the infringement of rights contained in ss. 19 to 22, the Act provides remedies in ss. 53 and following, including interim custody. Orders may exceptionally be issued against unnamed defendants ("John Doe, Jane Doe"), such as "street vendors".[267] These remedies include special measures at customs (s. 53.1), restitution/destruction (s. 53.1(7)) and, under s. 53.2, injunctions and the recovery of damages, including punitive damages (the French version makes clear the possibility of punitive damages), or profits, and the destruction of infringing goods. Exportation is possible. (See also s. 53.3 as to when goods can be (re-)exported in an unaltered state.)

The remedies available for the tort of passing off under s. 7 are essentially identical:[268] injunctions,[269] recovery of damages,[270] or recovery of profits.[271]

## (a) Injunctions Generally

Injunctions, usually in the form of a court order enjoining the defendant to stop an infringing activity (or, if *quia timet*, to prevent him from engaging in one), are an essential part of most intellectual property rights because those rights are generally presented as exclusive rights, or rights to "authorize or prohibit" a certain form of use of intellectual property, as, for example, a trade-mark, patented invention, or copyright work. By contrast, if only compensation were available and rightsholders could not stop in-

---

[266] (1987), 17 C.P.R. (3d) 126 (Man. Q.B.).

[267] See *Montres Rolex S.A. v. Balshin* (1992), [1993] 1 F.C. 236, 45 C.P.R. (3d) 174 (Fed. C.A.).

[268] See *Canadian Converters' Co. v. Eastport Trading Co.* (1968), [1969] 1 Ex. C.R. 493, 70 D.L.R. (2d) 149, 56 C.P.R. 204 (Can. Ex. Ct.).

[269] See *Centre Ice Ltd. v. National Hockey League* (1994), 53 C.P.R. (3d) 34, [1994] F.C.J. No. 68, 166 N.R. 44 (Fed. C.A.); and *A. Lassonde Inc. v. Island Oasis Canada Inc.* (2000), [2001] 2 F.C. 568, 273 N.R. 179 (Fed. C.A.).

[270] See, *e.g.*, *Marc-Aurele v. Ducharme* (1976), 34 C.P.R. (2d) 155 (Fed. T.D.).

[271] See, *e.g.*, *Ray Plastics Ltd. v. Canadian Tire Corp.* (1995), 62 C.P.R. (3d) 247 (Ont. Gen. Div.); and *Dubiner v. Cheerio Toys & Games Ltd.*, [1966] Ex. C.R. 801, 55 D.L.R. (2d) 420, 49 C.P.R. 155 (Can. Ex. Ct.).

fringements from occurring or continuing, their right would be reduced to a right to remuneration, the functional equivalent of a compulsory licence.

Injunctions are of two main types: permanent and interlocutory. Permanent injunctions are issued if the plaintiff proves his right and the infringement. The injunction order may remain in place until the exclusive right that was infringed by the defendant ceases to exist. Permanent injunctions are normally issued after a trial on the merits of a case. Interlocutory injunctions are issued during the pretrial phase. In fact, an action may begin with the issuance of a preliminary *ex parte* order (i.e., issued without informing the defendant). An interlocutory injunction is issued after a hearing where both parties are normally allowed to present some evidence, often only in written form, but not with the same scope as at a full trial.

The criteria used to decide whether an interlocutory injunction should be issued are well known.[272] There are two aspects to decide. One deals with the infringement, the other with the consequences of the order if issued. On the former element, the court must be satisfied that there is a "serious issue to be tried" (also known as the threshold test and it includes an analysis of the relative strength of the parties' case). In matters of trade-marks specifically, the plaintiff must not simply allege irreparable harm or, if relevant, likelihood of confusion. Evidence must be adduced to support the claim: "[A] court cannot infer, from a finding of confusion, the existence of a loss of goodwill or reputation. In order to be granted an interlocutory injunction, the moving party must produce concrete evidence of irreparable harm."[273] There may, however, be exceptional sets of facts where irreparable harm can be inferred from the nature of the infringement and the strength of the mark. The strength of the plaintiff's case on infringement may be measured as a multiplication of the chances that the defendant's conduct is infringing by the strength of the plaintiff's mark.[274]

In recent decisions in the United States,[275] courts have also weighed how the public interest would be affected by the issuance of the injunction.

---

[272] See *Turbo Resources Ltd. v. Petro-Canada Inc.*, [1989] 2 F.C. 451, 24 C.P.R. (3d) 1 (Fed. C.A.).

[273] *toronto.com v. Sinclair* (2000), [2000] F.C.J. No. 795, (sub nom. *Toronto.com v. Sinclair*) 6 C.P.R. (4th) 487, 2000 CarswellNat 1105 (Fed. T.D.). See also *ITV Technologies Inc. v. WIC Television Ltd.* (1997), [1997] F.C.J. No. 1803, 77 C.P.R. (3d) 495, 140 F.T.R. 302, 1997 CarswellNat 2505 (Fed. T.D.).

[274] Some commentators have argued in favour of a mathematical approach. See John Leubsdorf, "The Standard for Preliminary Injunctions" (1978) 91 Harv. L. Rev. 525-566. Such an approach, if applied mechanically, may not be realistic but it is useful to illustrate the underlying concept.

[275] See, e.g., *Amazon Inc. v. Barnes and Noble Inc.*, 239 F.3d 1343, 57 U.S.P.Q.2d 1747 (Fed. Cir., 2001), vacating and remanding 73 F.Supp.2d 1228, 53 U.S.P.Q. 2d 1115 (W.D. Wash., 1999).

In trade-mark cases, where protection is granted, at least in part, to protect the consumer's confidence in the source of a product or service, that consideration certainly seems relevant.

As to the second element (the consequences of the order), courts consider whether irreparable harm will be caused to the plaintiff (and the related inadequacy of damages),[276] and the balance of convenience, which one could perhaps call the balance of "inconveniences". The question is which party would suffer the most from the issuance (or not) of the injunction.

The relation between the elements of the test is not always clearly articulated. It seems fair to say, however, that a very strong infringement case should reduce the plaintiff's burden with respect to convenience, as if the two elements were combined on a sliding scale. As to irreparable harm, it is also important to bear in mind, as just mentioned, that most intellectual property rights are not simple rights to remuneration or compensation (and, in this way, are somewhat different from traditional tort principles) but rather rights to prevent use. In the case of trade-marks, the strength of the mark may be at stake. It thus is logical to link the strength of the plaintiff's case on infringement to the level of (irreparable) harm and inconvenience that must be shown. That said, injunctions remain equitable remedies and if a plaintiff waits too long before trying to obtain interlocutory relief, that will play in the defendant's favour, especially if the defendant has been using the mark or other protected object (copyright work, patented invention) for a significant amount of time. However, a prudent defendant should weigh the chances that the plaintiff may succeed on the merits (where delay is generally not available as a defence) and the damages that may be payable if that happens.

Courts have provided additional guidance on each element of the test. With respect to infringement, *i.e.*, the "serious question to be tried," it seems that this test is somewhat simpler to use and probably easier to pass than the "prima facie" (or "strong prima facie test") test previously applied.[277] In a case not involving intellectual property,[278] the Supreme Court explained the difference as follows:

---

[276] Which must be real and not speculative. See *Syntex Inc. v. Novopharm Ltd.* (1991), [1991] F.C.J. No. 424, 36 C.P.R. (3d) 129, 126 N.R. 114, 1991 CarswellNat 1113 (Fed. C.A.), leave to appeal to S.C.C. refused [1991] 3 S.C.R. xi (note) (S.C.C.).

[277] See *Syntex Inc. v. Apotex Inc.*, *supra*, note 148; and the discussion in *H.J. Heinz Co. of Canada v. Edan Foods Sales Inc.*, *supra*, note 241. The point is not crucial. The threshold or "serious question" test is now fairly well defined, independently of whether it is in fact a new test.

[278] *RJR-MacDonald Inc. v. Canada (Attorney General)*, [1994] 1 S.C.R. 311, 111 D.L.R. (4th) 385, 54 C.P.R. (3d) 114 (S.C.C.). See also *Metropolitan Stores*

Prior to the decision of the House of Lords in *American Cyanamid Co. v. Ethicon Ltd.*, [1975] A.C. 396, an applicant for interlocutory relief was required to demonstrate a 'strong *prima facie* case' on the merits in order to satisfy the first test. In *American Cyanamid*, however, Lord Diplock stated that an applicant need no longer demonstrate a strong *prima facie* case. Rather it would suffice if he or she could satisfy the court that 'the claim is not frivolous or vexatious; in other words, that there is a serious question to be tried'. The *American Cyanamid* standard is now generally accepted by the Canadian courts. . .

The relief the applicant seeks on the interlocutory motion must not be such as would effectively give it the relief to be sought at trial. Additionally, any delay or implied acquiescence (laches) will work against the plaintiff, as would any evidence of "dirty hands".[279] Finally, where the dispute affects some third person or the general public, or where the grant or refusal of the order can have serious public interest ramifications, the Court in its analysis must go *beyond* the ordinary balance of convenience test. If such broader consequences are likely, the motion cannot be treated as concerning only the immediate parties; the disadvantage to these third persons or to the public interest also must be weighed.[280] In appropriate circumstances, the plaintiff should provide an undertaking and/or security for potential damages sustained by the defendant, should the defendant prevail on the merits.

In *Turbo Resources Ltd. v. Petro-Canada Inc.*,[281] the Federal Court of Appeal reviewed the steps to be followed and gave examples of the "other factors" that a court may wish to consider:

Up to this point I have confined myself to selecting the appropriate threshold (or strength of case) test to be applied, and in seeing the extent to which that test has been satisfied in this case. In his *American Cyanamid* [*American Cyanamid Co. v. Ethicon Ltd.*, [1975] A.C. 396, [1975] 1 All E.R. 504 (H.L.)] formulation, Lord Diplock pointed out that other considerations are also to be

---

*(MTS) Ltd. v. Manitoba Food & Commercial Workers, Local 832*, (sub nom. *Manitoba (Attorney General) v. Metropolitan Stores Ltd.*) [1987] 1 S.C.R. 110, (sub nom. *Manitoba (Attorney General) v. Metropolitan Stores (M.T.S.) Ltd.*) 38 D.L.R. (4th) 321 (S.C.C.).

[279] See *Brewster Transport Co. v. Rocky Mountain Tours & Transport Co.*, *supra*, note 263.

[280] See *Gould v. Canada (Attorney General)*, [1984] 1 F.C. 1133, 13 D.L.R. (4th) 485 (Fed. C.A.), affirmed [1984] 2 S.C.R. 124 (S.C.C.); *Metropolitan Stores (MTS) Ltd. v. Manitoba Food & Commercial Workers, Local 832*, (sub nom. *Manitoba (Attorney General) v. Metropolitan Stores Ltd.*) [1987] 1 S.C.R. 110 (S.C.C.); and *Buffalo v. Canada* (1992), (sub nom. *Buffalo v. Canada (Minister of Indian Affairs & Northern Development)*) 57 F.T.R. 151 (Fed. T.D.).

[281] [1989] 2 F.C. 451, 24 C.P.R. (3d) 1 (Fed. C.A.).

weighed in the event a trial Judge concludes that there exists a serious question to be tried in the sense that it was neither frivolous nor vexatious. After discussing the appropriate threshold test, he proceeded to spell out these additional considerations when he says, at pp. 408-409:

> As to that, the governing principle is that the court should first consider whether, if the plaintiff were to succeed at the trial in establishing his right to a permanent injunction, he would be adequately compensated by an award of damages for the loss he would have sustained as a result of the defendant's continuing to do what was sought to be enjoined between the time of the application and the time of the trial. If damages in the measure recoverable at common law would be adequate remedy and the defendant would be in a financial position to pay them, no interlocutory injunction should normally be granted, however strong the plaintiff's claim appeared to be at that stage. If, on the other hand, damages would not provide an adequate remedy for the plaintiff in the event of his succeeding at the trial, the court should then consider whether, on the contrary hypothesis that the defendant were to succeed at the trial in establishing his right to do that which was sought to be enjoined, he would be adequately compensated under the plaintiff's undertaking as to damages for the loss he would have sustained by being prevented from doing so between the time of the application and the time of the trial. If damages in the measure recoverable under such an undertaking would be an adequate remedy and the plaintiff would be in a financial position to pay them, there would be no reason upon this ground to refuse an interlocutory injunction.
>
> It is where there is doubt as to the adequacy of the respective remedies in damages available to either party or to both, that the question of balance of convenience arises. It would be unwise to attempt even to list all the various matters which may need to be taken into consideration in deciding where the balance lies, let alone to suggest the relative weight to be attached to them. These will vary from case to case.
>
> Where other factors appear to be evenly balanced it is a counsel of prudence to take such measures as are calculated to preserve the status quo. If the defendant is enjoined temporarily from doing something that he has not done before, the only effect of the interlocutory injunction in the event of his succeeding at the trial is to postpone the date at which he is able to embark upon a course of action which he has not previously found it necessary to undertake; whereas to interrupt him in the conduct of an established enterprise would cause much greater inconvenience to him since he would have to start again to establish it in the event of his succeeding at the trial.

Save in the simplest cases, the decision to grant or to refuse an interlocutory injunction will cause to whichever party is unsuccessful on the application some disadvantages which his ultimate success at the trial may show he ought to have been spared and the disadvantages may be such that the recovery of damages to which he would then be entitled either in the action or under the plaintiff's undertaking would not be sufficient to compensate him fully for all of them. The extent to which the disadvantages to each party would be incapable of being compensated in damages in the event of his succeeding at the trial is always a significant factor in assessing where the balance of convenience lies; and if the extent of the uncompensatable disadvantage to each party would not differ widely, it may not be improper to take into account in tipping the balance the relative strength of each party's case as revealed by the affidavit evidence adduced on the hearing of the application. This, however, should be done only where it is apparent upon the facts disclosed by evidence as to which there is no credible dispute that the strength of one party's case is disproportionate to that of the other party. The court is not justified in embarking upon anything resembling a trial of the action upon conflicting affidavits in order to evaluate the strength of either party's case.

I would reiterate that, in addition to those to which I have referred, there may be many other special factors to be taken into consideration in the particular circumstances of individual cases. . . .

Risking the obvious dangers inherent in attempting to reduce a not uncomplicated formula to skeletal form, it appears nonetheless that the main features of each of these factors are as follows:

(a)    where a plaintiff's recoverable damages resulting in the continuance of the defendant's activities pending trial would be an adequate remedy that the defendant would be financially able to pay, an interlocutory injunction should not normally be granted;

(b)    where such damages would not provide the plaintiff an adequate remedy but damages (recoverable under the plaintiff's undertaking) would provide the defendant with such a remedy for the restriction on his activities, there would be no ground for refusing an interlocutory injunction;

(c)    where doubt exists as to the adequacy of these remedies in damages available to either party, regard should be had to where the balance of convenience lies;

(d)    where other factors appear to be evenly balanced, it is prudent to take such measures as will preserve the status quo;

(e)    where the evidence on the application is such as to show one party's case to be disproportionately stronger than the other's, this factor may be permitted to tip the balance of convenience in that party's favour provided the uncompensatable disadvantage to each party would not differ widely;

(g)    other unspecified special factors may possibly be considered in the particular circumstances of individual cases.

Courts may also issue "Anton Piller" orders (see the Remedies Section in Part I (Copyright)).

## VII. DOMAIN NAMES AND INTERNET-BASED INFRINGEMENT

A domain name is a unique identifier for an Internet site. Domain names are text-based addresses which "map to" lengthy numeric Internet protocol addresses. As an illustration of the terminology, for the online encyclopedia Wikipedia, the *URL* is http://www.wikipedia.org, the *domain name* is "wikipedia.org", the *subdomain* is "www," the *second level domain* is "wikipedia" and the *top level domain* is ".org". Top-level domains can be two-letter country codes (such as ".ca") or a general extension, such as ".com" or ".net." In recent years, trade-marks have been appropriated either as part of domain names or as invisible terms used in HTML known as "meta tags" that can be seen by search engines but not by people surfing the internet (unless they read the actual HTML coding).[282] Meta tags can be viewed in Firefox by choosing Page info, in Internet Explorer by choosing Source under the View menu, and in Netscape Navigator by choosing Page Source under the View menu. Meta tags, however, are declining in importance. Most Internet search engines now ignore or put little weight on meta tags because some web designers included the marks of a competitor's better known products or services in their own site's meta tags in order to place a site higher in search engine rankings or to include it in more search engine results and therefore increase the traffic to a site. The reasons that search engines are programmed to rely less on meta tags are the same reasons that make meta tags of interest to trade-mark law.

There are two types of cyber-predators: cyber-squatters and copy-cats. Cyber-squatters buy domain names with the general intention of selling them at a higher cost to the trade-mark owner. Copy-cats on the other hand, buy a domain name that is similar to that of a known brand and try to confuse the public and direct attention to their sites. They may simply copy the mark into their domain name or, knowing that internet users sometimes mistype, use variations of well known marks to lure unwary users to their site, in most cases either to sell pornography or competing products. This practice is referred to as typo-squatting.

---

[282] An interesting case dealing with those tags is *British Columbia Automobile Assn. v. O.P.E.I.U., Local 378, supra*, note 229.

When registering a domain name, the registrant must accept a binding arbitration clause which empowers recognized dispute-settlement providers to hear disputes between trade-mark holders and those registrants. In the case of general top-level domains (gTLDs), such as .com, .org and .net, the procedure is based on the Uniform Dispute Resolution Procedure (UDRP) adopted in 1999 by the Internet Corporation for Assigned Names and Numbers (ICANN), a private entity subject to the indirect control of the U.S. government that controls the assignment of domain names, including, ultimately, all national or country code domain names (cc TLDs, such as .ca for Canada, .uk for the United Kingdom, .fr for France, .tv for Tuvalu, etc.). Under the UDRP, which all registrars must also accept to be recognized by ICANN, if an arbitration panel orders the transfer or cancellation of a registration (the vast majority of complainants opt for a transfer), the registrar must comply.

The UDRP provides that to obtain the cancellation of a registration of its transfer, a trade-mark owner must show that the domain name is identical or confusingly similar to a trade-mark in which the complainant has rights; that the registrant has no rights or legitimate interests in respect of the domain name; and that the domain name has been registered and is being used in bad faith (Paragraph 4(a)).

On the first point, UDRP decisions show that both registered and common law marks may be invoked, though in the case of common law marks, significant evidence of use pre-dating the registration of the domain name is required. The confusing similarity is assessed according to normal trade-mark law principles.

If the complainant is successful on the first step, then to show legitimate interest, a registrant must be able to convince the panel that he or she either was authorized by the trade-mark owner to register or is otherwise making fair use of the name, for example for the purpose of criticism and with no commercial intent or motive whatsoever.

In addition to the above, the complainant must also show that the domain name has been registered and used in bad faith.

There are four situations in which the Policy deems that bad faith registration and use is present:

4(b) For the purposes of Paragraph 4(a)(iii), the following circumstances, in particular but without limitation, if found by the Panel to be present, shall be evidence of the registration and use of a domain name in bad faith:

(i)    circumstances indicating that the registrant has registered or the registrant has acquired the domain name primarily for the purpose of selling, renting, or otherwise transferring the domain name registration to the complainant who is the owner of the trademark or service mark or to a competitor of that complainant, for valuable consideration in excess of the registrant's documented out-of-pocket costs directly related to the domain name; or

(ii)   the registrant has registered the domain name in order to prevent the owner of the trademark or service mark from reflecting the mark in a corresponding domain name, provided that the registrant has engaged in a pattern of such conduct; or

(iii)   the registrant has registered the domain name primarily for the purpose of disrupting the business of a competitor; or

(iv)   by using the domain name, the registrant has intentionally attempted to attract, for commercial gain, Internet users to the registrant's web site or other on-line location, by creating a likelihood of confusion with the complainant's mark as to the source, sponsorship, affiliation, or endorsement of the registrant's web site or location or of a product or service on the registrant's web site or location.

In the absence of all four situations, a panel may still make a finding of bad faith if it is convinced that, at the time of registration the registrant knew about the complainant's mark (bad faith registration) and that the domain name is used (or not used) in a way that demonstrates bad faith.

UDRP proceedings do not exclude national courts, but they tend to be much faster (the entire proceeding takes less than sixty days) and less expensive because there are no hearings. The entire process is conducted via email.

In the case of disputes involving ".ca", the Canadian Internet Registration Authority (CIRA) adopted a procedure similar in many respects to the UDRP. It is known as the CIRA Domain Name Dispute Resolution Policy (CDRP). The main differences include a higher parallelism with Canadian trade-mark law, in particular the "use" requirement (see the Use of Trade-Mark section) and a more limited definition of what constitutes bad faith:

Registrant will be considered to have registered a domain name in bad faith *if, and only if:*

(a)   the Registrant registered the domain name, or acquired the Registration, primarily for the purpose of selling, renting, licensing or otherwise transferring the Registration to the Complainant, or the Complainant's licensor or licensee of the Mark, or to a competitor of the Complainant or the licensee or licensor for valuable consideration in excess of the Registrant's actual costs in registering the domain name, or acquiring the Registration;

(b)   the Registrant registered the domain name or acquired the Registration in order to prevent the Complainant, or the Complainant's licensor or licensee of the Mark, from registering the Mark as a domain name, provided that the Registrant, alone or in concert with one or more additional persons has engaged in a pattern of registering domain names in order to prevent persons who have Rights in Marks from registering the Marks as domain names; or

(c)    the Registrant registered the domain name or acquired the Registration primarily for the purpose of disrupting the business of the Complainant, or the Complainant's licensor or licensee of the Mark, who is a competitor of the Registrant.

Apart from these online arbitration proceedings, Canadian courts have also had to deal with various types of trade-mark (and copyright) infringement on the internet.

In *Saskatoon Star Phoenix Group Inc. v. Noton*,[283] the defendant had reproduced most of the content of the online version of the Saskatoon daily but replaced the advertisements with his own. This was found to be passing off.

In *PEINET Inc. v. O'Brien*,[284] the plaintiff was the regional internet provider in Prince-Edward Island. The plaintiff was incorporated as PEI-NET Inc. and its electronic address was peinet.pe.ca. The defendant, a former employee of the plaintiff, commenced a business as an internet provider. The defendant was assigned the domain name "pei.net" from an American registrar and briefly used it, but after the plaintiff complained, the defendant began to use isn.net and agreed to de-list pei.net. The court found that there was no passing off because the internet users would not be misled. In this early domain case, the court mistakenly put much emphasis on the difference between upper and lower case letters in domain names and the fact that the plaintiff's corporate name did not separate "pei" and "net" by a period.

In another case,[285] the Law Society of British Columbia, which operates websites under the domain names <lawsociety.bc.ca> and <lsbc.org>, alleged that the registration of domain names such <lawsocietyofbc.ca> and <lsbc.ca> and use of these domain names to direct people to an adult website (AL4A (Adult Links for Adults)) and later to the site of a political party was passing off. The British Columbia Supreme Court agreed as all three elements of the tort were present: the Law Society had goodwill; the domain name was a misrepresentation (with or without confusion); and there was damage to the Law Society's reputation, which is presumed if a misrepresentation case is made.

---

[283] (2001), 12 C.P.R. (4th) 4 (Sask. Q.B.).

[284] (1995), 61 C.P.R. (3d) 334 (P.E.I. T.D. [In Chambers]).

[285] *Law Society (British Columbia) v. Canada Domain Name Exchange Corp.*, *supra*, note 249.

In another British Columbia case, [286] an individual who was selling business application software at the web address <www.thesoftwareguy.com> alleged that a competing business launched at <www.thesoftwareking.com> constituted passing-off. Interestingly, both parties had previously been working for another software company, and both their sites resembled that of their former employer. The Court rejected a motion for an interlocutory injunction, correctly noting the weakness of the plaintiff's mark, composed of common words and, with respect to "software," a descriptive word.

In a 2001 case before the Ontario Court of Appeal,[287] Computer City, Inc. appealed a huge damages assessment against it for trade-mark infringement. The facts were summarized as follows by Carthy J.A.:

> The plaintiff, Pro-C Limited ('Pro-C'), recovered a judgment at trial for $450,000 in general damages and $750,000 in punitive damages for infringement of a trade-mark by the defendant, Computer City, Inc. The plaintiff's trade-mark 'Wingen', covering its software product, was adopted by the defendant in association with a non-competitive product (personal computers) sold in the United States. Pro-C used the trade-mark as the name of its website and when Computer City's American customers sought information or service they mistakenly arrived at Pro-C's website. Pro-C alleged that their site was so overwhelmed that it could not service its own customers and its business was ruined.
>
> Computer City's position on appeal is that the *Trade-Marks Act*, R.S.C. 1985 c.T-13 (the 'Act'), does not embrace the conduct complained of and that, in any event, no damages were proved. Pro-C cross-appeals for increased damages.
>
> Pro-C is a small Waterloo, Ontario, company operated from the home of its principal, selling source code generators for software to be used in the production of computer programs. Computer City is a large American corporation operating many retail stores across the United States and, at the relevant time, five stores in Canada.
>
> In 1994 Pro-C purchased the trade-mark WINGEN, registered in both Canada and the United States for 'computer programs used to generate programs for Windows.' The commercial purpose was to suggest an association with Microsoft's 'Windows' software. Pro-C was not alone with that thought. In 1996, Computer City developed an in-house line of computers that it called Wingen. From the outset of production of these computers the appellant was aware of

---

[286] *Software Guy Brokers Ltd. v. Hardy* (2004), [2004] B.C.J. No. 95, 32 C.P.R. (4th) 88, 2004 CarswellBC 97 (B.C. S.C.).

[287] *Pro-C Ltd. v. Computer City Inc.*, *supra*, note 176.

the registrations of the trade-mark Wingen owned by Pro-C. The computers were offered for sale in all the United States outlets but, due to costs in crossing the border, in none of the Canadian stores.

This litigation springs from the use of Internet websites rather than competition between products. Pro-C had an interactive website 'www.wingen.com' which it used to sell its software, transfer it to a purchaser and provide service. Computer City established a passive site 'www.computercity.com', used to advertise and provide product information.

Being a passive website, Computer City's site did not have interaction with customers — it used the site only to post information. A phone number was included for receiving orders but no sales were made directly to Canada or in Canada.

There is no directory for website names and a purchaser wishing information about a product would either guess the domain name or use keywords on a search engine. In this fashion many Computer City customers seeking information or service for their purchased computers mistakenly found their way to Pro-C's website. They saw the label Wingen on their units and sought out a site in that name rather than Computer City. Pro-C's evidence at trial was that over a period of some months it received over 100,000 hits (visits) per month by Computer City's customers. Because of the unwanted traffic to its website, Pro-C alleged that it could no longer service its clients or effectively sell its programs and that its business was destroyed. Its statement of claim is based solely on infringement of its trade-mark in Canada.

While damages could be shown, and the defendant was partly responsible, the question was whether the *Trade-marks Act* gave the plaintiff/respondent a cause of action to recover those damages. In particular, the case raised the question whether the defendant/appellant's passive use of the mark WINGEN constituted use within the meaning of the Act. The Court of Appeal allowed the appeal because passive "use" of a mark on a website does not constitute use as defined in the Act:

> Computer City's passive website could not constitute a use in association with wares because no transfer of ownership was possible through that medium.

> [. . .]

> The format for relief for this type of loss may exist outside the Act in proper circumstances. It is incidental that the plaintiff has a registered trade-mark. No wares competed in the marketplace and the damage, if damage there be, would have been the same if the name of the website did not have trade-mark protection. If a party intentionally or negligently causes injury and the ingredients for establishing a tort can be proved, then the new technology of the Internet and websites can be readily accommodated. It is much more sensible to apply tort

principles to accommodate new technologies than to distort statutory trade-mark rights.[288]

The reasoning seems correct: to "use" a mark on the internet, it must be used in the course of trade, and should thus enable or support some form of commercial transaction.

In cases of passive use, a person may rely on a UDRP (or CDRP) based proceeding (see above) if the use is within a domain name. It is unclear to what extent Canadian courts can order transfers, especially against regis-trars.[289] If the use is not in commerce and is not libellous or misleading, any remedy, if there is one in such a case, lies outside of trade-mark law.

In *itravel2000.com Inc. v. Fagan*[290] the owner of the trade-mark itravel, doing business online at www.itravel2000.com, successfully prevented the owner of the domain name itravel.ca, which had been registered by a person not in any way connected to the travel industry, from using or transferring that domain name. The court applied the usual three-part test for interloc-utory injunctions. The court did not comment on the first part of the test, namely whether registering "itravel" (which can be read as "I travel"), was necessarily or even probably an infringement of the plaintiff's mark. The court simply stated: "Based upon the materials filed, it is clear that this application is neither vexatious or frivolous. There is a serious issue to be tried. The issue relates to the ownership of the Internet domain name 'itravel.ca'." A similar finding was made in a case involving the mark YELLOWPAGES.[291] These cases led to orders to "freeze" domain names and, in the *Bell Actimedia* case, to order the defendant to produce documents, but not to transfer the domain name.[292] A plaintiff might consider combining a UDRP or CDRP proceeding to obtain a transfer with an action in federal or provincial court for damages and an injunction, but without asking for a transfer in the court action, which could lead to a dismissal of the UDRP complaint. In appropriate cases, a preliminary or interlocutory injunction could be sought to freeze the domain name, concurrently with a UDRP/CDRP proceeding.

---

[288] *Ibid.*

[289] *Molson Breweries, A Partnership v. Kuettner* (1999), 3 C.P.R. (4th) 479 (Fed. T.D.).

[290] (2001), (sub nom. *Itravel2000.com Inc. v. Fagan*) 197 D.L.R. (4th) 760, (sub nom. *Itravel2000.com Inc. v. Fagan*) 11 C.P.R. (4th) 164 (Ont. S.C.J.).

[291] *Bell Actimedia Inc. v. Puzo* (1999), 2 C.P.R. (4th) 289 (Fed. T.D.). See also *Tele-Direct (Publications) Inc. v. Canadian Business Online Inc.* (1997), 77 C.P.R. (3d) 23 (Fed. T.D.).

[292] See above note 289 and accompanying text.

In another Ontario case,[293] a British travel company, specializing in providing travel services and tours to and from Canada, and which operated the web site *www.canadian-affair.com,* alleged that the Defendant's registration and use of *www.canadianaffair.com* to sell pornographic services constituted both defamation and passing-off. On a motion to strike the statement of claim, the court had to decide whether the passing-off claim disclosed a valid cause of action. The test to apply at that stage is whether it is plain and obvious, or beyond doubt that the claim discloses no reasonable cause of action. The court accepted that there could be a valid claim, but expressed serious doubt as to deception.[294] Had the mark been registered, a claim under s. 22 could also have been made.

One of the inherent problems on the internet is jurisdiction. Since *Morguard Investments Ltd. v. De Savoye,*[295] the fundamental principle is that there must be a real and substantial connection between the subject matter of an action and the right of a court to assume jurisdiction over it. The question, of course, is what is a real and substantial connection on (not to. . .) the Internet. Certain cases have taken a very broad view of jurisdiction. For example, in *Alteen v. Informix Corp.,*[296] the Newfoundland Supreme Court asserted jurisdiction over a U.S. company because its stock had been made available to Canadian residents:

> [D]amage can be suffered in more than one place. The jurisdictional test for the place of a tort has been held to be the place where the damage is suffered, is assumed to be the place where the tort is committed so long as it was reasonably foreseeable that the product would be used or consumed where the plaintiff used or consumed it. *Moran v. Pyle National (Canada) Ltd.* (1973), [1975] 1 S.C.R. 393 (S.C.C.).

> Each of the individual Plaintiffs purchased the shares of the Defendant within the jurisdiction of Newfoundland where the Defendant no doubt could have reasonably foreseen that shares in the Defendant company would have been purchased. The Plaintiffs allege that the Defendant was well aware of the fact that Canadian citizens and, in particular, citizens within the jurisdiction of Newfoundland, purchased shares of the Defendant company, and so long as the Defendant had this knowledge, it could have reasonably foreseen that its actions could have resulted in damages to the stockholders. The Plaintiffs'

---

[293] *Airline Seat Co. v. 1396804 Ontario Inc.* (2000), 8 C.P.R. (4th) 12 (Ont. S.C.J.).

[294] Compare *Innersense International Inc. v. Manegre,* [2000] 9 W.W.R. 670, 265 A.R. 358, 7 C.P.R. (4th) 107 (Alta. Q.B.).

[295] [1990] 3 S.C.R. 1077, 76 D.L.R. (4th) 256, 52 B.C.L.R. (2d) 160, 15 R.P.R. (2d) 1 (S.C.C.).

[296] (1998), 164 Nfld. & P.E.I.R. 301, 507 A.P.R. 301, 21 C.P.C. (4th) 228 (Nfld. T.D.).

damages, which are outlined in the Plaintiffs' Statement of Claim, were obviously suffered within the jurisdiction of Newfoundland.

The Plaintiffs allege that the investing public were misled by the Defendant's financial performance in that the means by which the Defendant communicated its financial performances were through internationally accessible mediums. Public documents such as SEC filings, securities analysts' reports, and advisories about the company, press releases issued by the company, and media reports about the company, were all available to the Plaintiffs as a means of determining the financial future of this company. When the Defendant made these research tools available to the investing public, and, in particular, Newfoundland investors, they ran the risk of having legal action initiated against them should any of these financial performance claims be shown to have been made negligently or in such a manner as to be intentionally misleading. As to the Defendant's claim that it never made or issued any public statements to the Canadian financial or business press, the Plaintiffs state that any information disseminated by the various news wires and through the Internet are often picked up in news stories by the Canadian financial or business press.

Since the shares in question were purchased in Newfoundland, a fact the Defendant could have reasonably foreseen, following which they are alleged to have declined in value due to misdeeds of the Defendant, the jurisdictional test for the place of a tort is assumed to be the place where the tort is committed and damage suffered.

I conclude that this Court does have jurisdiction to try the case. Hence, the application for dismissal for want of jurisdiction fails.

By contrast, in *Easthaven Ltd. v. Nutrisystem.com Inc.*,[297] a case where the U.S. owner of the trade-mark SWEETSUCCESS (weight-loss products) was trying to prevent the use of the domain name sweetsuccess.com registered by a Barbados company, an Ontario Court refused to assert jurisdiction over a company simply because it was doing business in Toronto:

A domain name lacks a physical existence. The mere fact that it is registered through a corporation that happens to carry on business in Toronto does not give the domain name a physical existence in Ontario. A domain name is still simply a unique identifier for a particular internet site located on a particular computer. That computer may be located anywhere in the world and be unrelated to where the domain name is registered. The fact is that the internet is an

---

[297] (2001), 202 D.L.R. (4th) 560, 55 O.R. (3d) 334, 14 C.P.R. (4th) 22 (Ont. S.C.J.), additional reasons at (2001), 2001 CarswellOnt 3431 (Ont. S.C.J.), additional reasons at (2001), 2001 CarswellOnt 3693 (Ont. S.C.J.).

entity without conventional geographic boundaries. As Whitten J. observed in *Pro-C Ltd. v. Computer City Inc.* (Ont. S.C.J.[298]) at para. 1:

> The Internet, in reality a network of networks, has created a whole new territory independent of conventional geography. The conceptual location of this electronic interactivity available to us through our computers is oft referred to as 'cyberspace' [note omitted]. Unlike a 'real' territory with fixed borders, the Internet is constantly growing and at a phenomenal rate.

The question of how one determines jurisdictional issues when dealing with the internet or cyberspace is one which has only recently arisen and there is, consequently, little authority dealing with the issue. Indeed, I was not provided with any authorities by the parties on the issue — a fact that is perhaps not surprising given that there appear to be few authorities which have expressly dealt with the issue. This point was made by the U.S. Court of Appeals, Ninth Circuit, in *Panavision Intl., L.P. v. Toeppen*, 141 F.3d 1316 (U.S. 9th Cir. Cal., 1998) where Judge Thompson said, at p. 1320:

> Applying principles of personal jurisdiction to conduct in cyberspace is relatively new. 'With this global revolution looming on the horizon, the development of the law concerning the permissible scope of personal jurisdiction based on Internet use is in its infant stages. The cases are scant.' *Zippo Mfg. Co. v. Zippo Dot Com, Inc.*, 952 F. Supp. 1119, 1123 (W.D. Pa. 1997).

The decision in *Panavision* is helpful, however, because it does expressly address this issue albeit in the context of American procedure and legal concepts. The court in *Panavision* observed that personal jurisdiction could be founded on either general jurisdiction or specific jurisdiction. The court held that general jurisdiction could be found in such a case only if the person was domiciled in the jurisdiction or his activities there were 'substantial' or 'continuous and systematic'. In terms of specific jurisdiction, the court adopted a three-part test as follows, at p. 1320:

> (1) The nonresident defendant must do some act or consummate some transaction with the forum or perform some act by which he purposefully avails himself of the privilege of conducting activities in the forum, thereby invoking the benefits and protections of its laws; (2) the claim must be one which arises out of or results from the defendant's forum-related activities; and (3) exercise of jurisdiction must be reasonable.

[. . .]

---

[298] Which was reversed, though not on this point. See note 176.

I find the analysis of the U.S. Court of Appeals in *Panavision* to be helpful in my consideration of whether I should conclude that Ontario does have jurisdiction in the circumstances of this case. I can easily conclude that there is no general jurisdiction in this court over the defendant. Nutrisystem.com Inc. is not domiciled in Ontario nor is there any evidence that it has engaged in activities here that were substantial or continuous and systematic.

Increasingly, U.S. tort cases consider the need for the plaintiff to show that the defendant targeted an area located within the court's jurisdiction. In the above case, it is clear that Nutrisystem had not targeted Ontario. That case could perhaps have proceeded under the UDRP. There are specific provisions of U.S. trade-mark law that are particularly beneficial to trade-mark owners. These provisions form part of the *Anti-Cybersquatting Protection Act* (ACPA)[299] and may explain why many plaintiffs choose U.S. courts to sue non-U.S. defendants if they can establish a connection. It provides much broader protection than the UDRP, because it goes beyond simply domain names, and allows plaintiffs to recover statutory damages of not less than $1,000 and not more than $100,000 per domain name. One option to do so, accepted in some decisions, is that domain names are necessarily registered (ultimately) with Network Solutions, Inc.,[300] which is located in Virginia, thus giving courts of that State a reason to assert jurisdiction over any dispute involving domain names. Because all domain names are ultimately "residing" in Virginia, where the Internet "Root Server" and the company that operates it is located, by using *in rem* jurisdiction, as in the CNN case, courts in that State and the U.S. 4th Circuit may be able to assert jurisdiction over any dispute concerning domain names worldwide, and may be tempted to apply U.S. law to such disputes.

## VIII.  DISCUSSION QUESTIONS

**Q:**    A luxury leather goods company has been plagued by forgeries recently and as an anti-counterfeit measure has started to stamp its purses with the word "Aardvark." The word is printed in gold ink on the inside flap of the purse straps but is too small to be seen by the human eye unaided. The purse company has not publicly discussed this practice because they do not want the counterfeiters to stamp their forged purses with the same

---

[299] 15 U.S.C.A. § 1125(d).

[300] See, *e.g.*, *Barcelona.com, Incorporated v. Excelentisimo Ayuntamiento De Barcelona*, 330 F.3d 617, 67 U.S.P.Q. 2d 1025 (U.S. 4th Cir., 2003); and *Cable News Network, LP, LLLP v. CNNews.com*, 66 U.S.P.Q.2d 1057 (U.S. 4th Cir., 2003).

word. The company uses the word to identify authentic purses which originated from them. Is the word "Aardvark" a trade-mark?

**Q:**   Discuss whether the following marks would be registrable:

UMBRELLA for hand-held portable rain protection device
UMBRELLA for comprehensive insurance services
RAINY DAY for comprehensive insurance services
UMBRELLA for cat litter boxes with a privacy roof
UMBRELLA for computer mouse pads
UMLAB for citrus drinks

**A:**   Generic
Descriptive
Suggestive?
Suggestive
Arbitrary
Fanciful word

**Q:**   Galo, a toy company, has been selling coloured plastic building blocks. The blocks have an eight-stud design which allows the blocks to interlock with other blocks. Galo held a patent on the building blocks but the patent has expired. A rival company Maxi is marketing buckets of plastic building blocks with an almost identical shape. Galo argues it has an unregistered trade-mark in the eight-stud design. How would you rule in this case if you were the judge and what cases would you rely on?

**Q:**   A new luxury hotel in a large city in Canada is called the Library Hotel and is based on a library theme. The floors of the hotel and individual rooms are categorized according to a familiar library classification system. Under that system, alphabetical letters indicate broad categories ("P" for arts or "K" for law and political science) and individual texts are further designated within a category with alpha-numeric designators. A non-profit organization centrally administers the numbers in the library classification system and assigns new books specific numbers. The Library Hotel uses letters for each of its hotel rooms and decorates each hotel floor with decorations appropriate to the subject matter of the library classification scheme. On floor "K" the hotel has pictures of scales of justice, courthouse buildings, replicas of constitutions and gavels. On floor P, the hotel features sculptures and paintings. The non-profit system which administers the classification system has sued the Library Hotel for trade-mark infringement. You represent the Library Hotel and have been asked to develop an argument to defend against this claim.

**Q:**    MacWilliam's Restaurants is a famous fast-food restaurant chain which specializes in hamburgers, fried chicken and pizza. It has registered numerous trade-marks in relation to its restaurant services and its specialty food products, which all include the prefix "Mac." Recently, MacWilliam's Restaurant has expanded its menus to include health-food options such as salads, soy burgers, and grilled chicken. It includes health-related newsletters with nutrition and exercise advice in the bags of its health-food "combo" meals. MacWilliam's has been engaged in a large advertising campaign on its healthy food and commitment to reducing obesity in the country. Some of its restaurants sponsor morning walks. The walkers return to the restaurant for free juice and can order breakfast items (including both healthy and traditional offerings). A small consulting firm called "MacWellness" has just opened up with offices across the country for health-related counselling and classes. They offer personalized nutrition advice, preventative medical screenings, and classes on yoga and meditation. They are using the names "MacWellness," MacNutrition," and "MacHealthClub" on their business signs, in advertising, on the monthly pamphlets compiling health news, and on equipment that they sell for their classes (such as gym mats, yoga pants, exercise balls, water bottles, and exercise shirts). The company was founded by Charlie Campbell and Zinfel Zygot, two former employees of the national business consulting firm "MacKenzie." MacKenzie Company was founded by Arthur MacKenzie. Campbell and Zygot state that they are using the "Mac" prefix as a tribute to Arthur MacKenzie. MacWilliam's claims that "MacWellness" infringes its trade-marks. The CEO of MacWilliam's has emphasized MacWilliam's corporate plans to expand further into health and nutrition services on a global basis and cites the example of their healthy meals as one step in that corporate strategy.

**Q:**    A new Internet search engine company wants to use a picture of a Sherlock-Holmes figure with a tweed cape, and magnifying glass with the word "Sherlock" below the image as its trade mark for search engine services. What argument would you make to argue that this mark is *not* registrable?

**A:** One could argue that it is descriptive, not merely suggestive, because the idea of a detective is a common metaphor in the online industry for search functions.

**Q:**    A proprietary legal information database called LexMaxim, which uses "LEXMAXIM" in association with its subscription legal information database and legal information retrieval services objects to Librarian's use of "LEXNOTES" for his website on legal research. LexMaxim more broadly claims that any use of "lex" infringes its trademark.

**A:** Consider who the audience is for legal information. Lawyers may not interpret "lex" as a mark but as a general word meaning "law."

**Q:**    The General Counsel of EastJet, the well-known airline, comes to see you. He explains that East, which has been successful mostly east of Manitoba, wants to change its image to become a true national airline. They want to adopt the name Canadi*n Air, (the * can be either an a or an e, so that the name works in both official languages). EastJet asks you how they should proceed to protect their new name.

They also want to adopt a new logo, namely a red maple leaf on a white background, with two red stripes on each side (right & left) of the white square (same red as the maple leaf).

To make sure its advertising message gets maximum exposure, EastJet is also thinking of writing "We are better than Air Canada" on all its aircrafts.

A quick search in the Canadian Trade-Marks database at CIPO shows that when Canadian Airlines and Air Canada merged in 1999-2000, all trade-marks were transferred to Air Canada Inc. However, since 2001, all flights are operated exclusively under the mark "Air Canada".

If you are EastJet's intellectual property lawyer, how do you suggest they proceed?

If you are advising Air Canada, what could be done to prevent EastJet from implementing its proposed changes?

**Q:**    Given the high demand for "organic" products, Jean Poissonnier wants to start a business. He wants to open a grocery store in his province specializing in organic products (dairy products, meat, fish, fruits and vegetables, and grains). He is even thinking of launching his own line of homemade products under the brand name "Organic." He cannot decide on the name of his store and comes to consult with you. He has thought of several potential names for his grocery store, including "Bio Groceries," "Poissonnier," and "Mickey Mouse," since his five-year-old daughter, Camille, loves the Disney character Mickey Mouse (see image below). He is also thinking of using his wife's family name, which is "Loebeys." Jean knows that there is a major supermarket chain in the province called Loebeys, but he has heard that he has the right to use his wife's name.

Based on the *Trade-marks Act* and the relevant jurisprudence, consider the following questions and provide reasons for your responses.

a)    For his grocery business, can John use the name:
- "Bio Groceries"?
- "Poissonnier"?
- "Mickey Mouse"?

b)   For his "homemade" products, can John use the brand name "Organic"?

c)   Does Jean *have to* apply to register the brand name he has chosen? If he does not, will he be protected?

d)   Can John submit an application to register the brand names:
     - "Organic" for his homemade products?
     - "Mickey Mouse" for his business?

e)   Can Jean use and register the name "Loebeys"?

f)   If Jean begins to use and submits an application to register the brand name Loebeys, what might he expect on the procedural level?

g)   Jean calls you back a week later and tells you that after all he has decided to use "Camille Groceries." What must Jean do to register his brand name? (List the main steps only)

h)   Would the use of the image of Mickey Mouse in a written examination for a law school course violate the *Copyright Act* or the *Trade-marks Act*? Explain.

# *Chapter* 5: Patents

I. Introduction

II. Object of Protection

III. Application

IV. Term of Protection

V. Infringement

VI. Remedies

VII. Discussion Questions

## I. INTRODUCTION

### 1. Origin

According to Black's Dictionary, a patent is a grant of a privilege or property to an individual by the government.[1] The word "patent" originated in England and is derived from the Latin *patere*, a verb meaning "to be open." The British Crown released "letters patent" that is open letters (as opposed to the usual letters sealed with wax) informing the recipient (and the public) of the grant of privileges on an invention for a determined period. The *Statute of Monopolies* of 1623 put an end to the Royal prerogative allowing the King to grant discretionary patents and awarding sweeping control to the patentees. The *Statute* provided for an exclusive right to the "true and first" inventor for a period of 14 years.

A patent is thus essentially an exclusive right to use one's "invention" for a limited period of time, in exchange for its disclosure to the public. After the expiry of the term of protection, usually 20 years, the invention falls into the "public domain" and anyone can use it.

Michael Halewood explains in his article, *"Regulating Patent Holders, Local Working Requirements and Compulsory Licences at International Law,"* the historical evolution of patent law around the world and international agreements:[2]

> The earliest discovered patent legislation, the *Venetian Patent Act* of 1474, required the active exploitation of patents; otherwise, they were cancelled by the Venetian state. Likewise, the English *Statute of Monopolies*, 1623 mandated the working of the patent grant. The American *Patent Act* of 1790, provided

---

[1] *Black's Law Dictionary*, 8th ed. *s.v.* "letters patent".
[2] (1997) 35 Osgoode Hall L.J. 245-286.

what are now referred to as 'importation patents,' which gave Americans monopoly rights to import foreign technology, without any obligation to protect foreign inventors' rights. It has been held that, 'as far as the American Patent Act is concerned, there can be no doubt but that its primary raison d'être was to give an incentive for working new inventions locally.' The French Patent Law of 1791 also granted importation patents to work foreign inventions in France. In addition, the Patent Law revoked French patent grants if inventors attained a foreign patent in a subject matter originally patented in France.

By the middle of the nineteenth century, most industrialized countries had passed patent related legislation. As the discussion above indicates, patent law served, for the most part, to bolster domestic industrialization and provided very little by way of protection for foreign patents.

In 1883, the Union for the Protection of Industrial Property, produced the *Paris Convention*. [See the International Section.] This was the first multilateral treaty negotiation to standardize the treatment of intellectual property on an international scale.

## 2. Constitutional Ground

Patent law in Canada originated with the 1823 statute of Lower Canada and the 1826 statute of Upper Canada. The amended versions of these acts later formed the basis of the 1869 federal act. In Canada, the constitutional ground for patents can be found in s. 91(22) of the *Constitution Act, 1867*: "Patents of Invention and Discovery."[3] It is quite odd that the word "discovery" is in the wording of this section, since, as will be seen below, in fact discoveries are not protected by patent law.

## 3. Basic Principles

The Supreme Court summarized the underlying policy for the grant of patents in *Pioneer Hi-Bred Ltd. v. Canada (Commissioner of Patents)*[4] as follows:

In Canada the granting of a patent means the kind of contract between the Crown and the inventor in which the latter receives an exclusive right to exploit

---

[3] *Constitution Act, 1867* (U.K.), 30 & 31 Vict., c. 3, reprinted in R.S.C. 1985, App. II, No.5, online: Department of Justice Canada <http://laws.justice.gc.ca/en/const/index.html>.

[4] [1989] 1 S.C.R. 1623, 60 D.L.R. (4th) 223, 25 C.P.R. (3d) 257, 97 N.R. 185 (S.C.C.) at para. 23 [*Pioneer Hi-Bred* cited to S.C.C.]. See also *Barter v. Smith* (1876), 2 Ex. C.R. 455 (Can. Ex. Ct.).

his invention for a certain period in exchange for complete disclosure to the public of the invention and the way in which it operates.

This definition resembles the United States approach to patent law, which is enshrined in its Constitution:[5]

The Congress shall have Power : . . . To promote the Progress of Science and useful Arts, by securing for limited Times to Authors and Inventors the exclusive Right to their respective Writings and Discoveries.

The theory of patents is that they are a reward and incentive to invent something of value for the public (it is new and useful) *and* to disclose that invention to the public to spread knowledge and innovation. In exchange for disclosure, the patentee is granted a limited term monopoly for exclusive use of the invention. This bargain of legal protection in exchange for public disclosure is at the heart of patent law. Under traditional patent principles, patents are considered essential for a fast and effective development of technology. According to the orthodox view, "A patent grant rewards innovation in exchange for public disclosure, and thereby serves to foster and enhance the development and disclosure of new ideas and the advancement of scientific knowledge."[6] A patent is viewed as a contract between the inventor and the Crown. The inventor receives a monopoly for a certain period of time in exchange for a full disclosure of the invention. The nature of this bargain is explicitly utilitarian in the U.S. Constitutional provision for intellectual property: to encourage progress *by* securing an exclusive right to the inventor *for* a limited term. Potential inventors thus receive an *incentive* to invest in research and development and/or a *reward* for using their ingenuity to develop a new invention.

For example, in the case of pharmaceuticals, the patent-based monopoly allows pharmaceutical companies to charge a price for new drugs that not only reflects the cost to produce the "pill", which is usually minimal, but the immense sums invested in testing new molecules and, when the preliminary tests so warrant, to take them through several phases of animal and human clinical trials, and to repeat this process in every country where the regulatory approval process in place requires that such testing be done. Because a number of new compounds are developed and tested that do not

---

[5]  United States Const. art. I, § 8, cls. 1 and 8, online: U.S. House of Representatives: <http://www.house.gov/Constitution/Constitution.html>.

[6]  Stephen G. Kunin and Linda S. Therkorn, "Patent Issues Likely to Directly Affect The Development of the Agricultural and Microbial Biotech Industry Over the Next Five Years: Workshop on Future Public Policy And Ethical Issues Facing The Biotechnology Industry" (2004) 86 J. Pat. & Trademark Off. Soc'y 501.

make it to the clinical phase, pharmaceutical companies have to recoup those costs by selling the new drugs that make it to market. As a result, the cost of each new drug (taking into account all the above factors) is in the hundreds of millions of dollars. Because they are for-profit entities, these companies must also be able to generate profits. This contributes to the high cost of new pharmaceuticals. When a patent expires, other for-profit companies, sometimes referred to as "generic drug companies", may start to produce the drugs. Their cost is lower, as they do not incur the research costs involved in finding and initially testing new drugs or new applications for known drugs; however, their costs are not limited to the cost of producing the pills. They must also submit to regulatory approval, though in many countries their burden in that respect is considerably lower than that of "research-based" companies, and they incur significant legal fees. As we will see, a significant amount of cases in the area of patent law involve battles between research-based and generic companies, often as a strategy to keep generic drugs off pharmacy shelves for a little longer than the patent terms strictly provide.

There are ongoing debates as to the impact of asking the private sector to decide priorities based on profitability, which may lead to increased research on so-called lifestyle drugs as opposed to tropical or orphan diseases.[7] In addition, private companies generally keep their research data confidential and this may lead to inefficiencies in, for example, test duplication. An optimal mixture of private and publicly funded (and publicly available) research may constitute the best way forward. To ensure the success of the privately funded efforts, patents are necessary.

There is a controversy, however, as to the actual positive effect of patents in other industries. In recent years, a wave of patents has been issued on computer software in the United States, a wave that has thus far not hit Canada, where "pure" software patents are still unavailable (see the Computer Programs Section below). Many such patents are applied for in hopes of extracting rent from a third party and not, as in traditional patent theory, to actually exploit the invention (a phenomenon known as "patent trolls").

---

[7] According to MedicineNet.com, an orphan disease is a disease which has not been "adopted" by the pharmaceutical industry because it provides little financial incentive for the private sector to make and market new medications to treat or prevent it. An orphan disease may be:
1. A rare disease. According to U.S. criteria, an orphan disease is one that affects fewer than 200,000 people. (There are more than 5,000 such rare disorders.)
2. A common disease that has been ignored (such as tuberculosis, cholera, typhoid, and malaria) because it is far more prevalent in developing countries than in the developed world.

In addition, patents on business methods, in particular on the Internet (such as Amazon.com's "one-click" patent), have been somewhat controversial.

There has also been some measure of controversy with respect to the patentability of life forms and certain types of agricultural inventions. As discussed below (see the Life Forms Section below), there are several types of objections — legal, ethical and religious — to the patentability of so-called higher life forms. There are also concerns on a broader scale that patents may negatively affect food security, notably by using "terminator" genes that produce infertile crops,[8] or by limiting the means of developing nations to produce food at prices they can afford.[9]

In setting patent policy, governments must strike a balance between the need to provide proper incentives and rewards for inventors, so that new inventions are produced, and the need for others, including competitors, to continue to innovate and for the public to be able to benefit appropriately from inventions. Other policy considerations, such as the affordability of public health care, may also be relevant.[9a] There is thus theoretically an optimal protection level, which includes a proper term, appropriate criteria that set a threshold high enough to ensure that only "deserving" inventions" are protected, and finally a level of enforcing and constructing patent monopolies that is consonant with the above principles. In theory, this optimal level could be found by varying the criteria according to the type of invention, but international treaties have essentially removed that flexibility from national policy-makers (see the International Section). As noted recently by Professor Glynn Lunney:

> [I]f providing patent protection ensures the creation of a desirable information product and does so more efficiently than the plausible alternatives, such as direct government subsidies, the fact that the information product could have been more valuable still in the absence of the patent's protection has little practical significance. . . . To the extent that we provide the same protection to all information products that satisfy a uniform set of prerequisites, broader patent protection entails a trade-off between: (i) the social value of the additional information products broader protection ensures; and (ii) the reduced

---

[8]  See Cullen N. Pendleton, "The Peculiar Case of "Terminator" Technology: Agricultural Biotechnology and Intellectual Property Protection at the Crossroads of the Third Green Revolution" (2004) 23 Biotechnology L. Rep. 1.

[9]  See Michael R. Taylor & Jerry Cayford, "American Patent Policy, Biotechnology, and African Agriculture: The Case for Policy Change" (2004) 17 Harv. J.L. & Tech. 321.

[9a]  See *Bristol-Meyers Squibb Co. v. Canada (Attorney General)*, 2005 SCC 26.

social value associated with the preexisting information products protected more broadly than necessary to secure their discovery and disclosure.[10]

This debate over the optimal level of patent protection and differences between industries was also the subject of a blog[11] posting by well-known U.S. Judge Richard Posner, a member of the U.S. Court of Appeals for the Seventh Circuit and a senior lecturer at the University of Chicago Law School:

> The effects of patents on innovation are extremely complex, an important consideration being that when a field becomes blanketed by patents, as is happening with research tools, inventors are forced into what can be costly and protracted negotiations for licenses in order to be able to use and build on previous innovations. So we have to consider carefully what alternatives there are to patents for motivating innovation in pharmaceutical and other research.[12]

While patent laws treat all inventions alike, courts have tended to adapt those rules when applying patent legislation to different technologies. As was noted in respect of recent U.S. practice:[13]

> Patent law is a system of general rules that apply, with few exceptions, across technological boundaries. The *Patent Act* sets forth the basic requirements for patent validity — utility, novelty, nonobviousness, and adequate disclosure — in a technology-neutral manner. By its own statutory terms, then, patent law takes no account of the technology to which any particular patent is directed. Courts have adapted the general rules when adjudicating patent disputes however, in recognition of characteristics unique to particular technologies and industries. Perhaps the richest vein of technology-specific case law developed over several decades in the area of chemical compositions. In particular, the

---

[10] Glynn S. Lunney, Patent Law, "The Federal Circuit, and the Supreme Court: A Quiet Revolution" (2004) 11 Sup. Ct. Econ. Rev. 1 at 78.

[11] From "web log". A blog is a journal which is accessible on the web. Blogs are typically updated frequently and the entries are arranged with the most recent additions first. Law-related blogs are often referred to as "blawgs."

[12] Richard Posner, "Patenting Research Tools" Lessig Blog (25 August 2005, 10:07 a.m.), online: Lessig Blog <http://www.lessig.org/blog/archives/posner.shtml>.

[13] These comments are applicable in Canada, although as is explained below, The Canadian Intellectual Property Office has not been issuing patents on pure software, and thus courts have not had to deal with the same problems as their U.S. counterparts, or at least not to the same extent. Unlike copyright and trade-mark law, U.S. patent law is fairly similar to Canadian law. The patentability criteria are almost identical.

Court of Claims and Patent Appeals, the predecessor to the Federal Circuit,[14] adapted the doctrine of nonobviousness so that trivial and inconsequential modifications of prior art chemicals could be differentiated from modifications that produced structurally similar chemicals with unexpected new properties. A wooden rule would have grouped all chemical modifications that generated structurally similar compositions into the category of obvious inventions based on structural similarity alone. The court looked closely at the chemical technology instead, and crafted a more subtle doctrine. Importantly, the court considered not only the chemical structures themselves but also the areas in which the inventors applied their chemical inventions. Thus, for example, the discovery of an unpredictable and unexpected pharmaceutical activity could make a composition nonobvious despite its structural similarity to prior art chemicals.

More recently, the Federal Circuit has crafted particularized patent validity doctrines in the context of the two technological areas of biotechnology and software. As these two technologies have progressed in parallel, the court has applied the requirements of nonobviousness, enablement, and written description in strikingly different ways. In biotechnology, the Federal Circuit has established a remarkably low nonobviousness barrier such that even clear plans or methods in the prior art for production of the invention have not sufficed to invalidate a patent claim. The gentle treatment of biotechnology patentees with

---

[14] In 1982 the U.S. Congress passed the *Federal Courts Improvement Act* (FCIA), Pub. L. No. 97-164, 96 Stat. 25 (1982) (codified as amended in 28 U.S.C.). The FCIA created the Court of Appeals for the Federal Circuit (CAFC) through the merger of two courts, the Court of Claims and the Court of Customs and Patent Appeals. The CAFC's jurisdiction is not limited to patent appeals. The CAFC hears virtually all patent appeals from the district courts, as well as from the U.S. Patent and Trademark Office (USPTO) (see Rochelle Cooper Dreyfuss, "The Federal Circuit: a Case Study in Specialized Courts" (1989) 64 N.Y.U. L. Rev. 1). Two noted U.S. authors commented on the impact of the creation of a specialized court on applicants by comparing the Canadian and U.S. situations: "The results for Canada do not support the hypothesis that the creation of the patent court has been a significant factor in the growth in U.S. applications. Canadian applications were growing in step with U.S. applications and it seems unlikely that the increase in Canada is attributable to the creation of the patent court in the United States, unless U.S. firms have a practice of routinely applying for Canadian patents at the same time that they apply for U.S. ones. Contrary to the last suggestion, it does not appear that the increase in Canadian applications was the result primarily of an increase in applications filed by U.S. residents. Although we have data for only about twenty-four years starting in 1975, [our data] indicates that Canadian applications filed by non-U.S. residents grew at a rate comparable to all Canadian applications." (William M. Landes & Richard A. Posner, "An Empirical Analysis of the Patent Court" (2004) 71 U. Chi. L. Rev. 111 at 124-5).

respect to nonobviousness has stood in stark contrast to the stringent application of the doctrine in software cases, in which the court has strengthened the invalidating effect of prior art by relaxing its requirement of motivation to combine and its usual careful analysis of secondary considerations. On the other hand, the court has required more detailed disclosures in biotechnology patents than in software patents. In biotechnology cases, the court has required disclosure of actual structure, rather than a generalized description of the invention. In software cases however, the court has been satisfied with description of the inventions at the most abstract levels of program function, and has not required disclosure of the patentee's actual source code implementation.

While attention to the technological contexts of patent disputes has had the beneficial effect of fine-tuning patent law to the needs of different technologies, the proliferation of software technology potentially poses a new challenge as technologies converge. The problem is probably at its starkest in the areas where researchers are applying software to solve biotechnological problems in novel ways because such cases bring together technologies that the Federal Circuit has so far treated quite differently. The fields of research are numerous, and include bioinformatics database design, genetic search algorithms, protein structural science, and rational drug design. Patents have issued on aspects of all these fields, but none has yet been litigated. When a court eventually confronts a case of convergent technologies, it will have to decide which precedent is pertinent. In at least some of these new technological fields, it is not clear whether the software cases or the biotechnology cases are more instructive for questions of patent validity.[15] [footnotes omitted]

Because of the high degree of similarity between U.S. and Canadian patent legislation, U.S. developments are usually relevant in a Canadian context, though our courts have not always followed their American counterparts, as can be seen in the *Harvard College v. Canada (Commissioner of Patents)* (oncomouse) case,[16] which is discussed in the Life Forms Section below. In addition, the fact that many research and development efforts are led by multinational entities and that many fundamental rules of patent law are not enshrined in international trade treaties (see the International Section), have led our courts to consider the practice of other countries, including the United States, in deciding certain cases.

It is certain that technological developments will continue to pose new challenges for patent law and the courts that will be asked to uphold it:

---

[15] Amir A. Naini, "Convergent Technologies and Divergent Patent Validity Doctrines: Obviousness and Disclosure Analyses in Software and Biotechnology" (2004) 86 J. Pat. & Trademark Off. Soc'y 541 at 541-43.

[16] [2002] 4 S.C.R. 45 (S.C.C.).

As the field of technology continues to expand at a rate surpassed only by legislative inactivity, it will fall increasingly to the judiciary to adapt outgrown legal concepts to rapidly changing conditions, and to establish new boundaries between what, in a modern society, can properly be allowed to be the subject of a private monopoly and what, in the public interest, should be free from such monopolistic restrictions.[17]

## II. OBJECT OF PROTECTION

The patentability criteria can be summarized as follows: the nature of the "invention" must fall within the definition of "invention" in s. 2 of the *Patent Act* (patentable subject matter),[18] the invention must be "new", it must not be "obvious", and it must be "useful". The *Patent Act* defines "invention" in s. 2 as follows: "any new and useful art, *process, machine, manufacture* or *composition of matter,* or any *new* and *useful* improvement in any art, process, machine, manufacture or composition of matter." The definition is quite broad, as was noted by Mr. Justice Bastarache (for the majority) in *Harvard College v. Canada (Commissioner of Patents):*[19]

> [T]he definition of invention in the *Patent Act* is broad. Because the *Act* was designed in part to promote innovation, it is only reasonable to expect the definition of invention to be broad enough to encompass unforeseen and un-anticipated technology.

Here is a brief overview of these four concepts.

---

[17] Immanuel Goldsmith, "Patentable Subject-Matter: Traditional Subject-Matters" in Gordon F. Henderson, ed., *Patent Law of Canada* (Scarborough, Ont.: Carswell, 1994) 15 at 15-21.

[18] *Patent Act,* R.S.C. 1985, c. P-4, s. 2, online: Department of Justice Canada <http://laws.justice.gc.ca/en/p-4/text.html>.

[19] *Harvard College v. Canada (Commissioner of Patents),* [2002] 4 S.C.R. 45, 219 D.L.R. (4th) 577, 21 C.P.R. (4th) 417, 296 N.R. 1 (S.C.C.) at para. 158 [*Harvard College* cited to S.C.R.], citing *Free World Trust c. Électro Santé Inc.,* [2000] 2 S.C.R. 1024, (sub nom. *Free World Trust v. Électro Santé Inc.)* 194 D.L.R. (4th) 232, (sub nom. *Free World Trust v. Électro Santé Inc.)* 9 C.P.R. (4th) 168, (sub nom. *Free World Trust v. Électro Santé Inc.)* 263 N.R. 150 (S.C.C.) at para. 24 [*Free World Trust* cited to S.C.R.].

Table 1 — Summary of basic principles of patents

| SUBJECT-MATTER | USEFUL | NEW | NON-OBVIOUS |
|---|---|---|---|
| Process, Machine, Manufacture or "composition of matter" | Works as described and has a use (i.e., does something) | Must be new compared to *any* element of "prior art", *i.e.*, anything in existence prior to the invention | The invention must be the result of an inventive "spark" and not appear obvious to a person "skilled in the art" when considered in light of *all* elements of prior art |

Let us now look at each of these elements in detail.

## 1. Subject-Matter

### (a) Excluded Subject-Matter

To determine what constitutes acceptable subject matter, it is simpler to begin by considering what is not. Indeed, certain specific subject matters have been expressly excluded from patent protection. Section 27(8) of the *Patent Act* provides that: "No patent shall be granted for any mere scientific principle or abstract theorem." A distinction should be made between a discovery and an invention. A discovery adds to the amount of human knowledge, whereas an invention must produce some *tangible* result which is new and useful. Einstein's famous $E=mc^2$, which determined that the total energy of an object is its mass multiplied by the square of the speed of light, could not have been patented. Nor can a tree, a fungus or an animal "discovered" in a natural state during a scientific expedition. However, a practical application, such as a new drug or process made possible by that discovery, could be patentable:

> [A] principle cannot be the subject of a patent, and a claim to every mode or means of carrying this principle into effect would amount to a claim to a principle, for it was said in *Neilson v. Harford*[20], that there is no difference between a principle to be carried into effect in any way you will and claiming the principle itself. A patent may be granted for a principle coupled with a mode of carrying out this principle into effect, and it may be carried into effect under several patents operating in different ways and by different means.[21]

---

[20] (1841), 1 Web. Pat. Cas. 295.

[21] *Grissinger v. Victor Talking Machine Co.* (1928), [1929] Ex. C.R. 24 (Can. Ex. Ct.), affirmed (1930), [1931] S.C.R. 144, [1930] 4 D.L.R. 617 (S.C.C.). See also

In applying this distinction, courts have excluded from patentable subject matter natural phenomena, the so-called "laws of nature", scientific
principles, mathematical formulae or calculations made by a computer,
business systems, architectural plans, and even some biotechnical developments. Similarly, a patent will not be granted for an invention contrary
to the laws of nature. For example, a perpetual motion device can not be
patented for it violates the laws of nature. Such was the claim in *Otta v.
Canada (Patent Commissioner):*[22]

> The applicant is claiming a perpetual-motion device which runs counter to the
> natural laws of conservation of energy. A mechanical device cannot continue
> to operate without a source of external power even if there were no withdrawal
> of energy for other uses.

Professional skills and methods as well as business systems must be
excluded on the basis that a way of doing something is not patentable. Judge
Cattanach in the case *Lawson v. Commissioner of Patents*[23] explains the
reasoning behind this restriction:

> [P]rofessional skills are not the subject-matter of a patent. If a surgeon were to
> devise a method of performing a certain type of operation he cannot obtain an
> exclusive property or privilege therein. Neither can a barrister who has devised
> a particular method of cross-examination or advocacy obtain monopoly thereof
> so as to require imitators or followers of his methods to obtain a licence from
> him.

> It seems to me that a method of describing or laying out parcels of land in a
> plan of subdivision of a greater tract of land is the skill of a solicitor and
> conveyancer and that of a planning consultant and surveyor. It is an art which
> belongs to the professional field and is not a manual art or skill.

Methods of medical treatment are also unpatentable as such in Canada
(*e.g.,* a new surgical method),[24] but medical instruments may be patented.
There is a distinction to make between a method of medical treatment, such

---

*Application for Patent by Clorox Co., Re* (1989), 33 C.P.R. (3d) 160 (Can. Pat.
App. Bd. & Pat. Commr.).

[22] (1979), 51 C.P.R. (2d) 134 (Fed. C.A.). See also *Nogier, Re* (1984), (sub nom.
*Application of Nogier (New Patent No. 1,184,615), Re*) 6 C.P.R. (3d) 556 (Can.
Pat. App. Bd. & Pat. Commr.).

[23] (1970), 62 C.P.R. 101 (Can. Ex. Ct.) at 111.

[24] See, *e.g., Application for Patent by Regents of the University of Minnesota, Re*
(1988), (sub nom. *Regents of the University of Minnesota Patent Application,
Re*) 29 C.P.R. (3d) 42 (Can. Pat. App. Bd. & Pat. Commr.).

as the way a surgeon operates, which is not patentable, and an instrument, such as a machine used for laser eye surgery, which is patentable.[25] The Supreme Court held that the exclusion of methods of medical treatment did not apply to "a product apt to be used in connection with medical treatments."[26] In that case, it was a cream used with electrocardiograms. There is also a way to circumvent part of the "prohibition" by shifting the focus away from professional medical or surgical skills to a "method of use" of a medical or veterinary treatment.[27]

### (b)  Computer Programs

A category of much debate is computer programs. Computer programs involving a method of calculation are unpatentable since they are the mere application of mathematical concepts, which, as explained above, cannot be protected by patents. The case that is still viewed as a correct statement of Canadian law in that respect is *Schlumberger Ltd. v. Canada (Patent Commissioner)*:[28]

> This is an appeal from a decision of the Commissioner of Patents rejecting an application for a patent made by the appellant.
>
> The purpose of the alleged invention is to facilitate the exploration for oil and gas. That exploration is normally made by drilling boreholes through the geological formations thought likely to contain hydrocarbons and by passing instruments up and down those boreholes to effect various measurements of the characteristics of the soil. For reasons that need not be explained here, those measurements are not always very useful to geologists. However, the authors of the invention claimed by the appellant have discovered that those measurements may be combined and analyzed so as to yield more meaningful information. The appellant's application discloses a process whereby the measurements obtained in the boreholes are recorded on magnetic tapes, transmitted to a computer programmed according to the mathematical formulae set out in the specifications and converted by the computer into useful information produced in human readable form (e.g., charts, graphs or tables of figures).

---

[25] *VISX Inc. v. Nidek Co.* (1999), 3 C.P.R. (4th) 417 (Fed. T.D.), affirmed (2001), 207 F.T.R. 320 (note) (Fed. C.A.).

[26] See *Burton Parsons Chemicals Inc. v. Hewlett-Packard (Canada) Ltd.* (1974), [1976] 1 S.C.R. 555, 54 D.L.R. (3d) 711, 17 C.P.R. (2d) 97, 1 N.R. 553 (S.C.C.) [*Burton Parsons* cited to S.C.R.].

[27] See, *e.g., Application for Patent by Merck & Co., Re* (1992), 41 C.P.R. (3d) 52(Can. Pat. App. Bd. & Pat. Commr.).

[28] (1981), [1982] 1 F.C. 845, 56 C.P.R. (2d) 204 (Fed. C.A.), leave to appeal to S.C.C. refused [1981] 2 S.C.R. xi, 63 C.P.R. (2d) 261 (S.C.C.).

[. . .]

In order to determine whether the application discloses a patentable invention, it is first necessary to determine what, according to the application, has been discovered. Now, it is obvious, I think, that there is nothing new in using computers to make calculations of the kind that are prescribed by the specifications. It is precisely in order to make those kinds of calculations that computers were invented. What is new here is the discovery of the various calculations to be made and of the mathematical formulae to be used in making those calculations. If those calculations were not to be effected by computers but by men, the subject-matter of the application would clearly be mathematical formulae and a series of purely mental operations; as such, in my view, it would not be patentable. A mathematical formula must be assimilated to a 'mere scientific principle or abstract theorem' for which subsection 28(3) of the Act prescribes that 'no patent shall issue'. As to mental operations and processes, it is clear, in my view, that they are not the kind of processes that are referred to in the definition of invention in section 2. However, in the present case, the specifications prescribe that the calculations be made by computers. As a result, as I understand the appellant's contention, those calculations are not mental operations but purely mechanical ones that constitute the various steps in the process disclosed by the invention. If the appellant's contention were correct, it would follow that the mere fact that the use of computers is prescribed to perform the calculations prescribed in the specifications, would have the effect of transforming into patentable subject-matter what would, otherwise, be clearly not patentable. The invention of the computer would then have the unexpected result of giving a new dimension to the *Patent Act* by rendering patentable what, under the Act as enacted, was clearly not patentable. This, in my view, is unacceptable. I am of opinion that the fact that a computer is or should be used to implement discovery does not change the nature of that discovery. What the appellant claims as an invention here is merely the discovery that by making certain calculations according to certain formulae, useful information could be extracted from certain measurements. This is not, in my view, an invention within the meaning of section 2.

If the program does more than calculations — for example, produces a result according to the data recovered — the "system" may be patentable.[29] Furthermore, a system containing a computer and computer programs may be patentable as a whole.[30] There is, it seems, a growing tendency on the

---

[29] See *General Electric Co., Re* (1984), (sub nom. *Application for Patent of General Electric Co., Re*) 6 C.P.R. (3d) 191 (Can. Pat. App. Bd. & Pat. Commr.); and *Application for Patent of Tokyo Shibaura Electric Co. (Patent No. 1,197,919), Re* (1985), (sub nom. *Application for Patent of Tokyo Shibaura Electric Co., Re*) 7 C.P.R. (3d) 555 (Can. Pat. App. Bd. & Pat.Commr.).

[30] *Application of Vapor Canada Ltd., Re* (1985), 9 C.P.R. (3d) 524 (Can. Pat. App. Bd. & Pat. Commr.).

part of the Commissioner to distinguish *Schlumberger*[31] when a computer is used as part of an apparatus.[32]

The United States has taken a different position with regard to computer programs. In *State Street Bank & Trust Co. v. Signature Financial Group Inc.*,[33] the court decided a computer program used to implement a "business method" was patentable. The Court concluded in the affirmative:

> The [U.S.] Supreme Court has identified three categories of subject matter that are unpatentable, namely 'laws of nature, natural phenomena, and abstract ideas.' *Diehr*, 450 U.S. at 185. Of particular relevance to this case, the Court has held that mathematical algorithms are not patentable subject matter to the extent that they are merely abstract ideas. . . . In *Diehr*, the Court explained that certain types of mathematical subject matter, standing alone, represent nothing more than abstract ideas until reduced to some type of practical application, i.e., 'a useful, concrete and tangible result.' [This has come to be known as the mathematical algorithm exception. This designation has led to some confusion, especially given the Freeman-Walter-Abele analysis. By keeping in mind that the mathematical algorithm is unpatentable only to the extent that it represents an abstract idea, this confusion may be ameliorated.]
>
> Unpatentable mathematical algorithms are identifiable by showing they are merely abstract ideas constituting disembodied concepts or truths that are not 'useful.' From a practical standpoint, this means that to be patentable an algorithm must be applied in a 'useful' way. . . .
>
> Today, we hold that the transformation of data, representing discrete dollar amounts, by a machine through a series of mathematical calculations into a final share price, constitutes a practical application of a mathematical algorithm, formula, or calculation, because it produces 'a useful, concrete and tangible result' — a final share price momentarily fixed for recording and reporting purposes and even accepted and relied upon by regulatory authorities and in subsequent trades.
> [. . .]
>
> The question of whether a claim encompasses statutory subject matter should not focus on *which* of the four categories of subject matter a claim is directed to — process, machine, manufacture, or composition of matter — but rather

---

[31] See, *e.g., Motorola Inc. Patent Application No. 2,047,731, Re* (1998), 86 C.P.R. (3d) 76 (Can. Pat. App. Bd. & Pat. Commr.).

[32] See, *e.g., Western Geophysical Co. of America, Re* (1983), (sub nom. *Application of Western Geophysical Co. of America, Re*) 3 C.P.R. (3d) 386 (Can. Pat. App. Bd. & Pat. Commr.); and *Measurex Corp., Re* (1983), (sub nom. *Application for Patent of Measurex Corp., Re*) 10 C.P.R. (3d) 93 (Can. Pat. App. Bd.).

[33] 149 F.3d 1368, 47 U.S.P.Q.2d 1596 (U.S. Fed. Cir., 1998) at 1373 [*State Street Bank* cited to F.3d].

on the essential characteristics of the subject matter, in particular, its practical utility. [The Act] specifies that statutory subject matter must also satisfy the other 'conditions and requirements'. . . including novelty, nonobviousness, and adequacy of disclosure and notice. . . . For purpose of our analysis, as noted above, claim 1 is directed to a machine programmed with the Hub and Spoke software and admittedly produces a 'useful, concrete, and tangible result.'. . . This renders it statutory subject matter, even if the useful result is expressed in numbers, such as price, profit, percentage, cost, or loss.

### The Business Method Exception

As an alternative ground for invalidating the '056 patent . . . , the court relied on the judicially-created, so-called 'business method' exception to statutory subject matter. We take this opportunity to lay this ill-conceived exception to rest. Since its inception, the 'business method' exception has merely represented the application of some general, but no longer applicable legal principle, perhaps arising out of the 'requirement for invention' — which was eliminated by Section 103. Since the *1952 Patent Act*, business methods have been, and should have been, subject to the same legal requirements for patentability as applied to any other process or method. (some footnotes omitted)

The one-click purchase system developed by Amazon.com was also deemed patentable in the U.S.[34] A number of applications are pending in Canada, such as application No. CA 2246933, filed in September 1998 (Jeffrey P. Bezos et al., inventors), claiming, *inter alia*:

A method for placing an order to purchase an item, the order being placed by a purchaser at a client system and received by a server system, the method comprising: under control of the server system, receiving purchaser information including identification of the purchaser, payment information, and shipment information from the client system;

assigning a client identifier to the client system; associating the assigned client identifier with the received purchaser information; sending to the client system the assigned client identifier; and sending to the client system display information identifying the item and including an order button;

under control of the client system, receiving and storing the assigned client identifier; receiving and displaying the display information; and in response to the selection of the order button, sending to the server system a request to purchase the identified item, the request including the assigned identifier; and

---

[34] *Amazon Inc. v. Barnes and Noble Inc.*, 73 F.Supp.2d 1228, 53 U.S.P.Q. 2d 1115 (W.D. Wash., 1999), vacated by and remanded by 239 F.3d 1343, 57 U.S.P.Q.2d 1747 (Fed. Cir., 2001). After the Federal Circuit lifted the preliminary injunction, the parties reached a confidential settlement agreement.

under control of the server system, receiving the request; and combining the purchaser information associated with the client identifier included with the request to generate an order to purchase the item in accordance with the billing and shipment information whereby the purchaser effects the ordering of the product by selection of the order button.

It is clear that the above system is in fact computer code combined with a user's computer, Amazon.com's server and the Internet. Amazon.com cannot claim a patent on computers or the Internet, but is in fact claiming on its software as part of this "system", and the concept of online shopping.

CIPO[35] practice shows that patents are being issued on inventions resembling business models and/or computer software.[36] This evolution since *Schlumberger* prompted one commentator to write that:

> Canadian patent law has at last reached the point where software inventions are essentially considered patentable subject matter. While the Canadian Patent Office's 1995 guidelines appear to limit the scope of software patents to software-related inventions, in practice, few pure software applications are being rejected as unpatentable.[37]

The evolution since *Schlumberger* can be traced to two significant sets of documents. First, the publication in 1995 by CIPO of guidelines, as part of its Manual of Patent Office Practice, according to which software is patentable subject matter only when: (1) it is included in a new and useful process; and (2) it is integrated with another system that comprises patentable subject matter.[38] Second, there have been a number of decisions by the Patent Appeal Board allowing patents on software-based inventions. A case considered to be a turning point on this issue is *Motorola Inc. Patent Application No. 2,085,228, Re.*[39] In that decision the Board found that particular claims were not limited to a mere calculation because they included read-only memory coupled with a modification such that the claim was "necessarily limited to a specific configuration of at least one physical element." The decision

---

[35] Canadian Intellectual Property Office, online: CIPO <www.cipo.gc.ca>.

[36] See, *e.g.,* Microsoft patent No. CA 2107387, available on the CIPO website.

[37] Christopher Heer, "Software Patents with Inadequate Disclosure at the Canadian Patent Office" (2004) 62 U. Toronto Fac. L. Rev. 85.

[38] Industry Canada, Manual of Patent Office Practice (Practice Guide) (Ottawa: Patent Office, 2003), s. 16.08, online: Canadian Intellectual Property Office <http://strategis.ic.gc.ca/sc_mrksv/cipo/patents/mopop/mopop_dnld-e.html> [MOPOP].

[39] (1998), 86 C.P.R. (3d) 71 (Can. Pat. App. Bd. & Pat. Commr.).

stands for the principle that a novel algorithm, if embodied in firmware or hardware, will not be characterized as abstract. . . . [T]he principles that now emerge from Canadian jurisprudence with respect to software inventions are that software is only patentable when it is either: (1) incorporated into an otherwise patentable method, system or apparatus; (2) combined with a method or apparatus such that the combination is novel and non-obvious; or (3) itself the point of invention and applied to the technological arts such that exclusive rights are not granted to the underlying abstract algorithm.[40]

Unfortunately, because of the (understandable) hesitation of CIPO to "reverse" *Schlumberger*, patent agents who wish to abide by the Guidelines often end up using so-called "magic words" to pretend the invention is something other than software.

Given the globalization of intellectual property law (as noted by the minority in *Harvard College*[41]) and the cross-border nature of online shopping in North America, as well as the increasing use of software to make a number of machines and other devices "work", it may be that Canada will have to conduct a formal review of its jurisprudential exclusion with respect to the patenting of computer programs. Additionally, the requirement in Article 27(1) of the *TRIPS Agreement* (see the International section) that patents be available "in all fields of technology" tends to support the view that the exclusion of software *qua* software is inappropriate. If this is correct, then decisions as to the novelty, industrial applicability (utility), and presence of an inventive step (non-obviousness) of a program should be made case by case and not by excluding software as a class of unpatentable inventions *per se*.

## (c) Life Forms

A number of recent cases have brought the issue of patentability of certain life forms to the forefront of public debate. The issue is now fairly clear in Canadian law, based on several cases which have interpreted the definition of invention in s. 2 to determine whether life forms were within the scope of patentable subject matter.

In *Abitibi Co., Re*, the Patent Appeal Board recommended that "all new life forms which are produced en masse as chemical compounds and are prepared and are formed in such large numbers that any measurable quantity will possess uniform properties and characteristics" should come within

---

[40] C. Heer, *supra*, note 37 at 87.
[41] *Supra*, note 19.

statutory subject matter and listed all miro-organisms, yeasts, moulds, fungi, bacteria, actinomycetes, unicellular algae, cell lines, viruses or protozoa.[42]

In *Pioneer Hi-Bred Ltd. v. Canada (Commissioner of Patents)*,[43] the Federal Court of Appeal affirmed a decision of the Commissioner of Patents[44] that rejected a patent on a new variety of soybeans:

> Legislation designed to encourage, protect and reward the innovative efforts of human beings has existed in Canada since before Confederation and its application through all those years has given rise to numerous judicial pronouncements. Yet the problem raised by the present patent case, although a long-standing one and a by-product of a world-wide phenomenon, has never been submitted to a Canadian Court.

> The appeal is brought against a decision by the Commissioner of Patents whereby an application by the appellant for a grant of patent rights in a variety of soybean was refused. The appellant contends that the commissioner erred in determining that a strain of naturally grown plant derived by artificial cross-breeding is not an invention within the meaning of s. 2 of the *Patent Act*, R.S.C. 1970, c. P-4 (hereinafter the *Act*).

> It is not disputed that the refusal of the commissioner was consistent with traditional interpretation and application of patent legislation in this country. The assumption that life forms are not patentable subject-matter has been up to recent years so generally accepted that nobody would even have thought of disputing its validity in Court. Such an attitude may have arisen from an instinctive reaction to the apparent gap between animate and inanimate matter and it may have continued to prevail because it reflected the true state of the sciences and technological arts. Scientists had not succeeded in constructing or manufacturing living organisms and drawing the line between patentable and unpatentable subject-matter at the point where life begins was useful. But the spectacular advances realized recently in the bio-sciences and bio-technology could only but call into question this practice of excluding peremptorily living matter from the sphere of application of our patent legislation.

> In the United States, where the general patent legislation is similar to that of this country, the assumption that life forms are not patentable subject-matter has been rejected in two recent decisions, one of which being a decision by the Supreme Court itself. In 1980, in the now famous case of *Diamond v. Chakrabarty*, 447 U.S. 303, 206 U.S.P.Q. 193 (1980), the Supreme Court declared

---

[42] (1982), 62 C.P.R. (2d) 81 (Can. Pat. App. Bd. & Pat. Commr.) at 85-89.

[43] [1987] 3 F.C. 8, 14 C.P.R. (3d) 491 (Fed. C.A.), affirmed [1989] 1 S.C.R. 1623 (S.C.C.) at paras. 4-8, 12-14 [*Pioneer Hi-Bred* cited to F.C.].

[44] (1986), (sub nom. *Application for Patent of Pioneer Hi-Bred Ltd., Re*) 11 C.P.R. (3d) 311 (Can. Pat. App. Bd. & Pat. Commr.), affirmed (1987), 14 C.P.R. (3d) 491 (Fed. C.A.), affirmed [1989] 1 S.C.R. 1623 (S.C.C.).

valid patent claims for a man-made micro-organism capable of degrading four kinds of hydrocarbons.[45] In 1985, in *Ex Parte Hibbard*, the U.S. Board of Patent Appeals and Interferences, on the basis of the decision in *Chakrabarty*, acknowledged that hybrid seeds and hybrid plants could be patented under 35 U.S.C. 101, the United States general patent law, notwithstanding the provisions of the two specific Acts which had been adopted in the United States for the protection of plant breeders, the *Plant Protection Act*, 1930 and the *Plant Variety Act*, 1970.

In Canada, the assumption that living organisms are not patentable subject-matter has never been formally rejected by a Court of law but it has been under attack with some success before the Commissioner of Patents who recently, in a case quite similar to that of *Chakrabarty* in the United States, accepted an application for a yeast culture engineered to digest certain waste products in the effluent from a pulp and paper plant (*Re Abitibi Co.* (1982), 62 C.P.R. (2d) 80). In the present case, the attack against the traditional view is brought much further, and, interestingly enough, the subject-matter of the application is, as in *Ex Parte Hibbard* in the United States, a plant.
[. . .]

Even if those definitions were held to be applicable to a micro-organism obtained as a result of a laboratory process, I am unable to go further and accept that they can also adapt to a plant variety produced by cross-breeding. Such a plant cannot really be said, other than on the most metaphorical level, to have been produced from raw materials or to be a combination of two or more substances united by chemical or mechanical means. It seems to me that the common ordinary meaning of the words 'manufacture' and 'composition of matter' would be distorted if a unique but simple variety of soybean were to be included within their scope.

It is argued that the very nature of the patent system and the benefits that were expected therefrom should lead to the conclusion that Parliament intended the most open and favourable approach to its statute. Maybe so, but I do not think that such an approach would permit the interpreter to dispense with the necessity to respect the results suggested by a careful analysis of the terms used in the statute. Besides, speaking of the intention of Parliament, given that plant breeding was well established when the Act was passed, it seems to me that the inclusion of plants within the purview of the legislation would have led first to a definition of invention in which words such as 'strain', 'variety' or 'hybrid' would have appeared, and second to the enactment of special provisions capable of better adapting the whole scheme to a subject-matter, the essential characteristic of which is that it reproduces itself as a necessary result of its growth and maturity. I do not dispute the appellant's contention that those

---

[45] It is worth noting that this was a 5-4 decision, similar to the *Harvard College* decision by the Canadian Supreme Court (see below). [footnote not in original]

who develop new types of plants by cross-breeding should receive in this country, as they do elsewhere, some kind of protection and reward for their efforts but it seems to me that, to assure such result, the legislator will have to adopt special legislation, as was done a long time ago in the United States and in many other industrialized countries.

In sum, relying both on the common meaning of the words of the definition for 'invention' as it appears in the Act and on the legislative context in which they are found, in so far as the intention of Parliament may be derived therefrom, I am satisfied that the soybean variety developed by the appellant cannot be the subject-matter of a patent of invention.

The Supreme Court affirmed[46] and added an explanation of the type of technology involved:

[I]s this an invention within the meaning of the *Patent Act?*

More than a century ago Darwin developed the theory that only species and individuals that can adapt and acquire new characteristics can survive and reproduce. The same principle underlies the experiments which through genetic engineering now make possible adaptation to specific environments or new uses of known living organisms.

The real issue in this appeal is the patentability of a form of life. This is in fact a claim for a new product developed in the field of biotechnology, an area of activity taking in all types of techniques having a common purpose, 'the application of scientific and engineering principles to the processing of material by biological agents to provide goods and services' (see: A.T. Bull, G. Holt and M.D. Lilly, *Biotechnology: International Trends and Perspectives* (Paris: O.E.C.D., 1982) at p. 21). This is regarded by many as the latest technological system to be developed in the 20th century and the harbinger of a new era, and we must therefore be very cautious regarding the scope of our pronouncements.

Genetic engineering can occur in two ways. The first involves crossing different species or varieties by hybridization, altering the frequency of genes over successive generations. The main consequence of this intervention is to oppose within the same cell allelic genes, that is, opposing characteristics which replace each other alternately in the hereditary process, as a consequence of the alternate action of their dominant genes. Naturally, the genes only offer a reasonable prospect that the traits will be acquired from one generation to the next. It should further be remembered that acquiring a certain characteristic does not automatically mean developing that characteristic: some effects in gene devel-

---

[46] [1989] 1 S.C.R. 1623, 60 D.L.R. (4th) 223, 25 C.P.R. (3d) 257 (S.C.C.) at paras. 12-19 [*Pioneer Hi-Bred* cited to S.C.R.].

opment and the influence of environment can cause genetic mutation. It further appears that 'various studies have shown that mutations occur randomly in time and space, and have no connection with survival value' (N.M. Jessup, *Biosphere: A study of* Life (1970), at p. 294). There is thus human intervention in the reproductive cycle, but intervention which does not alter the actual rules of reproduction, which continue to obey the laws of nature.

This procedure differs from the second type of genetic engineering, which requires a change in the genetic material — an alteration of the genetic code affecting all the hereditary material — since in the latter case the intervention occurs inside the gene itself. The change made is thus a molecular one and the 'new' gene is thus ultimately the result of a chemical reaction, which will in due course lead to a change in the trait controlled by the gene. While the first method implies an evolution based strictly on heredity and Mendelian principles, the second also employs a sharp and permanent alteration of hereditary traits by a change in the quality of the genes.

The genetic engineering performed by Hi-Bred is of the first type. Hi-Bred obtained this new soybean variety by hybridization, that is by crossing various soybean plants so as to obtain a unique variety combining the desirable traits of each one. This is why, as the Hi-Bred patent application explains, selective reproduction was necessary after crossing: making the new line grow, keeping only plants with the desired characteristics and repeating the operation for a sufficient number of generations to ensure that the soybean plants will finally contain only genes having the ideal traits. In this connection I would mention that the passages included in evidence in the record of the Court by Hi-Bred give a good idea of the various procedures used to obtain improved soybean varieties.

The Hi-Bred argument rests on a particular characteristic of the reproductive cycle of the soybean. The male and female gametes are contained in the flower and are protected from almost any intrusion at the time of reproduction. 'Artificial' intervention is thus necessary to alter the cycle. The scope for 'natural' crossing is therefore almost nil. Appellant argued that human intervention and the innovative nature of this new variety are conclusive and allow it to 'qualify' for a patent under the *Patent Act*.

The intervention made by Hi-Bred does not in any way appear to alter the soybean reproductive process, which occurs in accordance with the laws of nature. Earlier decisions have never allowed such a method to be the basis for a patent. The Courts have regarded creations following the laws of nature as being mere discoveries the existence of which man has simply uncovered without thereby being able to claim he has invented them. Hi-Bred is asking this Court to reverse a position long defended in the case law. To do this, we would have, inter alia, to consider whether there is a conclusive difference as regards patentability between the first and second types of genetic engineering, or whether distinctions should be made based on the first type of engineering, in view of the nature of the intervention. The Court would then have to rule on the patentability of such an invention for the first time. The record contains no scientific testimony dealing with the distinction resulting from use of one engineering method rather than another or the possibility of making distinctions based on one or other method.

In view of the complexity presented by the question as to the cases in which the result of genetic engineering may be patented, the limited interest shown in this area by the parties in their submissions, and since I share the view of Pratte J. that Hi-Bred does not meet the requirements of s. 36(1) of the Act, I choose to dispose of this appeal solely on the latter point.

However, combining these discussions in *Pioneer Hi-Bred* and *Abitibi*, one could conclude that lower life forms, such as yeasts and fungi could be patented but not plants. The Supreme Court of Canada decided *Pioneer Hi-Bred* on the grounds that a deposit of a seed sample did not satisfy the disclosure requirement and thus the Court did not directly decide whether life forms are patentable subject matter *per se*. Then came the *Harvard College* case,[47] in which a split Supreme Court decided that "higher life forms," such as mice, but also plants (hence apparently confirming *Pioneer Hi-Bred*), could not be patented because they could not be considered manufactures or compositions of matter under s. 2. The case dealt with mice that were genetically altered to become more prone to developing certain forms of cancer, thus accelerating cancer research in laboratories. Harvard sought to patent the life form of the transgenically modified mouse and thus included the oncomouse itself in its patent claims. Its argument was that to protect its invention adequately, the mouse itself had to be patented in order to prevent others from buying and breeding the mice. The Commissioner allowed the patent claims on the method for producing the genetically altered mice but denied the patent claim on the animal itself. The litigation turned on whether the mouse was patentable subject matter within the *Patent Act*.

The majority of the Supreme Court did not disagree that the mice could be considered "compositions of matter," but decided that life was more than that, that it transcends matter:

[T]he question of whether a higher life form can be considered a 'manufacture' or 'composition of matter' approaches a pure determination of law. There is no disagreement in this case regarding the nature of the specific invention: if it is determined that higher life forms are 'manufacture[s]' or 'composition[s] of matter', then the oncomouse is an invention. The task is rather to determine

---

[47] *Harvard College*, *supra*, note 19.

whether Parliament intended the definition of invention to be interpreted broadly enough to encompass higher life forms. . .
[. . .]

The sole question in this appeal is whether the words 'manufacture' and 'composition of matter', in the context of the *Patent Act*, are sufficiently broad to include higher life forms. If these words are not sufficiently broad to include higher life forms, it is irrelevant whether this Court believes that higher life forms such as the oncomouse ought to be patentable. The grant of a patent reflects the interest of Parliament to promote certain manifestations of human ingenuity. As Binnie J. indicates in his reasons, there are a number of reasons why Parliament might want to encourage the sort of biomedical research that resulted in the oncomouse. But there are also a number of reasons why Parliament might want to be cautious about encouraging the patenting of higher life forms. In my view, whether higher life forms such as the oncomouse ought to be patentable is a matter for Parliament to determine. This Court's views as to the utility or propriety of patenting non-human higher life forms such as the oncomouse are wholly irrelevant.
[. . .]

Having considered the relevant factors, I conclude that Parliament did not intend to include higher life forms within the definition of invention found in the *Patent Act*. In their grammatical and ordinary sense alone, the words 'manufacture' and 'composition of matter' are somewhat imprecise and ambiguous. However, it is my view that the best reading of the words of the Act supports the conclusion that higher life forms are not patentable. As I discuss below, I do not believe that a higher life form such as the oncomouse is easily understood as either a 'manufacture' or a 'composition of matter'. For this reason, I am not satisfied that the definition of 'invention' in the *Patent Act* is sufficiently broad to include higher life forms. This conclusion is supported by the fact that the patenting of higher life forms raises unique concerns which do not arise in respect of non-living inventions and which are not addressed by the scheme of the Act. Even if a higher life form could, scientifically, be regarded as a 'composition of matter', the scheme of the Act indicates that the patentability of higher life forms was not contemplated by Parliament. Owing to the fact that the patenting of higher life forms is a highly contentious and complex matter that raises serious practical, ethical and environmental concerns that the Act does not contemplate, I conclude that the Commissioner was correct to reject the patent application. This is a policy issue that raises questions of great significance and importance and that would appear to require a dramatic expansion of the traditional patent regime. Absent explicit legislative direction, the Court should not order the Commissioner to grant a patent on a higher life form.

*(1) The Words of the Act*

The definition of invention in s. 2 of the *Patent Act* lists five categories of invention: art (*réalisation*), process (*procédé*), machine (*machine*), manufacture (*fabrication*) or composition of matter (*composition de matières*). The first three, 'art', 'process' and 'machine', are clearly inapplicable when considering claims directed toward a genetically engineered non-human mammal. If a higher life form is to fit within the definition of invention, it must therefore be considered to be either a 'manufacture' or a 'composition of matter'.

[T]he definition of invention in the *Patent Act* is broad. Because the Act was designed in part to promote innovation, it is only reasonable to expect the definition of invention to be broad enough to encompass unforeseen and unanticipated technology. I cannot however agree with the suggestion that the definition is unlimited in the sense that it includes 'anything under the sun that is made by man'. In drafting the *Patent Act*, Parliament chose to adopt an exhaustive definition that limits invention to any 'art, process, machine, manufacture or composition of matter'. Parliament did not define 'invention' as 'anything new and useful made by man'. By choosing to define invention in this way, Parliament signalled a clear intention to include certain subject matter as patentable and to exclude other subject matter as being outside the confines of the Act. This should be kept in mind when determining whether the words 'manufacture' and 'composition of matter' include higher life forms.

With respect to the meaning of the word 'manufacture' (*fabrication*), although it may be attributed a very broad meaning, I am of the opinion that the word would commonly be understood to denote a non-living mechanistic product or process. For example, the *Oxford English Dictionary* (2nd ed. 1989), vol. IX, at p. 341, defines the noun 'manufacture' as the following:

> [T]he action or process of making by hand. . . The action or process of making articles or material (in modern use, on a large scale) by the application of physical labour or mechanical power.

The *Grand Robert de la langue française* (2nd *ed. 2001), vol. 3, at p. 517,* defines thus the word '*fabrication*':

> [TRANSLATION]Art or action or manufacturing. . . . The manufacture of a technical object (by someone). Manufacturing by artisans, by hand, by machine, industrially, by mass production . . .

[. . .]

In my view, while a mouse may be analogized to a 'manufacture' when it is produced in an industrial setting, the word in its vernacular sense does not include a higher life form. The definition in *Hornblower v. Boulton* (1799), 8 T.R. 95, 101 E.R. 1285 (Eng. K.B.), cited by the respondent, is equally problematic when applied to higher life forms. In that case, the English courts defined 'manufacture' as 'something made by the hands of man' (at p. 1288). In my opinion, a complex life form such as a mouse or a chimpanzee cannot easily be characterized as 'something made by the hands of man'.

As regards the meaning of the words 'composition of matter', I believe that they must be defined more narrowly than . . . 'all compositions of two or more substances and . . . all composite articles'. If the words 'composition of matter' are understood this broadly, then the other listed categories of invention, including 'machine' and 'manufacture', become redundant. This implies that 'composition of matter' must be limited in some way. Although I do not express an opinion as to where the line should be drawn, I conclude that 'composition of matter' does not include a higher life form such as the oncomouse.

The phrase 'composition of matter' (*composition de matières*) is somewhat broader than the term 'manufacture' (*fabrication*). It is a well-known principle of statutory interpretation that the meaning of questionable words or phrases in a statute may be ascertained by reference to the meaning of the words or phrases associated with them (P.-A. Côté, *The Interpretation of Legislation in Canada* (3rd ed. 2000), at pp. 313-14. Also, a collective term that completes an enumeration is often restricted to the same genus as those words, even though the collective term may ordinarily have a much broader meaning (at p. 315). The words 'machine' and 'manufacture' do not imply a conscious, sentient living creature. This provides *prima facie* support for the conclusion that the phrase 'composition of matter' is best read as not including such life forms.
. . .

It also is significant that the word 'matter' captures but one aspect of a higher life form. As defined by the *Oxford English Dictionary, supra*, vol. IX, at p. 480, 'matter' is a '[p]hysical or corporeal substance in general. . . , contradistinguished from immaterial or incorporeal substance (spirit, soul, mind), and from qualities, actions, or conditions'. '*Matière*' is defined by the *Grand Robert de la langue française, supra*, vol. 4, p. 1260, as '[TRANSLATION] 'corporeal substance 'that is perceptible in space and has mechanical mass''. Although some in society may hold the view that higher life forms are mere 'composition[s] of matter', the phrase does not fit well with common understandings of human and animal life. Higher life forms are generally regarded as possessing qualities and characteristics that transcend the particular genetic material of which they are composed. A person whose genetic make-up is modified by radiation does not cease to be him or herself. Likewise, the same mouse would exist absent the injection of the oncogene into the fertilized egg cell; it simply would not be predisposed to cancer. The fact that it has this predisposition to cancer that makes it valuable to humans does not mean that the mouse, along with other animal life forms, can be defined solely with reference to the genetic matter of which it is composed. The fact that animal life forms have numerous unique qualities that transcend the particular matter of which they are composed makes it difficult to conceptualize higher life forms as mere 'composition[s] of matter'. It is a phrase that seems inadequate as a description of a higher life form.

[. . .]

Although he was referring specifically to crossbred plants and not to higher life forms in general, a similar point was made by Marceau J.A. in *Pioneer Hi-Bred* (F.C.A.), *supra*, at p. 14:

> It is argued that the very nature of the patent system and the benefits that were expected therefrom should lead to the conclusion that Parliament intended the most open and favourable approach to its statute. Maybe so, but I do not think that such an approach would permit the interpreter to dispense with the necessity to respect the results suggested by a careful analysis of the terms used in the statute. Besides, speaking of the intention of Parliament, given that plant breeding was well established when the Act was passed, it seems to me that the inclusion of plants within the purview of the legislation would have led first to a definition of invention in which words such as 'strain', 'variety' or 'hybrid' would have appeared . . . .

[. . .]

It is thus possible that Parliament did not regard crossbred plants and animals as patentable, not because they are higher life forms, but because they are better regarded as 'discoveries'. Unable to anticipate genetic alteration, Parliament would not have foreseen that higher life forms could be created in a manner reasonably understood as an invention. If this is the case, we should be wary of applying too broad or literal an interpretation of the phrase 'composition[s] of matter'. Even if higher life forms were more easily cognizable as 'compositions of matter', I still would find it difficult to conclude that the definition of 'invention' was intended to be sufficiently broad to include higher life forms.

Patenting higher life forms would involve a radical departure from the traditional patent regime. Moreover, the patentability of such life forms is a highly contentious matter that raises a number of extremely complex issues. If higher life forms are to be patentable, it must be under the clear and unequivocal direction of Parliament. For the reasons discussed above, I conclude that the current Act does not clearly indicate that higher life forms are patentable. Far from it. Rather, I believe that the best reading of the words of the Act supports the opposite conclusion — that higher life forms such as the oncomouse are not currently patentable in Canada.

*(2) The Scheme of the Act*

This interpretation of the words of the Act finds support in the fact that the patenting of higher life forms raises unique concerns which do not arise with respect to non-living inventions and which cannot be adequately addressed by the scheme of the Act. In *Pioneer Hi-Bred Ltd.* (F.C.A.), Marceau J.A. discussed the intention of Parliament to include crossbred plants in the following terms (at p. 14):

> . . . it seems to me that the inclusion of plants within the purview of the legislation would have led . . . to the enactment of special provisions capable of better adapting the whole scheme to a subject matter, the essential characteristic of which is that it reproduces itself as a necessary result of its growth and maturity. I do not dispute the appellant's contention that those who develop new types of plants by cross-breeding should receive in this country, as they do elsewhere, some kind of protection and reward for their efforts but it seems to me that, to assure such result, the legislator will have to adopt special legislation, as was done a long time ago in the United States and in many other industrialized countries.

Marceau J.A.'s observation in this regard is compelling. The patenting of higher life forms raises special concerns that do not arise in respect of non-living inventions. Unlike other inventions, biologically based inventions are living and self-replicating. In addition, the products of biotechnology are incredibly complex, incapable of full description, and can contain important characteristics that have nothing to do with the invention . . . . In my view, the fact that the *Patent Act* in its current state is ill-equipped to deal appropriately with higher life forms as patentable subject matter is an indication that Parliament never intended the definition of invention to extend to this type of subject matter.
[. . .]

Perhaps the most significant issue addressed by the [Canadian Biotechnology Advisory Council] is the patentability of human life. The CBAC recommends that if Canada decides to permit patents over higher life forms, human bodies at all stages of development should be excluded. It observes in this regard that although humans are also animals, no country, including Canada, allows patents on the human body. According to the CBAC, this understanding derives from the universal principle of respect for human dignity, one element of which is that humans are not commodities (see CBAC, *supra*, at p. 8).

The potential for commodification of human life arises out of the fact that the granting of a patent is, in effect, a declaration that an invention based on living matter has the potential to be commercialized. The commodification of human beings is not only intrinsically undesirable; it may also engender a number of troubling consequences. Many of the consequentialist concerns (i.e., the creation of 'designer human beings' or features) are directed at genetic engineering in general and not at patenting *per se*, and are perhaps better dealt with outside the confines of the *Patent Act* (see Schrecker, *supra*, at pp. 64-65). Nonetheless, there remains a concern that allowing patents on the human body will lead to

human life being reconceptualized as genetic information. A related concern is the potential for objectification. As noted by Schrecker, *supra*, at p. 62: '[t]o objectify something is implicit in treating it as a market commodity, but what is disturbing about objectifying a person or organism is not so much the exchange of money as it is the notion that a subject, a moral agent with autonomy and dignity, is being treated as if it can be used as an instrument for the needs or desires of others without giving rise to ethical objections'.
[. . .]

### (3) The Object of the Act

The respondent submits that the object of the *Patent Act* is to encourage and reward the development of innovations and technology. In its view, this objective supports a broad reading of the definition of invention that does not exclude any area of technology save for the statutory exclusion in s. 27(3).

There is no doubt that two of the central objects of the Act are 'to advance research and development and to encourage broader economic activity' (see *Free World Trust c. Électro Santé Inc.*, [2000] 2 S.C.R. 1024, 2000 SCC 66 (S.C.C.), at para. 42). As noted earlier, this does not, however, imply that 'anything under the sun that is made by man' is patentable. Parliament did not leave the definition of invention open, but rather chose to define it exhaustively. Regardless of the desirability of a certain activity, or the necessity of creating incentives to engage in that activity, a product of human ingenuity must fall within the terms of the Act in order for it to be patentable. The object of the Act must be taken into account, but the issue of whether a proposed invention *ought* to be patentable does not provide an answer to the question of whether that proposed invention *is* patentable. In addition, the manner in which Canada has administered its patent regime in the past reveals that the promotion of ingenuity has at times been balanced against other considerations. For example, under the former provisions of the *Patent Act*, a licence could be granted to manufacture a patented medicine seven years after the patent first appeared on the market. [. . .]

Based on the language and the scheme of the Act, both of which are not well accommodated to higher life forms, it is reasonable to assume that Parliament did not intend the monopoly right inherent in the grant of a patent to extend to inventions of this nature. It simply does not follow from the objective of promoting ingenuity that all inventions must be patentable, regardless of the fact that other indicators of legislative intention point to the contrary conclusion.
[. . .]

In *Chakrabarty*, [*Diamond v. Chakrabarty* (1980), 447 U.S. 303, 206 U.S.P.Q. 193, 100 S. Ct. 2204, 65 L. Ed. 2d 144 (U.S. Sup. Ct.)], a minority of four judges of the U.S. Supreme Court found that the passage of the 1930 *Plant Patent Act* and the 1970 *Plant Variety Protection Act* evidenced Congress's understanding that the *Patent Act* does not include living organisms. As noted, at p. 320:

> If newly developed living organisms not naturally occurring had been patentable under s. 101 [the equivalent to the definition of 'invention' in s. 2 of the Canadian *Patent Act*], the plants included in the scope of the 1930 and 1970 Acts could have been patented without new legislation. Those plants, like the bacteria involved in this case, were new varieties not naturally occurring.

The minority went on to note, at pp. 321-22:

> . . . the Court's decision does not follow the unavoidable implications of the statute. Rather, it extends the patent system to cover living material even though Congress plainly has legislated in the belief that §101 does not encompass living organisms. It is the role of Congress, not this Court, to broaden or narrow the reach of the patent laws. This is especially true where, as here, the composition sought to be patented uniquely implicates matters of public concern.

The majority of the court in *Chakrabarty* rejected the above argument, asserting that factors other than congressional intent to exclude higher life forms from the definition of invention were responsible for the passage of the Acts. In particular, the majority notes that, prior to 1930, the belief existed that plants, even those artificially bred, were products of nature for the purposes of the patent law. The second obstacle to patent protection for plants was the fact that plants were thought not amenable to the 'written description' requirement of the patent law. In enacting the *Plant Patent Act*, Congress addressed both of these concerns. The majority also addressed the passage of the 1970 *Plant Variety Protection Act* which, in its view, was passed to provide protection for sexually reproduced plants not covered by the 1930 *Act*.

Given that the *Plant Breeders' Rights Act* was passed following this Court's decision in *Pioneer Hi-Bred Ltd.* that the soybean variety in question was unable to meet the written description requirement of the *Patent Act*, the point of view of the majority in *Chakrabarty* may have merit in the Canadian context. In other words, it may well be that the *Plant Breeders' Rights Act* was passed not out of recognition that higher life forms are not a patentable subject matter under the *Patent Act*, but rather out of recognition that plant varieties deserve some form of intellectual property protection despite the fact that they often do not meet the technical criteria of the *Patent Act*.

[. . .]

*C.  Drawing the Line: Is it Defensible to Allow Patents on Lower Life Forms while Denying Patents on Higher Life Forms?*

The respondent notes that the Commissioner of Patents has since 1982 accepted that lower life forms come within the definitions of 'composition of matter' and 'manufacture' and has granted patents on such life forms accordingly. It adds that the *Patent Act* does not distinguish, in its definition of invention, between subject matter that is less complex (lower life forms) and subject matter that is more complex (higher life forms). It submits that there is therefore no evidentiary or legal basis for the distinction the Patent Office has made between lower life forms such as bacteria, yeast and moulds, and higher life forms such as plants and animals.

The patentability of lower life forms is not at issue before this Court, and was in fact never litigated in Canada. In *Abitibi Co.*, *supra*, the Patent Appeal Board, the Commissioner concurring, rejected the prior practice of the Patent Office and issued a patent on a microbial culture that was used to digest, and thereby purify, a certain waste product that emanates from pulp mills. The decision, in this regard, was based largely on the U.S. Supreme Court's decision in *Chakrabarty*, *supra*, and on the practice in Australia, Germany and Japan. Having noted that judicial bodies in these countries altered their interpretation of patentable subject matter to include micro-organisms, the Board observed, at p. 88: '[o]bviously the answer to the question before us, which once had seemed so clear and definite has become clouded and uncertain'. The Board was careful to limit the subject matter to which the decision would apply:

> . . . this decision will extend to all micro-organisms, yeasts, moulds, fungi, bacteria, actinomycetes, unicellular algae, cell lines, viruses or protozoa; in fact to all new life forms which are produced *en masse* as chemical compounds are prepared, and are formed in such large numbers that any measurable quantity will possess uniform properties and characteristics.

Though this Court is not faced with the issue of the patentability of lower life forms, it must nonetheless address the respondent's argument that the line between higher and lower life forms is indefensible. As discussed above, I am of the opinion that the unique concerns and issues raised by the patentability of plants and animals necessitate a parliamentary response. Only Parliament has the institutional competence to extend patent rights or another form of intellectual property protection to plants and animals and to attach appropriate conditions to the right that is granted. In the interim, I see no reason to alter the line drawn by the Patent Office. The distinction between lower and higher life forms, though not explicit in the Act, is nonetheless defensible on the basis of common sense differences between the two. Perhaps more importantly, there appears to be a consensus that human life is not patentable; yet this distinction is also not explicit in the Act. If the line between lower and higher life forms is indefensible and arbitrary, so too is the line between human beings and other higher life forms.

In their dissent, the four justices reviewed all the above arguments and added an "economic flavour" to their analysis:

The biotechnology revolution in the 50 years since discovery of the structure of DNA has been fuelled by extraordinary human ingenuity and financed in significant part by private investment. Like most revolutions, it has wide ramifications, and presents potential and serious dangers as well as past and future benefits. In this appeal, however, we are only dealing with a small corner of the biotechnology controversy. We are asked to determine whether the oncomouse, a genetically modified rodent with heightened genetic susceptibility to cancer, is an invention. The legal issue is a narrow one and does not provide a proper platform on which to engage in a debate over animal rights, or religion, or the arrogance of the human race.

The oncomouse has been held patentable, and is now patented in jurisdictions that cover Austria, Belgium, Denmark, Finland, France, Germany, Greece, Ireland, Italy, Luxembourg, The Netherlands, Portugal, Spain, Sweden, the United Kingdom and the United States. A similar patent has been issued in Japan. New Zealand has issued a patent for a transgenic mouse that has been genetically modified to be susceptible to HIV infection. Indeed, we were not told of any country with a patent system comparable to Canada's (or otherwise) in which a patent on the oncomouse had been applied for and been refused.

If Canada is to stand apart from jurisdictions with which we usually invite comparison on an issue so fundamental to intellectual property law as what constitutes 'an invention', the respondent, successful everywhere but in Canada, might expect to see something unique in our legislation. However, one looks in vain for a difference in definition to fuel the Commissioner's contention that, *as a matter of statutory interpretation*, the oncomouse is not an invention. The truth is that our legislation is not unique. The Canadian definition of what constitutes an invention, initially adopted in pre-Confederation statutes, was essentially taken from the United States *Patent Act of 1793*, a definition generally attributed to Thomas Jefferson. The United States patent on the oncomouse was issued 14 years ago. My colleague, Bastarache J., acknowledges that the fertilized, genetically altered oncomouse egg is an invention under our *Patent Act*, R.S.C. 1985, c. P-4 (para. 162). Thereafter, we part company, because my colleague goes on to conclude that the resulting *oncomouse*, that grows from the patented egg, is not itself patentable because it is not an invention. Subject matter patentability, on this view, is lost between two successive stages of a transgenic mouse's genetically pre-programmed growth. In my opinion, with respect, such a 'disappearing subject-matter' exception finds no support in the statutory language.
[. . .]

## A. Statutory Interpretation

The issue, in the words of s. 2 of the *Patent Act*, is whether the oncomouse that has been produced by a combination of genetic engineering and natural gestation is a 'composition of matter' that is new, unobvious and useful. If it is, then the President and Fellows of Harvard University, who funded the research, are entitled to a patent. . . .

While acknowledging, therefore, that the oncomouse is a 'composition of [genetic] matter', my colleague's contention is that the oncomouse is a 'composition of [genetic] matter' *plus* something else, undefined. The respondent, however, does not claim to have invented the 'plus'. Its sole claim is to have modified what my colleague describes as the 'genetic matter of which [the oncomouse] is composed', . . .

As will be explained more fully below, I believe that the extraordinary scientific achievement of altering every single cell in the body of an animal which does not in this altered form exist in nature, by human modification of 'the genetic material of which it is composed', is an inventive 'composition of matter' within the meaning of s. 2 of the *Patent Act*.
[. . .]

## B. International Scope of Intellectual Property Law

Intellectual property has global mobility, and states have worked diligently to harmonize their patent, copyright and trademark regimes. In this context, the Commissioner's approach to this case sounds a highly discordant note. Intellectual property was the subject matter of such influential agreements as the *International Convention for the Protection of Industrial Property* (*Paris Convention*) as early as 1883. International rules governing patents were strengthened by the *European Patent Convention* in 1973, and, more recently, the World Trade Organization *Agreement on Trade-Related Aspects of Intellectual Property Rights* (TRIPS) in 1994. Copyright was the subject of the *Berne Convention for the Protection of Literary and Artistic Works* in 1886, revised by the *Berlin Convention of 1908* and the *Rome Convention* of 1928. The *Universal Copyright Convention* was concluded in 1952. Legislation varies of course, from state to state, but broadly speaking Canada has sought to harmonize its concepts of intellectual property with other like-minded jurisdictions.

The mobility of capital and technology makes it desirable that comparable jurisdictions with comparable intellectual property legislation arrive (to the extent permitted by the specifics of their own laws) at similar legal results: *Galerie d'art du Petit Champlain inc. c. Théberge*, 2002 SCC 34 (S.C.C.) , at para. 6.
[. . .]

*C. The Commercial and Scientific Context*

Biotechnology is global in scope. Worldwide demand is expected to more than double from $20 billion in 1995 to $50 billion by 2005. Canada is a significant player. Statistics Canada reports that Canada's biotechnology sector in 1999 generated almost $2 billion in revenues, including $718 million in exports. These revenues are expected to exceed $5 billion in 2002. The Canadian Biotechnology Advisory Committee (CBAC), formed in 1999 to advise the federal government on these matters, recently reported that Canada has more biotechnology companies *per capita* than any other country: *Patenting of Higher Life Forms and Related Issues: Report to the Government of Canada Biotechnology Ministerial Coordinating Committee*, June 2002, p. 2. It was calculated by Ernst & Young in its *Seventh Annual European Life Sciences Report 2000*, that Canada is second behind the U.S. in terms of number of companies, third behind the U.S. and U.K. in revenues, and first in R&D *per* employee.

Genetic tests and 'engineered' products hold out the possibility of modifying genetic mutations that either cause a disorder (*e.g.*, Tay-Sachs disease, cystic fibrosis, Huntington's disease) or are responsible for increasing an individual's risk to develop, at some point during his or her lifetime, a particular disease (e.g., breast cancer). In addition, some research indicates a genetic element in some 'behavioural illnesses' such as schizophrenia, Alzheimer's, autism, attention-deficit hyperactivity disorder, and Tourette's syndrome. . .

*D. Financing Research and Development*

As this case demonstrates, even university research has to be paid for, and intellectual property rights are an important contributor.

We are told that in the United States (comparable statistics do not seem to be available in Canada), a health-related biotechnology product on average costs between 200 and 350 million dollars (U.S.) to develop, and takes 7 to 10 years from the research and development stage to bring it to market (*Biotechnology Use and Development — 1999*, Statistics Canada (March 2001), at p. 25). One would think it in the public interest to shorten the time and reduce the cost of research designed to minimize human suffering, and to reward those who develop research tools (such as the oncomouse) that might make this possible, provided the inventors disclose their work for others to build on.

Transgenic mice, including the oncomouse, have a role of potential importance. The evidence is that use of transgenic mice improves the effectiveness of the research that can be done, and shortens the time required to produce results. . . .

The CBAC report of June 2002 observed that healthcare is the major beneficiary of biotechnology. 'More than 90 percent of the advanced biotechnology products on the world market are related to health. It is expected that about three-quarters of global biotechnology demand will continue to be in this area' (*supra*, p. 2). Medical research inevitably relates to life, and its products will often impinge, directly or indirectly, on 'higher life forms'.

The practical *application* of biotechnology is in large measure the preoccupation of enterprises that need to profit from their successes to finance continued research on a broader front. These successes are few and far between (*Biotechnology Use and Development — 1999, supra*, at pp. 13-14). It seems Du Pont spent about US \$15 million to fund the oncomouse research . . .The patent system offers the only protection available for the intellectual product of this research, and thus, the only hope of a fair return against the great financial risks that investment in biotechnology entails.
[. . .]

### G.  The Interpretation of Section 2 of the Patent Act

The appellant Commissioner denies that a patent can be obtained in Canada for 'anything under the sun that is made by man' and I agree. He says that this expression, used in Congressional hearings in 1952, distinguishes the U.S. legislative history from ours, but this is not so, strictly speaking. A 1952 expression of opinion by a Congressional Committee almost 150 years after the definition was inserted into the U.S. *Patent Act* of 1793 is scarcely *contemporanea expositio*.

The check on the indiscriminate grant of patents lies in the established criteria of utility, novelty and non-obviousness. Those are the criteria judged by Parliament to be relevant to its statutory purpose, which is to encourage ingenuity by rewarding its disclosure. The expression 'composition of matter' was included in our patent laws prior to Confederation. It appears in 1824 in the Lower Canada statute entitled *An Act to promote the progress of useful Arts in this Province*, 4 Geo. 4, c. 25, and in Upper Canada two years later in *An Act to Encourage the Progress of Useful Arts within this Province*, 7 Geo. 4, c. 5. The 1826 Act included the terms 'manufacture' and 'composition of matter' in the preamble setting out its object:

> Whereas it is expedient for the encouragement of Genius and of Arts in this Province to secure an exclusive right to the Inventor of any New and Useful Art, Machine, Manufacture, or Composition of Matter . . .

Section 91(22) of the *Constitution Act, 1867*, assigned legislative competence in respect of 'Patents of Invention and Discovery' to Parliament which two years later defined patentable subject matter as follows:

Any person . . . having invented or discovered any new and useful art, machine, <u>manufacture, or composition of matter</u>, or any new and useful improvement on any art, machine, <u>manufacture or composition of matter</u>, not known or used by others before his invention or discovery thereof, or not being at the time of his application for a patent in public use or on sale in any of the Provinces of the Dominion with the consent or allowance of the inventor or discoverer thereof . . . [Emphasis added.]

(*Patent Act*, S.C. 1869, c. 11, s. 6)

The wording has not changed much in the intervening years, apart from dropping the reference to 'discovery'. . . .

It is common ground that to meet the subject matter criteria of the *Patent Act* the oncomouse must qualify as a 'composition of matter' or a 'manufacture'.

*(i)  'Composition of Matter'*

'Composition of matter' (*composition de matières*) is an open-ended expression. Statutory subject matter must be framed broadly because by definition the *Patent Act* must contemplate the unforeseeable. The definition is not expressly confined to inanimate matter, and the appellant Commissioner agrees that composition of organic and certain living matter can be patented. In the case of the oncomouse, the modified genetic material is a physical substance and therefore 'matter'. The fertilized mouse egg is a form of biological 'matter'. The combination of these two forms of matter by the process described in the disclosure is thus . . . a 'composition of matter'.

What, then, is the justification under the *Patent Act* for drawing a line between certain compositions of living matter (*lower* life forms) and other compositions of living matter (*higher* life forms)?

My colleague, Bastarache J., quotes from the *Oxford English Dictionary* (2nd ed. 1989) vol. IX, at p. 480, the entry that 'matter' is a '[p]hysical or corporeal substance in general . . . , contradistinguished from immaterial or incorporeal substance (spirit, soul, mind), and qualities, actions, or conditions', but this, of course, depends on context. 'Matter' is a most chameleon-like word. The expression 'grey *matter*' refers in everyday use to 'intelligence' — which is about as incorporeal as 'spirit' or 'mind'. Indeed, the same Oxford editors define 'grey matter' as 'intelligence, brains' (*New Shorter Oxford English Dictionary* (1993), vol. 1, p. 1142). The *primary* definition of matter, according to the *Oxford English Dictionary*, is '[t]he substance, or the substances collectively, out of which a physical object is made or of which it consists; constituent material' (at p. 479). The definition of '*matière*' in *Le Grand Robert*, quoted by my colleague, is to the same effect. The question, then, is what, in the Commissioner's view, is the 'constituent material' of the oncomouse as a physical entity? If the oncomouse is not composed of matter, what, one might ask, are such things as oncomouse 'minds' composed of? The Court's mandate is to approach this issue as a matter (that slippery word in yet another context!) of law, not murine metaphysics. In the absence of any evidence or expert assistance, the Commissioner now asks the Court to take judicial notice of the oncomouse, if I may use Arthur Koestler's phrase, as a 'ghost in a machine' but this pushes the scope of judicial notice too far. With respect, this sort of literary metaphor (or its dictionary equivalent) is an inadequate basis on which to narrow the scope of the *Patent Act*, and thus to narrow the patentability of scientific invention at the dawn of the third Millennium.

*L. Policy Arguments Against Granting a Patent for the Oncomouse*
[. . .]

The Court heard from a coalition of advocates opposed to the granting of a patent, including religious, environmentalist, agricultural, and non-profit research groups in addition to the concerns voiced by the Commissioner himself.

*(i)  The Religious Objection*

Some opponents object to scientists 'playing God'. A hint, perhaps, of their objection is reflected in the reasons of my colleague, Bastarache J., at para. 163:

> Although some in society may hold the view that higher life forms are mere 'composition[s] of matter', the phrase does not fit well with common understandings of human and animal life.

I do not think that a court is a forum that can properly debate the mystery of mouse life. What we know, in this case, is that the inventors were able to modify a particular gene in the oncomouse genome, and produce a new, useful and unobvious result. That is all we know about the mysteries of oncomouse life and, in my view, it is all we need to know for the purposes of this appeal.

*(ii)  The 'Lack of Regulatory Framework' Objection*

[M]uch of the Commissioner's argument turned on the lack of the regulatory framework that is necessary, he says, to address the ethical and scientific issues raised by genetic research. The argument is that because in his view genetic patents should be regulated, and because the *Patent Act* fails to do the job, Parliament cannot in 1869 have intended to grant patents for genetically engineered 'higher' life forms. My colleague, Bastarache J., accepts this argument . . . With respect, I do not agree.

First, we all probably have strong views that certain activities or things should be regulated. Some say contraceptive devices should not be patented because their use is immoral and unregulated. Others might wish to deny patents to environmentally risky chemical compositions for which, in their view, there is no adequate regulation. On the other hand, others feel that the use of potentially dangerous inventions like explosives and firearms should *not* be regulated. I do not think patents should be denied as a protest against perceived shortcomings in regulatory structures. The opponents of such patents should address themselves to Parliament, not the courts. . . .

Second, regulation necessarily follows, rather than precedes, the invention. No doubt most people would agree that nuclear technology requires regulation; yet the regulation could hardly have been anticipated in 1869, decades before Ernest Rutherford, while at McGill University, with Frederick Soddy, first formulated the theory of atomic disintegration. Prescription drugs are regulated, but the regulatory structure for new drug approval is not in the *Patent Act*. The grant of a patent does not allow the drug to be marketed. Nor should it. Health and safety are not, and never have been, the preoccupation of intellectual property legislation.

It is evident that there are as many areas of potential regulation as there are areas of invention. I think it is also evident that all of these regulatory regimes cannot and should not be put under the inadequate umbrella of the *Patent Act*. Parliament has shown a preference for using more specific statutes altogether outside the framework of patent law. This allows Parliament to tailor the statutory scheme and relevant incentives more precisely to the subject matters involved. Such collateral legislative activity, however, does not justify 'reading down' the definition of 'invention' in the *Patent Act*, in my opinion.

*(iii)  The 'Laws of Nature' Objection*

The appellant Commissioner rejected the oncomouse patent in part because the inventors exercised no control over the genetic characteristics of the mouse (hair colour, length of whiskers, etc.) except for the presence of the oncogene. Further, the Commissioner argued, the oncomouse is not reproducible *en masse* like bacteria. The trial judge upheld these objections. The animal resulting from the patented gene insertion process, he said, is 'completely unknown and unknowable' because the mouse's 'inherent genetic makeup' controls many characteristics and the whole mouse, *with the exception of the oncogene*, is completely independent of human intervention. This is true but not, in my opinion, relevant. The utility of the invention has nothing to do with the length of the mouse's whiskers. Its value, in terms of the patent, appears to reside wholly in the oncogene.
[. . .]

Counsel for the Commissioner says there is a world of difference between a fertilized single cell and the animal it becomes, but if the one is allowed, where is the cut-off point? At what point in the process of gestation does the fertilized single cell *cease* to be a 'composition of matter'? Counsel for the Commissioner says that growth from a single fertilized cell to the complete mouse has nothing to do with the inventors and everything to do with the 'laws of nature'. This is true (although each cell of the live mouse contains the genetic modification), but this is scarcely a fatal objection. The 'laws of nature' are an essential part of the working of many and probably most patented inventions. Patents on biotechnical processes such as fermentation, wholly dependent on the 'laws of nature', were first issued in the early 1800s. Pharmaceutical drugs utilize the normal bodily processes and functions of animals and humans and are not on that account regarded as less patentable. The anti HIV-AIDS drug AZT ingested orally would achieve nothing were it not circulated and processed through the body by the 'laws of nature'. Indeed, the AZT pill, like the oncomouse, could not be brought into existence without reliance on 'the laws of nature' in general and the processes of biochemistry in particular.

[. . .]

### (v)  Ordre Public or Morality

NAFTA and TRIPS each provide that contracting states may *exclude* from patentability inventions the exploitation of which would be contrary to *ordre public* (which seemingly equates to the protection of public security, the physical integrity of individuals as members of society, and the protection of the environment) or morality: *North American Free Trade Agreement Between the Government of Canada, the Government of the United Mexican States and the Government of the United States of America* (1992), Can T.S. 1994 No. 2 (entered into force January 1, 1994), art. 1709(2); *Agreement on Trade-Related Aspects of Intellectual Property Rights* (1994), 25 I.I.C. 209, art. 27(2). The exclusion presupposes a general rule of patentability. Parliament has amended the *Patent Act* to take account of each of these agreements, but has chosen not to include such an exclusion from patentability in the *Patent Act*.

The *European Patent Convention* contains an *ordre public* exclusion from patentability, and the corresponding European 'oncomouse' patent application was examined having specific regard to this exclusion. In its decision of April 3, 1992, the Examining Division of the European Patent Office stated the issue as follows:

> In the case at hand three different interests are involved and require balancing: there is a basic interest of mankind to remedy widespread and dangerous diseases, on the other hand the environment has to be protected against the uncontrolled dissemination of unwanted genes and, moreover, cruelty to animals has to be avoided. The latter two aspects may well justify regarding an invention as immoral and therefore unacceptable unless the advantages, i.e. the benefit to mankind, outweigh the negative aspects.

(*Grant of European patent No. 0 169 762 (Onco-mouse/Harvard)* (1992), OJ EPO 1992, 588, at pp. 591-92)

We do not possess such a 'balancing' test in our *Patent Act*, though some thought must have been given to it when Parliament 'opened up' the *Patent Act* for NAFTA and TRIPS-related amendments in 1994.

The Examining Division of the European Patent Office concluded that issuance of the oncomouse patent was *not* contrary to *ordre public* or public morality and further that '[i]f the legislator is of the opinion that certain technical knowledge should be used under limited conditions only it is up to him to enact appropriate legislation' (*ibid*, p. 591).

The European Community Directive on biotechnology (*Directive 98/44/EC of the European Parliament and of the Council of 6 July 1998 on the legal protection of biotechnological invention*) names specific inventions (human cloning, modifying germ line, commercial use of human embryos, and causing suffering to animals without substantial medical benefit to humans or animals) as contrary to *ordre public* or morality. If Parliament thinks it wise to spell out such a policy in the *Patent Act*, it will pass appropriate amendments.
[. . .]

### (vii)  Animal Rights

Animal rights supporters object to the fact that the oncomouse is deliberately designed to cause sentient beings to grow painful malignant tumours. Of course, whatever position is adopted under *patent* law, animals have been and will continue to be used in laboratories for scientific research. Pets are property. Mice are already commodified. Parliament may wish to address animal rights as a distinct subject matter. If the claim for the patent on the oncomouse itself is refused, the result will *not* be that Harvard is denied the opportunity to make, construct, use and sell the oncomouse. On the contrary, the result will be that *anyone* will be able to make, construct, use and sell the oncomouse. The only difference will be that Harvard will be denied the *quid pro quo* for the disclosure of its invention.

### (viii)  The Commodification of Human Life

Some critics argue that life and property rights are incompatible. Patents, they say, treat 'life' as a commodity that can be bought and sold, and therefore diminish the respect with which life ought to be regarded. Living entities become 'objects'.

The major concern is that human beings constitute a line that cannot be crossed. The CBAC agrees. But others argue that patenting *any* form of life puts us on a slippery slope. Today the oncomouse; tomorrow Frankenstein's creature. I do not agree. There is a qualitative divide between rodents and human beings. The broadest claim here specifically excepts humans from the scope of transgenic mammals. Moreover, for the reasons already expressed, I do not believe that the issue of patentability of a human being even arises under the *Patent Act*.

### (ix) Environmental Protection

Environmental concerns include the diversity of the gene pool and potential escape of genetically modified organisms into the environment. These are serious concerns which serious people would expect Parliament to address. The concerns, however, have little to do with the patent system. Patents or no patents, genetically engineered organisms have arrived in our midst. The genie is out of the bottle. . . . Patentability addresses only the issue of rewarding the inventors for their disclosure of what they have done. Larger questions are answered elsewhere.

### (x) Globalization

Anti-globalization groups object to the impact of broad patentability on developing countries, noting that research dollars and the beneficial effects of patented products are concentrated in developed countries. This criticism is, of course, first a broad attack on intellectual property rights generally and, second, a vote of no confidence in multilateral agreements such as TRIPS. The concerns of developing countries have received wide attention, and rightly so. A countervailing consideration is that the developing world may lose as much benefit as the economically developed world if excessive emphasis is placed on granting equitable access to inventions already made as opposed to continuing to offer adequate incentives for inventions to come. This too is an issue that does not arise for consideration on this appeal.

### (xi) Contrary Considerations

If a certain subject matter is unpatentable as a matter of law, inventors who do carry on inventing will gravitate toward alternative sources of protection. The most obvious would be trade secrets protection. The problem with this alternative, in terms of the public interest, is that the public would lose the *quid pro quo* of public disclosure that they receive under patent law.

Lacking legal protection against unauthorized appropriation of ideas, ingenious people may tend to hide and hoard the products of their ingenuity rather than disclose them for others to build on that knowledge. The 'hide and hoard' mentality was the very mischief the *Patent Act* was aimed at.

There are, in other words, many policy implications of *excluding* patent protection as well as the policy implications of inclusion relied upon by the appellant Commissioner. The balance between the competing interests is for Parliament to strike.

[. . .]

*M. Alleged Deficiencies in the Patent Regime*

There is much scholarly controversy in Canada over the role of intellectual property in biotechnology. . . Some thoughtful critics suggest that patents in this field may in fact deter rather than promote innovation: M. A. Heller and R. S. Eisenberg, 'Can Patents Deter Innovation? The Anticommons in Bio-medical Research' (1998), 280 *Science* 698; Gold, 'Biomedical Patents and Ethics: A Canadian Solution', *supra* [(2000) 45 McGill L.J. 413].

On a more technical level, it is pointed out that a 20-year patent is a very long time in the life cycle of biotechnology. A shorter patent life, with conditions more tailored to the industry, would, it is said, provide sufficient incentive. Then there are those who advocate the 'farmers' privilege' to avoid farmers being subject to patent enforcement in the case of the progeny of patented plants and animals. Others advocate protection for 'innocent bystanders' who inadvertently make use of a genetically engineered plant or animal, unaware of its being patented.

My colleague, Bastarache J., suggests that the *absence* of such provisions supports his conclusion that the oncomouse is unpatentable, but this approach, with respect, simply substitutes the Court's notion of good public policy for the judgment of Parliament, whose members are well aware of these and similar proposals. Parliament has had the *National Biotechnology Strategy* since 1983, renewed as the *Canadian Biotechnology Strategy: An Ongoing Renewal Process* fifteen years later in 1998, the work of the CBAC and *Proceed with Care: Final Report of the Royal Commission on New Reproductive Technologies* (1993).

[. . .]

*N. Conclusion*

In my view, the oncomouse is patentable subject matter.

More recently, in a decision which some may consider as backtracking somewhat from the majority's findings in *Harvard College*, the Supreme Court provided an "explanation" of the higher life form exclusion enunci-ated in *Harvard*. The case, *Monsanto Canada Inc. v. Schmeiser*,[48] dealt with the patentability of genetically altered canola seed ("Glyphosate-Resistant

---

[48] [2004] 1 S.C.R. 902, 239 D.L.R. (4th) 271, 31 C.P.R. (4th) 161, 320 N.R. 201 (S.C.C.) [*Schmeiser* cited to S.C.R.].

Plants") sold under the trade-mark "RoundUp Ready". Due to the genetic modification, farmers who use the modified seed can spray the herbicide RoundUp (also sold by Monsanto and containing the chemical glyphosate) which will not affect the canola. Most plants sprayed with a glyphosate herbicide do not survive, but a canola plant grown from seed containing the modified gene will survive. Roundup can be sprayed after the canola plants have emerged, killing all plants except the canola. This eliminates the need for tillage and other herbicides. It also avoids delaying seeding to accommodate early weed spraying. In the year 2000, approximately 20,000 farmers planted 4.5 to 5 million acres — nearly 40 percent of all canola grown in Canada — with "RoundUp Ready" seeds.

Monsanto requires a farmer who wishes to grow Roundup Ready Canola to enter into a licensing arrangement called a Technology Use Agreement (TUA). The licensed farmers must attend a Grower Enrolment Meeting at which Monsanto describes the technology and its licensing terms. By signing the TUA, the farmer becomes entitled to purchase Roundup Ready Canola from an authorized seed agent. They must, however, undertake to use the seed for planting a single crop and to sell that crop for consumption to a commercial purchaser authorized by Monsanto. The licensed farmers may not sell or give the seed to any third party, or save seed for replanting or inventory.

The TUA gives Monsanto the right to inspect the fields of the contracting farmer and to take samples to verify compliance with the TUA. The farmer must also pay a licensing fee for each acre planted with Roundup Ready Canola. In 1998, the licensing fee was $15 per acre.

Percy Schmeiser, a Saskatchewan farmer, had been caught using those seeds (95% of the canola on his land was of this variety); he argued the seeds had just been blown onto his land by wind, and that he had not used them in connection with RoundUp.

The Court had to determine whether the patented gene that made the canola resistant to glyphosate was valid. The majority found as follows:

> The appellant Schmeiser argues that the subject matter claimed in the patent is unpatentable. While acknowledging that Monsanto claims protection only over a gene and a cell, Schmeiser contends that the result of extending such protection is to restrict use of a plant and a seed. This result, the argument goes, ought to render the subject matter unpatentable, following the reasoning of the majority of this Court in *Harvard College v. Canada (Commissioner of Patents)*. ('*Harvard Mouse*'). In that case, plants and seeds were found to be unpatentable 'higher life forms'.

> This case is different from *Harvard Mouse*, where the patent refused was for a mammal. The Patent Commissioner, moreover, had allowed other claims, which were not at issue before the Court in that case, notably a plasmid and a

somatic cell culture. The claims at issue in this case, for a gene and a cell, are somewhat analogous, suggesting that to find a gene and a cell to be patentable is in fact consistent with both the majority and the minority holdings in *Harvard Mouse*.

Further, all members of the Court in *Harvard Mouse* noted in *obiter* that a fertilized, genetically altered oncomouse egg would be patentable subject matter, regardless of its ultimate anticipated development into a mouse (at para. 3, *per* Binnie J. for the minority; at para. 162, *per* Bastarache J. for the majority.).

Whether or not patent protection for the gene and the cell extends to activities involving the plant is not relevant to the patent's validity. It relates only to the factual circumstances in which infringement will be found to have taken place, as we shall explain below. Monsanto's patent has already been issued, and the onus is thus on Schmeiser to show that the Commissioner erred in allowing the patent: *Apotex Inc. v. Wellcome Foundation Ltd.*, [2002] 4 S.C.R. 153, 2002 SCC 77 (S.C.C.), at paras. 42-44. He has failed to discharge that onus. We therefore conclude that the patent is valid.
[. . .]

It is uncontested that Monsanto's patented claim is only for the gene and cell that it developed. This, however, is the beginning and not the end of the inquiry. The more difficult question — and the nub of this case — is whether, by cultivating plants *containing the cell and gene*, the appellants used the patented components of those plants. The position taken by Arbour J. [dissenting] assumes that this inquiry is redundant and that the only way a patent may be infringed is to use the patented invention in isolation.

This position flies in the face of century-old patent law, which holds that where a defendant's commercial or business activity involves a thing of which a patented part is a significant or important component, infringement is established. It is no defence to say that the thing actually used was not patented, but only one of its components.
[. . .]

Provided the patented invention is a significant aspect of the defendant's activity, the defendant will be held to have 'used' the invention and violated the patent. If Mr. Schmeiser's activities with Roundup Ready Canola plants amounted to use interfering with Monsanto's full enjoyment of their monopoly on the gene and cell, those activities infringed the patent. Infringement does not require use of the gene or cell in isolation.
[. . .]

The appellants' argument also ignores the role human beings play in agricultural propagation. Farming is a commercial enterprise in which farmers sow and cultivate the plants which prove most efficient and profitable. Plant science

has been with us since long before Mendel. Human beings since time imme-
morial have striven to produce more efficient plants. Huge investments of
energy and money have been poured into the quest for better seeds and better
plants. One way in which that investment is protected is through the *Patent Act*
giving investors a monopoly when they create a novel and useful invention in
the realm of plant science, such as genetically modified genes and cells.

Finally, many inventions make use of natural processes in order to work. For
example, many valid patents have referred to various yeasts, which would have
no practical utility at all without 'natural forces'. See *Abitibi Co., Re* (1982),
62 C.P.R. (2d) 81 (Can. Pat. App. Bd. & Pat. Commr.), in which the inventive
step consisted of acclimatizing a known species of yeast from domestic sewage
to a new environment, where it would then through its natural operation act to
purify waste from pulp plants.

The issue is not the perhaps adventitious arrival of Roundup Ready on Mr.
Schmeiser's land in 1998. What is at stake in this case is *sowing* and *cultivation*,
which necessarily involves deliberate and careful activity on the part of the
farmer. The appellants suggest that when a farmer such as Mr. Schmeiser
actively cultivates a crop with particular properties through activities such as
testing, isolating, treating, and planting the desired seed and tending the crops
until harvest, the result is a crop which has merely 'grown itself'. Such a
suggestion denies the realities of modern agriculture.

Inventions in the field of agriculture may give rise to concerns not raised in
other fields — moral concerns about whether it is right to manipulate genes in
order to obtain better weed control or higher yields. It is open to Parliament to
consider these concerns and amend the Patent Act should it find them persuasive.

Our task, however, is to interpret and apply the *Patent Act* as it stands, in
accordance with settled principles. Under the present Act, an invention in the
domain of agriculture is as deserving of protection as an invention in the domain
of mechanical science. Where Parliament has not seen fit to distinguish between
inventions concerning plants and other inventions, neither should the courts.

We conclude that the trial judge and Court of Appeal were correct in concluding
that the appellants 'used' Monsanto's patented gene and cell and hence infringed the *Patent Act*.

Interestingly, however, the Court did not award anything to Monsanto
because Schmeiser had not profited from the invention:

On the facts found, the appellants made no profits *as a result of the invention*.

Their profits were precisely what they would have been had they planted and harvested ordinary canola. They sold the Roundup Ready Canola they grew in 1998 for feed, and thus obtained no premium for the fact that it was Roundup Ready Canola. Nor did they gain any agricultural advantage from the herbicide resistant nature of the canola, since no finding was made that they sprayed with Roundup herbicide to reduce weeds. The appellants' profits arose solely from qualities of their crop that cannot be attributed to the invention.

On this evidence, the appellants earned no profit from the invention and Monsanto is entitled to nothing on their claim of account.

While *Monsanto Canada Inc. v. Schmeiser* may appear to be a reversal of *Harvard College*, this conclusion is incorrect. Certainly, in *Schmeiser* the Court seemed to accept the economic rationale to allow patents on new types of inventions (including modified genes in plants) which had been mentioned by the minority in *Harvard*. But those arguments had not been rejected by the majority in *Harvard College*. The *Harvard* conclusion that higher life forms per se are unpatentable still holds. It does not mean that inventions embedded in higher life forms are also unpatentable. In *Harvard*, the Supreme Court had not opposed the patentability of genetically modified plasmid[49] and the process to genetically modify a mouse so that it became susceptible to cancer. The claims relating to plasmid and process were found to be valid. Claims for the mouse itself were found to be invalid by the Patent Commissioner and that finding was upheld by the Court. In *Schmeiser*, the Court did not hold that the plant itself was patented but that one could patent modified genes and the resulting cells and that use of those modified genes and cells, whether in a laboratory or not, would infringe the patent.

The practical result is that many components of higher life forms, including proteins, genes and cells, can be patented, but entire organisms, such as plants and animals, cannot. Because one can infringe a patent in one of those components by "using" the higher life form in which it is embedded (see the Infringement section below), it may be that for the purposes of infringement it will prove to be a distinction without a difference.

The different procedural aspects of *Harvard College* and *Schmeiser* should also be noted. The *Harvard* litigation began as an appeal of the Commissioner's denial of the product claims in the patent application and was reviewed by the Supreme Court according to a correctness standard. By contrast, in the Monsanto infringement litigation, since a granted patent

---

[49] A plasmid may be defined in non-technical terms as DNA molecules often used as a vector ("carrier") for cloning.

is presumed valid (s. 43(2)), Schmeiser had the burden of proof to establish that the subject matter was not patentable.

## 2. Novelty

Once it is determined that a product or process falls within the realm of acceptable subject-matters, one must determine whether that product or process is "new". Novelty is defined in s. 28.2(1):

> The subject-matter defined by a claim in an application for a patent in Canada (the 'pending application') must not have been disclosed :
>
> (a)    *more than one year* before the filing date by the applicant, or by a person who obtained knowledge, directly or indirectly, from the applicant, in such a manner that the subject-matter became available to the public in Canada or elsewhere;
>
> (b)    *before the claim date* by a person not mentioned in paragraph (a) in such a manner that the subject-matter became available to the public in Canada or elsewhere;
>
> (c)    in an application for a patent that is filed in Canada by a person other than the applicant, and has a filing date that is before the claim date;
>
> (d)    . . . (a long subsection dealing with co-pending applications is omitted).

In other words this section provides a *"grace period"* for inventions. Once an invention has been made available to the public (by publication, sale, or use), anywhere in the world *by the applicant* or by a person who obtained knowledge, directly or indirectly, from the applicant, the inventor has one year to apply for a patent in Canada (and the United States). However, if at any time prior to the filing of the application, a person (other than the applicant or someone who has knowledge of the invention from the applicant) disclosed the invention anywhere in the world, the invention is no longer new. Finally, if two applications are filed in Canada for the same invention, the first to file will be entitled to the patent.

Note the two terms used in s. 28.2(c): *filing date* and *claim date*, both of which are defined in s. 2. The filing date is "the date on which the application is filed, as determined in accordance with section 28", *i.e.,* "the date on which the Commissioner receives the documents, information and fees prescribed for the purposes of this section or, if they are received on different dates, the last date." In other words, the filing date is the Canadian filing date. However, once an application is filed in a member country of the Paris Convention (see the International Section), the applicant has twelve months to file in other countries and receive the same date (28.4(5)) (known as a *"priority date"*) in all those countries. A "claim date" as defined in s. 2

is thus the "date of a claim in an application for a patent in Canada, as determined in accordance with section 28.1", which reads as follows:

> The date of a claim in an application for a patent in Canada (the "pending application") is the filing date of the application, unless
>
> (*a*)    the pending application is filed by
>> (i)    a person who has, or whose agent, legal representative or predecessor in title has, previously regularly filed in or for Canada an application for a patent disclosing the subject-matter defined by the claim, or
>> (ii)    a person who is entitled to protection under the terms of any treaty or convention relating to patents to which Canada is a party and who has, or whose agent, legal representative or predecessor in title has, previously regularly filed in or for any other country that by treaty, convention or law affords similar protection to citizens of Canada an application for a patent disclosing the subject-matter defined by the claim;
>
> (*b*)    the filing date of the pending application is within twelve months after the filing date of the previously regularly filed application; and
>
> (*c*)    the applicant has made a request for priority on the basis of the previously regularly filed application.
>
> (2) In the circumstances described in paragraphs (1) (*a*) to (*c*), the claim date is the filing date of the previously regularly filed application.

In other words, if a foreign applicant files in Canada within twelve months of the foreign filing and requests "priority", the "claim date" in Canada will be the date of the foreign filing. When applied to s. 28.2(c), this means that to be novel in Canada the actual Canadian filing date must be before someone else's (foreign) claim date.

It is worth noting that the one-year grace period is only available in Canada and the United States. Almost all other countries apply an absolute novelty standard, which means that any disclosure (whether by the applicant or another person), destroys the invention's novelty. In addition, s. 28.2 makes it clear that (a) a disclosure by a person other than the applicant (usually the inventor) or someone who has gained knowledge of the invention from the applicant will also void novelty; and (b) if two inventors file for the same invention, the first-to-file will be entitled to the patent. This is the rule applied in most countries, except the United States, which has a system known as "first-to-invent" (which Canada abandoned in 1989[50]). Under that system, if two applications are filed in respect of the same

---

[50] And further amended by S.C. 1993, c. 15, s. 33. See Michel H. Goulet, "Novelty Under Canada's Patent Act — A European Accent" (1999) 13 I.P.J. 83.

invention, a proceeding is launched to determine who the first inventor was. While this may sound fairer, it is also a long and extremely expensive process, and one which relies on documentary evidence to support an alleged date of invention, a system which tends to favor larger companies and laboratories. Additionally, a first-to-file system is an incentive to file quickly for patent protection, thus leading to a more rapid disclosure of new inventions consistent with the patent "bargain."

Once the appropriate date(s) to assess the novelty of an invention are determined,[51] the next step is to decide whether what was disclosed prior to that date was in fact the same invention.

In *Reeves Brothers Inc. v. Toronto Quilting & Embroidery Ltd.*,[52] the Federal Court set out two tests to determine whether the invention is new (an invention that is not new is said to have been "anticipated"):

> In brief, these inventions contemplate a flame lamination process which would do certain things to the surface of the foam without doing anything perceptible to the underlining body of the foam. The certain things which would be done to the surface of the foam are that the surface would be brought beyond its melting temperature (in a phenomenological sense as used in the subject patents rather than the scientific sense) to the burn-off point, thereby reducing the surface of the foam; and then by making use of the physical and chemical characteristics of the products of decomposition of the surface to laminate so as to get a strong and effective bond between the fabric and the remaining unchanged layers of cells of the foam by exerting only enough pressure to maintain contact between the fabric and the foam.
>
> This bond, the plaintiff submits is a chemical bond in part which is why the bond is effective.
> [. . .]

> *Prior art defences — Anticipation and obviousness*

[After reviewing prior patents, including one known as "Grom", the Court continues:]

> Contrary to Grom, the Reeves patents in suit teach the use of high temperature and minimal pressure to bond. They teach that isocyanates are present as a result of employing the Reeves process. Isocyanates are not present employing

---

[51] See, *e.g. Lubrizol Corp. v. Imperial Oil Ltd.* (1992), 98 D.L.R. (4th) 1, 45 C.P.R. (3d) 449 (Fed. C.A.), additional reasons at (1993), (sub nom. *Imperial Oil Ltd. v. Lubrizol Corp.*) 48 C.P.R. (3d) 1 (Fed. C.A.), leave to appeal to S.C.C. refused (1993), 104 D.L.R. (4th) vii (note) (S.C.C.).

[52] (1978), 43 C.P.R. (2d) 145 (Fed. T.D.).

the Grom process. Harrison also said that experiments indicated that the decomposition to form isocyanate groups does not begin to occur until the foam surface or parts of it reach temperatures of 250° C or more.

In discussing the nature of the bonding of the laminate by the Reeves process, Harrison said that while it is not possible by chemical analysis to be sure whether such bond between fabric and polyurethane is chemical or merely physical in nature, he was of the opinion that it was highly probable in flame lamination that chemical bonding takes place. As reasons for his opinion, he gave the following: (1) the strength of the bond; (2) the change of the bond strength with the passage of time; (3) that employing the acetone test 'the initial products of flaming of the surface are . . . soluble in acetone, but after a few hours these products revert to insoluble matter'; (4) by employing the ATR (attenuated total reflectance) technique; and (5) the fact that fuming attends the chemical process.

In differentiating between bonding as done by the Reeves process and as done by the Grom invention, Harrison said that chemical bonding is initiated by the isocyanate groups employing the Reeves process but that by employing the Grom invention there being no free isocyanate groups present at the surface of the foam, the bonding was purely physical in nature.
[. . .]

The question to be decided on the basis of this evidence, having regard to the state of the art, is: Was the Reeves (Dickey) alleged invention, in so far as claimed, new, that is, was it not anticipated? If the answer to this question is that the invention was new, or not anticipated, then was it obvious (that is, not involving an inventive step)? (In other words, the question of obviousness will only arise if there is no anticipation.)

As I understand it, in order that there may be a finding of anticipation, the prior art must (1) give an exact prior description; (2) give directions which will inevitably result in something within the claims; (3) give clear and unmistakable directions; (4) give information which for the purpose of practical utility is equal to that given by the subject patent; (5) convey information so that a person grappling with the same problem must be able to say 'that gives me what I wish'; (6) give information to a person of ordinary knowledge so that he must at once perceive the invention; (7) in the absence of explicit directions, teach an 'inevitable result' which 'can only be proved by experiments'; and (8) satisfy all these tests in a single document without making a mosaic. These tests are enunciated in the following cases: *Steel Co. of Canada Ltd. v. Sivaco Wire & Nail Co.* (1973), 11 C.P.R. (2d) 153 at pp. 189-92; *Pope Appliance Corp. v. Spanish River Pulp & Paper Mills Ltd.* (1929), 46 R.P.C. 23 at p. 54; *Lovell Mfg. Co. and Maxwell Ltd. v. Beatty Bros. Ltd.* (1962), 41 C.P.R. 18 at pp. 45-8, 23 Fox Pat. C. 112; *General Tire v. Firestone*, [1971] F.S.R. 417 at p. 444; *British Thompson-Houston Co. Ltd. v. Metropolitan-Vickers Electrical Co.*

*Ltd.* (1928), 45 R.P.C. 1 at pp. 22-4; *Letraset Int'l Ltd. v. Dymo Ltd.,* [1976] R.P.C. 65 at p. 75; *Xerox of Canada Ltd. et al. v. IBM Canada Ltd.* (1977), 33 C.P.R. (2d) 24 at pp. 46-8 and 49.

Employing these tests from the cases, in my view, considering the whole of the evidence, and particularly that commented upon and for the reasons given in respect to it, the known prior art neither individually nor in any reasonable combination would teach a person skilled in the art the invention described in the subject Reeves patents. The finding, therefore, is that there is no anticipation and this defence fails.

The test was also explicated by the Supreme Court in *Free World Trust:*[53]

> The legal question is whether the Solov'eva article contains sufficient information to enable a person of ordinary skill and knowledge in the field to understand, without access to the two patents, 'the nature of the invention and carry it into practical use without the aid of inventive genius but purely by mechanical skill' (H. G. Fox, *The Canadian Law and Practice Relating to Letters Patent for Inventions* (4th ed. 1969), at p. 127). In other words, was the information given by Solov'eva 'for [the] purpose of practical utility, equal to that given in the patents in suit'?: *Consolboard Inc. v. MacMillan Bloedel (Sask.) Ltd.,* [1981] 1 S.C.R. 504 (S.C.C.), *per* Dickson J. at p. 534, or as was memorably put in *General Tire & Rubber Co. v. Firestone Tyre & Rubber Co.,* [1972] R.P.C. 457 (U.K. H.L.), at p. 486:
>
>> A signpost, however clear, upon the road to the patentee's invention will not suffice. The prior inventor must be clearly shown to have planted his flag at the precise destination before the patentee.
>
> The test for anticipation is difficult to meet:
>
>> One must, in effect, be able to look at a prior, single publication and find in it all the information which, for practical purposes, is needed to produce the claimed invention without the exercise of any inventive skill. The prior publication must contain so clear a direction that a skilled person reading and following it would in every case and without possibility of error be led to the claimed invention.
>
> (*Beloit Canada Ltée/Ltd. v. Valmet Oy* (1986), 8 C.P.R. (3d) 289 (Fed. C.A.), *per* Hugessen J.A., at p. 297)

Anticipation (or absence of novelty) may thus be defined as the presence in a single element of prior art of a product or process containing all the

---

[53] *Supra,* note 19.

essential elements of the claimed invention, albeit not necessarily in the exact same form.[53a] Any significant difference must, however, be interpreted in the applicant's favor: if any difference in any of the essential elements could reasonably be said to leave a "possibility of error" for a person skilled in the relevant art or science, then the invention is new.[54]

One such example may be found in *Lightning Fastener Co. v. Colonial Fastener Co.*:[55]

> The patent relates to a locking device for separable slide fasteners, that is to say: fasteners consisting of two rows of co-operating elements (locking members) which are caused to engage with one another by the passage of a slider along the rows and are disengaged by the movement of the slider in the opposite direction. The appellant's invention is described as follows in the specification of the patent:
>
> According to this invention, a slider pull is provided adjacent its pivot with one or more fingers or lugs shaped to extend through a recess in the slider wing for direct engagement between locking members on one stringer or the lug may indirectly co-operate with said members through the aid of some other part of the slider. Preferably these lugs are spaced longitudinally and laterally to be engaged between locking members on each stringer.
>
> It is claimed that the finger or lug automatically moves by gravity into position, through the recess, between two of the co-operating fastener elements and thus provides locking means whereby the slider is retained against movement in either direction on the stringer. A feature is that by means of this device the movement of the slider may be prevented at any point along the stringer.
>
> The patent was applied for on the 26th of January, 1928, and was granted on the 16th of April, 1929.
>
> The infringing article is also a locking device for separable slide fasteners; . . .
>
> The respondents pleaded, amongst other things, that the appellant's patent was invalid because the invention was patented or described in printed publications more than two years before the application for the patent; and, at the trial,

---

[53a] The typical novelty-defeating disclosure takes the form of a publication. However, disclosure by use in public or sale (without a confidentiality undertaking) may also defeat novelty. See *Baker Petrolite Corp. v. Canwell Enviro-Industries Ltd.*, 2002 FCA 158, (2002), [2003] 1 F.C. 49, 211 D.L.R. (4th) 696, 17 C.P.R. (4th) 478 (Fed. C.A.).

[54] See, *e.g., Risi Stone Ltd. v. Groupe Permacon Inc.* (1995), 65 C.P.R. (3d) 2 (Fed. T.D.).

[55] [1933] S.C.R. 377, [1933] 3 D.L.R. 348 (S.C.C.).

reference was made to the fastener of M. Gabriel Fontaine, a patent for which was applied for in France, on the 14th of November, 1923, and granted on the 5th of March, 1924. A copy of the patent was produced, as also an enlarged model of the slider used in connection with that fastener. As described in the patent, in the Fontaine device, the pull of the slider is provided with two spaced lugs adjacent its pivot. When the stringers are drawn up through the channels of the slider, as soon as the pull is released, it comes down by force of gravity and the lugs are pressed against the fastener elements, immediately above the conical edges of the slider, where the fasteners are in engagement, thus offsetting the fasteners, retaining them against movement and preventing the slider from working in any direction.

The Fontaine fastener was primarily intended for use on footwear. But we can conceive of no reason why it could not equally be used on any number of other articles where fasteners are employed; and the point is that, in the Fontaine patent, the locking device disclosed is substantially similar, is designed for exactly the same purpose and the disclosure gives the same knowledge as the appellant's patent. [. . .]

[A]ll the essential points in the appellant's patent were already brought out in Fontaine's disclosure. . . .The lugs described by Fontaine have complete identity of function with those claimed by the appellant; and they perform that function substantially in the same way.

In that case, the Supreme Court provided a 'rule of thumb' to determine anticipation:

> '. . .what amounts to infringement, if posterior, should, as a general rule, amount to anticipation, if anterior.'[56]

Finding a new use of a known compound may be patentable subject-matter. The leading case on this point is *Shell Oil Co. v. Canada (Patent Commissioner)*:[57]

> The appellant applied for a patent on certain chemical compositions comprising chemical compounds mixed with an adjuvant. An adjuvant is simply a substance added to a prescription to facilitate the action of the principal ingredient. Some of the compounds were new but unpatented; others were old. The new

[56] *Ibid*, at 381 (per Rinfret J.). Quoted with approval by Dickson J. in *Consolboard Inc. v. MacMillan Bloedel (Sask.) Ltd.*, [1981] 1 S.C.R. 504, 122 D.L.R. (3d) 203, 56 C.P.R. (2d) 145, 35 N.R. 390 (S.C.C.) at 535 [*MacMillan Bloedel* cited to S.C.R.].
[57] [1982] 2 S.C.R. 536, 142 D.L.R. (3d) 117, 67 C.P.R. (2d) 1, 44 N.R. 541 (S.C.C.) [*Shell Oil* cited to S.C.R.].

compounds were initially included in the claim for patent but the claim in respect of them was subsequently withdrawn by the appellant.

The appellant describes its invention as 'the surprising discovery that compounds having a specific chemical structure have useful properties in respect of the regulation of the growth of plants'.
[. . .]

The appellant acknowledges that this discovery having been made there is nothing inventive in mixing these compounds with appropriate adjuvants. Indeed, it acknowledges that the adjuvants are inert carriers commonly used in compositions to be applied to plants. The 'invention', the appellant stresses, is the discovery of the usefulness of the compounds, old and new, as plant growth regulators and this is what it wants to protect by a patent on its chemical compositions.
[. . .]

It is not the process of mixing the old compounds with the known adjuvants which is put forward as novel. It is the idea of applying the old compounds to the new use as plant growth regulators; the character of the adjuvants follows inevitably once their usefulness for that purpose has been discovered. What then is the 'invention' under s. 2? I believe it is the application of this new knowledge to effect a desired result which has an undisputed commercial value and that it falls within the words 'any new and useful art'. I think the word 'art' in the context of the definition must be given its general connotation of 'learning' or 'knowledge' as commonly used in expressions such as 'the state of the art' or 'the prior art'. The appellant's discovery in this case has added to the cumulative wisdom on the subject of these compounds by a recognition of their hitherto unrecognized properties and it has established the method whereby these properties may be realized through practical application. In my view, this constitutes a 'new and useful art' and the compositions are the practical embodiment of the new knowledge.

The case which, in my view, is most closely analogous to this one is *Hickton's Patent Syndicate v. Patents and Machine Improvements Co.* (1909), 26 R.P.C. 339. The applicant in that case had an idea for equalizing the consumption of thread on lace-making machines by the process known as 'shogging'. There was nothing new about 'shogging'. It was a technique customarily employed in creating a pattern in the piece of lace being made. But it had not hitherto been thought of as a means of equalizing thread consumption. This was done by hand by interchanging the bobbins. It was clear on the evidence that once the idea was formed, no further inventive ingenuity was required in order to put it into effect. The plaintiff, who had obtained a patent on the idea and on its method of carrying it out, brought an action for infringement. The action was tried by Swinfen-Eady J. who held that although the idea of using the technique of 'shogging' to equalize thread consumption was new, there was no invention involved in carrying out the idea. The plaintiff's patent was accordingly invalid for want of subject-matter and its action failed. The plaintiff appealed and in allowing the appeal Cozens-Hardy M.R. said at p. 347:

> The learned Judge in his judgment states a proposition which, with the greatest possible respect, seems to me to be a great deal too wide. 'An idea may be new and original and very meritorious, but unless there is some invention necessary for putting the idea into practice it is not patentable'. That, I venture to say, is not in accordance with the principles which have hitherto been applied in Patent cases, and I do not think it ought to be recognised as the law. When once the idea of applying some well-known thing for a special and new purpose is stated, it may be very obvious how to give effect to that idea, and yet none the less is that a good subject-matter for a Patent.

In his concurring reasons, Fletcher Moulton L.J. was even more critical of the trial judge's statement. I quote from his reasons at the same page:

> After the judgment of the Master of the Rolls I do not intend to enter into the facts of the case, but I do wish to deal with the dictum of the learned Judge in the Court below, which really gives the ground for his decision. The Defendants contend that although the idea of traversing by 'shogging' in order to equalise is new, yet it is not proper subject-matter for a Patent as no invention whatever was necessary to carry it out. The learned Judge says: 'An idea may be new and original and very meritorious, but unless there is some invention necessary for putting the idea into practice it is not patentable.' With the greatest respect for the learned Judge, that, in my opinion, is quite contrary to the principles of patent law, and would deprive of their reward a very large number of meritorious inventions that have been made. I may say that this dictum is to the best of my knowledge supported by no case, and no case has been quoted to us which would justify it. But let me give an example. Probably the most celebrated Patent in the history of our law is that of *Bolton* and *Watt*, which had the unique distinction of being renewed for the whole fourteen years. The particular invention there was the condensation of the steam, not in the cylinder itself, but in a separate vessel. That conception occurred to *Watt* and it was for that that his Patent was granted, and out of that grew the steam engine. Now can it be suggested that it required any invention whatever to carry out that idea when once you had got it? It could be done in a thousand ways and by any competent engineer, but the invention was in the idea, and when he had once got that idea, the carrying out of it was perfectly easy. To say that the conception may be meritorious and may involve invention and may be new and original, and simply because when you have once got the idea it is easy to carry it out, that that deprives it of the title of being a new

invention according to our patent law, is, I think, an extremely dangerous principle and justified neither by reason, nor authority.

It seems to me that in *Hickton's Patent* the English Court of Appeal found that an idea was patentable notwithstanding the lack of any novelty in its implementation. No further invention was required in putting it into practice. As Lord Cozens-Hardy put it:

> When once the idea of applying some well-known thing for a special and new purpose is stated, it may be very obvious how to give effect to that idea, and yet none the less is that a good subject-matter for a Patent.

In my view, this is the thrust of the appellant's appeal to this Court. It says: 'I recognize that these compounds are old; I acknowledge that there is nothing inventive in mixing them with these adjuvants once their properties as plant growth regulators have been discovered; but I have discovered these properties in those old compounds and I want a patent on the practical embodiment of my invention'. I think he is entitled to receive it.

This new use (which is easier to demonstrate if it is in a different field as in *Shell Oil*[58]) of a known compound may be patentable, provided it meets the other patentability criteria of usefulness and nonobviousness. In the pharmaceutical area, the practice of "Swiss-style" claims that focus on new (medical) uses of a known substance (compound or composition) are commonplace. In Canada, such claims are patentable if they disclose a truly new industrial or commercial result. The patent should disclose clearly in the specification or claims the means for distinguishing the new use from the already known use.[59] When claiming a new use of an old article, care should be taken not to claim the old article.[60] Finding a new advantage for an old article is not patentable, if the use remains the same.[61]

Finding a new combination of known elements may also be patentable (provided it meets the usual criteria of utility and non-obviousness), but the jurisprudence distinguishes new combinations from simple aggregations. The distinction between a combination and an aggregation is that the latter is a simple juxtaposition, while the former produces a sum greater than the

---

[58]  See, e.g., *Application No. 144,173, Re* (1976), 44 C.P.R. (2d) 113 (Can. Pat. App. Bd. & Pat. Commr.).

[59]  See *Apotex Inc. v. Hoffmann-La Roche Ltd.* (1989), [1989] F.C.J. No. 321, 24 C.P.R. (3d) 289, 99 N.R. 198, 23 C.I.P.R. 1, 1989 CarswellNat 496 (Fed. C.A.).

[60]  See *Scott Paper Co. v. Minnesota Mining & Manufacturing Co.* (1981), 53 C.P.R. (2d) 26 (Fed. T.D.); and *Apotex Inc. v. Hoffmann-La Roche Ltd.*, supra.

[61]  See *Riello Canada Inc. v. Lambert* (1986), [1986] F.C.J. No. 243, 9 C.P.R. (3d) 324, 3 F.T.R. 23, 1986 CarswellNat 611 (Fed. T.D.), additional reasons at (1987), 15 C.P.R. (3d) 257 (Fed. T.D.).

parts individually. In a combination, there is, in modern parlance, a synergy between the combined elements. Put differently, the interaction among the elements must be a significant part of the invention as claimed.[62]

A problem related to novelty is known as "overclaiming". It may be found in various forms. In some cases the patentee tries to appropriate something that is known. The supposedly new invention closely resembles an invention previously disclosed or its practical utility, as in *Lightning Fastener Co.*[63] Overclaiming can result from claiming a monopoly over something disclosed in prior art or by using ambiguous terminology to describe the invention, in hopes that it will be construed favorably. In the application process, it is natural for an applicant to try to obtain as broad a monopoly as possible, but this comes with the inherent danger of claiming too much, which may result in a finding of anticipation. It is a difficult balancing act:

> [I]n many cases that an inventor is free to make his claims as narrow as he sees fit in order to protect himself from the invalidity which will ensue if he makes them too broad. From a practical point of view, this freedom is really quite limited because if, in order to guard against possible invalidity, some area is left open between what is the invention as disclosed and what is covered by the claims, the patent may be just as worthless as if it was invalid.[64]

A good statement of applicable principles is found in *Reliance Electric Industrial Co. v. Northern Telecom Ltd.*:[65]

> Plaintiffs are not entitled to claim broadly and then to introduce limitations into the claims in order to avoid the prior art. Counsel for the defendants cited many

---

[62] See *Crila Plastic Industries Ltd. v. Ninety-Eight Plastic Trim Ltd.* (1986), [1986] F.C.J. No. 425, 10 C.P.R. (3d) 226, 4 F.T.R. 165, 9 C.I.P.R. 237, 1986 CarswellNat 635 (Fed. T.D.), affirmed (1987), [1987] F.C.J. No. 1030, 18 C.P.R. (3d) 1, 81 N.R. 382, 16 C.I.P.R. 161, 1987 CarswellNat 735 (Fed. C.A.); *Therm-ionics Ltd. v. Philco Products Ltd.*, (sub nom. *Cutten-Foster & Sons Ltd v. Thermionics Ltd.*) [1943] S.C.R. 396, [1943] 3 D.L.R. 449, 3 C.P.R. 17 (S.C.C.); *Domtar Ltd. v. MacMillan Bloedel Packaging Ltd.* (1977), 33 C.P.R. (2d) 182 (Fed. T.D.), affirmed (1978), [1978] F.C.J. No. 906, 41 C.P.R. (2d) 182, 24 N.R. 85, 1978 CarswellNat 554 (Fed. C.A.).

[63] See *supra*, note 55 and compare with (1936), [1937] S.C.R. 36 (S.C.C.).

[64] *Burton Parsons Chemicals Inc. v. Hewlett-Packard (Canada) Ltd.*, *supra*, note 26.

[65] (1993), [1993] F.C.J. No. 132, 47 C.P.R. (3d) 55, (sub nom. *Reliance Electric Industrial Co. v. Northern Telecom Canada Ltd.*) 60 F.T.R. 208, 1993 CarswellNat 319 (Fed. T.D.), affirmed (1994), 55 C.P.R. (3d) 299 (Fed. C.A.). But see *Unilever PLC v. Procter & Gamble Inc.* (1995), [1995] F.C.J. No. 1005, 61 C.P.R. (3d) 499, 184 N.R. 378, 1995 CarswellNat 375 (Fed. C.A.).

authorities for this proposition and I will quote from her factum: Rand J. in *Noranda Mines Ltd. v. Minerals Separation North American Corp.* (1949), 12 C.P.R. 99 (S.C.C.), at page 199:

> ... we have a good example of the sort of thing mentioned by Earl Loreburn in *Natural Colour v. Bioschemes* (1915), 32 R.P.C. 256 at p. 266: 'Some of those who draft Specifications and Claims are apt to treat this industry as a trial of skill, in which the object is to make the Claim very wide upon one interpretation of it, in order to prevent as many people as possible from competing with the patentee's business, and then to rely upon carefully prepared sentences in the Specification which, it is hoped, will be just enough to limit the Claim within safe dimensions if it is attacked in Court.' As in *B.V.D. Co. v. Can. Celanese* [1937], 2 D.L.R. 481, S.C.R. 221, the claims are wide and general; and for the reasons there given, they cannot be restricted by the language of the disclosure.

Greene, M.R., in *Molins and Molins Machine Co., Ltd. v. Industrial Machinery Co., Ltd.* (1938), 55 R.P.C. 31 (C.A.), at page 39:

> But it is said that upon its true construction the claim must be read in a more limited sense in order to give effect to what is stated to be the sole object of the invention, namely, to remedy a defect which appears only at 'high speeds'. In other words, it is said that words must be imported into the claim limiting it to cases of what are called high speed machines, that is to say, machines capable of running at a high speed. That such a phrase, if it had appeared in the claim, might have been exposed to attack on the ground of ambiguity is, I think apparent; but I need not deal with that. It is sufficient for me to say that in my opinion there is no justification whatever for importing into the claim, drawn as it is in simple and direct language, a limitation extracted either from the language of the body of the specification or from the purpose at which the invention is aiming. It has been laid down over and over again that this method of construing a Patent Specification is inadmissible.

Lord Loreburn in *Ingersoll Sergeant Drill Co. v. Consolidated Pneumatic Tool Co.* (1908), 25 R.P.C. 61 (H.L), at page 83:

> The idea of allowing a patentee to use perfectly general language in the Claim and subsequently to restrict, or expand, or qualify what is therein expressed by borrowing this or that gloss from other parts of the Specification is wholly inadmissible.

Lord Russell of Killowen in *Electric and Musical Industries, Ld. et al. v. Lissen, Ld., et al.* (1938), 56 R.P.C. 23 (H.L), at page 41:

But I know of no canon or principle which will justify one in departing from the unambiguous and grammatical meaning of a claim and narrowing or extending its scope by reading into it words which are not in it; or which will justify one in using stray phrases in the body of a Specification for the purpose of narrowing or widening the boundaries of the monopoly fixed by the plain words of a claim.

Lord Justice Mark Romer in *British Hartford-Fairmont Syndicate, Ld. v. Jackson Bros. (Knottingley), Ld.* (1932), 49 R.P.C. 495 (H.L.), at page 556:

One may, and one ought to, refer to the body of the specification for the purpose of ascertaining the meaning of words and phrases used in the claims or for the purpose of resolving difficulties of construction occasioned by the claims when read by themselves. But where the construction of a claim when read by itself is plain, it is not, in my opinion, legitimate to diminish the ambit of the monopoly claimed merely because in the body of the Specification the Patentee has described his invention in more restricted terms than in the claim itself. The difference may well have been intentional, and created with the object - to use the words of Lord Loreburn in the Natural Colour Kinematrograph case -of holding in reserve a variety of constructions for use if the patent should be called in question, and in the meantime to frighten off those who might be disposed to challenge the patent.

Counsel for the defendants also noted that the above principles were cited with approval by Davis J. in *The B.V.D. Company, Limited v. Canadian Celanese Limited*, [1937] S.C.R. 221 , at page 237, by Thorson P. in *Lovell Mfg. Co. et al. v. Beatty Bros. Ltd.* (1962), 41 C.P.R. 18 (Ex. Ct.) , 34 and seq., and were quoted with approval by Urie J. of the Federal Court of Appeal in *Beecham Canada Ltd. v. Procter & Gamble Co.* (1982), 61 C.P.R. (2d) 1 at pages 8 - 11. In the case of *The B.V.D. Company, Limited v. Canadian Celanese Limited*, [1937] S.C.R. 221, at page 237, Davis J. stated:

In the Canadian patent involved in this appeal before us the inventor did not state in his claims the essential characteristic of his actual invention though it does appear in the claims in his British and United States patents. No explanation is offered. We are invited to read through the lengthy specification and import into the wide and general language of the claims that which is said to be the real inventive step disclosed. But the claims are unequivocal and complete upon their face. It is not necessary to resort to the context and as a matter of construction the claims do not import the context. In no proper sense can it be said that though the essential feature of the invention is not mentioned in the claims the process defined in the claims necessarily possesses that essential feature. The Court cannot limit the claims by simply saying that the inventor must have meant that which he has described. The claims in fact go far beyond the invention. Upon that ground the patent is invalid.

[. . .]

I think it is important, first of all, to set out my understanding of the law. The claims in a patent set out the invention on which the monopoly is claimed. A patentee obtains no monopoly on an invention which is described in the specifications if that invention is not claimed. Claims will often be more limited than the description of the invention contained in the body of the specification. I find it useful to refer to the oft-quoted explanation given by President Thorson in *Minerals Separation North Amer. Corpn. v. Noranda Mines Ltd.*, [1947] Ex.C.R. 306, at pages 352-3:

> By his claims the inventor puts fences around the fields of his monopoly and warns the public against trespassing on his property. His fences must be clearly placed in order to give the necessary warning and he must not fence in any property that is not his own. The terms of a claim must be free from avoidable ambiguity or obscurity and must not be flexible; they must be clear and precise so that the public will be able to know not only where it must not trespass by where it may safely go. If a claim does not satisfy these requirements it cannot stand. . . The inventor may make his claims as narrow as he pleases within the limits of his invention but he must not make them too broad. He must not claim what he has not invented for thereby he would be fencing off property which does not belong to him. It follows that a claim must fail if, in addition to claiming what is new and useful, it also claims something that is old or something that is useless.

The interpretation of the claims, and indeed of the patent as a whole, is a matter for the Court. The judge, in this regard, may be assisted by the evidence of an expert knowledgeable in the field. Such expert evidence may relate to matters such as the state of the act at the date of the patent, the meaning of technical terms and the working of the invention. When construing a patent, the claims are to be read in the context of the whole patent including the specifications and drawings. Overly technical interpretations should not defeat a patent claim. The patent should be given a purposive construction and be read with a mind willing to understand.

I find it useful to quote a summary of the law found in *Hughes and Woodley on Patents* (Butterworths, 1984) at page 390, paragraph 20:

> The specification of a patent is required to end with a claim or claims stating distinctively and in explicit terms the things or combinations that the applicant regards as new and in which he claims an exclusive property or privilege.

The claims define the scope of the monopoly and may be read with the disclosure in the earlier part of the patent in order to understand what the claims say, but it is the claims and claims alone that define the monopoly. The claims cannot be used to expand the invention as described in the disclosure.

The language in which a patentee has cast his claim has been referred to by the courts as a fence within which he claims protection from trespass and outside of which others are free to roam; whether infringement occurs depends on the final analyses on construction of the claim; if the claim is plain and unambiguous the courts are not to restrict or expend or qualify the scope of the invention by reference to the specification; resort to the specification is limited to assisting in comprehending the meaning of words or expressions contained in the claim but not to changing the meaning; a patent is to be construed as being addressed to a person killed in the art.

The claims must be looked at as if by a competent skilled workman at the date of the patent with a mind willing to understand and not by a mind desirous of misunderstanding. The Court should not be too astute or technical when construing claims, particularly in areas of insufficiency of description.

The nature of the invention must be found in the specification, and in particular, in the claim; they define the monopoly and are addressed to persons skilled in the art; the claims provide enlightenment as to what the invention really is, and define its scope, but the disclosure describes the invention. In construing a patent, the claims are the starting point. The claims alone define the statutory monopoly and the patentee has a statutory duty to state in the claims, what the invention is for which protection is sought. In construing the claims, recourse to the rest of the specification is: (1) permissible to assist in understanding the terms used in the claims; (2) unnecessary where the words are plain and unambiguous; and (3) improper to vary the scope or ambit of the claims.

(footnotes omitted)

A description of the applicable principles when construing claims, found in Goldsmith, *Patents of Invention* (Carswell, 1981), is also helpful (pages 222 - 223):

§221 The ambit or scope of the claims is a matter of law for the court. They must be supported by the disclosure, which must describe all the characteristics of an embodiment of the invention that arc set out in each claim respectively. The claims are to be construed with reference to the entire specification, and may thereby be limited in their scope. They are not to be read in any sense as isolated statements but are to be interpreted and explained in the light of the description contained in the body of the specification. This may have the effect either of validating a claim that would be too broad if considered apart from the limitations imposed upon it by the specifications, or of invalidating a claim by narrowing it down beyond the point of utility.

§222 But the principle that a claim is to be interpreted in the light of the description contained in the specification is not one of universal application and ought not to be applied in cases where a claim is expressed in simple and direct language or in wide or general terms whose mean is plain and unequivocal. If the words of the claim are plain and unambiguous it will not be possible to expand or limit their scope by reference to the body of the specification. But the specification must be considered in order to assist in comprehending and construing the meaning-and possibly the special meaning-in which the words or the expressions contained in the claims are used.

§223 In construing a technical term it is always proper and reasonable for a reader unfamiliar with the term to look at the specification to see whether the inventor has used it with a defined special meaning for the specification itself provides the dictionary by which the scope of effect of the terms in the claims are to be ascertained.

[footnotes omitted]

## 3. Utility

Another requirement that must be met in order to patent an invention is the utility test. It has two components: first, the invention must provide something of commercial or industrial usefulness and second, the patent must disclose an invention that works when put in practice according to the disclosure, as it would be understood and used by a person skilled in the art.[66] This requirement is known as operability. This second part of the test was explained as follows in *MacMillan Bloedel*,[67] where Dickson J., as he then was, explored the meaning of "not useful" in patent law. He said, quoting from *Halsbury's Laws of England*, (3rd ed.), vol. 29, at page 59:

---

[66] See *Reliable Plastics Ltd. v. Louis Marx & Co.* (1958), [1956-1960] Ex. C.R. 257, 29 C.P.R. 113 (Can. Ex. Ct.).

[67] *Supra*, note 56 at 525. See also *Goldfarb v. W.L. Gore & Associates Inc.* (2001), [2001] F.C.J. No. 208, 11 C.P.R. (4th) 129, 2001 CarswellNat 265 (Fed. T.D.), affirmed (2002), [2002] F.C.J. No. 1715, 23 C.P.R. (4th) 1, 298 N.R. 366, 2002 CarswellNat 4205 (Fed. C.A.), leave to appeal refused (2003), [2003] S.C.C.A. No. 39, 2003 CarswellNat 2038 (S.C.C.).

It means 'that the invention will not work, either in the sense that it will not operate at all or, more broadly, that it will not do what the specification promises that it will do'.

And in *X. v. Canada (Patent Commissioner)*:[68]

The test of utility of an alleged invention depends on whether by following the directions of the specification, the effects which the patentee professed to produce can be, in fact produced. In this application we are satisfied that which is described lacks utility because it is inoperable for the purpose for which it was designed.

The first part of the test may be viewed as a corollary of the characterization of patents as a contract between the inventor and the Crown, on behalf of "society" (see the Basic Principles Section). If the monopoly is the consideration from the inventor's viewpoint, the societal consideration is the disclosure of something of value in some way. This is also why the Patent Act requires a full disclosure of the invention (see in particular ss. 27(3) and (4)).

In *Northern Electric Co. v. Brown's Theatres Ltd.*,[69] the court stated this principle as follows:

An invention to be patentable must confer on the public a benefit. Utility as predicated of inventions means industrial value. No patent can be granted for a worthless art or arrangement. Here there is described and claimed something that lacks utility because it is inoperable for the purpose for which is was designed.

In the pharmaceutical area, *Tennessee Eastman Co. v. Canada (Commissioner of Patents)*[70] held that a product cannot be toxic at a therapeutic dosage for it fails the utility test.

There is no doubt that when a new substance is claimed as an invention of a 'medicine', it has to be shown that it is active and non-toxic in therapeutic doses. Otherwise the patent fails for lack of utility.

---

[68]  (1981), [1981] F.C.J. No. 1013, 59 C.P.R. (2d) 7, 46 N.R. 407, 1981 CarswellNat 740 (Fed. C.A.).

[69]  (1939), 1 C.P.R. 180 (Can. Ex. Ct.), affirmed [1941] S.C.R. 224, [1941] 2 D.L.R. 105, 1 C.P.R. 203 (S.C.C.). See also *Mailman v. Gillette Safety Razor Co.* (1932), [1932] S.C.R. 724, [1933] 1 D.L.R. 8 (S.C.C.).

[70]  (1972), [1974] S.C.R. 111, 33 D.L.R. (3d) 459, 8 C.P.R. (2d) 202 (S.C.C.).

In the same vein, a patent should not claim uses that impart no therapeutic value.[71]

*Burton Parsons Chemicals Inc. v. Hewlett-Packard (Canada) Ltd.*[72] is also relevant on that point. The Supreme Court held that the fact that one had to be a person skilled in the art in order to use the patent without causing harm did not render it non-useful.

The disclosure must include all essential elements of the invention to provide efficient use. Lack of an essential part of the invention would render the invention useless. Such was the case in *MacMillan Bloedel*.[73] If the patent fails to mention an essential component, the invention is not useful,[74] unless the failure concerns an element known in the art and obviously required for operability.[75]

Commercial success has been interpreted as a sign of usefulness,[76] and a lack thereof as a sign of non-usefulness.[77]

### (a) Sound Prediction

In certain cases, an applicant may be unable to state clearly that the invention is useful, but may be able to make a scientifically (or technologically) credible educated guess. In such cases, the doctrine of sound prediction may allow the applicant to meet the utility standard. In *Apotex Inc. v.*

---

[71] See *Société des usines chimiques Rhône-Poulenc v. Jules R. Gilbert Ltd.*, [1968] S.C.R. 950, 69 D.L.R. (2d) 353, 55 C.P.R. 207 (S.C.C.).

[72] *Supra*, note 26.

[73] *Supra*, note 56.

[74] See *Feherguard Products Ltd. v. Rocky's of B.C. Leisure Ltd.* (1994), [1994] F.C.J. No. 96, 53 C.P.R. (3d) 417, 72 F.T.R. 297, 1994 CarswellNat 1857 (Fed. T.D.), affirmed (1995), [1995] F.C.J. No. 620, 60 C.P.R. (3d) 512, 180 N.R. 346, 1995 CarswellNat 1908 (Fed. C.A.); and *Amfac Foods Inc. v. Irving Pulp & Paper Ltd.* (1986), [1986] F.C.J. No. 659, 12 C.P.R. (3d) 193, 72 N.R. 290, 9 C.I.P.R. 265, 1986 CarswellNat 637 (Fed. C.A.).

[75] See *Canadian Patent Scaffolding Co. v. Delzotto Entreprises Ltd.* (1978), 42 C.P.R. (2d) 7 (Fed. T.D.), affirmed on other grounds (1980), [1980] F.C.J. No. 117, 47 C.P.R. (2d) 77, 1980 CarswellNat 222 (Fed. C.A.), leave to appeal refused (1980), 47 C.P.R. (2d) 249 (S.C.C.).

[76] See *Prentice v. Dominion Rubber Co.*, [1928] Ex. C.R. 196 (Can. Ex. Ct.); *G. E. Prentice Manufacturing Co. v. Kenny*, [1931] Ex. C.R. 24, [1931] 2 D.L.R. 465 (Can. Ex. Ct.); and *Overend v. Burrow Stewart & Milne Co.* (1909), 19 O.L.R. 642 (Ont. C.A.).

[77] See *Electrolytic Zinc Process Co. v. French's Complex Ore Reduction Co.*, [1927] Ex. C.R. 94 (Can. Ex. Ct.), affirmed on other grounds [1930] S.C.R. 462, [1930] 4 D.L.R. 902 (S.C.C.).

*Wellcome Foundation Ltd.*,[78] the Supreme Court established the three elements of the doctrine of sound prediction:

> It was sufficient that at that time the Glaxo/Wellcome scientists disclosed in the patent a rational basis for making a sound prediction that AZT would prove useful in the treatment and prophylaxis of AIDS, which it did. For the Commissioner of Patents to have allowed Glaxo/Wellcome a patent based on speculation would have been unfair to the public. For him to have required Glaxo/Wellcome to demonstrate AZT's efficacy through the clinical tests required by the Minister of Health for approval of a new drug for medical prescription would have been unfair to Glaxo/Wellcome. The disclosure made in the patent was and is of real use and benefit to millions of HIV and AIDS sufferers around the world (irrespective of Glaxo/Wellcome's pricing policy for AZT, which it must be acknowledged has generated serious controversy in some countries, particularly in the developing world). The fact remains that Glaxo/Wellcome, by making the disclosure, has fulfilled its side of the bargain with the public, and is by law entitled to legal protection for what it has disclosed.
> [. . .]
>
> A patent, as has been said many times, is not intended as an accolade or civic award for ingenuity. It is a method by which inventive solutions to practical problems are coaxed into the public domain by the promise of a limited monopoly for a limited time. Disclosure is the *quid pro quo* for valuable proprietary rights to exclusivity which are entirely the statutory creature of the *Patent Act*. Monopolies are associated in the public mind with higher prices. The public should not be expected to pay an elevated price in exchange for speculation, or for the statement of 'any mere scientific principle or abstract theorem' (s. 27(3)), or for the 'discovery' of things that already exist, or are obvious. The patent monopoly should be purchased with the hard coinage of new, ingenious, useful and unobvious disclosures. The appellants' argument here is that the identification in March of 1985 of AZT as a treatment and prophylaxis for HIV/AIDS was a shot in the dark, a speculation based on inadequate information and testing, a lottery ticket for which the public in general and HIV and AIDS sufferers in particular have paid an exorbitant price. AZT works, but for reasons both unknown and unknowable by Glaxo/Wellcome at the time it filed its patent application, the appellants argue. A lucky guess is not, they say, patentable.
> [. . .]
>
> The *Patent Act* defines an 'invention' as, amongst other criteria, 'new and useful' (s. 2). If it is not useful, it is not an invention within the meaning of the Act.

---

[78] [2002] 4 S.C.R. 153, 219 D.L.R. (4th) 660, 21 C.P.R. (4th) 499, 296 N.R. 130 (S.C.C.) [*Wellcome Foundation* cited to S.C.R.].

It is important to reiterate that the only contribution made by Glaxo/Wellcome in the case of AZT was to identify a new use. The compound itself was not novel. Its chemical composition had been described 20 years earlier by Dr. Jerome Horwitz. Glaxo/Wellcome claimed a hitherto unrecognized utility but if it had not established such utility by tests or sound prediction at the time it applied for its patent, then it was offering nothing to the public but wishful thinking in exchange for locking up potentially valuable research turf for (then) 17 years. As Jackett C.J. observed in *Procter & Gamble Co. v. Bristol-Myers Canada Ltd.* (1979), 42 C.P.R. (2d) 33 (F.C.A.), at p. 39:

> By definition an 'invention' includes a 'new and useful process'. A 'new' process is not an invention unless it is 'useful' in some practical sense. Knowing a new process without knowing its utility is not in my view knowledge of an 'invention'.

Glaxo/Wellcome says the invention was complete when the draft patent application was circulated internally on February 6, 1985. Its argument here, as in the United States, was that the written description identified the drug and its new use sufficiently to give the invention 'definite and practical shape'. It taught persons skilled in the art how the invention could be practised. This, however, misses the point. The question on February 6, 1985 was not whether or how the invention could be practised. The question was whether AZT did the job against HIV that was claimed; in other words, whether on February 6, 1985, there was *any* invention at all within the meaning of s. 2 of the *Patent Act*.

Canadian case law dealing with inventorship has to be read keeping the particular factual context in mind. In *Christiani v. Rice*, [1930] S.C.R. 443, this Court held, *per* Rinfret J. (as he then was), at p. 454:

> . . . for the purpose of section 7 [now s. 27] 'it is not enough for a man to say that an idea floated through his brain; he must at least have reduced it to a definite and practical shape before he can be said to have invented a process'. [Emphasis added in original]

The claimed invention in that case was a process for manufacturing porous cement. The utility of porous cement was not in dispute. The question was how to make it, and who was the first to invent the process. In this case, Dr. Horwitz taught everyone how to make AZT. The question was what could usefully be done with it. In *Ernest Scragg & Sons Ltd. v. Leesona Corp.*, [1964] Ex. C.R. 649, Thorson P. held that if the invention related to an apparatus or process, it was sufficient if the apparatus had actually been built or the process used. The invention in that case was for 'Thermoplastic Yarns and Methods of Processing Them' (p. 659). AZT had been compounded and used in 1964, but not by Glaxo/Wellcome, and not in relation to HIV/AIDS. The invention claimed here related entirely to the new and hitherto unexpected use. Glaxo/Wellcome also cites *Owens-Illinois Inc. v. Keohring Waterous Ltd.* (1980), 52 C.P.R. (2d) 1 (F.C.A.), (leave to the Supreme Court of Canada refused, [1980] 2 S.C.R. ix), which dealt with an invention to harvest and process trees in the middle of a forest. The utility was obvious. The invention lay in the machine and its operation. Glaxo/Wellcome also relied upon two Canadian appeals to the Privy Council for the proposition that 'proof of utility is not required for there to be an invention' (factum para. 45): *Permutit Co. v. Borrowman*, [1926] 4 D.L.R. 285 (P.C.), and *C. G. E. Co. v. Fada Radio Ltd.*, [1930] 1 D.L.R. 449 (P.C.). In neither case was utility in doubt. *Permutit* dealt with a process for softening water and *Fada Radio* dealt with a radio tuning device. There may in such cases be some doubt about the commercial success of the invention, but utility in this context means useful for the purpose claimed, not commercial acceptance.

In the present case, by contrast, if the utility of AZT for the treatment of HIV/AIDS was unpredictable at the time of the patent application, then the inventors had not made an invention and had offered nothing to the public in exchange for a 17-year monopoly except wishful thinking.

Where the new use is the *gravamen* of the invention, the utility required for patentability (s. 2) must, as of the priority date, either be demonstrated or be a sound prediction based on the information and expertise then available. If a patent sought to be supported on the basis of sound prediction is subsequently challenged, the challenge will succeed if, *per* Pigeon J. in *Monsanto Co. v. Commissioner of Patents*, [1979] 2 S.C.R. 1108, at p. 1117, the prediction at the date of application was not sound, or, irrespective of the soundness of the prediction, '[t]here is evidence of lack of utility in respect of some of the area covered'.

3. The Limits of Sound Prediction

The evidence accepted by the trial judge showed that by March 16, 1985, Glaxo/Wellcome had sufficient information about AZT and its activity against HIV in human cells to make a sound prediction that AZT would be useful in the treatment and prophylaxis of HIV/AIDS in human beings. To the extent its claims went beyond the limits within which the prediction remained sound (e.g., in claiming treatment for human retroviruses other than HIV), the Federal Court properly struck them out.

Although the trial judge did not consider the doctrine of 'sound prediction' to be applicable in this sort of case, he seems to have applied it nevertheless when he decided that the claims did not exceed the invention, starting at para. 108. He also seems to have applied it when he upheld the patent claims for prophylaxis as well as treatment. At para. 292 he pointed out, in that connection, that 'demonstrated utility or reduction to practice is not a requirement under Canadian patent law' (emphasis added in original). Lack of <u>demonstrated</u> utility does not obviate the need for sound prediction.

The doctrine of sound prediction seems to have had its genesis in a comment by Lord MacDermott in *May & Baker Ltd. v. Boots Pure Drug Co.* (1950), 67 R.P.C. 23 (H.L.), at p. 50 (where, however, he rejected its application on the facts). It was connected to the requirement that the claims be 'fairly based' on the patent disclosure: *In re I. G. Farbenindustrie A. G.'s Patents* (1930), 47 R.P.C. 289 (Ch. D.), at pp. 322-23. The principle of 'fair basis' was later explicitly incorporated into the British *Patents Act, 1949,* 1949, c. 87, ss. 4(3) and 32(1)(*i*). While these specific provisions were repealed in 1977, the 'fair basis' doctrine seems still to be a force in British patent law; see Lord Hoffman in *Biogen Inc. v. Medeva PLC* , [1997] R.P.C. 1 (H.L.).

The doctrine of 'sound prediction' was given serious shape and substance by Graham J. in *Olin Mathieson Chemical Corp. v. Biorex Laboratories Ltd.* , [1970] R.P.C. 157 (Ch. D.). In that case the proposition was framed as follows, at p. 182:

> If it is really possible, according to the evidence, to make a sound prediction about a certain area, then prima facie it would be reasonable that the patentee should have a claim accordingly. . . .

The doctrine was explicitly received into our law in *Monsanto, supra.* In that case, the Court was confronted with a patent that included claims to numerous chemical compounds to inhibit premature vulcanization of rubber, but only three of the claimed compounds had actually been prepared and tested before the date the application was filed. The examiner rejected the claims to the untested compounds, holding that ''broad product claims must be adequately supported by a sufficient number of [tested] examples'' (p. 1111). The rejection was upheld by the Patent Appeal Board and the Federal Court, but this Court reversed on the basis that the 'architecture of chemical compounds' was no longer a mystery but, within limits, soundly predictable. Pigeon J. thus wrote, at pp. 1118-19:

> Although the report of the Board is quite lengthy, in the end with respect to claim 9 all it says after stating the principle with which I agree, is that a claim has to be restricted to the area of <u>sound prediction</u> and 'we are not satisfied that three specific examples are adequate'. As to why three is not enough nothing is said. In my view this is to give no reason at all in a matter which is not of speculation but of exact science. We are no longer in the days when the architecture of chemical compounds was a mystery. By means of modern techniques, chemists are now able to map out in detail the exact disposition of every atom in very complex mole-cules. It, therefore, becomes possible to ascertain, as was done in *Olin Mathieson*, the exact position of a given radical and also to relate this

position to a specific activity. It thus becomes possible to predict the utility of a substance including such radical. [Emphasis added in original]

Pigeon J. found persuasive a line of British patent cases including the decisions of the House of Lords in *May & Baker Ltd. & Ciba Ltd.'s Letters Patent*, *supra*, and *Mullard Radio Valve Co. v. Philco Radio & T.V. Corp. of Great Britain* (1936), 53 R.P.C. 323, as well as the Chancery Division judgment in *Olin Mathieson, supra*. Pigeon J. adopted a number of propositions stated by Graham J. in *Olin Mathieson*, a case dealing with claims to certain chemical derivatives for pharmaceutical use as tranquillizers, in their entirety, at pp. 1116-17:

> Where, then, is the line to be drawn between a claim which goes beyond the consideration and one which equiparates with it? In my judgment this line was drawn properly by Sir Lionel when he very helpfully stated in the words quoted above that it depended upon whether or not it was possible to make a sound prediction. If it is possible for the patentee to make a sound prediction and to frame a claim which does not go beyond the limits within which the prediction remains sound, then he is entitled to do so. Of course, in so doing he takes the risk that a defendant may be able to show that his prediction is unsound or that some bodies falling within the words he has used have no utility or are old or obvious or that some promise he has made in his specification is false in a material respect; but if, when attacked, he survives this risk successfully, then his claim does not go beyond the consideration given by his disclosure, his claim is fairly based on such disclosure in these respects, and is valid. [Emphasis added in original]

Adopting this admirably concise formulation, Pigeon J. drew the following conclusion at p. 1117:

> I have quoted again the passage quoted by the [Patent Appeal] Board because I consider the last sentence of the paragraph of some importance as it does clearly indicate what is meant by a 'sound prediction'. It cannot mean a certainty since it does not exclude all risk that some of the area covered may prove devoid of utility. It thus appears to me that the test formulated by Graham J. involves just two possible reasons for rejecting claims such as those in issue.
>
> 1.   There is evidence of lack of utility in respect of some of the area covered; [or]
> 2.   It is not a sound prediction. [Emphasis added in original]

Our Federal Court of Appeal subsequently applied the doctrine of 'sound prediction' in the context of a patent for a pharmaceutical product in *Ciba-Geigy AG v. Commissioner of Patents* (1982), 65 C.P.R. (2d) 73. In that case,

Thurlow C.J. upheld product and process claims in relation to certain 'new amines' useful in cardiac treatment, but added the qualification that what is predictable chemically may not be predictable pharmacologically, at p. 77:

> The predictability of a particular result seems to me to be essentially a question of fact, though in some situations it may be a matter of common knowledge. With respect to chemical reactions it is apparent from the foregoing that knowledge in the chemical art as to the predictability of chemical reactions has advanced considerably in the 50 years since *Chipman Chemicals Ltd. v. Fairview Chemical Co. Ltd.*, [1932] Ex. C.R. 107, was decided. The predictability of chemical reactions should not, however, be confused with predictability of the pharmacological effects and thus of the pharmacological utility of new substances. [Emphasis added in original]

Thurlow C.J. was not laying down as a matter of law that pharmacological utility cannot be predicted because, as he said, predictability is 'essentially a question of fact'. It will depend on the evidence. In *Beecham Group v. Bristol Laboratories Ltd.*, [1978] R.P.C. 153 (H.L.), for example, claims in respect of a semi-synthetic penicillin were invalidated as being little more than an announcement of a research project (p. 570). In that case, on the facts, Lord Diplock stated at p. 579:

> The evidence in the instant case is overwhelming that it is not yet possible to predict in advance what, if any, special therapeutic advantages will be possessed by a penicillin made to a particular formula. The only way to find out is to make it and discover what its therapeutic characteristics are by conducting extensive tests upon it *in vitro* and *in vivo*.

However, where, as here, the trial judge accepts on the evidence that the inventors *could* in fact make a sound prediction that an old compound (AZT) offers a hitherto unexpected utility in the treatment and prophylaxis of HIV/ AIDS, then (and only then) does their disclosure of 'the invention' offer real consideration for the monopoly benefits they seek.

The doctrine of 'sound prediction' balances the public interest in early disclosure of new and useful inventions, even before their utility has been verified by tests (which in the case of pharmaceutical products may take years) and the public interest in avoiding cluttering the public domain with useless patents, and granting monopoly rights in exchange for misinformation.
[. . .]

The doctrine of sound prediction has three components. Firstly, as here, there must be a factual basis for the prediction. In *Monsanto* and *Burton Parsons*, the factual basis was supplied by the tested compounds, but other factual underpinnings, depending on the nature of the invention, may suffice. Secondly, the inventor must have at the date of the patent application an articulable and 'sound' line of reasoning from which the desired result can be inferred from the factual basis. In *Monsanto* and *Burton Parsons*, the line of reasoning was grounded in the known 'architecture of chemical compounds' (*Monsanto*, at p. 1119), but other lines of reasoning, again depending on the subject matter, may be legitimate. Thirdly, there must be proper disclosure. Normally, it is sufficient if the specification provides a full, clear and exact description of the nature of the invention and the manner in which it can be practised: H. G. Fox, *The Canadian Law and Practice Relating to Letters Patent for Inventions* (4th ed. 1969), at p. 167. It is generally not necessary for an inventor to provide a theory of *why* the invention works. Practical readers merely want to know that it does work and how to work it. In this sort of case, however, the sound prediction is to some extent the *quid pro quo* the applicant offers in exchange for the patent monopoly. Precise disclosure requirements in this regard do not arise for decision in this case because both the underlying facts (the test data) and the line of reasoning (the chain terminator effect) were in fact disclosed, and disclosure in this respect did not become an issue between the parties. I therefore say no more about it.

It bears repetition that the soundness (or otherwise) of the prediction is a question of fact. Evidence must be led about what was known or not known at the priority date, as was done here. Each case will turn on the particularities of the discipline to which it relates. In this case, the findings of fact necessary for the application of 'sound prediction' were made and the appellants have not, in my view, demonstrated any overriding or palpable error.

## 4. Non-Obviousness

What is obvious? This is the question that patent application examiners and that courts faced with challenges to the validity of patents must answer frequently. It is perhaps the most difficult of the patent criteria to define and apply.

The non-obviousness test is now enshrined in the Act.[79] Section 28.3 reads as follows:

> The subject-matter defined by a claim in an application for a patent in Canada must be subject-matter that would not have been obvious on the claim date to a person skilled in the art or science to which it pertains, having regard to
>
> (*a*)   information disclosed more than one year before the filing date by the

---

[79] It was a deemed requirement in earlier jurisprudence. See *DeFrees v. Dominion Auto Accessories Ltd.* (1963), (sub nom. *De Frees v. Dominion Auto Accessories Ltd.*) [1964] Ex. C.R. 331, 44 C.P.R. 74 (Can. Ex. Ct.), affirmed [1965] S.C.R. 599, 47 C.P.R. 12 (S.C.C.).

applicant, or by a person who obtained knowledge, directly or indirectly, from the applicant in such a manner that the information became available to the public in Canada or elsewhere; and

(b)    information disclosed before the claim date by a person not mentioned in paragraph (a) in such a manner that the information became available to the public in Canada or elsewhere.

The threshold for of non-obviousness, also referred to in its "positive" version as the "inventive step" or ingenuity,[80] should not be put too high. "The test for obviousness is not whether anyone skilled in the art could have achieved the same result, but whether this particular invention would have been very plain to the unimaginative technician."[81] Very few inventions are unexpected discoveries. Practically all research work is done by looking in directions where the state of the art points.[82] Simplicity should not be mistaken for obviousness.[83] Moreover, it is easy in hindsight to overestimate how "obvious" something was at the time of invention.

Hugessen J.A.'s description of the concept of non-obviousness in *Beloit Canada Ltée/Ltd. v. Valmet Oy*[84] is perhaps the best in Canadian jurisprudence to date:

---

[80]    See *Cabot Corp. v. 318602 Ontario Ltd.* (1988), 20 C.P.R. (3d) 132 (Fed. T.D.). The determination whether an invention is obvious is sometimes referred to as the "Cripps" question. See *Creations 2000 Inc. v. Canper Industrial Products Ltd.* (1988), [1988] F.C.J. No. 656, 22 C.P.R. (3d) 389, 22 F.T.R. 180, 21 C.I.P.R. 87, 1988 CarswellNat 601 (Fed. T.D.), affirmed (1990), [1990] F.C.J. No. 1029, 34 C.P.R. (3d) 178, 124 N.R. 161, 1990 CarswellNat 1033 (Fed. C.A.):
"The test for inventiveness known as the 'Cripps question', which asks whether the invention was obvious to the man skilled in the art, in the light of the state of knowledge of the art, should be asked in Canada at the date of the invention. Although inventiveness may be presumed to exist where an invention has been a commercial success, it must be borne in mind that needs created through advertising and commercial success may be due to factors other than inventive ingenuity. The present invention demonstrated mechanical skill rather than inventiveness, and the patent under scrutiny was invalid for obviousness or lack of inventiveness."

[81]    *Bayer AG v. Apotex Inc.* (1995), 60 C.P.R. (3d) 58 (Ont. Gen. Div.), additional reasons at (1995), 62 C.P.R. (3d) 1 (Ont. Gen. Div.), affirmed (1998), (sub nom. *Bayer Aktiengesellschaft v. Apotex Inc.*) 82 C.P.R. (3d) 526 (Ont. C.A.), leave to appeal refused (1999), 84 C.P.R. (3d) v (S.C.C.).

[82]    *Farbwerke Hoechst A.G. Vormals Meister Lucius & Bruning v. Halocarbon (Ontario) Ltd.*, [1979] 2 S.C.R. 929, 104 D.L.R. (3d) 51, 42 C.P.R. (2d) 145, 27 N.R. 582 (S.C.C.).

[83]    See *Summers v. Abell* (1869), 15 Gr. 532 (U.C. Ch.); and *Overend v. Burrow Stewart & Milne Co.* (1909), 19 O.L.R. 642 (Ont. C.A.).

[84]    (1986), [1986] F.C.J. No. 87, 8 C.P.R. (3d) 289, (sub nom. *Beloit Can. Ltée/Ltd.*

The test for obviousness is not to ask what competent inventors did or would have done to solve the problem. Inventors are by definition inventive. The classical touchstone for obviousness is the technician skilled in the art but having no scintilla of inventiveness or imagination; a paragon of deduction and dexterity, wholly devoid of intuition; a triumph of the left hemisphere over the right. The question to be asked is whether this mythical creature (the man in the Clapham omnibus of patent law[85]) would, in the light of the state of the art and of common general knowledge as at the claimed date of invention, have come directly and without difficulty to the solution taught by the patent. It is a very difficult test to satisfy.
[. . .]

While the evidence of experts is, in my view, properly admissible even on an 'ultimate issue' question such as obviousness, it seems to me that it must be treated with extreme care.

Every invention is obvious after it has been made, and to no one more so than an expert in the field. Where the expert has been hired for the purpose of testifying, his infallible hindsight is even more suspect. It is so easy, once the teaching of a patent is known, to say, 'I could have done that'; before the assertion can be given any weight, one must have a satisfactory answer to the question, 'Why didn't you?'

In *Wessel v. Energy Rentals Inc.*,[86] Snider J. used this test and clarified some of the practical elements to be taken into account by the Court:

A helpful description of the skilled technician that this Court and experts giving evidence in this proceeding must contemplate when considering an allegation of obviousness was provided by Justice Hugessen for the Federal Court of Appeal in *Beloit Canada Ltd. v. Valmet Oy*. . .This test has been widely mentioned and followed by this Court.

---

v. *Oy*) 64 N.R. 287, 7 C.I.P.R. 205, 1986 CarswellNat 588 (Fed. C.A.), leave to appeal refused (1986), 69 N.R. 80 (note) (S.C.C.) [*Beloit Canada* cited to C.P.R.]. As of late 2004, the decision had been followed in at least 35 other Canadian cases, including *Diversified Products Corp. v. Tye-Sil Corp.* (1991), 35 C.P.R. (3d) 350 (Fed. C.A.).

[85] A British expression meaning a reasonable person or proverbial "man on the street" [footnote added].

[86] (2004), [2004] F.C.J. No. 952, 32 C.P.R. (4th) 315, 253 F.T.R. 279, 2004 CarswellNat 5614 (F.C.) [*Wessel* cited to C.P.R.]. See also *Procter & Gamble Pharmaceuticals Canada Inc. v. Canada (Minister of Health)* (2004), [2004] F.C.J. No. 374, 32 C.P.R. (4th) 224, 2004 CarswellNat 2894 (F.C.), affirmed (2004), 37 C.P.R. (4th) 289 (F.C.A.), leave to appeal refused (2005), 2005 CarswellNat 939 (S.C.C.).

In the case before me, I must determine whether a mythical skilled oilfield service technician would be led, based on the state of the art, to the claimed invention without conducting further experiments, serious thought or research (*Farbwerke Hoechst A.G. Vormals Meister Lucius & Bruning v. Halocarbon (Ontario) Ltd.* (1979), 42 C.P.R. (2d) 145 (S.C.C.), at 155; *Diversified Products Corp. v. Tye-Sil Corp.* (1991), 35 C.P.R. (3d) 350 (Fed. C.A.), at 365 -366; *SmithKline Beecham Pharma Inc. v. Apotex Inc.* (2001), 14 C.P.R. (4th) 76 (Fed. T.D.), at 99 -101, aff'd (2002), 291 N.R. 168 (Fed. C.A.)). Further, '[i]t is well-established that evidence of a 'mere scintilla of invention' is sufficient to support the validity of a patent.' (*Diversified Products, supra*). Therefore, the simplicity of an invention is not a bar to patent validity.

The invention before me is undeniably simple. However, its apparent simplicity does not lead inextricably to the conclusion that the Westmen trailer is obvious and not worthy of a patent. In my view, there are a number of factors that support a conclusion of inventiveness, in spite of the simplicity of the unit.

1. No prior similar units: Prior to the Westmen trailer, there were no trailers with this design being used in the industry. As stated by a number of the witnesses, prior to the invention, the power swivel equipment was shipped in a balanced fashion on the trailer, allowing no room for the drill collars. As a result, a second trailer or a much larger skid-mounted unit was required, thereby adding substantial cost to the transportation of these units. With the introduction of the trailer, Westmen was able to offer a better overall contract price for use of the power swivel unit. Mr. Scott Biluk and Mr. Dale Rangen, current or former employees of Energy Rentals, both acknowledged that the Westmen trailer was the first such unit that they had seen. Mr. Biluk went so far as to agree that he got the idea for the Energy Rentals trailer after he had seen the Westmen trailer in operation.

2. Commercial success: A factor that can support inventiveness is the commercial success of the invention. (*Diversified Products, supra*). And, Mr. Wessel's invention showed immediate commercial success. Within a very short time, he had 12 Westmen trailers on the road operating widely in Alberta and Saskatchewan. In one significant example, all of the producers in Brooks who had used his company's services converted to the use of the Westmen trailers.

3. Solution not 'plain as day': To be obvious, an invention must be 'plain as day' or 'crystal clear' (*Bayer AG v. Apotex Inc.* (1995), 60 C.P.R. (3d) 58 (Ont. Gen. Div.), at 80 -81, affirmed (1998), 82 C.P.R. (3d) 526 (Ont. C.A.); leave to appeal dismissed, (1999), [1998] S.C.C.A. No. 563 (S.C.C.)). That description does not fit the Westmen trailer. Mr. Wessel did not come easily to the invention; he designed and fabricated the trailer over a period of time hiding out in his workshop to prevent prying eyes from seeing the development of his invention. Mr. Neil McKay appeared as an expert. His expertise was uncontested and includes significant experience in regard to motor vehicle operation

and roadworthiness. He has spent over 30 years practising in his fields of expertise in Alberta. His testimony was that it would be 'very unusual' to mount permanently mounted equipment on one side of a trailer as opposed to both sides. He agreed that most of the time when people are designing a trailer 'they design it with permanently mounted equipment to be balanced without any additional load'.

4. 'Imitation is the sincerest flattery': Mr. Wessel, in 1998, had a falling out with one of his clients who had been using the Westmen trailer. This client, as explained by Mr. Biluk, approached Energy Rentals and said that he would contract with the company to use such a unit if they had one. From that request, Energy Rentals formed a team whose task was to develop a similar unit. Mr. Rangen acknowledged during cross examination that the goal of the team was to 'get around' Mr. Wessel's patent. After significant effort, the first Energy Rentals unit was placed on the road. The company built three more such units and acquired 9 more in a corporate acquisition. As with the Westmen trailers, these units are commercially successful. Leaving aside until later in this decision the question as to whether the Energy Rentals trailer infringes, the mere fact that the competitor took steps to copy the unit is indicative of the inventiveness of the Westmen trailer.

In summary, the Westmen trailer was an invention that was not intuitive, that took significant time and effort to develop, that demonstrated immediate commercial success and that was copied by a competitor. Cumulatively, the effect of these factors is 'simply irresistible' (*Beloit, supra,* at p. 296); the patent was inventive and not obvious.

The distinction between novelty and non-obviousness is important. When a patent is applied for, one must consider the prior art for two reasons: first the invention must be new (as of the relevant date — see the Novelty Section), which means that it must not have been disclosed in its entirety (i.e., all its essential elements) in a *single element* of prior art (prior patent, publication, etc.). Second, the invention must be non-obvious. Non-obviousness is judged by considering *all* of the relevant prior art and the question to ask is whether the average person skilled in the art concerned, if asked to solve the problem or find the solution that the inventor was searching for, would have found the solution disclosed in the application (or the patent if issued) obvious (at the relevant date as defined in s. 28.3, which, for Canadian applicants, is one year prior to the Canadian filing date). To quote again from Hugessen J.A. in *Beloit Canada Ltd. v. Valmet Oy* for a classic formulation of the difference between novelty and non-obviousness:[87]

---

[87] *Supra*, note 84.

While at times the trial Judge appears to be conscious of the need to keep the issues of obviousness and anticipation well distinct, there are a number of places, of which the phrase quoted in the preceding paragraph is an example, in which he seems to confound them. They are, of course, quite different: obviousness is an attack on a patent based on its lack of inventiveness. The attacker says, in effect, 'Any fool could have done that.' Anticipation, or lack of novelty, on the other hand, in effect assumes that there has been an invention but asserts that it has been disclosed to the public prior to the application for the patent. The charge is: 'Your invention, though clever, was already known.'

## III. APPLICATION

According to s. 27(1) of the Patent Act, the Commissioner shall grant a patent for an invention *to the inventor.* Much controversy can arise in determining who the inventor is.

## 1. The Inventor

Who is the inventor? It is the person who solves the problem and not the one who poses the problem. Merely presenting a problem to another person for a solution is not an act of "inventorship".[88] Maclean J.'s findings in *Gerrard Wire Tying Machines Co. v. Cary Manufacturing Co.* contain a good statement of the law:[89]

> Mr. Anglin very ably and ingenuously put forward the contention that a person who conceives an invention, and who is in a position if and when he chooses to produce a physical embodiment of his mental conception, is in law an inventor in this country. Mr. Anglin of course conceded that such a person might have great difficulty in establishing his invention by satisfactory evidence, but in this case he thought that difficulty had been overcome by Cary on the facts already related. This calls for some discussion as the contention is often advanced here. I cannot accept Mr. Anglin's proposition, as expressing the law, even with the evidence of the alleged, inventor as to the conception being accepted as proven, nor can I agree that a 'physical embodiment' of the conception, which was never disclosed would void the patent of a subsequent inventor who had first and effectively disclosed his invention. It must be

---

[88] *Procter & Gamble Co. v. Kimberly-Clarke of Canada Ltd.* (1991), [1991] F.C.J. No. 1273, 40 C.P.R. (3d) 1, (sub nom. *Procter & Gamble Co. v. Kimberly-Clark of Canada Ltd. (No. 4)*) 49 F.T.R. 31, 1991 CarswellNat 215 (Fed. T.D.) at 4 [C.P.R.].

[89] [1926] Ex. C.R. 170 (Can. Ex. Ct.) at 180-2. See also *Comstock Canada v. Electec Ltd.* (1991), [1991] F.C.J. No. 987, 38 C.P.R. (3d) 29, 45 F.T.R. 241, 1991 CarswellNat 207 (Fed. T.D.) [*Comstock Canada* cited to C.P.R.].

conceded I think, without qualification, that a mere conception of anything claimed to be an invention, that is concealed and never disclosed or published, is not an invention that would invalidate a patent granted to a subsequent inventor. To say that mere conception is invention or that a first inventor in the popular sense who has not communicated or published his invention is entitled to priority over a later invention accompanied by publication, and for which a patent was granted, or applied for, would I think throw this branch of our jurisprudence into such utter confusion as to render the law of little practical value owing to uncertainty. If this is the policy and meaning of the Patent Act, an inventor might safely withhold from the public his invention for years, while another independent but subsequent inventor of the same thing, who had secured or applied for a patent, and who had proceeded to manufacture and sell his invention without any knowledge of the undisclosed invention, would always be in danger if the prior inventor could secure a patent by merely proving an unpublished invention. The situation should not I think be changed by the production of drawings, plans, etc., evidencing the date of the prior invention, or even a physical embodiment of the invention by the alleged inventor. All this might be done and still be within the knowledge of the inventor alone, it having been kept a secret, and which so far as the public is concerned is no more effective publication than a mere conception uncommunicated to the public. There must be a publication or a use in public of a satisfactory kind in order to bar the claim of a subsequent inventor who discloses the same and first applies for a patent. The latter act is not perhaps necessary. What is publication is a question of fact, and each case must depend upon its own circumstances.

[. . .]

*It seems to me that the first inventor must and should mean in patent law, not the first discoverer or the first to conceive, but the first publisher, and publication is always a question of fact. That person must, however, be a true inventor, that is he must not have borrowed it from anyone else.* This principle was laid down in Great Britain by the courts there as early as 1776, and is there still accepted as expressing the law. In the case where a person who was first granted a patent was not in popular language the first inventor because somebody had invented it before him, but had not taken out a patent for it, it has been decided that the former was entitled to a grant provided the invention of the first inventor had been kept secret, or without being actually kept a secret had not been made known in such a way as to become part of the common knowledge or of the public stock of information. Therefore, the person who was in law held to be the first and true inventor was not so in popular language because one or more people had invented before him, but had not sufficiently disclosed it. *Plympton v. Malcolmson*, [1876] 3, Ch. Div. 531, at pp. 555, 556; *Dollonds Patent*, [1766] 1 W.P.C. 43; *Cornish v. Keene*, [1835] 1 W.P.C. 501; *Smith v. Davidson*, [1857] 19 Court of Sessions 691 at p. 698 (2nd Series); *Robertson v. Purdy*, [1906] 24 R.P.C. 273 at P. 290, *ex parte Henry*, [1872] 8 Chan. App. 167. While the general principles may be subject to qualification, depending upon the facts involved in any particular case, it seems to me they should he applied in this case. [. . .]

There is another point to which I must briefly refer. Mr. Anglin contended that there was not joint invention by Gerrard and Wright of the invention claimed by the plaintiff because an important part of the invention claimed was made by one of them only, and that the claim to joint invention in fact failing the application for a patent cannot in law be considered. The evidence satisfies me that both Gerrard and Wright had constantly been conferring together on the development of the shouldered wire and the appropriate machine with which to use it. I think the proper view in this connection is well stated in Walker on Patents, 5th Ed. at Sec. 46, which is as follows:

> Nor is a patent to joint inventors invalidated by the fact that one of them only first perceived the crude form of the elements and the possibility of their adaption to complete the result desired. In fact the conception of the entire device may be attributed to one, but if the other makes suggestions of practical value, which assist in working out the main idea and making it operative, or contributes an independent part of the entire invention which helps to create the whole, he is a joint inventor even though his contribution be of minor importance.[90]

As to whether failing to name one or more co-inventors in the application may invalidate the patent, it seems that the answer is negative, unless the omission is wilfully made for the purpose of misleading. By s. 53(1) and (2), a patent is void if any material allegation is untrue and the omission or addition is wilfully made for the purpose of misleading. In *Wellcome Foundation*,[91] the Supreme Court of Canada held that the names of the inventors can be "material" allegations under this section, but an error in inventors' names would invalidate the patent only if the omission or addition is wilfully made for the purpose of misleading.

> The trial judge concluded that Drs. Broder and Mitsuya were co-inventors, but that failure to include them in the patent was not a material misrepresentation that would invalidate the patent. In reaching this conclusion, he referred to the observation of Addy J. in *Procter & Gamble Co. v. Bristol-Myers Canada Ltd.* (1978), 39 C.P.R. (2d) 145 (F.C.T.D.) at p. 157 that 'it is really immaterial to the public whether the applicant is the inventor or one of two joint inventors as this does not got [*sic*] to the term or to the substance of the invention nor

---

[90] See also *Procter & Gamble Co. v. Bristol-Myers Canada Ltd.* (1978), 39 C.P.R. (2d) 145 (Fed. T.D.), affirmed (1979), [1979] F.C.J. No. 405, 42 C.P.R. (2d) 33, 28 N.R. 273, 1979 CarswellNat 798 (Fed. C.A.), leave to appeal refused (1979), 42 C.P.R. (2d) 33n (S.C.C.) [*Bristol-Myers* cited to C.P.R.].

[91] *Supra*, note 78.

even to the entitlement' (aff'd (1979), 42 C.P.R. (2d) 33 (F.C.A.)). At an earlier date, Thurlow J. had suggested in *Jules R. Gilbert Ltd. v. Sandoz Patents Ltd.* (1970), 64 C.P.R. 14 (Ex. Ct.), at p. 74, rev'd (on other grounds) *Sandoz Patents Ltd. v. Gilcross Ltd.* (1972), [1974] S.C.R. 1336, that 'allegations in the petition respecting anything other than the subject-matter of the claims in the patent as granted are not material'.

The appellants argue that, while as Addy J. says, it may be that the identity of the inventor is immaterial to the public in most instances, this is not necessarily true in all cases. Here, for example, the issue of 'entitlement' to the rewards of the AZT patent has created a significant public controversy. There were arguably important public policy ramifications to the issue of co-inventorship because of the contrasting mandates, objectives and funding sources of the institutions involved, in particular the NIH and the Glaxo/Wellcome corporate group. If indeed the NIH researchers had been 'co-inventors', and the NIH or the U.S. government had therefore held an ownership interest in the patent, there potentially could have been a significant effect on both the access to and the cost of the drug AZT across the world.

There is no need to consider the issue of materiality further in this case however, not only because of the conclusion that Drs. Broder and Mitsuya were not in fact co-inventors in this case, but also because there is no evidence whatsoever that the omission to name them was 'wilfully made for the purpose of misleading', as required by the concluding words of s. 53(1).

There are cases where one person thinks of something new but does not see its potential application. If someone else uses that idea and turns it into something useful, he or she will be considered the inventor because that person is responsible for the "invention." He or she must have reduced the invention to a definite and practical shape.[92] In other words, the inventor is the person who understands the utility of the invention, because patent law rewards the disclosure not of scientific achievements but of something useful:[93]

> Dr. Armstrong did not 'know' the invention in question in 1952 because he did not learn from his tests that fabrics could be satisfactorily conditioned in the dryer. By definition an 'invention' includes a 'new and useful process'. See s. 2 of the Patent Act. A 'new' process is not an invention unless it is 'useful' in some practical sense. Knowing a new process without knowing its utility is not in my view knowledge of an 'invention'. It follows that the learned

---

[92] See *Rice v. Christiani & Nielsen*, [1930] S.C.R. 443 (S.C.C.), affirmed [1931] A.C. 770 (Canada P.C.) at 454 [S.C.R.].

[93] *Bristol-Myers, supra*, note 90 at para 22 (Fed. C.A.). In this case, the utility was adding a conditioning agent to sheets to condition clothes in the dryer.

Judge's finding on the facts is a finding that amounts, in law, to a finding that Dr. Armstrong did not 'know' the invention in 1952.

## 2. Employees

If the inventor is an employee, the patent belongs to his or her employer if he or she was hired to invent and if he or she was hired to invent this type of thing or object for the employers' benefit. In *Comstock Canada*,[94] Muldoon J. provided a good overview of relevant cases and applicable principles, not without a certain element of dramatization:

> In relation to employees' inventions the general principle was established in *Bloxam v. Elsee*, (1825) 1 C. & P. 558 at p. 564, 171 E.R. 1316; *Bolxam v. Elsee* (1827) 6 B. & C. 169, 108 E.R. 415, where it was held by Lord Tenterdon that if a servant, while in the employ of his master, makes an invention, that invention belongs to the servant, not to the master; though if the master employs a skilful person for the express purpose of inventing, the inventions made by him will belong to the master so as to enable him to obtain the patent for them. [. . .]
>
> Is what the Comstock parties seek to do not akin to slavery? They seek to appropriate Hyde's work without paying any compensation. True enough, Hyde was not kept detained in bondage. He did not then know of the employer's intent to appropriate his work. Had he known, he most probably would have left his employer, as he was free to do. It is no less an unremunerated appropriation of Hyde's work just for the fact that it was attempted after his departure. What Comstock would accomplish if it were to deprive Hyde of his work and his property in his invention without agreed upon remuneration, would be the essence of slavery. Only the ancillary bondage would be missing, including the minions or instruments of intimidation for bondage and detention. Slavery, in effect, without overhead. That cannot be permitted.
>
> Electec and Hyde submit that the mere existence of an employer-employee relationship does not *per se* disqualify an employee from patenting for his own benefit an invention made by him during the course of his employment, even although the invention's subject-matter may be useful for his employers in their business. This is so, even although the employee may have made use of his employer's time and co-employees and material bringing his invention to completion and he may have allowed the employer to use the invention while in their employment: *Piper v. Piper* (1904), 3 O.W.R. 451 at 455 (C.A.); *Willards Chocolates Ltd. v. Bardsley* (1928), 35 O.W.N. 92 at 93 (H.C.J.);

---

[94] *Supra*, note 89. See also *Spiroll Corp. v. Putti* (1975), 64 D.L.R. (3d) 280, 22 C.P.R. (2d) 261 (B.C. S.C.), affirmed (1976), 77 D.L.R. (3d) 761, 29 C.P.R. (2d) 260 (B.C. C.A.).

*Spiroll v. Putti* (1975), 22 C.P.R. (2d) 261, 64 D.L.R. (3d) 280, [1975] W.W.D. 126 (B.C.S.C.); aff'd 29 C.P.R. (2d) 260, 77 D.L.R. (3d) 761, [1976] W.W.D. 150 (B.C.C.A.). The Court in *Willards Chocolates Ltd. v. Bardsley* gave judgment in the employer's favour. In *Fox, opt. cit.*, at pp. 302-03, it is stated that the Court there applied U.S.A. doctrine not acceptable in Canada. In footnote 161 on p. 303 is the assertion that the decision was obviously arrived at, on this point at least, *per incuriam.*

The only exceptions to the presumptions which favour the inventive employee, are: (1) an express contract to the contrary; or (2) where the person was employed for the express purpose of inventing or innovating: *Re Equator Mfg. Co., Ex p. Pendlebury*, [1926] 1 D.L.R. 1101 at 1105, 7 C.B.R. 472 29 O.W.N. 473 (S.C. in Bcky); *Devoe-Holbein Inc. v. Yam* (1984), 3 C.P.R. (3d) 52 at p. 67, 2 C.I.P.R. 229 (Que. S.C.); *Scapa Dryers (Canada) Ltd. v. Fardeau* (1971), 1 C.P.R. (2d) 199 (Que. S.C.) at p. 204; *W.J. Gage Ltd. v. Sugden* (1967), 51 C.P.R. 259, 62 D.L.R. (2d) 671, [1967] 2 O.R. 151 (H.C.J.); *Spiroll Corp. v. Putti.* Although a more senior employee may have a duty of good faith toward his employer, this notion alone does not impede the employee from claiming that the invention is his own. The Court should consider the nature and context of the employer-employee relationship, such as:

(a)    whether the employee was hired for the express purpose of inventing;
(b)    whether the employee at the time he has hired had previously made inventions;
(c)    whether an employer had incentive plans encouraging product development;
(d)    whether the conduct of the employee once the invention had been created suggested ownership was held by employer;
(e)    whether the invention is the product of the problem the employee was *instructed* to solve, i.e. whether it was duty to make inventions;
(f)    whether the employee's invention arose following his consultation through normal company channels (i.e. was help sought?);
(g)    whether the employee was dealing with highly confidential information or confidential work;
(h)    whether it was a term of the servant's employment that he could not use the ideas which he developed to his own advantage.

Counsel for the defendants, in his memorandum of fact and law, sets out the law in England, where, in the absence of a special contract, the invention of a servant, even though made in the employer's time and with the use of the employer's materials and at the expense of the employer, does not become the property of the employer.

However, when an employee hired *because of his inventive skills* creates something *in the ordinary course of his duties* so to create, the rights to an invention belong to the employer unless there is an agreement to the contrary. An abundant jurisprudence was cited to the Court in this regard, among which are: *Worthington Pumping Engine Co. v. Moore* (1903), 20 R.P.C. 41 (Ch. D.); *Edisonia Ltd. v. Forse*, (1908) 25 R.P.C. 546 (Ch. D.); *Mellor v. William Beardmore & Co.*, (1927) 44 R.P.C. 175 (Scotland C.A.); *Adamson v. Kenworthy, supra* (Ch. D.); *Vokes Ltd. v. Heather*, (1945) 62 R.P.C. 135 (C.A.); Leave to appeal to House of Lords denied; *Re Selz Ltd.'s Application* (1953), 71 R.P.C. 158; *Patchett v. Sterling Engineering Co.* (1955), 72 R.P.C. 50.

Caution must be exercised in applying this principle as was expressed in *Spiroll v. Putti*, a masterful review of jurisprudence performed by Mr. Justice Mc-Kenzie. He noted (at p. 273) that English jurisprudence has moved toward the U.S. view which tends to favour the employer as against the employee, thus: 'So there are two strains of cases - the older giving the rights to the employee unless the contrary is shown and the House of Lords gives the benefit to the employer unless the contrary is shown.' McKenzie J. then, upon analyzing the texts, noted (at p. 274): 'I read all of the cases discussed so far to have that message in common. In none of them do I find the notion that the mere fact of employment *ipso facto* obligates the employee to deliver up his invention to his employer.'

The trial judgment of McKenzie J. was unanimously upheld by the British Columbia Court of Appeal. Mr. Justice Robertson for that Court is reported (at p. 256-6) as follows:

> [I]t was no part of Putti's duty to make inventions . . . Putti was not employed as a designer or inventor.

> Such being the case, the rule applicable is the one stated in the same case [*Sterling Engineering Co. Ltd. v. Patchett*, [1955] A.C. 534, 72 R.P.C. 50 (H.L.)] by Lord Reid at p. 547, *viz.*, 'in the ordinary case the benefit of an invention belongs to the inventor'. To the same effect is the language of Eve, J. in *British Reinforced Concrete Engineering Co. Ltd. v. Lind*, (1917) 34 R.P.C. 101, that is quoted at the foot of p. 160 in *W.J. Gage Ltd. v. Sugden, supra*.

> With respect to the second proposition, I have in my passage numbered 3 already said all that I usefully can. In summary it is that, as under the employment contract Superior has no right to the invention and Putti must stand as its sole owner, no equitable right of ownership in Superior can be distilled from the relationship created by the contract. Further, even if that were not so, the facts do not support any finding that Putti's conduct was inconsistent with the good faith that he owed to Superior, or otherwise such as to make him a trustee of the invention for Superior or its assignee.

> I think that McKenzie J., was right and I would dismiss the appeal.

In the case at bar Hyde was open about his after-hours business carried on in Electec's name. It is extreme 'double-think' and nonsense to label Electec's insistent payment of the tooling invoice and dealings with Noma as fraud or any less species of duplicity on Hyde's part. On the contrary it was plain openness. Further, Barber snorted that he did not hire Hyde to be going about inventing.

The mere fact that an inventor held a senior position in a company at the time he invented does not deprive the inventor of his rights to the invention if that is not what he was hired to do: *Anemostat (Scotland) Ltd. v. Michaelis*, [1957] R.P.C. 167.

Where an individual, hired as a general manager of a design and manufacturing company, as a result of information gathered on a business trip sponsored by the employer, conceives and invents a design that might be used in association with the business of his employer, ownership of the invention is held by the employee. In determining the nature and scope of employment, where there is no written contract of employment, regard may be had to the wording of the newspaper advertisement seeking applicants for that position: *Re Selz Ltd.'s Application, supra*, at pp. 162-166 (per Lloyd-Jacob J. on appeal).

Comstock submits that it is an implied term in a contract of employment that any employee is a trustee for his employer of any invention made in the course of his duty as an employee, unless such an implied term is displaced by contrary agreement having legal effect. The meaning of implied term in this context is a term which is inherent in the nature of the contract which the law will imply unless the parties agree otherwise. Not so in Canada. The *Spiroll* case states the law. There is no such presumption permitting an employer to claw out of an employee's hand, without compensation, the fruits of his labour just by virtue of his employment. If the U.S. and English jurisprudence show such tendencies, so be it. In Canada, the law first looks, of course, to discover if the parties have concluded an objectively provable or reasonably inferred agreement about inventions. If there be no objectively proved agreement, as here, then the circumstances of the employment could indicate the correct result, by inference. Since Governor Simcoe, and later, however, the presumption in Canada operates in the direction of freedom, not slavery. In the absence of reliable *indicia*, the inventor keeps the benefit of the invention.

Comstock's counsel further posits that the level of an employee's duty of good faith to the employer is dependent upon the position of the employee within the employer's organization and the degree of responsibility and trust placed unto the employee. A manager's position is radically different from that of a mechanic (tradesman); a manager has a fundamental or fiduciary duty to extend all of his effort, skill, knowledge and inventive powers, in whatever way possible, to promote the efficiency and success of his employer and does not need to be specially directed or encouraged to do so.

*Worthington Pumping Engine Company v. Moore, supra,* at p. 49; *Edisonia Ltd. v. Forse, supra,* at pp. 550, 551 (last paragraph) and 552 (last paragraph); *Canadian Aero Service Limited v. O'Malley* (1973), 11 C.P.R. (2d) 206 at pp; 217-8 and 221-8, 40 D.L.R. (3d) 371, [1974] S.C.R. 592; *MacMillan Bloedel Ltd. v. Binstead* (1983), 22 B.L.R. 255 at p. 285, 14 E.T.R. 269, 20 A.C.W.S. (2d) 87 (B.C.S.C.).

Further, says Comstock, it is contrary to the utmost duty of good faith required of management employees for such an employee to usurp, for the employee's own private profit, a corporate opportunity which has been pursued and developed by the employer. This is particularly acute where the employee promoted or encouraged the employer to pursue and develop such opportunity. Equity demands, in modern commerce, that corporations, its promoters, directors and managers exercise obedience to norms of exemplary behaviour.

[. . .] In *Canadian Aero Service,* at p. 219, it is stated that 'the fiduciary relationship goes at least this far':

> . . .a director or a senior officer like O'Malley or Zarzycki is precluded from obtaining for himself, either secretly or without the approval of the company (which would have to be properly manifested upon full disclosure of the facts), *any property or business advantage* either *belonging to the company* or *for which it has been negotiating,* and especially is this so where the director or officer is a participant in the negotiations on behalf of the company.

> In my opinion, this ethic disqualifies a director or senior officer from usurping for himself or diverting to another person or company with whom or with which he is associated a maturing *business opportunity which his company is actively pursuing,* he is also precluded from so acting even after his resignation where the resignation may fairly be said to have been prompted or influenced by a wish to acquire for himself the opportunity sought by the company, or *where it was his position with the company rather than a fresh initiative* that led him to the opportunity which he later acquired.

> (Emphasis not in original text.)

Finally, the Court expressed a note of caution reported on p. 391 in the *Canadian Aero Service* case - that which is sometimes forgotten by counsel:

> In holding that on the facts found by the trial Judge, there was a breach of fiduciary duty by O'Malley and Zarzycki which survived their resignations I am not to be taken as laying down any rule of liability to be read as if it were a statute. The general standards of loyalty, good faith and avoidance of a conflict of duty and self-interest to which the conduct

of a director or senior officer must conform, must be tested in each case by many factors which it would be reckless to attempt to enumerate exhaustively. Among them are the factor of position or office held, the nature of the corporate opportunity, its ripeness, its specificness and the director's or managerial officer's relation to it, the amount of knowledge possessed, the circumstances in which it was obtained and whether it was special or, indeed, even private, the factor of time in the continuation of fiduciary duty where the alleged breach occurs after termination of the relationship with the company, and the circumstances under which the relationship was terminated, that is whether by retirement or resignation or discharge.

There are many substantial dissimilarities between this case at bar and the *Canadian Aero Service* case. Hyde was perhaps a 'senior officer' of Comstock, having been Manager, electrical department, Eastern Ontario Division at Comstock's office in Nepean, Ontario. Barber certainly never hired Hyde to design anything, and of course Comstock's business was that of an electrical contractor and, as the evidence discloses, most assuredly not a manufacturer or distributor of electrical fixtures, for its management wished to avoid any responsibility or liability in that regard. So Hyde on the one hand, and O'Malley and Zarzycki on the other were and are quite differently situated. Hyde had incorporated Electec long before he was employed by Comstock, and clearly not as a late-created vehicle in which to grab Comstock's business. If Hyde is alleged to have behaved surreptitiously in hiding Electec's existence from Barber, then Hyde went about it with less stealth than the proverbial bull in a china shop. Barber knew all along: he now regrets his lack of interest or his wilful blindness. On this, as on so many other matters herein when Hyde and Barber diverge in testimony the Court for all of the classical reasons accepts Hyde's testimony over Barber's. In cross-examination Hyde evinced some prickliness of temperament, but that did, and does, nothing to diminish his credibility whatsoever. Indeed that minor and infrequent demeanour enhanced the inherent plausibility of Hyde's testimony. In any event, the *Canadian Aero Service* judgment, which is not to be read like a statute, does not tell or toll against Hyde or Electec. No fiduciary duty was breached.
[. . .]

There was nothing secret about Hyde's conduct: he deceived no one. Electec was Hyde's corporation and his interest in it was no secret. Moreover, quite distinct from hiding his involvement, Hyde was insisting that Comstock and Noma recognize Electec and that Noma emboss Electec's name on the products invented and designed by Hyde. Binstead's flagrant, although purportedly secret and exposed, misbehaviour in the *McMillan Bloedel* case above cited does not tell against Hyde. Rather, it shows by contrast how open and above-board Hyde truly was, in all his dealings with, and apart from, Comstock, Barber, Dods, Noma and Drew. In light of the credible evidence here, policies and professional engineering handbooks and treatises count for nothing against

Hyde's professional or corporate conduct. To be sure they do count for something, but not against Hyde in these circumstances. These circumstances, given Comstock's diffidence about doing anything other than contracting, are rather akin to those in *Peso Silver Mines v. Cropper*, [1966] S.C.R. 673, 58 D.L.R. (2d) 1.

Upon review of all of the parties' material, the written arguments and the transcripts, as well as the exhibits, the Court is, after verifying references to testimony, exhibits and jurisprudence, persuaded to accept, ratify and adopt the oral and written arguments stated by Hyde's counsel.

Employers who rely on the existence of an employer-employee relationship run the risk that the presumption that the invention belongs to the actual inventor, namely the employee, will be used against them. It is only when employees are employed to invent and are employed because of their relevant skills that the employer can reasonably assume he or she will be the owner of the invention. Employers should seek to obtain in advance assignments of rights to inventions from their employees using valid and enforceable contracts. For inventions already invented, the same rule applies. It may be appropriate for an employer to agree in the contract to share some of the revenues generated by the invention with the employee/inventor.

### 3. Disclosure

A patent is a form of a contract providing protection in exchange for full disclosure:

> The description of the invention therein provided for is the *quid pro quo* for which the inventor is given a monopoly for a limited term of years on the invention. As Fox points out in *Canadian Patent Law and Practice* (4th ed.), p. 163, the grant of a patent is in the nature of a bargain between the inventor on the one hand and the Crown, representing the public, on the other hand. The consideration for the grant is twofold: 'first, there must be a new and useful invention, and secondly, the inventor must, in return for the grant of a patent, give to the public an adequate description of the invention with sufficiently complete and accurate details as will enable a workman, skilled in the art to which the invention relates, to construct or use that invention when the period of the monopoly has expired'.[95]

A few things must thus be present in the application. Section 27(3) of the Act states the requirements:

---

[95] *MacMillan Bloedel, supra*, note 56.

27(3) The specification of an invention must:

a)   correctly and fully describe the invention and its operation or use as contemplated by the inventor;

b)   set out clearly the various steps in a process, or the method of constructing, making, compounding or using a machine, manufacture or composition of matter, in such full, clear, concise and exact terms as to enable any person skilled in the art or science to which it pertains, or with which it is most closely connected, to make, construct, compound or use it;

c)   in the case of a machine, explain the principle of the machine and the best mode in which the inventor has contemplated the application of that principle; and

d)   in the case of a process, explain the necessary sequence, if any of the various steps, so as to distinguish the invention form other inventions.

The specification thus should fulfill two purposes: first, correctly and fully describe the invention so that at the end of the patent term a person skilled in the art who follows the instructions should be able to make use of the invention to produce the results that the invention is said to achieve; and second, state distinctly what the applicant regards as new and to which the applicant is claiming exclusive patent rights, so that the scope of the monopoly is clearly defined and others know the extent of the exclusive rights claimed. The monopoly cannot be larger than what the patent applicant claims is the "invention."

When writing a claim for a patent, some drafters often attempt to widen the scope of protection by using vague and ambiguous language. However, courts have little patience with this strategy. The House of Lords in *Natural Colour Kinematograph Co. v. Bioshemes Ltd.* indicated that nothing could excuse the use of ambiguous language when simple language could have been used.[96] These comments have been reiterated in several Canadian decisions. For example, in *Minerals Separation North American Corp. v. Noranda Mines Ltd.*,[97] the Privy Council noted:

> The law as to ambiguity is clear and their Lordships need only refer to a well known passage in the speech of Lord Loreburn in *Natural Colour Kinematograph Co. Ltd. v. Bioschemes Ltd.* (1915), 32 R.P.C. 256 where he says
>
> > It is the duty of a patentee to state clearly and distinctly, either in direct words or by clear and distinct reference, the nature and limits of what he

---

[96] (1915), 32 R.P.C. 256 (U.K. H.L.).

[97] (1952), 15 C.P.R. 133, 69 R.P.C. 81 (Canada P.C.). See also *R. v. Uhlemann Optical Co.* (1951), [1952] 1 S.C.R. 143, 15 C.P.R. 99 (S.C.C.); and *Burton Parsons Chemicals Inc. v. Hewlett-Packard (Canada) Ltd.*, reversed (1974), [1976] 1 S.C.R. 555 (S.C.C.).

claims. If he uses language which, when fairly read, is avoidably obscure or ambiguous, the Patent is invalid, whether the defect be due to design, or to carelessness or to want of skill. Where the invention is difficult to explain, due allowance will, of course, be made for any resulting difficulty in the language. But nothing can excuse the use of ambiguous language when simple language can easily be employed, and the only safe way is for the patentee to do his best to be clear and intelligible.

In Canada the requirements with regard to a specification are statutory. The relevant statute in this case is the *Patent Act, 1923*. Section 14(1) of that statute enacted with regard to a specification 'It shall end with a claim or claims stating distinctly the things or combinations which the applicant regards as new and in which he claims an exclusive property and privilege.' It was not argued that the law of Canada is less stringent than the law of the United Kingdom with regard to ambiguity of a claim.

## IV.  TERM OF PROTECTION

The protection term is set forth in s. 44 of the *Patent Act*. It provides a term of 20 years for patents filed on or after October 1st 1989. Prior to that date, the protection term was for 17 years. S. 44 should be read in conjunction with s. 55(1) and (2), which read as follows:

55(1) A person who infringes a patent is liable to the patentee and to all persons claiming under the patentee for all damage sustained by the patentee or by any such person, after the grant of the patent, by reason of the infringement;

(2) A person is liable to pay reasonable compensation to a patentee and to all persons claiming under the patentee for any damage sustained by the patentee or by any of those persons by reason of any act on the part of that person, after the application for the patent became open to public inspection under section 10 and before the grant of the patent, that would have constituted an infringement of the patent if the patent had been granted on the day the application became open to public inspection under that section.

The exclusive right of the patentee thus emerges fully only after the grant of the patent, not the filing date (or claim date if applicable). Because pending applications remain secret during the first eighteen months after filing (see s. 10), the patentee essentially has no right to enforce during that period since the *quid pro quo* of public disclosure in exchange for the limited monopoly is not fulfilled. Filing the application will protect his or her right as the first filer (against other potential inventors) and will start the examination process, hopefully leading to a grant. The principle that a patentee has no right during the "secret" period is expressed in respect of government-owned patents in s. 20(15).[98] There is an intermediate phase, namely the period of unknown duration between the opening of the application for inspection and the grant. During that period, third parties (here used in the sense of anyone not authorized by the patentee or by law) are on notice: they can read the application. They know the extent of the monopoly that may be granted to the applicant. However, there is no certainty that the patent will issue or that it will be granted as claimed. During that interim period, which may last several years but usually lasts between 12 and 24 months, those third parties do not have to pay "all damage" on accounting of profits (see the Remedy Section), but rather a reasonable compensation. The obligation applies "provided the patent is ultimately granted";[99] the Act uses the word "patentee" in s. 55(2) to make that clear.[100] It would be illogical to give an applicant a cause of action for a patent not yet issued, which he or she may never have if the patent does not issue. It would also constitute an incentive for applicants to delay the final decision in order to provide them with this separate cause of action.[101]

## V. INFRINGEMENT

### 1. Generally

A patent gives to the patentee the "exclusive right, privilege and liberty of making, constructing and using the invention and selling it to others to be used, subject to adjudication in respect thereof before any court of competent jurisdiction" (s. 42).

Section 43 of the Act provides that a patent is presumed valid "in the absence of any evidence to the contrary."[102] The presumption is rebuttable but any defendant trying to invalidate a patent has the burden of proof. The

---

[98] Certain applications may be kept secret for a period longer than the 18 months of regular applications (under s. 10) if certified as such by the Minister of National Defence (see ss. 20(7) to (9)).

[99] *Free World Trust v. Électro Santé Inc., supra,* note 19.

[100] The "patentee" as defined in s. 2 is "the person for the time being entitled to the benefit of the patent." See *671905 Alberta Inc. v. Q'Max Solutions Inc.* (2003), 27 C.P.R. (4th) 385 (Fed. C.A.), leave to appeal refused (2004), 30 C.P.R. (4th) vii (S.C.C.).

[101] See *Stamicarbon B.V. v. Urea Casale S.A.,* [2002] 3 F.C. 347, 17 C.P.R. (4th) 377 (Fed. C.A.), leave to appeal refused (2002), 303 N.R. 400 (note) (S.C.C.).

[102] See *Merck Frosst Canada Inc. v. Canada (Minister of National Health & Welfare)* (1998), 80 C.P.R. (3d) 110 (Fed. T.D.), additional reasons at (1998), 80 C.P.R. (3d) 575 (Fed. T.D.), affirmed (1999), (sub nom. *Merck Frosst v. Canada (Minister of National Health & Welfare)*) 86 C.P.R. (3d) 489 (Fed. C.A.).

presumption is a reflection of the fact that a patent is issued by the Commissioner after a thorough examination by an expert examiner and that decision is presumed to be well founded. For that reason, it is very difficult to invalidate a patent once it has been granted on issues that were already decided upon by the examiner, such as non-obviousness or utility, unless evidence can be adduced to show that the examiner's decision was based on flawed data. In *Ernest Scragg & Sons Ltd. v. Leesona Corp.*,[103] Thorson J. explained it as follows:

> The evidence required to rebut the presumption must be more than 'some evidence'. It must be credible evidence and substantial enough to satisfy the Court that the patent is invalid. In my opinion, the presumption of validity created by the section remains in effect unless the party attacking the patent shows to the satisfaction of the Court that it is invalid. Thus the section does impose on the party attacking the patent for invalidity the onus of showing that it is invalid and, in my opinion, the onus so imposed is not an easy one to discharge.

Courts are less reluctant to intervene in declaring a patent or part thereof (only certain claims of a patent can be invalidated) for anticipation, *i.e.*, lack of novelty, if the party alleging anticipation can bring to the court's attention an element of prior art not considered by the examiner.[104] In such a case, the court can place itself in the examiner's shoes instead of reviewing a decision already made. The standard of review is significantly different. If a person other than the patentee believes there is an element of prior art that the Office should have considered, it can also request a reexamination pursuant to s. 48.1.

### (a) Claim Construction Principles

Claim construction, a question of law, precedes the legal analysis of both validity and infringement. But the claims receive the "same interpretation for all purposes." The method and approach to claims construction invokes important policy considerations since the patentee asserts exclusive rights in the claims and from that language others should be able to predict what is "fenced off." In determining whether one or more claims of a patent

---

[103] [1964] Ex. C.R. 649, 45 C.P.R. 1, 26 Fox Pat. C. 1 (Can. Ex. Ct.) [*Scragg* cited to Ex. C.R.]; see also *Diversified Products Corp. v. Tye-Sil Corp.* (1991), 35 C.P.R. (3d) 350, 125 N.R. 218 (Fed. C.A.).

[104] Once a patent has been granted, anyone can obtain a copy of the application file cover or "wrapper", showing the actions taken by CIPO and the elements of prior art considered during the examination process.

have been infringed, courts must choose a method to interpret the language used in the claims, which delimit the extent of the patentee's monopoly:

> Patent claims are frequently analogized to 'fences' and 'boundaries', giving the 'fields' of the monopoly a comfortable pretence of bright line demarcation. Thus, in *Minerals Separation North American Corp. v. Noranda Mines Ltd.*, [1947] Ex. C.R. 306 (Can. Ex. Ct.), Thorson P. put the matter as follows, at p. 352:
>
>> By his claims the inventor puts fences around the fields of his monopoly and warns the public against trespassing on his property. His fences must be clearly placed in order to give the necessary warning and he must not fence in any property that is not his own. The terms of a claim must be free from avoidable ambiguity or obscurity and must not be flexible; they must be clear and precise so that the public will be able to know not only where it must not trespass but also where it may safely go.
>
> In reality, the 'fences' often consist of complex layers of definitions of different elements (or 'components' or 'features' or 'integers') of differing complexity, substitutability and ingenuity. A matrix of descriptive words and phrases defines the monopoly, warns the public and ensnares the infringer. In some instances, the precise elements of the 'fence' may be crucial or 'essential' to the working of the invention as claimed; in others the inventor may contemplate, and the reader skilled in the art appreciate, that variants could easily be used or substituted without making any material difference to the working of the invention. The interpretative task of the court in claims construction is to separate the one from the other, to distinguish the essential from the inessential, and to give to the 'field' framed by the former the legal protection to which the holder of a valid patent is entitled.[105]

One could adopt a literal reading on the basis that any monopoly should be interpreted restrictively and that any difference, however minute, between the language of the claim and the defendant's product or process is sufficient to avoid a finding of infringement. Historically, this approach was used in a number of cases.[106]

In Canada, a second approach known as the "purposive" or substantive construction, also known as the "teleological method" (from the Greek "teleos," which can be translated as "purpose") is preferred. The Supreme Court of Canada made it clear in *Whirlpool Corp. v. Camco Inc.*:[107]

---

[105] *Free World Trust, supra*, note 19, Binnie J.

[106] See note 15 and accompanying text.

[107] [2000] 2 S.C.R. 1067, 194 D.L.R. (4th) 193, 9 C.P.R. (4th) 129, 263 N.R. 88 (S.C.C.), reconsideration refused (2001), 2001 CarswellNat 283 (S.C.C.) [*Whirlpool* cited to S.C.R.].

In 1975, the respondent Whirlpool Corporation announced to the world an advance in clothes washing technology which the trial judge described as 'entirely new'. The nub of the improvement was to replace the traditional one-piece 'agitator' in the wash tub with a two-piece agitator consisting of a lower oscillating spindle with a rotating 'auger' attached to the top. By all accounts the two-piece 'dual action' agitator produced a more effective wash ('uniform scrubbing'). Whirlpool introduced these useful machines onto the North American market in the 1970s, and over the years sold millions of units to the clothes washing public. General Electric ('GE') and Maytag were somewhat envious of this invention, but moved quickly on expiry of the U.S. patents in 1995 to put their own dual action agitators on the market. Between 1995 and the date of trial, GE had sold in excess of 750,000 dual action machines. The respondents' complaint is that the appellants' machines were not only marketed in the United States but some of them were sold in Canada where the relevant patents had not yet expired.

The development work at Whirlpool resulted in three patents. Each, when issued, gave Whirlpool a 17-year monopoly[108] on manufacturing and marketing washing machines that incorporated the inventions as respectively claimed. The consumer market for large appliances is immense and this appeal brought together some of the major competitors for the purpose of alternatively denouncing or upholding the relevant patents owned by Whirlpool. The appellants say that the first two patents to issue covered the invention, and that the monopoly was improperly extended by the issuance of the third patent (which at trial they were held to have infringed). The third patent, the appellants say, ought for the most part never to have been granted and is to that extent invalid.

The practical impact of this argument is that if the most recent patent is invalid, the period of infringement is reduced by more than two years, and the compensation payable to Whirlpool would be greatly diminished. The appeal raises some important legal issues concerning the interpretation, validity and infringement of patents, but in the end, the appellants' case largely comes apart on the evidence (or lack of it) and the appeal must therefore be dismissed.

I. Facts

In the late 1960s, GE and its Canadian subsidiary, Camco marketed a range of washing machines across Canada that utilized what was known as a single action agitator, that is to say a single spindle sitting in a tub of water rotating its vanes back and forth to scrub the clothes. Similar machines were marketed by the respondents Whirlpool and Inglis, and by the appellants in the companion appeal, Maytag Corporation and its Canadian subsidiaries. The U.S. laboratories of the parent companies were at work trying to develop products that would give what advertising agencies call a 'new and improved wash' to heavy

---

[108] This was the term of protection issued prior to October 1, 1989. See s. 44.

household loads. Progress was uneven. Much research was done at Whirlpool and other manufacturers on the benefits of rigid vanes on the agitator versus flexible vanes (sometimes called 'flex vanes'). In the late 1960s, Whirlpool built a washer with flexible vanes for development purposes that mauled the clothes so badly it became known as 'the Golden Gobbler'. Maytag however developed a 'flex vane' unitary action machine in the late 1960s and the trial judge noted the evidence that '[i]t's been nothing but a satisfactory device' over the next 30 years ((1997), 76 C.P.R. (3d) 150, at p. 182). It did not tangle clothes unduly and was a great commercial success. By the end of the 1960s, the clothes washing machine trade in North America was thus familiar with one-piece agitators featuring rigid or flexible vanes, and understood that the 'yield' in the flex vanes could deliver an extra push to the laundry load to produce a better scrub. Indeed, the evidence was that Maytag obtained a 50 percent increase in wash loads by using flexible vanes rather than rigid vanes.

Eventually, Whirlpool came up with an ingenious dual action agitator that utilized the bottom portion of the shaft for the usual oscillating motion back and forth in the wash cycle, but added an upper sleeve that was designed to work as a helical auger. The auger rotated only in one direction like a post-hole digger, and propelled water and clothing downwards onto the oscillating vanes of the lower agitator which sent the laundry into a rollover tumble across the floor of the tub, upward along the side wall, thence back across the surface to the agitator (the 'toroidal motion').
[. . .]

## 2. The Claims in Suit

The '803 patent taught a double action agitator with a drive system which the trial judge described as 'unique'. There was no drive shaft. The upper part of the agitator was driven off the lower part by means of a clutch. Claim 1 sets out the broad description of the claimed monopoly as follows:

> 1. An agitator for a washing machine having a driven oscillating shaft, said agitator comprising: a first agitator portion capable of being mounted on said shaft by means of a locked, non-rotating connection and having an upper part, and a lower part provided with outwardly extending substantially vertically oriented vanes; a second agitator portion in the form of a sleeve having at least one outwardly extending, inclined vane, said sleeve being rotatably mounted on the upper part of the first agitator portion; and a one-way clutch located between the first and second agitator portions, the first agitator portion being adapted to drive said clutch and the second agitator portion being adapted to be driven by said clutch so that the rotation of the first agitator portion gives a positive rotation to the second agitator portion in only one direction of rotation of the first agitator portion, said inclined vane being inclined upwardly with respect to the direction of positive rotation of the second agitator

portion, and at least the lower parts of said vertically oriented vanes extending radially outwardly by a greater amount than said at least one inclined vane. [Emphasis added in original]

The abstract of the patent refers to an 'accessory comprising a sleeve which is securable to the barrel of the agitator ... having a vane means attachable thereto' (emphasis added). Further, a portion of the '803 disclosure talks about an 'agitator accessory ... easily removable from the agitator itself' (emphasis added). However, the claims themselves do not refer to the agitator sleeve as being either 'securable' or removable, and it is the claims, not the rest of the specification, that define the monopoly.

At trial, the respondents and appellants were agreed that the GE machines with flex vanes were covered by the '803 patent. They agreed that the only unresolved infringement issue under the '803 patent was whether or not 'the element identified as a 'sleeve'' was removable. As will be seen, the trial judge disagreed with both sides on the issue of claims construction. He concluded that the '803 technology as claimed employed rigid vanes only.

The appellants were also accused of infringing the '734 patent which explicitly stated that the vanes of the lower oscillator of the dual action agitator were flexible rather than rigid. The '734 patent disclosed the new 'continuous drive' claims. Claim 1 set out the broad monopoly claim as follows:

1. An agitator assembly for a clothes washing machine comprising:

a first agitator element,

a second agitator element,

drive means for driving said first agitator element in an oscillatory motion and for concurrently driving said second agitator element in an unidirectional rotary motion, said first and second agitator elements cooperating to circulate the contents of the machine in a toroidal rollover pattern within the washing machine, and means associated with said second agitator element for forcing articles adjacent thereto into the oscillatory path of said first agitator element and into said rollover pattern, said first agitator element having formed thereon flexible vanes which are free to flex in response to oscillatory motions of the agitator element, thereby to yieldingly engage fabrics deflected downwardly and lessening high impact loading of the first agitator element. [Emphasis added in original]

*3. The Litigation*

The appellants challenged the validity of both patents but adopted the fall-back position that if any infringement occurred, it was under the '803 patent. This allowed them to argue that the '803 patent included the flex vanes and that (apart from the continuous drive claims) there was nothing 'patentably distinct' to nourish the grant of the '734 patent. It argued that the intermittent drive claims in the '734 patent constituted an illegitimate effort to prolong the monopoly by an unjustified two additional years.

A similar action was subsequently initiated against Maytag and its Canadian subsidiaries. The claims against GE included both the 'intermittent' drive claims and the 'continuous' drive claims. The action against Maytag asserted only the intermittent claims.

The GE action proceeded to trial, it being agreed that the outcome of the GE action would govern the Maytag action as well, including all findings of fact and law at trial. The appeals were heard concurrently in the Federal Court of Appeal and in this Court.
[. . .]

A dispute over the internal workings of a washing machine is unlikely to fire everyone's imagination but, as with many intellectual property disputes, raises important legal issues and significant financial stakes.

Counsel for the respondents claims that his clients produced works of great ingenuity 'if not genius', and that the three patents were properly given in exchange for disclosure of these meritorious inventions. Counsel for the appellants suggest that while 'dual action' washing machines represented a useful advance on the prior art, Whirlpool was properly rewarded for its invention by the award of the '401 and '803 patents. Award of a third patent was excessive.

It is common ground that the bargain between the patentee and the public is in the interest of both sides only if the patent owner acquires real protection in exchange for disclosure, and the public does not for its part surrender a more extended monopoly than the statutory 17 years from the date of the patent grant (now 20 years from the date of the filing of the patent application). A patentee who can 'evergreen' a single invention through successive patents by the expedient of obvious or uninventive additions prolongs its monopoly beyond what the public has agreed to pay. The issue is whether Whirlpool's '734 patent falls into that condemned category.

The centrepiece of the attack by the appellants on the validity of the ' 734 patent is that the '734 patent constitutes 'double-patenting' because the invention set out in its intermittent drive claims corresponds with the invention set out in the claims of the earlier '803 patent. Alternatively, it was said that the use of flex vanes was well understood in the washing machine business from the 1960s onward, and even if the '803 patent contemplated (as held by the trial judge) only rigid vanes on the lower oscillator, the use of flexible vanes was an obvious and non-inventive variation that did not warrant patent protection. Either way, they say, the '734 patent is invalid.

The source of the error in the courts below, according to the appellants, is the approach to claims construction which the Federal Court has developed based initially on a misunderstanding and misapplication of the 'purposive construction' approach formulated by the House of Lords in *Catnic Components Ltd. v. Hill & Smith Ltd.*, [1982] R.P.C. 183. The appellants say the *Catnic* decision 'has had a detrimental impact throughout the Commonwealth jurisdictions, and in particular to a proper understanding of the common law of claim construction in Canada'. The appellants invite the Court to reject the *Catnic* approach, and to overrule the Federal Court cases that follow it, particularly *Eli Lilly & Co. v. O'Hara Manufacturing Ltd.* (1989), 26 C.P.R. (3d) 1 (F.C.A.). In this respect, however, I agree with the observation of William L. Hayhurst, Q.C., that '[p]urposive construction is nothing new, though Lord Diplock is credited with first using the expression in patent cases' (see Hayhurst, 'The Art of Claiming and Reading a Claim' in *Patent Law of Canada* (1994), edited by G. F. Henderson, Q.C., at p. 193).

The appellants, however, invite the Court to return to what they call a 'plain and unambiguous' meaning approach to claims construction. The plain and unambiguous meaning of the word 'vane' in the '803 patent, they say, is satisfied by either a flex vane or a rigid vane. Adoption of the *Catnic* 'purposive construction' approach at the initial stage of claims construction injects factual issues that are more appropriately left to the infringement analysis. If the attack on the validity of the '734 patent fails, the appellants seek a reversal of the finding that they infringed the 'continuous drive' claims of the '734 patent. They do not dispute infringement of the 'intermittent' drive claims.

These arguments resolve themselves into the following issues:

1.    What are the relevant principles of patent claims construction?
2.    Do the claims of the '803 patent, properly construed, include flexible vanes?
3.    If the '803 patent claims properly construed do not include flex vanes, is the '734 patent nevertheless invalid because of double patenting?
4.    If not, are the appellants liable for infringement of the 'continuous drive' claims?

*1. The Principles of Patent Claims Construction*

The content of a patent specification is regulated by s. 34 of the *Patent Act*. The first part is a 'disclosure' in which the patentee must describe the invention 'with sufficiently complete and accurate details as will enable a workman, skilled in the art to which the invention relates, to construct or use that invention when the period of the monopoly has expired': *Consolboard Inc. v. MacMillan*

*Bloedel (Sask.) Ltd.*, [1981] 1 S.C.R. 504, at p. 517. The disclosure is the *quid* provided by the inventor in exchange for the *quo* of a 17-year (now 20-year) monopoly on the exploitation of the invention. The monopoly is enforceable by an array of statutory and equitable remedies and it is therefore important for the public to know what is prohibited and where they may safely go while the patent is still in existence. The public notice function is performed by the claims that conclude the specification and must state 'distinctly and in explicit terms the things or combinations that the applicant regards as new and in which he claims an exclusive property or privilege' (s. 34(2))'. An inventor is not obliged to claim a monopoly on everything new, ingenious and useful disclosed in the specification. The usual rule is that what is not claimed is considered disclaimed.

The first step in a patent suit is therefore to construe the claims. Claims construction is antecedent to consideration of both validity and infringement issues. The appellants' argument is that these two inquiries — validity and infringement — are distinct, and that if the principles of 'purposive construction' derived from *Catnic* are to be adopted at all, they should properly be confined to infringement issues only. The principle of 'purposive construction', they say, has no role to play in the determination of validity, and its misapplication is fatal to the judgment under appeal.

It is true that in *Catnic* itself there was no attack on the validity of the patent. The litigation turned on issues of infringement. The patent in issue dealt with galvanized steel lintels for use in building construction. Lintels are structural members placed over openings such as doors and windows to support the building above. The patent taught an ingenious new type of lintel of sheet metal bent into a box-like 'lazy Z' shape that was light to handle and inexpensive to manufacture. The defendant knew of the plaintiff's product but was not familiar with the plaintiff's patent. The claims (of which they were unaware) taught that the lintel must have 'a second rigid support member *extending vertically* from or from near the rear edge of the first horizontal plate' (emphasis added). Vertical alignment would maximize the load-bearing capacity. For reasons unrelated to patent avoidance, the rigid support member in the defendant's product was inclined about eight degrees off vertical. The trial judge concluded that there was no literal infringement because the support did not extend precisely 'vertically', but that, since there was no material difference in function of the component part, there was, viewing the defendant's lintel as a whole, infringement of the 'pith and marrow' of the plaintiff's invention. The trial judge was reversed by a majority in the Court of Appeal but was subsequently avenged by restoration of his judgment by a unanimous House of Lords. Lord Diplock's description of purposive construction was as follows, at pp. 242-43:

> My Lords, a patent specification is a unilateral statement by the patentee, in words of his own choosing, addressed to those likely to have a practical interest in the subject matter of his invention (i.e. 'skilled in the art'), by

which he informs them what he claims to be the essential features of the new product or process for which the letters patent grant him a monopoly. It is those novel features only that he claims to be essential that constitute the so-called 'pith and marrow' of the claim. A patent specification should be given a purposive construction rather than a purely literal one derived from applying to it the kind of meticulous verbal analysis in which lawyers are too often tempted by their training to indulge. The question in each case is: whether persons with practical knowledge and experience of the kind of work in which the invention was intended to be used, would understand that strict compliance with a particular descriptive word or phrase appearing in a claim was intended by the patentee to be an essential requirement of the invention so that *any* variant would fall outside the monopoly claimed, even though it could have no material effect upon the way the invention worked.

The key to purposive construction is therefore the identification by the court, with the assistance of the skilled reader, of the particular words or phrases in the claims that describe what the inventor considered to be the 'essential' elements of his invention. This is no different, I think, than the approach adopted roughly 40 years earlier by Duff C.J. in *J.K. Smit & Sons Inc. v. McClintock*, [1940] S.C.R. 279. The patent in that case related to a method of setting diamonds in devices such as rotary drill bits for earth boring. Duff C.J., citing the earlier jurisprudence, put the focus on the inventor's own identification of the 'essential' parts of his invention, at p. 285:

> Obviously, the invention, as described by the inventor himself, involves the use of air suction to hold the diamonds in place while the molten metal is being introduced into the mold. There can be no doubt, in my mind, that as the inventor puts it, that is an *essential* part of his process. That part of his process is clearly not taken by the appellants. Adapting the language of Lord Romer, it is not the province of the court to guess what is and is not of the essence of the invention of the respondent. The patentee has clearly indicated that the use of air suction at that stage of the process is an essential, if not the essential, part of the invention described in the specification. [Emphasis added in original]

To the same effect is the judgment of Thorson P. in *McPhar Engineering Co. v. Sharpe Instruments Ltd.* (1960), [1956-60] Ex. C.R. 467 (Can. Ex. Ct.), at p. 525:

> Thus it is established law that if a person takes the substance of an invention he is guilty of infringement and it does not matter whether he omits a feature that is not *essential* to it or substitutes an equivalent for it. [Emphasis added in original]

The 'essential' elements approach was established in earlier English cases such as *Marconi v. British Radio Telegraph & Telephone Co.* (1911), 28 R.P.C. 181 (Ch. D.), at p. 217, referred to by Duff C.J. in *J. K. Smit* supra, and more recent pre-*Catnic* decisions in that country such as *Birmingham Sound Reproducers Ltd. v. Collaro Ltd.*, [1956] R.P.C. 232 (C.A.) and *C. Van der Lely N.V. v. Bamfords Ltd.*, [1963] R.P.C. 61 (H.L.), where Lord Reid, dissenting on the result, said at p. 76: 'you cannot avoid infringement by substituting an obvious equivalent for an *unessential* integer' (emphasis added in original).

The *Catnic* analysis therefore was not a departure from the earlier jurisprudence in the United Kingdom or in this country. It is no disrespect to Lord Diplock to suggest that at least to some extent he poured some fine old whiskies into a new bottle, skilfully refined the blend, brought a fresh clarity to the result, added a distinctive label, and *voilà* 'purposive construction'. In *Catnic*, as in the earlier case law, the scope of the monopoly remains a function of the written claims but, as before, flexibility and fairness is achieved by differentiating the essential features ('the pith and marrow') from the unessential, based on a knowledgeable reading of the whole specification through the eyes of the skilled addressee rather than on the basis of 'the kind of meticulous verbal analysis in which lawyers are too often tempted by their training to indulge' (*Catnic* supra, p. 243).

As stated, the Federal Court of Appeal applied the 'purposive construction' approach to claims construction in *O'Hara Manufacturing Ltd., supra,* and, with respect, I think it was correct to do so. The appellants' argument that the principle of purposive construction is wrong or applies only to infringement issues must be rejected for a number of reasons:

(a)    While *Catnic* supra, dealt with infringement, the court had first to determine the scope and content of the plaintiff's invention. Lord Diplock was careful to relate his discussion of the 'essential' features to the wording of the claims. It was these essential features considered without reference to specific issues of validity *or* infringement that constituted the 'pith and marrow of the claim'. He canvassed the possible existence of '*any* variant' of a 'particular descriptive word or phrase appearing in a claim' but was careful not to link his discussion of claims construction to the particular variant in the defendant's allegedly infringing lintel. Indeed, for emphasis, he italicized the word 'any' in '*any* variant'. A patent must not of course be construed with an eye on the allegedly infringing device in respect of infringement or with an eye to the prior art in respect of validity to avoid its effect: *Dableh v. Ontario Hydro,* [1996] 3 F.C. 751 (C.A.), at pp. 773-74. Claims construction cannot be allowed to become a results-oriented interpretation, but there is nothing in Lord Diplock's speech that would support such an erroneous approach.

(b)    Acceptance of the appellants' argument could result in a different claims construction for the purpose of validity than for the purpose of infringement (assuming purposeful construction is retained for infringement issues). However, it has always been a fundamental rule of claims construction that the claims receive one and the same interpretation for all purposes.

(c)  The orthodox rule is that a patent 'must be read by a mind willing to understand, not by a mind desirous of misunderstanding', *per* Chitty J. in *Lister v. Norton Brothers & Co.* (1886), 3 R.P.C. 199 (Ch. Div.), at p. 203. A 'mind willing to understand' necessarily pays close attention to the purpose and intent of the author.

(d)  Rejection of 'purposeful construction' would imply the embrace of a purposeless approach that ignores the context and use to which the words are being put. Purposeless construction was rejected by this Court long before *Catnic* supra, as in *Williams v. Box* (1910), 44 S.C.R. 1, *per* Idington J., at p. 10:

> If we would interpret correctly the meaning of any statute *or other writing* we must understand what those framing it were about, and the purpose it was intended to execute. [Emphasis added in original]

(e)  In fact, a patent is more than just 'other writing'. The words of the claims are initially proposed by the applicant, but they are thereafter negotiated with the Patent Office, and in the end are accepted by the Commissioner of Patents as a correct statement of a monopoly that can properly be derived from the invention disclosed in the specification. When the patent issues, it is an enactment within the definition of 'regulation' in s. 2(1) of the *Interpretation Act*, R.S.C., 1985, c. I-21, which says:

> 'regulation' includes an order, regulation, rule, rule of court, form, tariff of costs or fees, letters patent, commission, warrant, proclamation, by-law, resolution or other instrument issued, made or established
>
> (*a*)  in the execution of a power conferred by or under the authority of an Act, or
> (*b*)  by or under the authority of the Governor in Council; [Emphasis added in original]

A patent must therefore be given such interpretation according to s. 12 of the *Interpretation Act* 'as best ensures the attainment of its objects'. Intention is manifested in words, whose meaning should be respected, but words themselves occur in a context that generally provides clues to their interpretation and a safeguard against their misinterpretation. P.-A. Côté, in *The Interpretation of Legislation in Canada* (3rd ed. 2000), puts the matter succinctly when he writes, at p. 387, 'Meaning flows at least partly from context, of which the statute's *purpose* is an integral element' (emphasis added in original). To the same effect see *Rizzo & Rizzo Shoes Ltd., Re*, [1998] 1 S.C.R. 27, at para. 21.

These principles apply to claims construction by virtue of the *Interpretation Act*.

(f)    While the appellants express concern that 'purposive construction' may open the door to extrinsic evidence of intent, as is the case with certain types of extrinsic evidence in the United States, neither *Catnic* supra, nor *O'Hara Manufacturing Ltd., supra*, goes outside the four corners of the specification, and properly limit themselves to the words of the claims interpreted in the context of the specification as a whole.

(g)    While 'purposive construction' is a label introduced into claims construction by *Catnic* supra, the approach itself is quite consistent, in my view, with what was said by Dickson J. the previous year in *Consolboard* supra, on the topic of claims construction, at pp. 520-21:

> We must look to the whole of the disclosure and the claims to ascertain the nature of the invention and methods of its performance, (*Noranda Mines Limited v. Minerals Separation North American Corporation*, [1950] S.C.R. 36), being neither benevolent nor harsh, but rather seeking a construction which is reasonable and fair to both patentee and public. There is no occasion for being too astute or technical in the matter of objections to either title or specification for, as Duff C.J.C. said, giving the judgment of the Court in *Western Electric Company, Incorporated, and Northern Electric Company v. Baldwin International Radio of Canada*, [1934] S.C.R. 570, at p. 574, 'where the language of the specification, upon a reasonable view of it, can be so read as to afford the inventor protection for that which he has actually in good faith invented, the court, as a rule, will endeavour to give effect to that construction'.

Not only is 'purposive construction' consistent with these well-established principles, it advances Dickson J.'s objective of an interpretation of the patent claims that 'is reasonable and fair to both patentee and public'.

(h)    The appellants suggest that 'purposive construction' undermines the public notice function of the claims, and unfairly handicaps legitimate competition. The trial judge, they say, was able to salvage the '734 patent by narrowing the scope of the word 'vane' in the earlier '803 patent by a restrictive 'purposive' construction. However, purposive construction is usually criticized by accused infringers for tending to *expand* the written claims. In fact, purposive construction can cut either way. Here it enabled the appellants to escape infringement of the '803 patent. No doubt if the '734 patent had never been granted, the appellants would now be strongly advocating a narrow 'purposive construction' of the '803 patent, and of course the respondents would just as surely be advocating the contrary position. Purposive construction is capable of expanding or limiting a literal text, as Hayhurst, *supra*, points out at p. 194 in words that anticipate the trial judgment in this case:

> Purposive construction may show that something that might literally be within the scope of the claim was not intended to be covered, so that there can be no infringement. . . .

Similarly, two other experienced practitioners, Carol V. E. Hitchman and Donald H. MacOdrum have concluded that '[a] purposive construction is not necessarily a broader construction than a purely literal one, although it may be' ('Don't Fence Me In: Infringement in Substance in Patent Actions' (1990), 7 *C.I.P.R.* 167, at p. 202).

While the *Catnic* approach to claims construction has subsequently been held in England to be compatible with Article 69 of the *European Patent Convention*, it was not decided with reference to the *Convention. O'Hara Manufacturing Ltd.*, *supra*, does not represent a stealthy incorporation of the *Convention* into Canadian law. Indeed, as I have endeavoured to show, purposive construction has long been a theme in Canadian patent law, albeit not under that label.

Adopting the purposive construction approach, the court affirmed the Court of Appeal and trial judge findings that the patents had been infringed in spite of apparent differences in the vanes and the nature of the motion. The essential elements of the patent had been taken.

In determining whether a patent claim is infringed, it is the defendant's actions, not his or her intent, that the court must consider:

> What governs is what the infringer does, not what he intends: *Stead v. Anderson* (1846), 14 L.J.C.P. 250, 2 W.P.C. 156. Infringement occurs when the essence of an invention is taken. The principle to be applied was stated in *Lightning Fastener Co., Ltd. v. Colonial Fastener Co. Ltd.*, [1932] Ex. C.R. 89 *at p.* 98; reversed, [1933] 3 D.L.R. 791, [1933] S.C.R. 363; reversed, [1934] 3 D.L.R. 737, 51 R.P.C. 349 as follows:
>
> > In each case the substance, or principle, of the invention and not the mere form is to be looked to. It has been stated in many cases that if an infringer takes the principle and alters the details, and yet it is obvious that he has taken the substance of the idea which is the subject matter of the invention, and has simply altered the details, the Court is justified in looking through the variation of details and see that the substance of the invention has been infringed and consequently can protect the inventor. And the question is not whether the substantial part of the machine or method has been taken from the specification, but the very different one, whether

what is done by the alleged infringer takes from the patentee the substance of his invention.[109]

The relevant date to construe the claim (*i.e.*, the date at which the patent teachings are deemed communicated to the persons skilled in the art and whose knowledge is relevant at that point in time to understand such teachings) is the date on which they are open for inspection (under s. 10), normally 18 months after filing. As the Supreme Court stated in *Free-World Trust, supra*, note 19 at paras 53-54:

> The date of publication continues to be the critical date in England: Terrell, *supra*, at p. 106, although Lord Hoffman (as he now is) has observed that 'there is an important difference between the 1949 [*Patent Act*] and the 1977 [*Patent Act*]' which requires the date of application (or priority date) to become the critical date for certain purposes: *Biogen Inc. v. Medeva PLC*, [1997] R.P.C. 1 (H.L.), at p. 53. In that case the court was dealing with the sufficiency of disclosure, but some English judges have taken the cue to construe claims as of the date of application as well, e.g., *Dyson Appliances Ltd. v. Hoover Ltd.*, [2000] E.W.J. No. 4994 (QL) (Pat. Ct.), at para. 48(k). In Canada, Reed J. advocated a similar position in *AT & T Technologies Inc. v. Mitel Corp.* (1989), 26 C.P.R. (3d) 238 (F.C.T.D.), at p. 260, even in the absence of these statutory changes. While there may be some advantages to the establishment of a single critical date for multiple purposes including obviousness, sufficiency and claims construction, my view is that Canadian law does not support the date of application as the critical date for claims construction.

> There remains, however, a choice between the date of issuance of the patent and the date of its publication because under the former Act the date of issue and the date of publication were the same. Now, as a result of the obligations assumed by Canada under the *Patent Cooperation Treaty 1970* implemented by s. 10 of the new Act (S.C. 1993, c. 15, s. 28), the patent specification is 'laid open' 18 months after the effective date of the Canadian patent application. In my view, the same logic that favoured the date of issuance/publication as the critical date for claims construction under the former Act, favours the choice of the 'laid open' date under the new act. On that date, the invention is disclosed to the public, those interested have some ability to oppose the grant of the patent applied for, and the applicant for the patent is eventually allowed to claim reasonable compensation (s. 55(2)), provided the patent is ultimately granted, from and after the 'laid open' date. The public, the patentee, its competitors and potential infringers all have an interest and/or concern from that date forward. The notional skilled addressee has a text available for interpretation. In summary, public disclosure and the triggering of legal conse-

---

[109] *Computalog Ltd. v. Comtech Logging Ltd.* (1992), [1992] F.C.J. No. 609, 44 C.P.R. (3d) 77, 142 N.R. 216, 1992 CarswellNat 1011 (Fed. C.A.) [*Computalog* cited to C.P.R.].

quences on the 'laid open' date, as well as the policy considerations that underpinned the earlier case law, favour that date over the other possibilities as the critical date for the purpose of claims construction.

For purposes of construing claims the relevant date is the publication date, whereas for purposes of assessing validity or obviousness the relevant date is the claim date.

## (b) The Doctrine of Equivalents

In *Free World Trust*, a companion case to *Whirlpool*, the Supreme Court set out the test for patent infringement. As with the test for claims construction, the Supreme Court emphasized that it is important to formulate a test which will be fair and predicable for both the inventor and the public. To decide whether a patent is infringed, a court must first decide what its essential teachings are to a person skilled in the art. The method should not be used to unfairly broaden the monopoly, however:

> The appeal in this Court was essentially directed to the infringement issues. It has been established, at least since *Grip Printing & Publishing Co. v. Butterfield* (1885), 11 S.C.R. 291, that a patent owner has a remedy against an alleged infringer who does not take the letter of the invention but nevertheless appropriates its substance (or 'pith and marrow'). This extended protection of the patentee is recognized in Anglo-Canadian law, and also finds expression in modified form in the United States under the doctrine of equivalents, which is said to be available against the producer of a device that performs substantially the same function in substantially the same way to obtain substantially the same result: *Graver Tank & Manufacturing Co. v. Linde Air Products Co.*, 339 U.S. 605 (U.S. Ind. S.C. 1950), at p. 608[110].

> It is obviously an important public policy to control the scope of 'substantive infringement'. A purely literal application of the text of the claims would allow

---

[110] Binnie J. added in respect of that case a reference to a U.S. Supreme Court comment on the doctrine: "With respect to the United States, I mentioned earlier the seminal *Graver Tank* case in 1950. More recently, the United States Supreme Court revisited the doctrine of equivalents in *Warner-Jenkinson Co. v. Hilton Davis Chemical Co.*, 520 U.S. 17 (U.S. Ohio 1997), and concluded, *per* Thomas J., at pp. 28-9:

> We do, however, share the concern of the dissenters below that the doctrine of equivalents, as it has come to be applied since *Graver Tank*, has taken on a life of its own, unbounded by the patent claims. There can be no denying that the doctrine of equivalents, when applied broadly, conflicts with the definitional and public-notice functions of the statutory claiming requirement'."

a person skilled in the art to make minor and inconsequential variations in the device and thereby to appropriate the substance of the invention with a copycat device while staying just outside the monopoly. A broader interpretation, on the other hand, risks conferring on the patentee the benefit of inventions that he had not in fact made but which could be deemed with hindsight to be 'equivalent' to what in fact was invented. This would be unfair to the public and unfair to competitors. It is important that the patent system be fair as well as predictable in its operation.[111]

One risk that stems from the application of the *doctrine of equivalents*, according to which replacing an element in a claim with an equivalent thereof might still constitute an infringement, is that the monopoly will be broadened in unexpected ways, thus leading to a finding of infringement that a defendant did not foresee. The public is entitled to a reasonable degree of certainty as to the extent of the patentee's monopoly. Perhaps the best way to understand purposive construction is to ask what a person skilled in the art concerned would conclude, upon reading the patent claims, as to what the essential teachings of the patent are compared to the prior art. *Wenham Gas Co. v. Champion Gas Lamp Co.* stated:[112]

> [I]f the pith and marrow of the invention is taken it is no excuse to say that you have added something or, omitted something, even if the addition or omission be useful and valuable. The superadding of ingenuity to a robbery does not make the operation justifiable.

Adding along the same lines, *Lightning Fastener Co. v. Colonial Fastener Co.*:[113]

> It has been stated in many cases that if an infringer takes the principle and alters the details and yet it is obvious that he has taken the substance of the idea which is the subject matter of the invention, and has simply altered the details, the Court is justified in looking through the variation of details and see that the substance of the invention has been infringed and consequently can protect the inventor.

Against that backdrop, while courts are reluctant to simply disregard the words used in a claim to include all possible equivalents, they can do so in appropriate cases, as explained by the Federal Court of Appeal:[114]

---

[111] *Free World Trust, supra*, note 19 at paras. 28-9, Binnie J.

[112] (1891), 9 R.P.C. 49 (Eng. C.A.).

[113] [1932] Ex. C.R. 89 (Can. Ex. Ct.), affirmed [1933] S.C.R. 363 (S.C.C.), reversed (1934), 51 R.P.C. 349 (Canada P.C.).

[114] *Janssen Pharmaceutica Inc. v. Apotex Inc.* (2001), [2002] 1 F.C. 393, 203 D.L.R.

There are several issues to be decided on appeal. However, the essential issue for determination is whether, with respect to the critical acylation reaction necessary for making cisapride, the intramolecular reaction employed in the Torcan Process is an 'obvious chemical equivalent' of the intermolecular condensation reaction described and claimed in the Janssen Patent.
[. . .]

The Motions Judge began by construing claims 1 and 5 of the Janssen Patent. In doing so, he noted that a purposive construction should be given to the claims in light of the decision by the House of Lords in *Catnic Components Ltd. v. Hill & Smith Ltd.*, [1982] R.P.C. 183 (H.L.). [. . .]

The Motions Judge proceeded to restate some of the well-established principles of patent construction. Specifically, he noted that patent construction must be neither benevolent nor harsh, that it must be fair and reasonable to the patentee and the public, that it must be done with a mind willing to understand the invention and that it should endeavour to give the inventor protection for that which he has in good faith invented.

The Motions Judge also took note of the fact that at the time the Janssen Patent was filed, cisapride was a novel compound. In this connection, he observed that if it were not for the limitations contained in subsection 41(1) of the *Patent Act*, R.S.C. 1970, c. P-4 at the time of filing, cisapride could have been claimed in a product *per se* format, regardless of how the compound was made. Drawing support from the decision of Richard J. (as he then was) in *Pfizer Canada Inc. v. Apotex Inc.* (1997), 77 C.P.R. (3d) 547 (F.C.T.D.), the Motions Judge noted that because the types of reactions included in the Janssen Patent were general reactions known at the time of filing and because there was nothing inventive in the idea of using these reactions, the patentee could not have intended to be limited to the specific processes set forth in the claims. Rather, the process limitations were only included to comply with subsection 41(1) of the *Patent Act*. Given claim 5's coverage of the processes in claim 1 and all other obvious chemical equivalents, the Motions Judge determined that the specific process limitations in claim 1 could not be read as essential features.

Having considered the expert evidence adduced by the parties, the Motions Judge construed the Janssen Patent. At paragraph 58 of his reasons, he came to the following conclusion:

> In my view, on a purposive construction of the '847 [Janssen] Patent 'and construing the claims with a mind willing to understand the true essentials of the invention', the true purpose of the first process of claim

---

(4th) 105, 13 C.P.R. (4th) 410 (Fed. C.A.) [*Janssen* cited to F.C.]. In that case, the patent claim itself included the phrase and "all other obvious chemical equivalent processes."

1 is to make cisapride by the formation of the amide bond, and optionally, 0-methylation and/or preparing the cis isomer. With respect to claim 5 of the '847 [Janssen] Patent, it is my view that the claim claims cisapride when made or prepared by the first process of claim 1, i.e. formation of the amide bond, and optionally, 0-methylation and/or preparing the cis isomer, and by all other obvious chemical equivalents of the claim 1 process. [footnotes omitted]

The Motions Judge then turned to the issue of infringement. In doing so, he set out (at paragraph 59) the test established by Lord Diplock in *Catnic, supra* as restated by Hoffmann J. (as he then was) in *Improver Corp. v. Remington Consumer Products Ltd.*, [1990] F.S.R. 181 (Pat. Ct.) at 189:

1.     Does the variant have a material effect upon the way the invention works? If yes, the variant is outside the claim. If no, —

2.     Would this (i.e. that the variant had no material effect) have been obvious at the date of publication of the patent to a reader skilled in the art? If no, the variant is outside the claim. If yes, —

3.     Would the reader skilled in the art nevertheless have understood from the language of the claim that the patentee intended that strict compliance with the primary meaning was an essential requirement of the invention? If yes, the variant is outside the claim.

The Motions Judge added his view, based on *Novocol Chemical Manufacturing Co. v. MacFarlane*, [1939] Ex. C.R. 151 (Ex. Ct.), that where a variant performs the same function in substantially the same manner as the claimed process, it will constitute an equivalent.

In applying the *Catnic* test, the Motions Judge centred his analysis on the formation of the amide bond in the competing processes for making cisapride. In this connection, he framed the infringement issue (at paragraph 62) in this way:

It is undeniable, in my view, that the [Defendant's] amide bond is made in a manner analogous to the '847 [Janssen] Patent amide bond, *i.e.* by way of a nucleophilic acyl substitution reaction involving the non-bonded electrons of the nitrogen attacking the carbonyl carbon, which results in the displacement of an appropriate leaving group Y, to form the nitrogen-carbonyl carbon bond. There are a number of variants between the '847 [Janssen] Patent and the [Defendant's] Process, of which the principal is the use of an intramolecular acylation in lieu of an intermolecular acylation. The issue, therefore, is whether, by reason of these variants, the [Defendant's] Process falls outside the scope of the '847 [Janssen] Patent.

[. . .]

Adopting the analysis of Dr. Snieckus, the Motions Judge found that the only difference between the intramolecular reaction in the [Defendant's] Process and the intermolecular reaction described in the Janssen Patent was that in the former reaction, the two reactive groups (an amine and an ester) are part of the same molecule whereas in the latter reaction, they are part of different molecules. This difference had no effect on the nature of the reaction involved, which is determined by the nature of the reactive groups. Those groups were the same in each process.

The Motions Judge further accepted evidence that synthetic chemists have known for quite some time that they should consider intramolecular versions of an intermolecular reaction when planning a synthetic pathway. He also accepted evidence that the intramolecular reaction used in the [Defendant's] Process is well known and has been performed since 1937. Repeating his view that there is nothing in the Janssen Patent limiting the main reaction to an intermolecular one, the Motions Judge concluded that the intramolecular reaction in the [Defendant's] Process either falls within the scope of claim 1 of the Janssen Patent or constitutes an obvious chemical equivalent of the acylation reaction described in claim 1.
[. . .]

*Arguments on Appeal*

[. . .]

The other grouping of errors alleged by Apotex to have been committed by the Motions Judge includes a number of legal errors. These errors relate to the construction of the Janssen Patent and the application of the doctrine of equivalents in order to determine the issue of infringement. Apotex submits that the Motions Judge erred in concluding that, on a purposive construction, the Janssen Patent was not limited to the processes claimed therein and in particular was not limited to an intermolecular reaction. However, Apotex contends that what claim 1 does not include is not instructive as to the breadth of the claimed process. Rather, the applicable jurisprudence requires that claim 1 be construed on the basis of what is explicitly included in it. Contrary to the approach adopted by the Motions Judge, the language of claim 1 cannot be broadened by reference to the words 'all obvious chemical equivalents' in claim 5. Any obvious equivalence must be based on the explicit terms of claim 1.

On a proper construction of the Janssen Patent, therefore, Apotex contends that claim 1 only covers an intermolecular reaction. There is no evidence that the Janssen Patent contemplates an intramolecular reaction such as the one employed in the [Defendant's] Process. Indeed, in Apotex's submission, claim 1's silence on the possibility of an intramolecular reaction demonstrates that an intramolecular alternative is not at all obvious.
[. . .]

*Analysis*

*(A)  The Law of Patent Construction*

In order to verify the general allegation by Apotex that the Motions Judge erred
in construing the Janssen Patent, it is necessary to review, if only briefly, the
law applicable to patent construction. The recent decisions of the Supreme
Court in *Free World Trust c. Électro Santé Inc.*, [2000] 2 S.C.R. 1024, 2000
SCC 66, and *Whirlpool Corp. v. Camco Inc.*, [2000] 2 S.C.R. 1067, 2000 SCC
67, which were released after the decision being appealed, explain in comprehensive fashion the principles of patent construction which must be followed
in cases like the present appeal.
[. . .]

Construing a patent for the purposes of determining infringement is the next
step in the analysis. With the Supreme Court's decision in *Free World Trust*,
courts now have the benefit of a thorough road map to patent construction for
these purposes. In that decision, Binnie J. set out a series of propositions (at
paragraph 31) which must guide courts in determining infringement issues.
These propositions are the following:

(a)    The *Patent Act* promotes adherence to the language of the claims.
(b)    Adherence to the claims in turn promotes both fairness and predictability.
(c)    The claim language must, however, be read in an informed and purposive
       way.
(d)    The language of the claims thus construed defines the monopoly. There
       is no recourse to such vague notions as the 'spirit of the invention' to
       expand it further.
(e)    The claims language will, on a purposive construction, show that some
       elements of the claimed invention are essential while others are non-
       essential. The identification of elements as essential or non-essential is
       made:
       (i)    on the basis of the common knowledge of the worker skilled in
              the art to which the patent relates;
       (ii)   as of the date the patent is published;
       (iii)  having regard to whether or not it was obvious to the skilled reader
              at the time the patent was published that a variant of a particular
              element would *not* make a difference to the way in which the
              invention works; or
       (iv)   according to the intent of the inventor, expressed or inferred from
              the claims, that a particular element is essential irrespective of its
              practical effect;
       (v)    without, however, resort to extrinsic evidence of the inventor's
              intention.
(f)    There is no infringement if an essential element is different or omitted.

There may still be infringement, however, if non-essential elements are substituted or omitted. [emphasis added in original]

Proposition (e) underlined in the above excerpt from *Free World Trust* lies at the heart of the infringement analysis. That proposition recognizes that '[i]t would be unfair to allow a patent monopoly to be breached with impunity by a copycat device that simply switched the bells and whistles, to escape the literal claims of the patent' (*Free World Trust* at paragraph 55). Binnie J. succinctly explained the analysis necessary with respect to determining equivalence (at paragraph 55):

> For an element to be considered non-essential and thus substitutable, it must be shown either (i) that on a purposive construction of the words of the claim it was clearly not intended to be essential, or (ii) that at the date of publication of the patent, the skilled addressees would have appreciated that a particular element could be substituted without affecting the working of the invention, i.e., had the skilled worker at that time been told of both the element specified in the claim and the variant and 'asked whether the variant would obviously work in the same way', the answer would be yes: *Improver Corp. v. Remington*, supra, at p. 192. In this context, I think 'work in the same way' should be taken for our purposes as meaning that the variant (or component) would perform substantially the same function in substantially the same way to obtain substantially the same result.

Having reviewed the law of patent construction as comprehensively restated in the recent jurisprudence of the Supreme Court, it remains to determine whether the Motions Judge erred in applying that law as Apotex claims.

*(B) The Application of the Law by the Motions Judge*

Although the Motions Judge did not have the benefit of the Supreme Court's recent guidance when he construed the Janssen Patent, I am of the opinion, and both counsel in argument agreed on this, that he anticipated and applied the general approach expressed in the propositions laid down by Binnie J. in *Free World Trust*. Having employed the correct general principles, the decision of the Motions Judge to accept the evidence of Janssen's experts as an aid to his construction of the claims is entitled to some deference. In the circumstances, I am not persuaded that any palpable and overriding error was made by the Motions Judge in this respect and I therefore see no reason to interfere with his conclusion as to infringement.

Applying the purposive approach to patent construction, the Motions Judge construed the essentials of the Janssen Patent as follows (at paragraph 58):

In my view, on a purposive construction of the '847 [Janssen] Patent 'and construing the claims with a mind willing to understand the true essentials of the invention', the true purpose of the first process of claim 1 is to make cisapride by the formation of the amide bond, and optionally, 0-methylation and/or preparing the cis isomer. With respect to claim 5 of the '847 [Janssen] Patent, it is my view that the claim claims cisapride when made or prepared by the first process of claim 1, i.e. formation of the amide bond, and optionally, 0-methylation and/or preparing the cis isomer, and by all other obvious chemical equivalents of the claim 1 process. [footnotes omitted]

[. . .]

Nor am I persuaded that the Motions Judge applied the wrong test for equivalence. The allegation by Apotex that the Motions Judge reduced equivalence to the notion of 'effecting the same result' is nowhere substantiated on a reading of the decision under appeal. The Motions Judge applied the *Catnic* analysis as restated in Hoffmann J.'s three part test from *Improver, supra*. That test was endorsed by the Supreme Court in *Free World Trust*. The Motions Judge spoke of an equivalent as a process which 'performs the same function in substantially the same manner' as the claimed process (at paragraph 60). He also spoke of equivalence in terms of working in a similar manner to achieve the same result (at paragraph 70). This hardly amounts to defining an equivalent as a process which merely effects the same result as the claimed process. Indeed, the definition stated by the Motions Judge captures the essence of the Supreme Court's notion of equivalence as arising from the performance of substantially the same function in substantially the same way to obtain substantially the same result (*Free World Trust* at paragraph 55).

Applying the correct test for equivalence, the Motions Judge determined that Torcan's intramolecular acylation reaction was an obvious chemical equivalent of the intermolecular acylation reaction described in claim 1 of the Janssen Patent. I am not persuaded by the argument raised by Apotex that the Motions Judge misunderstood the concept of 'obviousness' in arriving at his conclusion. In my view, he did understand the test for obvious chemical equivalence as stated by Hoffmann J. in Improver and repeated by Binnie J. for the Supreme Court in *Free World Trust*, and he applied it properly.

Specifically, the question of equivalence supposes that the person skilled in the art is told of both the invention and the variant and asked whether the variant would obviously work in the same way (*Improver* at page 192, *Free World Trust* at paragraph 55). Apotex has ignored the particulars of this test in order to argue that the skilled person must view the variant as being obvious without being told of the variant's existence. This is not the correct approach but approximates the analysis for determining the obviousness of an invention in order to decide the issue of patent validity. However, the Motions Judge was not concerned with the inventiveness or validity of the Janssen Patent. He was concerned with deciding the issue of infringement, and he applied the correct notion of obviousness for the purpose of determining equivalence.

## (c) "Use" of a Patent

As noted above, s. 42 of the *Patent Act* gives the patentee the "exclusive right, privilege and liberty of making, constructing and using the invention and selling it to others to be used." It is therefore essential to determine what constitutes use of a patent.

To make a finding of infringement, a court must first construe the extent of the monopoly in the claims, as explained in the previous section, and then proceed to the infringement issue of determining whether the defendant "used" the claimed invention.[115]

In the simplest possible terms to answer what is "use" of a patent (under s. 42), from the patentee's point of view the question to ask is whether he or she was deprived, directly or indirectly, of the benefit of the monopoly as defined in the *Patent Act*. From the user's point of view, when read in conjunction with the bona fide experimental use defence (see the Defences Section below), an infringing use of the invention is use for a commercial purpose or for the direct or indirect purpose of making a profit.

The discussion in *Schmeiser*[116] is a fairly complete exposition of the law on the meaning of "use" under the *Patent Act,* and applies the principle from *Whirlpool* and *Free-World Trust* that the purpose of claim construction applies to both validity and infringement issues.

### (1) The Law on 'Use'

The central question on this appeal is whether Schmeiser, by collecting, saving and planting seeds containing Monsanto's patented gene and cell, 'used' that gene and cell. The onus of proving infringement lies on the plaintiff, Monsanto.

Infringement is generally a question of fact (see *Whirlpool*). In most patent infringement cases, once the claim has been construed it is clear on the facts whether infringement has taken place: one need only compare the thing made or sold by the defendant with the claims as construed. Patent infringement cases that turn on 'use' are more unusual. In those rare cases where a dispute

---

[115] An alternative approach would be to proceed in the reverse order, *e.g.,* by determining first that there was no "use" independently of the way the claims are construed, therefore making it unnecessary to analyze the breadth of the claims.

[116] See *supra*, note 48. The facts of the case are summarized in the text accompanying that note.

arises on this issue, as in this case, judicial interpretation of the meaning of 'use' in s. 42 of the Act may be required.

Determining the meaning of 'use' under s. 42 is essentially a matter of statutory construction. The starting point is the plain meaning of the word, in this case 'use' or '*exploiter*'. *The Concise Oxford Dictionary* defines 'use' as 'cause to act or serve for a purpose; bring into service; avail oneself of': *The Concise Oxford Dictionary of Current English* (9th ed., 1995), at p. 1545. This denotes utilization for a purpose. The French word '*exploiter*' is even clearer. It denotes utilization with a view to production or advantage: '*tirer parti de (une chose), en vue d'une production ou dans un but lucratif*; [. . .] [*u*]tiliser d'une manière advantageuse. . .': *Le Nouveau Petit Robert* (2003), at p. 1004.

Three well-established rules or practices of statutory interpretation assist us further. First, the inquiry into the meaning of 'use' under the *Patent Act* must be *purposive*, grounded in an understanding of the reasons for which patent protection is accorded. Second, the inquiry must be *contextual*, giving consideration to the other words of the provision. Finally, the inquiry must be attentive to the wisdom of the *case law*. We will discuss each of these aids to interpretation briefly, and then apply them to the facts of this case.

We return first to the rule of purposive construction. Identifying whether there has been infringement by use, like construing the claim, must be approached by the route of purposive construction: *Free World Trust c. Électro Santé Inc.*, [2000] 2 S.C.R. 1024, 2000 SCC 66. '[P]urposive construction is capable of expanding or limiting a literal [textual claim]': *Whirlpool, supra*, at para. 49. Similarly, it is capable of influencing what amounts to 'use' in a given case.

The purpose of s. 42 is to define the exclusive rights granted to the patent holder. These rights are the rights to full enjoyment of the monopoly granted by the patent. Therefore, what is prohibited is 'any act that interferes with the full enjoyment of the monopoly granted to the patentee': H. G. Fox, *The Canadian Law and Practice Relating to Letters Patent for Inventions* (4th ed., 1968), at p. 349; see also *Lishman v. Erom Roche Inc.* (1996), 68 C.P.R. (3d) 72 (F.C.T.D.), at p. 77.

The guiding principle is that patent law ought to provide the inventor with 'protection for that which he has actually in good faith invented': *Free World Trust* at para. 43. Applied to 'use', the question becomes: *did the defendant's activity deprive the inventor in whole or in part, directly or indirectly, of full enjoyment of the monopoly conferred by law*?

A purposive approach is complemented by a contextual examination of s. 42 of the *Patent Act*, which shows that the patentee's monopoly generally protects its business interests. Professor D. Vaver, in *Intellectual Property Law: Copyright, Patents, Trade-marks* (1997), suggests that the common thread among '(making, constructing and using the invention and selling it to others to be used)'. . . 'is that the activity is usually for commercial purposes — to make a profit or to further the actor's business interests . . .' (p. 151). This is particularly consistent with the French version of s. 42, which uses the word '*exploiter*'.

As a practical matter, inventors are normally deprived of the fruits of their invention and the full enjoyment of their monopoly when another person, without licence or permission, uses the invention to further a business interest. Where the defendant's impugned activities furthered its own commercial interests, we should therefore be particularly alert to the possibility that the defendant has committed an infringing use.

With respect for the contrary view of Arbour J., this does not require inventors to describe in their specifications a commercial advantage or utility for their inventions. Even in the absence of commercial exploitation, the patent holder is entitled to protection. However, a defendant's commercial activities involving the patented object will be particularly likely to constitute an infringing use. This is so because if there is a commercial benefit to be derived from the invention, a contextual analysis of s. 42 indicates that it belongs to the patent holder. The contextual analysis of the section thus complements — and confirms — the conclusion drawn from its purposive analysis. It is the reverse side of the same coin.

We turn now to the case law, the third aid to interpretation. Here we derive guidance from what courts in the past have considered to be use. As we shall see, precedent confirms the approach proposed above and it is of assistance as well in resolving some of the more specific questions raised by this case.

First, case law provides guidance as to whether patent protection extends to situations where the patented invention is contained within something else used by the defendant. This is relevant to the appellants' submission that growing *plants* did not amount to 'using' their patented *genes* and *cells*. Patent infringement actions often proceed in a manufacturing context. Case law has for that reason focussed on situations where a patented part or process plays a role in production.
[. . .]

By analogy, then, the law holds that a defendant infringes a patent when the defendant manufactures, seeks to use, or uses a patented part that is contained within something that is not patented, provided the patented part is significant or important. In the case at bar, the patented genes and cells are not merely a 'part' of the plant; rather, the patented genes are present throughout the genetically modified plant and the patented cells compose its entire physical structure. In that sense, the cells are somewhat analogous to Lego blocks: if an infringing use were alleged in building a structure with patented Lego blocks, it would be no bar to a finding of infringement that only the blocks were patented and not the entire structure. If anything, the fact that the Lego structure could not exist independently of the patented blocks would strengthen the claim, underlining the significance of the patented invention to the whole product, object, or process.

Infringement through use is thus possible even where the patented invention is part of, or composes, a broader unpatented structure or process. This is, as Professor Vaver states, an expansive rule. It is, however, firmly rooted in the principle that the main purpose of patent protection is to prevent others from depriving the inventor, even in part and even indirectly, of the monopoly that the law intends to be theirs: only the inventor is entitled, by virtue of the patent and as a matter of law, to the *full* enjoyment of the monopoly conferred.

Thus, in *Saccharin Corp. v. Anglo-Continental Chemical Works* (1900), 17 R.P.C. 307 (Ch. D.), the court stated, at p. 319:

> By the sale of saccharin, in the course of the production of which the patented process is used, the Patentee is deprived of some part of the whole profit and advantage of the invention, and the importer is indirectly making use of the invention.

> This confirms the centrality of the question that flows from a purposive interpretation of the *Patent Act*: did the defendant by his acts or conduct, deprive the inventor, in whole or in part, directly or indirectly, of the advantage of the patented invention?

In determining whether the defendant 'used' the patented invention, one compares the object of the patent with what the defendant did and asks whether the defendant's actions involved that object. In *Betts v. Neilson*, [1868] 3 Ch. App. 429 (Eng. Ch. App.) (aff'd by (1871), L.R. 5 H.L. 1), the object of the patent was to preserve the contents of bottles in transit. Though the bottles were merely shipped unopened through England, the defendant was held to have used the invention in England because, during its passage through that country, the beer was protected by the invention. Lord Chelmsford said, at p. 439:

> It is the employment of the machine or the article for the purpose for which it was designed which constitutes its active use; and whether the capsules were intended for ornament, or for protection of the contents of the bottles upon which they were placed, the whole time they were in *England* they may be correctly said to be in active use for the very objects for which they were placed upon the bottles by the vendors.

In fact, the patented invention need not be deployed precisely for its intended purpose in order for its object to be involved in the defendant's activity. It was not relevant in *Neilson* whether the invention had actually caused bottles to be preserved during shipping, in a situation in which they would otherwise have broken. As a further example, in *Dunlop Pneumatic Tyre Co. v. British & Colonial Motor Car Co.* (1901), 18 R.P.C. 313 (Pat. Ct.), the defendants placed on display at a car show a car with patented tires which they had intended to remove prior to sale, substituting other tires. The exhibition of the car with the patented tires was nonetheless held to be an infringing use. The common thread is that the defendants employed the invention to their advantage, depriving the inventor of the full enjoyment of the monopoly.

Moreover, as Lord Dunedin emphasized in *British United Shoe Machinery Co. v. Simon Collier Ltd.* (1910), 27 R.P.C. 567, *possession as a stand-by has 'insurance value'*, as for example in the case of a fire extinguisher. The extinguisher is 'used' to provide the means for extinguishment should the need arise. This is true, too, of a spare steam engine which is 'intended in certain circumstances to be used for exactly the purpose for which the whole machine is being actually used' (p. 572). Exploitation of the stand-by utility of an invention uses it to advantage.

In *Terrell on the Law of Patents* (15th ed., 2000), at para. 8.24, the authors observe that '[t]he word 'use'. . . would . . . seem to indicate making practical use of the invention itself'. In some circumstances, 'practical use' may arise from the stand-by utility resulting from mere possession of the invention, or from some other practical employment with a view to advantage. Use, and thereby infringement, are then established.

The general rule is that the defendant's intention is irrelevant to a finding of infringement. The issue is 'what the defendant does, not . . . what he intends': *Stead v. Anderson* (1847), 4 C.B. 806, 136 E.R. 724, at p. 736; see also *Hoechst Celanase International Corp. v. BP Chemicals Ltd.*, [1998] F.S.R. 586 (Pat. Ct.) at p. 598; *Illinois Tool Works Inc. v. Cobra Fixations Cie / Cobra Anchors Co.* (2002), 221 F.T.R. 161, 2002 FCT 829 (F.C.T.D.), at paras. 14-17; *Computalog Ltd. v. Comtech Logging Ltd.* (1992), 44 C.P.R. (3d) 77 (F.C.A.) at p. 88. And the governing principle is whether the defendant, by his actions, activities or conduct, appropriated the patented invention, thus depriving the inventor, in whole or part, directly or indirectly, of the full enjoyment of the monopoly the patent grants.

However, intention becomes relevant where the defence invoked is possession without use. Where the alleged use consists of exploitation of the invention's 'stand-by' utility, as discussed above, it is relevant whether the defendant intended to exploit the invention should the need arise.

Thus, possession was found to constitute 'use' in *Adair v. Young* (1879), 12 Ch. D. 13, where a ship's master was sued for infringement in relation to the presence of patented pumps on his ship. The ship's owners had fitted the ship with the pumps but were not named in the suit. The master had no power to remove the pumps and had never used them to pump water in British waters.

However, the court *held that the master intended to use the pumps if the need arose*. The court thus granted an injunction against use of the pumps to pump water.

Similarly, Fox states, *supra*, that '[*m*]ere possession of a patented article may amount to infringement where such possession is unlicensed and *where there is present the intention of user* to the detriment of the patentee, but not if there is no intention to use' (pp. 383-84) (emphasis added, footnotes omitted).

The onus of proving infringement would become impractical and unduly burdensome in cases of possession were the patent holder required to demonstrate the defendant's intention to infringe. As Professor Vaver explains, 'mere possession may not be use, but a business that possesses a patented product for trade *may be presumed either to have used it or to intend to use it, unless it shows the contrary*' (*supra*, at p. 151 (emphasis added)).

The classic case of *British United Shoe, supra*, suggests that mere possession of an object containing a patented ingredient or made by a patented process may not amount to 'use' if the defendant can show that the object is held without a view to advancing the defendant's interest. The defendant boot maker owned a machine containing a patented mechanism but was held not to have infringed the patent. The defendants did not use the patented part itself, as it was possible not to bring it into operation unless one wanted to do so. The court noted there was no question of the defendants' honesty (they had returned the patented part willingly when legal action commenced). In the court's view, '[t]he patented part . . . was . . . of no use to the Defendants and was put aside by them, and they never thought of using the patented part, nor was it appropriate to their trade' (p. 571). The court stated that there is a rebuttable presumption or 'ordinary inference' that a defendant in possession of an invention had either used it or had it for the future purpose of using it in an infringing manner (p. 571).

Commenting on *British United Shoe* in *Pfizer Corp. v. Ministry of Health* , [1965] A.C. 512 (H.L.), Lord Wilberforce observed that 'if it can positively be proved that the possession was innocent of any actual use or intention to use, the defendant will not be held to have infringed' (p. 572). Possession requires an 'additional ingredient' to make up an infringement (p. 572). In *Pfizer*, according to Lord Wilberforce, use arose from the transportation of patented articles (possession) with a view to trade (the additional ingredient). Where the patent holder shows that the defendant possessed the patented invention, it is up to the defendant to show the absence of the 'additional ingredient'.

Thus, a defendant in possession of a patented invention in commercial circumstances may rebut the presumption of use by bringing credible evidence that the invention was neither used, nor intended to be used, even by exploiting its stand-by utility.

The court does not inquire into whether the patented invention in fact assisted the defendant or increased its profits. This is the natural corollary of the finding in *Neilson* , *supra*, that it was not relevant to infringement whether the beer actually was preserved by the invention, and the finding in *Adair* , *supra*, that it was irrelevant whether the ship's master had profited from the presence of the pumps on the ship. The defendant's benefit or profit from the activity may be relevant at the stage of remedy, but not in determining infringement.

These propositions may be seen to emerge from the foregoing discussion of 'use' under the *Patent Act*:

1    'Use' or *'exploiter'*, in their ordinary dictionary meaning, denote utilization with a view to production or advantage.
2    The basic principle in determining whether the defendant has 'used' a patented invention is whether the inventor has been deprived, in whole or in part, directly or indirectly, of the full enjoyment of the monopoly conferred by the patent.
3    If there is a commercial benefit to be derived from the invention, it belongs to the patent holder.
4    It is no bar to a finding of infringement that the patented object or process is a part of or composes a broader unpatented structure or process, provided the patented invention is significant or important to the defendant's activities that involve the unpatented structure.
5    Possession of a patented object or an object incorporating a patented feature may constitute 'use' of the object's stand-by or insurance utility and thus constitute infringement.
6    Possession, at least in commercial circumstances, raises a rebuttable presumption of 'use'.
7    While intention is generally irrelevant to determining whether there has been 'use' and hence infringement, the absence of intention to employ or gain any advantage from the invention may be relevant to rebutting the presumption of use raised by possession.

## (d) Process Patents and Notice of Compliance Issues

A patent can protect a product, the process for making that product, or both. In the case of a process-only patent, it is sometimes difficult to determine which process was used by looking at the product. A presumption that can greatly help the holder of a process patent (i.e., a patent that protects a process rather than a product or device) is contained in s. 55.1:

In an action for infringement of a patent granted for a process for obtaining a new product, any product that is the same as the new product shall, in the absence of proof to the contrary, be considered to have been produced by the patented process.

This presumption was not viewed as displacing the onus in every case:

> It is the applicant which, as the initiator of the proceeding, has the carriage of the matter and bears the initial burden of proof. There may be some presumptions, such as section 43 of the *Patent Act*, which may help the applicant and have the effect of displacing the burden of proof. However, the presumption enacted by section 55.1 is not one of them. The applicant cannot expect to be able to make his case out of the mouth of the respondent.
>
> [. . .]
>
> Regarding the question of the burden of proof in these proceedings, Lilly submitted that it had the benefit of the statutory presumption found in section 55.1 of the *Patent Act*.
>
> [. . .]
>
> Amendments were made to this provision in 1993 as part of the *NAFTA Implementation Act*. It refers to 'an action for infringement', while article 1709(11) of the *North American Free Trade Agreement* refers to 'any infringement proceeding'. Lilly submits that, in light of *NAFTA*, the proceedings brought pursuant to section 6 of the *Regulations* should be construed to encompass an action for infringement and, accordingly, that it has the benefit of the statutory presumption in section 55.1. Whether the word 'action' in section 55.1 includes the type of proceeding envisaged by section 6, a summary application for judicial review, is not determinative since the proceeding referred to must be for infringement of a patent. Although the purpose of section 6 is to prevent the infringement of a patent, it is not a proceeding for a declaration of infringement of a patent pursuant to sections 54 and 55 of the *Patent Act*, but a proceeding for an order of prohibition against the Minister. This is so even if the allegation is one of non-infringement of a patent. Lilly has accepted that it has the overall burden of proof. However, it cannot, as it claimed, be assisted by the statutory presumption found in section 55.1 of the *Patent Act* in discharging this burden.[117] [footnotes omitted]

To understand the context of this interpretation, one must look at the process by which this presumption is used by research-based pharmaceutical companies to delay the issuance of a notice of compliance to generic drug companies (such a notice is required to allow them to sell medicines the patent on which has expired).[118] The process was explained as follows by the Federal Court of Appeal:

---

[117] *Eli Lilly & Co. v. Novopharm Ltd.* (1995), [1995] F.C.J. No. 632, 60 C.P.R. (3d) 417, 1995 CarswellNat 1869 (Fed. T.D.).

[118] See *Bayer AG v. Canada (Minister of National Health & Welfare)* (1993), [1993] F.C.J. No. 1106, 51 C.P.R. (3d) 329, 163 N.R. 183, 1993 CarswellNat 322 (Fed. C.A.); *Merck Frosst Canada Inc. v. Canada (Minister of National Health &*

In very abbreviated terms, the scheme permits drug manufacturers, who hold or are licensees under subsisting patents, to file a 'patent list' in respect of each drug for which they hold or obtain a notice of compliance (section 4[119]). The Regulations refer to anyone filing such a list as the 'first person'. In practice they will usually be brand name pharmaceutical manufacturers.

Thereafter, any other manufacturer (the 'second person' - in practice generic pharmaceutical companies) who wishes to apply for a notice of compliance in respect of the same drug must, unless he is prepared to wait until all outstanding patents have expired, make one of the allegations referred to in paragraph 5(1)(b),[120] in effect asserting that the first person is not the patentee or that the patent has expired or is invalid or would not be infringed by the second person if the notice of compliance were issued. That allegation is made to the Minister in the second person's new drug submission but notice of it must be served on the first person.

Up to this point there have been no court proceedings and, if none are taken, the Minister is entitled, after the expiry of 45 days, and assuming his public health and safety concerns under *The Food and Drug Regulations*[121] have been otherwise satisfied, to issue a notice of compliance to the second person.

Within that same 45 day period, however, section 6[122] allows the first person to apply to the court for an order prohibiting the Minister from issuing a notice of compliance (subsection 6(1)) and the court is directed to make such an order

---

*Welfare)* (1994), [1994] F.C.J. No. 518, 55 C.P.R. (3d) 176, (sub nom. *Merck Frosst Canada Inc. v. Canada (Minister of Health & Welfare))* 77 F.T.R. 81, 1994 CarswellNat 524 (Fed. T.D.); *Pharmacia Inc. v. Canada (Minister of National Health & Welfare)* (1994), (sub nom. *David Bull Laboratories (Canada) Inc. v. Pharmacia Inc.)* [1995] 1 F.C. 588, 58 C.P.R. (3d) 209, (sub nom. *David Bull Laboratories (Canada) Inc. v. Pharmacia Inc.)* 176 N.R. 48 (Fed. C.A.); and *Abbott Laboratories v. Canada (Minister of Health)* (2004), [2004] F.C.J. No. 708, 239 D.L.R. (4th) 627, 31 C.P.R. (4th) 321, 320 N.R. 37, 2004 CarswellNat 4911 (F.C.A.). The process was also discussed by the Supreme Court in *Eli Lilly & Co. v. Novopharm Ltd.*, [1998] 2 S.C.R. 129, 161 D.L.R. (4th) 1, 80 C.P.R. (3d) 321 (S.C.C.). There is, however, a defence to infringement when a patent is infringed "solely for uses reasonably related to the development and submission of information required under any law of Canada, a province or a country other than Canada that regulates the manufacture, construction, use or sale of any product." S. 55.2.

[119] Of the *Patented Medicines (Notice of Compliance) Regulations,* Canada SOR/93-133, as amended by SOR/98-166 and SOR/99-379.

[120] *Idem.*

[121] C.R.C., c. 870, as amended.

[122] See *supra*, note 119.

unless it finds one or more of the second person's allegations to be 'justified' (subsection 6(2)).

It has now been settled by the decision of this Court in *Bayer AG et al v. Canada (Minister of National Health and Welfare)*[123] that the proceedings launched by the first person are proceedings in judicial review and as such are governed by Part V.I of the *Federal Court Rules*.

In *Bayer, supra*, Mahoney J.A. also commented generally on the nature of section 6 proceedings as follows:

> The legislative scheme does not contemplate a proceeding by way of action. The person claiming patent rights must commence the proceeding within 45 days of being served with a notice of allegation and it is contemplated that the court will have resolved the matter within 30 months after that. Patent infringement actions simply do not proceed at a rate that would meet the legislative time frame. (When an extension of time that might delay final resolution of the application beyond 30 months is sought, the court will have to consider the impact of s. 55.2(4)(e) of the *Patent Act* and s. 7(5) of the Regulations on the discretion provided by Rule 1614.
>
> By merely commencing the proceeding, the applicant obtains what is tantamount to an interlocutory injunction for up to 30 months without having satisfied any of the criteria a court would require before enjoining issuance of a NOC. In particular, no liability as to damages arises from the application as would be imposed by the undertaking any court would require before making an interlocutory injunction. The liability for damages created by s. 8 of the Regulations pertains only to those incurred as a result of the NOC not issuing until after the patent has expired. That is by no means coextensive with the liability that arises on an undertaking exacted when an injunction is issued.
>
> The court has a clear duty to deal with an application expeditiously. Given that, in the scheme of the Regulations, it is the patentee who has both the carriage of the proceeding and the interest in its dilatory prosecution, departures from the schedule imposed by the Part V.1 rules ought not be routine.
> [at page 337]

Section 7[124] provides for a successive series of temporary prohibitions (in effect legislative interlocutory injunctions) for the period prior to and during the pendency of the proceedings under section 6 and extending for as much as

---

[123] See *supra*, note 118.
[124] See note 119.

thirty months from the date of the launching of the proceedings. Subsections 7(2) and 7(4) are particularly significant. Subsection 7(2) provides that the prohibition in paragraph 7(1)(e) shall cease upon the expiry of the patent or upon a judicial declaration of invalidity or non-infringement. Subsection 7(4), dealing presumably with a different situation, provides for the ending of the prohibition in the event that the first person's application is withdrawn or finally dismissed by the court. Subsection 7(5), in providing for judicial discretion to extend or shorten the 30 month period of prohibition, makes it plain that the proceedings are to be dealt with expeditiously.

The Regulations therefore may prolong the term of protection of pharmaceutical patents. This was viewed by research-based companies as a quid pro quo for s. 55.2 which allows generic companies to "work up" their submission to obtain their Notice of Compliance during the life of the patent. The Federal Court of Appeal decided on many occasions, however, that "when an action for patent infringement is available, the inability of a patent holder to access the automatic stay provisions in the *Patent Medicines (Notice of Compliance) Regulations* did not constitute irreparable harm."[125] In other words, if a patent is removed from the list ("Patent Register"), the patentee will not have the benefit of the automatic stay, but in the event of infringement by a competitor, it could bring an action for patent infringement. There is, therefore, no irreparable harm if the patentee is ultimately successful. Irreparable harm is a condition to obtain an interlocutory injunction (see the Remedy Section in the Trade-marks Part).

Using the same presumption, the Courts have held that importing a product produced outside Canada by a process which was patented in Canada could amount to infringement in Canada.[126]

---

[125] *Janssen-Ortho Inc. v. Canada (Minister of Health)* (2004), [2004] F.C.J. No. 750, 320 N.R. 161, 2004 CarswellNat 2724 (F.C.A.). See also *Bristol-Myers Squibb Canada Inc. v. Canada (Attorney General)* (2001), [2001] F.C.J. No. 16, 11 C.P.R. (4th) 539, 266 N.R. 141, 2001 CarswellNat 47 (Fed. C.A.).

[126] See *American Cyanamid Co. v. Charles E. Frosst & Co.*, [1965] 2 Ex. C.R. 355, 47 C.P.R. 215 (Can. Ex. Ct.); and *Saccharin Corp. v. Anglo-Continental Chemical Works* (1900), 17 R.P.C. 307 (Eng. Ch. Div.) at 319: "[b]y the sale of saccharin [an imported product], in the course of the production of which the patented process is used, the Patentee is deprived of some part of the whole profit and advantage of the invention, and the importer is indirectly making use of the invention." See also *Wellcome Foundation Ltd. v. Apotex Inc.* (1991), [1991] F.C.J. No. 1136, 39 C.P.R. (3d) 289, 1991 CarswellNat 213 (Fed. T.D.), additional reasons at (1992), 40 C.P.R. (3d) 361 (Fed. T.D.), reversed in part on other grounds (1995), [1995] F.C.J. No. 226, 60 C.P.R. (3d) 135, 187 N.R. 284, 1995 CarswellNat 119 (Fed. C.A.), leave to appeal to S.C.C. refused (1995), [1995] S.C.C.A. No. 142, 1995 CarswellNat 2830 (S.C.C.).

Another question relating to Notices of Compliance is the production of a pharmaceutical product that does not infringe a patent but for the approval of which one must rely on data submitted in respect of a patented product. In *Bristol-Myers Squibb Co. v. Canada (Attorney General)*,[127] the Federal Court of Appeal decided that the Notice of Compliance Regulations[128] did not allow the person who created such a product from obtaining a notice of compliance and, hence, from selling its product, in spite of the fact that the product itself does not infringe a patent.[129] The Supreme Court of Canada reversed, insisting on the need to balance patent rights against public health considerations and to maintain competition and innovation among pharmaceutical companies.[129a]

## 2. Defences

Invalidity of the patent is often the first line defence to patent infringement. However, as discussed above, the patent benefits from a presumption of validity. A finding of invalidity (for anticipation, obviousness or lack of utility or because the patent covers unpatentable subject-matter) is in fact a reversal of the Patent Office (CIPO) determination that the patent should be granted, unless new evidence can be adduced that the patent examiner did not consider[130] or it can be shown that the Commissioner applied the wrong test or erroneous data.[131] This defence is specifically mentioned in s. 59.

---

[127]   (sub nom. *Biolyse Pharma Corp. v. Bristol-Myers Squibb Co.*) [2003] 4 F.C. 505, 226 D.L.R. (4th) 138, (sub nom. *Biolyse Pharma Corp. v. Bristol-Myers Squibb Co.*) 24 C.P.R. (4th) 417, 303 N.R. 63 (Fed. C.A.), leave to appeal allowed (2003), 27 C.P.R. (4th) vi (S.C.C.).

[128]   *Patented Medicines (Notice of Compliance) Regulations*, SOR/93-133.

[129]   See also *Merck & Co. v. Canada (Attorney General)* (1999), [1999] F.C.J. No. 1825, 176 F.T.R. 21, 1999 CarswellNat 2461 (Fed. T.D.), affirmed (2000), (2000), (sub nom. *Merck & Co. v. Nu-Pharm Inc.*) 5 C.P.R. (4th) 138 (Fed. C.A.), leave to appeal refused (2000), 5 C.P.R. (4th) vii (S.C.C.).

[129a]   *Bristol-Meyers Squibb Co. v. Canada (Attorney General)*, 2005 SCC 26, *supra*, note 9a.

[130]   See above the Infringement: Generally Section and *Skelding v. Daly* (1940), 55 B.C.R. 427, 1 C.P.R. 247 (B.C. C.A.), affirmed on other grounds (1940), [1941] S.C.R. 184, [1941] 1 D.L.R. 305, 1 C.P.R. 257 (S.C.C.). But see *Glaxo-SmithKline Inc. v. Canada (Minister of Health)* (2003), [2003] F.C.J. No. 1151, 28 C.P.R. (4th) 307, 237 F.T.R. 218, 2003 CarswellNat 4875 (F.C.); and *Westaim Corp. v. Royal Canadian Mint* (2002), [2002] F.C.J. No. 1654, 23 C.P.R. (4th) 9, 224 F.T.R. 184, 2002 CarswellNat 3380 (Fed. T.D.).

[131]   See *Mills v. Canada (Commissioner of Patents)* (1988), [1988] F.C.J. No. 921, 22 C.P.R. (3d) 421, 21 C.I.P.R. 79, 1988 CarswellNat 600 (Fed. C.A.).

As mentioned above, a patented product or process may be used in relation with governmental regulatory submissions.[132]

The jurisprudence also recognizes a defence of *bona fide* experimental, non-commercial use. It is indirectly recognized in s. 55.2(6):

> For greater certainty, subsection (1) does not affect any exception to the exclusive property or privilege granted by a patent that exists at law in respect of acts done privately and on a non-commercial scale or for a non-commercial purpose or in respect of any use, manufacture, construction or sale of the patented invention solely for the purpose of experiments that relate to the subject-matter of the patent.

According to *Smith, Kline & French Inter-American Corp. v. Micro Chemicals Ltd.*,[133] limited experimental use, without a licence, of a patented article in experiments done in good faith is not a violation of the patent. The basis of this argument is that no damage is being suffered by the plaintiff and no profits are being generated by the defendant.

In *Dableh v. Ontario Hydro*,[134] the Federal Court of Appeal noted:

> The law does not regard testing to be an infringing use. Jessel M.R. summarized the law's perspective on the use of patented technology for testing purposes in *Frearson v. Loe*: [(1878), 9 Ch.D. 48 at 67]
>
> > Patent rights were never granted to prevent persons of ingenuity exercising their talents in a fair way. But if there be neither using nor vending of the invention for profit, the mere making for the purpose of experiment, and not for a fraudulent purpose, ought not to be considered within the meaning of the prohibition, and if it were, it is certainly not the subject for an injunction.
>
> This perspective has been accepted by the Supreme Court of Canada. In *Smith, Kline & French Inter-American Corp. v. Micro Chemicals Ltd.*, Hall J. stated:
>
> > The use Micro was making of the patented substance here was not for profit but to establish the fact that it could manufacture a quality product in accordance with the specifications disclosed in respondent's application for Patent No. 612204 ... Micro's experiments ... were not carried out for the purpose of improving the process but to enable Micro to produce it commercially as soon as the license it had applied for could

---

[132] See the Process Patents and Notice of Compliance Section and s. 55.2.

[133] (1971), [1972] S.C.R. 506, 25 D.L.R. (3d) 79, 2 C.P.R. (2d) 193 (S.C.C.).

[134] [1996] 3 F.C. 751, 68 C.P.R. (3d) 129, 199 N.R. 57 (Fed. C.A.), leave to appeal refused (1997), 74 C.P.R. (3d) vi (S.C.C.) [*Dableh* cited to F.C.].

be obtained. I cannot see that this sort of experimentation and preparation is an infringement.

In *Dableh*, the Court also noted that the defendant could not be held liable under the tort of inducement (of patent infringement) when the inducee had not himself infringed the patent.

Another defence applies to acts done in good faith prior to the claim date of the patent (under s. 10). The exception applies to pre-patent inventory.[135] Section 56(1) reads as follows:

> Every person who, before the claim date of a claim in a patent has purchased, constructed or acquired the subject matter defined by the claim, has the right to use and sell to others the specific article, machine, manufacture or composition of matter patented and so purchased, constructed or acquired without being liable to the patentee or the legal representatives of the patentee for so doing.

There have been a number of cases where the provision was interpreted, especially the meaning of "specific":

> In *Reeves Brothers Inc. v. Toronto Quilting & Embroidery Ltd.*, 43 C.P.R. (2d) 145, Mr. Justice Gibson was of the view that the key word in section 58 (now section 56) of the *Patent Act* was the word 'specific'. At page 163 of the decision, Gibson J. states that:
>
>> For a person to obtain the immunity given by s. 58, the person can only use or vend to others 'the specific article, machine, manufacture or composition of matter patented and so purchased, constructed or acquired before the issue of the patent therefor'.
>
> It would appear that the key word in s. 58[136] is 'specific'.
>
> Mr. Justice Gibson then goes on to write at page 164 that:
>
>> Counsel for the defendant submitted that this Court, in respect to the subject-matter of this case, should construe s. 58 of the *Patent Act* so as to find that the words 'specific article, machine, manufacture or composition of matter' are synonymous with the words 'unrestricted royalty free licence to use invention'. In other words, the word 'specific' if such submission was to be accepted, is in effect deleted.

---

[135] See *Merck & Co. v. Apotex Inc.* (2000), [2000] F.C.J. No. 1033, 8 C.P.R. (4th) 248, 258 N.R. 116, 2000 CarswellNat 1291 (Fed. C.A.).

[136] Now section 56.

In *Lido Industrial Products v. Teledyne Industries*, 57 C.P.R. (2d) 29, the Federal Court of Appeal also had occasion to examine section 58 (now section 56) of the *Patent Act*. At page 54 of the decision Urie J.A. writes as follows:

> Clearly s. 58 applies to a person other than the patentee who uses or sells an article or machine after the grant of patent. In this case the critical date is December 14, 1976. It must thus be determined as at that date, whether or not the specific articles or machines which the appellant used or sold were articles or machines that it purchased, constructed or acquired before the grant of patent. It is my view that because of its evident purpose s. 58 contemplates that the particular articles or machines must actually be in existence at the date of the grant to fall within its purview. As I see it, their actual existence at that date is essential to the application of the section.

Based on these authorities, it is therefore my view that Apotex may only sell or use the specific 'article' which it purchased prior to the issuance of the subject patents.

Consequently, Apotex may only use and sell to others the Lisinopril which it purchased in the form in which it was purchased. It is my view that s. 56 does not permit Apotex to use or sell its Lisinopril in a form other than that in which it was purchased. The clear words of s. 56 leave no doubt in my mind that it must be so.[137]

Another "defence" is known as "Gillette". It was first set out in *Gillette Safety Razor Co. v. Anglo-American Trading Co.*[138] and adopted in *Fero Holdings Ltd. v. Entreprises Givesco Inc.*[139] Essentially, this defense allows the defendant not to have to choose between arguing non-infringement and arguing invalidity of the patent, and it saves the court the need to make a final determination on either one. The defence is explained in *Fero Holdings* as follows by Pelletier J.:

> The motion for summary judgment is based on the Gillette defence, which permits judgment to be rendered in a patent case without the necessity of interpreting the patent itself. The defence is taken from *Gillette Safety Razor Co. v. Anglo-American Trading Co.* (1913), 30 R.P.C. 465 (H.L.) at 480 where the following appears:

---

[137] *Zeneca Pharma Inc. v. Canada (Minister of National Health & Welfare)* (1994), [1994] F.C.J. No. 179, 54 C.P.R. (3d) 538, 1994 CarswellNat 1917 (Fed. T.D.).
[138] (1913), 30 R.P.C. 465 (U.K. H.L.).
[139] (1999), [1999] F.C.J. No. 1310, 2 C.P.R. (4th) 32, 1999 CarswellNat 1609 (Fed. T.D.).

I am, therefore, of opinion that in this case the Defendants 'right to succeed can be established without an examination of the terms of the Specification of the Plaintiffs' Letters patent. I am aware that such a mode of deciding a patent case is unusual, but from the point of view of the public it is important that this method of viewing their right should not be overlooked. In practical life it is often the only safeguard to the manufacturer. It is impossible for ordinary member of the public to keep watch on all the numerous patents which are taken out and to ascertain the validity and scope of their claims. But he is entitled to feel secure if he knows that that which he is doing differs from that which has been done of old only in non-patentable variations, such as the substitution of mechanical equivalents or changes of material shape or size. The defence that 'the alleged infringement was not novel at the date of the plaintiff's Letters Patent' is a good defence in law, and it would sometimes obviate the great length and and expense of Patent cases if the defendant could and would put forth his case in this form, and thus spare himself the trouble of demonstrating on which horn of the well-known dilemma the plaintiff had impaled himself, invalidity or non-infringement.

If a defendant can show that his or her product or process is comparable to a product or process disclosed in some way prior to the claim date of the patent alleged to be infringed, then either the patent is invalid for anticipation or its claims must be interpreted as not preventing the defendant's use.

The defence of laches and acquiescence has had very little success in patent infringement cases. Essentially, a patentee can wait and file an action a day prior to the expiry of the patent. This will not affect the finding of infringement, but may influence the court's decision on the appropriate remedies, including damages.[140] Laches do not provide a cause of action, only a defence.[141] A long delay is also relevant at the interlocutory injunction stage. As was noted by Reed J.:

---

[140] See *Standal Estate v. Swecan International Ltd.* (1989), 28 C.P.R. (3d) 261, 27 F.T.R. 15, 25 C.I.P.R. 38 (Fed. T.D.): "In fixing a lump sum, I must consider that the defendants are, after all, as I have found, the guilty party, and that they have not shown much cooperation in providing documents to the accountant. On the other hand, I must also bear in mind that the plaintiffs themselves were guilty of procrastination in the prosecution of their action. Had they proceeded several years earlier, the task of the accountant and that of the presiding Judge would have been made easier."

[141] See *Combe v. Combe*, [1951] 1 All E.R. 767 (Eng. C.A.); *Bank of Montreal v. Glendale (Atlantic) Ltd.* (1977), 76 D.L.R. (3d) 303, 20 N.S.R. (2d) 216, 1 B.L.R. 279 (N.S. C.A.); *Saskatoon Credit Union Ltd. v. Central Park Enterprises Ltd.* (1988), 22 B.C.L.R. (2d) 89, 47 D.L.R. (4th) 431 (B.C. S.C.); and *Nintendo of America Inc. v. Battery Technologies Inc.* (2001), [2001] F.C.J. No. 914, 13 C.P.R. (4th) 102, 206 F.T.R. 71, 2001 CarswellNat 1223 (Fed. T.D.).

In general it is the effect of delay, not the fact of delay that precludes a party
from obtaining an interlocutory injunction. For example, effects which make
delay a reason for refusing an interlocutory injunction are: (1) the defendant
has prejudiced his position during the time of delay, as for example, through
the expenditure of money in developing a business; or (2) delay is evidence
that the plaintiff does not consider interdiction of the infringement an urgent
or pressing matter.[142]

It is worth noting that any person may apply to the Federal Court for
invalidation (or impeachment) of a patent (s. 60(1))[143] or for a declaration
that a process or article used or proposed to be used or any article made,
used or sold or proposed to be made, used or sold by him that might be
alleged by any patentee to constitute an infringement of an exclusive property or privilege granted thereby does not or would not constitute an infringement of the exclusive property or privilege (s. 60(2)). The applicant
must provide security for costs under s. 60(3).[144]

It is also important to bear in mind that there is a statutory limitation
period of six years (s. 55.01).

## 3. Compulsory Licences

A seldom used provision is s. 65, which reads as follows:

(1) The Attorney General of Canada or any person interested may, at any time
after the expiration of three years from the date of the grant of a patent, apply
to the Commissioner alleging in the case of that patent that there has been an
abuse of the exclusive rights thereunder and asking for relief under this Act.
(2) The exclusive rights under a patent shall be deemed to have been abused
in any of the following circumstances:

(a) and (b) [Repealed, 1993, c. 44, s. 196]
(c) if the demand for the patented article in Canada is not being met to an
adequate extent and on reasonable terms;
(d) if, by reason of the refusal of the patentee to grant a licence or licences on
reasonable terms, the trade or industry of Canada or the trade of any person or

---

[142] *ICI Americas Inc. v. Ireco Canada Inc.* (1985), 7 C.P.R. (3d) 1 (Fed. T.D.),
varied (1985), 8 C.P.R. (3d) 408 at 411 (Fed. T.D.), varied (1985), 8 C.P.R. (3d)
408 (Fed. T.D.). See also *Parke, Davis & Co. v. Laboratoire Pentagone Ltée*
(1963), 43 C.P.R. 42 (Que. S.C.), affirmed (1964), 44 C.P.R. 229 (Que. C.A.).

[143] Which can also be made as a counter-claim in an infringement action. See *Powell
Manufacturing Co. v. Balthes Farm Equipment Manufacturing Ltd.* (1979), 44
C.P.R. (2d) 30 (Fed. C.A.).

[144] See *Excalibre Oil Tools Ltd. v. Garay* (1999), 179 F.T.R. 313 (Fed. T.D.).

class of persons trading in Canada, or the establishment of any new trade or industry in Canada, is prejudiced, and it is in the public interest that a licence or licences should be granted;

(e) if any trade or industry in Canada, or any person or class of persons engaged therein, is unfairly prejudiced by the conditions attached by the patentee, whether before or after the passing of this Act, to the purchase, hire, licence or use of the patented article or to the using or working of the patented process; or

(f) if it is shown that the existence of the patent, being a patent for an invention relating to a process involving the use of materials not protected by the patent or for an invention relating to a substance produced by such a process, has been utilized by the patentee so as unfairly to prejudice in Canada the manufacture, use or sale of any materials.

The provision was invoked successfully in very few cases.[145] It was discussed by the Commissioner of Patents in his refusal of an application for a licence:

The basis of the Applicant's allegation that there has been an abuse in the circumstance described in paragraph 65(2)(c) is set out in paragraphs 22 to 27 of its application. Essentially, the applicant takes the position that the patented article in issue is the chemical compound enalapril maleate in bulk chemical form and that demand in Canada for bulk enalapril maleate is not being met because its acquisition and use are precluded by the patent and the Patentee's refusal to grant a licence to the Applicant. According to the Applicant, the relevant demand that is not being met in Canada is not a demand for enalapril maleate tablets for sale in Canada, but a demand for bulk enalapril maleate required for manufacture of finished tablets for export.
[. . .]

In my view, the term 'patented article' includes any article whose manufacture, use or sale without the consent of the patentee would infringe the exclusive rights granted to the patentee under section 42 of the Act. For a given patent there may be a large number of different articles whose manufacture, use or sale would infringe the patentee's exclusive rights and each of these could constitute a patented article for the purposes of paragraph 65(2)(c).

In the application, the only demand that the Applicant alleges as not being met is its own demand for bulk enalapril maleate. There is no allegation that there is any demand by anyone other than the Applicant that is not being met. The basis for the Applicant's allegation that its demand for bulk enalapril maleate is not being met is set out in paragraph 23 of the application:

---

[145] See *Puckhandler Inc. v. BADS Industries Inc.* (1998), 81 C.P.R. (3d) 261 (Can. Pat. App. Bd. & Pat. Commr.).

The demand in Canada for the patented article, the chemical compound ena-lapril maleate in bulk chemical form, is not being met by reason of the fact that the acquisition and use of the same are precluded by the Merck's Patent and Merck's refusal to grant a licence to Torpharm.

In this assertion, there is no indication that the Patentee ever refused to supply bulk enalapril maleate to the Applicant or that the Applicant had even made a request to the Patentee to be supplied with bulk enalapril maleate. [. . .]

In my view, the Applicant never asked the Patentee to supply it with bulk enalapril maleate; the Applicant only asked for a licence to purchase bulk enalapril, produce tablets in Canada and export the tablets from Canada. As the Applicant did not ask the Patentee to supply it with bulk enalapril maleate, I cannot see that there is any basis for concluding that there is any demand by the Applicant for bulk enalapril maleate that is not being met. Since there is no unmet demand by the Applicant and since, as noted above, there is no allegation in the application that there is any unmet demand by any other person, I find that there is no abuse under paragraph 65(2)(c) of the Act.

Although the above is sufficient for me to dismiss the Applicant's allegation that there has been an abuse under paragraph 65(2)(c) of the Act, I would point out that even if the facts in the present case could be construed as establishing a demand by the Applicant for bulk enalapril maleate that is not being met, I would still not be prepared to conclude that there has been an abuse under paragraph 65(2)(c). Paragraph 65(2)(c) of the Act is directed at ensuring that demand for patented articles in Canada is met. In my view, a demand for an article in Canada solely for the purpose of exporting that article would not fall within the scope of paragraph 65(2)(c); such a demand would in reality be a demand for the article in a foreign country but not in Canada [. . .].
[. . .]

I now turn to paragraph 65(2)(d) of the Act [. . .].

There are three elements to this species of abuse: there must be a refusal to grant a licence, there must be a prejudice, and it must be in the public interest that a licence be granted. If any one of elements is lacking, then abuse under paragraph 65(2)(d) of the Act will not have been made out. I will consider each in turn.

*Refusal to Grant a Licence*

In order to determine whether there has been a refusal by the Patentee to grant a licence on reasonable terms, I have carefully examined the correspondence between the two parties and the resulting actions taken.
[. . .]

On balance, I am not satisfied that the Applicant gave the Patentee sufficient time to consider the request for a voluntary licence. To my mind the onus is on the person seeking a licence to provide sufficient information to prompt a response. [. . .]

Notwithstanding the absence of a refusal to license by the Patentee, I have considered the second and third elements under paragraph 65(2)(d); namely, prejudice and public interest.

*Prejudice*

The Applicant submits that both it and the 'trade or industry in Canada' are unfairly prejudiced by the Patentee's refusal to provide the Applicant with the licence it seeks. In terms of prejudice to itself, the Applicant submits that it has it has already taken all the steps necessary to place itself in a position to export enalapril maleate tablets to the US for sale. If the Applicant is not in the US market when patent protection comes off on August 22, it argues that it will lose its opportunity to enter that market at a critical time. If the Applicant does not obtain a licence, it could consider manufacturing in the US; however, the regulatory process in the US would mean an 18 month delay in the Applicant entering the market and there are currently several other generic manufacturers ready to enter the market on August 22. In the words of the Applicant's President, another generic manufacturer entering the market 18 months after patent protection is lifted would be a 'non-event'.
[. . .]

[C]ontrary to the submissions of counsel, in order to demonstrate prejudice to the trade or industry of Canada, it is not enough to simply rely on the alleged prejudice to the Applicant. In *Robin Electric Lamp Co's Applications* [(1915), 32 R.P.C. 457], the court stated as follows:

> Again, the expression 'trade or industry' seems to me to be used in a wide sense just as we speak of the cotton trade, or industry, and the woollen trade or industry; so that <u>it is not enough to establish that a particular trader is unfairly prejudiced, it must be further proved that the trade or industry as a whole is thus affected.</u>

(emphasis added in original)

The construction of the phase 'trade or industry' in *Robin Electric* has been followed in subsequent cases. There is insufficient evidence before me upon which to conclude that the pharmaceutical trade and industry in Canada has been prejudiced by the Patentee's refusal to provide the Applicant with a licence and I find that such prejudice has not been established.

What about prejudice to the Applicant itself? With regard to the meaning of the phrase 'trade of any person', the court in *Brownie* stated as follows:

The next phrase is 'The trade of any person or class of persons trading in the United Kingdom.' This is, in my judgement, not capable of so wide an interpretation as the preceding phrase, for while the word 'trade' itself is of general import, the words that follow, 'of any person or class of persons trading in the United Kingdom,' especially when read with the phrase immediately following, must of necessity limit such generality to the *existing* trade of some person or class of persons.

(emphasis added in original) [*Re Application by Brownie Wireless Co.* (1929), 46 R.P.C. 457]

In *Canadian Patent Law and Practice*, Fox states that:

The term 'trade of any person on or class of persons trading in Canada' is not capable of so wide an interpretation as the preceding phrase and must be construed as referring to the existing trade of the applicant. This particular provision can, consequently, be of no benefit to an applicant who wishes to found a new business or extend an old one.

In my view, even if the fact that the Patentee did not respond to the Applicant's requests for a licence could be considered a refusal, I would not be prepared to find that such refusal caused prejudice to the Applicant's trade. On the basis of the authorities cited above, it is my view that the phrase 'trade of any person' must be construed as referring to the existing trade of any person. The opportunity which the Applicant seeks to pursue with respect to enalapril maleate is not part of the Applicant's existing trade. What the Applicant seeks to do in this case is, in the words of Fox, to 'extend' its business and, in my view, the Patentee's refusal to licence the Applicant in that circumstance cannot constitute prejudice to the trade of the Applicant within the meaning of the Act.

*Public Interest*

I now turn to the issue of public interest. The term 'public interest' is not defined in the Act or the Rules. Counsel for both parties submitted that in considering the issue of public interest, I should look not only at the interest of the Applicant and the Patentee, but at a broad range of interests, including the public in Canada generally. I agree with those submissions.

There is a dearth of helpful Canadian jurisprudence on the meaning of the words 'public interest'; however, what jurisprudence there is suggests that, in any given case, the meaning to be attributed to those words, or words having the same general meaning, should be determined by 'reference to the context and the objects and purposes' of the relevant statute. In my view, the notion of public interest in section 65(2)(d) requires me to weigh and balance the various competing interests at play, i.e. both those interests which would favour the granting of a compulsory licence and those which would run counter to the granting of such a licence.

I have already discussed the possible prejudice the Applicant may suffer if it does not obtain the licence it seeks. It would clearly be in the Applicant's interest to obtain a licence and, as the Applicant's interest is part of the public interest, that fact should go on the side of the balance which would favour granting a compulsory licence to the Applicant. In considering the issue of public interest, I have attempted to gain an understanding of the extent to which the Applicant's interests would be impacted by the grant or refusal of a licence. In that regard, I note that the evidence indicates that the Applicant employs approximately 300 people in its existing manufacturing operations and that it would add 10 to 15 positions if it were to obtain the licence it seeks. In assessing the impact that this decision will have on the Applicant's interests, I think that it is important to be mindful of those facts and the size of the Applicant's opportunity with respect to enalapril maleate, relative to the Applicant's overall operations. As noted above, it is clear that if the Applicant does not obtain a licence in this case, it will be deprived of the opportunity to exploit a new product market. However, the impact of the refusal would clearly not be such as to place the Applicant's survival as a viable commercial entity in jeopardy. I state the foregoing, not because it is my view that an applicant under section 65 (2)(d) must establish that it will fail if it does not obtain a licence, but rather to try to gauge the order of magnitude of the impact of this decision on the Applicant's interests.

[. . .]

What of the interests of the consuming Canadian public? As noted, if the Applicant were granted a licence, it would use it to service markets other than Canada. That being said, in another way, in my view, the Canadian public would be ill-served by the issuance of a compulsory licence to the Applicant. To understand this point, I think it is important to understand the rational for the existence of the patent system. As described in a leading text on the subject of patents:

> At no time in English history were all monopolies regarded as anathema. . . . If they were for the good of the realm their propriety was never questioned; indeed, if the grant covered a new trade or article it was not considered to be a monopoly. From this theory evolved the principle that a new invention or the setting up of a new manufacture was a laudable thing and that a grant of exclusive privilege to its introducer by an exercise of the Crown prerogative was a beneficial act. . ..
>
> (emphasis added in original)[Fox, *Canadian Patent Law and Practice* (4th ed.)]

In my view, it is upon precisely the basis articulated by Fox in the preceding passage that patent and patent law exist in Canada today. Parliament, in passing the Act, clearly recognized that a patentee can under that Act restrict others from using its invention. That limitation is, in effect, a restraint on trade. Notwithstanding that fact, Parliament saw fit to create patent rights. In my view, it must be assumed that Parliament considered it to be in the public interest to have a patent system in this country which would encourage research and innovation by granting patentees certain rights.

If I were to construe the public interest in the manner advocated by the Applicant, the patent system in this country could, in certain ways be undermined. This point was addressed in a decision of a former Commissioner of Patents in *E. C. Walker & Sons v. Lever Bias Machine Corporation*[(1953), 20 C.P.R. 61]. In that case, a Canadian manufacturer, Walker, had sought a compulsory licence to permit it to use a machine to produce certain kinds of tape. The patentee was a U.S. corporation. It had provided two of the patented machines and the related manufacturing process to a Canadian company and the Canadian market was being amply supplied with the kind of tape at issue. In rejecting Walker's application, the Commissioner stated as follows:

If I were to interpret the provisions of s. 65(2)(e) in the manner suggested by Walker & Sons, I am very much afraid that we would establish a practice whereby no one holding a patent could ever be sure that he is not abusing his rights by refusing a licence to a competitor and this especially in the case of a patent for a process or one for a machine to make a known product. The owner of a particularly successful patent could work his patent and sell the product thereof cheaper than his competitor and in such case the competitor would be able to prove prejudice to his trade and obtain a licence. The position of an exclusive licencee would be impossible and the effect of such a licence would be nullified. Competitors would wait until a product was well established on the market and then they would secure a compulsory licence and reap the benefit of any pioneering work done by others.

I agree with the views of the Commissioner in *Walker* and adopt them as my own for the purposes of this decision. In my view, the interests of maintaining a strong and predictable patent system weigh against the granting of a compulsory licence to the Applicant.

As noted above, the notion of public interest contemplates a weighing and balancing of various competing interests. The process requires that the relevant interests first be identified. Once identified, the various interests must be assessed. Finally, all of these interests must be placed on the scale so that a determination of the public interest may be made. This last step in the process requires the exercise of judgement, given that the competing interests cannot be assigned precise arithmetic values. Having proceeded through the foregoing steps, it is my view that, on balance, it would not be in the public interest to grant the Applicant a compulsory licence in this matter. In my view, the interests of the Applicant that support the granting of a licence to the Applicant are simply not sufficient to offset the competing interests on the other side on the balance.

### (c)  Abuse under Subsection 65(1)

Finally, I turn to the third ground of abuse advanced by the Applicant; namely, that the Patentee is exercising its patent right for no *bona fide* purpose and that this is an abuse under subsection 65(2) of the Act.

Counsel for the Applicant argued that even if I were not satisfied that the circumstances of this case and that the conduct of the Patentee fell within any of the deemed abuse provisions in subsection 65(2) of the Act, I could nevertheless find, under subsection 65(1), that the Patentee had abused its patent. Counsel submitted that the deeming provisions in subsection 65(2) are not exhaustive and cited a number of cases in which the courts have considered deeming provisions in various pieces of pieces of legislation, including the *Criminal Code*, the *Canada Labour Code* and the *National Transportation Act*.

Notwithstanding counsel's able argument, I am unable to accede to the proposition that subsection 65(2) of the Act is not exhaustive of the instances where abuse can be found to exist. In a number of cases dealing with abuse applications under the Act and its U.K. statutory counterpart, the courts have held that, to succeed on an abuse application, an applicant must demonstrate that the facts it relies on satisfy the requirements of one of the deeming paragraphs in relevant legislation. For example, in *Celotex Corp. v. Donnacona Paper Company Limited*, [[1939] Ex. C.R. 128] the Exchequer Court of Canada considered an appeal of a decision of the Commissioner of Patents. In describing the abuse provisions of the Act, the Court stated as follows:

> Sec. 65(1) provides that any person interested may at any time after the expiration of three years from the date of the grant of the patent apply to the Commissioner alleging, in the case of that patent, that there has been an abuse of the exclusive rights thereunder, and asking for relief under the Act. There are six classes of cases in which monopoly rights are to be deemed to be abused. These classes are not mutually exclusive; but unless the circumstances relied upon fall within one or the other of the classes, no relief can be granted under the section.

(emphasis added in original)

Similar statements have been made by courts in other cases[146] and in the leading text on the subject of patents. In light of the views expressed in the referenced authorities, it is my view that subsection 65(2) is exhaustive in delineating the

---

[146]  See, for example, *McKechnie Brothers Ltd. for Compulsory License in Respect of Certain Letters Patent, Re* (1934), 51 R.P.C. 461 at 466; *Brownie Wireless Co., Re* (1929), 46 R.P.C. 457 at 471-472 (footnote in original).

instances in which abuse may be found to exist and therefore the Applicant's argument under subsection 65(1) of the Act must fail.[147]

A parallel procedure, though much broader in scope, can be found in s. 32 of the *Competition Act*:[148]

(1)    In any case where use has been made of the exclusive rights and privileges conferred by one or more patents for invention, by one or more trade-marks, by a copyright or by a registered integrated circuit topography, so as to

(a)    limit unduly the facilities for transporting, producing, manufacturing, supplying, storing or dealing in any article or commodity that may be a subject of trade or commerce,

(b)    restrain or injure, unduly, trade or commerce in relation to any such article or commodity,

(c)    prevent, limit or lessen, unduly, the manufacture or production of any such article or commodity or unreasonably enhance the price thereof, or

(d)    prevent or lessen, unduly, competition in the production, manufacture, purchase, barter, sale, transportation or supply of any such article or commodity,

the Federal Court may make one or more of the orders referred to in subsection (2) in the circumstances described in that subsection.

*32(2) Orders*

The Federal Court, on an information exhibited by the Attorney General of Canada, may, for the purpose of preventing any use in the manner defined in subsection (1) of the exclusive rights and privileges conferred by any patents for invention, trade-marks, copyrights or registered integrated circuit topographies relating to or affecting the manufacture, use or sale of any article or commodity that may be a subject of trade or commerce, make one or more of the following orders:

(a)    declaring void, in whole or in part, any agreement, arrangement or licence relating to that use;

(b)    restraining any person from carrying out or exercising any or all of the terms or provisions of the agreement, arrangement or licence;

(c)    directing the grant of licences under any such patent, copyright or registered integrated circuit topography to such persons and on such terms and conditions as the court may deem proper or, if the grant and other

---

[147] *Torpharm Inc. v. Merck & Co.* (2000), 9 C.P.R. (4th) 520 (Can. Pat. App. Bd. & Pat. Commr.).

[148] R.S.C. 1985, c. C-34, s. 32.

remedies under this section would appear insufficient to prevent that use, revoking the patent;

(d)    directing that the registration of a trade-mark in the register of trade-marks or the registration of an integrated circuit topography in the register of topographies be expunged or amended; and

(e)    directing that such other acts be done or omitted as the Court may deem necessary to prevent any such use.

*32(3) Treaties, etc.*

No order shall be made under this section that is at variance with any treaty, convention, arrangement or engagement with any other country respecting patents, trade-marks, copyrights or integrated circuit topographies to which Canada is a party.

## VI. REMEDIES

There are four stages in the examination of an alleged patent infringement, and remedies vary accordingly:

(a)    Someone inadvertently or otherwise acquired the subject mater defined by the patent claims;

(b)    Someone used the invention between its claim date (*i.e.* its Canadian filing date or priority date if filed in a treaty country as defined by s. 28.1 — see the International Section) and its publication date;

(c)    Someone used the invention after its publication (under s. 10) but before the grant of the patent; and

(d)    Someone used the invention after the grant and before the expiry of the term of protection.

There are different liability regimes that apply to the above situations. Under situation (a), the purchaser might use or sell to others specific articles purchased prior to the claim date (s. 56(1)). If the invention can be discovered by simple reverse engineering by looking at a product available prior to the claim date, a question may also be raised as to the patent's novelty and thus its validity, especially if, as would normally be the case, the invention was made available prior to the claim date by a person other than the inventor or a person who obtained knowledge of the invention from the applicant — see s. 28.2(1)(b)).[148a]

---

[148a] See *Baker Petrolite Corp. v. Canwell Enviro-Industries Ltd.*, *supra*, note 54a.

For the time period in the situation described under (b), the *Patent Act* is silent. A combined reading of s. 42, which refers to the date of the *grant*, and the limited liability regime applicable between publication and the grant under s. 55(2) (see below), would lead one to the conclusion that the patentee has no right to a remedy for a violation occurring between the filing date and the publication date. This is also consonant with the principles concerning innocent infringement.[149] It would be unfair to impose liability on a person who had no way of acquiring knowledge that a patent had been applied for, which theoretically happens on the publication (or "laid open") date.[150] If an applicant had put a defendant on notice of a pending application prior to its publication and provided sufficient information about the claimed invention, the application of the innocent infringement doctrine would no longer apply. However, to impose liability prior to the publication of the application is hard to reconcile with the wording of ss. 42 and 55(2).

In the situation described under (c), the patentee and persons claiming under him are entitled to a reasonable compensation for damage sustained by them after publication but before the grant of the patent. This right is contingent on the issuance of the patent.[151] Elements to be taken into account in determining a reasonable level of compensation would include the actual damages suffered by the patentee and profits made by the defendant, and whether in addition to the "constructive notice" that takes place on the "laid open" date, the defendant was in fact put on notice by the patentee of the pending application.

After the grant, in the time period described in situation (d), the patentee and persons claiming under him are entitled to "all damage" sustained by them or, if they so elect, to an accounting of profits.[152]

The *Patent Act* refers to "all damage sustained by the patentee"[153] in s. 54, and to orders enjoining the party from further use, manufacture or sale of the subject matter and "for and respecting inspection or account" in s. 57(1). The Supreme Court has noted that courts have discretion as to the method of determining the monetary compensation for patent infringement.

---

[149] See *British United Shoe* in *Pfizer Corp. v. Ministry of Health*, [1965] A.C. 512 (U.K. H.L.).

[150] See *Free World Trust, supra*, note 19.

[151] See *idem* and *Stamicarbon B.V. v. Urea Casale S.A.*, [2002] 3 F.C. 347, 17 C.P.R. (4th) 377, 284 N.R. 295 (Fed. C.A.), leave to appeal refused (2002), 303 N.R. 400 (note) (S.C.C.).

[152] S. 55(1). See also *Schmeiser, supra*, note 48.

[153] And "to all persons claiming under the patentee". *See 671905 Alberta Inc. v. Q'Max Solutions Inc.*, [2003] 4 F.C. 713, 27 C.P.R. (4th) 385, 305 N.R. 137, 241 F.T.R. 160 (note) (Fed. C.A.), leave to appeal refused (2004), 330 N.R. 392 (note) (S.C.C.).

In addition, delivery up[154] or destruction[155] of the infringing products may be ordered.

Under s. 20(1)(b) of the *Federal Courts Act*,[156] the Federal Court of Canada has exclusive jurisdiction to impeach or annul any patent (see also s. 60 of the *Patent Act*). Under s. 20(2) of the same Act, the Federal Court has concurrent jurisdiction with provincial courts in all cases in "which a remedy is sought under the authority of an Act of Parliament or at law or in equity respecting any patent of invention. . ." (see also s. 54(2) of the *Patent Act*). When a contract dispute (e.g., an alleged licence) is raised by the defendant, the Federal Court has jurisdiction, but not if a counter-claim is made on that basis.[157]

The criteria applicable to interlocutory injunctions are discussed in the Infringement section of the Trade-Marks Part. In brief, courts must assess the strength of the parties' case (whether there is a serious question to be tried); the degree of harm which will occur to the plaintiffs if the injunction is not granted and occurring to the defendant if it is (considering irreparable harm and the balance of convenience) and any equitable considerations (delay, unfair or unreasonable conduct). Summary judgment may be granted.[158] However, summary judgment is normally not granted where there is an issue as to the patent's validity[159] or a serious technical issue[160] or disagreement about material facts.[161]

---

[154] See, *e.g., Baxter Travenol Laboratories of Canada Ltd. v. Cutter (Canada) Ltd.* (1980), 52 C.P.R. (2d) 163 (Fed. T.D.), affirmed in part on other grounds (1983), 68 C.P.R. (2d) 179 (Fed. C.A.), leave to appeal refused (1983), 72 C.P.R. (2d) 287 (S.C.C.); and *Clinton Wire Cloth Co. v. Dominion Fence Co.* (1907), 11 Ex. C.R. 103 (Can. Ex. Ct.), affirmed by (1907), 39 S.C.R. 535 (S.C.C.).

[155] See, *e.g., Energy Absorption Systems Inc. v. Y. Boissonneault & fils Inc.* (1990), [1990] F.C.J. No. 330, 30 C.P.R. (3d) 420, 33 F.T.R. 96, 1990 CarswellNat 780 (Fed. T.D.).

[156] R.S.C., 1985, c. F-7.

[157] See *Jagna Ltd. v. Transpavé Inc.* (1997), [1997] F.C.J. No. 1204, 79 C.P.R. (3d) 467, 146 F.T.R. 2, 1997 CarswellNat 2651 (Fed. T.D.).

[158] See, *e.g., Hudson Luggage Supplies Inc. v. Tormont Publications Inc. / Éditions Tormont Inc.* (1995), [1995] F.C.J. No. 1748, 65 C.P.R. (3d) 216, 109 F.T.R. 18, 1995 CarswellNat 760 (Fed. T.D.); *Heffco Inc. v. Dreco Energy Services Ltd.* (1997), [1997] F.C.J. No. 403, 73 C.P.R. (3d) 284, 127 F.T.R. 286, 1997 CarswellNat 659 (Fed. T.D.); and *G.D. Hanna Inc. v. L.S. Display Systems Inc.* (1998), [1998] F.C.J. No. 132, (sub nom. *G.D. Hanna Inc. (Hanna Design) v. L.S. Display Systems Inc.*) 78 C.P.R. (3d) 456, 1998 CarswellNat 243 (Fed. T.D.).

[159] See *Pallmann Maschinenfabrik GmbH Co. KG v. CAE Machinery Ltd.*

Damages can be given for loss of profits. An accounting of the defendant's profits is also possible, if the plaintiff so elects,[162] but remains in the court's discretion,[163] as does the method for its calculation.[164] A delay in bringing the action argues against granting an accounting of profits.[165] Punitive damages are possible, even though the *Patent Act* does not mention them specifically because of the court's inherent jurisdiction; however, they are rarely awarded. One example is *Eli Lilly & Co. v. Apotex Inc.*[166] in which Evans J.A. contemplates that possibility:

> If, at the end of the infringement proceeding, Apotex is found, both to have infringed Lilly's patent, and to have misconducted itself prior to the issue of the NOC, it would be open to the Judge to award punitive damages or solicitor-client costs.

---

(1995), [1995] F.C.J. No. 898, 62 C.P.R. (3d) 26, 98 F.T.R. 125, 1995 CarswellNat 149 (Fed. T.D.).

[160] See, *e.g.*, *Hayden Manufacturing Co. v. Canplas Industries Ltd.* (1996), [1996] F.C.J. No. 766, 68 C.P.R. (3d) 186, 115 F.T.R. 20, 1996 CarswellNat 744 (Fed. T.D.).

[161] See *Jim Scharf Holdings Ltd. v. Sulco Industries Ltd.* (1997), [1997] F.C.J. No. 1488, 77 C.P.R. (3d) 156, 1997 CarswellNat 2121 (Fed. T.D.), affirmed (2000), [2000] F.C.J. No. 1103, 7 C.P.R. (4th) 383, 2000 CarswellNat 1470 (Fed. C.A.).

[162] The election can probably be made after discovery of the defendant. See *Apotex Inc. v. Merck & Co.* (2002), [2002] F.C.J. No. 840, 19 C.P.R. (4th) 460, 219 F.T.R. 259, 2002 CarswellNat 1275 (Fed. T.D.), reversed in part (2003), [2003] F.C.J. No. 1034, 26 C.P.R. (4th) 278, 307 N.R. 364, 2003 CarswellNat 3425 (Fed. C.A.).

[163] See *Johnson Controls Inc. v. Varta Batteries Ltd.* (1984), [1984] F.C.J. No. 239, 80 C.P.R. (2d) 1, 53 N.R. 6, 3 C.I.P.R. 1, 1984 CarswellNat 581 (Fed. C.A.), leave to appeal to S.C.C. refused (1984), 56 N.R. 398n (S.C.C.).

[164] See *Wellcome Foundation Ltd. v. Apotex Inc.*, [2001] 2 F.C. 618, 11 C.P.R. (4th) 218, 267 N.R. 109 (Fed. C.A.), leave to appeal to S.C.C. refused (2001), [2001] S.C.C.A. No. 192, 2001 CarswellNat 1776 (S.C.C.).

[165] See *Unilever PLC v. Procter & Gamble Inc.* (1993), [1993] F.C.J. No. 117, 47 C.P.R. (3d) 479, 60 F.T.R. 241, 1993 CarswellNat 355 (Fed. T.D.), affirmed (1995), [1995] F.C.J. No. 1005, 61 C.P.R. (3d) 499, 184 N.R. 378, 1995 CarswellNat 375 (Fed. C.A.); *Teledyne Industries Inc. v. Lido Industrial Products Ltd.* (1979), 45 C.P.R. (2d) 18 (Fed. T.D.), varied (1981), [1981] F.C.J. No. 703, 57 C.P.R. (2d) 29, 1981 CarswellNat 561 (Fed. C.A.), leave to appeal to S.C.C. refused (1981), 59 C.P.R. (2d) 183 (S.C.C.).

[166] (2000), [2000] F.C.J. No. 1905, 9 C.P.R. (4th) 439, 266 N.R. 339, 2000 CarswellNat 2795 (Fed. C.A.); *Lubrizol Corp. v. Imperial Oil Ltd.* (1992), [1992] F.C.J. No. 1110, 98 D.L.R. (4th) 1, 45 C.P.R. (3d) 449, 150 N.R. 207, 1992 CarswellNat 1049 (Fed. C.A.), additional reasons at (1993), (sub nom. *Imperial Oil Ltd. v. Lubrizol Corp.*) 48 C.P.R. (3d) 1 (Fed. C.A.), leave to appeal refused (1993), 50 C.P.R. (3d) v (note) (S.C.C.).

In *Profekta International Inc. v. Lee*,[167] Linden J.A. reviewed applicable cases as follows:

> The appellant takes issue with both the quantum of general damages and with the refusal to award exemplary damages.
>
> In *Woelk v. Halvorson* (1980), 114 D.L.R. (3d) 385, at pp. 388-89, the Supreme Court of Canada held that, in order to justify appellate intervention with the assessment of quantum of damages, there must be some evidence, *inter alia*, of a wrongly applied principle of law or the award reached must be 'wholly erroneous'. This standard is applicable, even where no *viva voce* evidence has been presented, in order to respect the 'autonomy and integrity of the trial process', (see *Schwartz v. R.*, [1996] 1 S.C.R. 254, at pp. 278-79, per Cory J.). The assessment of damages in patent infringement actions proceeds on the principle that the infringer ought to be made pay that which he or she would have paid if he or she had entered into a legitimate licensing agreement with the patent holder, (see *General Tire & Rubber Co. v. Firestone Tyre & Rubber Co.*, [1975] 2 All E.R. 173 (H.L.), per Lord Wilberforce). This principle has been adopted and applied in this Court, (see *Consolboard Inc. v. MacMillan Bloedel (Sask.) Ltd.* (1983), 74 C.P.R. (2d) 199 (F.C.A.), per Heald J.). [. . .]
>
> On the issue of exemplary damages, the Supreme Court of Canada has held in *Hill v. Church of Scientology of Toronto*, [1995] 2 S.C.R. 1130, at pp. 1208-1209, (per Cory J.), that such damages should only be awarded in cases 'where the combined award of general damages and aggravated damages would be insufficient to achieve the goal of punishment and deterrence'. This approach has been recently followed in this Court (see *Lubrizol Corp. v. Imperial Oil Ltd.* (1996), 197 N.R. 241 (F.C.A.)). According to Cory J. in *Hill*, the question which this Court must ask, in reviewing the Motions Judge's refusal to award exemplary damages, is: 'was the misconduct of the defendant so outrageous that punitive damages were rationally required to act as deterrence?'

*J.M. Voith GmbH v. Beloit Corp.*[168] teaches that if the infringement is on part of a product that was sold, the accounting of profits may be for the entire product if its sale is dependant on the presence of the infringing component:

> Two questions must be addressed in deciding this issue. First, whether the patentee is entitled to an assessment of the whole article sold where its patented

---

[167] (1997), [1997] F.C.J. No. 527, 75 C.P.R. (3d) 369, 214 N.R. 309, 1997 CarswellNat 721 (Fed. C.A.).

[168] (sub nom. *Beloit Canada Ltd. v. Valmet-Dominion Inc.*) [1997] 3 F.C. 497, (sub nom. *Beloit Canada Ltd. v. Valmet-Dominion Inc.*) 73 C.P.R. (3d) 321, (sub nom. *Voith (J.M.) GmbH v. Beloit Corp.*) 214 N.R. 85 (Fed. C.A.).

article forms only part of the whole article. Second, if the first is answered in the affirmative, then it must be determined whether Beloit, in the case at bar, is entitled to an assessment based upon sales of the press sections with other components.

With respect to the first issue, the Supreme Court of Canada in *Lightning Fastener Co. v. Colonial Fastener Co.*[[1937] S.C.R. 36], held that there may be instances when a patentee may be entitled to damages based upon the whole article of which the patented article forms a part. In that instance, the Court awarded damages not just for the infringed article, the stringers, but for the completed article, the fasteners. The Court reached this conclusion on the basis that the stringers were only of importance in their use with the fasteners. In coming to this conclusion the Court adopted the principle established in *Meters Ltd. v. Metro Gas Meters Ltd.* [(1911), 28 R.P.C. 157 (C.A.)] where, at pages 41-42, Kerwin J. (as he then was), stated for the Court:

> . . . the Court of Appeal had to consider the amount of damages the plaintiff was entitled to where the defendant infringed the plaintiff's patents, one of which related to a particular kind of cam and spindle for opening the gas valve in a prepayment gas meter, and the other of which was for a particular kind of crown wheel in a like meter. *It had been shown before the Master and Eve J., . . . , that the plaintiff would have sold many more meters but for the defendant's intervention*, and it was, therefore, awarded 13s.4d. for the loss of profits on each of such meters.
>
> [Emphasis added in original]

Similarly in *Beloit Canada Ltée/Ltd. v. Valmet Oy* [(1992), 45 C.P.R. (3d) 116 (F.C.A.)], this Court stated at page 119, with respect to a discovery issue in the reference, that it could

> . . . see no reason in principle why a patentee, whose property has been wrongly appropriated through infringement, should not recover *all* the profits, direct and indirect, derived by the infringer from his wrongful infringement:

This Court went on to note that,

> Questions as to whether any proportion of the profits earned by the defendant on the sales of non-infringing parts of paper machines was due to such machines have infringing press sections incorporated into them, and the amounts thereof, if any, are difficult questions of fact.

Accordingly, this Court in *Beloit Canada Ltée/Ltd. v. Valmet Oy* [(1995), 61 C.P.R. (3d) 271 (F.C.A.)] upheld the Trial Judge's refusal to award profits on the entire machines containing infringing press sections. This Court wrote at page 278 that the 'question is wholly one of fact'. At page 279 it observed that the 'judge made very strong findings of fact' and then cited the following portion of the Trial Judge's reasons:

> Based on the evidence, I am unable to conclude that any of the profit realized by Valmet on the sale of the four paper machines in question was derived as a result of its wrongful infringement of the plaintiff's patent. The facts clearly show there were numerous reasons why the defendant was successful in its bid for the sale of those machines. None of them, in my view, are in any way related to the infringing press section.

Based upon the jurisprudence, in our view the first question should be answered in the affirmative. A patentee is entitled to damages assessed upon the sale of non-infringing components when there is a finding of fact that such sale arose from infringing the patented component.

The remaining question is whether the Trial Judge correctly determined that Beloit was entitled to damages based upon sales of other components with the press components. At pages 37 and 38, the Trial Judge wrote:

> I cannot accept the defendant's contention that an award of damages to the plaintiff should be limited to the press section of a paper machine and not beyond, in those instances where the defendants actually sold an entire machine. The case law does not support a restriction of the measure of damages to the loss of profits attributable to the patented article itself. *If, in the normal course of a patentee's trade, the patented article is sold by itself, this may well be all he is entitled to. However, where the patented article is not always or necessarily sold by itself, it is reasonable to assume that the damage to the patentee lies, not merely in loss of profits attributable to the article itself, but in selling the articles in which he trades, in the present case, paper machines with triple nip press sections.* Indeed this was the position taken by the Supreme Court of Canada in *Colonial Fastener Co. Ltd. et al. v. Lightning Fastener Co. Ltd.. . . .*

> The end result is that at the reference, the plaintiff must show what profit it would have made on the sale of the three machines sold by the defendant VDI to Corner Brook Pulp & Paper Limited, Donohue Malbaie Inc., and Repap N.B. Inc., respectively, the two press section rebuilds sold by the defendant Voith to Canadian International Paper (Gatineau) and to British Columbia Forest Products, and the one press section sold by the defendant VDI to Great Lakes Forest Products Limited, all of which have been found to infringe the patent.

[Emphasis added in original]

We are unable to agree with the Trial Judge's statement that 'where the patented article is not always or necessarily sold by itself, it is reasonable to assume damages to the patentee lies. . . in selling the articles in which he trades. . .' As shown in the preceding review of the jurisprudence, the scope of damages to which a patentee is entitled is not based upon an assumption but rather on a finding of fact. The reasons for the Trial Judge do not, in our respectful view, contain a specific finding based on evidence that non-infringing components parts of machines were sold because the infringing press sections were sold with them. We must conclude from the record, therefore, that the Trial Judge erred in directing that VDI must pay damages based on other components with which the press sections were sold rather than on the press sections alone.

For an examination of how pre-and post-judgment interest should be calculated, see *Consolboard Inc. v. MacMillan Bloedel (Saskatchewan) Ltd.*,[169] and *J.M. Voith GmbH v. Beloit Corp.*[170]

## VII. DISCUSSION QUESTIONS

**Q:**    Frieda has been looking for a way to organize her class notes, which she writes by hand on loose pieces of paper. She doodles a design one day during a lecture that will hold pieces of paper together using a curved fine piece of metal with chewing gum on the end. Frieda wants to patent this design. The gum keeps the paper clip from sliding off in her bookbag. Her friend Sceptical Cecilia says she can't patent a paper clip with gum on the end of it because paper clips are an old idea. Is Cecilia correct? Cecilia takes one of the gum-topped paper clips and uses it to hold up sprouting herbs when the plants are too delicate to stand up on their own. Can Cecilia patent her method of stabilizing young plants?

**Q:**    Eric the explorer discovers a new bird while he is out trekking in the mountains, which he names a Dobo. Can Eric patent his discovery? Alissa creates a new bird through genetic modification of a blue jay. Can Alissa patent her created bird? Pierre researches the Dobo and learns that it naturally consumes dandelions and does not harm the surrounding vegetation. Can Pierre patent use of the Dobo as a weed-eater? Wanda improves Alissa's bird by training it to make a loud cackling noise when intruders come near a residential house to scare off burglars. Can Alissa patent her bird-training method?

---

[169] (1982), 63 C.P.R. (2d) 1 (Fed. T.D.), varied (1983), [1983] F.C.J. No. 710, 74 C.P.R. (2d) 199, 50 N.R. 161, 1983 CarswellNat 501 (Fed. C.A.).

[170] *Supra*, note 168.

**Q:**    Joe is a sociologist and has been researching architecture's effect on promoting or hindering social interactions among strangers. His research shows that wide staircases with deep stairs in large public buildings promote conversations. He wants to patent his research finding so that he can get a royalty from any architect who uses that design feature in public buildings. Is this idea patentable? Harold is from the engineering department and talks to Joe about his research. Harold comes up with a method to add marble extensions to grand staircases in existing museums and university buildings to get the social benefits that Joe has identified. Can Harold patent his engineering method?

**Q:**    The famous mathematician Fermat told his friends that he had just solved a great riddle in math. He wrote out some clues to the mathematical puzzle, but unfortunately he died before he could write out a full answer as he had planned. Many enthusiasts and academic specialists tried to solve the riddle over the next hundred years but none could. Many published articles discussed the gaps that were still unanswered. Last month, Anastasia solved the full riddle. She wrote the mathematical proof down. Can she patent her answer to this mathematical problem?

**Q:**    Technology Company has just designed a device that allows physicians and health services staff to speak to one another in hospitals. The device is called Transponder. The device is the first working version of the transponders which were featured in the *Star Trek* television show, a science-fiction show which was set in the future in the 23rd century. The devices are worn on hospital uniforms and have an effective range through the whole hospital building and surrounding property. The devices are an improvement over the existing two-way walky-talky technology which also allow two-way communications. Can the device be patented?

**Q:**    Your client, Ms. WidgetMaker, comes to see you as a renowned patent expert. She explains that she has just invented a new garbage bag. The top part of the new bag has the shape of two elongated strips of plastic, each with a hole big enough to slide a hand in. This allows users of the bag to tie the bag without a separate tie, and to carry the bag using the "handles" formed by the holes.

To differentiate her product from other bags, Ms. WidgetMaker wants to produce purple bags. She also explains that she added a "lace" pattern at the top of the plastic strips. She thought it would make the bags look nicer.

A search of the Patent database at CIPO reveals that garbage bags with elongated strips are already patented (since 1987). You also know that the idea of making holes in the side of a box or container is not new. But you cannot find a patent on a bag that contains both features.

Suggest an optimal strategy to protect Ms. WidgetMaker's intellectual property.

**Q:**    A new cloning procedure has just been invented. It is used to clone large animals (such as horses and cows). This new process succeeds (that is, an embryo is produced) in 50% of the attempts, while the processes used previously failed in 90% of cases. The embryos are to be used mainly for scientific experiments (for example, to develop new medications or test genetic modifications).

Based on the *Patent Act* and relevant jurisprudence, is this new process patentable? List the relevant criteria and explain how each of them applies to this new process.

Are the animals produced by this process patentable? Explain.

**Q:**    Scientists discovered that a type of moth whose larvae live and grow in birch tress (usually resulting in the death of the tree) are repelled by potato skins. By genetically engineering individual cells of the birch tree to add potato genes, they were able to create a type of birch that is resistant to the bug.

Are the new birch trees containing the genetically modified cells patentable? Can the invention be protected in any way under the *Patent Act*? Would someone unknowingly cutting a birch tree on his property containing the genetically engineered cells infringe the patent? Why? Under what circumstances could infringement arise?

# *Chapter* 6: **Confidential Information**

I. Introduction

II. Object of the Protection

III. Employees

IV. Breach of Duty of Confidence, Elements and Defences

V. Remedies

VI. Information Submitted to Government

VII. Discussion Question

## I. INTRODUCTION

In patent law, the bargain requires that the patentee publicly disclose the invention in exchange for a limited term exclusive right with respect to the invention. Patent law provides a limited confidentiality period. During a period of 18 months following the filing of a patent application, the application remains secret. The inventor or patent holder may benefit from the fact that actual or potential competitors do not have access to the contents of the application to gain market-share or further develop the product or process concerned. But there are situations, however, in which a person may not wish to disclose information at all or where patent law is otherwise inadequate or inappropriate and where a person may want an alternative legal protection. Lists of clients or prices, for example, have value to the extent that they stay secret. In some cases, it may be that obtaining a patent is not possible, or that even if a patent were obtained, it would be fairly easy to circumvent or difficult to enforce. This is often the case with process patents, in spite of the presumption found in s. 55.1 of the *Patent Act*.[1] In other cases, a decision may be made not to apply for a patent because of its limited duration. Had the formula for Coca-Cola® been patented, assuming of course it could have been patentable at the time of its creation, the protection would have lapsed several decades ago. By maintaining its secrecy, its value has remained intact.

---

[1] "In an action for infringement of a patent granted for a process for obtaining a new product, any product that is the same as the new product shall, in the absence of proof to the contrary, be considered to have been produced by the patented process."

With patent law, it is a condition of acquiring a patent that the invention not have been publicly disclosed (see Novelty in Patents section), but it is a condition of the grant of the patent that the patent be publicly disclosed after 18 months. Under confidential information law, the confidential nature of the information is a prerequisite for legal protection and the information must continue to be secret in order to maintain legal protection. Confidential information should be distinguished from other intellectual property because the benefit to the public from enforcing the protection is more oblique.

The law of confidential information is a mixture of contract law (*e.g.*, non-disclosure agreements), torts (*e.g.*, conversion), trusts (*e.g.*, breach of a fiduciary duty), and statutory provisions that protect certain forms of confidential information (*i.e.*, information disclosed to government as part of a regulatory approval process). There is no unified statutory regime to protect confidential information. Confidential information is one of the oldest of intellectual property rights, with roots that can be traced back to Hammurabi's Code and Roman law. A more recent lineage for Canadian confidential secrets law can be found in equity in cases that protected unpublished documents, as for example in the case of *Pope v. Curl*,[2] where it was decided that a person had a right to maintain the confidentiality of an undisclosed manuscript. A right of a similar nature exists today in s. 3 of the *Copyright Act*, which provides authors of unpublished work with the exclusive right to publish such works.[3] As La Forest J. stated in *R. v. Sanelli*:

> [I]t has long been recognized that this freedom not to be compelled to share our confidences with others is the very hallmark of a free society. Yates J., in *Millar v. Taylor* (1769), 4 Burr. 2303, 98 E.R. 201, states, at p. 2379 and p. 242:
>
>> It is certain every man has a right to keep his own sentiments, if he pleases: he has certainly a right to judge whether he will make them public, or commit them only to the sight of his friends.[4]

This policy that people should have a right to control when confidences are disseminated similarly underlies the law of confidential information. For individuals, privacy concerns are at their strongest where aspects of an individual's identity are at stake, such as in the context of information "about one's lifestyle, intimate relations or political or religious opinions."[5] In the

---

[2] (1741), 2 Atk. 342, 26 E.R. 608.

[3] See *Le Sueur v. Morang & Co.* (1911), 45 S.C.R. 95 (S.C.C.); and *R. v. Bellman*, [1938] 3 D.L.R. 548 (N.B. C.A.).

[4] (sub nom. *R. v. Duarte*) [1990] 1 S.C.R. 30 (S.C.C.) at 53-54.

[5] *Thomson Newspapers Ltd. v. Canada (Director of Investigation & Research)*, [1990] 1 S.C.R. 425 (S.C.C.) at 517-18.

commercial context, businesses have strong concerns about controlling confidences with respect to such information as client lists, technical specifications, product recipes, etc.

The protection of confidential information is generally considered as a form of intellectual property. A number of international treaties treat it as such. Article 10*bis* of the *Paris Convention* (see the International Section) provides that member countries (including Canada) must "assure . . . effective protection against unfair competition" and further that "any act of competition contrary to honest practices in industrial or commercial matters constitutes an act of unfair competition." This would apply, for example, to industrial espionage. The WTO *TRIPS Agreement* (see the International Section) is even clearer. Article 39 provides as follows:

> 1.  [. . .]Members shall protect undisclosed information in accordance with paragraph 2 and data submitted to governments or governmental agencies in accordance with paragraph 3.

> 2.  Natural and legal persons shall have the *possibility of preventing* information lawfully within their control *from being disclosed* to, *acquired by, or used by* others without their consent in a *manner contrary to honest commercial practices*[6] so long as such information:

>> (a)  is secret in the sense that it is not, as a body or in the precise configuration and assembly of its components, generally known among or readily accessible to persons within the circles that normally deal with the kind of information in question;
>> (b)  has commercial value because it is secret; and
>> (c)  has been subject to reasonable steps under the circumstances, by the person lawfully in control of the information, to keep it secret.

> 3.  Members, when requiring, as a condition of approving the marketing of pharmaceutical or of agricultural chemical products which utilize new chemical entities, the submission of undisclosed test or other data, the origination of which involves a considerable effort, shall protect such data against unfair commercial use. In addition, Members shall protect such data against disclosure, except where necessary to protect the public, or unless steps are taken to ensure that the data are protected against unfair commercial use. [emphasis added]

---

[6] For the purpose of this provision, "a manner contrary to honest commercial practices" shall mean at least practices such as breach of contract, breach of confidence and inducement to breach, and includes the acquisition of undisclosed information by third parties who knew, or were grossly negligent in failing to know, that such practices were involved in the acquisition.

A first step in examining Canadian law is to consider whether confidential information is in fact "property". In *R. v. Stewart*,[7] the Supreme Court discussed whether confidential information was property for the purposes of theft under the *Criminal Code*:

> It can be argued — as Professor Weinrib does in 'Information and Property' (1988), 38 U.T.L.J. 117 — that confidential information is property for the purposes of civil law. Indeed, it possesses many of the characteristics of other forms of property: for example, a trade secret, which is a particular kind of confidential information, can be sold, licensed or bequeathed, it can be the subject of a trust or passed to a trustee in bankruptcy. In the commercial field, there are reasons to grant some form of protection to the possessor of confidential information: it is the product of labour, skill and expenditure, and its unauthorized use would undermine productive efforts which ought to be encouraged. As the term 'property' is simply a reference to the cluster of rights assigned to the owner, this protection could be given in the form of proprietary rights. The cases demonstrate that English and Canadian civil law protect confidential information. However, the legal basis for doing so has not been clearly established by the courts. Some cases have treated confidential information as property, and thus have entitled the owner to exclude others from the use thereof: *Aas v. Benham*, [1891] 2 Ch. 244 (C.A.); *Exchange Telegraph Co. v. Gregory & Co.*, [1896] 1 Q.B. 147 (C.A.); *Exchange Telegraph Co. v. Central News Ltd.*, [1897] 2 Ch. 48; *Exchange Telegraph Co. v. Howard* (1906), 22 T.L.R. 375 (Ch. Div.). On the other hand, the courts have recognized certain rights with respect to confidential information in the guise of an equitable obligation of good faith: *Peter Pan Manufacturing Corp. v. Corsets Silhouette Ltd.*, [1963] 3 All E.R. 402 (Ch. Div.); *Saltman Engineering Co. v. Campbell Engineering Co.*, [1963] 3 All E.R. 413n (C.A.); *Argyll v. Argyll*, [1965] 2 W.L.R. 790 (Ch. Div.); *Pre-Cam Exploration & Development Ltd. v. McTavish*, [1966] S.C.R. 551; *Seager v. Copydex Ltd.*, [1967] 2 All E.R. 415 (C.A.); *Boardman v. Phipps*, [1967] 2 A.C. 47 (H.L.); *Fraser v. Evans*, [1968] 3 W.L.R. 1172 (C.A.)
>
> It appears that the protection afforded to confidential information *in most civil cases arises more from an obligation of good faith or a fiduciary relationship than from a proprietary interest*. No Canadian court has so far conclusively decided that confidential information is property, with all the civil consequences that such a finding would entail. The case law is therefore of little assistance to us in the present case.
>
> *It is possible that, with time, confidential information will come to be considered as property in the civil law* or even be granted special legal protection by statutory enactment. Even if confidential information were to be considered as property under civil law, it does not however automatically follow that it qualifies as property for the purposes of criminal law. Conversely, the

---

7   [1988] 1 S.C.R. 963, 50 D.L.R. (4th) 1, 39 B.L.R. 198, 21 C.P.R. (3d) 289, 19 C.I.P.R. 161, 85 N.R. 171 (S.C.C.) [*Stewart* cited to S.C.R.].

fact that something is not property under civil law is likewise not conclusive for the purpose of criminal law. Whether or not confidential information is property under the *Criminal Code* should be decided in the perspective of the criminal law.

In *Oxford v. Moss* (1978), 68 Cr. App. R. 183, the Divisional Court had to decide whether confidential information was 'intangible property' for the purposes of the *Theft Act, 1968*. A student was accused of stealing an examination paper that he hoped to return without being detected. After considering a number of civil authorities dealing with the subject of confidential information, Smith J. wrote (at pp. 185-86):

> Those are cases concerned with what is described as the duty to be of good faith. They are clear illustrations of the proposition that, if a person obtains information which is given to him in confidence and then sets out to take an unfair advantage of it, the courts will restrain him by way of an order of injunction or will condemn him in damages if an injunction is found to be inappropriate. It seems to me, speaking for my part, that they are of little assistance in the present situation in which we have to consider whether there is property in the information which is capable of being the subject of a charge of theft. In my judgment, it is clear that the answer to that question must be no.

In civil law, the characterization of something as property triggers a series of legal consequences. That characterization has the same effect under the criminal law, although the consequences are somewhat different. If confidential information is considered as property for the purposes of the theft section, other sections of the *Criminal Code* relating to offences against property may also apply: ss. 27 (use of force to prevent commission of offence), 38 (defence of movable property), 39 (defence with claim of right), 302 (robbery), 312 (possession of property obtained by crime), 350 (disposal of property to defraud creditors), 616 (restitution of property), 653 (compensation for loss of property) and 654 (compensation to bona fide purchasers). For example, let us assume a person obtains confidential information by the commission of a crime, such as theft if it were possible. If, after having memorized the information, that person is incapable of erasing it from his memory, he could, one might argue, be charged with an offence under s. 312 of the *Criminal Code* for each day that he is unable to forget the information.

Furthermore, the qualification of confidential information as property must be done in each case by examining the purposes and context of the civil and criminal law. It is understandable that one who possesses valuable information would want to protect it from unauthorized use and reproduction. In civil litigation, this protection can be afforded by the Courts because they simply have to balance the interests of the parties involved. However criminal law is designed to prevent wrongs against society as a whole. From a social point of view, whether confidential information should be protected requires a weighing of interest much broader than those of the parties involved. As opposed to the alleged owner of the information, society's best advantage may well be to favour the free flow of information and greater accessibility by all. Would society be willing to prosecute the person who discloses to the public a cure for cancer, although its discoverer wanted to keep it confidential? [emphasis added]

*Stewart* does not answer the question whether confidential information is property for the purposes of private law, and seems to indicate that the qualification of such information as property *may happen*.

By contrast, in an important decision concerning an ex-employee's obligation not to disclose confidential information belonging to an ex-employer, the Ontario Court of Appeal wrote:

> At the time when some of these successive improvements were originated by Ashton while he was with the appellant company, they are, *I think, to be regarded as trade secrets which were the exclusive property of the appellant,* [former employer]for whom Ashton was a trustee. It is trite to state that a secret once disclosed is no longer a secret. If the improvements, devices and developments made to the continuous form press of the appellant company while Ashton was in its employ, and the method in which the component parts of the machine in question were assembled, also the design and improvements to the various other machines used in finishing the continuous forms, became known to others who were interested in the construction or sale of such presses and supplementary machines, that is to say, became known to the trade, the character of secrecy with which these devices and improvements were formerly surrounded would disappear.[8] [emphasis added]

The Court also quoted with approval *Triplex Safety Glass Co. v. Scorah*,[9] in which Farwell J. stated:

> [A]part altogether from any express covenant, [. . .] any invention or discovery made in the course of the employment of the employee in doing that which he was engaged and instructed to do during the time of his employment, and during working hours, and using the materials of his employers, *is the property of the employers* and not of the employee, and [. . .] having made a discovery or invention in course of such work, the employee becomes a trustee for the employer of that invention or discovery, and he is therefore as a trustee bound to give the benefit of any such discovery or invention to his employer.

---

[8]  *R.L. Crain Ltd. v. Ashton* (1949), [1950] O.R. 62, [1950] 1 D.L.R. 601, 11 C.P.R. 53 (Ont. C.A.) [*Crain* cited to D.L.R.] [*Crain*]. See also *Abernathy v. Hutchison* (1825), 3 L.J. Ch. 209, 47 E.R. 1313.
[9]  (1937), [1938] Ch. 211 (Eng. Ch. Div.) at 217.

One could also point to the *Canadian Institutes of Health Research Act*,[10] s. 26(1)(f) of which reads as follows:

> The Canadian Institutes of Health Research may, for the purpose of achieving its objective,
>
> [. . .]
>
>> (f) license, assign, sell or otherwise make available any patent, copyright, industrial design, trade-mark, *trade secret or other like property right* held, controlled or administered by the CIHR;

However, as the definition of property is a provincial matter under s. 92(13) of the *Constitutional Act, 1867*, it is unlikely that this characterization in a federal statute would carry much weight.

While the definitive case on this point may not have been written, the Supreme Court's analysis in *Cadbury Schweppes*[11] of the legal effect of treating information as property lays a strong foundation. It notes that the main impact of a characterization of confidential information, such as trade secrets, as property lies in the remedies available, a distinction that is also relevant when deciding whether protection (outside of property) is based in equity or tort:

> The argument that confidential information is property for some purposes is made by Professor A. S. Weinrib in 'Information and Property' (1988), 38 *U.T.L.J.* 117. In *R. v. Stewart*, [1988] 1 S.C.R. 963 (S.C.C.), this Court concluded that whatever may be the property status of information in other contexts, information is not property for purposes of the theft provisions of the *Criminal Code*. [. . .]
>
> The respondents' characterization of confidential information as property is controversial. Traditionally, courts here and in other common law jurisdictions have been at pains to emphasize that the action is rooted in the relationship of confidence rather than the legal characteristics of the information confided. See, for example, Holmes J. in the United States Supreme Court in *E. I. Du Pont De Nemours Powder Co. v. Masland*, 244 U.S. 100 (U.S. Pa. 1917) at p. 102:
>
>> The word property as applied to . . . trade secrets is an unanalyzed expression of certain secondary consequences of the primary fact that

---

[10] S.C. 2000, c. 6, online: Department of Justice Canada <http://laws.justice.gc.ca/en/c-18.1/text.html>.

[11] *Cadbury Schweppes Inc. v. FBI Foods Ltd.*, [1999] 1 S.C.R. 142, 167 D.L.R. (4th) 577, 42 B.L.R. (2d) 159, 83 C.P.R. (3d) 289, 235 N.R. 30 (S.C.C.) [*Cadbury Schweppes* cited to S.C.R.].

the law makes some rudimentary requirements of good faith. Whether the plaintiffs have any valuable secret or not the defendant knows the facts, whatever they are, through a special confidence that he accepted. The property may be denied but the confidence cannot be. Therefore the starting point for the present matter is not property . . . but that the defendant stood in confidential relations with the plaintiffs, or one of them.

The same point was made in the High Court of Australia, *per* Deane J., in *Moorgate Tobacco Co. v. Philip Morris Ltd.* (1984), 156 C.L.R. 414 (Australia H.C.) at p. 438:

Like most heads of exclusive equitable jurisdiction, its rational basis does not lie in proprietary right. It lies in the notion of an obligation of conscience arising from the circumstances in or through which the information was communicated or obtained.

See also *Federal Commissioner of Taxation v. United Aircraft Corp.* (1944), 68 C.L.R. 525 (Aust. H.C.), *per* Latham C.J., at pp. 534-35; *Macri v. Miskiewicz* (1991), 39 C.P.R. (3d) 207 (B.C. S.C.); varied at (1993), 50 C.P.R. (3d) 76 (B.C. C.A.), *per* Southin J.A., at p. 83.

Whether the cause of action is described as *sui generis* or equitable does not change its preoccupation with the violation of a confidence. It is nevertheless true that the nature of the information may influence the appropriate remedy. The respondents rely on the much-quoted (and often criticized) analogy drawn by Lord Denning M.R. in *Seager v. Copydex Ltd. (No. 2), supra,* in which he analogized compensation for breach of confidence to damages for conversion of property, at p. 719:

Now a question has arisen as to the principles on which the damages are to be assessed. They are to be assessed, as we said, at the value of the information which the defendant company took. If I may use an analogy, it is like damages for conversion. Damages for conversion are the value of the goods. Once the damages are paid, the goods become the property of the defendant. A satisfied judgment in trover transfers the property in the goods. So, here, once the damages are assessed and paid, the confidential information belongs to the defendant company.

*Seager v. Copydex Ltd. (No. 2)* was referred to by La Forest J. in *Lac Minerals,* at p. 671. In that case, Lord Denning addressed issues regarding remedies that arose out of the decision on liability in *Seager v. Copydex Ltd.(No. 1), supra.* The facts regarding liability in that case are as follows. The plaintiff had invented a carpet grip. It was not patented. In the course of negotiations for a potential production and marketing agreement with Copydex, the plaintiff described his invention in detail. No agreement was concluded. The defendant subsequently marketed a carpet grip which the court considered a copy of the plaintiff's invention, albeit innocently, by a process of what was called 'un-conscious plagiarism'. No injunction was awarded, yet the defendant was required to pay the plaintiff the 'market value' of the information it had wrong-fully, though innocently, misappropriated. Having paid the compensation, Lord Denning's view was that 'the confidential information belongs to the defendant company' (p. 719).

*Seager v. Copydex Ltd. (No. 2)* presents some theoretical difficulties in terms of equitable doctrine. Equity could not operate on the 'guilty conscience' of the defendant in that case because the defendant's conscience was apparently clear. Despite the finding at p. 417 of *Seager v. Copydex Ltd. (No. 1)* that '[t]he coincidences are too strong to permit of any other explanation' except plagia-rism, the court held the defendant morally blameless. While Lord Denning characterized the cause of action as 'equitable' (at p. 417), the lack of uncon-scionable conduct may have led the court to emphasize the value of the infor-mation misappropriated rather than to focus on the misappropriation itself. It should also be noted that in *Phipps v. Boardman*, [1967] 2 A.C. 46, decided two years before *Seager v. Copydex Ltd. (No. 2), supra*, the House of Lords in a divided decision held that confidential information could properly be char-acterized as a property interest for purposes of the law of trusts. In that case, the trustee profited from confidential information to benefit both the trust and himself. The question was whether the information thus misappropriated was an asset of the trust, thus rendering the trustee liable to disgorgement of his portion of the profit. The House concluded that it was, and disgorgement was ordered. The decision was grounded in trust law rather than property law. In *Re Keene*, [1922] 2 Ch. 475 (C.A.), a secret formula was considered to be an asset that passed to the trustee in bankruptcy.

I do not think that the respondents' reliance on intellectual property law is of much assistance here. It ignores 'the bargain' that lies at the heart of patent protection. A patent is a statutory monopoly which is given in exchange for a full and complete disclosure by the patentee of his or her invention. The disclosure is the essence of the bargain between the patentee, who obtained at the time a 17-year monopoly on exploiting the invention, and the public, which obtains open access to all of the information necessary to practise the invention. Accordingly, at least one of the policy objectives underlying the statutory remedies available to a patent owner is to make disclosure more attractive, and thus hasten the availability of useful knowledge in the public sphere in the public interest. As pointed out by Hugessen J.A. in *Smith, Kline & French Laboratories Ltd. v. Canada (Attorney General)*, [1987] 2 F.C. 359 (Fed. C.A.) at p. 366, entrepreneurs in the food industry frequently eschew patent protection in order to avoid disclosure, and thus perhaps perpetuate their competitive advantage beyond the 17-year life span of a patent. We are told that the secrecy of the Coca-Cola recipe has apparently endured for decades. If a court were to award compensation to the respondents on principles analogous to those ap-plicable in a case of patent infringement, the respondents would be obtaining the benefit of patent remedies without establishing that their invention meets the statutory criteria for the issuance of a patent, or paying the price of public disclosure of their secret.

The reluctance of common law courts outside the United States to treat trade secrets as a species of property or quasi-property has been criticised: see, e.g., M. Chromecek and S. C. McCormack, *World Intellectual Property Guidebook* (1991), wherein it is observed at p. 3-27:

> Not all information can be property; only confidential information can. Confidentiality is a condition sine qua non of the information's proprietary status. This view is fully consistent with the essence of other intellectual property rights, patents, copyrights, industrial designs, trade marks, or even personality rights, the value of which lies not in their possession but in the owner's ability to exclude others from exploiting them.

I agree, of course, with the author's emphasis on confidentiality. Breach of confidentiality is the gravamen of the complaint. When it comes to a remedy, however, I do not think a proprietary remedy should automatically follow. There are cases (as in *Lac Minerals*) where it is appropriate. But equity, with its emphasis on flexibility, keeps its options open. It would be contrary to the authorities in this Court already mentioned to allow the choice of remedy to be driven by a label ('property') rather than a case-by-case balancing of the equities. In some cases, as Lord Denning showed in *Seager v. Copydex Ltd. (No. 2), supra*, the relevance of the specific quality of the information to a remedy will not be its property status but its commercial value. In other cases, as in *Lac Minerals*, the key to the remedy will not be the 'property' status of the confidence but the course of events that would likely have occurred 'but for' the breach. Application of the label 'property' in this context would add nothing except confusion to the task of weighing the policy objectives furthered by a particular remedy and the particular facts of each case. In the present case, the trial judge considered the confidential information to be nothing very special, and that 'but for' the breach the respondents would in any event have faced a merchantable version of Caesar Cocktail in the market place within 12 months. On these facts, a 'proprietary' remedy is inappropriate.

E. *Relevance of Tort*

At least one commentator (Professor P. M. North in 'Breach of Confidence: Is There a New Tort?' (1972), 12 *J.S.P.T.L.* 149, at pp. 163-65), has suggested that Lord Denning was moving toward the development of a new tort that would provide 'some form of common law protection of interests in confidential information by way of damages analogous to the statutory protection provided in the fields of patents, copyright and designs' (p. 170). In *Seager v. Copydex Ltd. (No. 2), supra*, Winn L.J., at p. 721, said 'the basis on which damages are to be recovered in this case is a tortious basis'. The United Kingdom Law Commission recommended the creation of a statutory tort in its report on *Breach of Confidence* (Law Com. No. 110, Cmnd. 8388 1981), at p. 151, para. 6.105, *et seq.* Events in England have not moved in this direction. The House of Lords has subsequently affirmed that actions for breach of confidence are equitable in nature: see the *Spycatcher* case, *supra*.

Nevertheless, tort principles could have a potential impact in a breach of confidence case on the rules governing the assessment of equitable compensation. It is well established that equitable rules may produce a more generous level of compensation than their counterparts in tort.

## II. OBJECT OF THE PROTECTION

There is no formal definition in Canadian law, but the criteria enunciated in the *TRIPS Agreement* (Art. 39(2)) (see the International Section), to which Canada is party since January 1, 1995, reflects a generally accepted standard, namely:

the information must

- be secret;
- have value because of its secrecy; and
- have been subject to reasonable steps under the circumstances to keep it secret.

On the first criterion, the *TRIPS Agreement* codifies the notion of *relative secrecy* that is applicable here ("secret in the sense that it is not, as a body or in the precise configuration and assembly of its components, *generally known among or readily accessible* to persons *within the circles that normally deal* with the kind of information in question"). The notion of secrecy applicable here is different from the notion of secrecy in patent law, which is linked to novelty. While in patent law a single public disclosure destroys novelty, for confidential information courts will take steps to maintain a relative degree of secrecy if it is still useful to do so.

> Clearly a claim that the disclosure of some information would be a breach of confidence is not to be defeated simply by proving that there are other people in the world who know the facts in question besides the man as to whom it is said that his disclosure would be a breach of confidence and those to whom he had disclosed them ... It must be a question of degree depending on the particular case, but if the relative secrecy remains, the plaintiff can still succeed.[12]

---

[12] *Franchi v. Franchi*, [1967] R.P.C. 149 (U.K.). See also *Attorney-General (United Kingdom) v. Wellington Newspapers Ltd.*, [1988] 1 N.Z.L.R. 129.

As noted by Paul Lavery:

> It is, of course, true that in the present age, with the radical improvement of communication technology, information published in one location will enter the public domain in another location very quickly. . . . This does not, however, contradict the general principle that information known to the few will not destroy the confidentiality of information which is not known by the many. . . Whether a publication of information will be such as to destroy confidentiality will depend on the facts of the case, the type of publication made and the nature of the industry within which such publication is made.[13]

A number of American courts have also held that publication does not necessarily put material into the public domain.[14]

To determine whether information is confidential and entitled to protection, courts consider *objective* factors such as markings (where appropriate), limits to access and physical protection measures of the information (locks, security, etc.), and whether confidentiality agreements were signed, especially before access by anyone not bound by an implied obligation (*e.g.* fiduciary duty), etc. In *Air Atonabee Ltd. v. Canada (Minister of Transport)*, a case involving disclosure to a governmental entity, Mackay J. evaluated the context, purposes, and circumstances for compiling and communication the information, by considering specifically whether "(a) the content of the record [is] such that the information it contains [was] *not available from sources otherwise accessible by the public* or . . .could *not be obtained by observation or independent study* by a member of the public acting on his own, (b) that the information originate[d] and [was] communicated in a *reasonable expectation of confidence* that it would not be disclosed, and (c) that the information [was] communicated, whether required by law or supplied gratuitously, in a relationship [. . .] that [was] either a *fiduciary relationship* or . . . not contrary to the public interest, and which relationship will be fostered for public benefit by confidential communication."[15]

---

[13]  P. Lavery, "Secrecy, Springboards and the Public Domain" (1998) 20:3 *Eur. Int. Prop. Rev.* 93-97.

[14]  See, e.g., *K2 Ski Co. v. Head Ski Co.*, 506 F.2d 471 (9th Cir., 1974). Since K2, however, which interpreted California law, adoption of the *Uniform Trade Secrets Act* changed the law in part. Interestingly, the *UTSA* states that the purpose of an injunction in this context is to "eliminate the commercial advantage that a person would obtain through misappropriation." See *Warman Intern. Ltd. v. RM-Holz, Inc.*, 977 F.2d 594 (9th Cir., 1992).

[15]  (1989), [1989] F.C.J. No. 453, 27 C.P.R. (3d) 180, 1989 CarswellNat 585 (Fed. T.D.) at 202 [C.P.R.]. See also *Merck Frosst Canada Inc. v. Canada (Minister of National Health)* (2000), [2000] F.C.J. No. 1281, 2000 CarswellNat 1702 (Fed. T.D.), affirmed 2002 FCA 35 (Fed. C.A.).

In a commercial context, absent a contract, courts may use equitable remedies and find, *e.g.,* that a constructive trust exists even in the absence of a fiduciary duty, when confidential information is disclosed.[16]

## 1. Trade Secrets

Are trade secrets simply a form of confidential information? Broadly speaking, the answer is yes. Trade secrets, usually a secret method, formula or process, can be considered a form of confidential commercial or technical information. As noted by Gill J.:

> In *R.L. Crain Ltd. v. Ashton* (1948), [1949] O.R. 303 (Ont. H.C.), Chevrier J. accepted the following definitions of trade secrets, at 388-89:
>
>> 1st. A trade secret ... is a property right, and differs from a patent in that as soon as the secret is discovered, either by an examination of the product or any other honest way, the discoverer has the full right of using it ... *Progress Laundry Co. v. Hamilton*, 270 S.W. 834, 835, 208 Ky. 348.
>>
>> 2nd. A trade secret is a plan or process, tool mechanism or compound known only to its owner and those of his employees to whom it is necessary to confide it. *Cameron Mach. Co. v. Samuel M. Longdon Co.*, N.J. 115 A. 212, 214; *Victor Chemical Works v. Iliff*, 132 N.E. 806, 811, 299 Ill. 532.
>>
>> 3rd. The term 'trade secret', as usually understood, means a secret formula or process not patented, but known only to certain individuals using it in compounding some article of trade having a commercial value, and does not denote the mere privacy with which an ordinary commercial business is carried on. *Glucol Mfg. Co. v. Shulist*, 214 N.W. 152, 153, 239 Mich. 70.
>>
>> 4th. A trade secret may consist of any formula, pattern, device, or compilation of information which is used in one's business, and which gives him an opportunity to obtain an advantage over competitors who do not know or use it. A trade secret is a process or device for continuous use

---

[16] See *International Corona Resources Ltd. v. Lac Minerals Ltd.*, (sub nom. *LAC Minerals Ltd. v. International Corona Resources Ltd.*) [1989] 2 S.C.R. 574, (sub nom. *LAC Minerals Ltd. v. International Corona Resources Ltd.*) 61 D.L.R. (4th) 14, 44 B.L.R. 1, (sub nom. *LAC Minerals Ltd. v. International Corona Resources Ltd.*) 26 C.P.R. (3d) 97, 101 N.R. 239, 35 E.T.R. 1 (S.C.C.) [*Lac Minerals*].

in the operation of the business. The subject matter of a trade secret must be secret. Restatement, Torts, 757.[17]

In other cases, courts have relied on the dictionary meaning, *i.e.*, "a formula, pattern, process or device that is used in one's business and that gives an advantage over competitors who do not know it or use it."[18] Indeed, if a company is taking steps to keep a formula or process secret, one can assume it is because it would have value for its competitors or that its disclosure would remove an advantage it has over those competitors.

Parties to a contract often define the scope of the obligation of secrecy. Care should be taken if the expression "trade secret" or "confidential information" is used in a contract in a sense that differs from its ordinary meaning.[19]

Many cases have noted that s. 20(1) of the *Access to Information Act*[20] lists a number of categories of information that the government can refuse to disclose, including "trade secrets". Subsection 20(1) provides as follows:

20. (1) Subject to this section, the head of a government institution shall refuse to disclose any record requested under this Act that contains

(*a*) trade secrets of a third party;

(*b*) financial, commercial, scientific or technical information that is confidential information supplied to a government institution by a third party and is treated consistently in a confidential manner by the third party;

(*c*) information the disclosure of which could reasonably be expected to result in material financial loss or gain to, or could reasonably be expected to prejudice the competitive position of, a third party; or

(*d*) information the disclosure of which could reasonably be expected to interfere with contractual or other negotiations of a third party.

The expression "trade secret' used in sub. (a) is distinguished from commercial or technical confidential information. Courts have tended to consider that, for the purposes of that *Act*, "trade secret" should be defined narrowly:

---

[17] *Ebco Industries Ltd. v. Kaltech Manufacturing Ltd.* (1999), 1999 CarswellBC 2289 (B.C. S.C. [In Chambers]).

[18] *Western Electrical Co. v. Minister of National Revenue*, [1969] C.T.C. 274 (Can. Ex. Ct.).

[19] See *Noreco Inc. v. Laserworks Computer Services Inc.* (1994), 57 C.P.R. (3d) 461, 136 N.S.R. (2d) 309 (N.S. S.C.).

[20] R.S.C. 1985, c. A-1, online: Department of Justice Canada <http://laws.justice.gc.ca/en/a-1/text.html>.

[I]n the context of subs. 20(1) trade secrets must have a reasonably narrow interpretation since one would assume that they do not overlap the other categories: in particular, they can be contrasted to 'commercial . . . confidential information supplied to a government institution . . . treated consistently in a confidential manner. . .' which is protected under para. (*b*). In respect of neither [paras.] (*a*) nor (*b*) is there a need for any harm to be demonstrated from disclosure for it to be protected. There must be some difference between a trade secret and something which is merely 'confidential' and supplied to a government institution. I am of the view that a trade secret must be something, probably of a technical nature, which is guarded very closely and is of such peculiar value to the owner of the trade secret that harm to him would be presumed by its mere disclosure.[21]

This narrower definition seems specific to the context of that Act and should thus not be used in other dissimilar contexts.

## III. EMPLOYEES

As was noted by the Ontario Court of Appeal in the *Crain* case,[22] ex-employees cannot use or disclose secrets belonging to an ex-employer. The employer has the burden to show that the employees knew that the information was secret.[23] In addition, courts take into account whether a confidentiality agreement was signed by the employee and will not impose as high an obligation when no such agreement exists,[24] except in certain cases involving senior managers. While all employees have a duty to act in good faith towards an ex-employer, senior managers have a fiduciary duty and will thus be held to a much higher standard, especially if a person in such a position voluntarily leaves her employment and uses a business opportunity belonging to the former employer.

---

[21] *Société Gamma Inc. v. Canada (Secretary of State)* (1994), [1994] F.C.J. No. 589, 17 B.L.R. (2d) 13, (sub nom. *Société Gamma Inc. v. Canada (Department of the Secretary of State)*) 56 C.P.R. (3d) 58, 79 F.T.R. 42, 1994 CarswellNat 1301 (Fed. T.D.). See also *Canadian Tobacco Manufacturers' Council v. Minister of National Revenue* (2003), [2003] F.C.J. No. 1308, 28 C.P.R. (4th) 139, 239 F.T.R. 1, 2003 CarswellNat 4362 (Fed. T.D.).

[22] See *supra*, note 8.

[23] See *Corp. scientifique Claisse inc. c. Instruments Katanax inc.* (2004), 2004 CarswellQue 1120 (Que. S.C.).

[24] See *Excelsior, cie d'assurance-vie c. Mutuelle du Canada (La), cie d'assurance* (1992), [1992] A.Q. No. 1854, 1992 CarswellQue 801 (Que. C.A.).

In *Canadian Aero Service Ltd. v. O'Malley*,[25] the Supreme Court held that senior officers owed the same duty to their corporate employer as directors and that such duty continued after termination of employment. The duty was described as one of loyalty, good faith, avoidance of conflict of duty and self-interest.

A useful and quite thorough overview of leading cases is contained in a 1999 decision by the British Columbia Court of Appeal.[26] The case involved a mid-level manager (office supervisor) who had left her employment and immediately started working for a competitor of the plaintiff. She had not signed any agreement concerning non-competition or confidentiality. Hall J.A. wrote for the Court:

> This sort of problem is not a novel one in the law. It has its origins in the field of contract law, but it also involves a fairly significant overlay of equitable principles.

> [. . .]

> There was no covenant in this case. However, from that field of the law came the development of the area we are here concerned with, namely, the duties of an employee to a former employer. Absent any express contractual terms, the law has developed to provide that a former employee will not be at liberty to act in an unfair way to a former employer. Whether it be called a fiduciary duty, a duty of good faith or a duty of confidence, the theme running through this whole area of the law is that in appropriate circumstances, a former employee may be found to have breached an enforceable duty owed to a former employer and may be successfully sued for injunctive relief or for damages.

> Clearly, an employee has duties to a present employer not to divulge trade secrets or to work against the interests of his or her employer but the duty is not just limited to current employment. After leaving employment, an employee may be obligated not to pursue certain activities to the detriment of the former employer. For instance, it has been usually reckoned to be unfair conduct to permit a former employee to take with him or her customer lists to use for solicitation of business or to divulge trade secrets or to seek to appropriate maturing business opportunities of the former employer. On the other hand, I

---

[25] (1973), [1974] S.C.R. 592 (S.C.C.). See also *Sherelco inc. c. Laflamme* (1992), 1992 CarswellQue 1301 (Que. S.C.); and *157079 Canada Inc. c. Ste-Croix,* [1988] R.J.Q. 2842 (Que. S.C.); *Sun Drilling Products Corp. v. Garrett* (1999), 37 C.P.C. (4th) 356 (Alta. Q.B.); *Provincial Plating Ltd. v. Steinkey* (1997), 162 Sask. R. 241 (Sask. Q.B.); and *Polar Bear Rubber Ltd. v. Brothers Industrial Supply Ltd.* (1998), [1999] 1 W.W.R. 522, 128 Man. R. (2d) 105 (Man. Q.B.), affirmed (1998), [1999] 7 W.W.R. 633, 131 Man. R. (2d) 292 (Man. C.A.).

[26] *Barton Insurance Brokers Ltd. v. Irwin* (1999), 63 B.C.L.R. (3d) 215, 170 D.L.R. (4th) 69, 84 C.P.R. (3d) 417 (B.C. C.A.) [*Barton Insurance* cited to D.L.R.].

suppose to avoid what might otherwise be a condition of almost involuntary servitude, it has long been held that an employee is free to compete for custom with a former employer. As usual in human affairs, the difficulty is in the details and it is often difficult to know where to draw the line.

We were favoured with a very extensive canvass of numerous authorities in the comprehensive argument of counsel for the appellant. It was argued, as I earlier observed, that the trial judge fell into error by categorizing Ms. Irwin as a 'mere employee' who would not be subject to a fiduciary duty to her former employer.

At 42 B.C.L.R. (3d) 176, the trial judge said this:

> In trying to balance the competing interests of fairness to the employer and allowing the employee to work in a competitive marketplace, the courts have considered as important and worthy of protection the knowledge a senior manager obtains of the structure and philosophy of the company, rather than the piecemeal and compartmentalized information available to an employee.
>
> Here, Ms. Irwin was not an employee of the kind of Mr. Mountjoy (see *Edgar T. Alberts Ltd.*, [*infra* para 23]). She had minor supervisory duties and no dealing with or responsibility for anything beyond the branch. In fact, it is not the 'branch manager' aspect of her job that led to her ability to compete with her former employer upon her departure. It was the day-to-day contacts she made as a producer that stood her in good stead when she went to Porter and McMillan. Even there, although she did manage to come up with a substantial list of names, it could only have been a small part of her overall portfolio when the respective values of the commissions are compared.
>
> In short, Ms. Irwin was, for the purposes of this case, a mere employee. As such, she owed her employer a duty not to take client lists and confidential information, insofar as these items were recorded in documents and not to make unfair use of the information she acquired while employed by Howat/Barton. She was, however, entitled to recall the people she had dealt with, aided by a telephone book, and ask them if they wished to do business with her in her new location.

I am not of the view that the trial judge fell into error in her analysis of the situation in this case. Many and varied fact patterns will fall to be analyzed in cases in this area. It should not be forgotten that the relationship of employer and employee is based on contract. If some restriction on an employee's scope of action post employment is thought to be desirable, then perhaps an enforceable covenant could be obtained by the employer. There is considerable jurisprudence on the limits of the enforceability of this class of covenant.

In some cases, courts have found that a fiduciary duty may be invoked to prevent threatened or existing conduct of an ex-employee concerning the business of his or her former employer. It is not necessary to go further back in time than the case of *Canadian Aero Service Ltd. v. O'Malley* (1973), 40 D.L.R.

(3d) 371 (S.C.C.), to examine the development in this country of these principles. That case was substantially different from the case at bar in that it involved the appropriation of a maturing business opportunity. The case is useful, however, in that it draws distinctions among persons who are employed at differing levels of responsibility. In the *Canadian Aero* case, the employees were the former president and vice-president of Canadian Aero. After leaving the employment of Canadian Aero, the two defendants, through a corporate vehicle, acquired a large surveying contract that they had previously been pursuing on behalf of Canadian Aero. Their former employer, Canadian Aero, sued them and their corporation. Canadian Aero was not successful either at trial or in the Ontario Court of Appeal, and it appealed to the Supreme Court of Canada. Laskin J., as he then was, delivered the judgment of the Supreme Court reversing the decisions in the lower courts. The core conclusion of the Court is found in the following passage commencing at p. 381:

> Like Grant, J., the trial Judge, I do not think it matters whether O'Malley and Zarzycki were properly appointed as directors of Canaero or whether they did or did not act as directors. What is not in doubt is that they acted respectively as president and executive vice-president of Canaero for about two years prior to their resignations. . . . They were 'top management' and not mere employees whose duty to their employer, unless enlarged by contract, consisted only of respect for trade secrets and for confidentiality of customer lists. Theirs was a larger, more exacting duty which, unless modified by statute or by contract (and there is nothing of this sort here), was similar to that owed to a corporate employer by its directors.

> . . . . .

> Although they were subject to supervision of the officers of the controlling company, their positions as senior officers of a subsidiary, which was a working organization, charged them with initiatives and with responsibilities far removed from the obedient role of servants.
> It follows that O'Malley and Zarzycki stood in a fiduciary relationship to Canaero, which in its generality betokens loyalty, good faith and avoidance of a conflict of duty and self-interest. Descending from the generality, the fiduciary relationship goes at least this far: a director or a senior officer like O'Malley or Zarzycki is precluded from obtaining for himself, either secretly or without the approval of the company (which would have to be properly manifested upon full disclosure of the facts), any property or business advantage either belonging to the company or for which it has been negotiating; and especially is this so where the director or officer is a participant in the negotiations on behalf of the company.
> An examination of the case law in this Court and in the Courts of other like jurisdictions on the fiduciary duties of directors and senior

officers shows the pervasiveness of a strict ethic in this area of the law. In my opinion, this ethic disqualifies a director or senior officer from usurping for himself or diverting to another person or company with whom or with which he is associated a maturing business opportunity which his company is actively pursuing; he is also precluded from so acting even after his resignation where the resignation may fairly be said to have been prompted or influenced by a wish to acquire for himself the opportunity sought by the company, or where it was his position with the company rather than a fresh initiative that led him to the opportunity which he later acquired.

Perhaps the primary significance of the *Canadian Aero* case to this area of the law lies in the fact that it was relied upon in the leading case of *Edgar T. Alberts Ltd. v. Mountjoy* (1977), 16 O.R. (2d) 682, 79 D.L.R. (3d) 108 a decision of the Ontario High Court. This case involved, as does the case at bar, former employees of an insurance agency. One of the defendants in the case, Mountjoy, had been the general manager of the agency for upwards of twenty years, and had been a company director for over ten years prior to his resignation in 1974. When he left, he took with him another defendant, a salesman named Butt who had been employed by the plaintiff for about five years. The facts concerning the new operation started by Mountjoy are set out at p. 683 of the report:

> The defendant Mountjoy immediately established his own insurance brokerage business, operating from his home in Metropolitan Toronto and about July 12, 1974, engaged the defendant Butt in this business, although such employment was earlier discussed with Butt on July 5, 1974. Another employee of the plaintiff, Mrs. Wright, who had been the defendant Mountjoy's secretary for 30 years, left the plaintiff's employ on July 12, 1974, and joined the defendants' new business almost at once. The business established by the defendant Mountjoy was, for the purposes of this litigation, regarded as identical to that carried on by the plaintiff. The defendants proceeded at once, after they respectively established and joined the business, to solicit for and did obtain from many customers of the plaintiff, the general insurance business of those clients.

Estey C.J.H.C., as he then was, reviewed at some length earlier cases both in England and in Canada that established that an employee was generally entitled to solicit former customers after leaving employment. Estey C.J.H.C. did not in the course of his analysis overlook the dictum of Lord Atkinson in *Herbert Morris Ltd. v. Saxelby*, [1916] 1 A.C. 688 (H.L.) at p. 702, where His Lordship observed that an employer is entitled not to have his old customers 'by solicitation or such other means enticed away from him'. Estey C.J.H.C. noted at p. 687 that *Saxelby* was a covenant case and observed that:

From the preceding portions of the judgment it is difficult to determine whether his Lordship, in the above quotation, is dealing with a legal principle at large or whether the remarks are confined to the particular terms of the restrictive covenant before the Court.

After pointing out that an insurance agency was quite vulnerable to solicitations of customers by ex-employees, the judge went on to consider the principles enunciated in the *Canadian Aero* case. He said this at p. 692:

> I do not believe it to be an extension of the principles established in *Canadian Aero* to apply those principles in the disposition of the issues arising herein. If it were indeed to be an extension, the basis for so doing can be found later in the judgment of Laskin, J., at p. 610 S.C.R., p. 384 D.L.R.:
>
> > What these decisions indicate is an updating of the equitable principle whose roots lie in the general standards that I have already mentioned, namely, loyalty, good faith and avoidance of a conflict of duty and self-interest. Strict application against directors and senior management officials is simply recognition of the degree of control which their positions give them in corporate operations, a control which rises above day-to-day accountability to owning shareholders and which comes under some scrutiny only at annual general or at special meetings. It is a necessary supplement, in the public interest, of statutory regulation and accountability which themselves are, at one and the same time, an acknowledgement of the importance of the corporation in the life of the community and of the need to compel obedience by it and by its promoters, directors and managers to norms of exemplary behaviour.
>
> If any further authority be required for the accountability of senior management offending such rules, reference may be had to the remarks of Lord Russell of Killowen, *Regal (Hastings)*, [*Regal (Hastings) Ltd. v. Gulliver*, [1942] 1 All E.R. 378], at p. 389.
>
> In this case the defendant Mountjoy stood in a fiduciary relationship to the plaintiff and there was accordingly imposed upon him a 'larger, more exacting duty' than a duty simply to respect his former employer's trade secrets and the confidentiality of its customer lists.
>
> As well, where a defendant of lower rank such as the defendant Butt might have claimed immunity from the duties attaching to a fiduciary, he lost that advantage in joining with Mountjoy in the new business venture which successfully diverted the business opportunity of his former employer and fixed him with the same fiduciary duty as Mountjoy.

Estey C.J.H.C. found both defendants liable in damages for the sum of $12,500.00 and apportioned $10,000.00 of the liability to Mountjoy and $2,500.00 to Butt.

The *Mountjoy* case is often cited as setting forth the governing principles in this class of case. The ratio I take from it is that persons occupying positions of directors or senior management may be found to be subject to a continuing fiduciary duty to a former employer. Such a duty often encompasses a prohibition on solicitation of former customers. However, other employees will not necessarily be so restrained. I infer from the reasons of Estey C.J.H.C. that if Butt alone had been a defendant and had not been associated in the new venture with Mountjoy, he might well have escaped liability.

Counsel for the appellant referred in argument to the decision of the English Court of Appeal in *Faccenda Chicken Ltd. v. Fowler*, [1986] 1 All E.R. 617. *Faccenda* on its facts is not necessarily favourable to the position of the appellant but I understood that counsel referred us to that case because of the reference therein at p. 625 to the above quoted dictum of Lord Atkinson in the *Saxelby* case. In my view, it is to be seriously doubted that it is the current law of this country that all former employees are to be restrained on pain of damages from soliciting customers of the former employer. Unless a defendant is found to be a key employee or director or as perhaps was found to be the situation in the Manitoba case of *Hudson's Bay Co. v. McClocklin* (1986), 42 Man. R. (2d) 283 (Q.B.), when an employee is in effect 'the whole show', a fiduciary duty preventing solicitation of former customers will not usually be found to exist.

I believe that the senior management or director distinction is clearly illustrated by the case of *W.J. Christie & Co. v. Greer* (1981), 121 D.L.R. (3d) 472 (Man. C.A.). In that case, a senior management employee who was also a director of the former employer was found to have breached his fiduciary duty by solicitation of clients both before and after resignation. Speaking for the court, Huband J.A. said at p. 477, after referring to the *Mountjoy* case:

> There is nothing to prevent an ordinary employee from terminating his employment, and normally that employee is free to compete with his former employer. The right to compete freely may be constrained by contract. It would be improper, too, for an employee to purloin trade secrets or confidential information, including customer lists. But it is different for a director/officer/key management person who occupies a fiduciary position. Upon his resignation and departure, that person is entitled to accept business from former clients, but direct solicitation of that business is not permissible. Having accepted a position of trust, the individual is not entitled to allow his own self-interest to collide and conflict with fiduciary responsibilities. The direct solicitation of former clients traverses the boundary of acceptable conduct. (my emphasis)

Although this court in its decision expressly refrained from deciding whether the facts disclosed a breach of fiduciary duty in the case of *57134*

*Manitoba Ltd. v. Palmer* (1989), 37 B.C.L.R. (2d) 50, it was held therein that the conduct of the main defendant was by any standard unfair and ought to attract an award of damages. The headnote discloses the facts and findings:

> The defendant P. worked for the plaintiff in a sales capacity from 1971 to 1979. Over time he took on some managerial duties as business expanded in western Canada and by 1979 he was responsible for the plaintiff's Vancouver branch, although subject to considerable head office control. After being advised that the Vancouver branch would have to be trimmed back in order to improve its profitability, P. gave 30 days' notice of resignation. During that period he joined the defendant S. Ltd. and induced some of his fellow employees to do the same. He copied and removed some of the plaintiff's client lists and order records; diverted maturing business opportunities to his new employer and, after joining that company, embarked on a systematic course of soliciting the plaintiff's customers. Ten months later, P. left S. Ltd. and formed a new company, the defendant C. Co., which took over the business the plaintiff had taken to S. Ltd. The plaintiff brought an action against all of the defendants for damages. The trial judge found that P. had breached his fiduciary duty to the plaintiff and held S. Ltd. liable for the damages suffered by the plaintiff while P. was in its employ. No award was made for the loss of a secret discount which a supplier had terminated after P. had requested the same discount for S. Ltd. S. Ltd. appealed the judgment and the plaintiff cross-appealed on damages.
>
> Held - Appeal and cross-appeal dismissed.
>
> Having regard to the totality of his activities after leaving the plaintiff, P. was clearly in breach of his general duty of good faith to that company. By any standard, his activities were unfair. Without regard to the question whether he was a fiduciary, he thus rendered himself liable for the damage which he thereby caused to his former employer.

In that case, that defendant was described as a general manager. He was obviously very much a key employee in the company's local operations. I note from p. 55 of that judgment that Esson J.A. specifically notes that it might have been permissible for the ex-employee to solicit former customers if he had done so fairly. Esson J.A. said:

> I also think it doubtful that, assuming he did become subject to the strict ethic of the fiduciary, he would have been precluded from soliciting Mayers' customers after he went to work for a competitor had he done that fairly. A clear statement on the point is to be found in one of the American authorities referred to in the judgment of Laskin J. in *Can. Aero, Raines v. Toney*, 313 S.W. 2d 802 (Ark. S.C., 1958). The passage quoted by Laskin J. at pp. 386-87 deals with the responsibilities of 'corporate fiduciaries' who resign to form a competing enterprise. The concluding statement in that passage is:

But they can use in their own enterprise the experience and knowledge they gained while working for their corporation . . . They can solicit the customers of their former corporation for business unless the customer list is itself confidential.

I do not suggest that Laskin J. in *Can. Aero* adopted that statement of the law but, on the other hand, I cannot read his judgment as rejecting it. The passage was quoted by Laskin J. without disapproval although, as appears in the last paragraph on p. 387, he thought that the trial judge in *Can. Aero* had erred in referring to it as supporting the view that the liability of directors or senior officers is limited to contracts obtained "in the course of their duties as such".

It is true, as Mr. Fraser submits, that a number of later decisions in other provinces provide some support for his submission. Some of those cases have found employees of humble degree, although none perhaps as humble as Mr. Palmer, to be subject to the 'strict ethic' and have found those employees to have breached their duty by soliciting the customers of their former employer for business. The most prominent of those cases is the decision of Estey C.J.H.C. (as he then was) in *Edgar T. Alberts Ltd. v. Mountjoy* (1977), 16 O.R. (2d) 682, 2 B.L.R. 178, 36 C.P.R. (2d) 97, 79 D.L.R. (3d) 108. An appellate decision which takes somewhat the same approach is *W.J. Christie & Co. v. Greer*, [1981] 4 W.W.R. 34, 14 B.L.R. 146, 59 C.P.R. (2d) 127, 121 D.L.R. (3d) 472, 8 Man. R. (2d) 269, a decision of the Court of Appeal of Manitoba.

None of the decisions relied on by Mr. Fraser on this question are binding on this court but this is not the right case in which to decide whether they should be followed. The point simply does not arise. It does not matter whether Mr. Palmer was in that select group subject to the rule of the strict ethic. As with any employee, he was subject to the general duty of good faith owed by any employee to his employer.

. . . . .

*Having regard to the totality of his activities after leaving Mayers, Palmer was clearly in breach of his general duty of good faith towards that company. Assuming he had the right to solicit customers, he only had the right to do so fairly. By any standard his activities were unfair. It is therefore futile to consider whether, had he acted fairly towards Mayers, he would have been nevertheless restricted from soliciting its customers.* [Hall J.A.'s emphasis)

I note that in his judgment, his Lordship referred to a passage from the headnote in *Faccenda Chicken*, which passage appears to suggest a former employee will not usually be prohibited from canvassing former customers. The judgment of Esson J.A., in my opinion, lends no support to the appellant in the present case.

The key employee or senior management analysis was also fundamental to the finding of liability in *Tree Savers International Ltd. v. Savoy* (1991), 81 Alta. L.R. (2d) 325 (Q.B.), affirmed on this point, (1992), 87 D.L.R. (4th) 202 (C.A.). This was a case which the appellant Barton strongly relied on. It was found there that one S. was a key employee and after he and another employee left the plaintiff on two weeks' notice and began soliciting former customers, the two were found liable to the plaintiff's former employer for breaches of fiduciary duty. After referring to the *Mountjoy* case, the trial judge, Gallant J. made the following findings at pp. 329-30:

> In this case, TSI had only about 20 employees, of which Savoy, Deringer, and Albert Roesch and Bruce Cherewyk, the principals of TSI, were four. Those employees operated from three locations in Alberta, namely, Calgary, Red Deer, and Grande Prairie. Savoy was sales manager of TSI and was the only employee at Calgary. About 90 per cent of TSI's business was directed through the offices of oil well owners and operators at Calgary. Savoy had been employed with TSI since 1985. When he arrived, he brought his own customer list with him. There is no doubt in my mind that, due to the high turnover rate in personnel in the industry, by April 21, 1989, the day of Savoy's departure, the up-to-date customer list bore little or no resemblance to the one he brought to TSI. By April 21, 1989, the customer list had become TSI's customer list. An example of the comprehensiveness of a customer list is shown in Ex. 1, tab 33, which comprises about 95 pages. In some cases about 100 contact persons are shown for some owners or operators. In addition, while employed by TSI, Savoy developed special TSI lists for Christmas gifts to be delivered to special contact persons of the owners or operators. Savoy developed and maintained up-to-date knowledge of those contact persons and he maintained personal contact with them. He knew their needs and wants in the isolation tool and frachead business. He knew of the upcoming job possibilities. Because of his personal relationships, he was given an opportunity to quote on the jobs. While TSI had published price lists, Savoy had wide powers to discount list prices, and he did so. And he had the power to do so without interference within those broad limits. If he felt that deeper discounts were to be given, Roesch and Cherewyk deferred to his views, which demonstrates the extended power that Savoy enjoyed with respect to pricing. He was, to a great extent, autonomous in his position. The extraordinary power that he enjoyed at TSI was further exemplified by a requirement that he be sent copies of all proposed invoices to be sure that they did not conflict with his discounting policies and quotations. *No one else in the firm had his up-to-date customer lists or had but a small portion of his knowledge of the customer contact persons or customers' needs and wants or the upcoming job opportunities. Savoy enjoyed liberal expense accounts and club memberships for client promotion. He had extraordinary power to affect the interests of his employer, and his employer relied on and was de-*

*pendent on his loyal performance and was vulnerable to the exercise of*
*his power, and he knew, or should have known, of such reliance and*
*vulnerability. I find that he was a key employee who owed a fiduciary*
*duty to TSI.* [Hall J.A.'s emphasis]

The same analysis can be said to be applicable to the decision in the
Alberta case of *Anderson, Smyth & Kelly Customs Brokers Ltd. v. World Wide*
*Customs Brokers Ltd.* (1996), 39 Alta. L.R. (3d) 411 (C.A.). I am not sure that
I would necessarily agree with the proposition that virtually any employee
could be found to be a fiduciary (if that is what is suggested in the following
passage) at p. 417:

> The Trial Judge approached the issue of Kelly's fiduciary obligation
> from the standpoint of his position as an employee with a limited duty.
> The law has moved away from the use of formal and recognized rela-
> tionships as limiting the circumstances in which fiduciary obligations
> may be found. The substance of the relationship between the parties is
> critical, not the nomenclature used to describe it. There are now few
> obstacles to characterizing an employee as a fiduciary of his employer.
> As noted by the Supreme Court of Canada in *Guerin v. R.* (1984), 13
> D.L.R. (4th) 321, there is no comprehensive list of standard relationships
> giving rise to fiduciary obligations. At p. 341 Dickson J. (as he then was)
> said:
>
>> It is sometimes said that the nature of fiduciary relationships
>> is both established and exhausted by the standard categories of
>> agent, trustee, partner, director, and the like. I do not agree. It is
>> the nature of the relationship, not the specific category of actor
>> involved that gives rise to the fiduciary duty.

However, I consider that the following passage from p. 420 is supportable
on the authorities:

> I am unable to agree with the reasoning of the Trial Judge which
> appears to ignore the distinction between the duty of fidelity and good
> faith owed to employers by all employees (including fiduciaries), and
> the higher duty springing from the existence of a fiduciary duty. While
> mere employees leaving their employment are not (in the absence of
> contract or some other consideration) prohibited from soliciting their
> former employer's clients for their direct or indirect benefit, the same is
> not true of employees who are fiduciaries. Such employees have a duty
> not to solicit their employer's clients upon departure. Thus, after finding
> Kelly to be 'an integral part of the Plaintiff's Edmonton operation', and
> characterizing him as a 'key employee' (A.B. 596), the Trial Judge
> should, in my view, have held him accountable to the Appellant on the
> basis of the higher fiduciary standard.

The senior management-key employee finding was also essential in my view to the findings of liability made in *Canadian Industrial Distributors Inc. v. Dargue* (1994), 20 O.R. (3d) 574 (Ont. Gen. Div.) and *Quantum Management Services Ltd. v. Hann* (1989), 69 O.R. (2d) 26 (Ont. H.C.), both Ontario Court trial judgments.

I believe a useful review of the competing considerations in this area is to be found in the judgment of Skipp L.J.S.C. in *TOS Insurance Services Ltd. v. Dale & Co.*, [1988] B.C.J. No. 504 (QL) [summarized 9 A.C.W.S. (3d) 252]. The defendant L. was an account executive, which I take to be a salesperson, who had been employed by the plaintiff insurance broker firm for several years. The defendant left the employ of the plaintiff and joined another insurance brokerage firm. He began to solicit clients of the plaintiff and the former employer applied for an injunction prohibiting such activity. Skipp L.J.S.C. refused the injunction. His reasoning is, I believe, a useful statement of applicable principles:

> . . . an employer is protected against unfair competition resulting from a breach by a former employee who stood in a fiduciary position while the courts may refuse to intervene where the effective result would be to make the former employee a captive of the employer: *Tomenson, Saunders Whitehead Ltd. v. Baird et al.* (1980) 7 C.C.E.L. 176 (Ont. S.C.).
>
> As to where the line is to be drawn, I respectfully adopt the comments of Spencer J. in *57134 Manitoba Ltd. v. Palmer, Smith Paper Ltd. and Classic Packaging Corp.* (1985) 65 B.C.L.R. 355 at 359-60:
>
>> I am of the opinion that the imposition of the sort of fiduciary duty found in *Can. Aero Service Ltd. v. O'Malley, supra,* is not to be tested so much by what the defendant did not do with the former employer . . . but rather by what he did. Nominal titles are not determinative. The court must examine the actual level of functions and responsibility held by the employee.

Counsel conceded that Lishanko was not 'top management'. What material there is indicates that Lishanko was a junior employee with TOS. His responsibility was limited to serving a certain subgroup of the plaintiff's total clientele.

It is clear that persons holding senior employee positions cannot directly solicit business from customers of their former employer. It is equally clear that a departing junior employee is entitled to compete with his former employer and may bring to his new business the knowledge and skills acquired while with his former employer. This is subject to the caveat that an ex-employee is not entitled to disclose or make use of confidential information, including customer lists, belonging to his former employer: *W.J. Christie & Co. Ltd. v. Greer et al.* (1981) 121 D.L.R. (3d) 472 (Man. C.A.); *Alberts et al. v. Mountjoy et al..* (1977) 79 D.L.R. (3d) 103 (Ont. H.C.); *Tomenson, Saunders, supra.*

The onus is on the plaintiff to show that the defendant breached his duty to the plaintiff and thus may be liable in damages. As Estey C.J.H.C. noted in *Alberts v. Mountjoy, supra*, at p. 113:

> It appears from the law as enunciated in these authorities that whether or not an ex-employee may solicit customers of his employer turns upon the narrow question as to whether or not the solicitation is from a list of customers or clients removed from the ex-employer's premises, as against solicitation based upon the memory of the ex-employee.

Injunctions have been obtained against former employees who took or made a copy of their employer's entire customer list: *Hudson's Bay Company McClocklin* (17 June 1986, Man. Q.B., 8601-11194, Jewers J.); *Gemologists International Inc. v. Gem Scan International Inc.* (4 April 1986, Ont. H.C., 7162/85, Montgomery J.). However, where the only material retained is a list of clients that the employee dealt with, some courts have declined to grant an injunction: see *Tomenson, Saunders*, supra.

The protected information need not be contained in a document or other tangible form, but can include information memorized by the former employee: *Monarch Messenger Services Ltd. v. Houlding* (1984) 5 C.C.E.L. 219 (Alta. Q.B.). However, in *Tomenson, Saunders*, supra, Keith J. observed that (at p. 189):

> I am further of the opinion that the fact that the names and telephone numbers of some of the individuals with whom the defendants had been dealing while in the employ of the plaintiff were readily at hand by reference to the personal diaries of the defendants which they quite properly took with them, is of no consequence. I haven't the slightest doubt that the defendants could very easily have compiled a new book of such names and telephone numbers from memory and reference to the telephone directory.
>
> In the result therefore, I am satisfied that these defendants were entitled to compete with their former employer as they did. They were making no unfair use of the knowledge they had gained while in the employ of the plaintiff, nor were they in breach of any fiduciary obligation.

It is difficult, if not impossible, to reconcile *Monarch* and *Tomenson*. While neither is binding upon this court, I prefer the *Tomenson* case as it recognizes the competing interests that a court must consider.

*Monarch Messenger Services Ltd. v. Houlding* (1984), 5 C.C.E.L. 219 (Alta. Q.B.), referred to in *TOS Insurance*, was a judgment of the Alberta trial court wherein a messenger who had considerable contact with customers was found liable to his former employer for improper use of confidential information, including customer names, rates charged and a general knowledge of the business practices of customers. I prefer the reasoning and conclusions of Keith J. in the *Tomenson* case [*Tomenson Saunders Whitehead Ltd. v. Baird* (1980), 7 C.C.E.L. 176 (Ont. H.C.J.)] to the conclusions reached in *Monarch*.

## IV. BREACH OF DUTY OF CONFIDENCE, ELEMENTS AND DEFENCES

The test for whether there has been a breach of confidence, as described by the Supreme Court in *Lac Minerals*[27] involves establishing three elements: 1) the information conveyed was confidential (evaluated on an objective standard); 2) the information was communicated in a relationship of confidence (express, implied by customs, or implied by law (fiduciary relationship, relationships such as employees, joint ventures, etc.); and 3) the information was misused by the party to whom it was communicated. Defences include consent, that the information was no longer confidential, and that the disclosure was compelled by law.

## V. REMEDIES

The doubts that remain as to whether confidential information is "property" under Canadian law (outside of criminal matters where the Supreme Court has ruled that it is not for purposes of theft) in turn leads to uncertainty as to the available remedies. Retaining physical "embodiments" of the information (plans and other writings, lists, computer disks, etc.) normally would constitute conversion. The courts may order seizure of those objects as property of the plaintiff.

The same may not be true of intangible information, and certainly not of information "stored" only in a person's (*e.g.* an ex-employee) head.

Remedies in such cases are more often based on equitable considerations (see the Employees section). In *Lac Minerals*, the Supreme Court held that a constructive trust was an appropriate remedy. An injunction may be issued to prevent (further) disclosure, if there is still sufficient relative secrecy to warrant such an order, and subject to applicable equitable defences. An employee will not be enjoined not to use professional skills or similar information.

Damages may also be awarded and, as indicated in *Cadbury Schweppes*, "tort principles could have a potential impact in a breach of confidence case

---

[27] *Supra*, note 16.

on the rules governing the assessment of equitable compensation. It is well established that equitable rules may produce a more generous level of compensation than their counterparts in tort."[28] Punitive damages may be awarded.[29]

The existence of an express covenant does not preclude reliance on a concurrent or alternative tortious liability. The same is also true of reliance on a common law duty of care that falls short of a specific obligation or duty imposed by the express terms of the contract. However, a concurrent or alternative liability in tort would not be admitted where it would permit a plaintiff to circumvent a contractual exclusion or limitation of liability.[30]

As a corollary, any contract that purports to limit liability should be very clear.[31]

## VI.  INFORMATION SUBMITTED TO GOVERNMENT

Article 39(3) of the *TRIPS Agreement* and 1711 of *NAFTA* (see the International Section) impose on Canada an obligation to protect confidential information submitted as part of a regulatory approval process (e.g., prior to the marketing of a new pharmaceutical product).

Article 1711(5) establishes the obligation to maintain the confidentiality of the information submitted:

> If a Party requires, as a condition for approving the marketing of pharmaceutical or agricultural chemical products that utilize new chemical entities, the submission of undisclosed test or other data necessary to determine whether the use of such products is safe and effective, the Party *shall protect against disclosure* of the data of persons making such submissions, where the origination of such data involves considerable effort, except where the disclosure is necessary to protect the public or unless steps are taken to ensure that the data is protected against unfair commercial use.

Article 1711(6) of *NAFTA* creates a non-reliance obligation as well:

---

[28] *Supra*, note 11.

[29] See *Franklin Supply Co. v. Midco Supply Co.* (1995), 33 Alta. L.R. (3d) 362 (Alta. Q.B.).

[30] *Central & Eastern Trust Co. v. Rafuse*, (sub nom. *Central Trust Co. v. Rafuse*) [1986] 2 S.C.R. 147, (sub nom. *Central Trust Co. v. Rafuse*) 31 D.L.R. (4th) 481, 34 B.L.R. 187, (sub nom. *Central Trust Co. v. Rafuse*) 69 N.R. 321, (sub nom. *Central Trust Co. v. Rafuse*) 75 N.S.R. (2d) 109 (S.C.C.), varied (sub nom. *Central Trust Co. v. Rafuse*) [1988] 1 S.C.R. 1206 (S.C.C.).

[31] See *Bauer v. Bank of Montreal*, [1980] 2 S.C.R. 102, 110 D.L.R. (3d) 424, 32 N.R. 191, 10 B.L.R. 209 (S.C.C.).

Each Party shall provide that for data subject to paragraph 5 that are submitted to the Party after the date of entry into force of this Agreement, *no person* other than the person that submitted them may, without the latter's permission, *rely on such data in support of an application for product approval during a reasonable period of time* after their submission. For this purpose, a reasonable period shall normally mean not less than five years from the date on which the Party granted approval to the person that produced the data for approval to market its product, taking account of the nature of the data and the person's efforts and expenditures in producing them. Subject to this provision, there shall be no limitation on any Party to implement abbreviated approval procedures for such products.

The question that arises most frequently in that context is whether a "generic" drug manufacturer can request a marketing approval after the expiry of a patent by proving the bioequivalence of its product with a previously-approved (patented) product, and thus benefit from the test data (and efforts) expended by the original manufacturer showing that the product is safe.

In *Bayer Inc. v. Canada (Attorney General)*,[32] the Federal Court rejected Bayer's argument that in so doing, the Minister of Health was "relying" on the test data. The Federal Court of Appeal, in affirming Evans. J. (as he then was), stated:

> Where a manufacturer of a new drug is not the innovator but is a competitor of the innovator, that competing manufacturer may file an Abbreviated New Drug Submission (ANDS) comparing its product with the innovator's product where the two products are pharmaceutically equivalent and bioequivalent. In the case of a competitor's product which is being compared with the innovator's product, safety tests and evidence of clinical effectiveness may not be required as the safety and effectiveness may be demonstrated by comparison with the innovator's product.
>
> The issue is whether, when a competitor of an innovator seeks approval of the safety and effectiveness of its product by comparing it with the innovator's product, there is examination and reliance by the Minister on the confidential detailed safety reports and evidence of clinical effectiveness originally filed by the innovator with the government. If so, the innovator will be entitled to at least five years of protection from competition.
>
> The appellant's argument is that whenever a subsequent manufacturer (herein a 'generic manufacturer', although it could also be a brand name competitor of the innovator), files an ANDS for the purpose of establishing the safety and effectiveness of its product by comparing its product with an innovator's product on the basis that its product is the pharmaceutical and bioequi-

---

[32] (1998), [1999] 1 F.C. 553 (Fed. T.D.), affirmed (1999), 87 C.P.R. (3d) 293 (Fed. C.A.), leave to appeal refused (2000), 259 N.R. 200 (note) (S.C.C.).

valent of the innovator's product, the Minister must explicitly or implicitly have examined and relied upon confidential information originally filed by the innovator with the Minister in its NDS for its Notice of Compliance.

The appellant says that on this interpretation of subsection C.08.004.1(1)[33], the Minister may not issue a Notice of Compliance to the generic manufacturer earlier than five years after the date of issuance of the Notice of Compliance to the innovator for its product. Evans, J. rejected this interpretation of the regulation. We are in agreement with his detailed and persuasive reasons and add the following only to address the specific arguments made before this Court.

When a generic manufacturer files an ANDS, the safety and effectiveness of the generic product may be demonstrated by showing that the product is the pharmaceutical and bioequivalent of the innovator's product. If the generic manufacturer is able to do so solely by comparing its product with the innovator's product which is being publicly marketed, the Minister will not have to examine or rely upon confidential information filed as part of the innovator's NDS. In such case, the minimum five year market protection referred to in the regulation will not apply.

On the other hand, if, in order to be satisfied of the safety and effectiveness of the generic product, the Minister examines and relies upon information filed by the innovator in its NDS, the minimum five year market protection for the innovator will apply. This is because the safety and effectiveness of the generic product will only be established by reference to confidential information provided to the Minister by the innovator. It is only this use of that confidential information by the Minister on behalf of the generic manufacturer that gives rise to the minimum five year protection from competition for the innovator.

The appellant says that whenever an ANDS is filed by a generic manufacturer comparing the generic product with the innovator's product, the Minister must implicitly be examining and relying upon the confidential information filed by the innovator in its NDS. We do not read subsection C.08.004.1(1) in this way. To do so would be to interpret it as invariably providing a minimum five years of market protection to an innovator when an ANDS is filed by a generic manufacturer. Rather, the regulation contemplates that the Minister may or may not examine and rely upon confidential information filed by the innovator. The appellant's argument reads out of the regulation the option given to the Minister as to whether or not to examine and rely on the confidential information filed by the innovator.

The Regulatory Impact Analysis Statement accompanying the amended regulations at issue provides a further indication that the intention of the regulation is that the confidential information filed by the innovator may or may not be examined and relied upon. The statement reads in part:

> In the case where the Drugs Directorate intends to rely on the data of the innovator to support safety and efficacy claims, and this would result in

---

[33] Of the *Food and Drugs Regulation*, C.R.C. 1978, c. 870.

a delay in the issuance of the NOC, the Drugs Directorate will notify the second-entry manufacturer in advance of the review. The Drugs Directorate will give the second-entry manufacturer the option of supplying additional information to support the claim without relying on the data previously submitted by the innovator. If the manufacturer wishes to supply the required information directly, in accordance with the policy on management of information, the manufacturer will avoid the application of this provision.

The government's policy appears to be that where the Minister intends to rely on data of the innovator to support the safety and efficacy claims of the generic manufacturer, thereby giving rise to the minimum five year protection from competition for the innovator, the generic manufacturer will be given the option of supplying additional information in order to avoid the Minister relying on information supplied by the innovator. If the generic manufacturer takes this option and satisfies the Minister, there will be no examination or reliance on the innovator's information and the minimum five year protection from competition will not apply. The appellant's interpretation would preclude this option to the generic manufacturer.

As Evans, J. pointed out, the appellant's argument would require that the Court read into the regulation the word 'indirectly' or some other modifier to capture the idea that whenever a generic manufacturer files an ANDS comparing its product to an innovator's product, that there is implicit examination and reliance on the confidential information previously submitted by the innovator in its NDS. The Court cannot read words into the regulation.

The regulation provides for a sequential process; first, the filing of the ANDS by the generic manufacturer; second, and after the filing of the ANDS, examination of the information filed by the innovator; and third, reliance by the Minister on that information in issuing a Notice of Compliance to the generic manufacturer. Only if all three steps are applicable, does the minimum five year market protection provided by the regulation apply. There is no implied examination or reliance.

*Is subsection C.08.004.1(1) consonant with sections 5 and 6 of Article 1711 of the NAFTA?*

The appellant argues that subsection C.08.004.1(1) was enacted because of the requirement of Article 1711 of the North American Free Trade Agreement of December 17, 1992 and that subsection C.08.004.1(1) must be interpreted in a manner consonant with the NAFTA. Article 1711 is entitled 'Trade Secrets'. . . . Section 5 requires that Canada protect against the disclosure of undisclosed test or other data submitted for the purpose of determining whether the use of a product is safe and effective when the origination of the data involves considerable effort. Section 6 provides that with respect to such confidential data, no person other than the person submitting the data shall rely on that confidential data in support of an application for product approval for a reasonable period of time i.e. normally not less than five years. Subject to this requirement, there is no limitation on Canada implementing an abbreviated approval procedure on the basis of bioequivalence and bioavailability studies.

The NAFTA provisions are intended to protect trade secrets. If the generic manufacturer exercises the option of having the Minister examine the confidential information filed by the innovator in support of its application for a Notice of Compliance, it is, in effect, relying on that information within the meaning of section 6 of Article 1711. It is apparent that if confidential data is not relied upon, the trade secrets provisions of the NAFTA are not applicable. Specifically, if a generic manufacturer is able to establish the safety and effectiveness of its product on the basis of bioequivalence or bioavailability studies without the Minister having to examine and rely upon confidential data filed by the innovator, there is no reason or justification for the minimum five year protection from competition. This interpretation of subsection C.08.004.1(1) is consonant with section 5 and 6 of Article 1711 of the NAFTA.

*Distinction between patent protection and trade secret protection*

Appellant's counsel concedes that subsection C.08.004.1(1) is not a provision that provides patent protection, but that is indeed the essence of his argument. If a generic manufacturer compares its product to an innovator's product solely on the basis of public information, providing the innovator with protection from competition for a minimum of five years is tantamount to granting it the protection a patent would provide. Put another way, even if the Minister did not examine and rely on the innovator's confidential information, the innovator would be entitled to the minimum of five years protection from competition. The words of subsection C.08.004.1(1) cannot be construed to yield such a result.

Subsection C.08.004.1(1) of the *Food and Drug Regulations* and Article 1711 of the NAFTA deal with confidential information or trade secrets, a concept separate and distinct from patents. It is understandable that an innovator should not have to face immediate competition from a competitor based on the competitor being able to produce a product using proprietary confidential information of the innovator. Section 5 of Article 1711 of the NAFTA calls this 'unfair commercial use' of the confidential data. That 'unfair commercial use' is restricted by subsection C.08.004.1(1) even in the absence of a patent protecting the innovator's product from competition. Obviously, where there is no commercial use of confidential data, subsection C.08.004.1(1) and Article 1711 do not provide or require that the innovator be protected from competition because no confidential information or trade secrets are being examined or relied upon in bringing the generic product to the market.

*Conclusion*

Subsection C.08.004.1(1) and sections 5 and 6 of Article 1711 of NAFTA are responsive to the requirement on innovators of pharmaceutical products of having to disclose confidential proprietary information to the government. They provide for the use of that confidential or trade secret information by the government on behalf of the generic manufacturer and when that occurs, the minimum five year protection from competition for the innovator applies. Where the government does not use that confidential or trade secret information on behalf of the generic manufacturer, the provision is not applicable.

Some factors and practices help to characterize business information as "confidential": restricting access to and circulation of information within a company; using physical and technological security devices; logging photocopiers and restricting access to photocopy machines; explaining confidential information to employees and using exit interviews to notify employees of continuing obligations with respect to continuing information; and having non-employees sign non-disclosure agreements.

## VII.  DISCUSSION QUESTION

**Q:** A company which manufactures food products has a secret recipe for a soup and has come to you for advice about legally protecting it. Discuss a detailed strategy to ensure that the soup recipe is protected as confidential information. Recommend both things that the company should do and things that it should avoid doing.

# *Chapter* 7: **Plant Varieties**

I. Introduction

II. The Application Process

III. Scope and Duration of Rights

IV. Infringement and Remdies

V. Discussion Questions

## 1. INTRODUCTION

Plant varieties are protected under *sui generis* legislation known as the *Plant Breeder's Rights Act*.[1] The Act protects new plant varieties. Section 2 defines "plant variety" as "any cultivar, clone, breeding line or hybrid of a prescribed category of plant that can be cultivated". All plants, including many fruit (*e.g.* apples and strawberries), vegetables (*e.g.,* peas, potatoes) and grain products (*e.g.,* oats, wheat) are eligible for protection, while algae, bacteria and fungi are not.

The Plant Breeder's legislation provides alternative intellectual property protection for plant varieties. New plant varieties are expensive and time consuming to develop but are hard to qualify for patent protection, particularly where the variety results from cross-breeding rather than genetic modification. The *Plant Breeder's Rights Act* is specifically tailored to promoting and protecting new plant varieties.

The variety must be new. Novelty, in this context, is determined by three characteristics, namely:

(a) [. . .] by reason of one or more identifiable characteristics, [the variety is] clearly distinguishable from all varieties the existence of which is a matter of common knowledge at the effective date of application for the grant of the plant breeder's rights respecting that plant variety;

(b) is stable in its essential characteristics in that after repeated reproduction or propagation or, where the applicant has defined a particular cycle of reproduction or multiplication, at the end of each cycle, remains true to its description; and

(c) is, having regard to the particular features of its sexual reproduction or vegetative propagation, a sufficiently homogeneous variety.[2]

---

[1] S.C. 1990, c. 20, online: Department of Justice Canada <http://laws.justice.gc.ca/en/P-14.6/text.html>.

[2] *Ibid.,* s. 4(2).

Section 4(3) defines the expression "sufficiently homogeneous variety" used in s. 4(2)(c) as "a variety that, in the event of its sexual reproduction or vegetative propagation in substantial quantity, any variations in characteristics of plants so reproduced or propagated are predictable, capable of being described and commercially acceptable."

In simpler terms, a variety can be protected if:

1.    it is *new* (usually means not previously sold);
2.    *different* (from other varieties);
3.    *uniform* (all plants in the variety are the same); and
4.    *stable* (each generation of the plant is the same).

In the only reported case dealing directly with the Act,[3] which dealt not with infringement but with a change of denomination of a protected variety, Muldoon J. of the Federal Court explained the Act's purpose as follows:

Plant breeders' rights are a form of intellectual property right under the *Plant Breeders' Rights Act*. The holder of the plant breeders' rights has the exclusive right to sell and produce the protected variety in Canada, to sell the variety's propagating material, to use the variety in commercially producing another variety, to use the variety in producing ornamental plants or cut flowers, and to license a third party to use the variety.

A proponent of a new seed variety may apply to the Commissioner of the Plant Breeders' Rights Office for plant breeders' rights. Once the rights are granted, the selected denomination must be used when selling propagating materials. Subection 2(1) of the *Plant Breeders' Rights Act* defines 'propagating material' as 'any reproductive or vegetative material for propagation, whether by sexual or other means, of a plant variety, and includes seeds for sowing and any whole plant or part thereof that may be used for propagation.'

When a particular variety's applicant has been granted plant breeders' rights, it is an offence under the *Plant Breeders' Rights Act* to sell propagating material of that variety under a different denomination.

Although the intellectual property rights associated with breeding plants are created under the *Plant Breeders' Rights Act*, the import, export, advertising and sale of plant varieties fall under the *Seeds Act* and its associated *Regulations*. [. . .]

---

[3] *University of Saskatchewan v. Canada (Commissioner of the Plant Breeders' Rights Office)*, [2001] 3 F.C. 247, 11 C.P.R. (4th) 348, (sub nom. *University of Saskatchewan v. Plant Breeders' Rights Office (Commissioner)*) 201 F.T.R. 173 (Fed. T.D.) [*University of Saskatchewan* cited to F.C.].

c. Development Process for a New Plant Variety

The uncontradicted affidavit evidence in this case describes how a new barley variety is developed. The plant breeder must first develop a potential malt barley variety. The plant breeder assigns a number to the variety based on the plant breeder's own internal system.

If the malt barley variety exhibits exceptional merit, the plant breeder then enters it into wide-scale cooperative trials to determine its agronomic characteristics such as yield, maturity, lodging, and disease resistance. These trials are conducted by an association of plant breeders, universities, private organizations and Agriculture Canada. Typically, the cooperative trials take three years to complete.

During the co-operative trials, the variety is assigned a number by the test co-ordinator. Using a designation system which has been in use for more than twenty years, the varieties are designated 'TR' for two row varieties and 'BT' for six row varieties. The digits following the first two letters are numbers which are later recycled in unrelated trials.

After three years of agronomic evaluation and two years of small scale malting and brewing quality testing, the variety may be registered under the *Seeds Act* and testing occurs on a larger scale. The practice in Canada is to register the malting barley variety initially under the *Seeds Act* using the numerical code from the co-operative tests as the denomination. This is a critical stage of the commercialization process. Before this large scale testing, the amount of seed is limited, and brewing and malting facilities have not tested the variety in commercial quantities. The malting and brewing industry in Canada generally requires a minimum of two years of commercial plant testing before including a new variety in its ingredient list.

The large scale testing requires more seed, and some seed must therefore be sold to seed growers. Because the *Plant Breeders' Rights Act* prohibits any sale of seed before the application for plant breeders' rights, the rights are obtained at this stage.

Generally, a plant breeder will assign the variety a permanent name only after at least two years of large scale testing and only after commercial acceptance of the variety. The malt, grain and seed marketers can then develop brand recognition. For example, in the case at bar, the designation TR133 was renamed CDC Kendall after three years of testing. Under the *Seeds Act*, this name change is relatively routine. Typically, the designations also include an institution identifier which signals the plant breeder who developed the seed.

d. The Case at Bar

On June 21, 1995, the applicant registered a variety of two-rowed malting barley under the denomination TR133 with the Variety Registration Office pursuant to the *Seeds Act*.

On March 17, 1997, the applicant was granted plant breeders' rights under the *Plant Breeders' Rights Act* for a barley variety with the same denomination TR133.

On November 28, 1997, the applicant changed the variety's denomination with the Variety Registration Office from TR133 to CDC Lager. The applicant mistakenly assumed that the Variety Registration Office would advise the Plant Breeders' Rights Office of the change because they are in the same building and are both part of the Canadian Food Inspection Agency. However, each office operates independently, and the denomination change was never registered with the Plant Breeders' Rights Office.

[. . .]

In 1998 and 1999, the applicant paid the annual registration fee to the respondent under the denomination TR133 pursuant to the *Plant Breeders' Rights Act*.

In January 2000, the respondent discovered that the applicant was selling TR133 [. . .]. On January 27, 2000, Valerie Sisson, Commissioner of the Plant Breeders' Rights Office, wrote to Dr. Bryan Harvey, the Vice-President of Research at the University of Saskatchewan, and notified him that the variety known as TR133 was registered under the *Plant Breeders' Rights Act*, but that the variety known as CDC Kendall denomination was not:

[. . .]

PBR was granted on March 17, 1997 to the University of Saskatchewan for the barley variety designated 'TR 133' [. . .].

[. . .]

It is an offence to wilfully designate any propagating material of a variety for the purpose of selling it by using a denomination different from the denomination approved by the Commissioner (Subsection 53(2) of the *PBR Act*). A corporation that commits such an offence is liable on summary conviction to a fine of up to twenty-five thousand dollars or on conviction on indictment to a fine the amount of which is in the discretion of the court (Subsection 53(5) of the *PBR Act*).

[. . .]

Purpose of the Act

The *Plant Breeders' Rights Act* allows plant breeders legally to protect new varieties of plants. Plant varieties may be covered under the legislation for a period of up to 18 years. All plant species, except algae, bacteria and fungi, are eligible for protection. The owner of a new variety who receives a grant of rights has exclusive rights over the use of the variety, and can protect the new variety from exploitation by others. The intent of the legislation is to stimulate plant breeding in Canada, to provide Canadian producers with better access to foreign varieties and to facilitate the protection of Canadian varieties in other countries.

The holder of plant breeders' rights has the exclusive right to sell and produce a variety in Canada, to sell its propagating material, to use the variety in commercially producing another variety, to use the variety in producing ornamental plants or cut flowers, and to license a third party to use the variety.

The purpose of the *Plant Breeders' Rights Act* is conceived primarily in terms of establishing entitlements to parties, and not as a delicate balancing between different constituencies. Although there is an international aspect to plant breeders' rights because Canada is a signatory to the *International Convention for the Protection of New Varieties of Plants*, the legislation contemplates protecting Canadian plant breeding interests at home and abroad.

## II. THE APPLICATION PROCESS

According to ss. 7 and 9 of the Act and applicable regulations, applications to protect plant varieties are submitted to the Plant Breeders' Rights Office (PBRO), which is part of the Canadian Food Inspection Agency (CFIA). The application must contain a proposed denomination for the variety (see s. 14), a brief summary of how the variety is distinct from all varieties known in Canada; a description of the origin and breeding history of the variety; a statement of uniformity and stability; a sample of propagating material; particulars of where the variety will be maintained throughout the duration of the rights (see s. 30), and the methods to be used for maintaining the variety; data concerning any previous commercial use of the variety; and documentation supporting ownership. The PBRO may request additional information.

After the PBRO has completed its examination, comparative photographs and results of tests and trials, a description of the variety is published in the *Plant Varieties Journal*. Any person may file an objection and both the applicant and the person making the objection are given an opportunity to be heard (s. 22). The objection must be filed within six months of the publication of the application.

## III. SCOPE AND DURATION OF RIGHTS

According to s. 5(1), the holder of a plant breeders' right has the exclusive right (*a*) to sell, and produce in Canada for the purpose of selling, propagating material, as such, of the plant variety;

(*b*) to make repeated use of propagating material of the plant variety in order to produce commercially another plant variety if the repetition is necessary for that purpose;

(*c*) where it is a plant variety to which ornamental plants or parts thereof normally marketed for purposes other than propagation belong, to use any such plants or parts commercially as propagating material in the production of ornamental plants or cut flowers; and

(*d*) to authorize, conditionally or unconditionally, the doing of an act described in paragraphs (*a*) to (*c*).

The *Act* limits the right of s. 5(1)(a) and (b) to commercial use. There-fore, farmers may save and use their own seed of protected varieties without infringing on the holder's rights. This is usually referred to as the "farmer's privilege." However, some recent cereal plant varieties contain a so-called "terminator" gene that does not allow reuse of seeds and forces farmers to purchase new seeds for every crop. In areas other than ornamental and cut flowers, protected varieties may be used for breeding and developing new plant varieties.

The applicant also can propose a name for the new variety, subject to the approval of the Commissioner (s. 14).

Plant Breeders' Rights are granted for a period of up to 18 years (s. 6), effective from the date of issue of the rights certificate. At any time during this period the holder may surrender the rights on the variety. To maintain the protection, annual fees must be paid. There is also an obligation to maintain the variety (s. 30).

Compulsory licensing of plant varieties is possible. According to s. 32, the Commissioner of Plant Breeders' Rights can issue a non-exclusive compulsory license and require the holder of the plant breeder's rights to make propagating material available to the holder of the compulsory licence. Under s. 32(2), the Commisioner must endeavour to secure that

(a) the plant variety is made available to the public at reasonable prices, is widely distributed and is maintained in quality; and

(b) there is reasonable remuneration, which may include royalty, for the holder of the plant breeder's rights respecting the plant variety.

Prior to issuing such a license, the holder of a PBR must be given an opportunity to be heard (s. 32(5)).

## IV.  INFRINGEMENT AND REMEDIES

The Provincial and Federal Court have jurisdiction (ss. 42 and 43). However, the Federal Court has exclusive jurisdiction, on application of the Commissioner or of any interested person, to order that any entry in the register be struck out or amended or to invalidate a plant breeder's right (s. 43).

An infringer is liable for "all damages" under s. 41. Subsection 41(2) allows for a competent court to grant orders:

> [B]y way of injunction and recovery of damages and generally respecting proceedings in the action and, without limiting the generality of the foregoing, may make an order
>
> (*a*)  for restraint of such use, production or sale of the subject-matter of those rights as may constitute such an infringement and for punishment in the event of disobedience of the order for that restraint;
>
> (*b*)  for compensation of an aggrieved person;
>
> (*c*)  for and in respect of inspection or account; and
>
> (*d*)  with respect to the custody or disposition of any offending material, products, wares or articles.

Defences include (apart from a factual defence based on an absence of infringement), the fact that the right should not have been granted (*e.g.*, because the holder did not comply with the Act, especially ss. 4 and 7) or that the holder failed to maintain the variety as provided for in s. 30 (see s. 46). In cases involving equitable remedies, the usual defences are available (*e.g.*, laches, unclean hands).

Criminal offences are also included but have never been invoked in any reported case (s. 53).

## V.  DISCUSSION QUESTIONS

**Q:** Discuss the advantages or disadvantages of applying for plant variety protection instead of a patent? Compare and contrast the scope and availability of plant variety and patent protection? In which case would a patent for a plant be available? For part(s) of a plant? Could a patent and plant variety protection be available for the same new variety?

# *Chapter* 8: Integrated Circuit Topographies

I. *Integrated Circuitry Topography Act*

II. Discussion Question

## I. *INTEGRATED CIRCUITRY TOPOGRAPHY ACT*

The U.S. government adopted specific, *sui generis* intellectual property legislation called the *Semiconductor Chip Protection Act* to protect the "mask" of topography of integrated circuits (or "computer chips") because it believed that copyright protection would be ineffective and patent protection unavailable in many cases. Given that the U.S. legislation only protected foreign "chips" from countries that adopted similar protection, and as required under NAFTA (see the International section) and then the TRIPS Agreement, Canada adopted its own *sui generis* legislation, the *Integrated Circuit Topography Act*, which came into force in 1993.[1] The Act defines "topography" as follows (s. 2):

> the design, however expressed, of the disposition of
>
> > (*a*) the interconnections, if any, and the elements for the making of an integrated circuit product, or
> >
> > (*b*) the elements, if any, and the interconnections for the making of a customization layer or layers to be added to an integrated circuit product in an intermediate form.

In simpler terms, a topography is a representation of the way in which the elements and interconnections are spatially related to one another.

As to the nature of the protection, it was explained as follows by Industry Canada:[2]

> A topography will qualify as original if it is developed through the application of intellectual effort, and if it is not produced by the mere reproduction of all, or a substantial part, of another topography. The Act does not protect pre-existing topographies which are commonplace among topography designers or integrated circuit product manufacturers.

---

[1] S.C. 1990, c. 37.

[2] Canadian Intellectual Property Office, *A Guide to Integrated Circuit Topographies* (January 2001), <http://www.strategis.ic.gc.ca/sc_mrksv/cipo/ict/ict_gd_main-e.html>.

The legislation permits owners of registered topographies to exclude others from:

- reproducing a protected topography or any substantial part of one;
- manufacturing an integrated circuit product incorporating the topography or a substantial part of one;
- importing or commercially exploiting (which includes the sale, lease, offering or exhibiting for sale or lease, or other commercial distribution) a topography or a substantial part of one, or of an integrated circuit product that embodies a protected topography or a substantial part of one;
- importing or commercially exploiting an industrial article which incorporates an integrated circuit product that embodies a protected topography or a substantial part of one.

The Act protects registered integrated circuit topographies for up to 10 years. The term begins on the filing date of the application for registration. The term ends on December 31 of the tenth year after the year of the first commercial exploitation or the year of the filing date, whichever is earlier.

. . .

The Act provides for the full range of civil remedies, including injunctions, damages and punitive damages. . . .

Because of changes in the design of computer chips, the Act, which was seldom used, is now almost obsolete. There are no reported cases under the Act.

## II. DISCUSSION QUESTION

**Q:** Compare and contrast the protection of topographies and the protection of computer chips that may be available under other intellectual property rights.

# *Chapter* 9: International Intellectual Property

I. Substantive Instruments

II. Other Instruments

III. The Role of Intellectual Property Treaties in Domestic Law

IV. Discussion Questions

The increasing scope and nature of international regulation of intellectual property in recent years has left little leeway to Canadian policymakers, especially with the entry into force on January 1, 1995, of the *Agreement on Trade-Related Aspects of Intellectual Property Rights* as part of the Uruguay Round of Multilateral Trade Negotiations, which gave birth to the World Trade Organization (WTO).[1]

International intellectual property norms can be grouped into three categories: substantive instruments that set minimum norms; instruments designed to harmonize the description of goods and services for purposes of registration; and finally instruments that create multilateral registration mechanisms and authorities. The non-discrimination concept of national treatment—treating foreign rightsholders no less favorably than one's nationals—is an important concept underlying these agreements, found for example in Art. 3(a) of the *Paris Convention*,[2] in Art. 5 of the *Berne Convention*,[3] and in Art. 3 of the *TRIPS Agreement*. We will examine the first category of treaties, with a special emphasis on the *TRIPS Agreement*,[4] and then briefly look at the other categories. In the last section, we will look at how Canadian courts have relied on international intellectual property treaties in interpreting Canadian law.

---

[1] *Agreement Establishing the World Trade Organization, Annex 1C: Agreement on Trade-Related Aspects of Intellectual Property Rights*, 15 April 1994, 1869 U.N.T.S. 299, online: WTO <http://www.wto.org/english/docs_e/legal_e/27-trips_01_e.htm> [*TRIPS* or *TRIPS Agreement*].

[2] *Paris Convention for the Protection of Industrial Property*, 20 March 1883, 828 U.N.T.S. 305, as last revised at the Stockholm Revision Conference 14 July 1967, online: WIPO <http://www.wipo.int/treaties/en/ip/paris/trtdocs_wo020.html> [*Paris Convention*].

[3] *Berne Convention for the Protection of Literary and Artistic Works*, 9 September 1886, 828 U.N.T.S. 221, as last revised 24 July 1971, online: WIPO <http://www.wipo.int/treaties/en/ip/berne/trtdocs_wo001.html > [*Berne Convention*].

[4] As will become apparent below, this Agreement is more significant because of its scope and its enforceability.

The protection of foreign copyright works and the criteria used to determine whether a work will be protected under the *Copyright Act*[5] are discussed in the Copyright part (Foreign Works and Points of attachment section).

## I. SUBSTANTIVE INSTRUMENTS

There are sixteen multilateral instruments in this category, although only eight have a significant impact on Canadian legislation. They are:

- The *Paris Convention*;
- The *Berne Convention*;
- The *International Convention for the Protection of Performers, Producers of Phonograms and Broadcasting Organizations*;[6]
- The *TRIPS Agreement*;
- The *North American Free Trade Agreement*, chapter 17;[7]
- The *WIPO Copyright Treaty*;[8]
- The *WIPO Performances and Phonograms Treaty*;[9] and
- The International Convention for the Protection of New Varieties of Plants (UPOV).[9a]

The other eight instruments in this category, which will not be discussed, are:

---

[5] *Copyright Act*, R.S.C. 1985, c. C-42, online: Department of Justice Canada <http://laws.justice.gc.ca/en/c-42/text.html>.

[6] *The International Convention for the Protection of Performers, Producers of Phonograms and Broadcasting Organizations*, 26 October, 1961, 496 U.N.T.S. 43, as amended in Geneva, 1985, online: WIPO <http://www.wipo.int/treaties/en/ip/rome/trtdocs_wo024.html> [*Rome Convention*].

[7] *North American Free Trade Agreement Between the Government of Canada, the Government of Mexico and the Government of the United States*, 17 December 1992, Can. T.S. 1994 No. 2, (entered into force 1 January 1994), online: International Trade Canada: <http://www.dfait-maeci.gc.ca/nafta-alena/agree-en.asp> [*NAFTA*].

[8] *WIPO Copyright Treaty*, 20 December 1996, 36 I.L.M. 65, online: WIPO <http://www.wipo.int/treaties/en/ip/wct/trtdocs_wo033.html > [*WCT*].

[9] *WIPO Performances and Phonograms Treaty*, 20 December 1996, 36 I.L.M. 76, online: WIPO <http://www.wipo.int/treaties/en/ip/wppt/trtdocs_wo034.html > [*WPPT*].

[9a] Of 1961. Revised in 1972, 1978 and 1991. Canada is party to the 1978 Act. The 1991 Act limits farmers' rights to reuse seed and allows dual protection (patent and plant variety).

- *Brussels Convention Relating to the Distribution of Programme-Carrying Signals Transmitted by Satellite*;
- *Convention for the Protection of Producers of Phonograms Against Unauthorized Duplication of Their Phonograms* (*Geneva Phonograms Convention*);
- *Madrid Agreement for the Repression of False and Deceptive Indications of Source on Goods*;
- *Nairobi Treaty on the Protection of the Olympic Symbol*;
- *The Patent Law Treaty* (*PLT*);
- *Trademark Law Treaty* (*TLT*);
- *Treaty on the International Registration of Audiovisual Works* (*Film Register Treaty*) ; and the
- *Treaty on Intellectual Property in Respect of Integrated Circuits* (*Washington Treaty*).

As of January 1, 2005, Canada was *not* party to the *Brussels Convention*, the *Geneva Phonograms Convention*, the *Madrid Agreement*, the *Nairobi Treaty*, the *TLT*, the *Film Register Treaty* or the *Washington Treaty*. Also as of January 1, 2005, the *PLT* had not entered into force, but Canada is a signatory.[10]

Canada is, however, party to the treaties mentioned in the first group, except, as of January 1, 2005, the *WCT* and *WPPT*; but the government had announced its intention to ratify these treaties in the near future. They were also mentioned by Justice LeBel in *SOCAN* as relevant in interpreting Canadian law:[11]

> Although Canada has not ratified the treaty [*WCT*], this does not mean that it should not be considered as an aid in interpreting the [Copyright] Act.

---

[10] The PLT deals mostly with administrative issues. A treaty on substantive patent issues (known as "Substantive PLT" or "SPLT") is also under negotiation.

[11] *Society of Composers, Authors & Music Publishers of Canada v. Canadian Assn. of Internet Providers*, (sub nom. *Socan v. Canadian Assn. of Internet Providers*) [2004] 2 S.C.R. 427, (sub nom. *SOCAN v. Canadian Assn. of Internet Providers*) 240 D.L.R. (4th) 193, (sub nom. *SOCAN v. Canadian Assn. of Internet Providers*) 32 C.P.R. (4th) 1, 322 N.R. 306 (S.C.C.) at 484-85 [*SOCAN* cited to S.C.R.]. Another statement endorsing the use of international agreements which have not been adopted as law as interpretive aids is that of McGillis J. in *Krazy Glue Inc. v. Grupo Cyanomex S.A. de C.V.* (1992), 45 C.P.R. (3d) 161 (Fed. T.D.): "The Paris Convention has not been adopted as a law of Canada and may only be used as an interpretative aid in circumstances where ambiguity exists in the Trademarks Act, R.S.C. 1985, c. T-13." See also s. 6 below.

## 1. The Paris Convention

The *Paris Convention* was signed in 1883 and entered into force on July 7, 1884. It had two main objectives: (a) extend to all member nations the principle of national treatment (*i.e.,* the obligation to treat foreign nationals no less favourably than nationals) and (b) guarantee minimum standards of protection for patents and trade-marks.

As member countries increased their level of protection and started to coordinate the evolution of their national laws, it became possible to increase the level of harmonization and to agree to rules designed to facilitate the acquisition of patent and trade-mark rights in foreign countries. These changes to the Convention were made at revision conferences held in various cities, all held in Western Europe. The last such conference was held in Stockholm in 1967. There have been no revisions since then and it is unlikely that there will be, due to the complex, unanimity-based process of revision conferences. Such consent among 168 countries (as of October 1, 2004) on any issue is unlikely.

Canada became party to the *Paris Convention* for the first time in 1925 and ratified the 1967 Stockholm Act (or version) on May 26, 1996.[12]

The Convention is administered by the World Intellectual Property Organization (WIPO), which was created at the 1967 Stockholm Conference by the adoption and entry into force of the *Convention Establishing the World Intellectual Property Organization,* which Canada ratified with effect as of June 26, 1970. Because of the foreseen difficulty in revising the Convention, WIPO member States have adopted separate instruments, such as the *Trademark Law Treaty* (adopted in 1994) and the *PLT* (adopted in 2000). But the international intellectual framework was also considerably modified by the entry into force of the *TRIPS Agreement* on January 1, 1995, but in a different forum, namely the World Trade Organization (WTO). That Agreement is discussed below.

Without going into too much detail,[13] it is important to note that the *Paris Convention* contains four sets of provisions:

A)   Rights and obligations of Paris Union members and establishment of Union:

---

[12] With respect to the substantive provisions contained in Articles 1 to 12. Canada had previously adhered to the administrative provisions only (articles 13 to 30) on July 7, 1970.

[13] A detailed analysis of the 1967 text of the Convention may be found in G. Bodenhausen, *Guide to the Paris Convention* (Geneva: BIRPI, 1969).

- Art. 6*ter*, which protects armorial bearings, flags and State emblems
- Art. 12-24, which govern the administrative operation of the "Paris Union", i.e., the Union composed of all States party to the Convention. Art. 12 obliges member States to create a national industrial property office, such as the Canadian Intellectual Property Office (CIPO);
- Art. 26-30, which govern the entry into force and revision of the Convention.

B)   Requirements or authorization to legislate in certain areas

In the area of patents:

- Art. 4D, providing a one-year time period to file foreign patent applications, thus allowing time for translation, paperwork, etc. This so-called "right of priority" is also governed by Article 4 (see below under D)
- Art. 4G(2), concerning the division of patent applications;
- Art. 5A(2) concerning the abuse of patent rights;
- Art. 5*bis*(2) allowing members to restore patents which lapsed for failure to pay the required fees.

And in the area of trade-marks:

- Art. 6*bis*(2) providing protection for well-known marks;
- Art. 6 *septiès*(3) dealing with agents;
- Art. 10*bis*(1) requiring States to provide protection against unfair competition;
- Art. 10*ter* requiring protection against false indications and other unlawful acts concerning trade-marks;

And finally two general provisions, applicable to all forms of industrial property (trade-marks, patents, utility models — where national law so provides, such as the United States — and industrial designs):

- Art. 11, which provides for temporary protection of industrial property rights in respect of goods exhibited at an international exhibition; and
- Art. 25, containing a general obligation to give effect to the Convention in national law.

C)    Provisions regulating the substantive law of industrial property requiring the application of domestic laws

- Art. 2 and 3, which provide for national treatment (see above);
- Art. 9 and 10, dealing with remedies in the area of trade-marks, including seizure (Art. 9(3)). Such remedies are also applicable to false indications of source (Art. 10(1)).

D)    Provisions regulating substantive law of industrial property regarding rights and obligations of private parties. These provisions may be directly applicable in the national law of certain countries. This is not the case in Canada (see s. 6 below).

General provisions:
- Art. 1, containing a definition of industrial property;
- Art. 5, which regulates the obligation to exploit (or "work") industrial property rights and the issuance of compulsory licenses;
- Art. 5*bis*, providing a grace period to pay applicable fees;

In the area of patent law:
- Art. 4, concerning the right of priority;
- Art. 4*bis*, providing that each (national) patent is independent of patents issues in other countries;
- Art. 4*ter*, which provides inventors with the right to be mentioned in the patent;
- Art 4*quater*, which limits the member States' power to refuse of annul patents;
- 5*ter*, dealing with patent infringement where a patented device forms part of a vessel, aircraft or "land vehicle"
- 5*quarter*, concerning process patents;

In the area of trade-marks:
- Art. 6, providing for the registration and independence of trade-marks;
- Art. 6*quater*, concerning the assignment of trade-marks;
- Art. 6*quinquiès*, dealing with the registration of foreign trade-marks;
- Art. 6*septiès*, dealing with trade-mark agents;
- Art. 7, providing for the exclusion of the nature of the goods as a bar to the registration of a mark;
- Art. 8, protecting trade names;

- Art. 10(2), dealing with false indications of source and providing an interest in pursuing same;
- Art. 10*bis*(2) and (3), defining acts of unfair competition.

It should be noted that while the scope of the *Paris Convention* appears quite broad, the language used in fact provides significant flexibility to the member States. In addition, while Art. 28 theoretically provides for recourse to the International Court of Justice, this mechanism was never used. This means that member States cannot legally force other members to implement the Convention.

Three examples taken from the trademark-related provisions of the Convention will suffice to show the relative normative weakness of this instrument:

Article 6*bis*(1) The countries of the Union undertake, [. . .] to refuse or to cancel the registration, and to prohibit the use, of a trademark which constitutes a reproduction, an imitation, or a translation, liable to create confusion, *of a mark considered by the competent authority of the country of registration or use to be well known in that country* as being already the mark of a person entitled to the benefits of this Convention and *used for identical or similar goods.* These provisions shall also apply when the essential part of the mark constitutes a reproduction of any such well-known mark or an imitation liable to create confusion therewith.

Art. 7bis(1) The countries of the Union undertake to accept for filing and to protect *collective marks* belonging to associations the existence of which is not contrary to the law of the country of origin, even if such associations do not possess an industrial or commercial establishment.

(2) *Each country shall be the judge* of the particular conditions under which a collective mark shall be protected and may refuse protection if the mark is contrary to the public interest. [Emphasis added.]

Finally, Art. 9, which seems not to contain any enforceable obligation, provides:

9(1) All goods unlawfully bearing a trademark or trade name shall be *seized* on importation into those countries of the Union where such mark or trade name is entitled to legal protection.

(2) Seizure shall likewise be effected in the country where the unlawful affixation occurred or in the country into which the goods were imported.

[. . .]

(5) If the legislation of a country *does not permit seizure on importation,* seizure shall be replaced by prohibition of importation or by seizure inside the country.

(6) If the legislation of a country permits neither seizure on importation nor prohibition of importation nor seizure inside the country, then, until such time as the legislation is modified accordingly, these measures shall be replaced by the actions and remedies available in such cases to nationals under the law of such country. [Emphasis added.]

In addition, there are significant gaps in the Convention. Among the most notable omissions, one could mention:

- Term of protection;
- The definition of patentability criteria;
- The extent of patent rights;
- Conditions surrounding the issuance of compulsory licenses;
- Rules governing the examination of trade-mark applications;
- Protection of service marks (as marks);
- Very limited rules on ownership and enforcement.

Most of these issues were addressed in the *TRIPS Agreement* (see below). Others, mostly those of an administrative nature or related to the examination and application process, are dealt with in the *PLT* of 2000 (not in force as of April 1, 2005) and the *TLT* of 1994, which entered into force on August 1, 1996. The *TLT* contains provisions regulating the contents and language of an application (exhaustive list); provisions concerning service; filing dates; applications in several classes (division etc.); signatures, recordal of ownership changes; and an initial term of protection of 10 years (renewals are possible). Revisions to the *TLT* under consideration in 2004 would regulate licences and the form of communications (with trade-mark offices), and provide procedures for cases where time limits provided in national laws are not complied with, such as extension, continued processing of applications, and the reinstatement of applications when the failure to comply with a time limit is deemed unintentional.

## 2. The Berne Convention

The Convention signed at Berne, Switzerland in 1886 was the copyright equivalent of the *Paris Convention*. It established the principle of national treatment (see above) in the area of copyright and began a process of harmonization of national copyright laws, which continued at the six revision conferences of that Convention, the last one being the one held in Paris in 1971. Reference is thus made to the "*Paris Act*" of the *Berne Convention* so as not to be confused with the *Paris Convention*. For the reasons explained above with respect to the *Paris Convention*, it is unlikely that a new act or version of the *Berne Convention* will ever be adopted. However, as we will see below, two new conventions were adopted under the aegis of WIPO in December 1996.

Canada became party to the *Berne Convention* for the first time in 1928 and ratified the *Paris Act* of 1971 on June 26, 1998.

Unlike the *Paris Convention*, the *Berne Convention* contains essentially two types of provisions, namely those of a substantive nature, and those concerning the administration of the Berne Union, *i.e.,* the Union composed of all countries party to the Convention. Here is a quick glance at the Convention's content:[14]

First, the Convention contains a number of general provisions:

- Art. 2 defines the expression "literary and artistic works" by providing a list of categories of the types of works that should be protected. It also allows member countries to require fixation; protect translations, adaptations, arrangements and collections (compilations); exclude or limit the copyright protection of official texts (as is the case in the United States), news, and works of applied art.
- Art. 2*bis* allows limitations on the protection of political and "legal" speeches;
- Art. 3 and 4 define the so-called "attachment factors" according to which the protection of foreign works under the Convention is based, such as the nationality of author or the place of publication of work.
- Art. 5 protects national treatment;
- Art. 6 provides that a member may limit the protection of nationals of another member that does not adequately protect its own authors.
- Art. 6*bis* protects the moral rights of integrity and authorship;
- Art. 7 and 7*bis* provide a term of protection which in most cases is of life of the author plus 50 years.

The Convention also contains a number of general provisions, including a provision on ownership of cinematographic (audiovisual) works (art. 14*bis*), the enforcement of copyright (art. 15), including seizure of infringing copies (art. 16); and provisions allowing member States to make bilateral

---

[14] A more complete explanation may be found in M. Ficsor, *Guide to the Copyright and Related Rights Treaties Administered by WIPO and Glossary of Copyright and Related Rights Terms* (Geneva: WIPO, 2004).

other agreements to increase the level of protection guaranteed by the Convention (art. 19 and 20). Finally, the protection of works in existence at the time a country adheres to the Convention is governed by Art. 18.

Then the Convention defines the rights that form part of the Convention's copyright "bundle":

- The right of reproduction (Art. 9);
- The right of translation (Art. 8, 11 and 11*ter*) and the right of adaptation (art. 12 and 14)
- The right of public performance and communication to the public (Art. 11 and 11*bis*)
- The right of "public recitation" and communication to the public of a recitation;
- The *"droit de suite"* or right to obtain a share on the resale of a work of art (art. 14*ter*), if national legislation so provides (which is not the case in Canada).

The Convention also permits certain exceptions:

- quotations and illustrations used for teaching (Art. 10); reproduction by the press, the broadcasting or the communication to the public by wire of articles published in newspapers or periodicals on current economic, political or religious topics, and of broadcast works of the same character (Art. 10*bis*);
- Compulsory licensing for broadcasting and retransmission (Art. 11*bis*(2))
- Compulsory licensing for the reproduction of musical works on sound recordings (Art. 13).

Articles 1 and 22-38 are of an administrative nature and will not be discussed here.[15]

Because the Convention was last revised before the massive use of personal computers, digital carriers for music and images (*e.g.*, CDs and DVDs) and the Internet, a number of countries felt the norms had to be updated. Part of that update was effected by the 1994 *TRIPS Agreement*

---

[15] Article 1 has a dual nature. While mostly administrative in that its purpose is to "establish" the Union, it is also substantive in that it states the purpose of the Union, namely to "protect the rights of authors in their literary and artistic works." Article 37(3) is also relevant: it provides that in case of discrepancy, the French version of the Convention prevails. The Convention also contains an Appendix with special provisions for developing countries. It is seldom used and will not be discussed here.

(see below), while the two WIPO Treaties of 1996 (see below) were adopted to adapt the international copyright framework to the Internet.

### 3. The Rome Convention (1961)

The *Rome Convention*, to which Canada became party on June 4, 1998,[16] protects the rights of music performers, sound recording ("phonogram") producers, and broadcasting organizations. While it is fairly flexible in the way it can be implemented,[17] it essentially provides an obligation on member countries to implement the following rights:

> For music performers, the minimal protection shall include the possibility of preventing the broadcasting and the communication to the public, without their consent, of their performance; the fixation, without their consent, of their unfixed performance; and the reproduction, without their consent, of a fixation of their performance if the original fixation itself was made without their consent or if the reproduction is made for purposes different from those for which the performers gave their consent (Art. 7).
>
> For record producers, member countries must provide the right to authorize or prohibit the direct or indirect reproduction of their phonograms (Art. 10).

Member States must also provide an obligation imposed on broadcasters to pay an equitable remuneration to performers, producers or both for the use of music in broadcasts (Art. 12). This right, implemented by s. 19 of the *Copyright Act,* led to the imposition of a tariff by Canada's Copyright Board.[18]

Finally, the *Rome Convention* provides certain minimum rights for broadcasters: the right to authorize or prohibit the rebroadcasting of their broadcasts; the fixation of their broadcasts; the reproduction of fixations, made without their consent, of their broadcasts; and the communication to the public of their television broadcasts if such communication is made in places accessible to the public against payment of an entrance fee (subject to conditions in national law—see s. 21(1)(d) of the *Act*).

---

[16] 78 countries were party to this Convention as of October 1, 2004, but not the United States. While U.S. law provides full protection for sound recordings under copyright law, it does not protect performances and broadcasts under that law. U.S. protection at a level below that of the Convention is available under different federal and state statutes and doctrines. The U.S. *Copyright Act* also does not provide for equitable remuneration for broadcasts (see below).

[17] See *Guide to the Rome Convention and the Phonograms Convention* (Geneva: WIPO, 1981).

[18] *SOCAN-NRCC Pay Audio Services Tariff (1997-2002)*, Canada Gazette, Part I, March 16, 2002.

## 4. The TRIPS Agreement

### (a) History[19]

The *TRIPS Agreement*, together with the 1968 Stockholm Conference that adopted the revised Berne and Paris Conventions and created the World Intellectual Property Organization (WIPO), was the most significant milestone in the development of intellectual property in the twentieth century. Its scope was much broader than that of any previous international agreement, covering not only all areas already (sometimes only partly) protected under previous agreements, but also giving new life to treaties that failed and protecting for the first time rights that did not benefit from any multilateral protection. In addition, and some would say perhaps more importantly than its broad coverage, the *TRIPS Agreement* enshrined detailed rules on one of the most difficult and, for rights holders, painful aspects of intellectual property rights: enforcement.

In 1986, members of the *General Agreement on Tariffs and Trade*, the predecessor organization of the WTO, launched the "Uruguay Round of Multilateral Trade Negotiations" at Punta del Este (Uruguay).[20] The Declaration that launched the Round, which ended at a meeting in Marrakech in April 1994, after a number of near failures, contained the following negotiating mandate in respect of intellectual property:

> In order to reduce the distortions and impediments to international trade, and taking into account the need to promote effective and adequate protection of intellectual property rights, and to ensure that measures and procedures to enforce intellectual property rights do not themselves become barriers to legitimate trade, the negotiations shall aim to clarify GATT provisions and elaborate as appropriate new rules and disciplines.
>
> Negotiations shall aim to develop a multilateral framework of principles, rules and disciplines dealing with international trade in counterfeit goods, taking into account work already undertaken in GATT.
>
> These negotiations shall be without prejudice to other complementary initiatives that may be taken in the World Intellectual Property Organization and elsewhere to deal with these matters.[21]

---

[19] For a complete historical analysis, see Daniel Gervais, *The TRIPS Agreement: Drafting History and Analysis,* 2nd ed. (London: Sweet & Maxwell, 2003).

[20] *General Agreement on Tariffs and Trade*, 30 October 1947, 58 U.N.T.S. 187, Can. T.S. 1947 No. 27, (entered into force 1 January 1948), online: WTO <http://www.wto.org/english/docs_e/legal_e/gatt47_01_e.htm> [*GATT 1947*].

[21] Document MIN.DEC of September 20, 1986, pp. 7-8.

In comparing this text with the *TRIPS Agreement*, the work accomplished between Punta del Este and Marrakech becomes readily apparent: the broadest and most extensive multilateral agreement in the field of intellectual property, covering basically the entire area and adding enforcement, acquisition and most-favoured nation obligations to new and existing rules and incorporating those rules in what could be considered the only truly effective and binding dispute settlement mechanism between States, was negotiated on the basis of a limited initial mandate.

The negotiation was difficult for many reasons, including the fact that the GATT Secretariat and many, if not most, of the negotiators, in particular those from developing countries, had little if any expertise in intellectual property.

The playing field was clearly delineated. Industrialized countries had their vision of the basic parameters and scope of a future *TRIPS Agreement*. A number of key issues divided their proposals, however, and later entered the list of "North-North" issues to be resolved. Other proposals targeted mostly developing countries and their reaction made it abundantly clear that the negotiations would not be easy.

Most of the initial North-North issues remained unsettled in the final agreement.[22] But the developing countries' proposal was all but forgotten, except for two Articles which were supposed to reflect their concerns, namely Articles 7 and 8. Developing countries were also given more time to implement *TRIPS*.

The *TRIPS Agreement* was formally adopted as Annex 1C of the *Final Act Embodying the Results of the Uruguay Round of Multilateral Trade Negotiations*, at Marrakech (Morocco) on April 15, 1994. It entered into force on January 1, 1995. Article 64 of the Agreement provided for a general transition period of one year. The Agreement entered into force with respect to the more industrialized WTO Members on January 1, 1996. The Agreement entered into force with respect to the developing countries as of January 1, 2000, although these Members could delay the protection by patents of product inventions in "areas of technology not so protectable (i.e. by patent) in its territory" (such as pharmaceuticals) until January 1, 2005, subject to the other provisions of *TRIPS* (e.g. on national treatment, most-favoured nation, enforcement and acquisition of rights) and to the "mailbox" protection provisions of Article 70(8) and the obligation to provide "exclusive marketing rights" contained in Article 70(9). Least-developed WTO Members benefit from a transitional period until January 1, 2006 to apply the Agreement (except for a few provisions, especially national treat-

---

[22] This included at the time issues such as the level of protection of biotechnological inventions, the protection of geographical indications for wines and spirits and national treatment provisions on private copying levies.

ment), with possible extensions by the TRIPS Council. Such an extension (until 2016) on the introduction of patent protection for pharmaceutical products was granted to least-developed WTO members at the Doha (Qatar) Ministerial Conference in November 2001.

At that Conference, which followed a very public failure of the Conference held in Seattle, Washington, the year before, a new Round was launched. The *Ministerial Declaration* contains very few provisions dealing with intellectual property. It calls on members to complete negotiations on the Uruguay Round's unfinished business (many of the North-North issues, including the protection of geographical indications). Otherwise, however, the language of the *Doha Declaration* is a measure of the sea change since 1994.[23] In the three paragraphs concerning the *TRIPS Agreement*, there are scant opportunities for demands of increased intellectual property protection. Paragraph 17 states that TRIPS should be implemented "in a manner supportive of public health, by promoting both access to existing medicines and research and development into new medicines and, in this connection, are adopting a separate declaration." In the following paragraph, the *Doha Declaration* addresses a mostly North-North issue, the completion of the negotiations on geographical indications on wines & spirits. Paragraph 19, which is perhaps the most famous of the Declaration, instructs the TRIPS Council to:

> [E]xamine, *inter alia*, the relationship between the TRIPS Agreement and the Convention on Biological Diversity, the protection of traditional knowledge and folklore, and other relevant new developments raised by members pursuant to Article 71.1. In undertaking this work, the TRIPS Council shall be guided by the objectives and principles set out in Articles 7 and 8 of the TRIPS Agreement and shall take fully into account the development dimension.

In other words, apart from the possible increase in protection of names of wines & spirits as a result of negotiations on a multilateral register foreseen in the second paragraph, the *Doha Declaration* essentially reflects the concerns of developing countries. The first paragraph insists on the balance between the need for access to intellectual property and its protection. It may serve as a philosophical underpinning for ongoing discussions.

The third paragraph is, however, the most significant for at least two main reasons. First, together with the separate declaration on the *TRIPS Agreement* and Public Health also adopted at Doha, it led to the adoption of a Decision of the WTO General Council on August 30, 2003 on Imple-

---

[23] WTO, *Ministerial Declaration*, 14 November 2001, online: WTO <http://www.wto.org/english/thewto_e/minist_e/min01_e/mindecl_e.htm>    [*Doha Declaration*].

mentation of paragraph 6 of the *Doha Declaration* on the *TRIPS Agreement* and public health. This Decision will allow, under certain conditions, WTO members to export generic versions of drugs used to treat diseases such as HIV to countries that can neither afford nor manufacture these pharmaceuticals.[24]

The third paragraph is also important because of its mention of the *Convention on Biological Diversity*.[25] The *CBD*, signed by 168 countries as of October 1, 2004, is important not because of its normative content, which is rather weak in the areas that overlap with the *TRIPS Agreement*, but rather because it opened the door to the inclusion of *TRIPS* in a broader normative framework. The most often mentioned provision of the *CBD* in its relations with *TRIPS* is Article 8(j) concerning in situ conservation. This Article reads as follows:

> Each Contracting Party shall, <u>as far as possible</u> and <u>as appropriate</u>:
>
> (j)   <u>Subject to its national legislation</u>, respect, preserve and maintain knowledge, innovations and practices of indigenous and local communities embodying traditional lifestyles relevant for the conservation and sustainable use of biological diversity and promote their wider application with the approval and involvement of the holders of such knowledge, innovations and practices and encourage the equitable sharing of the benefits arising from the utilization of such knowledge, innovations and practices. [Emphasis added.]

In spite of the numerous "outs", the *CBD* may be important in the Doha context in its insistence on the need to bring holders of traditional knowledge (TK) into the picture of international intellectual property.[26] This is reinforced by the specific mention of traditional knowledge and folklore in the *Doha Declaration*.

The changing face of international intellectual property is also evidenced by the reference in the *Doha Declaration* to Arts. 7 and 8 of the *TRIPS Agreement, i.e.*, the two provisions inserted originally to reflect the concerns of developing countries. Though they have been given little regard

---

[24] Canada was the first country to take advantage of this Declaration by the adoption of the *Act to amend the Patent Act and the Food and Drugs Act (the Jean Chrétien Pledge to Africa)*, S.C. 2004, c. 23, which received Royal Assent on May 14, 2004, but has yet to enter into force.

[25] *The Rio de Janeiro Convention on Biological Diversity*, 14 June 1992, 31 I.L.M. 818, (entered in force 29 December 1993), online: Secretariat of the Convention on Biological Diveristy <http://www.biodiv.org/convention/articles.asp> [*CBD*].

[26] See the chapter on traditional knowledge in the Advanced Materials.

up to now in dispute-settlement proceedings in the WTO (see below the "dispute-settlement" section), these two provisions could be given a somewhat higher normative profile in future disputes because of what is a possible "special status" in the Doha text. Article 7 is cut from the same tree as paragraph 17 of the *Doha Declaration* (*i.e.*, the first of the three dealing with TRIPS). It reads as follows:

> The protection and enforcement of intellectual property rights should contribute to the promotion of technological innovation and to the transfer and dissemination of technology, to the mutual advantage of producers and users of technological knowledge and in a manner conducive to social and economic welfare, and to a balance of rights and obligations.

A similar concern is voiced of course by many people in industrialized countries as well as developing ones. Many argue that it is wrong to think that, in all cases, more intellectual property protection is necessarily better. There is an increasing recognition that, while intellectual property is necessary at least in certain areas to justify enormous research and development expenditure (pharmaceutical patents are a good example), the optimal configuration of intellectual property norms cannot be ascertained on the basis of available empirical data. The pre-TRIPS historical development of norms was a haphazard process and does not offer sufficient economic, social or philosophical justifications for continuing along the same path without further analysis. In parallel, many countries argue that major industrialized countries only adopted high protection norms *after* they had developed economically.[27] They also argue that many "free*r* trade" measures demanded by industrialized countries relate to goods with a high ideational or informational content, areas in which it is often harder for smaller or developing economies to compete. At the same time, trade barriers are maintained on goods on which they could compete, such as agricultural products and textile products.

All this is now reinforced by views emerging within industrialized countries not only about the possible negative impact of imposing too-high protection norms on developing countries but also on the development of a vibrant technological and creative culture. One can point to movements such as open source software and to creative commons in the field of

---

[27] This is, roughly, the debate between the Development theorists (according to whom development will follow the putting in place of a normative framework as well as a judicial and administrative infrastructure that mirror those of industrialised nations) and the Dependency theorists, who argue that adopting those high-protection standards in developing countries will lead to increased economic dependency of those countries.

copyright, and to analyses of the sometimes poor social value of letting only the market dictate the path of innovation. Indeed, leaving it entirely to the market by giving monopolies to market-driven innovation may mean more money to fight baldness or erectile difficulties than tropical or orphan diseases. Companies decide, unsurprisingly given legal and economic structures, based on how they can maximize profit, not on the societal value of their investments. This also means that countries may be tempted to "socially engineer" their intellectual property regime.

## (b) The Logic of the *TRIPS Agreement*

The TRIPS negotiators had a choice. They could have tried to reinvent the intellectual property wheel and in some cases tried to do so. For example, detailed provisions on the protection of layout-designs of integrated circuits were tabled in 1990. Certain scholars proposed replacing existing forms of protection with more economically efficient ones. This would have had advantages, of course, at least from a theoretical point of view: redesigning the protection from scratch, unencumbered by previous rules and practices. But the disadvantages far outweighed any possible gains. Some of the world's largest industries (pharmaceutical, agri-food, computer software, entertainment, luxury goods) depend on effective protection of their intellectual property rights to survive. Moreover, each and every legitimate business relies in part on intellectual property to flourish, if only because its name or trade mark is protected. A complete change of the intellectual property framework could have wreaked havoc in forcing each company to adapt. The transition cost would have been enormous. Industries, inventors, creators, policy makers, courts, administrative and enforcement authorities would probably have had to make unreasonable efforts to understand and apply the new forms of protection. TRIPS negotiators were thus wise to opt for an updating of existing rules. Looking at the *Paris Convention*, the *Berne Convention*, the *Rome Convention* and the *Treaty on Intellectual Property in Respect of Integrated Circuits* (which never entered into force), they came to the following conclusions:

- Few rights had to be created anew, as those conventions offered a very good basis and in most cases relied on decades of recognised practices; however, in respect of many existing rights, binding clarifications were required. In addition, some new rights were necessary (e.g. a rental right and right in respect of geographical indications);
- Some of the exceptions and limitations contained in those conventions were no longer necessary or justified;

- Provisions on enforcement had to be added to address one of the main lacunae of existing conventions;
- There was a need for a binding dispute settlement mechanism in the field of intellectual property;
- Some additional specific rules would be useful, such as the application of the most-favoured nation principle, rules facilitating acquisition procedures, and transparency requirements with regard to laws, rules and other practices.

Based on these perceptions, negotiators used existing conventions as a logical point of departure. As a first step, they looked at each one and decided which provisions should be incorporated into the future *TRIPS Agreement*. All of the substantive provisions of the Paris and Berne Conventions (with the exception of Article 6*bis* of the latter) and the *Washington Treaty* (with the exception of a provision on compulsory licenses) were thus incorporated by reference. The second step was to add the necessary new rights, seen in the addition of provisions on rental rights, geographical indications, trade-marks and service marks, and on the protection of confidential information, although this latter issue is presented as a simple extension of existing obligations in respect of unfair competition. However all the above provisions cover a fairly small part of the *TRIPS Agreement* as such. In fact, most of the provisions in Parts I and II either clarify existing obligations (sometimes increasing the level of protection) or restrict the possibility of using limitations or exceptions.

Once this had been achieved, the standards were in place. Negotiators, continuing along the same logical line, then added an entirely new set of rules on enforcement. There was no precedent for this in the field of intellectual property at the multilateral level. Provisions were thus drafted on the basis of concerns expressed by industry experts and other interested parties.

The final pieces of the puzzle could then be added, including more precise rules on acquisition and, more importantly, provisions bringing *TRIPS* under the general WTO dispute settlement umbrella, known as the integrated dispute settlement system. All that was missing were usual provisions on entry into force, including protection of existing subject matter, and transitional periods on institutional arrangements. *TRIPS* was complete.

### (c) *TRIPS* Dispute-Settlement

Contrary to treaties administered by WIPO, such as the Paris, Berne and Rome Conventions,[28] the *TRIPS Agreement* is part of the WTO framework. As such, when countries disagree about the implementation or application of the Agreement, they can have recourse to the WTO binding dispute-settlement mechanism. Under this mechanism, when WTO members disagree, a panel composed of trade experts is appointed. The panel's decision may be appealed to a standing Appellate Body. The final decision (of the panel or Appellate Body, as the case may be), enters into force once adopted by the assembly of WTO members, but adoption is automatic unless members agree not to adopt the decision. If a member is found not to be in compliance, it is usually given a certain delay to implement changes to its national legislation. If it fails to do so, the other party may impose trade sanctions, including in an unrelated area of trade.

As a result of complaints filed by the European Union and the United States,[29] Canada was forced to amend its *Patent Act*. It had to reconsider the term of protection of patents[30] and remove an exception that allowed generic drug manufacturers to start manufacturing a patented product up to six months prior to the expiry of the patent, thus allowing them to start marketing immediately after the expiry date of the patent (the so-called "stockpiling exception").[31] An exception contained in s. 55.2(1) allowing use of a patent to submit information required under law (*e.g.,* to obtain marketing approval for a generic) was maintained.

### (d) The Substantive Content of *TRIPS*

The *TRIPS Agreement* covers all areas already protected under the Paris, Berne and Washington agreements and extends protection to rights that had not previously been protected under multilateral agreements. Further, *TRIPS* details enforcement rules. The *acquis* of the Berne and Paris Conventions constituted the basis on which the *TRIPS* negotiations proceeded. The perceived shortcomings of existing instruments became the agenda for the negotiations.

---

[28] The Rome Convention is jointly administered by WIPO, UNESCO and the International Labour Office (ILO).

[29] *Canada – Patent Protection of Pharmaceutical Products*, Report of the Panel, WTO document WT/DS114/R of March 17, 2000; and *Canada – Term of Patent Protection*, Report of the Appellate Body, WTO document WT/DS170/AB/R of Sept. 18, 2000.

[30] See 2001, c. 10, s. 1.

[31] See 2001, c. 10, s. 2.

### (e) General Provisions

Articles 2 (1) and 9 (1) of *TRIPS* require that members comply with the substantive provisions of the Paris and Berne Conventions. These two Articles have the effect of imposing the obligations contained in those provisions to countries not party to the Conventions, while integrating all WTO Members in the *TRIPS* framework, notably as regards dispute settlement. These provisions were drafted so as to create a positive obligation to comply, that is, to take the necessary steps to bring national legislation in line with the relevant provisions of the *Paris Convention*. As regards the *Berne Convention*, the Agreement adds that states shall not have rights or obligations under *TRIPS* "in respect of the rights conferred under Art. 6*bis* of that Convention or of the rights derived therefrom", *i.e.,* the moral right. Added to the obligation to comply with the Paris and Berne Conventions is a provision indicating that the contents of Part II (sector-specific norms) of the *TRIPS Agreement* do not derogate from existing obligations.

Articles 3 and 4 guarantee national treatment and, for the first time in a multilateral intellectual property treaty, most-favoured-nation treatment (where benefits accorded nationals of a specific foreign country must be extended to nationals of other Contracting States). As regards national treatment, the main difference between the *TRIPS Agreement* and earlier WIPO-administered agreements is that the actual practice of states can now be tested before a WTO dispute-settlement panel. This may apply, for example, in the copyright field to levies paid only to national rightsholders, a difficult issue which surfaced at the end of the Uruguay Round.

Article 6 excludes from dispute settlement the question of "exhaustion of rights," otherwise known as "parallel importation," i.e. the importation of goods lawfully manufactured in another country and generally intended for distribution in that other country.

### (f) Copyright

Article 10 of the *TRIPS Agreement* is the first provision in any multilateral instrument to confirm the protection of computer programs by copyright. Although laws in many countries had been amended as early as 1990 to include computer programs in the list of protected works, the extent of the protection was still unclear. As regards databases and other "compilations," Art. 10 (2) confirms the application of copyright law to databases. Given the EU move towards *sui generis* protection, however, it is likely that the scope of copyright protection in databases will tend to shrink, at least in territories where *sui generis* protection exists.[32]

---

[32] EC, *Council Directive 96/9/EC of the European Parliament and of the Council*

Article 11 establishes a rental right on computer programs and films. A similar right in respect of sound recordings is provided in Art. 14 (4).

## (g) Trade-Marks

Article 15 (1) is another important first at the multilateral level as it defines the expression "trade mark." The definition is very broad and does not limit the types of signs that may be considered a trade-mark. Instead the focus is on distinctiveness, which one could fairly call a universal criterion, although its application differs from one system to another. Where the signs are not inherently capable of distinguishing the relevant goods or services (e.g. the shape or packaging of certain products), registrability is required but may be made dependent on distinctiveness acquired through use. In addition, registrability may be limited to visually perceptible marks, thus probably excluding from mandatory registration olfactory and sound marks. In comparing this provision with Article 6*quinquies*B, and recognizing the principle that a mark duly registered in its country of origin should be registered, a mark should thus be examined on its individual merits and proper instructions given accordingly to examiners (particularly as regards to countries not party to the *Paris Convention* that are or will become WTO Members).

Another key element of the definition is that it includes service marks. This is a major improvement on Article 6*sexies* of the *Paris Convention*, which only contained what is often considered a mere "wish" to that effect.

Article 16 (1) requires WTO members to grant the owner of a registered mark the exclusive right to prevent third parties from using the mark in the course of trade for goods or services that are identical or similar to those in respect of which the mark is registered, where such use would result in a likelihood of confusion. The provision adds a presumption of likelihood of confusion when an identical sign is used for identical goods or services.

Article 18 establishes a minimum seven years term for the validity of the initial registration of a mark and renewals thereof. *TRIPS*, in keeping

---

*of 11 March 1996 on the Legal Protection of Databases*, [1996] O.J. L. 077/20, online: EUROPA <http://europa.eu.int/smartapi/cgi/sga_doc?smartapi!celexplus!prod!DocNumber&lg=en&type_doc=Directive&an_doc=1996&nu_doc=9> which provides for a "a right for the maker of a database which shows that there has been qualitatively and/or quantitatively a substantial investment in either the obtaining, verification or presentation of the contents to prevent extraction and/or re-utilisation of the whole or of a substantial part evaluated qualitatively and/or quantitatively, of the contents of that database".

with principles established in other agreements in this field, provides for indefinite renewals, as long as conditions for renewal are met.

### (h) Geographical Indications

The *TRIPS Agreement* is the first multilateral text dealing with geographical indications as such, and may be rightly considered an important first step in this difficult field. Given its groundbreaking nature, this section of the Agreement begins with a definition of what constitutes a geographical indication. This should be welcomed because definitions are crucial to distinguish geographical indications from the notion of "indication of source" and that of "appellation of origin."[33] At first glance Art. 22 (1) resembles Art. 2 of the Lisbon Agreement, yet it differs from Lisbon on a number of points: (1) appellations of origin under the Lisbon Agreement are necessarily geographical names of a country, region, or locality, while geographical indications under TRIPS are any indication pointing to a given country, region or locality; (2) appellations of origin under Lisbon designate a product, while a geographical indication under TRIPS identifies a good; (3) Lisbon limits appellations to the quality and characteristics of a product, while TRIPS also mentions its reputation; (4) finally, appellations of origin refer to a geographical environment, including natural and human factors, while TRIPS uses a more general concept of "geographical origin."

Under Art. 23 (1), using a geographical indication identifying wines or spirits for wines and spirits not originating in the place indicated by the indication is prohibited. There is no need here to show that the public might be misled or that the use constitutes an act of unfair competition. Art. 23 (4) requires that negotiations be undertaken in the TRIPS Council to establish an international notification and registration system for geographical indications for wines.

---

[33] *Madrid Agreement for the Repression of False or Deceptive Indications of Source on Goods*, 14 April 1891, 828 U.N.T.S. 389, as amended July 14, 1967, art. 1(1), online: WIPO <http://www.wipo.int/treaties/en/ip/madrid/trtdocs_wo032.html> [*Madrid Agreement*], which deals with indications of source and provides for seizure on importation. *The Lisbon Agreement for the Protection of Appellations of Origin and their International Registration*, 31 October 1958, 923 U.N.T.S. 205, as revised at Stockholm on July 14, 1967, and as amended on September 28, 1979, online: WIPO <http://www.wipo.int/lisbon/en/legal_texts/lisbon_agreement.htm> [*Lisbon* Agreement], which deals solely with appellations of origin. In the same vein, one should mention also the *Convention on the Use of Appellations of Origin and Denominations of Cheeses*, signed at Stresa, Italy, on June 1, 1951.

### (i) Industrial Designs

There are only two provisions of the TRIPS Agreement dealing with industrial designs, but their impact on the protection of industrial designs could be significant. Article 25 (1) creates an obligation on WTO Members to protect all designs that are "new or original." The two criteria are not cumulative. The second sentence allows WTO members to apply an "objective" criterion of novelty as opposed to a subjective one. The expression "independently created" in the first sentence of the Article is directed to what one could call "subjective novelty," in the sense that the design must not have been copied from or imitate an existing design; the possible exclusion of "known designs or combinations of known designs features" is clearly an objective criterion. In other words, the former is closer to copyright-type tests, while the latter resembles the "prior art novelty" of patents. Again, the need to reflect various conceptions of the protection of industrial designs had to be taken into consideration. Negotiators sought to achieve the overarching objective: to ensure an adequate level of protection of industrial designs. Finally, the last sentence of this Article does allow WTO Members to exclude design dictated essentially by technical or functional considerations. This may apply to the definition of "originality" in this context, which seems to refer to choices made by the designer other than those dictated by such considerations. Since the exclusion is optional, so-called "utility design" protection remains possible, an issue of considerable importance to the car-part industry.

### (j) Patents

The patent section of the *TRIPS Agreement* was one of the most difficult to negotiate. It involved a number of key North-North as well as North-South issues. The result is impressive, in that the scope and coverage of the section are comprehensive, and makes TRIPS the most important multilateral instrument in this field.

Article 27 (1) requires that patents be available in all fields of technology, based on the three usual criteria, i.e. novelty, industrial applicability and involving an inventive step. Combined with the explicit inclusion of both product and process inventions and the part of the last sentence which prohibits any distinction concerning the field of technology, one might say that a general principle of eligibility to be patented is established.

Another important element is the elimination of discrimination "as to the place of invention." This may concern more directly the United States,[34]

---

[34] Traditionally, the first-to-invent system has been presented as being fair because

which insisted on maintaining its so-called "first-to-invent" system, as opposed to the "first-to-file" system.

Article 27(2) contains a serious restriction to the general principle of eligibility to be patented: a WTO member may exclude inventions from patentability based on a risk that their commercial exploitation within its territory could endanger the *ordre public* or morality within the territory of the WTO member concerned. Examples given are the protection of human, animal or plant life or health. Avoiding serious prejudice to the environment is also a ground for exclusion from patentability. It is difficult to predict how broadly those exceptions will be interpreted. Concepts of "serious prejudice" and *ordre public* are not very precise. That said, *ordre public* is well known in civil law systems and refers to the fundamentals from which one cannot derogate without endangering the institutions of a given society. An objective justification must exist. It is also worth noting that Art. 27 (2) seems to require exclusions of specific inventions rather than entire categories of inventions.

Article 31 deals with what are traditionally referred to as compulsory licences. It sets specific conditions for the grant, but does not list or define the cases where a licence may be granted, except for semiconductor technology. Negotiators weighed both options and preferred to leave open the cases where compulsory licensing (defined here as use by governments or by third parties authorised by governments) may be allowed. Instead, they established strict safeguards. The first such principle is that licences must be granted only on a case-by-case basis. Compulsory licences under which certain categories of inventions automatically become eligible for a licence would seem to violate this provision. Article 31 constitutes a detailed checklist for WTO members. The compulsory licence may be granted provided that the following conditions are met, subject to a few exceptions: (1) the need for prior negotiation with the rightholder; (2) the duration of the compulsory licence is limited; (3) the scope is similarly limited; (4) as regards semi-conductor technology, compulsory licences may be granted only for public non-commercial use or to remedy an anti-competitive practice; (5) with respect to general licensing terms, compulsory licences must be non-exclusive and non-assignable; (6) compulsory licences must be limited to supply of the domestic; (7) adequate remuneration of the right-

---

a patent is granted (assuming the conditions are met) to the person who actually invented it first. Contrary to first-to-file, however, this may involve long and costly debates in the case of conflicting applications. This is why advocates of first-to-file insist on the efficiency of the system. In addition, under s. 104 of the U.S. patent law, evidence of inventive acts was restricted to the territory of the United States and foreign applicants were "not permitted to prove a date of invention which antedates their foreign filing date."

holder is required; and (8) judicial or similar review must be available. There are special rules concerning dependent patents (*i.e.* where use of a patent requires the authorisation to use a prior patent).

Article 33 establishes a minimum term of protection that cannot end less than 20 years calculated from the filing date.

### (k)  Integrated Circuits

The main issue was to internationalize the *sui generis* protection of masks or layout-designs of semi-conductor chips already found in a number of national laws. Such a scheme had been established in the Washington Treaty, but that Treaty never entered into force, owing mainly to a provision on compulsory licensing which a number of industrialized countries considered unacceptable. There were basically four specific points on which amendments to the Washington Treaty were proposed: scope of the rights, innocent infringement, compulsory licensing and term of protection. The reference to the relevant Articles of the Treaty explicitly excludes the provision dealing with compulsory licensing.

### (l)  Undisclosed Information

The protection of confidential information in the *TRIPS Agreement* will no doubt be useful for industries that must obtain regulatory marketing approval and must submit confidential data to governmental authorities in order to obtain such approval. It is also the first multilateral instrument dealing in any detail with the protection of what in various national laws might be called "trade secrets," "confidential information" or the like, and is often protected not by specific intellectual property legislation but by general civil law standards. This field is not regulated in multilateral conventions, apart from the general obligations in respect of unfair competition found in Article 10*bis* of the *Paris Convention*. The expression used in the Agreement, that is, "undisclosed information", was chosen to avoid referring to a expression linked to a given legal system.

Article 39(2) defines the actual scope of the obligation, by specifying the conditions governing any disclosure of the information concerned, namely: (1) the information is secret in the sense that it is not, as a body or in the precise configuration and assembly of its components, generally known among or readily accessible to persons within the circles that normally deal with the kind of information in question; (2) the information has commercial value because it is secret; (3) the information must have been subject to reasonable steps, under the circumstances, by the person lawfully in control of the information, to keep it secret.

## (m) Enforcement

The enforcement of rights in this context refers to their application before administrative and judicial authorities. This section of the *TRIPS Agreement* is clearly one of the major achievements of the negotiation. Before *TRIPS*, provisions dealing with enforcement of rights were basically general obligations to provide for legal remedies and, in certain cases, seizure of infringing goods.[35] Otherwise, the question was left entirely up to national legislation.

The enforcement section starts with general principles applicable to all enforcement actions. Those principles should help in ensuring fair and transparent procedures. In most cases it guarantees a right of judicial review. Article 42 is quite important. It provides for the existence of civil judicial proceedings covering all the rights protected under the *TRIPS Agreement*. It also includes a prohibition of overly burdensome requirements concerning mandatory personal appearances. In certain jurisdictions, only the chief executive may represent a legal person. This is unreasonable for routine judicial proceedings. The Article also guarantees the right to present all relevant evidence to substantiate one's claims.

According to Art. 44, injunctions must be available. They are defined as "an order to desist from an infringement, *inter alia*, to prevent the entry into the channels of commerce in their jurisdiction of imported goods that involve the infringement of an "intellectual property right." The measure must be available "immediately after customs clearance" of the goods. While this Article applies to infringements that have started, urgent (provisional) orders are also provided for under Art. 50 (1)—see below.

Article 46 provides that judicial authorities must have the authority to order that seized goods be disposed of outside the channels of commerce (e.g. given to the rightholder or to a charitable organization). Destruction must also be possible unless "contrary to existing constitutional requirements." The same principle applies to materials and implements, subject to the rule of proportionality. It would seem that in case of professional infringement industries, at least the seizure and removal of materials and implements should be ordered. Article 46 also addresses specifically the question of certain counterfeit goods to which an infringing mark is affixed, e.g. garments and travel accessories, sometimes in a country different from that of manufacture of the goods. If simple removal of the mark is allowed, the (professional) infringer takes very little chance: he just waits for the

---

[35] See Arts. 9, 10, 10*bis* and 10*ter* (1) of the *Paris Convention, supra,* note 2, Art. 16 of the *Berne Convention, supra,* note 3 and Art. 8 of the *Lisbon Agreement, supra,* note 33.

next shipment of infringing logos, etc., and starts again. The general rule is clearly established: this is not permitted.[36]

Article 50 is one of the most important of the enforcement Part. It provides for *inaudita altera parte* (also known as "ex parte") action, which is often the only effective means of combating piracy and counterfeiting. Professional infringers seldom remain available to pay damages and costs awarded on the merits of a case. Measures mentioned here must be available quickly and be effective. Any time delays or other conditions contained in national law that diminish the effectiveness of provisional measures could come under WTO scrutiny. Preventive injunctions must be available in respect of "qualified acts," i.e. acts that require the authorization of the rightsholder or other clearance. The wording used here focuses on the effect of the measure, rather than the time-frame. While it does not expressly mandate the availability of injunctions before any infringement has taken place (but only to stop new or further infringement from occurring), it would seem that injunctions should in principle be available even where an infringement has not yet started. Similar measures must be available to preserve evidence "in regard to" the alleged infringement.

To the arsenal of civil and provisional measures contained in previous Articles, Art. 51 and following add border measures. At least in respect of pirated copyright and counterfeit trade-marked goods, a procedure must be made available before a "competent" authority to a rightsholder to lodge an application for suspension of the release of goods. Since no such procedure existed in many WTO member countries before the entry into force of the *TRIPS Agreement*, negotiators included detailed provisions on the procedure and the way in which a suspension should be carried out. A detailed procedural framework is provided.

Finally, Art. 61 provides for criminal measures, which are often considered as an essential ingredient of the fight against organized infringement. The obligation here is to apply criminal measures in cases of wilful trade mark counterfeiting and copyright piracy on a commercial scale. The criminal remedies must include fines and/or imprisonment at a level sufficient to deter the accused and other professional infringers (see also under Art. 41).

### (n) Protection of Existing Subject-Matter

The *TRIPS Agreement* contains two main rules concerning the protection of existing subject-matter. The first rule is simple: acts that took place before the date of application of the Agreement do not give rise to obliga-

---

[36] Unless justified under Art. 41 (5).

tions for the member on the territory of which those acts occurred. This is non-retroactivity.

The second set of rules is more complex. The principle is that the *TRIPS Agreement* applies to all subject-matter existing on the "date of application" of the Agreement, provided such subject-matter meets or comes to meet the criteria for protection under *TRIPS*. There are a number of specific exceptions, however. To name just a few important ones: as regards copyright, Art. 18 of the *Berne Convention* (which may be called a "relative retroactivity provision") applies. Article 18 also applies mutatis mutandis to related rights. A number of special rules apply to patents, including an obligation for WTO Members that did not, as of January 1, 1995, make available patent protection for pharmaceutical and agricultural chemical products to (1) provide for the filing of applications for patents for such inventions (the so-called "mail-box" applications); (2) apply to these applications the criteria for patentability laid down in the Agreement as if they had applied at the date of filing (or any applicable priority date); and (3) provide patent protection in accordance with *TRIPS* as from the date of grant and for the remainder of the patent term for those applications that meet the criteria for patentability. In addition, where a pharmaceutical or agricultural chemical product is the subject of such a black-box application, exclusive marketing rights shall be granted for the shortest of (1) a period of five years after marketing approval is granted or (2) the period until the grant or rejection of the patent and provided certain conditions are met.

## 5. *NAFTA*

Chapter 17 of the *North American Free Trade Agreement* deals with intellectual property. Its main structure was taken from *TRIPS*, although a number of specific differences were introduced, many of which affected Canadian legislation. For example, *NAFTA* does not contain the "public interest" statement of objectives and principles;[37] it modifies the conditions

---

[37] Articles 7 and 8 of *TRIPS* were inserted to allay the concerns of developing nations. They are as follows:

*Article 7 (Objectives)*

The protection and enforcement of intellectual property rights should contribute to the promotion of technological innovation and to the transfer and dissemination of technology, to the mutual advantage of producers and users of technological knowledge and in a manner conducive to social and economic welfare, and to a balance of rights and obligations.

*Article 8 (Principles)*

1. Members may, in formulating or amending their laws and regulations, adopt measures necessary to protect public health and nutrition, and to

of grant of patent compulsory licenses,[38] restricts other exceptions to patent rights, provides for the protection of pharmaceutical test data[39] and provides for a possible extension of the patent term to compensate for regulatory approval processes.[40] Annex 313 of *NAFTA* also contains a list of protected geographical indications (such as Tequila and Mescal, Tennessee and Kentucky Bourbon and Canadian Whiskey).[41]

## 6. The *WIPO* Treaties

On December 20, 1996, two treaties were signed under the aegis of WIPO, namely the *WIPO Copyright Treaty* and the *WIPO Performances and Phonograms Treaty*. As of January 1, 2005, Canada had not ratified the treaties but had announced its intention of doing so in the near future. The *WCT* entered into force on March 6, 2002, after the deposit by thirty States of their instruments of accession or ratification. The *WPPT* entered into force under similar conditions on May 20th of the same year.

The treaties were dubbed the "Internet treaties" because they created a right[42] to make protected material[43] available to the public "by wire or

---

promote the public interest in sectors of vital importance to their socio-economic and technological development, provided that such measures are consistent with the provisions of this Agreement.

2. Appropriate measures, provided that they are consistent with the provisions of this Agreement, may be needed to prevent the abuse of intellectual property rights by right holders or the resort to practices which unreasonably restrain trade or adversely affect the international transfer of technology."Art. 1704 of *NAFTA* is a rough equivalent of the second paragraph of Art. 8. There are no equivalents of Article 7 or 8(1) of *TRIPS* in *NAFTA*.

[38] *Supra*, note 7, Art. 1709 (10).

[39] *Ibid.*,Art. 1711(6).

[40] *Ibid.*, Art. 1709 (12).

[41] A more complete overview of the differences between *TRIPS* and *NAFTA*, and a discussion of Canada's implementation of the latter agreement can be found in Ron J. Corbett. "Impact of NAFTA and TRIPS on Intellectual Property Rights Protections in Canada and the United States" (2000), 6 *NAFTA: L. & Bus. Rev. Am.* 591.

[42] Arguably, the right of making available is only one form of the right of communication to the public.

[43] That is, works protected by copyright, performances fixed on phonograms and the phonograms (sound recordings) themselves. The rights are granted to authors, performers and producers (makers), respectively.

wireless means, in such a way that members of the public may access them from a place and at a time individually chosen by them".[44]

The treaties also create obligations to protect "rights management information," defined as "information which identifies the work, the author of the work, the owner of any right in the work, or information about the terms and conditions of use of the work, and any numbers or codes that represent such information, when any of these items of information is attached to a copy of a work or appears in connection with the communication of a work to the public."[45] More controversial, the treaties also obligate states to "provide adequate legal protection and effective legal remedies against the circumvention of effective technological measures that are used by authors in connection with the exercise of their rights under this Treaty or the Berne Convention and that restrict acts, in respect of their works, which are not authorized by the authors concerned or permitted by law."[46]

The provision is controversial first because of its language. The exact meaning of what constitutes adequate protection and an effective remedy is unclear. Additionally, it seems strange at first glance to mandate the protection of only "effective technological measures," because presumably, if such measures are effective, they will not require protection. A largely accepted interpretation is that the measures must be reasonably effective.[47] The type of technologies targeted by this provision are sometimes referred to as Rights Management Systems, or Digital Rights Management (DRM),[48] and include simple measures such as password-protected access to technological locks that prevent users from copying or transmitting protected material, or both. The *WCT* refers to "effective technological measures that are used by authors in connection with the exercise of their rights under this Treaty or the Berne Convention and that restrict acts, in respect of their works, which are not authorized by the authors concerned or permitted by law." As such, one could conclude that if the use does not infringe copyright, then protection of the technological measures is not mandated. While this seems a reasonable interpretation of the treaty language, there is no require-

---

[44] *WCT, supra*, note 8, art. 14 and *WPPT, supra*, note 9, art. 10 (performances) and 14 (phonograms).

[45] *WCT, supra*, note 8, art. 10. A parallel provision was included in the *WPPT, supra*, note 9, art. 19.

[46] *WCT, supra*, note 8, art. 11 and *WPPT, supra*, note 9, art. 18.

[47] On this point and for a complete history of the treaties, see Mihály Ficsor, *The Law of Copyright and the Internet* (Oxford Univ. Press, 2001).

[48] See D. Gervais, "Copyright and eCommerce", chapter in Melvin Simensky, Lanning Bryer, Neil J. Wilkof, *Intellectual Property in the Global Marketplace*, 2001 Suppl. (New York: Wiley, 2002).

ment that a "key" to unprotect the material be made available to perform, for example, an act exempted from the rightsholder's reach by fair dealing or other exemptions, in the same way that the *Copyright Act* does not *expressis verbis* prohibit the use of non-negotiable contracts (including "clickwrap") to oblige users to waive recourse to fair dealing or other exceptions. Second, the *WCT* and *WPPT* can be implemented in many different ways. While the right to prevent circumvention can be granted as an accessory to copyright, which logically it is, it can also be granted as a stand-alone right, decoupled from copyright (and exceptions thereto). This also means that the right to circumvent may belong to and be exercised by a person other than the copyright holder, thus adding a level of right to be cleared prior to lawful use.[49] This seems to be the approach taken in U.S. law, where the anti-circumvention legislation was adopted as part of the 1998 *Digital Millennium Copyright Act*.[50] This Act is controversial also because of its application to objects other than traditional copyright "works". In *Lexmark International, Inc. v. Static Control Components, Inc.*,[51] a laser printer manufacturer sued a supplier of toner cartridge refurbishing equipment under the *DMCA*, seeking to enjoin the manufacture and marketing of a microchip that enabled unauthorized toner cartridges to work in the plaintiff's printers by circumventing an authentication sequence. The Sixth Circuit vacated the district court's decision to grant an injunction and remanded the case. In *Chamberlain Group, Inc. v. Skylink Technologies, Inc.*,[52] a manufacturer of garage door openers invoked the *DMCA* in an effort to prevent a competing company from selling replacement transmitters. The Federal Circuit upheld the lower court's grant of summary judgment in favour of the competitor. In a much publicized case in 2003, the Recording Industry Association of America tried to use the *DMCA* to issue "private" subpoenas to force Internet Service Provider (ISP) Verizon to disclose the names of its subscribers who had been "sharing" music files. Verizon successfully challenged the subpoena in the D.C. Circuit.[53]

---

[49] See D. Gervais and A. Maurushat, "Fragmented Copyright, Fragmented Management: Proposals to Defrag Copyright Management" (2003), 2 *Can .J. of L. & Tech* 15-34.

[50] Pub. L. No. 105-304, 112 Stat. 2860 [*DMCA*]. This Act was the subject of at least 50 law review articles since its entry into force.

[51] 253 F.Supp.2d 943 (E.D. Ky., 2003), vacated and remanded by 387 F.3d 522, 72 U.S.P.Q. 2d 1839 (6th Cir., 2004), rehearing denied, rehearing *en banc* denied, cert. denied U.S. Sup. Ct. June 2005.

[52] 292 F.Supp.2d 1040 (N.D. Ill., 2003), affirmed 381 F.3d 1178, 72 U.S.P.Q. 2d 1225 (Fed. Cir., 2004), cert. denied 125 S.Ct. 1669 (U.S. Sup. Ct. 2005).

[53] *Recording Industry Association of America, Inc. v. Verizon Internet Services, Inc.*, 351 F.3d 1229 (D.C. Cir., 2003), cert. denied 125 S.Ct. 309, 125 S.Ct. 347 (U.S. Sup. Ct. 2004).

The *DMCA* exempts ISPs from liability for copyright infringement but imposes a "notice and take down' procedure according to which rights-holders in copyright content can force an ISP to "take down" (remove access to) content they consider infringing. The operator of the website to which access is denied can challenge the notice by following an elaborate procedure. In the *SOCAN* decision, Mr. Justice Binnie seemed to imply that an obligation to act in a similar fashion may already exist for Canadian ISPs:

> [T]o the extent the host server provider has notice of copyrighted material posted on its server, it may, as the Board found, 'respond to the complaint in accordance with the [Canadian Association of Internet Providers] Code of Conduct [which] may include requiring the customer to remove the offending material through a 'take down notice'' (at p. 441). If the host server provider does not comply with the notice, it may be held to have *authorized* communication of the copyright material, as hereinafter discussed.[54]

## II. OTHER INSTRUMENTS

As mentioned in the introduction to this Part, there are two other types of treaties in the field of intellectual property, namely instruments designed to harmonize the description of goods and services for purposes of registration, and instruments that create multilateral registration mechanisms and authorities.

In the first category, one could mention the:

- *Locarno Agreement Establishing an International Classification for Industrial Designs*;[55]
- *Nice Agreement Concerning the International Classification of Goods and Services for the Purposes of the Registration of Marks*;[56]

---

[54] *SOCAN, supra*, note 11 at para. 110.

[55] *Locarno Agreement Establishing an International Classification for Industrial Designs*, 8 October 1968, 828 U.N.T.S. 435, as last revised on 28 September 1979, online: WIPO <http://www.wipo.int/treaties/en/classification/locarno/trtdocs_wo014.html>.

[56] *Nice Agreement Concerning the International Classification of Goods and Services for the Purposes of the Registration of Marks*, 15 June 1957, 550 U.N.T.S. 45, as last revised 28 September 1979, online: WIPO <http://www.wipo.int/treaties/en/classification/nice/trtdocs_wo019.html>.

- *Strasbourg Agreement Concerning the International Patent Classification*;[57] and the
- *Vienna Agreement Establishing an International Classification of the Figurative Elements of Marks.*[58]

Canada is only party to the *Strasbourg Agreement* (since June 11, 1996) which, as its name indicates, provides a uniform classification for classes of invention. This makes it easier to find inventions in a particular field.

With respect to multilateral registration mechanisms, there are five worth mentioning here, namely the

- *Budapest Treaty on the International Recognition of the Deposit of Microorganisms for the Purposes of Patent Procedure*;[59]
- *Hague Agreement Concerning the International Deposit of Industrial Designs*;[60]
- *Lisbon Agreement for the Protection of Appellations of Origin and their International Registration*;[61]
- *Madrid Agreement Concerning the International Registration of Marks*;[62] and the

---

[57] *Strasbourg Agreement Concerning the International Patent Classification*, 24 March 1971, 1160 U.N.T.S. 483, as last revised 28 September 1979, online: WIPO <http://www.wipo.int/treaties/en/classification/strasbourg/trtdocs_wo026.html> [*Strasbourg Agreement*].

[58] *Vienna Agreement Establishing an International Classification of the Figurative Elements of Marks*, 12 June 1973, 1863 U.N.T.S. 317, as last revised 1 October 1985, online: WIPO: <http://www.wipo.int/treaties/en/classification/vienna/trtdocs_wo031.html >.

[59] *Budapest Treaty on the International Recognition of the Deposit of Microorganisms for the Purposes of Patent Procedure*, 28 April 1977, 1861 U.N.T.S. 361, as amended 26 September 1980, online: WIPO <http://www.wipo.int/treaties/en/registration/budapest/trtdocs_wo002.html > [*Budapest Treaty*].

[60] *Hague Agreement Concerning the International Deposit of Industrial Designs*, 6 November 1925, Industrial Property Laws and Treaties, Multilateral Treaties, text 4-001, online: WIPO <http://www.wipo.int/hague/en/legal_texts/wo_has0.htm >.

[61] *Lisbon Agreement for the Protection of Appellations of Origin and their International Registration*, 31 October 1958, 923 U.N.T.S. 205, as last revised 28 September 1979, online: WIPO <http://www.wipo.int/lisbon/en/legal_texts/lisbon_agreement.htm >.

[62] *Madrid Agreement Concerning the International Registration of Marks*, 14 April 1891, 828 U.N.T.S. 389, as last amended 28 September 1979, online: WIPO <http://www.wipo.int/madrid/en/legal_texts/trtdocs_wo015.html>.

  •     *Patent Cooperation Treaty (PCT).*[63]

   Canada is party to the *Budapest Treaty* (since September 21, 1996); and the *PCT* (since January 2, 1990). The *PCT* is heavily used by patent applicants in the 123 member States (as of October 1, 2004).[64] It allows applicants to file a single application[65] and to designate the national or regional offices where they may be interested in obtaining a patent. Because of *PCT* procedures, applicants can delay making a decision about this so-called "national phase" of their application for 30 months after the initial filing. This may allow them to seek financing or test the market for the invention.

   Canada was also considering joining the Madrid system, created under both the *Madrid Agreement Concerning the International Registration of Marks* of April 14, 1891 (as revised) ("Agreement") and the *Protocol Relating to the Madrid Agreement Concerning the International Registration of Marks* ("Protocol") signed at Madrid on June 28, 1989, which came into operation on April 1st, 1996. Under this system, the trade-mark applicant names offices other than in her country of origin (the office of origin and offices named must be from countries party to Protocol or Agreement). The application is sent to WIPO by the Office of origin and WIPO then notifies other named offices. A refusal must be notified to the applicant within 12 months (Agreement) or 18 months (Protocol). A longer time period is possible if an opposition is filed. The international registration remains dependent on maintaining the registration in the country of origin for the first five years. Under the Madrid system, the applicant can file a single application (and updates) in a single language.

## III. THE ROLE OF INTELLECTUAL PROPERTY TREATIES IN DOMESTIC LAW

   Canadian courts have relied on provisions of treaties, including in one case a treaty which Canada had not (yet) ratified, to interpret Canadian intellectual property statutes.

---

[63] *Patent Cooperation Treaty*, 19 June 1970, 1160 U.N.T.S. 231, last revised 3 October 2001, online: WIPO <http://www.wipo.int/pct/en/texts/articles/atoc.htm> [*PCT*].

[64] A complete description of the PCT and related procedures is available online: WIPO <http://www.wipo.int/pct/en/>.

[65] The Canadian Intellectual Property Office (CIPO) became the only competent International Searching Authority (ISA) and International Preliminary Examining Authority (IPEA) for international applications filed on or after July 26, 2004 by nationals and residents of Canada; the amount of the search fee is $1,600.

In *Harvard College v. Canada (Commissioner of Patents),*[66] Mr. Justice Binnie of the Supreme Court wrote the following in his dissent:

> Intellectual property was the subject matter of such influential agreements as the *International Convention for the Protection of Industrial Property (Paris Convention)* as early as 1883. International rules governing patents were strengthened by the *European Patent Convention* in 1973, and, more recently, the World Trade Organization *Agreement on Trade-Related Aspects of Intellectual Property Rights* (TRIPS) in 1994 (1869 U.N.T.S. 299). Copyright was the subject of the *Berne Convention for the Protection of Literary and Artistic Works* in 1886, revised by the *Berlin Convention* of 1908 and the *Rome Convention* of 1928. The *Universal Copyright Convention* was concluded in 1952. Legislation varies of course, from state to state, but broadly speaking Canada has sought to harmonize its concepts of intellectual property with other like-minded jurisdictions.
>
> The mobility of capital and technology makes it desirable that comparable jurisdictions with comparable intellectual property legislation arrive (to the extent permitted by the specifics of their own laws) at similar legal results: *Théberge v. Galerie d'Art du Petit Champlain inc.*, [2002] 2 S.C.R. 336, at para. 6.
>
> [. . .]
>
> NAFTA and TRIPS each provide that contracting states may *exclude* from patentability inventions the exploitation of which would be contrary to *ordre public* (which seemingly equates to the protection of public security, the physical integrity of individuals as members of society, and the protection of the environment) or morality: *North American Free Trade Agreement Between the Government of Canada, the Government of the United Mexican States and the Government of the United States of America* (1992), Can T.S. 1994 No. 2 (entered into force January 1, 1994), art. 1709(2); *Agreement on Trade-Related Aspects of Intellectual Property Rights* (April 15, 1994), 1869 U.N.T.S. 299, art. 27(2). The exclusion presupposes a general rule of patentability. Parliament has amended the *Patent Act* to take account of each of these agreements, but has chosen not to include such an exclusion from patentability in the *Patent Act.*
>
> The *European Patent Convention* contains an *ordre public* exclusion from patentability, and the corresponding European 'oncomouse' patent application was examined having specific regard to this exclusion. In its decision of April 3, 1992, the Examining Division of the European Patent Office stated the issue as follows:

---

[66] [2002] 4 S.C.R. 45, 219 D.L.R. (4th) 577, 21 C.P.R. (4th) 417, 296 N.R. 1 (S.C.C.) [*Harvard College* cited to S.C.R.].

> In the case at hand three different interests are involved and require balancing: there is a basic interest of mankind to remedy widespread and dangerous diseases, on the other hand the environment has to be protected against the uncontrolled dissemination of unwanted genes and, moreover, cruelty to animals has to be avoided. The latter two aspects may well justify regarding an invention as immoral and therefore unacceptable unless the advantages, i.e. the benefit to mankind, outweigh the negative aspects.

> (*Grant of European patent No. 0 169 762 (Onco-mouse/Harvard)* (1992), OJ EPO 1992, 588, at pp. 591-92)

We do not possess such a 'balancing' test in our *Patent Act*, though some thought must have been given to it when Parliament 'opened up' the *Patent Act* for NAFTA and TRIPS-related amendments in 1994. [emphasis in original]

In its recent *Monsanto Canada Inc. v. Schmeiser*[67] decision, the Supreme Court referred to the *TRIPS Agreement* to interpret a process patent claim in favour of the patentee:

> Monsanto's process claims are likewise valid. The method claims for making transgenic glyphosate-resistant plant cells should be valid because an invention may be a 'process': *Tennessee Eastman, supra*. A process claim may be valid even where the subject matter it manufactures is not patentable, for example, because it is obvious: *F. Hoffmann-Laroche & Co. v. Commissioner of Patents*, [1955] S.C.R. 414; or it constitutes unpatentable subject matter: *Harvard College, supra*.
>
>       The second part of the method—the regeneration of the plant cell into a plant—may, however, seem more problematic. However, since this process involves substantial human intervention and does not follow the 'laws of nature' as would natural asexual or sexual reproduction, I conclude that this part of the process would likewise be patentable. The Patent Commissioner in *Harvard College, supra*, found that the process of creating a transgenic cell culture that had the intermediate step of 'allowing said embryo to develop into an adult animal' was patentable as a process claim. This conclusion is consistent with the policy of the Patent Office: *Patent Office Manual, supra*, at para. 16.05, and with art. 27(3)(b) of the *Agreement on Trade-Related Aspects of Intellectual Property Rights (TRIPS)*, 1869 U.N.T.S. 299 (being Annex 1C of the *Marrakesh Agreement Establishing the World Trade Organization*, 1867 U.N.T.S. 3).

[. . .]

---

[67] [2004] 1 S.C.R. 902, 239 D.L.R. (4th) 271, 31 C.P.R. (4th) 161, 320 N.R. 201 (S.C.C.) [*Schmeiser* cited to S.C.R.].

In *Harvard College, supra*, both the majority and the minority called for Parliament's intervention on the issue of patenting higher life forms. As things stand, my conclusion on the scope of Monsanto's patent claims that is determinative of both validity and infringing use is not contrary to art. 27(1) of *TRIPS* whereby Canada has agreed to make patents available for any invention without discrimination as to the field of technology.

[. . .]

Allowing gene and cell claims to extend patent protection to plants would render this provision of *TRIPS* meaningless. To find that possession of plants, as the embodiment of a gene or cell claim, constitute a 'use' of that claim would have the same effect as patenting the plant. Therefore, my conclusion on both the scope of the claims and the scope of use is consistent with Canada's international obligations under *TRIPS*."

In *SOCAN*, Justice LeBel referred not only to the Berne Convention, to which Canada is a party, but also to the *WCT* to interpret the *Copyright Act*:

The only question is whether Parliament intended the Act to have effect beyond Canada. The principle of territoriality operates at the level of a rebuttable presumption that Parliament does not intend the Act to operate beyond Canada's borders. Moreover, copyright law is territorial in nature and thus limited to its enacting State. The territoriality principle has been incorporated into a number of international treaties, to which Canada is a signatory: see e.g. *Berne Convention for the Protection of Literary and Artistic Works*, 1886 ('*Berne Convention*'); *Agreement on Trade-Related Aspects of Intellectual Property Rights*, 1994 ('TRIPS') (1869 U.N.T.S. 299) ; World Intellectual Property Organization *Copyright Treaty*, 1996 ('*WCT*'); and World Intellectual Property Organization *Performances and Phonograms Treaty*, 1996 ('*PPT*').

Article 5 of the *Berne Convention* calls for the territorial treatment of copyright; however, the *Berne Convention* does not specifically address the communication of works over the Internet. Canada is a signatory to the *WCT*, but it is not yet party to the treaty; it has yet to ratify it. The Board refused to interpret the Act in light of the *WCT* because the *WCT* is 'not binding in Canada since it has been signed but not ratified by the Canadian Government' (at p. 448). I disagree. Although Canada has not ratified the treaty, this does not mean that it should not be considered as an aid in interpreting the Act. Article 8 of the *WCT* provides:

[Right of Communication to the Public]

Without prejudice to the provisions of Articles 11(1)(ii), 11*bis*(1)(i) and (ii), 11*ter*(1)(ii), 14(1)(ii) and 14*bis*(1) of the Berne Convention, authors of literary and artistic works shall enjoy the exclusive right of authorizing any communication to the public of their works, by wire or wireless means, including the making available to the public of their

> works in such a way that members of the public may access these works from a place and at a time individually chosen by them. [Emphasis added.]

The purpose of art. 8 of the *WCT* is to harmonize domestic copyright laws in the party States with respect to the right of communication of copyrighted works. We should not ignore that fact.

As McLachlin C.J. recently held, even though international norms are generally not binding without domestic implementation, they are relevant in interpreting domestic legislation: see *R. v. Sharpe*, [2001] 1 S.C.R. 45, 2001 SCC 2, at para. 175. Parliament is presumed not to legislate in breach of a treaty, the comity of nations and the principles of international law. This rule of construction is well established: see *Daniels v. White*, [1968] S.C.R. 517, at p. 541. Although the *Copyright Act* has not yet been amended to reflect the signing of the *WCT*, I believe this cannon of interpretation is equally applicable to the case at bar.

How to interpret the meaning of 'communicate' in s. 3(1)(*f*) in the context of the Internet so as to best respect the principle of territoriality in the *Berne Convention*? In my opinion, the host server test adopted by the Board has the benefit of clearly complying with the territoriality requirement of international copyright law. It also accords with the *WCT* communication right (art. 8), which includes 'the making available to the public of their works in such a way that members of the public may access these works from a place and at a time individually chosen by them'; copyrighted works are made available on the Internet when they are posted on a host server. Before they are posted on a host server, they are not available to the public.[68]

The reference made by Justice LeBel to the "breach of a treaty, the comity of nations and the principles of international law" is interesting. While the first condition does not apply (because Canada had not ratified the *WCT* at the relevant time), the last two are open to discussion. The *WCT* entered into force on March 6, 2002 (i.e., during the *SOCAN* case), and as of October 1, 2004, it had been ratified by 48 States. One may question whether, both because of its relative novelty and the breadth of ratifications, not following the *WCT* does indeed constitute a violation of rules on comity or principles of international law, in the latter case customary law. Because of Canada's stated intention to ratify the Treaty,[69] however, the reference remains relevant.

---

[68] *Supra*, note 2.

[69] See *Supporting Culture and Innovation: Report on the Provisions and Operation of the Copyright Act*. Oct. 2002. Available online at <http://strategis.ic.gc.ca/epic/internet/incrp-prda.nsf/en/rp00866e.html>.

It is interesting to note that in an anterior decision in *BMG Canada Inc. v. John Doe*,[70] von Finckenstein J. arrived at what seems to be the opposite conclusion to that of Mr. Justice LeBel, precisely because Canada had not ratified the *WPPT*:

> The exclusive right to make available is included in the *World Intellectual Property Organization Performances and Phonograms Treaty*, (WPPT), 20/ 12/1996 (CRNR/DC/95, December 23, 1996), however that treaty has not yet been implemented in Canada and therefore does not form part of Canadian copyright law.[71]

In *CCH Canadian Ltd. v. Law Society of Upper Canada*,[72] the Supreme Court again referred to the *Berne Convention* in its analysis of the history and purpose of copyright law:

> The idea of 'intellectual creation' was implicit in the notion of literary or artistic work under the *Berne Convention for the Protection of Literary and Artistic Works* (1886), to which Canada adhered in 1923, and which served as the precursor to Canada's first *Copyright Act*, adopted in 1924. See S. Ricketson, *The Berne Convention for the Protection of Literary and Artistic Works: 1886-1986* (1987), at p. 900. Professor Ricketson has indicated that in adopting a sweat of the brow or industriousness approach to deciding what is original, common law countries such as England have 'depart[ed] from the spirit, if not the letter, of the [Berne] Convention' since works that have taken time, labour or money to produce but are not truly artistic or literary intellectual creations are accorded copyright protection: Ricketson, *supra*, at p. 901.

The Federal Court of Canada has also used intellectual property treaties in a number of cases to interpret Canadian law. In a 1999 case,[73] the Trial Division had to decide whether provisions from trade agreements, including

---

[70] [2004] 3 F.C.R. 241, 239 D.L.R. (4th) 726, 32 C.P.R. (4th) 64 (F.C.) [*BMG Canada* F.C. cited to F.C.R.], affirmed 2005 FCA 193, [2005] F.C.J. No. 9858 (FCA).

[71] *Ibid.*, at para. 25. The Federal Court of Appeal dismissed the appeal but expressly declined to confirm the conclusions reached by von Fickenstein J. on copyright issues.

[72] [2004] 1 S.C.R. 339, 236 D.L.R. (4th) 395, 30 C.P.R. (4th) 1, 317 N.R. 107 (S.C.C.) [*CCH Canadian* cited to S.C.R.].

[73] *Pfizer Inc. v. R.*, (sub nom. *Pfizer Inc. v. Canada*) [1999] 4 F.C. 441, (sub nom. *Pfizer Inc. v. Canada*) 2 C.P.R. (4th) 298, (sub nom. *Pfizer Inc. v. Canada (Minister of National Health & Welfare)*) 171 F.T.R. 211 (Fed. T.D.), affirmed (1999), [1999] F.C.J. No. 1598, (sub nom. *Pfizer Inc. v. Canada (Minister of National Health & Welfare)*) 250 N.R. 66, 1999 CarswellNat 2125 (Fed. C.A.) [*Pfizer* cited to F.C.].

*TRIPS*, could be used by a private party (Pfizer) to obtain a remedy against the government:

> The basis for the relief claimed by Pfizer is article 33 of the *Agreement on Trade Related Aspects of Intellectual Property Rights* (the 'TRIPS Agreement') which requires member countries to provide a minimum term of protection for all patents not less than twenty years from the filing date of a patent application. Since Pfizer applied for the '815 patent on October 30, 1980, Pfizer claims under the TRIPS Agreement an expiry date of October 30, 2000.
>
> The TRIPS Agreement is one of the agreements annexed to the *World Trade Agreement (WTO Agreement)* which Pfizer says by the provisions of the *Final Act Embodying the Results of the Uruguay Round of Multilateral Trade Negotiations* ('the Final Act'), Canada agreed in section 2(a) thereof to submit, as appropriate for the consideration of their respective competent authorities with a view to seeking approval of the *WTO Agreement* in accordance with their procedures. Pfizer also relies upon the provisions of the *Marrakesh Agreement* establishing the World Trade Organization specifically in article XVI.4 thereof which provides that each member shall ensure the conformity of its laws, regulations and administrative procedures with its obligations as provided in the annexed agreements (the *Marrakesh Agreement*). Against this background and in this context, the Parliament of Canada enacted the *World Trade Organization Implementation Act* ('*WTO Implementation Act*') in 1994.
>
> The defendants based their motion to strike on three grounds.
>
> First, the defendants say, on the basis of sections 5 and 6 of the *WTO Implementation Act*, the aggregate effect of which is to bar any person from commencing any type of legal action under either the Act itself or the underlying *WTO Agreement* without the consent of the Attorney General, that the plaintiffs' action is barred, said consent having not been given in this case.
>
> Second, the defendants submit that the provisions of an agreement between Canada and any foreign state are implemented into Canadian domestic law only insofar as they are explicitly enacted in legislation passed in the ordinary way by Parliament and further submit that no enactment exists amending the *Patent Act*, to grant to the plaintiffs the patent term claimed in the statement of claim occurred.

[. . .]

The introductory part of the *WTO Implementation Act* contains definitions including a definition of 'Agreement' which reads as follows:

> 'Agreement' means the Agreement establishing the World Trade Organization, including
>
>> (a) the Agreements set out in Annexes 1A, 1B, 1C, 2 and 3 of that Agreement and

> (b) the Agreements set out in Annex IV to that Agreement that
> have been accepted by Canada. . . .

The *TRIPS Agreement* is contained in Annex 1(c).

[. . .]

Sections 5 and 6, under the heading 'General' contain the statutory bars upon which the defendants rely. They read:

> 5. No person has any cause of action and no proceedings of any kind shall be taken, without the consent of the Attorney General of Canada, to enforce or determine any right of obligation that is claimed or arises solely under or by virtue of Part I or any order made under Part I.
> 6. No person has any cause of action and no proceedings of any kind shall be taken, without the consent of the Attorney General of Canada, to enforce or determine any right or obligation that is claimed or arises solely under or by virtue of the Agreement.

Part I, as noted, is headed 'Implementation of Agreement Generally'. Section 8 is headed 'Approval of Agreement' and simply reads:

> 8. The Agreement is hereby approved.

[. . .]

Part II, headed 'Related and Consequential Amendments', contains amendments to a large number of federal statutes in respect of which Parliament had constitutional authority on a division of legislative power basis.

A close examination of the specific Part II *WTO Implementation Act* amendments is revealing. Such an examination demonstrates that Parliament did not resort to a single method of implementation. Specificity is the hallmark of Part II. The nature of the required Parliamentary intervention varied according to the circumstances. I have in mind factors such as the nature of a specific obligation contracted for by Canada, the characteristics of existing federal statutory or regulatory requirements (are the prescriptions contained in a statute or in a regulation), the need for flexibility and the presence of federal authority mandated to administer on a case-by-case basis contracted obligations (a good example of such a federal authority is the Canadian International Trade Tribunal which decides, on the ground so to speak, dumping, subsidies and other cases).

[. . .]

[T]he *Patent Act* was amended in Part II. Existing sections 44 and 45 previously amended in 1993 were not further amended. Only two changes were made to the *Patent Act*. The definition of 'country' was amended to include a member of the WTO. Section 19.1 of the Act was amended to provide that the Commissioner may not, under section 19, authorize any use of semi-conductor technology other than a public non-commercial use.

In terms of intellectual property, I note the *Trade-marks Act* was extensively amended with reference made to the TRIPS Agreement.

**Analysis**

*(a)  Has the WTO Agreement been legislated into domestic law*

To succeed in their declaration that the term of the '815 patent is October 20, 2000, the plaintiffs must establish the *WTO Agreement* which annexes the *TRIPS Agreement* has been legislated into domestic law through the *WTO Implementation Act*. Pfizer argues that this is so through the combined effect of the purpose clause which is to implement the *WTO Agreement*, the approval clause whereby the *WTO Agreement* is approved and Canada's commitments under the *Final Act* and the *Marrakesh Agreement*.

In so submitting, Pfizer seems to accept the distinction between treaty making and treaty implementation. Pfizer also accepts the proposition that many treaties cannot be implemented without alteration to the internal law of Canada which can only be done by the enactment of legislation to alter that domestic law. See Peter Hogg, *Constitutional Law of Canada*, 4th ed. pages 293 and 294; *Capital Cities Communications Inc. v. Canada (Radio-Television & Telecommunications Commission)* (1977), [1978] 2 S.C.R. 141 (S.C.C.) at 173 where Laskin C.J. said this:

> Indeed, if the contention of the appellants has any force under its first submission it can only relate to the obligations of Canada under the Convention towards other ratifying signatories. There would be no domestic, internal consequences unless they arose from implementing legislation giving the Convention a legal effect within Canada.

The *WTO Agreement* is an international agreement to which sovereign states are the only parties. The central issue in this case is whether Parliament, in enacting the *WTO Implementation Act*, gave legal effect or translated into federal law that Agreement as a whole and, in particular, its annexed *TRIPS Agreement* or section 33 thereof.

Defendants refer to a number of cases including Reference *Re Weekly Rest in Industrial Undertakings Act and other Acts, Canada (Attorney General) v.*

*Ontario (Attorney General)*, [1937] 1 D.L.R. 673 (Canada P.C.) and a recent case cited by Guthrie J. in *UL Canada Inc. v. Quebec (Procureur Général)*, May 16, 1999, (1999) J.Q. No. 1540, for the proposition that a simple approval by Parliament does not operate to legislate an international agreement into federal law. In the *UL Canada Inc.* case, Guthrie J. considered whether the *North American Free Trade Agreement Implementation Act* and the *WTO Implementation Act* made the international agreements domestic law, whether federal or provincial. . . .

Guthrie J., at paragraph 95, [decided the issue of] the *WTO Implementation Act* to the effect the *WTO Agreement* was not made part of federal law.

Pfizer counters principally with the case of *Orelien v. Canada (Minister of Employment & Immigration)* (1991), 135 N.R. 50 (Fed. C.A.). Mahoney J.A., at page 58, considered the international law agreements which involved the *Fourth Geneva Convention*.

In my view, much guidance to answer the central question considered here is derived from the recent Supreme Court of Canada judgment in *Vancouver Island Railway, An Act Respecting, Re*, [1994] 2 S.C.R. 41 (S.C.C.).

The issue before the Court was whether a federal statute had given statutory force to the *Dunsmuir Agreement* such that the provisions of the *Dunsmuir Agreement* were, in effect, the provisions of the federal statute itself.

The *Dunsmuir Agreement* was a schedule to a federal Act. Section 2 of the federal Act with respect to the *Dunsmuir Agreement* said:

> The agreement, . . . is hereby approved and ratified, and the Governor in Council is authorized to carry out the provisions thereof according to their purport.

[. . .]

Iacobucci J. said this at page 110:

> I do believe, however, that simple 'ratification' or 'confirmation' of a scheduled agreement, without more, is equivocal in terms of the required legislative intention.

As a factor in discovering Parliamentary intent, Iacobucci J. took into account the fact that the federal Act repeated parts of the *Dunsmuir Agreement* in the text of the statute. He said this at page 111:

> The *Dominion Act* simply confirms and ratifies the Dunsmuir Agreement, authorizes the Governor in Council to carry out the contract, and proceeds, in several of its provisions, to recount specifically clauses from that contract (ss. 4, 5, 6, 8, and 9). If the Dunsmuir Agreement was intended to have statutory force, I would find this repetition of contractual provisions in the text of the *Dominion Act* to be inexplicable.

I have come to the conclusion it is plain and obvious that Parliament did not legislate into federal domestic law the *WTO Agreement* and, in particular, section 33 of the *TRIPS Agreement*, which is essential to the success of Pfizer's declaration.

Parliament, in my view, manifestly indicated its intention as to how it was implementing the *WTO Agreement* and its annexed *TRIPS Agreement* or any part thereof. Parliament gave legal effect to its WTO obligations by carefully examining the nature of those obligations, assessing the state of the existing federal statutory and regulatory law and then deciding the specific and precise legislative changes which were required to implement the *WTO Agreement*.

The term of a patent is a matter governed by the *Patent Act*. Parliament did not change the provisions of sections 44 and 45 of that Act to provide what Pfizer is seeking. Statutory change was required and Parliament did not make that change. Whether Parliament, in doing so, was in breach of its international obligations is not material to the question before me. The *WTO Agreement* has procedures, government to government, to deal with a question of that nature.

To accede to Pfizer's argument would, in my view, make redundant and negate the entire overall structure and approach taken by Parliament to implement the WTO obligations through the *WTO Implementation Act*. By analogy to what Iacobucci J. said in *Vancouver Island Railway, An Act Respecting, Re, supra*, if Parliament had intended the *WTO Agreement* to have statutory force, it would not have enacted Part II of the *WTO Implementation Act* in the detailed and careful manner it did.

[T]he defendants' motion to strike is granted, Pfizer's statement of claim in this action is struck and its action is dismissed with costs.

In a different case involving the same parties,[74] the Court of Appeal did not accept a submission based on the *TRIPS Agreement*, the *Paris Convention* and the intellectual property provisions of *NAFTA* to judicially amend the *Patented Medicine (Notice of Compliance) Regulations*:[75]

I am of the view that there is no need to resort to these instruments in this case. I base this conclusion on the long-established jurisprudence that while Parliament is presumed not to intend to legislate contrary to international treaties or general principles of international law, this is only a presumption: where the legislation is clear one need not and should not look to international law. (See, e.g. *Daniels v. White*, [1968] S.C.R. 517 (S.C.C.), at 541; *Schreiber v. Canada (Attorney General)*, 2002 SCC 62 (S.C.C.) at para. 50). The appellants nevertheless say this principle has been modified by the Supreme Court in *National Corn Growers Assn. v. Canada (Canadian Import Tribunal)*, [1990] 2 S.C.R. 1324 (S.C.C.). They take that case to mean that 'international treaties are always

---

[74] *Pfizer Canada Inc. v. Canada (Attorney General)*, [2003] 4 F.C. 95, 224 D.L.R. (4th) 178, 24 C.P.R. (4th) 1, 301 N.R. 376 (Fed. C.A.), leave to appeal refused (2003), 27 C.P.R. (4th) vi (S.C.C.).

[75] SOR/93-133.

a proper aid to be used to interpret domestic legislation'. But in that case Gonthier J. put it thus:

> If the convention may be used on the correct principle that the statute is intended to implement the convention then, it follows, the latter becomes a proper aid to interpretation, and, more especially, may reveal a latent ambiguity in the text of the statute even if this was 'clear in itself' .... (pages 1371-2)

(See also *Pushpanathan v. Canada (Minister of Employment & Immigration)*, [1998] 1 S.C.R. 982 (S.C.C.) at para. 51)

[. . .]

[T]he Paris Convention does not, as I understand it, confer immediate enforceability in Canada of a patent applied for or obtained in another member country. While it gives certain priorities to its holder in prosecuting a Canadian patent application, that holder or its affiliate must still apply in Canada for a patent before being able to enforce it here.

## IV. DISCUSSION QUESTIONS

**Q:** Could Canada impose a compulsory license (*i.e.,* without the rights-holder's consent, but subject to the payment of adequate compensation) in the following cases without being in violation of its international obligations:

— A licence allowing all Canadian Internet users to upload to and download from the Internet files containing protected music?
— A licence allowing all Canadian university, college and high school students to download, copy and use anything they can find on the Internet as long as it is related to their studies? Would this include copies of files of scanned textbooks?
— A licence allowing a private Canadian company to manufacture a cancer-fighting pharmaceutical that the government wanted to make available but that the patent owner did no want to sell into Canada?
— A licence allowing the use of the "Starbucks" mark on coffee shops operated by the National Capital Commission in the Ottawa area?

**Q:** In the four situations above, could an exemption be imposed (*i.e.,* a right to use without requiring either an authorization or adequate compensation)?

**Q:** Discuss the following statement by Mr. Justice Lebel in *Society of Composers, Authors & Music Publishers of Canada v. Canadian Assn. of Internet Providers* :

> Canada is a signatory to the [WIPO Copyright Treaty], but it is not yet party to the treaty; it has yet to ratify it. The Board refused to interpret the Act in light of the WCT because the WCT is "not binding in Canada since it has been signed but not ratified by the Canadian Government" (at p. 448). I disagree. Although Canada has not ratified the treaty, this does not mean that it should not be considered as an aid in interpreting the Act. Article 8 of the WCT provides:
>
> > Without prejudice to the provisions of Articles 11(1)(ii), 11bis(1)(i) and (ii), 11ter(1)(ii), 14(1)(ii) and 14bis(1) of the Berne Convention, authors of literary and artistic works shall enjoy the exclusive right of authorizing any communication to the public of their works, by wire or wireless means, including the making available to the public of their works in such a way that members of the public may access these works from a place and at a time individually chosen by them. [Emphasis added.]
>
> The purpose of art. 8 of the WCT is to harmonize domestic copyright laws in the party States with respect to the right of communication of copyrighted works. We should not ignore that fact.
>
> As McLachlin C.J. recently held, even though international norms are generally not binding without domestic implementation, they are relevant in interpreting domestic legislation: see *R. v. Sharpe,* [2001] 1 S.C.R. 45, 2001 SCC 2 (S.C.C.), at para. 175. Parliament is presumed not to legislate in breach of a treaty, the comity of nations and the principles of international law. This rule of construction is well established: see *Daniels v. White* , [1968] S.C.R. 517 (S.C.C.), at p. 541. Although the Copyright Act has not yet been amended to reflect the signing of the WCT, I believe this cannon of interpretation is equally applicable to the case at bar.
>
> How to interpret the meaning of "communicate" in s. 3(1)(f) in the context of the Internet so as to best respect the principle of territoriality in the Berne Convention? In my opinion, the host server test adopted by the Board has the benefit of clearly complying with the territoriality requirement of international copyright law. It also accords with the WCT communication right (Art. 8), which includes "the making available to the public of their works in such a way that members of the public may access these works from a place and at a time individually chosen by them"; copyrighted works are made available on the Internet when they are posted on a host server. Before they are posted on a host server, they are not available to the public.

# *Chapter* 10: Intellectual Property Overlaps

I. Copyright and Trade-Marks and Protection of Image

II. Copyright and Industrial Designs

III. Copyright and Topographies

IV. Patents and Copyright

V. Trade-Marks and Industrial Designs

VI. Patents and Trade-Marks

VII. Discussion Questions

There is no hierarchy to the various intellectual property statutes. As a result, conflicts and overlaps do arise. That happens partly because a single tangible object can give rise to more than one intangible right and because the various intellectual property rights protect different things. In such cases, courts try to interpret the statutes so each of their objectives can be met and generally will not allow using one type of protection to extend a form of protection that is available under another statute (known as back-door protection). For example, one cannot use a trade-mark on a patented invention, or copyright in drawings included as part of a patent, to extend patent protection.

Each of the intellectual property rights has a bargain/exchange that is underwritten by policy and theory and tampering with that bargain throws the system off balance. A key part of the bargain is the length of the term of protection, and the related requirement that the object of the protection be freely useable by others after the expiry of such term.

There are, however, a few cases where courts have in fact combined two forms of protection (during their respective terms) to achieve a more complete protection. These decisions are often based in part on equitable considerations. The best example is the protection of fictional characters, for which the protection available under Canadian law is achieved by combining copyright and trade-marks.

## I. COPYRIGHT AND TRADE-MARKS AND PROTECTION OF IMAGE

An interesting case on the relationship between copyright and trade-marks is *Mihaljevic v. British Columbia*,[1] which involved "Expo 86". The province of British Columbia had registered EXPO 86 and EXPO as official marks, while a local business person had registered copyrights for designs using "Expo" and "Expo 86" for souvenir items. The business person argued that he had copyright in the phrases themselves, but the court refused to recognize "Expo" as copyrightable subject matter. The province meanwhile was unsuccessful in its bid to monopolize the number 86, with the court ruling that the digits "designate a year in the life of the world which simply must be lived or endured and cannot be avoided by the living."[2]

### 1. Fictional Characters

Perhaps the most fertile interplay between copyright and trade-marks is with fictional characters. Fictional characters can be based in prose (such as Jane Eyre or Holden Caulfield), visual (in two- or three-dimensions) (such as Charlie Brown or Garfield), or audio-visual media (such as Buffy the Vampire Slayer). Fictional characters are protected under copyright, trade-mark, unfair competition law, contract and appropriation of personality. Each doctrine protects different aspects of a fictional character depending on the objective of that law. Thus, while copyright protects the original expression of the literary or artistic creations, trade-mark law protects fictional characters as indicators of the source of a good or service.

Fictional characters are an increasingly important and valuable asset. They are both cultural and commercial commodities. These properties have economic value through character merchandising (lunchboxes, key chains, calendars, etc.), which value is increased through the multiple media outlets in which these figures can appear (including, for example, books, television, film, Internet DVDs, etc.). Fictional characters also have significant expression and identity value to the public as they become integrated into the popular lexicon. The more visible and more recognizable a character, the more stories and more media in which they can appear, including both authorized (officially licensed apparel, for example) and unofficial uses (such as fan sites on the Internet). Copyright and trade-mark owners must

---

[1] (1988), [1988] F.C.J. No. 738, 23 C.P.R. (3d) 80, 1988 CarswellNat 211 (Fed. T.D.), affirmed (1990), [1990] F.C.J. No. 963, 34 C.P.R. (3d) 54, 116 N.R. 218, 1990 CarswellNat 226 (Fed. C.A.), leave to appeal refused (1991), 135 N.R. 79 (note) (S.C.C.) [*Mihaljevic* cited to C.P.R.].

[2] *Ibid.* at para 22.

strategize how to protect the legal rights in these characters without alienating the popular fan base to which the characters appeal.

### (a) Copyright Protection for Fictional Characters

Elements of the fictional characters include their name, physical appearance, and character traits. Copyright law protects the original expression in the fictional character, and not all of these elements are part of copyrightable subject matter. There is no separate category for fictional characters under the Canadian *Copyright Act,* but the characters can fall within existing categories of copyrighted works, including literary works, dramatic works (including motion pictures) and artistic works (drawings and artistic craftsmanship). An example of a pictorial or graphic character is Mickey Mouse; of a literary fictional character is Anne of Green Gables or Robinson Crusoe; and of an audio-visual character is Bart Simpson.

There has been a sustained debate as to whether fictional characters *per se* are copyrightable as independent works, or rather, if characters are protected as part of the larger work in which they appear. In the latter case, there would be infringement with the fictional character if someone reproduces a substantial part of the larger work in which they appear. The preferable view is that fictional characters can be independently copyrighted.

In *Preston v. 20th Century Fox Canada Ltd.,*[3] MacKay J. considered the plaintiff's claim of copyright infringement against Fox and Lucasfilm, the producers of the Star Wars film *Return of the Jedi,* alleging that they had infringed his copyright in his "Space Pets" script and the Olak and Ewok characters featured therein. Preston claimed the Ewok creatures in the film were based on the alien furry space creatures (of the same name) that he created in his script, which he claimed had been sent to George Lucas. Lucasfilm noted it was standard practice to return all unsolicited scripts and to shield Lucas from any incoming mail. MacKay J. found no substantial similarity between the two scripts. In considering whether the Ewok character was independently copyrightable, MacKay J. reviewed both U.K. and U.S. case law. MacKay J. suggested that under Canadian copyright law a literary fictional character could be separately protected, but held that these characters were not sufficiently delineated and thus the mere similarity in the two characters' names did not constitute infringement.

One American test to which MacKay J. refers is an influential U.S. test for fictional characters described by Judge Learned Hand in *Nichols v.*

---

[3] (1990), [1990] F.C.J. No. 1011, 33 C.P.R. (3d) 242, 1990 CarswellNat 205 (Fed. T.D.), affirmed (1993), [1993] F.C.J. No. 1259, 53 C.P.R. (3d) 407, 164 N.R. 304, 1993 CarswellNat 2391 (Fed. C.A.).

*Universal Pictures Corp.*[4] That test provides that the "less developed the characters, the less they can be copyrighted; that is the penalty an author must bear for marking them too indistinctly."[5] The test, in other words, attempts to define when a fictional character is "expression" and not merely an idea, while acknowledging the elusive nature of the inquiry: "Nobody has ever been able to fix that boundary [between protectable expression and unprotected idea] and nobody ever can."[6] An author can get copyright in their expression of a mouse but not of all cartoon mice; likewise, an author could have copyright in the original expression of *a* superhero but not a monopoly of all superheroes. By focusing on how well delineated a character is, the test incorporates "originality," in the sense that a developed character suggests the author's skill and judgment, and a public notice function, since a well delineated character can be recognized and others will be better able to predict how to use stock character features without trespassing on the copyright of a particular fictional character.

There are curiosities about the copyright tests and their application to fictional characters. First, the *type of medium* that the character is in can affect the scope of protection. Generally, courts have been more likely to find infringement with respect to pictorial depictions than with literary characters. This may be partly accounted for by evidentiary factors; one can compare two visual representations with greater confidence than the intangible and subjective "image" that a purely literary description of a fictional character (which may concentrate on that character's subconscious more than physical appearance) calls up. By corollary, similarities in two graphic characters' appearances are more likely to be infringing than similarities in two characters' personality traits. Thus, graphic characters can even be protected where look-alike characters are used but with radically different personality traits. In a famous example from the United States, *Walt Disney v. Air Pirates*,[7] characters which physically resembled various Disney cartoon figures, but with greatly disparate character traits, were held to be infringing the Disney characters. In that case, Mickey, Minnie, Goofy, Donald Duck and friends appeared in an adult comic book which depicted these characters as counter-establishment participants in a promiscuous drug culture. The general rule for graphic characters seems to be that visual similarity, even absent a similarity of personality and behaviour, will infringe: with respect to Donald Duck, one could (somewhat facetiously) generalize, "if it *looks* like a duck. . .," it infringes.

---

[4] 45 F.2d 119 (2nd Cir., 1930).
[5] *Ibid.* at 121.
[6] *Ibid.*
[7] 345 F. Supp. 108 (1972), modified 581 F.2d 751 (9th Cir., 1978).

With literary characters, comparing mental images conjured up by prose narratives to see if one character substantially reproduces another poses a difficult challenge for judges analyzing infringement. As a result, fictional characters in narratives that feature introspective and enigmatic characters may be less likely to be protected under copyright than a character who has a few but memorable quirks, even though more briefly and sketchily represented, because it is harder to determine that another character substantially reproduces the first character's sub-conscious. It is particularly hard to determine when a fictional character visually represented by one person is the same character (that is, substantially similar) as a character that another person described with words and therefore infringing.

### (b)  Copyright and Trade-Mark Convergence

Because s. 3 of the *Copyright Act* provides that reproduction in *any material form* infringes copyright, three-dimensional figures based on two-dimensional figures can infringe copyright if they are substantially similar. The copyrighted expression of a two-dimensional fictional character (from a comic strip, for example) can be infringed by a three-dimensional reproduction of that figure (a stuffed animal toy, for example). By illustration, in *King Features Syndicate Inc. v. O. & M. Kleemann Ltd.*,[8] a defendant who made dolls and brooches of Popeye was held to have infringed the plaintiff's copyrighted artistic work in the Popeye comic strip.

In another case involving Popeye, *King Features Syndicate Inc. v. Lechter*,[9] King Features owned the Canadian copyright for the Popeye comic strip, including both drawings and the text. The best known character from that comic strip was, of course, Popeye. Sometimes "Popeye" was used as the title for the strip, but at other times the strip appeared with the title of "Thimble Theatre." The defendant was a wholesale and retail dealer in watches and jewellery. The defendant advertised and sold watches which had Popeye and three other characters, Wimpy, Olive Oyl and Sweetpea, on their dial face. The defendant registered the trade-mark for POPEYE. King Features alleged infringement of their copyright design, in the design of the watches, advertising, packages, and character names. Plaintiffs had their own watches as well which featured the four Popeye characters. The defendants admitted their initial watch designs infringed copyright by reproducing the plaintiff's characters on the dial face. Another issue arose with respect to whether the *title* of a fictional character was protected under copyright. Generally, titles cannot be copyrighted independently. However,

---

[8] [1941] A.C. 417 (U.K. H.L.).
[9] [1950] Ex. C.R. 297 (Can. Ex. Ct.).

s. 2 of the *Copyright Act* provides that a copyrighted work includes the title when the title is original and distinctive. The title is not an independently copyrightable work (although it may be a fit subject for trade-mark protection) but reproducing the title could infringe copyright if it constitutes taking a substantial part of the copyrighted work. The court here found that the use of the word "Popeye," *with the characters*, was an infringement of the copyrighted work. When the title was linked with the reproduction of the artistic depictions of characters, it was a reproduction of a substantial part of the work. The defendants subsequently marketed different watches which used look-alike figures, such as a "Popeye-ish" character, sporting a sailor jacket and a red hat, but missing the authentic Popeye's characteristic pipe and some other features. The court concluded the defendant was deliberately trying to design a character that would avoid infringement but still be recognizable by consumers, and since the characters were so similar and there was no evidence of independent creation, the "look-alike" characters infringed copyright, even without appearing under the character name of "Popeye."

This case points to a common problem of convergence (or confusion) between copyright and trade-mark principles in these fictional character infringement cases. Fictional characters frequently raise issues of both copyright and trade-mark law. For example, in *Cie générale des établissements Michelin - Michelin & Cie v. CAW-Canada*,[10] Michelin brought both copyright and trade-mark actions against a union which was reproducing and using the Bibendum tire character on its union recruiting posters. Although copyright law is supposed to protect original expression, and trade-mark law to protect distinctive marks which indicate the source of particular goods or services, courts often consider in the *copyright* analysis whether characters are *recognizable* and *distinctive*, which is more properly considered as a trade-mark issue. The concept of substantially similar reproduction under copyright law and the concepts of recognition, distinctiveness, and likelihood of confusion of trade-mark law are not always addressed separately. As the result in the *Michelin* case illustrates, where Michelin was successful on the copyright claim but not the trade-mark analysis, it is important to consider the copyright and trade-mark policies and legal requirements separately.

---

[10] (1996), [1997] 2 F.C. 306, (sub nom. *Cie Générale des Établissements Michelin-Michelin & Cie v. C.A.W.-Canada*) 71 C.P.R. (3d) 348, (sub nom. *Cie Générale des Établissements Michelin-Michelin & Cie v. C.A.W.-Canada*) 124 F.T.R. 192 (Fed. T.D.) [*Michelin*].

## 2. The Tort of Misappropriation of Personality

By contrast to fictional characters, the image, likeness, name or signature of a famous person can also be protected. In most cases, courts will rely on the tort of misappropriation of personality, which recognizes that others can wrongfully take aspects of a person's personality and reflects the commercial reality that image, particularly of celebrities, has economic value. The tort is a hybrid of privacy and property interests and, while there is no concise definition, it involves taking aspects of someone else's personality (such as name, reputation or likeness) for commercial gain without that person's permission. Some provinces include the tort in provincial privacy legislation and other provinces have developed the tort in common law.

The tort of misappropriation of personality was analyzed as follows by the Ontario Court of Appeal, in a case involving the use of a football player's image to advertise a car:[11]

> A member of a professional team, by the very nature of his participation in a professional sport in a public stadium, exposes himself to public view directly by people in the stadium and indirectly to the general public outside the stadium when the game is broadcast by television. Obviously, the image of the respondent Krouse along with that of the other players would be telecast at those moments in which he participated in telecast games, in association with pictures of the products of the telecast sponsors. Equally inevitably, the respondent Krouse, as indeed the evidence showed here, would find his likeness printed in newspapers and sporting publications at least in the area in which he performed as a football player. This exposure would be anticipated and encouraged by the team and by players such as the respondent, and the commercial success of the team owners who pay their salaries is dependent upon such public exposure. Indeed the object, value, and purpose of professional sport is to attract the public in the greatest numbers possible to the game, and in the final analysis the owners and, presumably, the players will reap rewards proportionate to the numbers thus attracted. It therefore follows that Krouse and the other participants by the clearest implication authorize and invite the communications media to photograph and write about their exploits. The photograph in question was taken, as I have said, by a photographer who was issued a 'press pass' by the respondent's employers for the purpose of photographing the game for possible use by the press.
>
> Apart from promoting the success of the institution of professional football by directing the public's attention to its activities, the individual participants' notoriety and success rise and fall by the publicity given their individual exploits. Thus it is not surprising that the respondent did not include amongst

---

[11] *Krouse v. Chrysler Canada Ltd.* (1973), 1 O.R. (2d) 225, 40 D.L.R. (3d) 15, 13 C.P.R. (2d) 28 (Ont. C.A.) at 20-31 [*Krouse* cited to D.L.R.].

the appellants the photographer or any news media which might have printed
or telecast the photograph of the respondent or a report of the football game in
which the respondent participated.

The question therefore arises as to what limitations, if any, the respondent
can impose on the use of pictures taken of him during a football game. These
events have been partially anticipated by a clause in the contract between the
respondent and the Hamilton Tiger Cats Football Club, which provides as
follows:

> 19. The parties agree that the Club shall have the exclusive right to
> permit any person, firm or corporation to display, for publicity or com-
> mercial purposes, pictures of the player without the player receiving
> remuneration therefor, and the player shall not allow either gratuitously
> or for remuneration, any pictures of the player to be used for any publicity
> purposes without the consent in writing of the Club first had and obtained.

No claim is made that the appellants have procured a breach of this or any
contract.

Counsel for the appellants in a thorough review of the authorities in this
country, the United Kingdom and the United States, which directly or by
analogy have dealt with the issues herein arising, submitted:

> (a) Heretofore such actions would be tried in libel, but none of the
> authorities would qualify the plaintiff in these circumstances;
> (b) Actions for 'passing-off' similarly would not avail the plaintiff be-
> cause there was no common field of endeavour between the plaintiff
> and the defendants, there being no evidence that the plaintiff was in
> the business of selling automobiles;

and therefore there is no cause of action known to our law vested in the
respondent.

The respondent founded his claim on the existing principles of trespass
and seeks to apply those principles to the relatively new field of commerce in
which persons such as professional athletes enjoy large incomes from the
possibilities of exploiting the publicity value of their notoriety and personality.
Unfortunately, to date these claims have been confined to very isolated cases
which can be explained on other grounds: *Dixon v. Holden* (1869), L.R. 7 Eq.
488 (later disapproved by the Court in *Prudential Ass'ce Co. v. Knott* (1875),
10 Ch. App. 142); *Routh v. Webster* (1847), 10 Beav. 561, 50 E.R. 698.

The essence of the facts and of the issue arising can be stated as follows:
in producing the Spotter the appellants sought to appeal to followers of football
by providing an attractive and handy device for the better enjoyment of a
televised football game. The appellants have produced this device as a medium
for the advertisement of their automobiles. To attract the attention of the public
a photograph of an interesting event in an actual football game has been
included in the device. The photograph shows players, including the respondent

who alone can be identified by the number in the Spotter if the viewer recognizes his uniform colours as those of the Hamilton team. The simple question put to the Court is: 'Is this actionable by the respondent against the appellants?'

In the classification of claims such as those made herein by the respondent Krouse, the Courts have not been slow either to adapt or extend the ancient principles of law so as to apply them to new conditions prevailing in the community. As was stated by Judson, J., in *Fleming v. Atkinson*, [1959] S.C.R. 513 at p. 535, 18 D.L.R. (2d) 81 at p. 99:

> I can think of no logical basis for this immunity and it can only be based upon a rigid determination to adhere to the rules of the past in spite of changed conditions which call for the application of rules of responsibility which have been worked out to meet modern needs. It has always been assumed that one of the virtues of the common law system is its flexibility, that it is capable of changing with the times and adapting its principles to new conditions.

If any proper base be required for these judicial practices, reference can be made to *Pasley et al. v. Freedman* (1789), 3 T.R. 51, 100 E.R. 450, where Ashhurst, J., stated at p. 63:

> Where cases are new in their principle, there I admit that it is necessary to have recourse to legislative interposition in order to remedy the grievance; but where the case is only new in the instance, and the only question is upon the application of a principle recognized in the law to such new case, it will be just as competent to Courts of Justice to apply the principle to any case which may arise two centuries hence as it was two centuries ago; if it were not, we ought to blot out of our law books one fourth part of the cases that are to be found in them.

The respondent in this Court and below sought to found his claim on several recognized principles to which Courts in the past have resorted where one person with or without the motive of gain has in some way put to use another's name or, for want of a better word, another's personality. Sometimes the action has succeeded in contract, sometimes in tort, and sometimes on some vague theory of property law.

The appropriation of one's image by photography was first dealt with in the Courts in England on the basis of an implied contract not to use the negative produced by the defendant for any commercial purpose without the authority of the person photographed: *Pollard v. Photographic Co.* (1888), 40 Ch.D. 345; *Corelli v. Wall* (1906), 22 T.L.R. 532; *Palmer v. National Sporting Club, Ltd.* (1906), 2 MacG. C.C. 55 (Ch.D.); *Sports & General Press Agency, Ltd. v. 'Our Dogs' Publishing Co. Ltd.*, [1917] 2 K.B. 125.

Sometimes the Courts have sought to find the answer to a claim of appropriation of one's personality in the field of defamation. In *Tolley v. J.S. Fry & Sons, Ltd.*, [1931] A.C. 333, the plaintiff, a prominent amateur golfer, recovered damages for the unauthorized use of his photograph in an advertisement by the defendant of its products which it was held would lead the public to believe that the plaintiff had been paid for this use of his image (when in fact he had not), with the result that his amateur standing, which was of considerable value to him, would be in jeopardy. The respondent Krouse is, of course, in a diametrically opposite position, namely, he is asserting the right to compensation for the use of his image by another for commercial purposes. While this case is of no assistance in the disposition of the issue herein arising, it does illustrate the extent to which customs of the community and commercial practices change so radically over a relatively short period of time, sometimes requiring modification in the application of recognized legal doctrines to meet these new circumstances.

*Clark v. Freeman* (1848), 11 Beav. 109, 50 E.R. 759, is a more drastic illustration of changing times. In that case, a plaintiff physician was unable to obtain an injunction against the defendant, who is advertising a remedy for gout, claimed that the plaintiff, an eminent physician, prescribed the defendant's medicine for this ailment. Lord Langdale in giving judgment did not believe that the plaintiff physician had been seriously injured in his reputation by such false statements by the defendant and indeed concluded that in any event persons of the station of the plaintiff must accept such exposure as the price of eminence. At p. 118, his Lordship stated:

> Other persons try to avail themselves of their names and reputations for the purpose of making profit for themselves; that unfortunately continually happens.

At one time an attempt was made to establish a property right in a name so as to preclude its appropriation by another for his commercial advantage. This claim was advanced in *Dockwell v. Dougall* (1899), 80 L.T. 556; *McCulloch v. Lewis A. May (Produce Distributors), Ltd.*, [1947] 2 All E.R. 845, and *Walter v. Ashton*, [1902] 2 Ch. 282 at p. 293. Momentary success was realized in *Dixon v. Holden* (1869), L.R. 7 Eq. 488, as noted earlier.

A more imaginative basis for this type of action has been explored in the United States where the Courts of New York, for example, found a plaintiff in circumstances not unlike those affecting the respondent in the present proceedings had a right to enjoin the use of his photograph and name on the basis of a violation of his right to publicity: *Haelan Laboratories Inc. v. Topps Chewing Gum* (1953), 202 F. 2d 866. Shortly thereafter the Courts of California declined to extend such a right of action to California law: *Strickler v. National Broadcasting Co.* (1958), 167 F. Supp. 68. Sometimes this type of claim was classified as a breach of privacy and more recently and accurately as breach of the right to publicity. Neither the Courts of England or of this country have as yet recognized such a right.

The learned trial Judge has founded the claim of the respondent in the tort of passing-off. Traditionally the Courts have restricted this doctrine to proceedings where the plaintiff and defendant are competing in a common trade or are each commercially associated in a common sector of the commercial world: *King Features Syndicate Inc. v. Lechter* (1950), 12 C.P.R. 60, [1950] Ex. C.R. 297, 10 Fox Pat. C. 144, and *McCulloch v. Lewis A. May (Produce Distributors), Ltd., supra.* The basis of the actionable wrong of passing-off is misrepresentation 'for any business purpose as to the origin of goods or services which the defendant proposes to or does deal in or employs in the course of business . . .': Fleming, *Law of Torts*, 4th ed. (1971), at p. 627. The confinement of the doctrine of passing-off to these principles formed the basis of the judgment of the House of Lords in *McCulloch v. Lewis A. May (Produce Distributors), Ltd.*, where a well-known broadcaster of children's programmes was unable to restrain a manufacturer of breakfast cereals who used the broadcaster's name as the trade name under which the breakfast cereal was marketed. The House of Lords found that no property existed in the name of the broadcaster, and inasmuch as there was no common field of activity between the plaintiff broadcaster and the defendant manufacturer, there was no action for the tort of passing-off.

It has been argued that the Australian High Court in *Henderson et al. v. Radio Corp. Pty. Ltd.*, [1969] R.P.C. 218, has deleted the requirement of a common field of undertaking from the action of passing-off. In that proceeding the plaintiffs, professional dance instructors, succeeded in enjoining the defendant record manufacturer from selling a dance music recording package in a wrapper on which was printed a photograph of the two plaintiffs dancing. If the case need be distinguished from the case now before us, it may be done on the essential differences in fact. There the plaintiffs carried on an extensive commercial undertaking as dancing instructors and the product sold by the defendant was recorded dance music. The recording of the defendant and the services rendered by the business of the plaintiff appealed to the same sector of the buying public. The association of well-known dancers with a supply of dance music would no doubt associate the plaintiff with the defendant's product so as to enable the latter to gain some immediate trade advantage. The buyer of the record could reasonably be taken to assume participation in some way by the plaintiffs in the production of the recording, although such was not the case in fact. In short, the plaintiffs and the defendant were engaged in a common commercial field, whereas the broadcaster and the cereal manufacturer in *McCulloch v. Lewis A. May (Produce Distributors), Ltd.*, were not.

C.J. Evatt, in giving judgment in the Court of Appeal stated in *Henderson et al. v. Radio Corp. Pty. Ltd.*, [1969] R.P.C. 218 at p. 231:

> The general effect in a shop display is to give prominence to the Hendersons and their dancing: which could easily lead to deception of possible purchasers.'

His Lordship continued at p. 232:

> . . . we are of opinion that the proper finding is that the class of persons for whom the record was primarily intended would probably believe that

the picture of the respondents on the cover indicated their recommendation or approval of the record . . .

The representation that the respondents recommended the record is
an inducement to buy it. The recommendation can only be attributed to
the respondents in their capacity of professional dancers, that is, a recommendation made in the course of their professional activities, and
means that as professional dancers they have associated themselves with
the appellant in promoting sales of the record, and that amounts to a
connexion, in respect of the marketing of the record, between the business of the respondents and the business of the appellant.

The Court, at p. 234, found that in fact the plaintiff's and the defendant's
businesses were competitive.

After a careful review of the evidence and with the greatest respect to the
learned trial Judge, I have concluded that in this case *the tort of passing-off
would appear to have no application to the claim of the respondent because
the buying public would not buy the products of the appellant on the assumption
that they had been designed or manufactured by the respondent, nor would the
public be understood to have accepted the Spotter as being something designed
and produced by the respondent.* Finally, the Spotter was not produced by the
appellants to be passed off on the public in competition with a similar product
marketed by the respondent.

The position of the respondent Krouse is different from the positions of
the several plaintiffs who have in the past asserted the variety of claims that I
have here attempted to classify. Krouse, by reason of his profession as a
professional athlete, has developed a notoriety which is a by-product of his
athletic proficiency. It is doubtless true that his notoriety is smaller in degree
and of lesser commercial significance than that of other professional athletes,
including, perhaps, some of his own teammates. If he has a right known to the
law, however, the difference in commercial value runs to damages and not to
the presence or absence of a cause of action. Thus, I have approached the
respondent's position on the basis that he is a well-known professional athlete,
and while he may be a player of lesser public following than others, he is
certainly prominent in the field of professional sport in the eyes of those
following football in this Province, and that he has the same rights, if any, as
those enjoyed by the better-known personalities in professional sport.

The appellants were not passing out the Spotter as a public service. In a
calculated fashion they incurred the expense of producing the Spotter for the
avowed purpose of improving the sales of their automobiles. In designing the
Spotter to include the representation of an identifiable football player, in this
case the respondent, they must be taken to have included the football action
picture deliberately, either to attract the public to the Spotter as a ready identification device which could be tested on the spot with reference to No. 14, or
to make the Spotter immediately attractive to the eyes of the potential automobile buyers, so as to lure thereby the recipient of the Spotter into a study of
the products of the appellants in the hope of inducing him thereafter to purchase

an automobile of the appellant Chrysler's manufacture. Perhaps the appellants had both objects in mind.

Such a use of the respondent's image certainly does not suggest an express endorsement by him of the represented products of the appellants as in the case of athletes who appear on television or in the newspaper advertisements driving automobiles and praising their qualities. Nor does it appear to be an endorsement by implication or inference of the automobiles of the appellants. Had the respondent been depicted standing by or sitting in an automobile such an inference might arise, but I do not believe that a reasonable inference of endorsement or approval by the respondent of the appellants' products can be drawn from the presence of the respondent in the photograph included on one side of the Spotter.

It therefore remains to be determined whether the use of the respondent's image by the appellants in this way *is a wrongful appropriation, and therefore as urged by counsel a trespass against the respondent's right to realize, if he can, a commercial advantage from the notoriety which professional athletes in our community and in these times possess.*

Trespass would not in any case appear to be the appropriate basis for any such alleged wrongful appropriation since such a wrong would fall within the classification of an action on the case, or in more recent legal history in an action for trover or conversion in its modern form. Thus, the plaintiff must prove both injury and damages if he is to succeed in the action. In that connection I note that the evidence indicates that after the issuance of the writ of summons herein the respondent Krouse was able to realize some slight tangible benefit from the commercial community by licensing the use of his image or personality.

*There is indeed some support in our law for the recognition of a remedy for the appropriation for commercial purposes of another's likeness, voice or personality. Tolley v. J.S. Fry and Sons Limited, supra,* although based in the law of libel does in the end protect a public athletic figure from invasion of or aggression against his status as an athlete by commercial interests for their gain. *Thus far the Courts in this country and the United Kingdom have declined to found an award on any broad basis such as appropriation of personality or even an injury to the latent power of endorsement.* Even in the United States such judgments, as have been granted, are largely based on statute. Indeed, the right first recognized in this general area of the law, the right to privacy, has been held by the Court of Appeals of the State of New York not to apply to the incidental telecasting without authorization of a professional entertainer on a commercial television programme: *Gautier v. Pro-Football, Inc.* (1952), 304 N.Y. 354. There is, of course, no privacy legislation in Ontario. The authorities in this branch of the law have been collected and reviewed by D.L. Mathieson in 'Comments', 39 *Can. Bar Rev.* 409 (1961).

I, therefore, conclude from the foregoing examination of the authorities in the several fields of tort related to the allegations made herein that the *common law does contemplate a concept in the law of torts which may be broadly classified as an appropriation of one's personality.* Assuming the existence of such a wrong in our law, it remains to be determined whether the respondent has established that the appellants have committed such a wrong and have thereby damaged the respondent.

It is clear from the evidence and by the slightest exercise of judicial notice that our community to date recognizes by contract the right of the professional athlete and persons otherwise in the public eye to commercialize on their notoriety. The law of contract is regularly invoked to make the personal attributes which are attached to such people by the community, the subject of commerce. On the other hand, it is equally clear that professional sport, either at the entrepreneurial or participant's level, invites the widest possible coverage and publicity from the communications media. The photograph on the Spotter was taken pursuant to authorization granted by the CFL and the Hamilton team for such publicity purposes. The licence so granted has not been restricted expressly or by implication to the mere reporting of the football games themselves. Newspapers, magazines and television regularly produce articles, features and discussions about the game of football, past and present, and an almost endless flow of facts and speculations concerning individual games and participating players. In these general commentaries the reader or the viewer is also exposed to events occurring in games and in or about the lives of the participating professional athletes, all with at least the tacit approval of those who apparently benefit from such publicity, namely, the owners of the teams, and the individual players. Exposure would appear to be the life-blood of professional sport. Thus, in the real world of professional sport and promotional publicity in the communications media, some minor loss of privacy and even some loss of potential for commercial exploitation must be expected to occur as a by-product of the express or implied licence to publicize the institution of the game itself. In my view, that is what has happened in this case.

[. . .]

The danger of extending the law of torts to cover every such exposure in public not expressly authorized is obvious. Progress in the law is not served by the recognition of a right which, while helpful to some persons or classes of persons, turns out to be unreasonable disruption to the community at large and to the conduct of its commerce. Much of this publicity will in reality be a mixed blessing involving the promotion of the game itself, but at the same time resulting in some minor or theoretical invasion of a player's individual potential for gainful exploitation. By way of illustration, a sports report on television might expose a motion or still picture of one or more well-known players immediately before or after the telecasting of a commercial message by an enterprise not associated with the telecasting of football games. The public in our community would not consider any players so represented on the screen as thereby endorsing the products advertised on the same programme, nor would a viewer reasonably associate in any other way the players so depicted and the product mentioned in the programme's commercial messages. Thus, it would be a gross exaggeration to say that the usefulness of the player's name or image in some form of commercial exploitation in the advertising world was thereby diminished. The use by the appellants of the respondent's image in this case is in no way parallel to the use of a hockey player's signature on a hockey stick, or of a photograph of a professional athlete driving an automobile of the advertisers. Aside from the laws of defamation, the Courts have not heretofore found it appropriate to bring acts of the kind complained of in the particular facts of this proceeding within the purview of the law of torts.

As I have indicated, there may well be circumstances in which the Courts would be justified in holding a defendant liable in damages for appropriation of a plaintiff's personality, amounting to an invasion of his right to exploit his personality by the use of his image, voice or otherwise with damage to the plaintiff, but after a careful review of the evidence in the present action, I have come to the conclusion that the respondent has not demonstrated any infringement by the appellants of any legal right of the respondent. I would, therefore, allow the appeal with costs, set aside the judgment in appeal, and direct that judgment issue in place thereof dismissing the action with costs.[12] [emphasis added; footnotes omitted]

The tort was invoked successfully in *Athans v. Canadian Adventure Camps Ltd.*[13] The "signature image" of a well-known water-skier, George Athans, had been copied and published as a line drawing in a brochure prepared for advertising a summer camp for children. The defendants intended to depict a water-skier in action, since water-skiing was an important part of the camp program. The court, on the basis of *Krouse*, awarded $500 in damages.[14]

In a case opposing the estate of Tim Horton, a famous Toronto Maple Leafs hockey player, to a donut company that now bears his name, the court added that "the gravamen of the [*Krouse*] tort is the usurpation of the plaintiff's right to control and market his own image. Implicit in this is the protected right of the celebrity to profit from the use of his or her personality and to decide how that profit is to be earned."[15] The court applied a "sales v. subject" distinction to balance the individual's interest in personality rights with the public interest in expression; under this standard, the use of a persona for a commercial object ("sales') would be actionable but the use

---

[12] *Ibid.* (per Este J.A.). See also *Holdke v. Calgary Convention Centre Authority* (2000), 265 A.R. 381 (Alta. Prov. Ct.).

[13] (1977), 17 O.R. (2d) 425, 80 D.L.R. (3d) 583, 34 C.P.R. (2d) 126 (Ont. H.C.).

[14] See also *Joseph v. Daniels* (1986), 4 B.C.L.R. (2d) 239, 11 C.P.R. (3d) 544 (B.C. S.C.); *Gould Estate v. Stoddart Publishing Co.* (1996), 30 O.R. (3d) 520, 74 C.P.R. (3d) 206 (Ont. Gen. Div.), affirmed (1998), 39 O.R. (3d) 545 (Ont. C.A.), leave to appeal refused (1999), 82 C.P.R. (3d) vi (S.C.C.).

[15] *Horton v. Tim Donut Ltd.* (1997), 75 C.P.R. (3d) 451 (Ont. Gen. Div.), affirmed (1997), 104 O.A.C. 234 (Ont. C.A.) at 459 [C.P.R.].

of a persona as the "subject" (for example, in a biography) would be protected free expression.

A combination of copyright, trade-mark, and tort law is used to protect real persons or personae created by actors. Sometimes all three forms of protection may be combined (*e.g.*, copyright in a script or set sketches, trade-mark use of a person's name or image, and the tort of misappropriation), although usually only one or two are applicable. It is important to distinguish the underlying rationale for this protection from the rationale underlying the tort of invasion of privacy in cases involving the use of an *unknown* person's name or likeness without that person's authorization. With invasion of privacy, the damage suffered is a significant reduction in the person's anonymity and sphere of privacy.[16] That loss of privacy may in fact prove to be economically valuable but it affects the person's day-to-day activities and is a loss of control and autonomy. In the case of a famous person or persona, unauthorized reuse is a form of rent dissipation.[17] In other words, someone is (mis-)using a famous person's name or likeness in a way that is likely to affect the famous person's ability to maximize "celebrity income." Both torts involve a loss of autonomy and control.

Where a human actor is identified strongly with a single fictional character "persona", as for example with Minnie Pearl, Pee Wee Herman or Groucho Marx, that person may have legal rights in the character through appropriation of personality law. By comparison, where an actor or actress portrays a fictional character, but that character is merely one role among many for the actor, the actor usually cannot use the appropriation of personality tort to recover for personal injuries resulting from someone else reproducing the character they portray. However, the rights holder(s) for that character can bring copyright and trade-mark actions for infringement.

Other sources to protect aspects of personality include moral rights and performers' rights (see the Copyright section), confidential information, invasion of privacy tort law, trade-mark and passing off, and contract law.

## II. COPYRIGHT AND INDUSTRIAL DESIGNS

The overlap between copyright and industrial designs is the only one to be regulated in the applicable statutes. It is possible in some circumstances to have protection under both copyright and industrial design law.

---

[16] See *Cohen c. Queenswear International Ltd.* (1989), [1989] Q.J. No. 893, [1989] R.R.A. 570 (Que. S.C.).

[17] See *Cranston v. Canadian Broadcasting Corp.* (1994), 2 C.C.E.L. (2d) 301 (Ont. Gen. Div.).

The *Copyright Act* and the *Industrial Design Act* use similar definitions of "design" in s. 2. The *Industrial Design Act* also specifies that it does not protect those features of a useful article that are solely utilitarian, defined as "a function other than merely serving as a substrate or carrier for artistic or literary matter."[18] Nor does it protect methods of manufacture.

Section 64 of the *Copyright Act* describes the scope of copyright in relation to industrial designs:[19]

Where copyright subsists in a design applied to a useful article or in an artistic work from which the design is derived and, by or under the authority of any person who owns the copyright in Canada or who owns the copyright elsewhere,

(*a*) the article is reproduced in a quantity of more than fifty, or
(*b*) where the article is a plate, engraving or cast, the article is used for producing more than fifty useful articles,

it shall not thereafter be an infringement of the copyright or the moral rights for anyone

(*c*) to reproduce the design of the article or a design not differing substantially from the design of the article by

(i) making the article, or
(ii) making a drawing or other reproduction in any material form of the article, or

(*d*) to do with an article, drawing or reproduction that is made as described in paragraph (*c*) anything that the owner of the copyright has the sole right to do with the design or artistic work in which the copyright subsists.

---

[18] *Copyright Act* R.S.C. 1985, c. C-42, s. 64 (1), online: Department of Justice Canada <http://laws.justice.gc.ca/en/C-42/index.html> and *Industrial Design Act*, R.S.C. 1985, c. I-9, s.2, online: Department of Justice Canada <http://laws.justice.gc.ca/en/I-9/text.html>. See *DRG Inc. v. Datafile Ltd.* (1991), [1991] F.C.J. No. 144, 35 C.P.R. (3d) 243, 117 N.R. 308, 1991 CarswellNat 1123 (Fed. C.A.). A substrate or carrier would be paper, holiday greeting cards, posters etc.

[19] It is interesting to compare the two linguistic versions of this provision, bearing in mind that both have equal value under the *Official Languages Act*, R.S., 1985, c. 31, s.13. n This version of s. 64 applies to designs created after June 8, 1988 (see s. 64(1) and (4) and *Milliken & Co. v. Interface Flooring Systems (Canada) Inc.* (2000), [2000] F.C.J. No. 129, 5 C.P.R. (4th) 209, 251 N.R. 358, 2000 CarswellNat 177 (Fed. C.A.) [*Milliken* cited to C.P.R.].

(3) Subsection (2) does not apply in respect of the copyright or the moral rights in an artistic work in so far as the work is used as or for

> (*a*) a graphic or photographic representation that is applied to the face of an article;
> (*b*) a trade-mark or a representation thereof or a label;
> (*c*) material that has a woven or knitted pattern or that is suitable for piece goods or surface coverings or for making wearing apparel;
> (*d*) an architectural work that is a building or a model of a building;
> (*e*) a representation of a real or fictitious being, event or place that is applied to an article as a feature of shape, configuration, pattern or ornament;
> (*f*) articles that are sold as a set, unless more than fifty sets are made; or
> (*g*) such other work or article as may be prescribed by regulation.

In order for it not to infringe, the copyright owner has to have authorized the making of more than 50 articles. Where a copyrighted design is applied to a useful article,[20] and the person who owns the copyright authorizes it being reproduced in quantities greater than 50, then after those 50 are reproduced, it does not infringe copyright if someone else reproduces the design by making the *article* or any reproduction in material form of the article, or anything else the copyright owner would otherwise have sole right to do in respect of the article. Section 64(3) specifies that articles in a set should be counted as one unit, so that more than fifty *sets* will lead to a loss of copyright protection. The fact that reproducing a *design* applied to an article is not an infringement of copyright or moral rights where the article is reproduced in more than 50 units is a strong incentive to apply for industrial design protection. (The rationale for the registration process was discussed in the Industrial Designs section.)

In *Milliken*,[21] the Federal Court of Appeal explained that under s. 64, a difference should be made between designs applied to an article, and those applied to a "useful" article:[22]

> The words in the definition of design are 'in a finished article' not, as the appellants argue, in a 'finished useful article.' The omission of the word 'useful' in the definition of design was not accidental. The words 'article' and 'useful

---

[20] It should also be noted that the exception applies to a "useful article" defined in s. 64(1) of the *Copyright Act* (as in s. 2 of the *Industrial Designs Act*) as an article that has a utilitarian function, *i.e.*, a "function other than merely serving as a substrate or carrier for artistic or literary matter." The expression is also used, though not defined, in s. 13 of the *Trade-Marks Act* (see the Trade-Marks and Industrial Designs section *infra*.)

[21] *Idem.*

[22] See *supra*, note 19 at 218-19 [emphasis added].

article' are separately defined, 'article' being quite general and 'useful article' being more specific. 'Useful article' means an article that has a 'utilitarian function'. 'Utilitarian function' is defined, in part, as a 'function other than merely serving as a substrate or carrier for artistic or literary matter.' *It is clear that the general term 'article' includes useful articles and articles that are not useful articles. Thus a finished article in the definition of design need not be a useful article. Therefore, whether an artistic work is or is not a design is not dependent upon it having been applied to a useful article.* Had that been the case, I think the adjective 'useful' would have been included in the definition of 'design' rather than the adjective 'finished'.

This conclusion is consistent with subsection 64(2), which states that it will not infringe copyright to reproduce designs which are applied to useful articles in specified circumstances. The opening words of subsection 64(2) that 'Where copyright subsists in a design applied to a useful article . . .' show, first, that copyright may subsist in a design and, second, that contrary to the appellants' argument, the creation of the design may pre-exist its application to a useful article. By necessary implication, if a design may be applied to a useful article, the existence of that design may be independent of the useful article. *Had Parliament intended that for the purposes of subsection 64(2), a design does not come into existence until is actually applied to a useful article, words to that effect would have been used.*

The appellants point to the words in subsection 64(2) '. . . or in an artistic work from which the design is derived . . .' to argue that the artistic work and the design are necessarily different and that prior to application to a useful article, the work is an artistic work and only becomes a design when applied to the useful article. While these words indicate that the artistic work and design may be different, they are not necessarily so. These words contemplate the situation in which a design applied to a useful article is not the artistic work itself but is derived from the artistic work. The words 'in an artistic work from which the design is derived' do not mean that a design does not come into existence until applied to a useful article.

In summary, the *Copyright Act* provides that copyrighted articles lose their copyright protection when they are designs lawfully applied to a useful article (*e.g.*, a boat, a chair) and there are more than 50 units of them. In that case, subject to the formalities provided therein, the *Industrial Design Act* will protect the visual elements of designs (that "appeal to and are judged solely by the eye") that are applied to manufactured objects. It is important to note that once 51 copies have been made with the copyright owner's consent, copyright protection in the article is lost, whether or not industrial design protection is applied for.[23]

---

[23] See *Bayliner Marine Corp. v. Doral Boats Ltd.*, [1986] 3 F.C. 421, 10 C.P.R. (3d) 289, 67 N.R. 139 (Fed. C.A.), leave to appeal to S.C.C. refused (1986), [1986] S.C.C.A. No. 358, 1986 CarswellNat 1262 (S.C.C.) [*Bayliner*].

Section 64(3) provides exceptions to the exceptions. In spite of the above, copyright continues to subsist in the following even where more than fifty copies are made:

- A trade-mark design;
- Labels;
- Architectural work that is building or model of building;
- Textile design; but the clothing loses copyright protection;
- Character merchandising: real or fictitious being, event or place that is applied to article as feature of shape
- Graphic Design on face of article;

If the owner of copyright did not consent to the mass production of more than 50 articles, copyright still applies in the design, but not to the article.

Section 64.1 of the *Copyright Act,* in keeping with the above-mentioned principles, adds a number of exceptions which permit people to use functional features of a work without infringing copyright:

> The following acts do not constitute an infringement of the copyright or moral rights in a work:
>
> (*a*) applying to a useful article features that are dictated solely by a utilitarian function of the article;
>
> (*b*) by reference solely to a useful article, making a drawing or other reproduction in any material form of any features of the article that are dictated solely by a utilitarian function of the article;
>
> (*c*) doing with a useful article having only features described in paragraph (*a*), or with a drawing or reproduction made as described in paragraph (*b*), anything that the owner of the copyright has the sole right to do with the work; and
>
> (*d*) using any method or principle of manufacture or construction.

While s. 64 limits copyright protection in a design applied to a useful article when more than 50 copies of the useful article are made, s. 64.1 allows use of the utilitarian functions of an article. A person will not infringe if she can show that a feature applied to an article was "dictated solely by a utilitarian function of the article." It is important to note that this exception is limited by the word "solely" in subs (a) and (b). The presence of functional elements in a protected design will not be sufficient to defeat copyright protection if non-utilitarian features are copied.[24] This may apply, for ex-

---

[24] See *Northwest Marine Technology Inc. v. Crosby* (1996), 75 C.P.R. (3d) 491 (B.C. S.C.).

ample, to certain spare parts for automobiles and trucks which have an aesthetic component in addition to meeting required safety standards.

As explained in *CCH Canadian Ltd. v. Law Society of Upper Canada*,[25] copyright protects creative choices, defined as non-mechanical, non trivial choices. Choices dictated solely by utilitarian (as defined in the Act) considerations are thus excluded from copyright protection. This is essentially what s. 64.1 codified.[26]

A good example of the overlap is found in *Bayliner*.[27] The plaintiff made plans for a boat and then made what is called a "plug," *i.e.*, a three-

---

[25] [2004] 1 S.C.R. 339, 236 D.L.R. (4th) 395, 30 C.P.R. (4th) 1, 317 N.R. 107 (S.C.C.). See the discussion on Originality in the Copyright Section.

[26] The section was added to the Act in 1988. This may have been in reaction to the decision of the House of Lords in *British Leyland Motor Corp. v. Armstrong Patents Co.*, [1986] A.C. 577 (U.K. H.L.), which held the following:

> It seems to me that when one is considering machinery which is not the subject of any patent protection, it is unnecessary and may be misleading to introduce the concept of an implied licence. The owner of a car must be entitled to do whatever is necessary to keep it in running order and to effect whatever repairs may be necessary in the most economical way possible. To derive this entitlement from an implied licence granted by the original manufacturer seems to me quite artificial. It is a right inherent in the ownership of the car itself. To curtail or restrict the owner's right to repair in any way may diminish the value of the car. In the field of patent law it may be right to start from the patentee's express monopoly and see how far it is limited by exceptions. In the field of law applied to machinery which enjoys no patent protection, it seems to me appropriate to start from a consideration of the rights of the owner of the machinery and then to see how far the law will permit some conflicting legal claim to impinge upon those rights. I can see no reason to doubt that any owner of a BL car might exercise his right to repair the car, whenever the exhaust pipe needs replacement, by producing an exact copy of the original pipe in his own workshop or by instructing the local blacksmith to do the same.

This is not an altogether different conclusion than the one reached in *Galerie d'art du Petit Champlain inc. c. Théberge*, [2002] 2 S.C.R. 336, (sub nom. *Théberge v. Galerie d'Art du Petit Champlain inc.*) 210 D.L.R. (4th) 385, (sub nom. *Théberge v. Galerie d'Art du Petit Champlain inc.*) 17 C.P.R. (4th) 161, (sub nom. *Théberge v. Galerie d'art du Petit Champlain inc.*) 285 N.R. 267 (S.C.C.) at para. 33, where the majority held that a case opposing a painter (artist) to the owner of legally produced posters of one of his paintings demonstrated "the basic economic conflict between the holder of the intellectual property in a work and the owner of the tangible property that embodies the copyrighted expressions."

[27] See *supra*, note 23. At the time, s. 46 (now 64) of the *Copyright Act* read as follows: "This Act does not apply to designs capable of being registered under

dimensional rendering of the boat based on the designs. Plastic moulds were made from that plug. The defendant, rather than go through the cost of designing a boat from scratch, used the plaintiff's *boat* itself to come up with the defendant's design for a boat. In other words, the defendant bought boats, stripped them down, and used those as the superstructure for its own boats. They added aesthetic features copied from the plaintiff's boats. The plaintiff claimed the defendant had infringed copyright in its drawing designs. The Federal Court of Appeal found that the plaintiff's boat design should have been registered. The plaintiff intended to produce more than 50 boats from his design, and those boats were made from an industrial process. In so finding the Court noted the following:

> It is, I think, pertinent to observe that this case is concerned with the statutory monopoly accorded by the *Copyright Act*. It is not concerned with unfair competition or issues of commercial morality.
>
> The designs disclosed by the plans in issue are, in my opinion, designs capable of being registered under the *Industrial Design Act* within the meaning of s. 46 of the *Copyright Act* and are not excluded from the operation of that provision by s. 11 of the Industrial *Designs Rules*. The plans themselves are not, therefore, subject of copyright.[28]

Absent the exception in s. 46 (now 64), copying from a three-dimensional version of the two-dimensional copyrighted design can infringe the plans, as would producing plans of a three-dimensional design. The second work may itself be original in certain circumstances (if it is not a mere copy and the second author added creative choices), but still infringing for reproducing a substantial part of the original work.

---

the Industrial Design Act, except designs that, though capable of being so registered, are not used or intended to be used as models or patterns to be multiplied by any industrial process." It had to be read in conjunction with rule. 11(1) of the Industrial Designs Rules (C.R.C. 1978, c. 964), which reads as follows:

> A design shall be deemed to be used as a model or pattern to be multiplied by any industrial process within the meaning of section 46 of the *Copyright Act*,
>
> (a) where the design is reproduced or is intended to be reproduced in more than 50 single articles, unless all the articles in which the design is reproduced or is intended to be reproduced together form only a single set as defined in subsection 2; and
>
> (b) where the design is to be applied to(i)printed paper hangings,(ii)carpets, floor cloths, or oil cloths manufactured or sold in lengths or pieces,(iii) textile piece goods, or textile goods manufactured or sold in lengths or pieces, and(iv) lace, not made by hand.

[28] *Supra*, note 23 at paras. 18 and 19.

In *Import-Export René Derhy (Canada) inc. c. Magasins Greenberg ltée*,[29] the Quebec Court of Appeal explained the difference between ss. 64(2) and (3). The case dealt with a vest sold under the name "BARBITAL" on which an artistic design had been sewn. The Court found that while the vests were not protected by copyright (under s. 64(2)), taking only the sewn design and applying it to a different article did infringe copyright, because the work was listed in s. 64(3) "textile design".

In other cases, s. 64(2) was found to apply to a "portal crane,"[30] but not to tax forms,[31] football coupons,[32] pictograms,[33] and design plans.[34] Whether jewellery is a "useful" article under s. 64(2) is currently being considered by the courts.[35]

## III. COPYRIGHT AND TOPOGRAPHIES

The *Copyright Act* provides a specific exception for topographies (see the Topographies Section). Section 64.2(1) reads as follows:

> This Act does not apply, and shall be deemed never to have applied, to any topography or to any design, however expressed, that is intended to generate all or part of a topography.

## IV. PATENTS AND COPYRIGHT

There are some perhaps counter-intuitive lines drawn between copyright and patents. Software, for example, is treated as a literary work under copyright rather than as patentable subject matter.

One of the most significant overlaps between patent and copyright is patent drawings. Most patents contain one or more drawings of an example of an object embodying the invention. These drawings are artistic works and protected as such under the *Copyright* Act. Can the copyright protection

---

[29] (2004), [2004] J.Q. No. 2705, 2004 CarswellQue 566 (Que. C.A.).

[30] See *Harnischfeger Corp. of Canada v. Kranco Inc.* (1991), [1991] B.C.J. No. 2993, 39 C.P.R. (3d) 81, 1991 CarswellBC 1185 (B.C. S.C.).

[31] See *U & R Tax Services Ltd. v. H & R Block Canada Inc.* (1995), [1995] F.C.J. No. 962, 62 C.P.R. (3d) 257, 97 F.T.R. 259, 1995 CarswellNat 1343 (Fed. T.D.).

[32] See *In the Matter of the Application of Littlewoods Pools, Ltd., to Register a Design* (1949), 66 R.P.C. 309 (U.K.).

[33] See *2426-7536 Quebec Inc. v. Provigo Distribution Inc.* (1992), 50 C.P.R. (3d) 539(Que. S.C.)

[34] See *idem*.

[35] See *Pyrrha Design Inc. v. 623735 Saskatchewan Ltd.* (2004), [2004] F.C.J. No. 2084, 2004 CarswellNat 4660 (F.C.A.).

for the drawings be used to extend the patent protection?[36] By corollary, is the copyright term in drawings reduced or waived when the drawings are filed as part of the patent application?

One should note, first, that the *Patent Act* encourages people to make information public. This is why the *Act* requires the applicant to "correctly and fully describe the invention and its operation or use as contemplated by the inventor" and "set out clearly the various steps in a process, or the method of constructing, making, compounding or using a machine, manufacture or composition of matter, in such full, clear, concise and exact terms as to enable any person skilled in the art or science to which it pertains, or with which it is most closely connected, to make, construct, compound or use it."[37] Copyright does not have the same purpose. Even unpublished works are protected. Its purpose it to prevent people from reproducing copyrighted works, such as drawings, or a substantial part thereof.

The conflict between the two forms of protection was raised in a number of court cases. In *Burnaby Machine & Mill Equipment Ltd. v. Berglund Industrial Supply Co.*,[38] Walsh J. wrote:

> On the present motion defendants argue, inter alia, that a valid copyright registration cannot be obtained for the drawings incorporated in a patent registration in order to attempt to obtain protection for machinery made from the drawing long after the patent for the machinery itself has expired. As authority for this reference was made to the case of *Catnic Components Ltd. et al. v. Hill & Smith Ltd.*, [1978] F.S.R. 405 at pp. 427-8, in which Mr. Justice Whitford stated:
>
> > 'In my view, by applying for a patent an accepting the statutory obligation to describe and if necessary illustrate embodiments of his invention, a patentee necessarily makes an election accepting that, in return for a potential monopoly, upon publication, the material disclosed by him in the specification must be deemed to be open to be used by the public, subject only to such monopoly rights as he may acquire on his application for the patent and during the period for which his monopoly remains in force, whatever be the reason for the determination of the monopoly rights. If this be correct, and even if I were wrong in the view which I have expressed that 'D3' and 'D4' do not infringe, upon publication, the plaintiffs must be deemed to have abandoned their copyright in drawings the equivalent of the patent drawings.'

---

[36] See J.P. Mikus, "Of Industrious Authors and Artful Inventors: Industrial Works andSoftware at the Frontier of Copyright and Patent Law", (2004) 18 *I.P.J.* 187.

[37] *Patent Act*, R.S.C. 1985, c. P-4, ss. 27(2) and (3), online: Department of Justice Canada: <http://laws.justice.gc.ca/en/p-4/text.html>.

[38] (1984), 81 C.P.R. (2d) 251 (Fed. T.D.).

In *Rucker Co. v. Gavel's Vulcanizing Ltd.*,[39] the plaintiff had copyright in engineering designs in safety valve for oil rigs. The engineering designs were protected by copyright. The plaintiff later filed for a patent and included drawings. The drawings in the patent application were not identical to the copyrighted engineering designs, but they both related to the subject matter of the patent. The plaintiff claimed that the defendant infringed his patent and infringed his copyrighted designs. The Court (also Walsh J.) concluded as follows:

> [T]o give the wide interpretation sought by defendant to copyright protection for the drawings would defeat the time limitation provided for in the *Patent Act*. Most mechanical patents have drawings in connection therewith and the drawings can readily be copyrighted, but when patent infringement protection is no longer available to the owner of the patent it is not desirable that he should be able to extend this protection by application of the *Copyright Act* to the drawings from which the physical object covered by the patent was constructed, and thereby prevent anyone else from manufacturing the same device, even without the use of the drawings. I strongly believe that it was not the intention of Parliament nor from a practical view is it desirable that the *Patent Act,* the *Copyright Act,* and the *Industrial Design Act* should be interpreted so as to give overlapping protection.

These decisions seem to stand for the proposition that one waives copyright in drawings submitted with a patent application. A contrary view was taken by the Quebec Superior Court in *R. c. Boutin,*[40] where the Court found that the two forms of protection were independent and should be interpreted as such.

There may be a way to reconcile these cases. Because one of the main purposes of the *Patent Act* is to inform the public of an invention and to let them use it, either during the patent term in the very limited ways allowed under the Act or after the expiry of the term of protection, it would be reasonable to conclude that drawings submitted as part of a patent application are subject to an implied licence, allowing anyone to use them in ways connected to the use of the patented invention. Beyond that licence, the drawings retain copyright protection. It is similarly clear that, while the normal rule is that making a three-dimensional object from a two-dimensional drawing would normally infringe the copyright in the drawings, one does not, also on the basis of an implied licence, infringe copyright in patent drawings by making the patented invention after the expiry of the patent.

---

[39] (1985), [1985] F.C.J. No. 1031, 7 C.P.R. (3d) 294, 6 C.I.P.R. 137, 1985 CarswellNat 571 (Fed. T.D.), varied (1987), 14 C.P.R. (3d) 439 (Fed. T.D.) at para. 34 [*Rucker* cited to C.P.R.].

[40] (1997), [1997] A.Q. No. 3111, 1997 CarswellQue 909 (C.Q.).

This interpretation accords with the conclusion that if drawings filed with a patent application were made by someone other than the applicant and stolen or otherwise used without the artist's authorization, it would still be an infringement of copyright. However, when the drawings are filed voluntarily by the copyright holder or with her consent, the Patent Office as well as third parties are impliedly licensed to use such drawings and make the three-dimensional object (if any) described as the invention after the expiry of the patent term. It is a necessary part of submitting a patent application. The applicant knows in advance that the application will be published 18 months after filing, that it will be included in searchable databases, and that it will be read (and in most cases copied and/or communicated for that purpose) by third parties to determine whether they could be infringing, and after the expiry of the patent, to learn its teachings, which at that point form part of the public domain.

Once the patent term expires, the drawings in the patent application can be used for purposes related to the patented invention; copyright, in other words, cannot be used to subvert the patent objective of public disclosure. However, the expiration of the patent term does not undermine the copyright and *its* purposes. Thus, the drawings are still protected against unauthorized reproduction for purposes that are not related to patent disclosure. This is also assuming that the patent applicant owned the copyright in the drawings.

Another area of potential overlap is software and software-based inventions. As discussed in the Patent section, it is still difficult to obtain patent protection in Canada for software and software-based inventions, such as Internet business models. While software code and the visual/audiovisual output generated while running a program can both be protected under copyright (subject to the usual requirements, including minimal originality), obtaining a patent may confer a broader form of protection on the method of doing something which uses a computer or network of computers than the protection conferred by copyright on the exact implementation (code). In a situation where both a patent and copyright were obtained for software, courts should carefully separate the two forms of protection and not prolong the life of a patent under the guise of copyright, while at the same time not reducing copyright protection applicable to the code and (audio)visual output available under copyright law.

## V. TRADE-MARKS AND INDUSTRIAL DESIGNS

The overlap between trade-marks and industrial designs is regulated in part by statute. Section 13 of the *Trade-Marks Act* reads as follows:

> (1) A distinguishing guise is registrable only if

(*a*) it has been so used in Canada by the applicant or his predecessor in title as to have become distinctive at the date of filing an application for its registration; and

(*b*) the exclusive use by the applicant of the distinguishing guise in association with the wares or services with which it has been used *is not likely unreasonably to limit the development of any art or industry.*

(2) No registration of a distinguishing guise *interferes with the use of any utilitarian feature embodied in the distinguishing guise*

(3) The registration of a distinguishing guise may be expunged by the Federal Court on the application of any interested person if the Court decides that the registration *has become likely unreasonably to limit the development of any art or industry.* [emphasis added]

The overlap between trade-marks and industrial design law is neither entirely regulated nor prohibited. The Act prohibits the grant of trade-mark *registration* (or expungement of same) when a guise *is "likely unreasonably to limit the development of any art or industry,"* but that does not prevent recourse to common law protection.

The purpose is clear. As noted by MacGuiguan J.A. in *Remington Rand Corp. v. Philips Electronics N.V.*:

Whatever the portion of the sales market in question, registration of a primarily functional mark is a restraint on manufacturing and trade, since it effectively amounts to a patent or industrial design in the guise of a trade mark.[41]

In a 2003 decision,[42] the Federal Court considered the overlap in deciding whether one could protect subject matter as a distinguishing guise under trade-mark law after the registration as an industrial design for the same subject matter had expired. This case involved a sloped roof design for outside garbage containers that was intended to foil attempts by wild animals to open the lids. The design had been registered as an industrial design but the registration had expired. Kelen J. reviewed applicable law and concluded that trade-mark and industrial design are not mutually exclusive protections:

---

[41] (1995), [1995] F.C.J. No. 1660, 64 C.P.R. (3d) 467, 191 N.R. 204, 1995 CarswellNat 1846 (Fed. C.A.), leave to appeal to S.C.C. refused (1996), [1996] S.C.C.A. No. 78, 1996 CarswellNat 3160 (S.C.C.) at 476 [*Remington Rand* cited to C.P.R.]. See also *WCC Containers Sales Ltd. v. Haul-All Equipment Ltd.* (2003), [2003] F.C.J. No. 1266, 28 C.P.R. (4th) 175, 238 F.T.R. 45, 2003 CarswellNat 5181 (F.C.) [*WCC Containers* cited to C.P.R.].

[42] *WCC Containers Sales Ltd. v. Haul-All Equipment Ltd., ibid* at paras. 60-64.

The genesis of WCC's argument can be found in an article from Mr. Gordon J. Zimmerman, a Canadian intellectual property lawyer, entitled 'Extending the Monopoly? The Risks and Benefits of Multiple Forms of Intellectual Property Protection' (2001) 17 C.I.P.R. 345 at pp. 347, 364-367. At page 347 of his article, Mr. Zimmerman summarized his rationale for prohibiting the issuance of a distinguishing guise trade-mark if the same design has previously been the subject of an industrial design registration:

> There is, however, a very good argument for disallowing trade-mark protection in aesthetic features previously protected by a now-expired industrial design, because essentially the same thing is sought to be protected by each. The owner's reputation in association with the design may grow free of competition during the term of the design registration; to allow unlimited trade-mark protection following expiry of the design registration may well unreasonably limit development of the relevant art or industry. Unreasonableness may flow from reneging on the promise to dedicate the design to the public following expiry of the design registration.

Neither the *Trade-marks Act* nor the *Industrial Design Act* contain a statutory provision that prohibits the scenario outlined by Mr. Zimmerman. This can be contrasted with section 64 of the *Copyright Act*, R.S.C. 1985, c. C-42 as amended, which removes articles with a utilitarian function from the scope of copyright protection and thereby prevents overlapping protection with the *Industrial Design Act*. The solution proposed by Mr. Zimmerman is to derive a statutory basis from paragraph 13(1)(b) by finding that it is unreasonable to extend the industrial design monopoly by means of a distinguishing guise. WCC also claims this prohibition can be founded in paragraph 18(1)(b). It argues that after the term of an industrial design registration expires, the design becomes dedicated to the public and cannot be considered distinctive, the design being neither 'adopted to distinguish' nor 'actually distinguishing' the holder's wares from those of others. In support of this proposition, WCC has submitted an affidavit dated November 15, 2001 from Mr. David J. French, a Canadian intellectual property lawyer, in which he deposed at paragraph 35:

> Mere sale of products on an exclusive basis during the monopoly period afforded by an industrial design registration would not necessarily be indicative of the use of a distinguishing guise as a trademark as much as it would be indicative of the advantage afforded by the industrial design monopoly. Indeed, it could be that exclusive use established during a period of monopoly would not meet the 'distinctiveness' requirement as envisioned by the trademark legislation since upon expiration of the industrial design right the design is dedicated to the public. As well, the use of a design pursuant to a statutory monopoly would not be use by the applicant *as a trademark*, but rather as an aesthetic design that appeals to and is judged solely by the eye, as required by the definition of a

design under section 23 of the *Industrial Design Act*. [Emphasis in original]

This deposition is not evidence, but argument.

The respondent disagrees with WCC's dedication to the public argument and submits that if an industrial design is capable of functioning as a distinguishing guise and acquires distinctiveness, then it may also be registered as a trade-mark. The respondent's argument relies upon the opinions of several distinguished authors, including Dr. Harold Fox and Mr. Roger T. Hughes, to support its position. Ultimately, the interpretation adopted by the respondent can be traced back to two English cases in which it was determined that registration as a trade-mark and a design are not mutually exclusive: *Re United States Playing Card Company's Application*, [1908] 1 Ch. 197; and *Sobrefina S.A.'s Trademark Application*, [1974] R.P.C. 672 (Ch. D.). Whitford J. in *Sobrefina* stated at pp 680-681:

> I am for my own part unable to reach the conclusion that a device which may be registrable as a design cannot be used as a trade mark. . . Many trade marks are in fact of such a nature that they could undoubtedly be registered as designs. . . . Many trade marks may also enjoy double protection not only by way of registration as a trade mark and by way of registration as a design but also under the *Copyright Acts*. I think myself that it is important to have this in mind, that whatever the rights and wrongs of this particular application may be the registrations to which I have already referred, for example the siphon and the Coca Cola bottle, do indicate acceptance by the Trade Marks Registry in the past of registrations of what can be considered as being device marks, the device marks in question in fact being representations of containers.

Picking up on Whitford J.'s final point in this paragraph, the respondent points out that registration of the same design as an industrial design and a distinguishing guise is a long-standing practice in Canada. The respondent has identified the traditional Coca-Cola Bottle, the Haig & Haig 'pinch' bottle and the J-Cloth Box as three such designs. The respondent claims that any change in the system would wreak havoc on the manufacturing industry.

I cannot accede to WCC's argument for the following reasons. First, legislative responsibility rests with Parliament and it has not chosen to make industrial design protection and trade-mark protection mutually exclusive. In light of its decision to explicitly limit the overlapping of industrial design protection and copyright protection, it must be presumed that it did not feel it was necessary to create a similar barrier between the *Industrial Design Act* and the *Trade-marks Act*. Second, as the respondent has demonstrated, it has been the long-held position of the courts not to prohibit the registration of a design as a trade-mark even if it has already enjoyed the protection of an industrial design registration. Third, neither paragraph 13(1)(b) nor the concept of distinctiveness create the needed foundation for this restriction. They narrow the scope of trade-mark protection and limit its applicability to designs; but if a design can fit within the constraints of the *Trade-marks Act*, then it is entitled to registration. Fourth, it is not within the competency of this Court to read-in the restriction sought by the applicants. Therefore, I conclude the respondent's trade-mark cannot be expunged because of the respondent's earlier industrial design registration.

The Court did, however, find that the alleged trade-mark was functional and allowed the mark to be expunged for that reason. The Court seems to have correctly concluded that if a distinguishing guise which meets the required distinctiveness criterion contains non-functional elements, those elements may be protected under trade-mark law independently of whether an industrial design was applied for. In the same vein, any analysis of infringement under either the *Industrial Design Act* or the *Trade-marks Act* (or related common law doctrines) must similarly proceed independently.

## VI. PATENTS AND TRADE-MARKS

Trade-mark law permits an indefinite term of protection, so one concern is that trade-mark law not be used to extend the limited term patent protection on functional aspects indefinitely. Conflicts between patents and trade-marks arise most frequently when a potential distinguishing guise under trade-mark law includes functional aspects subject to patent law protection. In *Kirkbi AG v. Ritvik Holdings Inc. / Gestions Ritvik Inc.*, Sexton JA for the majority emphasized that trade-mark law should not be used to extend the time-limited protection which patents accord the functionality of the invention itself:

> The purpose or policy behind applying this doctrine of functionality is to ensure that no one indirectly achieves the status of patent holder through the guise of a trade-mark. If the mark has a primarily functional use and is granted trade-mark protection, which can be perpetual, then it is providing something which a patent for the same product could not provide because patent protection cannot be perpetual. The protection of function and design is what a patent does. It would be abusive and unfair to the public and to competitors to allow a person to gain the benefits of a patent and a monopoly when merely holding a trade-mark, especially when the person otherwise could not obtain a patent or when the person merely holds a patent that has expired. A person could achieve this patent-like monopoly because a trade-mark gives to its holder the right of exclusive use in association with the wares in order to highlight the source of those wares. It should be explained what I mean by 'exclusive use'—the holder of a trade-mark can exclusively use the mark to distinguish its goods.[43]

---

[43] (2003), [2003] F.C.J. No. 1112, 228 D.L.R. (4th) 297, 26 C.P.R. (4th) 1, 2003

One of the most complex areas where intellectual property rights overlap is when the shape of an article has become a distinguishing guise under the *Trade-marks Act* while being protected by a patent. The classic case on this point is *Remington Rand* involving a three-head design for razors:[44]

> It is common ground, and was so stated by the trial judge, that the invalidity of a trade mark registration on the basis of functionality has no express statutory basis and has to be found in the case law, beginning with *Imperial Tobacco Co. v. Registrar of Trade Marks*, [1939] 2 D.L.R. 65, [1939] Ex. C.R. 141. In that case registration was sought for a cellophane outer wrapper for tobacco in all its forms with a narrow coloured band extended around the package. Registration was refused by the registrar on the grounds that the coloured band performed the function of indicating where the tear strip was located, thus facilitating the opening of the wrapper, and that, such wrapper being in use by other manufacturers, it would not identify the wares wrapped as those of the applicant. The mark was not treated as a distinguishing guise but as a design mark. Maclean P. held (at pp. 67-8):
>
>> It seems to me that the trade mark applied for was intended to replace the patents referred to [which he had found to be to the same effect] if they should be found to be invalid, as they were. In my opinion any combination of elements which are primarily designed to perform a function, here, a transparent wrapper which is moisture proof and a band to open the wrapper, is not fit subject-matter for a trade mark, and if permitted would lead to grave abuses. The introduction of a coloured strip or strand might be a good mark in some cases, particularly where it is practically impossible otherwise to mark the goods.

It should be noted that Maclean P. referred to 'elements which are primarily designed to perform a function'.

The Supreme Court of Canada had occasion to consider a similar issue in *Parke, Davis & Co. v. Empire Laboratories Ltd.* (1964), 43 C.P.R. 1, 45 D.L.R. (2d) 97, [1964] S.C.R. 351, 27 Fox Pat. C. 67, where differently coloured bands encircling capsules containing pharmaceuticals, and placed where the two halves of a capsule were joined, were found to have a functional use. Noel J. at trial had dismissed actions against the owners of other banded capsules for infringement and passing-off. Hall J. delivered the unanimous reasons for decision of the court (at p. 6):

> The validity of the trade marks may, in my view, be disposed of on the ground that the coloured bands have a functional use or characteristic and cannot, therefore, be the subject of a trade mark.

---

CarswellNat 3408 (F.C.A.), leave to appeal allowed (2004), 30 C.P.R. (4th) vii (S.C.C.) at para 41 [*Kirkbi* cited to D.L.R.].

[44] *Remington Rand, supra*, note 41 at 471, 473-78.

The law appears to be well settled that if what is sought to be registered as a trade mark has a functional use or characteristic, it cannot be the subject of a trade mark. With respect, I agree with Maclean P., when, in *Imperial Tobacco Co. of Canada Ltd. v. Registrar of Trade Marks*, [1939] 2 D.L.R. 65 at p. 67, [1939] Ex. C.R. 141 at p. 145, he said:

> 'In my opinion any combination of elements which are primarily designed to perform a function, here, a transparent wrapper which is moisture proof and a band to open the wrapper, is not fit subject-matter for a trade mark, and if permitted would lead to grave abuses.'

[. . .]

The issue came to this court in *Samann v. Canada's Royal Gold Pinetree Mfg. Co.* (1986), 9 C.P.R. (3d) 223, 8 C.I.P.R. 307, 65 N.R. 385 which dealt with expungement proceedings in relation to trade marks for air fresheners in automobiles, each carrying the representation of an evergreen tree. Heald J.A. looked closely at *Imperial Tobacco, Parke, Davis and Elgin Handles* and decided that, as far as physical functionality was concerned, those cases were distinguishable on the facts, since the trial judge had found that it was the combination of the air freshener in the evergreen tree and a plastic wrapper that was possessed of functionality. As for ornamental functionality, Hughes was distinguishable (at p. 231):

> Similarly that case is distinguishable on its facts from the case at bar. It stands for the proposition that it is not permissible to convert what is merely an ornamental design into a trade mark. On this record, it is not possible to conclude that the marks in issue were merely or solely ornamental. I agree with the appellant's counsel that it is likely that any design mark will have some ornamental features. However, the circumstance will not, per se, render a mark unregistrable so long as it possesses the essential requirements for registrability.

It is clear from these words that Heald J.A. adopted a narrow-rule approach to functionality: some functionality is permissible.

I believe that *Pizza Pizza Ltd. v. Canada (Registrar of Trade Marks)* (1989), 26 C.P.R. (3d) 355, 24 C.I.P.R. 152, [1989] 3 F.C. 379 (C.A.), which follows the same approach, gives a clearer indication of what functionality is permissible. The issue there was whether a telephone number, which was used for all Toronto-area outlets, was registrable as a trade mark for a pizza take-out business. The registrar and the trial judge had both held that such a numerical combination was not registrable.

The most focused reasons for judgment were the concurring ones of Pratte J.A., who held that the only kind of functionality that was alien to the registration of a trade mark was that which made a mark part of the wares. The whole substance of Pratte J.A.'s opinion is as follows (at pp. 356-7):

> Counsel for the respondent tried to support the decision of the Trial Division . . . on only one ground, namely, that a telephone number is not registrable as a trade mark because, according to the jurisprudence [*Parke, Davis and Elgin Handles*] a mark that is primarily designed to perform a function cannot be the subject of a trade mark. This position, in my view, reveals a complete misunderstanding of that jurisprudence. In those cases, the marks that were held to be functional were, in effect, part of the wares in respect of which registration was sought so that the registration of those marks would have granted the applicant a monopoly on functional elements or characteristics of their wares; the applicants would, in effect, have obtained patents under the guise of trade marks. The situation here is entirely different. The trade mark applied for by the appellant is not functional in that sense; for that reason, its functional character does not make it 'not registrable'.

[. . .]

If functionality goes either to the trade mark itself (*Imperial Tobacco*, and *Parke, Davis*) or to the wares (Elgin *Handles*), then it is essentially or primarily inconsistent with registration. However, if it is merely secondary or peripheral, like a telephone number with no essential connection with the wares, then it does not act as a bar to registration.

The weighty reason for this conclusion was clearly specified by Pratte J.A. If a mark is primarily functional as 'part of the ware,' the effect would be to grant applicants for registration 'a monopoly on functional elements or characteristics of their wares'. This would be effectively to create a patent or industrial design rather than a trade mark: 'the applicants would, in effect, have obtained patents under the guise of trade marks'. In my view, that would be precisely the consequence of registration of the design trade mark in the case at bar. I cannot therefore agree with the trial judge that the design marks 'contain no functional elements or components'. Rather, they have an intrinsic reference to the principal functional feature of the Philips shaver, its cutting heads, which they depict. If this were a mere representation, it could not have the effect of preventing the appellants from producing a similar shaver with a different design mark. But the respondent agrees—indeed insists—that this is the effect of its registration of the design mark.

Moreover, I am not persuaded by the trial judge's alternative conclusion that there was no evidence that 'utilitarian functionality dictated the design of the triple headed shaver'. Shaver heads in general are utilitarian in nature, and the trial judge found that the 'equilateral triangular configuration is one of the better designs for a triple headed shaver'. Here, the shaver heads are functional and the three-headed equilateral triangular configuration is functional. The design mark, by depicting those functional elements, is primarily functional. [. . .]

The appellants must therefore succeed as to the design mark.

The issue as to the distinguishing guise trade mark is entirely one of first impression, since none of the cases cited has pronounced on the question. The British or American case law is also of no assistance because such a statutory concept is unknown in their law. I believe, however, that, despite the uncharted state of the law, the matter can be resolved on the basis of the *Pizza Pizza* decision.

Section 2 of the Act [*Trade-marks Act*, R.S.C. 1985, c. T-13] defines 'trade- mark', *inter alia*, as 'a mark that is used by a person for the purpose of distinguishing or so as to distinguish wares or services manufactured, sold, leased, hired or performed by him from those manufactured, sold, leased, hired or performed by others'. Urie J.A. held in Pizza Pizza that the telephone number in question was a mark held by a corporate person used for the purpose of distinguishing wares manufactured or sold by it, which distinguishes such wares from those sold by others. It is therefore clear from the definition section of the Act, from the holding of Urie J.A., and indeed from all the case law, that the essence of a trade mark is to distinguish the wares of a registered owner from those sold by others.

[. . .]

The essence of a distinguishing guise is thus identical with that of a design mark in that it serves to distinguish the wares of a registered owner from those sold by others.

It is clear that every form of trade mark, including a distinguishing guise, is characterized by its distinctiveness. A distinguishing guise, therefore, not being different in essence from a design mark, must be governed by the same considerations of functionality as a design mark, since the public policy basis is the same, viz., to distinguish wares from those of competitors, by monopolizing, not the wares, but the mark as used in relation to them. The trial judge may have been correct in stating that 'a distinguishing guise necessarily possesses a functional element or component' (although I wonder about, say, a bottle shape which might not even be ornamental), but to the extent that such functionality relates primarily or essentially to the wares themselves it will invalidate the trade mark.

The distinguishing guise in the case at bar is in my opinion invalid as extending to the functional aspects of the Philip shaver. A mark which goes beyond distinguishing the wares of its owner to the functional structure of the wares themselves is transgressing the legitimate bounds of a trade mark.

Another interesting case is *Dominion Lock Co. v. Schlage Lock Co.*[45] Schlage had applied for a trade-mark for original keys with a specific key

---

[45] (1961), 22 Fox Pat. C. 102 (Reg. T.M.).

design (a bow on the top of the key). The competitor companies objected because they wanted to supply blank replacement keys to locksmiths in that design because industry practice is for the locksmith to use the shape of the key as a way to locate the correct blank. The Registrar of Trade-marks concluded as follows:

> The attacks on the application, although stated under three or more heads appear to me to resolve themselves into the two questions implicit in Section 13(1)(a) and (b), that is, whether the mark was distinctive at the time of filing the application, and secondly whether the exclusive use by the applicant of the mark is likely unreasonably to limit the development of any art or industry.

> [. . .]

> Part of the evidence of the opponents was directed to showing that key blanks generally resembling the trade mark of the present application had been sold in Canada in considerable quantities by persons other than the applicant, before the date of filing the present application. Among other arguments on behalf of the applicant, it was strongly argued that original keys for door locks and key blanks are quite different wares and that original keys are sold to the general public whereas key blanks are sold to locksmiths. In my opinion the evidence shows that this is not a realistic distinction.

> Secondly, it has been established to my satisfaction that it is a common procedure that key blanks are frequently made with outline shape such that they match the outline shape of original keys of different manufacturers of keys and locks, and that locksmiths use such outline shapes to select blanks, or perhaps more precisely speaking, to narrow down the selection of blanks.

> Accordingly, looking at all the evidence, I have come to the conclusion that the applicant's trade mark was not distinctive when the application was filed, and that it is not registrable for the further reason that it does not meet the test of Section 13(1)(b). The application is therefore refused pursuant to Section 37(8) of the *Trade Marks Act*.[46]

In *Thomas & Betts Ltd. v. Panduit Corp.*,[47] the Plaintiff manufactured a cable tie with an oval shape and had a patent on it but the patent term had expired. The defendants started to manufacture a cable tie which was virtually identical to plaintiff's cable design. The plaintiff claimed the defendant was infringing its common law trade-mark rights in the distinctive

---

[46] *Idem.* See also *Gillette Canada Inc. v. Mennen Canada Inc.*, (sub nom. *Calumet Manufacturing Ltd. v. Mennen Canada Inc.*) (1991), [1991] F.C.J. No. 1253, 40 C.P.R. (3d) 76, 1991 CarswellNat 1110 (Fed. T.D.).

[47] [2000] 3 F.C. 3, 185 D.L.R. (4th) 150, 4 C.P.R. (4th) 498, 252 N.R. 371 (Fed. C.A.), leave to appeal to S.C.C. refused (2000), [2000] S.C.C.A. No. 105, 2000 CarswellNat 2568 (S.C.C.) [*Thomas & Betts* cited to F.C.].

shape of the head of the cable tie and passing off its goods. The defendant argued that the plaintiff could not extend the length of the patent term by claiming trade mark rights in the expired patent's design.

The Federal Court of Appeal in *Thomas & Betts* analyzed the overlap as follows:

> After referring to subsection 27(3) of the *Patent Act* and to various cases dealing with patent law, the Motions Judge then reached a conclusion with respect to the trade-mark asserted by T & B in this trade-mark case without making any reference to the *Trade-marks Act*. This is an incorrect approach. One can simply not on the one hand conclude as the Motions Judge did, and correctly in my view, that the *Patent Act* and the *Trade-marks Act* must co-exist, and on the other hand attempt to reconcile them having only regard to one of them.
>
> The practical effect of the impugned decision is to tell a patentee that even though it never claimed nor had a specific monopoly with respect to the preferred embodiment of the invention described in the patent application, yet in exchange for the monopoly granted to it by the patent with respect to the invention, the public, when allowed to copy the *invention* at the expiry of the patent, can automatically use any guise depicted or described in the preferred embodiment which was never part of the monopoly to start with.
>
> I have found no authority for such a proposition which, reduced to its simplest or extended to its extreme, would mean that any element described or depicted in the preferred embodiment—regardless of whether it is claimed or of its importance to the claimed invention—is automatically as a matter of law and without further inquiry disqualified from trade-mark protection.
>
> As noted by Christopher Wadlow in *The Law of Passing-Off*, 2d ed. (London, Sweet & Maxwell, 1995) at 367,
>
>> It is more difficult for a plaintiff to prove that a mark has become distinctive of him when he has enjoyed a legal, natural or *de facto* monopoly of the goods in question [. . .] It is wrong to say that distinctiveness cannot be acquired during a period of monopoly, but proof of acquired distinctiveness may be harder to come by, especially for a mark which has a low inherent capacity to distinguish. There is no rule of law that because goods were once patented the name or get-up given to them by the patentee can be copied with impunity. [. . .] (My emphasis.)
>
> During the existence of the Schwester patent, T & B could not have used patent law to prevent a competitor from making a cable-tie that used a different invention but which also featured an oval-shaped head. The patentee never had a monopoly over the oval-shaped head, and it would therefore be unfair to later prevent it, as a matter of law, from asserting a trade-mark right with respect to the oval-shaped head. This would be tantamount to retroactively extending or mischaracterizing the expired patent-monopoly to include the oval-shaped head.

On the other hand, it would be unfair to the public if a patentee could, after the expiry of its patent, use the *Trade-marks Act* to give itself a monopoly over the shape of its invention when that shape is so closely related to the invention as to be for all practical purposes an element essential to making full use of the invention.

It is precisely to solve this dilemma that the *Trade-marks Act* comes into play and this is precisely why this Court, in interpreting that Act, has ensured that it not be used to perpetuate a patent monopoly that would otherwise have expired. The solution retained by this Court is the doctrine of functionality. I need only refer to *Remington Rand Corp. v. Philips Electronics N.V.* (1995), 64 C.P.R. (3d) 467 F.C.A.), where MacGuigan J. A. after observing that:

> It is common ground [. . .] that the invalidity of a trade mark registration on the basis of functionality has no express statutory basis and has to be found in the case law [. . .] (at 471)

He went on to confirm the 'narrow-rule approach to functionality: some functionality is permissible', (at 474) first adopted by President Maclean in *Imperial Tobacco Co. v. Registrar of Trade Marks*, [1939] Ex. C.R. 141, [1939] 2 D.L.R. 65 in these words:

> [. . .] In my opinion any combination of elements which are primarily designed to perform a function [. . .] is not fit subject-matter for a trade mark, and if permitted would lead to grave abuses [. . .] (cited to Ex. C.R. at 145)

MacGuigan J.A. also endorsed, at 476, the view expressed by Pratte J.A. in *Pizza Pizza Ltd. v. Canada (Registrar of Trade Marks)*, [1989] 3 F.C. 379 (F.C.A.), that

> [i]f a mark is primarily functional as 'part of the ware', the effect would be to grant applicants for registration 'a monopoly on functional elements or characteristics of their wares' [and that] 'the applicants would, in effect, have obtained patents under the guise of trade marks' [. . .]

and he went on to deal with the distinguishing guise at issue in the *Remington Rand* case, *supra* at 478:

> [. . .] The trial judge may have been correct in stating that 'a distinguishing guise necessarily possesses a functional element or component' (although I wonder about, say, a bottle shape which might not even be ornamental), but to the extent that such functionality relates primarily or essentially to the wares themselves it will invalidate the trade mark.
>
> The distinguishing guise in the case at bar is in my opinion invalid as extending to the functional aspects of the Philip shaver. A mark which goes beyond distinguishing the wares of its owner to the functional

structure of the wares themselves is transgressing the legitimate bounds of a trade mark.

In the case at bar, the Motions Judge erred in focussing on the 'invention' under the *Patent Act* rather than on the 'wares' under the *Trade-marks Act*. The validity of the patent was not at issue nor was its specific scope as compared with a competing device. The issue in the action is whether the oval-shaped head was a distinguishing guise within the meaning of the *Trade-marks Act*. In addressing that issue, which is partly and perhaps essentially one of fact, the Motions Judge would have had to examine the very facts of the case in the light of trade-marks principles, including the doctrine of functionality. It may be that at the end of a trial a judge would reach the conclusion, with respect to the specific issue of functionality, that the description or depiction of the oval-shaped head as a preferred embodiment of the invention was evidence, perhaps conclusive evidence, of functionality, but any such conclusion would be premature in this case at the stage of a motion for summary judgment.

As a result, the Motions Judge was in no position to dismiss the action brought by T & B under the *Trade-marks Act* on a motion for summary judgment. He was obviously led astray by Panduit's decision not to argue before him the 'functionality' ground it had raised in writing in its Motion for summary judgment. Whatever reasons Panduit might have had in abandoning that ground, which was the first ground on which it originally based its attack, the Motions Judge could not decide the merit of the action brought by T & B without applying general trade-mark principles to the wares at issue and without examining the doctrine of functionality.

A word, in closing, on the use of American jurisprudence by Canadian courts when dealing with patent and trade-mark cases. I need only repeat here what I had said in *Tele-Direct (Publications) Inc. v. American Business Information, Inc.*, [1998] 2 F.C. 22 (F.C.A.), leave to appeal dismissed by the Supreme Court of Canada at S.C.C. No 26403 (21 May 1998). It is permissible for Canadian courts to find some assistance in authoritative United States courts decisions, provided that Canadian courts proceed very carefully in doing so. Where, as here, the legal issue is the very issue that has been argued by the same parties in a U.S. Court, it may be useful to have regard to the particular decision rendered.

In this respect, the Denlow decision on which the Motions Judge relied has since been overturned by the U.S. Court of Appeals for the Seventh Circuit on March 4, 1998 (reported at 138 F.3d 277 (7th Cir. 1998). I have examined with interest that decision. It is remarkably well articulated and it contains some eloquent statements of policy and principle which are highly persuasive. I note, however, that the *Lanham Act* (15 U.S.C. sec. 1051 et seq.), which is the American counterpart of our *Trade-marks Act* is differently drafted and that the doctrine of functionality, mentioned expressly in the *Lanham Act* for the first time in 1998, may not have evolved in the United States the same way it has in Canada. I will therefore say no more than that I take some comfort from the approach adopted by the Court of Appeals and that there is a fortunate similarity in the end result achieved.

The patent protection monopoly on functional elements of an invention is finely calibrated. It has a limited term of protection. Trade-mark law, by contrast, allows potentially perpetual protection. Courts thus are careful that the exclusive rights to a trade-mark do not give the owner exclusive rights to the functional elements of the associated product. Trade-mark law should not be used to "evergreen" a patent (*i.e.* perpetuate the patent monopoly after the term would otherwise expire).[48] Just as the intangible rights of copyright are separate from the tangible rights in the physical object that embodies that expression, here the rights of the trade-mark owner in the exclusive use of the object are separate from the rights in the functional elements. The courts have prevented inventors who coin a new word to describe their invention from also claiming that word as an exclusive trade-mark after the patent term expires because it is "attempting by registering the name of the patented product to prolong the patent monopoly."[49] Thus, the inventors of "shredded wheat" and "linoleum" could not get trade-mark rights in those terms because they were the name of the general product itself.[50] (See Prohibited or Invalid Trade-Marks section in Trade-Marks).

For the same reasons, therefore, one cannot control the functional or utilitarian elements by getting a trademark in distinguishing guise. This is provided for explicitly in s. 13(2) of the *Trade-marks Act*: "No registration of a distinguishing guise interferes with the use of any utilitarian feature embodied in the distinguishing guise."

Recently, the Federal Court of Appeal considered the doctrine of functionality at length in *Kirkbi AG*, a case involving the relationship between distinguishing guise trade-marks and patent law.[51] The plaintiffs had held patents on LEGO interlocking children's toy building blocks, but the patents had expired. The blocks were designed with eight studs on the top of each brick and corresponding tubes underneath. This system enabled the bricks to be locked together vertically and laterally. The plaintiffs brought a passing off action, under s. 7(b) of the *Act*, against the defendants who made blocks of a similar configuration except that they were oversized for younger children and did not grip to other blocks as tightly. The plaintiffs claimed the shape of the eight-stud block as an unregistered distinguishing guise

---

[48] *Kirkbi AG, supra,* note 43 at para. 43.

[49] *Canadian Shredded Wheat Co. v. Kellogg Co.,* [1938] 2 D.L.R. 145, 55 R.P.C. 125 (Ontario P.C.) at 150 [*Canadian Shredded Wheat* cited to D.L.R.].

[50] *Canadian Shredded Wheat, ibid,* and *Linoleum Manufacturing Co. v. Nairn* (1878), 7 Ch. D. 834 (Eng. Ch. Div.).

[51] *Kirbi AG, supra,* note 43.

trade-mark. The majority of the Federal Court of Appeal ruled that the block design was "primarily functional" and therefore was not valid as a trade-mark.

The above cases teach a conclusion consonant with the implied licence approach applicable to copyright drawings contained in patent applications (see above), though in this context the result is achieved simply by applying the statute. Trade-mark law will not extend to protect the utilitarian feature of a distinguishing guise. However, if a guise acquires the required degree of distinctiveness and is not purely functional, its protection under trade-mark law remains unaffected by the expiry of a related patent. By the same token, if the invention described in the expired patent can be reproduced without copying the non-utilitarian (*i.e.*, aesthetic) aspects of the patentee's product, there will be no violation of either the (expired) patent or the trade-mark.

In summary, the results in the case law involving overlaps between intellectual property rights affirm two principles: first, to the extent possible and consistent with the statutory provisions, there should be legal protection for each aspect of each intellectual property right as long as it does not conflict with the purpose of another intellectual property right and there is no specific override specified in legislation; and second, that intellectual property rights protect different aspects so that any particular tangible object can implicate more than one intangible intellectual property right.

## VII.  DISCUSSION QUESTIONS

### Overlaps

**Q:** Assume the federal government has created a national clown registry where professionally licensed clowns can submit illustrations and/or photographs of their signature clown faces. Bill Board is a professional clown who performs as "Mopey Mobey." Board registers his face design for Mopey Mobey, which consists of blue cheeks, yellow polka dots on the forehead, red tear drops near the eyes, and a green frown. A Canadian toy company uses Mopey Mobey's clown face without Board's permission as an image on its new line of children's toys. Has the company infringed the tort of misappropriation of personality? What factors would you consider? Would the Mopey Mobey face be a copyrightable work? What copyright requirement(s) might not be met?

**Q:** A world famous Oscar® winning actress, Gwyn Gardner, has just had a baby and has named her infant daughter "Grapefruit." Gwyn and her baby have received enormous press coverage and photographs of mother and child have appeared in many news articles and in association with the promotion of Gwyn's new movie where she stars as a new mother. The baby's name has been widely reported in celebrity-themed news coverage. Florence Fan has avidly followed Gardner's career and is president of the local chapter of the Gwyn Gardner fan club. Fan is pregnant and has written on her club's bulletin board that she plans to name her baby Grapefruit as a tribute to Gardner. Gardner hears about this and wants to trade-mark the name "Grapefruit" to prevent other people from naming their babies "Grapefruit." She comes to you, her intellectual property lawyer, for advice as to whether this is possible. She would like you to specify the arguments that Fan might make in support of her right to name her daughter "Grapefruit" and wants you to evaluate the likelihood of success of each side's arguments. Gardner also mentions that she has heard about a tort called "misappropriation of personality." She wants to know if someone taking her baby's name could fit within the scope of this tort.

**Q:** Andy Adaptor has designed a new software program to make movies more "family friendly." The program removes swear words and offensive violence or sexual contents in a movie and substitutes inoffensive words, like "darn" or "good grief," for the swear words, and replaces the violent or sexual scenes in a movie with scenes such as natural landscapes or children playing that could fit in a variety of genres.

> Is the software program copyrightable?
> Does the resulting movie have copyright? What factors would be considered? If so, who is the author?
> Does the resulting movie infringe the copyright of the original movies, and if so, what rights are infringed?
> Does the resulting movie infringe moral rights?
> Is this fair dealing?
> Is the software program patentable?
> Is the movie patentable?

**Q:** Fifi has written a high-pitched tape of music for dogs. The music cannot be heard by humans but dogs can hear it and enjoy the songs.

> Can the songs be copyrighted?
> Does a "musical work" need to be perceptible/readable by humans?
> Could the tape be patented if Fifi was the first to come up with the idea?

**Sample Exam Questions**

**Q:** If you go to a county fair in eastern Ontario, you may have a chance to see a singer called Shania Twin. Ms. Twin sings only the songs that her idol, the famous country singer Shania Twain from Timmins, sings. Ms. Twin is usually accompanied by a four-man band (guitar, bass, drums, and fiddle).

In addition to singing Shania Twain's songs, Ms. Twin wears clothes and make-up exactly like Shania Twain's and imitates as faithfully as possible her voice, her patter between songs, her dance steps, and the way she moves on stage.

Members of the audience often record Ms. Twin's performances on videotape.

Discuss the aspects of intellectual property concerning Ms. Twin's shows. Is Ms. Twin infringing intellectual property rights? Which ones? (Explain.) Does Ms. Twin have any right whatsoever? Does someone else have rights to assert?

**Q:** Louis, an old friend who is finishing his degree in chemistry, comes to see you in your law office. He thinks he has come up with the invention of the century. He wants to manufacture and sell a product that he's thinking of calling "5000 Flushes." He wants to compete with an existing product on the market called "2000 Flushes," a tablet that is placed in the toilet tank and dissolves slowly. The time it takes this tablet to dissolve is about one month, and since the average North American family uses the toilet 2,000 times a month, the product is called "2000 Flushes." But even in the tank of an unused toilet, the tablet would dissolve in 30 days. The technology used to create the "2000 Flushes" product is known as "super compression."

Louis explains to you that the technology he has invented, and named "hyper compression," is a tablet that dissolves only when the toilet is used, since the dissolution is activated by the movement of water when the toilet is flushed. He has calculated that with a water temperature of 20°C, his tablet will last for 5,000 uses – whence the name "5000 Flushes."

a)    *Discuss all aspects relating to use of the names "2000 Flushes" and "5000 Flushes" in Canadian trade-mark law, given that the name "2000 Flushes" is a brand name registered in Canada. In particular, can Louis use the brand name "5000 Flushes"? How can he protect this brand name? If the owner of the brand name "2000 Flushes" wants to oppose the use of the brand name "5000 Flushes," when and how must he do it? What arguments could Louis use to defend himself?*

**b)**    *What intellectual property rights can Louis use to protect his technology? Explain and describe all relevant criteria that apply to this case. (If there is more than one possibility, discuss all the means that Louis could use.)*

**Q:**   A Canadian software company, PointSource has a new product "Spam Stop." Spam Stop is software to filter unsolicited commercial email and to direct email from unreliable sources into a special folder separated from the regular inbox. The software successfully filters 75% of unsolicited commercial email. It incorrectly blocks 5% of email that is not "spam" and prevents the user from receiving it.

The Canadian company Cormel has been marketing a canned luncheon meat made of spiced ham using the name Spam for fifty years. Fifty years ago, Cormel invented and successfully patented the process to make spiced meat. The process ingeniously used small bits of ham that would otherwise go to waste and formed them into an edible product that could be easily sliced. In 1955, Cormel registered "spam" as a trade mark in Canada for use with spiced meat. On the can labels and in advertising, the company describes the product as simply, "Spam." Cormel's patent expired over 20 years ago. Other companies now make and market spiced meat products, sometimes using "spam" as a general term to refer to such meat products. Cormel's lawyers send these companies a stern letter which warns that "spam" is a registered trade-mark. Comedians use the term "spam" to mock any product that uses low-grade cuts of meat in sandwich meat.

Cormel uses a picture of a pig snout and the word spam in distinctive script writing on its cans of Spam and in its advertising. Cormel has a catchy jingle in its television and radio advertising with a voice that repeats, "Spam, Spam, Spam, Spam, Spam, Spam, Spam, Spam, Spam, Superlative Spam." The song jingle was originally written by a Cormel employee who was hired to write advertising slogans for the company.

On the packaging and advertising for "Spam Stop," PointSource uses a picture of a pig snout and the word spam in the same font that Cormel uses, surrounded by a circle with a red slash through it. PointSource also puts the same picture on a stop sign (an eight-sided figure with a red field). The text on the advertising and the software packaging states, "Stop people from spam, spam, spamming you. Superlative protection."

Cormel has given up trying to stop people from using the word "spam" to describe unsolicited commercial email. The company thinks that references to junk email as "spam" won't hurt the company's intellectual property.

You have been approached by PointSource as someone who specializes in Canada in intellectual property law.

**a)**    *Discuss the copyright rights that Cormel might have and whether PointSource is infringing any of those rights. Consider applicable remedies and defences in your answer.*

**b)**    *Discuss the statutory or common law trade-mark rights Cormel might have and whether PointSource is infringing any of those rights. Consider applicable remedies and defences in your answer.*

**c)**    *Could PointSource register the proposed trade-mark "SPAM STOP" for use with its email filtering software? Explain your reasons. Identify any problems and discuss strategies to fix them so PointSource could register a mark for their product.*

**Q:** Spiritual Sylvia is a Canadian software designer. She has written a computer program to help people improve their yoga exercise. Yoga is an ancient art comprised of a course of related exercises and postures that promote physical body control, mental discipline and spiritual well being. Spiritual Sylvia first learned yoga from an instruction manual titled "Enlightened Yoga." The book is in the public domain. The book factually describes how to do more than 100 different moves and illustrates yoga postures using artwork that is more that 500 years old. Each of the individual body postures described in the book has been practiced for hundreds of years.

Sylvia's idea is to use a computer and a digital camera to take digital images of people as they perform yoga. The software program that she has written analyses the digital images of people's body positions and movements. The program produces a printed report advising people how to improve their yoga postures so as to lower their heart rate and blood pressure, and put less stress on their joints. The program also designs a new twenty-minute routine that is customized for each person's body type and strength. For each person, the program selects the best yoga postures, and the most appropriate sequence and timing of the movements. The computer program generates instructional word text to explain the sequence of movements in each custom routine and provides computer generated illustrations of what each person would look like as they do each part of the custom routine.

Computer generated imaging is a known technique but it has not been applied to physical exercise or physical therapy before. Each of the individual yoga postures is familiar to people who practice yoga, but the custom routines generated by the computer program are new. Spiritual Sylvia has not told anyone about her computer program yet. She hopes she can successfully market this idea since there are no other comparable computer programs on the market. Sylvia thinks that offering custom yoga routines might be a good business model for a health club. She has heard that patents provide strong legal protection.

*Spiritual Sylvia comes to you to seek advice on whether she could get a patent, copyright, and/or some other intellectual property protection for her computer program. Explain fully and advise Sylvia what intellectual property rights, if any, she should pursue in Canada, the likelihood of success, and any strategies that might improve her chances for successfully protecting her idea through intellectual property law.*

**Q:** Bob Lawlace is an entrepreneur specializing in get-rich-quick projects. For Thanksgiving, he bought a wholesale bulk order of FORMALPOULTRY brand turkeys. FormalPoultry is a well-known brand that is marketed in large Canadian grocery store chains. The plastic wrapping around the frozen turkeys is tied off with a 4" rectangular laminated paper label at the top. The label shows a comic scene of turkeys in formal attire at a dinner party. The label originally showed turkeys at the dining table dressed in flowery hats. A few years ago FORMALPOULTRY started to update their labels by having the turkeys wear tiaras and top hats. FORMALPOULTRY has been marketing their turkeys across Canada for fifty years. They registered the flowery hat trade-mark ten years ago. FORMALPOULTRY turkeys come from Genetic Research Labs.

In October, Genetic Research Labs finished experiments on turkeys with a plumpogene that increases the white breast meat and keeps the meat juicy during cooking. A group of animal advocates and small farmers vigorously opposes genetically modified food. They have been passing out flyers in front of the Genetic Research's laboratory complex. The flyers have a picture of turkeys at a dinner table with their chairs pulled back from the table and their wings crossed in protest. They also designed an animated doll in the figure of a turkey with crossed wings that shouts out protests. The turkey doll comes with a computer chip which controls its movements and the phrases that it says.

When the bulk order of frozen FORMALPOULTRY turkeys arrived, Bob pasted on new labels over the laminated tie off. The new label reads, "Bob's Original Fine Gourmet Free Range Organic poultry." The labels covered over information about the original manufacturer and the FORMALPOULTRY name. Bob marked up the price by 50% and sold them to small health food and gourmet specialty stores. In Ontario the turkeys were sold with Bob's new labels attached. For transportation to the rest of the country, Bob hired a refrigerator truck. Bob got a good deal on the price of the shipping because the truck was an older model. The refrigeration unit broke on the truck and the turkeys spoiled. When the frozen turkeys started to thaw, Bob's labels peeled off and the original manufacturer information and FORMALPOULTRY name could be read. People who bought the turkeys in Vancouver were hospitalized with food poisoning. In Regina, people who bought the turkeys noticed they smelled funny. They served omelets for Thanksgiving dinner and cursed FORMALPOULTRY.

Despite the pesky setback outside of Ontario, Bob was encouraged by the profits in Ontario. Bob wrote a pamphlet about his successful marketing venture. Bob is also interested in patenting his turkey profit idea and is considering developing software that will automatically create fake labels in the appropriate size.

Phil L. Eagle saw Bob's pamphlet and decided to set up a website that would have information on culinary holiday scams. Thinking Bob would like the publicity, Phil scanned and uploaded Bob's pamphlet on to his website, www.eagle.com. Phil also collected fifty other authors' pamphlets. One was written by a prisoner as a therapeutic exercise in a twelve-step program to seek forgiveness for having sold moldy fruitcakes to a nursing home. Three other pamphlets were written by provincial governmental employees as material for a prosecutors' seminar on how to litigate con artists. Phil found those on the official government sites and copied them. One pamphlet had ten simple points. The first point, typical of the rest, stated, "cheating is fun and free." Another pamphleteer was more elaborate. Jane Bluff had a full-page title for her pamphlet featuring her invented word "jabluff." Jabluff now has some popularity among local teenagers who bought Jane's pamphlet in a kiosk in front of the local music store.

Phil arranged the pamphlet materials on his website alphabetically according to the type of food in the scheme ("t" for turkeys, "f" for fruit-cakes. . .). Phil called the book length collection "Food for Thought and Profit." Phil was not satisfied with the website, thinking it lacked a certain punch. When his home page starts, the voice of Marta Perfect, a famous host of a daytime show on home cooking and decorating, says her signature line "this is a good thing."

1. *Bob arrives at your law office. He is excited about getting as much intellectual property as he can. Advise Bob about his options and anything he should be concerned about.*

2. *Bob is also irritated about Phil L. Eagle's use of Bob's pamphlet. Bob is so mad about what Phil has done that he wants you to file a suit against Phil. Bob thinks other people might be equally as irritated with Phil's website and that Phil could be bankrupted. He would like you to give him a memo about eagle.com.*

3. *Genetics Research Lab goes to their in-house legal department. They are worried about their intellectual property strategy. Their stock has plummeted since the media reported about Formal-Poultry food poisoning, the holiday omelet scandal, and the turkey protesters. They would like to ensure that their brand reputation recovers. They are also thinking they might be more profitable if*

*they could patent their turkeys, or constituent parts such as genes or cell lines. Another company already has a patent on the plumpogene for "poultry including chickens, pheasant, and Cornish hens."*

4. *The protest group is wondering if they have any intellectual property rights in their flyers or their animated turkey doll.*

**Q:** Face Figures is a Canadian company which designs, manufactures, and sells action figures. Action figures are toy dolls for both adults and children. This year they have launched a new product of custom personalized action figures under the product line name of "Everyone is a Hero." Customers send in photos of someone's face to the company. Face Figures manufactures a customized toy doll to resemble the person in the photograph. The personalized action figures are expensive and so far only a few people have purchased them. Most people order likenesses of themselves.

Lisa Mona is a famous Canadian actress known for her smile. For her thirtieth birthday, Lisa Mona's friends sent in a picture of the actress to Face Figures and placed an order for a personalized action figure. The photographic portrait that Lisa's friends used was commissioned by Lisa and she had paid the photographer ahead of time in dollars for the photograph. Lisa Mona did not sign a contract with the photographer. Face Figures fulfilled the order by creating and sending the custom doll to Lisa Mona's friends who gave it to Lisa Mona as a gift for her birthday. Lisa Mona did not like the doll that her friends surprised her with, but she thanked her friends politely.

To promote the new product line of "Everyone is a Hero," Face Figures is using pictures of the personalized action figures that the company has already custom made for customers' orders. This saves money since the company does not have the expense of creating new dolls just for advertising purposes. The pictures appear on Face Figures's web site, catalogue, and on the packaging for other Face Figures products. The Lisa Mona doll is prominently featured in the advertising. Lisa Mona's name is not used in the advertising but the doll is a very good likeness of the celebrity, especially as she appeared in the photograph, and Lisa Mona has a recognizable face. News and gossip items about her appear regularly in the press and television.

Face Figures received a lot of calls from Lisa Mona fans who saw the picture of the doll and want to buy one. The company is now selling more copies of the Lisa Mona doll which are identical to the one that the company originally made to fulfill the order of Lisa's friends. Face Figures has made and sold fifty-five dolls. The company is marketing the doll as the "Mona Smile Doll."

Lisa Mona sees the web site and calls her lawyer. Lisa Mona complains that they are taking her image without payment and she says her image is her property. She mentions she finds the whole idea of her face on a doll creepy, but she should be the one who gets any profits if the dolls are going to be marketed. "It's my face," she says. Lisa Mona's lawyer sends a letter to Face Figures demanding that they cease marketing the doll.

Face Figures comes to you as an expert in intellectual property law. The company does not want to have to stop selling these profitable dolls unless there is no other alternative.

    **a)**    *You are asked to research whether Face Figures has infringed any intellectual property Lisa Mona may have and, if so, the remedy that a court would be likely to award. Provide specifics with respect to each intellectual property right that Lisa Mona might have, the possible infringing actions of Face Figures, and any defences and remedies. Assume that the case is heard in Ontario.*

    **b)**    *Identify any intellectual property rights that Face Figures might have and design a strategy to protect those rights.*

**Q:** Brooke Garamond is an employee of the *Ottawa Times* newspaper. Her employment contract specifies that her employment duties are to edit the newspaper copy for the "Style and Entertainment" section of the newspaper. Brooke's job is to check for grammar, word choices, and sentence structure.

Outside of her specified work-day hours, Brooke has designed a new typeface font design. The design is for the twenty-six letters of the alphabet, in upper case and lower case and Roman and italic letters, as well as the digits from zero to nine. She has called the typeface Sophisticated Garamond. Brooke wants the name of the typeface to include her surname. "Garamond," however, is the general name for a family of typefaces which have the qualities and characteristics of light, airy, clean, classic lines. (This sentence is typed in "Garamond".) "Garamond" has been in use as a general term for this family of fonts since the French designer Claude Garamond designed an innovative typeface in the sixteenth century. **Brooke's typeface design has intricate and heavy lines, like this.**

Brooke has also created a computer program for the typeface design. The program allows the font to be used with standard word-processing programs and controls how the typefaces are displayed on the computer screen. The program also installs the typeface design so that a personal computer can be used as a label-maker machine.

*You are a lawyer in Canada specializing in intellectual property law. Brooke comes to you to ask about her intellectual property rights. Brooke would like as wide a protection from intellectual property law as possible and would like you to research intellectual property protection relating to her typeface design and computer program. She would like to receive a royalty every time someone uses her font. She thinks her font design could be very profitable because people would have to pay her whenever they write letters or numbers that are intricate and heavy like her typeface. She would like to call her typeface Sophisticated Garamond and prevent others from using similar names for typefaces. She also wonders if she could get rights in her computer program and if she might have intellectual property rights in any written documents and materials which a user creates with the assistance of her computer program.*

*Discuss what intellectual property rights, if any, Brooke might have or could acquire in Canada and describe a strategy to protect these rights and to protect Brooke against infringement of her rights. Address the likelihood of success, and any strategies that might improve her chances for success-fully protecting her idea through intellectual property law. Identify any problems and discuss strategies to fix them or the recommendations you would make to Brooke. Explain fully.*

**Q:** Finn Sparkle is a specialist in firework displays. Firework displays require a fine appreciation of colour, timing, and three-dimensional space. There is a lot of creativity and judgment, based on experience, involved in designing firework displays. Many people appreciate the artistry and aes-thetic value of Sparkle's fireworks displays. Sparkle is currently working on a 20-minute firework display which will commemorate the Governor General's anniversary. Sparkle comes to your law firm which specializes in intellectual property law in Canada. Sparkle is fed up with his competitors watching his firework displays and then selling the same shows, with the same colours, type of fireworks, and timing, to the competitors' customers. He complains that fireworks are his art and that they are stealing his ideas. He is particularly concerned that this 20-minute masterpiece which he is working on for the Governor General's festivities be protected.

You are an associate at the law firm where Sparkle is a client and have been asked to write a research memorandum which will advise Sparkle whether he can protect his firework displays under Canadian intellectual property law and if so how. You have been asked to consider the following issues.

   **a)**   *Sparkle would like to get copyright protection for his firework display. Evaluate whether the copyright could be registered. To do so, you will need to identify any copyrightable material Sparkle might have and select the best choice(s) of work or subject matter of neighbouring rights to describe it under the* Copyright Act. *You will also need to ensure the other requirements for copyright are met. Explain your strategy fully. Advise Sparkle whether he is likely to meet the requirements for copyright and, if so, what* *actions by his competitors would infringe his copyright. Consider applicable remedies and defences in your answer.*

**b)**    *Sparkle would also like to pursue trade-mark protection. Sparkle thinks it would be effective if he could his use a three-second distinctive firework display which he personally designs as his trade-mark. The firework display would spell out "SPARKLE" in firework lights and come immediately before all of his firework displays. It would stay in the sky for approximately one minute. Sparkle has not yet done this in one of his fireworks displays but has the ability to design lights that would spell out a word in this way. Explain fully whether Sparkle could register this three-second "SPARKLE" display as a mark in relation to Sparkle's firework design services and/or the fireworks as a ware. Address whether Sparkle now has any common law rights and/or what he should do to acquire common law rights. Identify any problems and discuss strategies to fix them.*

**Q:** Bell Graham has compiled a list of cell numbers belonging to subscribers from different wireless providers. Graham had to spend many weeks tracking down the information. Graham arranges the names alphabetically. Is Graham's compilation of these telephone numbers a copyrightable work?

Assume that Graham's alphabetical list includes several names of Irish and Scottish origin with prefixes of O', Mc, and Mac. The list also includes many surnames beginning with variations of "von" "van" and "de". Graham researches how to alphabetize these names and concludes there is no single approved alphabetizing method and no consensus among professional indexers as to how to arrange such surnames. Graham spends quite a bit of time to craft a logical procedure for alphabetizing.

*Is the alphabetized compilation of these names ordered using Graham's procedure a copyrightable work? If Graham writes up a manual to describe his alphabetizing method is that a copyrightable work? If someone reads the manual and uses Graham's scheme to alphabetize a list golf courses does that list infringe Graham's copyright (if any)? Could Graham patent his alphabetizing procedure?*

# INDEX

**Adaptation** *See* **Infringement of copyright**

**Authorization** *See* **Infringement of copyright**

*Berne Convention*, 536-539 *See also* **International intellectual property**, substantive instruments

**Canadian Internet Registration Authority (CIRA)** *See also* **Domain names and internet-based infringement**
    CIRA Domain Name Dispute Resolution Policy (CDRP), 325-326
        bad faith, more limited definition of, 325-326

**Computer programs**, 350-355 *See also* **Patents** *and* **Integrated circuit topographies**

**Confidential information**
breach of duty of confidence: elements and defences, 512
discussion question, 518
employees, 499-512
    ex-employees not to use or disclose secrets belonging to ex-employer, 499
    senior officers having duty of loyalty, good faith, avoidance of conflict of duty, 500-507
        duty not to divulge trade secrets, 500
        key employee or senior management analysis, 505-509, 510
    senior managers having continuing fiduciary duty, 499, 501, 502-503, 504, 505, 509
    senior officers having same duty as corporate directors, 500
    whether solicitation of former customers permitted, 503-504, 505, 508, 511-512
government, information submitted to, 513-518
    *NAFTA* and obligation to maintain confidentiality, 513-514, 516-518
    patent protection vs. trade secret protection, 517
    question arising in context of generic drug manufacturer, 514-516
        impact of *NAFTA* provisions protecting against disclosure of trade secrets, 516-518
        proof of bioequivalence of product with previously patented product, 514-516
            whether reliance on test data and safety reports filed by innovator, 514-516
introduction, 485-495
    benefit in not disclosing information, 485
    freedom not to be compelled to share confidences with others, 486

nature of information influencing appropriate remedy, 492-494
    equitable cause of action, whether, 492-494
patent law having limited confidentiality period, 485
    patent publicly disclosed after 18 months, 486
protection of confidential information being form of intellectual property, 487
    *Paris Convention*, 487
    WTO *TRIPS Agreement*, 487
right to control when confidences disseminated, 486-487
tort, relevance of, 486, 494-495
whether confidential information being "property", 488-492
    characterization as property, laying foundation for, 490-492
        trade secrets, 490-492
    private law, for purposes of, 490
object of protection, 495-499
    criteria in *TRIPS Agreement*, 495-496
        context, purposes and circumstances, 496
        objective factors, 496
        relative secrecy, 495
    trade secrets, 497-499
        *Access to Information Act*, categories of information under, 498-499
            "trade secrets" defined, 498-499
        secret method, formula or process, 497-498
remedies, 512-513
    concurrent or alternative tortious liability, 513
    damages, 512-513
    equitable considerations, 512
    seizure of objects, 512


**Copyright** *See also* **Infringement of copyright**
assignment/transfer of copyright, 46-47
    moral right, assignment of, 47
    reversion, 47
    tangible property vs. intangible expression, 46-47
    collective management, 116-126
    general regime, 119-121
        collective management of various rights, 119-121
        tariffs, 121
    overview, 116-118
        advantages, 116
        categories of collective societies or organizations, 117
        "collective society" defined, 116-117
        full voluntary system, 117-118
            SOCAN, 118-119
    private copying, 122-126
        Canadian Private Copying Collective (CPCC), 122

   digital age, 122-126
     exception allowing copying of music for private use, 122-126
       "audio recording medium" ordinarily used by individual
       consumers, 123-124
         CDs "ordinarily used", 123
         DVDs not "ordinarily used", 123
         interpretation of s. 80, 124
         "ordinarily used", meaning of, 123-124
       "medium", scope of, 124-126
          digital audio recorders, 124-126
          Internet downloads on portable device, 126
   retransmissions and certain uses by educational institutions, 121-122
     "particular cases regime", 121-122
common law and civil law traditions and copyright, 10-12
   *Copyright Act* both creating and being definitive of rights, 12
   "*droit d'auteur*" including elements of both economic and moral rights, 11
     rights stemming from intellectual effort or activity, 11
   "*droit d'auteur*" vs. copyright, 11-12
     Supreme Court jurisprudence emphasizing economic aspects of
     copyright, 11-12
   economic rights associated with common law tradition, 10, 11
   moral rights descending from civil law tradition, 10-11
   copyright philosophy and idea of "balancing", 3, 12-13
   authors' rights and users' rights, balance between, 12
   digital copyright, balance for, 13
   promoting dissemination of works vs. obtaining just reward for creator, 12-13
     excessive control by holders of copyright unduly limiting utilization, 13
database protection, 127-128
   whether non-original databases should be protected, 128
discussion questions, 129-140
   artistic works, 134
   dramatic works, 132-133
   fair dealing, 138-139
   infringement, 137-138
   literary works, 132
   moral rights, 137
   multiple issues, 139-140
   musical works, 133-134
   originality, 129-131
   originality and authorship, 136-137
   photographs, 134-135
   photographs and architectural works, 135-136
   tangible vs. intangible, 129
   translations, 132
foreign works and points of attachment, 126-127

introduction, 7-13
    *Copyright Act* regulating copyright in Canada, 7-9, 10
        *Berne Convention* and *Universal Copyright Convention*, adhering to, 10
        copyright law being purely statutory law, 8
        creating rights and obligations, 7-8
        revision ongoing in three-phase process, 8
        rights protected, 8-9
            economic rights, 8-9
            "moral" rights, 8, 9
    United States *Copyright Act*, 9-10
        fundamental differences, 9-10
ownership, 38-46
    collective works, 45-46
    Crown copyright, 44
    employees, 39-42
        employees and meaning of publication, 40-42
            authors of newspaper articles retaining right to control article, 40-41
        generally, 39-40
    introduction, 38-39
        interview and journalist's contribution, 38-39
            oral statements alone not recognized as literary creations, 38-39
    joint ownership, 44-45
        whether music and lyrics distinct or whole "song" authored jointly, 45
    photography, 42-43
        owner of "plate" deemed to be "author" of photography, 42-43
        plate paid for by third party, 42-43
            agreement to contrary, 43
            third party being first owner of copyright, 42-43
protection, terms of, 47-48
    life of author plus 50 years, 47-48
related rights, 114-116
    neighbouring rights, 114-115
        performers' rights, 114-115
        producers' rights, 115
registration, 113-114
    assignments and licences, 114
    optional registry in Canada, 113
    presumption respecting copyright and ownership, rebuttable, 113
        certificate of registration serving as evidence to contrary, 113
work, 13-38
    architectural works, 37
    artistic works, 33-34
        definition, 33
        objective expression, 33
    compilations, 37-38

originality assessed with respect to selection or arrangement, 37-38

dramatic works, 30-32

definition, 30-31

"fixation", meaning of, 14-15

ideas vs. expression, 15-16

literary works, 25-30

computer programs, 27-28

future of computer program protection by copyright, 28-30

generally, 25-26

quality, 26-27

quantity, 27

musical works, 32-33

originality, 16-25

Canada's middle way, 21-25

creativity standard of originality being too high, 22

effort and labour but neither mechanical nor trivial, 22, 23

*Feist* standard of originality, 21, 22, 23-24

measuring creative choices, 23

"modicum of creativity" approach, 23

level of originality almost indistinguishable from "modicum of creativity" approach, 23-24

standard in *CCH* essentially identical to *Feist* standard, 24-25

main theories, 17-21

creativity as criterion for originality, 19-20

*Feist* standard of originality in U.S., 20-21

modicum of creativity, 18

"skill, labour and judgment", 17-18, 19

"recipe" approach, 19

photographs, 34-36

change of medium not sufficient to render product original, 36

original expression, 36

"work", meaning of, 13-14


**Domain names and internet-based infringement** *See also* **Infringement of trade-names**

arbitration clauses and proceedings, 324-326

Canadian Internet Registration Authority (CIRA), 325-326

dispute-settlement providers empowered to hear disputes, 324

Uniform Dispute Resolution Procedure (UDRP), 324-325

general top-level domains (gTLDs), utilized by, 324

Canadian Internet Registration Authority (CIRA), 325-326

CIRA Domain Name Dispute Resolution Policy (CDRP), 325-326

bad faith, more limited definition of, 325-326

courts dealing with infringement on internet, 326-330

passive "use" of mark on website not constituting "use", 328-329

remedies beyond trade-mark law, 329-330

whether Act creating cause of action to recover damages, 327-328
whether tort of passing off committed, 326-327
cyber-predators, 323
copy-cats, 323
cyber-squatters, 323
jurisdictional issues, 330-333
*Anti-Cybersquatting Protection Act* (ACPA) providing broader protection, 333
doing business within jurisdiction not sufficient, 331-333
real and substantial connection, 330
stock of company available to Canadian residents, 330-331
whether defendant targeted area located within court's jurisdiction, 333
passive use, 328-329
terminology, 323
"domain names", 323
meta tags, 323
top-level domains, 323
Uniform Dispute Resolution Procedure (UDRP), 324-325
cancellation of registration, 324-325
domain name identical or confusingly similar to trade-mark, 324
domain name registered and used in bad faith, 324-325
finding of bad faith, 325
situations in which deemed bad faith, 324-325
email, process conducted by, 325
registrant having no rights or legitimate interests in domain name, 324
general top-level domains (gTLDs), utilized by, 324
ICANN, adopted by, 324


**Fictional characters**, 576-580 *See also* **Overlaps of intellectual property**
*Harvard Mouse* case, 360-379, 380-381, 383-384 *See also* **Patents**, object of protection, life forms


**Industrial design** *See also* **Overlaps of intellectual property**
discussion questions, 164
infringement, remedies and defences, 158-164
activities constituting infringement, 163
defences, 164
exclusive right provided by registration, 158
pattern or representation applied to ornamenting of article, 160
remedies, 163
similarity, determining, 158-161
*Cimon* test, 160, 162
design as whole viewed through eyes of consumer, 161
eye of Court, 158, 159, 161-162
side-by-side comparison, 158-159, 162-163
"substantially different" test, 158-159, 160, 161-163

        application of test, 162-163
        explanation of test, 161-162
introduction, 141-142
    *Industrial Design Act* definitions, 141-142
marking, 157
object of protection, 142-155
    aesthetic aspects of design protected, 143
        ornamental features, 143
    aesthetic designs applied to useful articles, 142, 144
    function and shape completely overlap, where, 143
    functional aspects of design not protected, 142-143
    originality, 149-155
        declaration of originality, 154
        design applied to "ornamenting" of article, 153-154
        design objectively different from preceding designs, 149-151
            requirement of novelty, 150, 151
        intellectual activity in originating something, 152
        novelty test, closer to, 155
        substantial originality, 154-155
    protected pattern vs. underlying object, 143-144
    visual appeal, 145-149
        design visible to consumers, 145-149
            design appealing to eye of customers, 148-149
            functional aspects of design, 146, 148
            where design features hidden, 147, 148
        functional objects capable of aesthetic design, 145, 146-147
registration, ownership and term of protection, 155-157
    assignment or exclusive licence, 157
    certificate of registration as prima facie evidence, 155
    ownership, 156-157
        employee, 156-157
    protection valid for ten years, 157
    publication of design, 155-156
        "publication" defined, 155-156


**Infringement of copyright** *See also* **Copyright**
adaptation and translation, 56-60
    adaptation and traditional knowledge, 59-60
    adaptation being subject to copyright and enjoying its own protection, 58-59
    adaptation right and derivative work, 56-57
    derivative work, concept of, 57-58
        *Berne Convention*, 57
        "recast, transformed or adapted", 58
authorization, 60-68
    context of CRIA/Peer-to-peer (P2P) litigation, 64-68
        availability of file for other P2P users being form of distribution, 67

communication to public, 65, 66-67
    communication by virtue of Internet being "telecommunication", 66-67
    file transmitted, when, 66, 67
    "passive authorization" analysis, 64
        P2P user generally not having duty to supervise other Internet users, 64
        whether P2P user actually passive, 64-65
            passive/dual use analysis, 64
    section 80 exception and downloading, 65-66
        distribution not included, 67
        PC as allowable medium, 65
            hard drive as "audio recording medium", 65, 66
        private use, 65-66
    uploading and downloading as infringement, 65
    vicarious and contributory infringement under U.S. law, 67-68
        Napster users "sharing" protected music files, 68
        VCR capable of substantial non-infringing use, 67-68
  introduction, 60-63
    notion of authorization, sequential analysis of, 63
        active or passive authorization, 63
    photocopy service not constituting authorization, 62-63
    providing means to infringe alone not constituting authorization, 61-62
        control-based test, 61
        whether technology having substantial non-infringing use, 61-62
    "sanction, approve or countenance", meaning of, 60-61
communication to public/public performance, 54-56
  "perform in public", 54-55
  "public" defined, 55
  transmission of musical works on Internet, 55-56
criminal sanctions, 104-112
  *Criminal Code*, s. 42, 104-106, 112
  offering materials for sale that infringed copyright, 107-108
    whether defendants acting "knowingly", 107-109
        actual or subjective state of mind, 108-109
        "intentionally or recklessly", 109
  "renting out" infringing copies, 106-107
    elements of offence, 106-107
  selling infringing copies, 109-112
    proof of knowledge, 111-112
    whether strict liability offence, 110-111
defences, principal, 74-80
  idea, not its expression, taken, 74-77
    "abstraction-filtration-comparison" test, 75-76, 77
    idea/expression merger, 77
    "scenes à faire", 77

            use of flowchart or structure, 76-77
        ignorance of existence of protection, 80
        "insubstantial part" taken, 77-80
            context in which material used, 80
            determined by quality and not quantity, 77-79
                essential melody of musical march, 77-79
            impact on potential market, 79
            substantial similarity, 79-80
        licence or consent, existence of, 80
        no "copy" or other restricted act, 74
defences, statutory, 80-98
    fair dealing, meaning of, 84-88
        comparative analysis of Canada and U.S. systems, 86-88
        criteria in Canada for determining fairness, 84-85, 86
            Canadian courts having more flexibility, 85, 86
            comparison with U.S. criteria, 85
        criteria in U.S. for determining fair use, 85-86
        high degree of parallelism between criteria in Canada and U.S., 86
        "research" given broad interpretation, 84
    hierarchy of exceptions, 81-84
        "fair dealing" having special status among exceptions, 81-83
            whether "fair dealing" being "inferior" in status, 82-83
        "research" given broad interpretation, 83
        "users' rights" vs. authors' rights, 82-83
            users having right to deal fairly with protected work, 83
    impacts of *CCH*'s approach, other possible, 88-90
        fair dealing vs. "normal" exceptions, 88
            fair dealing broadly interpreted, 88
        fairness requirement, satisfying, 89
        "research or private study", scope of, 89-90
        sequential analysis, 89
            fairness of conduct determined first, 89
    other exceptions, 97-98
        absence of motive of gain, 97
        educational institutions, 97
        incidental inclusion, 98
        "small exceptions", 97-98
        user-specific exceptions, 97
    parody and "public interest" defence, 90-96
        Canadian cases and freedom of expression as defence, 90-92
        function of exceptions considered in broader societal context, 95-96
        U.K. case and public interest and public's right to information, 92-95
            freedom of expression able to trump copyright protection, 93
            public interest defence recognized, 93-95
discussion questions, 137-139
    fair dealing, 138-139

infringement, 137-138
moral rights, 137
general aspects, 48-50
exclusive rights of author, 48-49
"produce or reproduce the work or any substantial part thereof", 49
general infringement rule, 50
technology and "distance" performance, 49-50
moral rights, 69-72
civil law concept of *droit d'auteur*, 69
common law "copyright", 69-70
economic rights, 69-70
right to be associated with work, 69
right to integrity of work, 69-70
modification of artistic creation, 70, 71-72
mutilation of work, 71-72
objective evaluation of prejudice, 70, 71-72
not distort, mutilate or otherwise modify, 69-71
remedies, 98-104
"Anton Piller" orders, 103-104
criteria for obtaining order, 104
equitable remedies, 98-99
accounting of profits, 98-99
Mareva injunction, 104
punitive damages, 99-101
factors, 101
seizure of infringing goods, 103-104
"Anton Piller" orders, 103-104
statutory damages, 101
summary judgment, 101-102
general principles, 102
rental, 60
reproduction, 50-54
introduction, 50-53
act of copying inferred from similarities between both works, 52
causal connection between copyright work and infringing work, 51-52
independent creation not copy, 50-51
substantial part of work copied, 50
"to produce or reproduce", meaning of, 52-53
transformation to another medium would infringe copyright, 53
"unconscious" reproduction considered copy, 51
parallel importation, 54
publication, 53-54
secondary violation of copyright, 72-73

**Infringement of patent** *See also* **Patents**
claim construction principles, 427-441

interpretation of language used, 427-428
literal reading, 428
"purposive" or substantive construction or "teleological method", 428-440
    date of publication being relevant date for construing claims, 440-441
    *Whirlpool Corp.* "dual action agitators" case, 428-440
        basis of litigation, 431-433
        claims in suit, 430-431
        defendant's actions, not intent, that court considering, 439-440
        facts, 429-430
        principles of patent claims construction, 433-440
            purposive construction, 434-439
                benefits of purposive construction, 436-439
                "essential" elements approach, 435-436
compulsory licences, 465-474
    *Competition Act*, parallel procedure under, 473-474
    provision seldom invoked, 465-466
    refusal of application for licence by Commissioner of Patents, 466-473
        abuse under s. 65(1) of Act, 472-473
        prejudice, issue of, 468-469
        public interest, issue of, 469-471
            balancing of competing interests, 469-471
defences, 460-465
    *bona fide* experimental non-commercial use, 461-462
    *Gillette* defence, 463-464
    good faith acts prior to claim date of patent, 462-463
        pre-patent inventory, sale of, 462-463
            "specific" article, meaning of, 462-463
    invalidity of patent, finding of, 460
    laches and acquiescence having limited success, 464-465
equivalents, doctrine of, 441-449
    application of doctrine, 446-448
        essential elements vs. non-essential elements, 446-448
    *Catnic* test, 444-445, 448
    public policy considerations, 441-442
    purposive construction approach, 443-444, 445, 446-448
    what constituting essential teachings of patent to person skilled in art, 441-442, 444-445, 448
        *Catnic* test, 444-445, 448
    generally, 426-427
patent presumed valid, 426-427
    rebuttal of presumption requiring credible evidence, 426-427
    process patents and notice of compliance issues, 455-560
presumption that same product produced by patented process, 455-459
    presumption not displacing burden of proof on applicant, 456
use of presumption by research-based pharmaceutical companies, 456-459

delaying issuance of notice of compliance to generic drug companies, 456-459

orders prohibiting issuance of notice of compliance, 457-459

where patent infringement action, patent holder unable to access automatic stay, 459

remedies, 474-481

damages for loss of profits, 477, 478-481

accounting of profits, 477, 478-479

patentee entitled to damages assessed on sale of non-infringing component, 479, 480

where infringement on part of product, 478-481

discretion of court, 475-476

Federal Court having concurrent jurisdiction with provincial courts, 476

Federal Court having exclusive jurisdiction to impeach or annul patent, 476

four situations of alleged patent infringement, 474-475

remedies varying according to situation, 474-475

interlocutory injunctions, 476

punitive damages, 477-478

summary judgment, 476

"use" of patent, 449-455

intention of user, relevance of, 453-454

meaning of "use", 450

contextual examination, 450-451

commercial purposes, 451

purposive construction, 450

mere possession not necessarily amounting to "use", 454-455

"practical use" of invention, making, 453

propositions, summary of, 455

where invention contained within something that was not patented, 451-452

whether defendant's actions involved object of patent, 452-453


**Infringement of trade-marks** *See also* **Trade-marks**

domain names and internet-based infringement, 323-333

arbitration clauses and proceedings, 324-326

Canadian Internet Registration Authority (CIRA), 325-326

dispute-settlement providers empowered to hear disputes, 324

Uniform Dispute Resolution Procedure (UDRP), 324-325

general top-level domains (gTLDs), utilized by, 324

Canadian Internet Registration Authority (CIRA), 325-326

CIRA Domain Name Dispute Resolution Policy (CDRP), 325-326

bad faith, more limited definition of, 325-326

courts dealing with infringement on internet, 326-330

passive "use" of mark on website not constituting "use", 328-329

remedies beyond trade-mark law, 329-330

whether Act creating cause of action to recover damages, 327-328

whether tort of passing off committed, 326-327

cyber-predators, 323
    copy-cats, 323
    cyber-squatters, 323
jurisdictional issues, 330-333
    *Anti-Cybersquatting Protection Act* (ACPA) providing broader protection, 333
    doing business within jurisdiction not sufficient, 331-333
    real and substantial connection, 330
    stock of company available to Canadian residents, 330-331
    whether defendant targeted area located within court's jurisdiction, 333
passive use, 328-329
terminology, 323
    "domain names", 323
    meta tags, 323
    top-level domains, 323
Uniform Dispute Resolution Procedure (UDRP), 324-325
    cancellation of registration, 324-325
        domain name identical or confusingly similar to trade-mark, 324
        domain name registered and used in bad faith, 324-325
            finding of bad faith, 325
            situations in which deemed bad faith, 324-325
        email, process conducted by, 325
        registrant having no rights or legitimate interests in domain name, 324
    general top-level domains (gTLDs), utilized by, 324
    ICANN, adopted by, 324
generally, 285-286
infringement of any mark, 296-317
    common law, 296-311
        tort of passing off, 296-311
            elements of passing off, 303, 310-311
            general principles, 303-305
            history and purpose, 296-302
                principles expanded, 301-302
                protection of public, 297, 299, 302
                protection of trade-mark owner, 302
                role of passing off, 298-299
                unfair competition, species of, 299-301
            purposes of action, 305-310
                protection of customers, 307-310
                protection of manufacturers, 305-307
    section 7 "codification", 311-317
        constitutionality of subsections in doubt, 312
        defences, 316-317
        subsection 7(a), 312
            elements to prove, 312

subsection 7(b) being codification of tort of passing off, 312-313

subsection 7(c) constituting extension of tort of passing off, 313-314

subsection 7(d) requiring false or misleading designation, 314-315

    *Competition Act*, invoked in conjunction with, 315

    *Criminal Code*, relevance of, 316

    limited constitutional validity, 315

subsection 7(e) unconstitutional, 312

text of s. 7, 312

infringement of registered marks, 286-295

depreciation of goodwill, 289-295

    "depreciate the value", 290-292

        broader interpretation adopted, 291-292

        more restrictive interpretation, 292

    "depreciation", notion of, 294-295

        not equivalent to U.S. concept of "dilution", 296

    "goodwill" defined, 289

    union's "use" of employer's logo not prevented, 292-293

    "use", meaning of, 292-293, 294

parallel importation, 295

right to use, 286-288

    confusing trade-mark, 287, 288

        defendant "sold, distributed or advertised wares or services", 287

    defences, 288

    "exclusive right to use", 286, 287

    mechanism of ss. 19 and 20, 287

    "throughout Canada", right valid, 286

remedies, 317-323

generally, 317

injunctions generally, 317-323

    interlocutory injunction, 318-319

        criteria used in determining whether to issue injunction, 318-320

            irreparable harm, 318, 319

            public interest, 318-319

            "serious issue to be tried", 318, 319-320

        other factors considered, 320-323

            main features of factors, 322-323

        relation between elements unclear, 319

    permanent injunction, 318

**Integrated circuit topographies**

discussion question, 528

*Integrated Circuitry Topography Act*, 527-528

computer chips, 527

nature of protection, 527-528

"topography" defined, 527

**International intellectual property**
discussion questions, 573-574
domestic law, role of intellectual property treaties in, 562-573
 court not accepting treaties to judicially amend *Patented Medicine Regulations*, 572-573
 referral to *Berne Convention* and *WCT* to interpret *Copyright Act*, 565-567
  whether not following *WCT* constituting violation of rules on comity, 566-567
 referral to *Berne Convention* in analysis of history and purpose of copyright law, 567
 referral to *TRIPS Agreement* to interpret process patent claim, 564-565
 reliance on treaties in interpreting Canadian statutes, 562-564
 whether *TRIPS Agreement* could be used by private party to obtain remedy, 567-572
  issue whether *WTO Agreement* legislated into domestic law, 568, 570-572
introduction, 529-530
 three categories of norms, 529
other instruments, 560-562
 instruments creating registration mechanisms, 529, 561-562
  *Budapest Treaty*, 561, 562
  Madrid system, 561, 562
  *Patent Cooperation Treaty (PCT)*, 562
 instruments harmonizing description of goods and services for registration, 529, 560-561
substantive instruments, 530-560
 *Berne Convention*, 536-539
  copyright "bundle" rights, 538
  exceptions, 538
  general provisions, 537-538
  norms updated by *TRIPS Agreement*, 538-539
 generally, 530-531
  sixteen multilateral instruments, 530-531
 *NAFTA*, 556-557
 *Paris Convention*, 532-536
  domestic law, requiring application of, 534
  flexibility to members, 535
  normative weakness of instrument, 535-536
   trade-mark related provisions, 535-536
  notable omissions, 536
   addressed in *TRIPS Agreement*, 536
  requirements or authorization to legislate in certain areas, 533
   patents, 533
   trade-marks, 533
  revision conferences, 532
  rights and obligations of members, 532-533

rights and obligations of private parties, 534
    patent law, 534
    trade-marks, 534-535
World Intellectual Property Organization (WIPO) administering Convention, 532
    member states adopting separate instruments, 532
*Rome Convention* (1961), 539
    minimum rights for broadcasters, 539
    obligation imposed on broadcasters to pay equitable remuneration, 539
    protection of performers, producers and broadcasting organizations, 539
*TRIPS Agreement*, 540-556
    confidential or undisclosed information, 553
    copyright, 548-549
    dispute-settlement, 547
        WTO binding dispute-settlement mechanism, 547
    enforcement, 554-555
        border measures, 555
            pirated copyright and counterfeit trade-marked goods, 555
        criminal measures, 555
        disposal of seized goods, 554
        *ex parte* action, 555
        general principles ensuring fair and transparent procedure, 554
        injunction, 554
        judicial review, right of, 554
        preventive injunctions in respect of "qualified acts", 555
    general provisions, 548
        national treatment guaranteed, 548
    geographic indications, 550
        wines and spirits, 550
    history, 540-545
        *Doha Declaration*, 542-543
            Convention on Biological Diversity (CBD), mention of, 542, 543
                opening door to inclusion of *TRIPS* in broader normative framework, 543
            promotion of technological innovation and dissemination of technology, 544-545
            reflecting concerns of developing countries, 542, 543
            supportive of public health, 542
            traditional knowledge and folklore, specific mention of, 542, 543
        GATT launching Uruguay Round of negotiations, 540-541
            broad mandate in respect of intellectual property, 540-541
        pre-*TRIPS* historical development of norms being haphazard process, 544
        *TRIPS Agreement* formally adopted, 541-542

transitional period, 541-542
integrated circuits, 553
industrial designs, 551
logic of *TRIPS Agreement*, 545-546
    existing conventions used as point of departure, 546
    necessary new rights added, 546
    new set of rules on enforcement, 546
    *TRIPS* brought under WTO dispute settlement umbrella, 546
    updating of existing rules preferred, 545-546
        conclusions deduced, 545-546
patents, 551-553
    compulsory licenses, 552-553
    elimination of discrimination "as to the place of invention", 551-552
    patents available for all fields of technology based on usual criteria, 551
    restriction where endanger *ordre public* or morality, 552
protection of existing subject-matter, 555-556
    applying to all subject-matter existing on "date of application" of Agreement, 556
        exceptions, 556
        special rules, 556
substantive content of *TRIPS*, 547
trade-marks, 549-550
    "trade-mark" broadly defined, 549
        distinctiveness, focus on, 549
        service marks included, 549
*WIPO* Treaties, 557-560
"Internet treaties", 557-558
"rights management information", protection of, 558
states to provide adequate legal protection and effective remedies, 558-559
    anti-circumvention right as accessory to copyright or stand-alone right, 559
        U.S. *Digital Millennium Copyright Act (DMCA)*, 559-560
            case involving replacement transmitters, 559
            case where microchip enabling unauthorized toner cartridges, 559
            Internet Service Providers (ISPs) forced to "take down" content, 560
right to prevent circumvention of effective technological measures, 558, 559
    measures reasonably effective, 558
    password-protected access to technological locks, 558
    whether protection required where use not infringing copyright, 558-559

*WIPO Copyright Treaty (WCT)*, 557, 566-567
*WIPO Performance and Phonograms Treaty (WPPT)*, 557

**Internet-based infringement** *See* **Domain names and internet-based infringement**

**Life forms** *See* **Patents**, object of protection

**Moral rights** *See also* **Infringement of copyright**
civil law concept of *droit d'auteur*, 69
common law "copyright", 69-70
    economic rights, 69-70
right to be associated with work, 69
right to integrity of work, 69-70
    modification of artistic creation, 70, 71-72
        mutilation of work, 71-72
        objective evaluation of prejudice, 70, 71-72
    not distort, mutilate or otherwise modify, 69-71

*NAFTA*, 556-557 *See also* **International intellectual property**

**Novelty**, 384-399 *See also* **Patents**, object of protection

**Overlaps of intellectual property**
copyright and industrial designs, 590-597
    *Copyright Act* describing scope of copyright relating to industrial designs, 591-592
    copyright continuing to subsist where more than 50 copies in certain instances, 594
    copyright owner required to authorize reproduction of more than 50 copies, 592
        copyright protection lost where designs applied to useful article and more than 50 units, 593
    "design" defined similarly in both Acts, 591
    designs applied to article vs. designs applied to "useful" article, 592-593
        useful article having utilitarian purpose, 593
    example of overlap, 595-596
    functional features of work, use of, 594
    utilitarian functions of article, use of, 594-595
copyright and topographies, 597
copyright and trade-marks and protection of image, 576-590
    fictional characters, 576-580
        copyright and trade-mark convergence, 579-580
            common problem of convergence of principles, 580
            three dimensional figures based on two-dimensional figures, 579
            whether title of fictional character protected, 579-580

       title with characters infringing copyright, 580
    copyright protection for fictional characters, 577-579
        fictional characters capable of being independently copyrighted, 577
        graphic characters protected where visual similarity, 578
        literary characters less likely protected, 579
        type of medium being factor, 578
        U.S. test that less developed characters are less copyrighted, 577-578
        when fictional character becoming expression, 578
    generally, 576-577
    personality, misappropriation of, 581-590
        football player's image used to advertise car, 581-589
            passing-off appearing to have no application, 584-586
            wrongful appropriation of personality recognized as tort, 587-589
                danger of extending law of torts to cover exposure in public, 588-589
        gravamen of tort being usurpation of person's right to control own image, 589-590
            "sales vs. subject" distinction, 589-590
        invasion of privacy distinguished, 590
        persona created by actors, where, 590
        "signature image" of well-known water skier copied and published, 589
        tort being hybrid of privacy and property interests, 581
discussion questions, 614-624
    overlaps, 614-615
    sample exam questions, 616-624
introduction, 575
patents and copyright, 597-600
    conflict raised in number of court cases, 598-599
    patent drawings, 598-600
        use of drawings when patent term expiring, 600
        whether waiver of copyright in drawings submitted with patent application, 599-600
            reconciling conflicting cases, 599-600
    software and soft-ware based inventions, 600
patents and trade-marks, 604-614
    article becoming distinguishing guise while protected by patent, 604, 605-606
    distinguishing guise invalid as transgressing bounds of trade-mark, 608, 613
    functionality, doctrine of, 613-614
    functional aspects subject to patent law protection, where, 604, 605-608, 613
    trade-mark application for keys with specific design, 608-609

trade-mark law not to be used to extend time-limited patent protection, 604, 613-614

whether applicant extending patent term by claiming trade mark rights, 610-613

trade-marks and industrial designs, 600-604

    *Trade-Marks Act* prohibiting registration where guise limiting development of art, 600-601, 602-604

    industrial design protection and trade-mark protection not mutually exclusive, 603-604

    prohibition not preventing recourse to common law protection, 601

**Overview**

"intellectual property", meaning of, 1-2

  definition (WIPO), 1-2

  intellectual property vs. tangible property, 1

    non-exclusive, 1

    non-rivalrous, 1

  protection, scope of, 2

  statutes and other laws, 2

justifying intellectual property, 2-4

  balancing dissemination of works and obtaining just reward, 3

  economic ability to exploit and profit from idea, 3

    promoting circulation of ideas and intellectual production, 3

  hiding and hoarding idea not desirable result, 3

  "non-rivalrous" and "non-exclusive", 2-3

    Jefferson's description of these qualities, 2

  public domain, 4

    access creating more intellectual activity, 4

theories of intellectual property, 4-5

  labour theory, 4

    common law jurisdictions, 4, 5

    intellectual property being reward and incentive for work, 4

    "value-added" theory, 4

  personality theory, 4-5

    civil law jurisdictions, 5

    natural rights arising from creator's relationship with idea, 4-5

    original ideas and expression being integral part of creator's identity, 4

  right to protection of interests and right to access to creation, 5

*Paris Convention*, 532-536 *See also* **International intellectual property**

**Passing off** *See* **Infringement of trade-marks** *and* **Trade-marks**, constitutional ground

**Patents** *See also* **Infringement of patent**

application, 413-425

disclosure, 423-425

  application requirements, 423-424

  patent protection in exchange for full disclosure, 423

  purposes of specifications, 424

  simple language to be used, 424-425

  vague and ambiguous language invalidating patent, 424-425

employees, 417-423

  assignment of employee's rights to invention suggested, 423

  employer's patent if employee hired to invent thing for employer's benefit, 417-419

    considerations concerning employer-employee relationship, 418

    exceptions favouring inventive employee, 418, 419-421

    general principle, 417-419

    where employee hired because of inventive skills, 418-419, 423

  managerial employee not necessarily deprived of rights to invention, 420-422

inventor, 413-417

  co-inventors, 415-416

    failure to name co-inventor not invalidating patent unless willful, 415-416

      issue of materiality, 415-416

  who constituting inventor, 413-417

    co-inventors, 415-416

    first publisher of invention, 414

    person not borrowing from anyone else, 414

    person reducing invention to definite and practical shape, 416-417

    person solving problem, 413

    whether joint invention, 415

discussion questions, 481-483

introduction, 339-347

  basic principles, 340-347

    balancing incentives for inventors and need for others to innovate, 343

      "deserving inventions", ensuring, 343

    computer software and extracting rent from third party, 342

    life forms and agricultural products, patentability of, 343

      legal, ethical and religious objections, 343

    optimal level for patent protection, 343-344

    patentee granted limited term monopoly for exclusive use, 341

      monopoly in exchange for public disclosure, 341

    pharmaceuticals example, 341-342

      debate over priorities being based on profitability, 342

    reward and incentive to invent and to disclose invention, 341

    rules adapted when applied to different technologies, 344-347

      biotechnology and low nonobviousness barrier, 345-346

      chemical composition modifications and subtle doctrine of nonobviousness, 344-345 convergent technologies, where, 346

             software and stringent application of doctrine, 345, 346

             summary, 346-347

         underlying policy for grant of patent, 340-341

         U.S. developments usually relevant, 346

     constitutional ground, 340

     origin of patents, 339-340

object of protection, 347-413

     non-obviousness, 408-413

         description of concept, 409-411

         factors supporting conclusion of inventiveness, 411-412

         novelty vs. non-obviousness, 412-413

         test for obviousness enshrined in Act, 408-409

         threshold for non-obviousness not put too high, 409

     novelty, 384-399

         "anticipation" defined, 388-389

         claim date, 384-385

            where foreign filing, 385

         disclosure voiding novelty, 385

         filing date, 384

         first-to-file system in Canada, 385, 386

         first-to-invent system in U.S., 385-386

         priority date where foreign filing, 384, 385

         grace period of one year, 384, 385

         new combination of known elements possibly patentable, 393-394

            new combinations vs. simple aggregations, 393-394

         new use of known compound being patentable subject matter, 390-393

            "Swiss-style" claims focusing on new medical uses patentable, 393

         "novelty" defined, 384

         "overclaiming", 394-399

            claiming monopoly over something disclosed in prior art, 394

            principles applicable, 394-399

                claim construed with reference to entire specification, 398-399

                claim failing where something that was old claimed, 397

                claim given unambiguous and grammatical reading, 396, 398

                court not diminishing or extending ambit of monopoly claimed, 396

         tests to determine whether invention new, 386-390

            "anticipation" defined, 388-389

            test for anticipation being difficult to meet, 388

            whether alleged invention not anticipated, 387

            whether finding of anticipation, 387-388

            whether significant difference, 389-390

     overview, 347-348

     subject matter, 348-384

         computer programs, 350-355

Canadian Patent Appeal Board allowing patents on software-based inventions, 354-355

CIPO practice and guidelines, 354

    inventions resembling business models and/or computer software, 354

computer program used to implement "business method" patentable in U.S., 352-354

    business method exception, 352-353

    one-click purchase system, 353-354

globalization possibly leading to review of jurisprudential exclusion, 355

method of calculation being unpatentable, 350-351

"system" patentable where computer part of apparatus, 351-352, 354-355

excluded subject matter, 348-350

    medical treatment, methods of, 349-350

        method vs. instrument, 349-350

    "mere scientific principle or abstract theorem", 348-349

        discovery vs. invention, 348-349

    professional skills and methods and business methods, 349

life forms, 355-384

    genetically altered canola seed case: explanation of higher life form exclusion, 379-383

        conclusion compatible with *Harvard Mouse* case, 283-384

            components of higher life forms patentable, 383

            genetically modified plasmid and process being patentable, 383

        cultivating plants containing cell and gene amounting to infringement, 381-382

        damages for infringement not awarded as defendant not profiting, 382-383

        farmers licensed to grow modified seed, 380

        *Harvard Mouse* case distinguished, 380-381

patent for gene and cell developed, 381

    *Harvard Mouse* case: higher life forms not patentable, 360-379

        dissent adding "economic flavour" to analysis, 369-379

            commercial and scientific context, 371

            deficiencies in patent regime, alleged, 379

            financing research and development, 371-372

            international scope of intellectual property law, 370

            interpretation of s. 2 of *Patent Act*, 372-374

                "composition of matter", 373-374

            oncomouse patentable in other jurisdictions, 369

            policy arguments, 374-379

                animal rights, 377

                commodification of human life, 377-378

contrary considerations, 378-379
environmental protection, 378
globalization, 378
"lack of regulatory framework" objection, 374-375
"laws of nature" objection, 375-376
ordre public or morality, 376-377
religious objection, 374
genetically altered mouse used for cancer research, 360
lower life forms patentable: defensibility of drawing line, 360,
368-369
not considered manufactures or compositions of matter, 360-
363
"composition of matter", meaning of, 363-364
"invention", definition of, 362
"manufacture", meaning of, 362-363
object of Act, 366-367
scheme of Act, 364-366
soybeans, patent rejected on new variety of, 356-360
Federal Court of Appeal, 356-358
Supreme Court of Canada and types of genetic engineering,
358-360
change in genetic material by alteration of genetic code,
359
intervention by crossing different species by
hybridization, 358-360
hybridization not patentable, 359-360
whether life forms within scope of patentable subject matter, 355-
356
utility, 399-408
commercial or industrial usefulness, 399, 400-401
conferring benefit on public, 400
pharmaceutical having therapeutic value, 400-401
operability, 399-400
sound prediction, 401-408
elements of doctrine of sound prediction, 402-404, 407-408
articulable and "sound" line of reasoning, 407-408
factual basis, 407
proper disclosure, 408
limits of sound prediction, 404-407
meeting utility standard, 401-402
term of protection, 425-426
"secret" period, no right during, 425-426
intermediate phase, 426
term of 20 years, 425

**Personality, misappropriation** *See* **Overlaps of intellectual property**

**Plant varieties**
application process, 523
discussion questions, 525
infringement and remedies, 525
    damages, 525
    defences, 525
introduction, 519-523
    novelty determined by three characteristics, 519-520
        criteria in simpler terms, 520
        "sufficiently homogeneous variety" defined, 519-520
    *Plant Breeders' Rights Act*, 519-520
        alternative intellectual property protection for new plant varieties, 519
        development process for new plant variety, 521
        novelty determined by three characteristics, 519-520
        purpose of Act, 520, 522-523
rights, scope and duration of, 523-524
    commercial use, 524
    compulsory licensing, 524
    period of up to 18 years, 524


**_Rome Convention_ (1961)**, 539 *See also* **International intellectual property**


**Trade secrets** *See* **Confidential information**


**Trade-marks** *See also* **Infringement of trade-marks**
discussion questions, 333-337
introduction, 165-192
    constitutional ground, 167-188
        federal jurisdiction, 167-168
            regulation of trade and commerce, 167-168
        tort of passing off, 168-188
            constitutional validity of s. 7(a), 186-188
                *Asbjorn* findings minimized, 186-187, 188
            constitutional validity of s. 7(b), 178-186
                civil remedy required to be genuinely integral with regulation, 179-180
                enforcement required to be intimately connected to regulation, 183-184
                nature of action under s. 7(b), 182-183
                validity of s. 7(b) as *intra vires*, 184-186
            constitutional validity of s. 7(e), 168-178
                scope of s. 7 as bearing on its validity, 173-175
                scope of s. 7 generally, 172-173
                scope of s. 7(c), 171
                scope of s. 7(d), 171
                scope of s. 7(e), 171-172

section 7(e) declared *ultra vires*, 168, 178, 188
validity of s. 7(e), 175-178
"codification" of tort in *Trade-marks Act*, s. 7, 168
provincial jurisdiction, 168
summary, 188
origin, 165-167
differentiation of brands, 167
exclusive right to use mark in association with designated good or service, 167
informational purpose of trade-marks, 166
"mental link" between product or service and given mark, 166
protecting "goodwill" associated with mark, 166
*Trade-marks Act*, purpose of, 165
purpose and theory of protecting trade-marks, 189-192
primary purposes, 189, 192
purpose and policy of trade-mark law, 189-191
private right to ownership, 190-191
exclusive right, 191
registration of mark actually used, 190-191
public right to competition, 190
rationale for tort of passing off, 189-190
licences and assignments, 284-285
object of protection, 192-275
clearly descriptive trade-marks, 217-246
generally, 217-231
clearly descriptive or deceptively misdescriptive, 225-227, 231
"clearly descriptive", test for, 225-226
"deceptively misdescriptive", test for, 226
English or French language limitation, 225, 226-227
certain exceptions, 227
clearly descriptive trade-mark vs. suggestive trade-mark, 220-223, 231
distinctive requirement, 217, 219-220
distinctiveness through use, 219
inherently distinctive marks, 219
principles applicable, 219-220
first impression of hypothetical purchaser test, 218-219
mark considered in its totality, 223-224
clearly descriptive where common word(s), 223-224
mark not using common word, 224
whether word elements "dominant", 223
first impression of prospective consumer, 223
prohibition under s. 10 where mark becoming descriptive by usage, 217, 231
suggestive trade-mark, example of, 225
suggestive trade-marks registrable, 217

surname not registrable where primarily surname of individual, 227-231

    Japanese surname not recognizable as surname, 227-229
    "primarily", application of word, 229-231
    surname in directory not primarily known as surname, 229-230
loss of distinctiveness, 238-246
    confusion/deception resulting from transfer, 239-241
        change of ownership creating confusion, 240
    confusion between distinctive marks, notion of, 246
    different products using same trade-mark diluting trade-mark, 242-243, 245
    licensee not adequately indicating ownership, 238-239
    licensee's use attributable to owner, 239
    mark becoming generic, 244-245
        whether word becoming completely descriptive, 244-245
    non-distinctive mark struck from register, 245
    outsourcing without informing consumers, 243-244
    single-source rule, 238, 241-242
        "single entity" qualification, 241-242
    source of goods guaranteed, 241
    trade-mark deemed transferable, 239
place of origin, 231-235
    alcoholic beverage cases, 233-235
    bar to registration, not usage, 235
    first impression of average consumer test, 232-233
        liberal interpretation of test, 232-233
    protected "geographic indications", 235
secondary meaning, 235-238
    acquired distinctiveness, significance of, 235-236, 237
    coined words tending to more inherently distinctive, 236
    distinctive of its owner, 235, 236
    inherently distinctive or actually distinguishing, 238
    prohibition under s. 10 where word becoming descriptive by usage, 237-238
        word resembling recognizable designation of origin, 237-238
    "single source", mark indicating, 235
    strong link between product or service and mark, 236
company names, 197-198
    whether trade-name causing confusion with trade-mark, 198
confusion, 257-275
    conclusion largely factual matter, 261-262
    confusion analysis, review of, 272-274
    confusion test applying to likely consumer, 262-263
    consumer confusion preventing registration, 257-258
    five criteria considered in determining whether likelihood of confusion, 258-259

language as factor in confusion, 263-270

    anglophone, francophone and bilingual consumers considered, 266-269

    average bilingual consumer considered, 263-264

    language becoming cause of confusion, 264-266

        *Boy Scouts of Canada* case, 264-266

    other languages of consumers not relevant at present time, 269-270

        growing number of communities speaking foreign languages, 270

length of use, 258, 260

nature of commerce, 258, 260-261

part of mark confusing, where, 270-271

products starkly different, where, 272-275

    whether different conclusion with growing trend to use cartoon characters, 275

resemblance, degree of, 258, 261

strength of mark, 258, 259

type of merchandise and service, 258, 260

generally, 192-197

    functional elements not protected, 194

    "mark" defined, 192-193

        *Trade-marks Act*, 193

        TRIPS Agreement, 192-193

    "proposed trade-mark" concept, 194

    sensory indicators qualifying as protected marks, 195-197

    *Trade-marks Act* definitions, 193-194

        "certification mark", 193

        "distinguishing guise", 193-194

        "mark" not defined, 195

        "proposed trade-mark", 194

        "trademark", 193

    visual perceptibility requirement, 195-197

        unusual marks, 197

official marks, 212-216

    objective of official marks scheme, 212-213

    "national trade-mark", 216

        agri-food industry, 216

    official marks "adopted" rather than "registered", 213

    prior registered mark protected, 213-214

    "public authority" making request, 213, 215-216

        "public authority" defined, 215-216

            Canadian Olympic Association, 215

    public notice of adoption, 213-215

        official mark prevailing over pending application, 214-215

prohibited or invalid trade-marks, 246-257

    foreign marks, 254-257

"distinctive character" as criteria for registration, 254-257
 assessed as of date of application, 257
 comparison with distinctiveness standard, 255-256
 use in Canada not required where inherently distinctive, 256-257
names, 253-254
 names of persons when names become distinctive, 253
 prohibition of mark which "falsely" suggesting connection with individual, 253-254
  "consent" limitation, 253
 use of own name as trade-name, 254
prohibitions under s. 9, 246-249
 against "adoption", 246, 248, 249
 types of prohibitions, 249
prohibitions under s. 10, 248-249
 against adoption and use, 248-249
prohibitions under s. 12, 249-253
 "relative" prohibition, 249
 whether mark with functional aspects clearly descriptive, 252-253
 whether word clearly descriptive to extent that not usable as trade-mark, 250-252
proposed trade-marks, 198
well-known trade-marks, 198-212
 confusion, likelihood of, 209-212
  nature of wares and nature of trade, 211-212
 marks "made known" in Canada, 200-203, 209
  advertisement in "printed publication circulated in Canada", 200-202
   "printed publication", meaning of, 201-202
  broadcasts received by Canadian source, 202-2003
  distribution in Canada, 200
 protection of well-known international trade-marks, 198-200
 registration by owner of mark, 200
 tort of passing off, 203-209
  confusion with mark of U.S. company operating in same field, 203-207
  deliberate deception, protection from, 205, 206
  misappropriation of goodwill, 207-208
  unfair competition, 205
registration, 279-284
 expungement, 282-284
  application by "interested person", 283-284
   "interested person", meaning of, 283-284
  Federal Court having jurisdiction to order that register entries be struck, 283
  notice to owner requiring proof of use, 282

removal of unused registered marks, 282

special circumstances justifying retention of trade-mark, 282-283

generally, 279

impact of registration on previous users, 281

procedure, 280-281

advantages of registration, 281

application, 280

certificate of registration, 280

opposition proceedings, 280

publication of application, 280

who able to file for registration, 279

"use" of trade-mark, 275-279

central concept, 275

updated or revised mark, use of, 278-279

"use" defined, 275-276

important aspects of definition, 276

use of mark for services, 277

use of mark for wares, 277

"user" of mark being "source", 278

distributor where trade-mark distinctive of distributor, 278

manufacturer being user in typical product distribution chain, 276

*TRIPS Agreement*, 192-193, 495-496, 540-556 *See also* **International intellectual property**, substantive instruments

**Utility**, 399-408 *See also* **Patents**, object of protection